CONQUERING
WITH CHRIST

CONQUERING
WITH CHRIST
A Commentary on the Book of Revelation

IAN A. FAIR

Abilene Christian University Press

CONQUERING WITH CHRIST

A Commentary on the Book of Revelation

Copyright 2011 by Ian A. Fair

ISBN 978-0-89112-294-4

LCCN 2011033451

Printed in the United States of America

THE TEXT ADOPTED IN THE COMMENTARY

The basic text adopted in this commentary is that of the *New International Version*.

The following copyright reference pertains to the use of the New International Version (NIV) in this commentary.

"Scripture taken from HOLY BIBLE, NEW INTERNATIONAL VERSION®. Copyright © 1973, 1978, 1984 by International Bible Society. Used by permission of Zondervan Publishing House."

Where necessary, the NIV text has been compared to the text of the *Revised Standard Version*, Copyright © 1971 by Zondervan Publishing House. On occasion, where indicated, the Revised Standard Version has been used.

The Greek text upon which many comments have been based is *The Greek New Testament*, edited by Barbara Aland, Kurt Aland, Johannes Karavidopoulos, Carlo M. Martini, and Bruce Metzger, 4th Revised Edition. © United Bible Society, 2001. In order to keep this commentary readable by the non Greek scholar Greek words have been presented transliterated into the English alphabet. This tends to be cumbersome but is necessary in light of the need to keep this commentary readable.

LIBRARY OF CONGRESS CATALOGING-IN-PUBLICATION DATA

Fair, Ian A.

A commentary on the book of Revelation / Ian A. Fair.

   p. cm.

ISBN 978-0-89112-294-4

1. Bible. N.T. Revelation--Commentaries. I. Title.

BS2825.53.F35 2011

228.07--dc23

2011033451

Cover design by Rick Gibson

Interior text design by Sandy Armstrong

For information contact:

Abilene Christian University Press

1626 Campus Court

Abilene, Texas 79601

1-877-816-4455 toll free

www.abilenechristianuniversitypress.com

11 12 13 14 15 16 / 7 6 5 4 3 2 1

Contents

Preface 7

Introduction 11

Chapter 1   The Prologue (1:1–20) 71

Chapter 2   The Seven Letters: The Church in Imperfection—Part 1.
Ephesus, Smyrna, and Pergamum (2:1–2:17) 105

Chapter 3   The Seven Letters: The Church in Imperfection—Part 2.
Thyatira, Sardis, Philadelphia, and Laodicea (2:18–3:22) 131

Chapter 4   The Heavenly Scene: God is Ultimately in Control of
the Universe (4:1–11) 157

Chapter 5   The Scroll: God's Plan for Handling the Problem of Evil
is Revealed in and by Christ (5:1–14) 171

Chapter 6   The Seven Seals: Christ Reveals God's Plan for Dealing
with Evil (6:1–8:6) 183

Chapter 7   The Seven Trumpets: Warning Judgments on the Ungodly
—Repent (8:7–11:19) 213

Chapter 8   The Seven Mystic Figures: The High Point and Summary of
Revelation (12:1–14:20) 249

Chapter 9   The Seven Bowls of Wrath: The Consummated Judgments
(15:1–16:21) 281

Chapter 10   The Authority of God Over Evil Exercised (17:1–20:15) 305

Chapter 11   The New Order of Things:
The Church in Perfection (21:1–22:5) 355

Chapter 12   The Epilogue (22:6–21) 373

Chapter 13   The Meaning and Relevance of Revelation 385

Glossary 391

Bibliography 413

Notes 417

Preface

I am indebted to several people and scholars for shaping my thoughts on Revelation and for encouraging me to write this commentary.

First, I became spellbound by Revelation during a course at Abilene Christian College in 1966 while a student under Dr. J W Roberts.[1] For the first time Revelation made sense. Under Dr. Roberts' critical yet enlightening exposition, the book no longer appeared as a mysterious and strange work of esoteric symbols and confusing terms and language. Dr. Roberts' disciplined exegetical and scholarly approach treated the book in its own historical, religious, cultural, and literary contexts. Revelation became a real book with a real message to real people. This appealed to me, and I was hooked on Revelation. The required text for the course, published only the year before I took the course under Dr. Roberts, was G. B. Caird's *The Revelation of St. John the Divine*. This fine commentary reinforced Robert's exposition and through the years has been a continuing guide in my study of Revelation. I have since learned to take issue with both Caird and Roberts at certain points, but not often.

Second, as a result of ongoing study culminating in the Ph. D. degree in theology, and being invited in 1978 to join the faculty of my alma mater, Abilene Christian University, I have been teaching university courses on Revelation for thirty years at both the undergraduate and graduate levels. It has been with a keen sense of honor and obligation that I have been able to continue the fine tradition of exegetical study in Revelation so ably established by my mentor, J W Roberts.

Third, over the years my students and others who know of my interest in Revelation, have stressed the need for a study guide in some form for congregational Bible class use, coupled to a commentary that is solid enough to challenge serious students and teachers. Without wishing to cast a negative reflection on several excellent studies on Revelation presently available, this work is written with the hope that it will provide resources suitable for a serious student seeking references and guidance for personal study as well as for use in Bible class teaching.

Fourth, an invitation to accompany Dr. Bill Humble of Abilene Christian University on a tour of Western Turkey and the seven cities of Revelation became a journey into the life of real people and the living church in Asia in the first century of Christianity. The visit resulted in the publication of a series of video lessons and a study guide on the Seven Cities of Revelation. What was initially a scholarly archaeological experience resulted in a passion to understand the theology that defined the living faith of the church in the first and subsequent centuries which empowered them to defy the awesome might of Rome. My professional academic interest has been challenged to find relevance for the church in the twenty-first century as it faces similar threats today. This trip heightened my concern for a commentary that is biblically and theologically sound, readable by the average church member, and focused on a theology that is relevant today.

Fifth, I am indebted to several outstanding scholars whose research has resulted in a rich repository of resources for the study of Revelation: to J W Roberts' class notes, journal articles, and other materials used in his lectures; to G. B. Caird's fine commentary, *The Revelation of St. John the Divine*; to Isbon T. Beckwith's old, yet comprehensive commentary, *The Apocalypse of John* (reprinted by Baker Book House); to Adela Yarbro Collins's scholarly research and publications, notably her doctoral work, *The Combat Myth in the Book of Revelation*, and her two studies, *Crisis and Catharsis* and *The Apocalypse*; to Elisabeth Schüssler Fiorenza's fine contributions to the field of Revelation studies, notably her *Revelation*; to John J. Collins's continued research in apocalyptic literature, and to his excellent study, *The Apocalyptic Imagination*; to George W. E. Nickelsburg's fine study, *Jewish Literature between the Bible and the Mishna*; to Andrei Orlov and his research and publications on Slavonic Enoch and the Enoch-Metatron Tradition; to Leon Morris' two fine books, *Apocalyptic* and *The Revelation of John*; to Robert H. Mounce's *The Book of Revelation*; to Richard Bauckham's *The Climax of Prophecy* and *The Theology of the Book of Revelation*; to David E. Aune's three-volume commentary *Revelation*; to G. K. Beale, *The Book of Revelation*; and finally to Grant R. Osborne, *Revelation*. It will not take the reader long to identify my deep indebtedness to these fine scholars and their excellent research in the field of Jewish apocalyptic and pseudepigraphical studies.

Sixth, for their insightful editing of my manuscript I am indebted to Dr. Andrei Orlov, professor of New Testament at Marquette University, and Dr. Gary Holloway, professor of Bible at Lipscomb University, and Carolyn Thompson of Abilene Christian University.

Finally, I wish to express my appreciation to two librarians in the Brown Library at Abilene Christian University, Gary Oliver and Craig Churchill, both theologians in their own right, good friends, and excellent research librarians.

I am also indebted to Dr. Royce Money, chancellor of Abilene Christian University, for his support of the publication of this commentary and providing funds necessary for a project of this size.

This book is dedicated to the memory of J W Roberts, my memorable teacher of Revelation at Abilene Christian College in 1967, to my wife, June, whose patience and support through the years has encouraged me to persist with this project in the midst of many other daily tasks, and to my three sons, Deon, Nigel, and Douglas who through their Christian example and life for Jesus have been a constant encouragement to me to complete this study.

My prayer is that this book will introduce many readers to the fascinating world of apocalyptic eschatology, inviting them to join the chorus of the four living creatures and twenty-four elders of Revelation 4 who night and day sing the praises of our God and his Son Jesus who have provided us with a magnificent victory over Satan and his agents. I pray that this study will bring glory to Jesus and contribute to the acceptance of his present reign in God's eternal kingdom, and that it will challenge many to understand that Jesus is already reigning here on earth.

Finally, my hope is that this study will help Christians understand and realize every day the victory over Satan God has provided for us in Christ.

Introduction

Modern readers often have difficulty understanding this magnificent two-thousand-year-old book. This is mostly due to a failure to set the book in its unique historical, literary, and theological contexts. This introduction explains what I consider to be the "ground rules" that are absolutely essential for a study of this magnificent piece of literary theology. We will examine in some detail the historical, literary, and theological factors that are crucial to understanding and interpreting the strange, often mysterious language and message of Revelation. We will also examine the difficult style of proleptic apocalyptic eschatology adopted by John in Revelation. Since the meaning of this unusual literary genre and the importance of setting Revelation in its historical and theological context form the basis of much of the discussion in the commentary, it is essential that the reader of Revelation be familiar with the symbolism and style of this genre. The introduction will also cover the traditional introductory matters of provenance, date, audience, writer, and structure.

Key Texts and Thoughts

"Now war arose in heaven, Michael and his angels fighting against the dragon; and the dragon and his angels fought, [8]but they were defeated and there was no longer any place for them in heaven. [9]And the great dragon was thrown down, that ancient serpent, who is called the Devil and Satan, the deceiver of the whole world—he was thrown down to the earth, and his angels were thrown down with him. [10]And I heard a loud voice in heaven, saying, *"Now the salvation and the power and the kingdom of our God and the authority of his Christ have come*, for the accuser of our brethren has been thrown down, who accuses them day and night before our God. [11]And they have conquered him by the blood of the Lamb and by the word of their testimony, for they loved not their lives even unto death."* 12:7-11

"Behold I send you out as sheep in the midst of wolves . . . Beware of men; for they will deliver you up to councils, and flog you in their synagogues, and you will be dragged before governors and kings for my sake, to bear testimony before them and the Gentiles. . . . *A disciple is not above his teacher. . . . it is enough for the disciple to be like his teacher. . . . So have no fear of them; And do not fear those who kill the body but cannot kill the soul*; rather fear him who can destroy both soul and body in hell. . . . he who does not take his cross and follow me is not worthy of me. . . . *he who loses his life for my sake will find it."* Matt. 10:16-39

"What then shall we say to this? If God is for us, who can be against us? . . . . Who shall separate us from the love of Christ? Shall tribulation, or distress, or persecution, or famine, or nakedness, or peril, or sword? . . . *No in all these things we are more than conquerors through him who loved us.* For I am sure that neither death nor life, nor angels, nor principalities, nor things present, not things to come, nor powers, nor height, nor depth, nor anything else in all creation, will be able to separate us from the love of God in Christ Jesus our Lord." Rom. 8:31-39.

"I am writing to all Christians, and I give injunctions to all men, that I am dying willingly for God's sake, if you do not hinder it. I beseech you, be not 'an unseasonable kindness' to me. Suffer me to be eaten by the beasts, through whom I can attain to God. I am God's wheat, I am ground by the teeth of wild beasts that I may be found pure bread of Christ. Rather entice the wild beasts that they may become my tomb, and leave no trace of my body, that when I fall asleep I be not burdensome to any. *Then shall I be truly a disciple of Jesus Christ*, when the world shall not even see my body. Beseech Christ on my behalf, that I may be found a sacrifice through these instruments."[Ignatius, Bishop of Antioch, *Ignatius to the Romans*, IV, *The Apostolic Fathers*, trans Kirsopp Lake (Cambridge, MA.: Harvard University Press, 1998), 1:231]

THE GIST OF REVELATION

John wasted no time in telling his audience what Revelation is all about. Revelation 1:1-3 explicitly states that the message which God gave Jesus to pass on to his servants was that certain things in the life of the church *"must soon take place"* for *"the time is near."* It is only with great difficulty that one can project this simple straightforward statement, and these urgent and imminent things, into the church's far distant future. Revelation must therefore be about *things that God predicted were soon to take place.* The gist of Revelation must therefore be an explanation of what these things must be, and how the church was to relate to them.

Church history affords us a clear picture of what happened in the life of the churches in Asia in John's imminent future. The early church historian Eusebius (263–339) records that shortly after the establishment of the church a burgeoning persecution broke out from two directions: one from a frustrated Judaism and Synagogue, the other from Rome in the form of provincial governors' attempts to maintain peace in the Roman provinces. Eusebius' *Historia Ecclesiastica*,[1] which covers much of the first three centuries of church history, graphically describes the struggles of the church in its early years in the context of impending and growing persecution.

Persecution would not have surprised the early church since Jesus himself had warned his disciples that opposition and persecution would be brought against them by their families, neighbors, and ruling powers. Jesus had warned his disciples:

> "You must be on your guard. You will be handed over to the local councils and flogged in the synagogues. On account of me you will stand before governors and kings as witnesses to them. [10] And the gospel must first be preached to all nations. [11] Whenever you are arrested and brought to trial, do not worry beforehand about what to say. Just say whatever is given you at the time, for it is not you speaking, but the Holy Spirit. [12] Brother will betray brother to death, and a father his child. Children will rebel against their parents and have them put to death. [13] All men will hate you because of me, but he who stands firm to the end will be saved. " (Mark 13:9-13)

Speaking of the sufferings and persecution experienced by the young Thessalonian church, Paul had encouraged them to persist in their faith because "You know quite well that we were destined for them" (1 Thess. 3:3), namely, suffering and persecution. The citations from Romans 8 and Ignatius of Antioch at the outset of this introduction tell the story of how church leaders in the first and early second centuries of Christianity countered this persecution. Paul encouraged the church in Rome to see that with God, Jesus, and the Holy Spirit on their side they would be more than conquerors in the face of persecution as long as they kept their faith in God. Ignatius obviously took Jesus' and the apostles' admonition seriously and faced persecution and martyrdom with a confident faith. Revelation stands at the threshold of this era of trial and persecution, calling Christians to faithfulness in Jesus without compromise.

Most commentators realize that they face a serious challenge in unraveling the many confusing messages contained in this "mysterious" book. Grant R. Osborne, speaking for all serious readers of Revelation, observes that "The Apocalypse is a difficult book to interpret."[2] Unfortunately, the mysterious message of Revelation has been made even more mysterious and confusing by centuries of speculative interpretation. J. Ramsey Michaels adds an amusing tongue-in-cheek observation by Ambrose Bierce, *The Devil's Dictionary*: "REVELATION, *n*. A famous book in which St. John the Divine concealed all that he knew. The revealing is done by commentators, who know nothing." Michaels adds: "We who presume to write commentaries on the book of Revelation need to take Bierce's words to heart so as not to take our own words or opinions too seriously."[3]

It is unfortunate that the message of Revelation has been complicated and hidden by confusing millennial rhetoric through the centuries. The millennial rhetoric chosen by many as the vehicle for conveying the meaning of Revelation is more confusing than Revelation itself. G. B. Caird observes: "From the time of the millenarian Papias to the present day it [Revelation] has been the paradise of fanatics and sectarians, each using it to justify his own peculiar doctrine and so adding to the misgivings of the orthodox. And in modern times scores of commentaries have been written on it so diverse as to make the reader wonder whether they are discussing the same book."[4]

With sensitivity to the challenge of interpreting this magnificent literary and theo-logical work, I have taken up the challenge in the belief that we have in Revelation one of the most essential messages for churches and Christians in the twenty-first century.

Richard Bauckham speaks to this challenge: "One of the problems readers of the New Testament have with Revelation is that it seems an anomaly among other New Testament books. They do not know how to read it. Misinterpretations of Revelation often begin by misconceiving the kind of book it is."[5] The publisher's note to Bauckham's book, *The Theology of the Book of Revelation*, observed: "The Book of Revelation is a work of profound theology. But its literary form makes it impenetrable to many modern read-ers and open to all kinds of misinterpretations. . . . It calls on Christians to confront the political idolatries of the time and to participate in God's purpose of gathering all the nations into his kingdom. Once Revelation is properly grounded in its original context it is seen to transcend that context and speak to the contemporary church."[6]

Bauckham begins his major theological study of Revelation, *The Climax of Prophecy*, with this observation: "The Apocalypse of John is a work of immense learn-ing, astonishingly meticulous literary artistry, remarkable creative imagination, radical political critique, and profound theology. . . . close attention to the literary composition of the work is essential."[7] In his *Theology of the Book of Revelation* Bauckham observed: "The opening verses of Revelation seem to indicate that it belongs not to just one but to three kinds of literature."[8] I concur with Bauckham, but add that it is not only an appropriate understanding of the genre of Revelation that is essential to correct reading of this great book. It is also essential that we let the book stand in its own first-century historical context, and that we understand the crises already breaking into the life of the churches in Asia. This commentary will strive to keep interpretation securely anchored in these essential contexts before attempting to make application to contemporary situations.

It is essential therefore that we begin with John's introductory verses (1:1–3) to observe how he sets his message firmly within the struggles of the first-century churches in Asia. We will then be able to draw from these fundamental theological principles what John wished to convey to his readers. Only then will we be able to translate the message and principles of Revelation to our times.

Revelation 1:1–3 clearly pictures God warning his church of a crisis about to break in on them. He cautions the seven churches to be prepared, for the price of Christian discipleship will be high. Although the message of Revelation is couched in the context of a severe crisis about to break in on the churches, the message is not focused simply on persecution and martyrdom. *Revelation's message is a triumphant one of victory in Christ.* The message is that the God who had triumphed over Satan at Jesus' crucifixion, and who had raised Jesus from the dead, would not abandon his church in its hour of crisis. God has always been faithful to saints who die for their faith. He will not fail them in their impending crisis. Their sovereign God would raise the conquered saints, triumphing over death, transforming their "defeat" into a magnificent victory, for as of old he is a loving God whose "steadfast love abides forever"(Ps. 136, Lam. 3:22–24). The substance of Revelation is that through an uncompromising faith in Jesus believers would be "more than conquerors" (Rom. 8:35–39) and win a victory over their enemies.

The gist of Revelation, then, is a message set in the context of churches in the Roman province of Asia toward the close of the first century in which Christians were called to an uncompromising faith in Jesus. John paints a dramatic picture of the Jewish synagogue[9] and Rome becoming the agents of Satan in Satan's attempts to defeat God's purpose in the church. The message of Revelation promises Christians that through their unwavering faith in Jesus (which would possibly, perhaps inevitably, culminate in their martyrdom) God would give them a triumphant victory over Satan and Rome. Revelation assures the saints that by their martyrdom and consequent resurrection they would be vindicated and share in the messianic reign of Christ. Death for Jesus would not be defeat, but a triumphant victory in which the saints would reign over the nations completely and fully with Christ.

The Abiding Allure and Challenge of Revelation

Even though Revelation was not early accepted into the Christian canon in some quarters, it was readily accepted by many of the early second-century churches. Although the Apostolic Fathers appear to have little knowledge of Revelation,[10] the work was widely cited by the mid to late second century. Papias (ca. 130), Justin Martyr (ca. 130), Irenaeus (ca. 135), Melito, Bishop of Sardis (ca. 175), Theophilus of Antioch in Syria (ca. 180), and Tertullian of Carthage in Africa (ca. 190) all made repeated positive reference to Revelation. A fragment of the *Muratorian Canon* (ca. 190) includes Revelation, indicating that at least the Western church of the late second century accepted Revelation as canonical.

It was not long, however, before clouds of uncertainty concerning the canonicity of Revelation began to appear on the horizon. A second-century church leader, Montanus (ca. 170) of Pepuza in Phrygia (modern Turkey) and founder of a charismatic movement later named after him (Montanism), claimed to be miraculously empowered by the Holy Spirit. Thus empowered, he claimed to speak oracles from God. Central to his teaching was a view that the New Jerusalem would descend within his lifetime in Pepuza. Revelation was one of Montanus' favorite texts. The Montanists met with immediate opposition from mainstream orthodox churches, with several synods being held in Asia Minor to resolve the Montanist heresy. These synods resulted in the eventual excommunication of the Montanists. The impact of this on Revelation was the raising of serious questions regarding the reliability of the book.

In addition to Montanist problems, a heretical group known as the Alogoi[11] rejected Revelation as a "vulgar and fanciful" work, not in keeping with the central teachings of the New Testament. Since the Montanists sought biblical grounds from Revelation 20 for their radical views regarding Pepuza, the Alogoi spoke out vehemently against Montanism and the Montanist's favored text, Revelation. Regarding Alogoi objections to the Montanists' views of Revelation, Hippolytus referred to an influential church leader in Rome named Caius who claimed that Revelation was written by the Gnostic heretic, Cerinthus. It is not certain whether Caius was one of the Alogoi, but his arguments seem to indicate such affinity. Revelation thus faced further opposition from the orthodox churches in view of presumed Gnostic origins.

As a result of the Montanist predilection for Revelation, and the Gnostic rhetoric that developed around the Alogoi's and Caius' arguments, the canonicity of Revelation came under serious question by mainstream orthodox churches, especially in the East.

Although Revelation was readily accepted by part of the Western church, the Alexandrian church also questioned its orthodoxy and use. Along with the Alexandrian church, some in the Eastern churches were reluctant to include Revelation in their canon of authoritative texts. In spite of these serious questions regarding the inclusion of Revelation in the canon, the work gradually was accepted into the canon of orthodox churches. It seems that the primary reluctance was its unusual literary style and the fact that it became a favored text of questionable church movements. Although it was initially accepted by certain sectors of the church as helpful, albeit unorthodox in style, it continued to be viewed as a controversial element in the canonization of the New Testament. Eusebius (ca. 330) classified Scripture into the three categories: "accepted," "rejected," and "disputed." He included Revelation under the category of "disputed," thus opening the way for a centuries-long uneasiness with Revelation. As we shall notice below, the second-century reluctance to accept Revelation fully did not change in the centuries immediately following Eusebius.

In the fourth century the great scholar Jerome (ca. 400), although recognizing the value of Revelation, opened the door to further speculation. Jerome wrote: "The Apocalypse of John has many secret words. I am saying less than the book deserves. It is beyond all praise; for multiple meanings lie hidden in each single word."[12] Jerome's suggestion of "secret words" and "multiple meanings" within Revelation suggested to some that Revelation could be applied in various ways to almost any theological persuasion. The unfortunate reference to "multiple meanings" within Revelation continues, even in the twentieth-century, to encourage subjective speculation and to help make Revelation a springboard for almost any and every strange doctrinal view. As a result, Revelation has been viewed askance or ignored with some embarrassment by many even within Christian orthodoxy.

As an illustration of this embarrassment, Martin Luther accepted Revelation into his canon but ignored it since, in his opinion, it neither taught Christ nor recognized him in its teachings. John Calvin likewise ignored Revelation, writing commentaries on twenty-six books of the New Testament but ignoring the twenty-seventh. Even the great twentieth-century New Testament scholar Rudolf Bultmann questioned Revelation's benefit, relegating it to the periphery of Christian doctrine.

In spite of these concerns and dismissals, Revelation exhibits an abiding allure. Hardly a decade passes without several new commentaries or studies appearing on the stage of theological scholarship. Its language continues to mystify and its idiom confuses. Its interpretations are so diverse that one, in agreement with Caird, sometimes wonders whether some commentators are working with the same biblical text.

With the recent advent of increased scholarly research in the fields of apocalyptic writings and Jewish mysticism, scholars have given fresh attention to Revelation as a viable arena of research. Increased interest in extra-biblical literature has provided scholars a rich repository of resources previously unavailable. Discoveries of rich literary deposits such as the Dead Sea Scrolls and the library of Gnostic texts at Nag Hammadi have opened doors to rewarding research opportunities. Renewed interest in the pseudepigraphical and apocryphal texts has likewise stimulated interest in the literary genre akin to Revelation.[13]

Allan McNicol observes regarding apocalyptic that although Revelation is the first instance in ancient literature where a literary piece refers to itself as apocalyptic, the genre was well formed and understood long before the writing of Revelation.

> In common speech, the word apocalypse [Greek *apokalypsis*] refers to extreme crisis situations ending in a train-wreck type of event. This is a complete misrepresentation of the nature and function of an ancient apocalypse. Although Revelation may be the first instance in ancient literature where a literary work actually calls itself an apocalypse (1:1), by no means is this the first time that we find in ancient literature writings that claim to unveil divine secrets and the course of history. The prophets were taken by inspiration into heavenly places and the councils of God's advisors, focusing on problems in Israel. . . . This information was always limited in scope. God chose not to reveal to humans all divine counsel and wisdom. . . . Later certain scribes claimed to have access to the wisdom of great sages of the past such as Enoch, Baruch, and Ezra. They believed the sages had made trips into the heavenly world accompanied by angels and learned about the universe, the state of the dead, and the end times. Written accounts of this legacy were very common not only among the Jews but throughout the Greco-Roman world. To the ancients, such writing as 1 Enoch provided insight into unknown matters and built hope that there existed a transcendent realm guaranteeing ultimate justice and order in the universe.[14]

It is encouraging to note, furthermore, that with the increased scholarly attention being given to the historical, sociological, and literary environment of texts such as Revelation, a broad if not concise consensus has been building in regard to the meaning of this biblical book.[15] Unfortunately, the repeated failure of sensational prophetic predictions regarding the "signs of the times" to reach historical fulfillment and the bankruptcy of predictions of an imminent apocalyptic end continue to cause skepticism regarding the possibility of a reasonable interpretation of Revelation. Pop millennial theology continues to focus on the sensational rather than the real theology of this book. Futurist and dispensational focus on the end times has shifted the central message of Revelation away from the immediate faith crises faced by the first-century churches in Asia, and away from the magnificent triumphant theological message of Revelation, to predictions of a sensational, cataclysmic end of the world. Much modern speculative "apocalyptic" theology focuses more on fearful predictions and speculations of the end times than on the encouraging victory of faith over evil.[16]

In addition to the many sensational apocalyptic schemes conveyed by the popular media, the confusing array of dispensational and millennial timetables adds to the

problem. Without a firm anchor in a recognized historical and literary context, and without a reasonable understanding of the figurative and impressionistic idiom encountered
in Revelation and similar texts, we find ourselves without adequate checks and balances
that insure against speculative and sensational interpretations.

UNDERSTANDING REVELATION

Contrary to the tendency of many popular interpreters of Revelation to prematurely
apply the text to contemporary situations, thus turning Revelation into a support
mechanism for some sensational "fulfillment of prophecy" theology, this commentary
is written under the conviction that Revelation must first address its own historical and
sociological context, and do so within its own literary genre or type. Only then may
one appropriately apply its theology to contemporary situations. Failure to first seek
Revelation's meaning within its own unique context will inevitably lead to a distortion
of its message.

Most scholars today[17] believe that Revelation was written towards the close of the
first century to Christians living under severe political, social, and religious stress in the
Roman province of Asia Minor. A commitment to this historical and sociological perspective must become an *essential framework* for the interpretation of Revelation. Colin
Hemer cites H. B. Swete (1907) regarding the fundamental importance of understanding
this historical and sociological context:

> The book of [Revelation] starts with a well-defined historical situation, to
> which reference is made again at the end, and the intermediate visions which
> form the body of the work cannot on any reasonable theory be dissociated
> from their historical setting. The prophecy arises out of local and contempo-
> rary circumstances; it is, in the first instance at least, the answer of the Spirit to
> the fears and perils of the Asian Christians towards the end of the first century.
> Hence all that can throw light on Asia about 70–100 A.D., and upon Christian
> life in Asia during that period, is of primary importance to the student of the
> Apocalypse.[18]

Hemer adds: "Swete is surely right in stressing the importance of the historical approach
to the book, and the letters to the seven churches constitute the section in which the
historical situation is most explicit and approachable. *Here is the key to the easiest lock in
an admittedly difficult text* (italics mine)."[19]

A brief note concerning models of interpretation is apropos at this point in light of
these observations that an historical-critical foundation is essential to a sound interpretive model of Revelation. Michaels observes that "Modern historical critical scholarship
has assumed that it [Revelation,] is indeed about the author's sociological world." He
adds that this is typically defined as the preterist approach. While he operates within
a basic historical-critical approach, Michaels, however, does see in Revelation some
grounds for a futurist mindset.[20] Osborne adds that "The consensus interpretation among
nonevangelicals [sic] is preterist. In the SBL [Society of Biblical Literature] seminar it

is assumed that the book uses a future orientation not to describe future reality but to challenge the situation of the original readers."[21]Without at this stage engaging debate over the various models of interpretation, we note that Caird, Morris, Metzger, Beasley-Murray, Beale, Mounce, Boring, Aune, and Beckham all work out of a basic historical-critical model which sets Revelation in its original historical context. Commenting on the eclectic approach of Beale, Morris, Mounce, and others which combines a preterist (historical critical) model with idealist and futurist interests, Osborne observes that his own approach is in some agreement with the idealist model of Beale except that Beale does not permit the futurist approach to take a central place in his model.

My approach to Revelation will be to set it primarily in its historical, sociological, and literary contexts (a moderate preterist model) while exploring John's intriguing use of the apocalyptic genre in a proleptic inaugurated apocalyptic eschatology[22] to demonstrate that God will judge the church's enemies in the present with the severity of the future final judgment. This is an eclectic approach which combines the historical, literary, apocalyptic, dramatic, and idealist approach in a philosophy of history model of interpretation.[23] My argument is that without setting the message of Revelation in its historical, sociological, and literary context one faces the danger of reading into Revelation one's own context and presuppositions, thus disengaging Revelation from its original context and message. We now turn our attention to this historical and literary background.

A BRIEF POLITICAL HISTORY OF THE ROMAN PROVINCE OF ASIA UP TO THE AGE OF CONSTANTINE

John gives us some indication of the context of Revelation by observing that Revelation was written to seven churches in the Roman province of Asia, namely, Ephesus, Smyrna, Pergamum, Sardis, Philadelphia, and Laodicea. Unfortunately, as Michaels aptly observes, "Revelation gives us little information about the *actual* social world in which it was written."[24] Asia Minor was what we know today as Western Turkey. Hence, we already have two items that set the scene for understanding this book: one, that it was written in the first century (we learn this from early church historical references to Revelation, and most contemporary scholars are comfortable with this date[25]), and two, that it was written to Christians living in the Roman province of Asia. Already, we have established some preliminary parameters for the interpretation of the book.

We have no certain knowledge of when Christianity first entered the Roman province of Asia. From Acts 2 we know that there were Jews from Cappadocia, Pontus, and Asia present when Peter preached his epoch-making sermon on the day of Pentecost, but beyond that we have no certain knowledge of the roots of Christianity in this area. These Diaspora Jews from Asia mentioned in Acts 2 were among the first converts to Christ after his death and resurrection. They may have returned home with the Christian gospel. Some years later, around 49–52 , however, we do know that Paul entered the Roman province of Asia on his second missionary journey (Acts 15:36), and during his third missionary journey (ca. 53–57) he was active evangelistically in Ephesus and Luke records that "all the residents of Asia" (certainly a hyperbole, but a meaningful one) had heard the gospel (Acts 19:10) by the time of his writing Luke-Acts. We know that churches were established in several cities during Paul's third missionary effort.

The history of the region was rich in saga, reaching back to the third millennium B.C. The chronicles of Asia have been glorified by legendary accounts of the mighty Hittite nation (1850–1200 B.C.), and ancient Troy has become part of Western legend through Homer's *Iliad* and *Odyssey*. The magnificent stories of the Hittites and the captivating *Iliad* and *Odyssey* form part of the rich ancient heritage of the Asia we enter centuries later at the close of the first century with the writing of Revelation. These legends and tales of early history provide a living background to the region of the seven cities of Revelation and inform us that the region already had a rich history reaching back long before our New Testament era.

In the sixth century B.C., legend has it that Croesus, king of Lydia was the richest man in the world. His ill-informed attack on Cyrus, king of Persia, and consequent defeat at the Halys River resulted in two centuries of Persian occupation of Asia. The Persian occupation was finally brought to an end by the victorious campaigns of Alexander the Great of Macedon in the fourth century B.C. These fascinating stories are woven into the fabric of the history of Revelation's Sardis and its surrounding countryside. The Asia of Revelation had a rich and interesting history long before we encounter Sardis, Ephesus, and the other cities of Revelation; this history impacts the story of the seven cities in a dramatic manner and has colored John's description of Jesus' message to the seven churches.[26]

Alexander the Great and the Seleucid dynasty that followed him established a sophisticated culture in what the Macedonian Greeks would have considered a "barbarian" area. Greek would eventually become the primary language and Greek philosophy the dominant world-view. As an outgrowth of Alexander's conquests a new phenomenon, a Hellenistic society became the established mindset of Asia Minor. This Hellenistic culture was to play a centuries-long role in the development of the New Testament church and its Scriptures, and on the missionary outreach of the church.

In 133 B.C. Rome finally overcame the descendants of Alexandrian conquest, the Seleucid rulers of Asia Minor, and the area became a Roman province. By the time John penned Revelation, Asia Minor had already become an influential and vital part of the Roman Empire. Cities like Pergamum, the Roman capital of the province, and Ephesus, the striking port of the region, became important centers of Roman rule, culture, and influence. It was to these important Roman centers, especially Ephesus, that the Apostle Paul gravitated during his missionary activity. Ephesus soon developed into the hub of Christian missionary expansion and influence under the Apostle Paul and his co-workers, and later in the century under the Apostle John.

Following the fall of Jerusalem in 70, and a succession of Jewish-Roman clashes in Judea and the surrounding region, the churches of Palestine began to fall behind the churches in Asia in both numbers and influence. Clearly, Asia had become a major center of Christian influence at the close of the first century.

By Paul's day, Ephesus had become one of the foremost cities in the Roman world, certainly a city vital to the Roman Province of Asia. As a major seaport, Ephesus was a vibrant commercial center, a principal seat of the Roman imperial cult, the site of the magnificent temple of Artemis, and home of several pagan mystery cults. Ephesus was a thriving cultural center with a growing library that was eventually to become one of the most esteemed libraries of the ancient world. Ephesus was rivaled in Asia only by Pergamum, the capital city of the Roman province of Asia.

Pergamum, "the flower of Hellenistic culture," was recognized as the most distinguished city of the region with a magnificent citadel perched upon a mountain overlooking fertile plains. With its own outstanding library, second only to the library of Alexandria, and the world-renowned Asklepion medical complex, Pergamum was a thriving center of Hellenistic culture and civilization and also of the burgeoning Roman imperial cult.

Each of the other cities addressed by John in Revelation had a uniqueness and significance that demonstrated the sophisticated culture found in this area at the close of the first century. Smyrna, the birthplace of Homer, and itself a significant seaport with an impressive stadium and theater, was acclaimed as the most beautiful city of the Roman world. Philadelphia, built by King Attalus II in honor of his brother, with its wide and fertile plain, was a thriving agricultural center. Thyatira, possibly the least important city of the seven, was nevertheless a thriving commercial, industrial, and marketing center. Sardis, with its legendary history dating back to Croesus, was a city of wealth and fame. Laodicea, located at the junction of two major imperial trade routes, with a famous medical school, was the wealthiest city in the Roman province of Asia. Each of the seven cities of the Roman province of Asia could lay claim to fame in its own right, and each of the cities reflects the past glory of the region.

By the close of the first century, the Roman province of Asia ranged east to west from Galatia to the Aegean Sea, and north to south from the Bosphorus to the Mediterranean—an area some two hundred fifty square miles. Geographically, the region in which the seven cities of Revelation were located was a beautiful and fertile region of mountains and rich river plains. Agriculture thrived, lumber was plentiful, and the region was rich in mineral deposits. At the close of the first century the population was estimated to be approximately 4.6 million.[27] William Ramsay adds that it was the wealthiest region of the whole Roman Empire.[28]

The mixed ethnic and cultural nature of the population of Asia in the first century of Christianity not only opened doors to the rapid spread of Christianity, but also presented challenges to church leaders striving to develop and maintain Christian identity and unity. Although the common language of Asia at the time of John's writing was predominantly Greek, the region was home to many other ethnic and national groups. Lydians, Persians, Hittites, as well as a fairly large Jewish population had in various degrees been absorbed into the cosmopolitan flavor of the region. A fairly large number of Romans also made their home in proconsular Asia. Each of these groups contributed to the rich social and religious fiber of the communities.

The Jews built their synagogues in the cities and through their high moral code made a significant impact on the moral character of the populace. Being a national religion, Judaism was tolerated by the Romans as long as it respected the Roman hegemony and caused no political turmoil. The Greeks with roots all the way back to ancient Troy provided a broad pantheon of gods. Asian fertility cults blended with other pagan practices to provide an immoral sexual character to the texture of society that was in sharp contrast to the Jewish-Christian ethic. The temples to Artemis at Ephesus, Apollo at Didyma, and Zeus and Athena at Pergamum stood out prominently as testimony to the richness of the religious syncretism of the area. The medical cult of Asklepios operated a temple-hospital in Pergamum that was second only to the great Asklepion and temple cult at Delphi in Greece. But it was the burgeoning Roman imperial cult and forceful nature of Emperor Domitian that was most prominent and most threatening to the Christians living in Asia at the close of the first century. The Roman imperial cult, and other Roman divinities were prominently and powerfully enshrined in magnificent temples that dominated every major city in the Roman province of Asia.[29]

ROMAN PERSECUTION OF JUDAISM AND THE CHURCH, 70–100[30]

It is not possible to understand Revelation without an appreciation of the relationship between the Jewish-Christian faith and the Roman imperial cult at the turn of the first and second centuries. Roman conquerors were beneficent in permitting their subjugated peoples to continue with their national religions as long as they were not a threat to the religious and political fiber of the empire, and as long as they respected the Roman pantheon of divinities. By nature, the Romans were syncretistic in their attitude toward religion. They continued through the years of their national expansion to add divinities to their pantheon of gods. As long as these new religions and divinities did not threaten the political unity provided by *pax Romana*, they were tolerated.

This created problems for the Jews and Christians who were expected by their political overlords to pay appropriate respect to the emperor. Often the demands to fulfill Roman civic responsibility required paying homage to the imperial cult and Roman divinities, including obeisance to the Roman Emperor as a divine being. The history of Roman-Jewish clashes is well documented in the Jewish apocryphal, apocalyptic, and pseudepigraphical traditions of the period 160 B.C. to A.D. 100. Neither the Jews nor the Christians would compromise their faith in the one and only God—Jehovah for the Jews and for the Christians, their messiah, Jesus. For a while, especially prior to the destruction of Jerusalem in 70, the Romans tolerated the Jewish faith as a national religion. Christianity was initially tolerated along with Judaism since it was viewed by the Romans as part of the Jewish national faith. However, following the destruction of Jerusalem (ca. 66–70), the Jews began to distance themselves from all association with the Christians. Their reasons for this were both religious and political. The Jews maintained that Christians had no part in their Jewish national religion. They charged that Christians were a group of independent followers of a renegade Jewish king, Jesus, and that they were in reality opposed to Judaism and all other religions, including the Roman pantheon. This charge led to official opposition from the Roman magistrates, especially in the Roman provinces where political peace was considered a measure of the success of the Roman governor. By the time of the close of the first century of the Christian era sporadic Roman persecutions were already breaking out in the Roman provinces, or were just over the horizon.

The Romans were not by nature opposed to the Christians. In many cases they treated them with great fairness. At times, however, when Christians were identified as threats to the national peace or *pax Romana*, they often faced official or social persecution. In many instances, as was apparently the case in Smyrna and Philadelphia, this Roman opposition was aroused by Jewish charges that Christians were a threat to Rome. The persecutions were localized within the Roman provinces. Eusebius points out that there was no universal persecution of the church in the first century.[31]

However, increasing Judean Jewish opposition to Roman rule (that led to the destruction of Jerusalem and the siege and tragic mass suicide at Masada), and firm Christian rejection of the demands of the Roman imperial cult resulted in a growing Roman dissatisfaction with the "recalcitrant" Jews and stubborn Christians. Increasing Jewish "rebellions" and Christian inflexibility finally led to some forms of "official" provincial and finally national Roman imperial persecution. It was also commonly perceived that conversion to Judaism or Christianity meant a conversion to a way of life that was openly alien to Greco-Roman culture. This led to anti-Semitic attitudes among segments of the Roman governing class. Similar hostile attitudes developed toward the Christians who were likewise perceived to be opposed to Roman cultured lifestyle. Rejection of the Roman pantheon of gods in some instances resulted in Christians being accused of practicing an atheistic religion. Furthermore, the misunderstood Christian practice of "eating the body of Jesus" in the Eucharist (Lord's Supper) was perceived by cultured Romans to be a strange and repugnant form of cannibalism. Such charges of atheism, ethical rejection of pagan religious practices, and misconceptions of the "cannibalistic" ceremony of the Christian Eucharist lead to a "cultured" rejection of the Christian faith as both sociologically and religiously inferior to the Roman cultus.[32]

It was primarily toward the close of Domitian's reign (81–96) that the cultural and religious rejection of the Christian faith became an "organized" threat that finally escalated into open persecution of Christians. Domitian was not one to tolerate what he perceived to be civic or religious disobedience. His growing sense of self-importance and demands to be honored as a divine being stood in sharp contrast to the simplicity of the Christian faith and confession of Jesus as Lord. The Roman confession "Caesar is Lord" stood as an open denial of the Christian confession "Jesus is Lord." W. H. C. Frend observes: "We can trace a growing megalomania from *circa* 86 onwards when Domitian appears to have persuaded himself that he was "Deus et dominus", and ordered his courtiers and poets to greet him as such . . . . It was under Domitian that the practices of taking an oath by the Emperor's genius, of offering libation and incense before his statue, and addressing him as *Dominus* grew up."[33]

Such emperor "worship" was not unique to the first century, for we can trace emperor veneration and worship to the conquests of Alexander the Great (ca. 330 B.C.). It was Domitian, however, who for the first time made emperor "worship" a matter of *pax Romana*. Refusal to honor him as *Deus et dominus* (Lord and God) was interpreted not only as a religious insult, but also politically perceived to be treason. "It seems evident that Domitian's lust for self-importance entailed stricter control over acceptance of foreign religions by Roman citizens, especially when this might detract from respect to be paid to his own majesty."[34] Christians faced a real threat when the demand to confess "Domitian is Lord" became part of the accepted social norm, for to Christians this amounted to nothing short of blasphemy (13:5, 15) and denial of the faith. To the Christians, there could be no compromise; they would confess none other than "Jesus is Lord."

As observed above, the persecutions encountered in Asia and the other Roman provinces in the late first and early second centuries were related more to specific seats of provincial government and provincial problems than to official state legislation. Although Christians and Jews on several occasions were expelled from Rome (possibly under Tiberius in 19 and then by Claudius in 49—Acts 18:2), it was not an official policy of Rome to persecute the Christians. In Rome itself no aggressive program of persecution against the Christians seems to have been the practice in the first century.

When we move from Rome to the Roman provinces like Asia and Judea in the closing years of the first century, we encounter a politically charged situation. With the failure of the economy and ineffective administration of state affairs, considerable social instability developed. Any activity that could be interpreted as discrediting the state or the emperor was severely suppressed. Christian denial of the lordship of the Caesar could not be tolerated. Official opposition and various forms of persecution were inevitable.[35]

There is considerable discussion among commentators regarding the role that persecution played in the crises faced by the churches in Asia at the close of the first century.[36] Osborne cites Yarbro Collins, L. L. Thompson, D. L. Barr, J. Nelson Kraybill, Elisabeth Schüssler Fiorenza, and Helmut Koester as some who play down the centrality of persecution in the crises faced by the churches in Asia in the first century. I would add Kenneth Cukrowski to this list. Each of these in one or another manner locate the crises of the church more in social and economic issues, and compromise with the pagan culture as the basis of the problems addressed in Revelation. I agree with Osborne that Collins and others have overstated their case. Certainly the social and economic issues were present, but the underlying concern seems to be opposition and persecution from the provincial powers, the Roman imperial cult, aided by the Jewish Synagogue. The almost two-century history of apocalyptic literary outcry against Rome or "Kittim" (a euphemism for Rome) indicates Jewish and Christian concerns over Roman oppression.[37]

Almost within a decade of Domitian's reign and the writing of Revelation, the Roman emperor Trajan (111) responded to a request from Pliny, one of his provincial governors regarding how to deal with Christians. Although a legal and financial expert, Pliny had little political experience as governor. How to handle the Christians was becoming a frustrating problem for him. Pliny therefore appealed to Emperor Trajan for advice. His letter to Trajan has become one of the most interesting documents from Roman antiquity on the persecution of Christians. Pliny was convinced that Christianity was "an extravagant and depraved superstition, intolerable perhaps, but not to be regarded as conspiracy." Frend observes that Pliny had applied the normal Roman sacrifice test in which the accused were required to offer a libation of incense and wine before the imperial statue and venerate the emperor. Furthermore, Pliny wrote he had "ordered the accused 'to curse Christ' – none of which acts . . . those who are really Christians can be forced into performing." Trajan's response to Pliny was that Pliny should not search out Christians, but if Christians were denounced as traitors for their failure to confess allegiance to the state, and this was proven to be true, "they were to be given the chance of repentance and recantation, 'that is, by worshiping our gods'. . . they were not to be sought out."[38] In spite of this apparently lenient decision by Trajan, open denial of "Caesar as Lord," and the contrary confession "Christ is Lord," continued to be unacceptable to the Roman mind, and thus an offence punishable by death.

The poignant tradition surrounding the martyrdom of the aged Bishop Polycarp of Smyrna (ca. 155) within sixty years of the writing of Revelation, recorded so movingly by Eusebius in his *Ecclesiastical History*, documents both the Roman provincial and Jewish Synagogue opposition to Christians.

It is apparent from the tone of Revelation that the Roman Christian situation in Asia toward the close of the century was deteriorating rapidly. A violent period of Roman opposition and persecution was both inevitable and imminent. God was consequently warning the churches of a serious challenge to their faith. The message of Revelation, therefore, calls the church to an uncompromising and radical faith in Jesus as Lord. Revelation warns against venerating the person of the emperor as deity, even if this denial resulted in their death as martyrs.

THE SOCIO-RELIGIOUS AND POLITICAL ENVIRONMENT OF THE CHURCH IN ASIA AT THE CLOSE OF THE FIRST CENTURY

There is a tendency in Revelation studies to focus almost exclusive attention on the rising clash between the Roman imperial cult and Christianity toward the close of the first century. Alongside this problem were several other socio-religious issues. Yarbro Collins and Kenneth Cukrowski have both drawn attention to this. Collins identifies these issues as "conflict with the Jews," "mutual apathy toward neighboring Gentiles," "conflict over wealth," and the "general social unrest in Asia," in addition to "precarious relations with Rome."[39] Cukrowski along similar lines concludes: "In general, the threat of death because of the emperor cult seems *overestimated*, while the influence of the emperor cult on the daily life of early Christians is *underestimated*."[40]

ISSUES ADDRESSED IN THE BOOK OF REVELATION

Our brief survey of both the Roman political and secular history and the religious history of Christianity in Asia Minor at the time of writing Revelation reveals that the church in Asia Minor was about to enter a difficult time of opposition from its pagan cultural and Roman political environment, as well as a burgeoning alienation from the synagogue and its Jewish heritage. Brooding clouds of suffering, persecution, and oppression were developing and moving into view. With this in mind, God warned the church through his prophet John that certain crises were about to break in on the church. God was

encouraging them to heed carefully the warnings of John's prophetic writing. The imminence and significance of these crises, and God's warnings in the message of Revelation,
we will develop in detail in the commentary on 1:1–3.

How Did John Choose to Convey God's Message to the Churches in Asia, and How Should We Hear it Today?

We began this portion of our study by stressing the obvious: the literary style (genre or
idiom) of Revelation is indeed strange to the modern Western mind and vastly different
from the remainder of the New Testament. As a result this great resource of Christian faith
is often overlooked in the teaching program of the church because of its "strangeness" and
"remoteness." This is unfortunate since the message of Revelation, although set in the
context of the struggles of the church under Rome in the closing years of the first century,
is both timely and relevant for Christians living today in a post-modern secular world.

The strangeness of the literary style and idiom of Revelation often prompts
Christians to ask questions like, "How does this ancient book speak to us across two
thousand years and across cultures vastly different from ours today?" and "How relevant
can an ancient book be to an age two thousand years removed from its original setting?"[41]

Although Christians in the twenty-first century should be more sensitive to figurative or symbolic language, this has not always been the case. The recent popularity of
Tolkien's *Lord of the Rings* trilogy and C. S. Lewis' *Chronicles of Narnia*[42] have stimulated
interest in this type of literary experience. In opposition to this, the tendency of some
entrenched conservative or fundamentalist Christians has been to miss the significance
and power of the rich symbolism of Revelation and to over literalize its language. For
some, it is as though figurative or symbolic language is appropriate for secular thought,
but not for conveying spiritual truth.[43]

Revelation stands deeply imbedded in a Jewish Christian literary tradition that had
surfaced whenever the Jews or Christians were faced with suffering and oppression.[44]
Modern scholars refer to the apocalyptic literary genre adopted by John in conveying
this unique message of triumph over suffering, opposition, and persecution as prophetic
apocalypticism. We will notice below that this genre or tradition is characterized by an
extreme form of symbolic, figurative, and dramatic idiom, and that it projects its message onto a timeless cosmic stage, not in the form of an historical narrative. Failure to
understand this figurative and mythological genre, and to type its genre as an historical
narrative to be interpreted literally removes its theological impact from its literary and
theological context.

Revelation is to the modern Western mind a unique literary genre, a highly impressionistic nonliteral symbolic means of communication, significantly distinct from the
remaining New Testament documents. Revelation, nevertheless, stands within a Jewish
and Christian literary tradition with which the church in the first century was very familiar. Revelation must therefore be interpreted within that Jewish-Christian tradition and
not within sensational contemporary end-of-the-world interests. When Revelation is

interpreted within contemporary sensationalized concerns it becomes isolated from its unique theological tradition, as well as from its original historical setting.

Unfortunately the unique apocalyptic genre of Revelation is neither understood nor appreciated by modern societies of North America and much of Western Europe that have not experienced firsthand cultural or political oppression and social rejection. Jews living in Europe, Africans living under Apartheid South Africa, and African Americans living in the United States have as minority oppressed peoples understood this and have produced apocalyptic forms of expression in songs, poetry, and literature. The language of apocalyptic is the language of the oppressed, not of the powerful or the oppressor. That the apocalyptic genre was understood by John's audience is obvious since both Judaism and Christianity were at the time minority and somewhat oppressed cultures with a rich heritage of apocalyptic literature. Furthermore, it must have been readily understood by the church in Asia in the first century since John chose to address the church in that genre. The literary genre of apocalyptic had its roots in the era of 200 B.C. to A.D. 200 when first the Jews were oppressed by their Seleucid and later by their Roman overlords. The same situation was later encountered by Christians, who along with the Jews were oppressed "minority" cultures. This fact makes it difficult for those living today in a Western "majority" culture to appreciate the genius of apocalyptic. Failure to apply a cross cultural hermeneutic that transcends the gulf between the oppressed and the oppressor will result in frustration for most Americans and Western Europeans over the mysterious idiom of apocalyptic. Because of this, radical, sensational interpretations of Revelation removed from the oppressive historical setting of the churches in Asia tend to overlook the powerful dynamic of apocalyptic.

Several elements surface when we explore the question, how does Revelation communicate its message to us today? We now turn briefly to these.

First, as we have already seen, Revelation is written within and to a specific historical and social context, addressing a specific theological or religious problem, and using a unique literary style.

Second, the apocalyptic literary genre adopted by John provides a meaningful vehicle by which the message of Revelation is powerfully conveyed. Understanding the genius of the apocalyptic literary genre assists one in determining the theological message of the text. We are assisted in the study of this genre by examining texts of a similar literary form within the biblical canon and in the extra-canonical apocalyptic literature.[45] An impressive and extensive library of this extra-biblical literature has become available to biblical scholars providing striking new research opportunities.

Third, the internal *structure* of the text itself also clarifies or reinforces this process of determining the theological intention or message of the text. Biblical writers adopted a variety of literary structures and formulae in shaping their texts in a form that would express powerfully the theological intent of their writing. More will be said in the context of our exposition of the use of the chiastic structure and use of formula statements which John uses effectively in presenting his message.[46]

Fourth, John's prophetic apocalyptic style points to a pessimistic-optimistic dichotomy that frames his theological message. What we have learned from a literary analysis of the apocalyptic genre reveals a theological message pessimistic about history but optimistic about God's divine intervention in history in behalf of his people. The function of this dichotomy is that it calls for an uncompromising faith in God's *Heilsgeschichte*, or plan of salvation.

Careful analysis of the text of Revelation reveals that John considers his writing to be part of the biblical prophetic tradition. John does not refer to Revelation as an apocalyptic work, but it soon becomes apparent to the discerning reader that it is a prophetic work rich in the apocalyptic tradition. The apocalyptic tradition is evidenced by the titles of certain commentaries as in Isbon T. Beckwith's commentary on Revelation, *The Apocalypse of John* (1919), and Yarbro Collins, *The Apocalypse* (1979). It has thus traditionally been the practice of some scholars to refer to Revelation as an Apocalypse.[47] Revelation is apocalyptic in the sense that its hope lies not in man's ability to change his circumstances, but solely in God's power to deliver. It is prophetic in that it announces a crisis that is shortly to break in fully on the churches (cf 1:1-3).

Unlike the popular historical narrative with which Western readers are familiar, Revelation is a highly symbolic and impressionistic drama.[48] John couches his message in cosmic visions, and incorporates images drawn from a rich Jewish literary heritage which are not readily familiar to the modern Western reader. Contrary to popular literalist or fundamentalist traditions, Revelation was not intended to be interpreted literally. Revelation's literary style "paints kaleidoscopic impressionistic" pictures by drawing on and combining familiar Old Testament images and resetting them in a new apocalyptic context. Through this symbolic impressionism (which is common to the poetic tradition) Revelation conveys its message in a dramatic visionary style. Revelation and apocalyptic share little with the modern historical narrative, especially in regard to history. Although apocalyptic literature is set in a historical context (as is Revelation), apocalyptic does not tell its story in historical constructs but in non-historical, symbolic constructs. Furthermore, Revelation and apocalyptic's visions are not intended to be sequential as in an historical narrative but a kaleidoscopic repetition of images in dramatic scenes, with each series of visions building on previous visions, all the while interlocked and developing a new theme in a "rebirth of images."[49] "Intertextuality is the use by one text of the words, ideas, or images of one or more other texts. Revelation recycles images and even quotations from Daniel, Isaiah, Ezekiel, and elsewhere, all the while creating something entirely new."[50] The rebirth of images or intertextuality becomes a common literary device in John's brilliant use of Old Testament words and images.

The Writing of Revelation

I have argued above that the apocalyptic *genre* of a text is as essential to understanding its message as is the discipline of historical criticism in determining the *historical context* of the text. *How* the writer has approached the socio-religious historical concerns of his community, and *how* he has sought to communicate the significance of those circumstances is of vital importance to understanding a text. One way of writing theology is to construct an historical narrative around events, as in Acts of the Apostles in which Luke has stressed the theological impact of the events in the narrative in an apologetic form. Another form of sacred literature already prevalent in Christian circles was the gospel in which the message was set in a broad historical framework whose interest was not simply chronology but theology. John could have adopted the familiar Christian epistolary style of Paul and others, but because of the unique message he was developing he parted with the familiar Christian epistolary form. Although Revelation does contain some striking epistolary similarities, the formal epistle does not provide an adequate vehicle for John's message. The familiar poetic genre of the Psalms was obviously readily available to John, and although he incorporated poetry in his message, his preferred medium was not poetry, as powerful as this style might be. Because of the nature of the problems addressed in Revelation, John chose to set his message in a well-recognized Jewish form of literary expression which we have identified as *apocalyptic eschatology*. As we consider this literary genre we must turn to the discipline of literary criticism and be aware of the vast library of literature upon which John draws.

JOHN'S USE OF LITERARY SOURCES IN REVELATION

Even a cursory analysis of John's literary style reveals his literary genius. Revelation is a superb piece of creative theological writing. Not only does John have a stunning message to proclaim, but he proclaims it in a dynamic and striking manner. As he drew on a vast resource of images and literary expressions that would be clearly understood by his readers, he blended them together as a skilled author into a series of new impressionistic visions and images. John dipped his theological paint brush into his vast literary palette and painted a series of visionary images depicting the cosmic struggle between Satan and his agents (Rome) and God and his agents (the church). The images and colors that John used to paint his picture were drawn from a deep and well-known Jewish literary tradition. It is this Jewish literary tradition, and John's use of it, that we now briefly explore.[51]

The Old Testament

A careful reading of Revelation discloses a wide range of references to the Old Testament. Scholars differ on how many times John returns to the Old Testament for his literary images, but counts range from four hundred to a thousand times. In twenty-two chapters and 406 verses there are at least four hundred Old Testament citations or allusions. That is at least one Old Testament reference for every verse in Revelation! What we encounter in Revelation is a stunning tapestry of Old Testament images and concepts.

A further intriguing fact is that John never quotes an Old Testament verse or expression precisely. He refers to the Old Testament, uses its images and thought, but does not quote directly from it. His style in using the Old Testament is, however, in keeping with some Jewish traditions.[52] We will notice below that John uses his images in a variety of different stylish, analogous, and impressionistic ways.

John's use of the Old Testament in Revelation bears close similarity to what is commonly known as a *midrashic* or *pesher* style in which the writer draws parallel or analogous theological messages from an Old Testament text and applies them to the new setting he is addressing. In this the writer of the new text often states that what he is addressing is a fulfillment of an Old Testament text. The fulfillment could be an historical time line fulfillment or an analogous theological fulfillment. We find this to be a strategic hermeneutic key to Matthew's Gospel, where R. H. Gundry has demonstrated this in regard to several fulfillment passages.[53] Gundry argues convincingly that the term fulfillment can have several uses, which we will shortly discuss.[54]

In good *midrashic* style, John often refers to an Old Testament situation or person, knowing that his readers would be familiar with what was going on in the Old Testament. He then makes a comparative point or theological statement drawn from his Old Testament citation. On several occasions, John refers to the plagues of Moses in Egypt. What he is doing is making a parallel theological statement from his Old Testament reference. We might say that John's use of the Old Testament is intended to conjure up theological allusions or points which he wishes to drive home in Revelation. When John cites an Old Testament passage or prophetic piece, he is not making the reference in Revelation a historical or temporal fulfillment of the Old Testament prophesy, but one which has parallel theological implications.

A common mistake made by futurists adopting a literalist interpretation of the Old Testament, as in Dispensational views, is seeing the connection between the Old Testament and Revelation as a normal historical time line fulfillment rather than as a *midrashic, analogous, theological fulfillment* or application of the Old Testament reference or citation to a new analogous or parallel situation.

I agree with Beale, Gundry, and many scholars that John uses the Old Testament stylistically. His references do not conform well either to the Hebrew text or the Septuagint (LXX, the Greek translation of the Hebrew Old Testament that was the common Old Testament version used by the writers of the New Testament). For example, it seems most likely that John has in some instances translated the Hebrew to maintain contact with the Hebrew idiom but not to be in direct agreement with the LXX. For this reason some have claimed that the Greek in Revelation is vulgar Greek or at least Greek that uses "barbarous idiom."[55] The issue is that John, in translating some Hebrew phrases, maintained the Hebrew idiom and vulgarized the Greek in the process. This practice, however, was not uncommon, being similar in approach to the Aramaic translations of the Targums and in keeping with Midrashic practices. What I perceive in Revelation is John's theological use of the Old Testament, not an inferior knowledge of the Greek language or a literal view of the connection of some Old and New Testament references.

Such use of Old Testament images in new ways was common in most apocalyptic and pseudepigraphical literature, though to unaccustomed eyes it may appear that the writer is not using the sacred text faithfully. Readers of this literary tradition would not be disturbed by this practice, knowing full well what the writer was doing.[56]

John's use of the Old Testament is more typological or thematic than temporal fulfillment. One might say that John makes allusions to the Old Testament and draws on its images and idiom as he paints impressionistic paintings for dramatic effect. Caird refers to John's stylistic use of his sources as manifesting a "brilliant lucidity and compelling power."[57] Beale summarizes John's use of fulfillment statements in Revelation under several categories which he describes as literary prototypes. These prototypes he identifies as thematic, analogical, indirect, universalization, inverted, and stylistic.[58] We might add a typological prototype to Beale's list. I conclude with the suggestion that the Old Testament forms a rich idiomatic or typological palette from which John drew as he painted powerful new dramatic visions that convey many of the meanings found in the Old Testament narratives in a new theological context.

Although John's use of the Old Testament is broad, he favored Psalms, Isaiah, Jeremiah, Ezekiel, Daniel, Joel, and Zechariah. Scholars are divided in their opinion as to whether Ezekiel or Daniel predominates. Both, along with the Psalms, form a major background to John's theological use of the Old Testament.

Three texts in particular should become familiar to the student of Revelation. They are Psalm 2, Ezekiel 1:1-3:3, and Daniel 7. John returned repeatedly to the images of these three texts as he wove them into a powerful message of victory for the saints in the first century. The student of Revelation must become familiar with the theological message of these three texts, for they feature prominently in the theological message and imagery of Revelation.

The New Testament

Interestingly, John does not make significant use of the New Testament as a literary source. This should not surprise us since the literary style and purpose of the other New Testament books is significantly different from Revelation. Some sections of the New Testament are similar in style to Revelation, drawing on apocalyptic genre, but the major literary style of most of the New Testament is vastly different form Revelation. Among the New Testament sections that draw on the apocalyptic genre are Matthew 23–25, Mark 13, Romans 1:18–32 and 8:18–39, and 1 and 2 Thessalonians. It is obvious that the New Testament has many references to impending persecution, and that Käsemann is not far from the point when he observes that apocalyptic was "the mother of all Christian theology."[59] In agreement with Käsemann, D. N. Freedman observes that "the controlling factor in the literature of the New Testament is apocalyptic."[60] One will naturally find woven throughout Revelation many of the major Christian theological images such as the death, burial, and resurrection of Jesus, and the description of Jesus as the Lamb of God; but as a source John makes minor use of the remaining books of the New Testament. We should note, however, that the Christian literary corpus was not yet fully developed when Revelation was penned.

The Apocrypha, Pseudepigrapha, and Apocalyptic Tradition

Without some awareness and understanding of the apocryphal, pseudepigraphical, and apocalyptic traditions and literary resources the student of Revelation is severely handicapped. This would not have been a problem for Christians living in the first century, for they would have been well acquainted with these writings since they were the religious writings of their day. The apocryphal, pseudepigraphical, and apocalyptic literature were a mixture of Jewish and Christian writings, most of which were produced under conditions of persecution and trials very similar to those about to be faced by the churches in Asia to whom Revelation was addressed. It was only natural that John would draw heavily from these resources since they spoke in the language of suffering and persecution that would be meaningful to those facing similar trials. (See the glossary for a list of apocryphal writings.)

Literary Criticism

Although we will lean heavily on the discipline of literary criticism in our exploration of the message of Revelation, the Christian perspective is that John was operating under the empowering guidance of the Holy Spirit.[61] John's "inspired" instructions were to write a book in the form of an urgent and dramatic "letter" to be delivered to the church in the Roman province of Asia. The doctrine of inspiration is certainly a key factor underlying the Judeo-Christian view of Scripture, and essentially that of Revelation. It was also a characteristic of many apocalyptic seers that their visions were the result of divine inspiration.

Of vital importance to the message of Revelation is the understanding that its message originated in the mind and purpose of God, who through angelic beings revealed to John certain crises that would shortly occur in the experience of the churches in Asia. Under the inspiration of the Holy Spirit, John was empowered to see these things in a series of dramatic visions and to record these visions and their interpretation accurately, meaningfully, and in a trustworthy manner. Notice these comments relating to the inspiration of Revelation from the opening and closing verses of Revelation:

> The Revelation of Jesus Christ, which God gave him to show to his servants what must soon take place; he made it known by sending his angel to his servant John, who bore witness to the word of God and to the testimony of Jesus Christ, even to all that he saw. . . ." (1:1–2)
> He who was seated on the throne said, "Write this down, for these words are trustworthy and true." (21:5)[62]

I must stress, however, that claims to inspiration do not negate individual creative style and vocabulary nor the sources the "inspired" writer chose to draw on to illustrate his message. Any writer functioning under the empowerment of the Holy Spirit, however this was understood, was still free to adopt his own literary form of expression, resources, and vocabulary.

As John wrote his inspired message to the churches and recorded his visionary experience, profusely illustrated with references to Old Testament persons and events and a supporting library of Jewish religious symbols, we immediately become aware John's remarkable literary acumen. The dramatic style of Revelation indicates an author of rare ability and creativity, even literary genius. Bauckham observes that "The Apocalypse of John is a work of immense learning, astonishingly meticulous literary artistry, remarkable creative imagination, radical political critique, and profound theology." He adds, "The book of Revelation is an extraordinary complex literary composition" and in a footnote to this comment observes: "The more Revelation is studied in detail, the more clear it becomes that it is not simply a literary unity, but actually one of the most unified works in the New Testament."[63] Revelation is not simply a religious work, but is an astonishing piece of literary creativity by an author writing out of the depths of human crises and experience. We cannot overstate the view that Revelation is a strikingly brilliant, stylistically complex theological and literary achievement by an author of unique sensitivity and giftedness.

The careful student of Revelation soon becomes aware of John's brilliant blending of the clear historical crises faced by the church, his revelatory empowerment by the Holy Spirit, the profoundly religious principles he espouses, and the literary genre upon which he leans. The synergistic skill he exhibits as he blends together his rich palette of resources into one of the theological masterpieces of the Bible is nothing short of stunning.

Writing in the visionary literary genre of prophetic apocalypticism, John places the impending historical crises faced by the churches in Asia in the context of a gripping war between the saints of heaven and the powers of this world. Yarbro Collins identifies John's style in Revelation as "combat language" or "combat mythology,"[64] while Bauckham speaks of "The Apocalypse as a Christian War Scroll."[65] The climactic message of this drama is that the saints, shortly to be involved in a brutal and seemingly impossible struggle with Rome, Satan, and other worldly powers, will through Jesus triumphantly overcome the awful traumas and sufferings of the demonic powers of this world that at times seem to be beyond human resolution. The message of Revelation conveyed by the well-known literary genre of apocalyptic is one of divine victory through Christ.

The language of this cosmic "combat mythology" becomes a key ingredient to the literary style adopted by John. Illustrative of this are the passages in Revelation 12:7–12, already cited above, in which a war arose in heaven between Michael and his angels and the dragon (Satan) and his angels. John also describes a "beast" that is "allowed to make war on the saints and to conquer them" (16:12—16). Again, John will speak of a battle at Mount Megiddo (Armageddon –Anglicized from *Har Megiddo*, the Hebrew for the Mount of Megiddo). Finally, John predicts the resurgence of evil among the nations of Gog and Magog as they surround the camp of the saints before being finally defeated (20:7–10). War imagery permeates the book, but the war imagery, although describing a real war in which the saints are engaged, is "mythological" in the sense that it is described in cosmic imagery. In striking parallel to this concept of a war between the righteous and the forces of evil, the Qumran Covenanters of Dead Sea Scroll renown treasured a document which we now know as *The War Scroll* (1QM, 4QM).

John paints a magnificent picture of God in all his glory reigning in his kingdom through Jesus, the Lamb. God has raised this sacrificial Lamb from the dead to reign as king in his glorious, eternal kingdom. All who are willing to die for their faith in God's crowning victory in the Lamb will through their martyrdom share fully in the Lamb's victory and reign. They will be "more than conquerors through him who loved us" (Rom. 8:37). The study of Revelation, therefore, demands a careful analysis of this "combat mythological"[66] literary style in order to understand the message which to us seems beyond understanding, yet to John's readers in the first century was profoundly enriching and encouraging. Yarbro Collins sums this up well:

> It must be clear by now that I regard careful attention to the original historical context as the essential foundation of the interpretation of any text. Such attention is especially important for the book of Revelation. . . . Although I believe that the historical methods are essential, I do not think that they are fully adequate to the task of exploring the mystery of the meaning of the text. . . .
>
> The book of Revelation is not only an artifact of a specific place and time, a historical document; it is also a literary creation, a work of great artistic beauty and power. As aesthetic literary critics and philosophers have reminded us so often, a great work of literary art has a dynamic union of form and content. The content or message is best grasped in and through the form. Thus the historical approach must be complimented also by literary sensitivity and by aesthetic literary-critical methods.[67]

REVELATION IS A PROPHETIC APOCALYPTIC DRAMA

On several occasions above I have mentioned that John expressed himself in a highly dramatic fashion, using symbols drawn from the Old Testament and a vast library of Jewish images. The setting of John's visions in a cosmic dimension reinforces that we are reading a cosmic drama played out on a vast heavenly set, and not an historical narrative. It is essential, therefore, that the message be understood and interpreted in the context of a play or drama acted out on this cosmic stage. This drama is arranged in two major acts with several sub-sets within each act. Revelation is not a gospel, an epistle, or a historical narrative, but a spectacular "theatrical" presentation in the form of a cosmic drama incorporating a number of literary forms.

Apocalypse or Apocalyptic

The influence of this unique literary genre of apocalyptic on Revelation has occasioned considerable focus in scholarly journals and publications on the nature and impact of apocalyptic on Revelation. Substantial attention has been devoted to the whole corpus of biblically related writings falling within this field.[68] From these studies it is apparent from the many apocalyptic images and expressions in Revelation that John's work should be considered primarily within the literary horizons of apocalyptic. As a literary stylist, John drew heavily on the dramatic impact and theology of the apocalyptic genre as he weaved his interesting and challenging work.

Several striking claims regarding apocalyptic heighten the importance of understanding this genre. Ernst Käsemann observed that "Apocalyptic . . . was the mother of all Christian theology."[69] R. H. Charles, the great English scholar of apocalyptic, pseudepigrapha, and apocrypha, observed in similar vein that apocalyptic is "the parent of Christianity."[70] D. N. Freedman maintained that apocalyptic was "the controlling factor in the literature of the New Testament."[71] Although these views may tend to overstatement, they do emphasize the significance of this genre for New Testament studies in general, and in particular for Revelation. Leon Morris has observed that "It is plain that apocalyptic ideas were more widely held in New Testament times than has always been realized."[72]

So what exactly is apocalyptic? What do its strange images and idiom mean? And how does it relate to the Christian message? Furthermore, how does it convey its message? A thoughtful answer to these questions is crucial to understanding Revelation. Unless one is able to stand in the shoes of the apocalyptist, one will not be able to fully understand Revelation—or if Käsemann and others are even remotely accurate, even the New Testament.

The Term Apocalyptic

The term *apocalyptic*, although readily adopted in studies of Revelation, is not itself without problems. A number of scholars question whether the term has real meaning or relevance. Chief among them is Klaus Koch who argues that he comes away from the term "confused," "perplexed," and "embarrassed."[73] John Collins responds that one reason for the reaction against apocalyptic is that "Theologians with a more rational bent are often reluctant to admit that such material played a formative role in early Christianity. There is consequently a prejudice against the apocalyptic literature which is deeply ingrained in biblical scholarship."[74] Although scholars influenced by Koch have attempted to do away with the term, its unique character and powerful influence on the thought of generations has entrenched it as a durable literary category, especially in the realm of Revelation studies.

The English term apocalyptic is primarily derived from the Greek word, *apokalupsis*, meaning "a discovery, a disclosure, an uncovering, a revelation." It is, however, more appropriately understood as an adjective describing some noun, for example, as in "apocalyptic literature." Due to common use, the adjective has become a noun describing a particular genre of communication most often encountered in the form of literature, or a manner of conceptualizing and describing a unique worldview. Questions are raised as to whether it should be understood as describing a manner of speaking, a literary genre (apocalyptic literature), an interpretation of history (apocalyptic or eschatological history), a description of a reactionary social movement, or simply as a way of thinking.[75] Perhaps it is best to understand the term *apocalyptic* in reference to a mindset or a way of interpreting the destiny of the world which expresses itself dramatically in a literary form. Minear argues that it certainly was the manner of thinking "of virtually all members of the first generation church." Developing this thought further, Minear contends that Christianity was a movement whose root system was deeply imbedded in apocalyptic thinking.[76]

Apocalyptic in scholarly biblical terms most often has reference to the literary genre developed by Jewish or Christian communities of believers facing seemingly insurmountable faith crises. This genre thrived early among Jews under the Seleucid and Roman occupation of Judea and the Mediterranean world, and later among Christians in the first two hundred years of church history. It is commonly held that the apocalyptic genre reached its zenith between the years 200 B. C. and 200 A. D. Many scholars find early roots of apocalyptic thinking among the Babylonian dualistic cultures. The church of the first century, although it had much to celebrate in the grace of God and the power of the cross, found itself as Jesus had predicted in an increasingly hostile world (Matt. 10:24-31). Offering the peace of God, Christianity had taken root in an unfriendly and antagonistic world in which peace was often only a remote hope. Some theological explanation for the existence of evil in a world that believers held was created and controlled by an omnipotent God had to be found. This explanation lay in the dualism of the apocalyptic genre which predicted the final overcoming of evil by a supreme God.

The first crisis the emerging church had to face was the opposition of Judaism. Jesus had himself been rejected by his own people mostly because he had run contrary to the messianic plans of the Jewish leaders (John1:11). He had prophesied that his disciples would meet similar opposition (Matt. 10:24, 25): "A disciple is not above his teacher. . . . If they have called the master of the house Beelzebul, how much more will they malign those of his household." As predicted, almost immediately after the establishment of the church, the disciples faced fierce resistance from the Jewish rulers and elders. In short order Stephen was stoned as a martyr "and on that day a great persecution arose against the church in Jerusalem" (Acts 7:54–8:2). Saul of Tarsus, "breathing threats and murder against the disciples of the Lord," received authority from the high priest to persecute the church as far afield as Damascus (Acts 9:1). It is ironic that the first major opposition to the fulfillment of God's saving plan should come from within his own people.

The pagan world, however, was not far behind Judaism in its hostility toward God's saving activity. Although there was no immediate, formalized Roman persecution of the church, it was not long before Christians were confronted by an increasingly hostile pagan and Roman world. Acts records how in city after city local civic leaders for one reason or another turned on Paul and the early Christian missionaries. Typical of this was the uproar in Philippi where Paul was imprisoned under the false charge that he advocated "customs which were not lawful for Romans to accept or practice" (Acts 16:21), and at Ephesus Demetrius the silversmith saw in Paul a threat to the local pagan deity, Artemis, and the lucrative business surrounding the temple of Artemis (Acts 19:23).[77]

Minear summed this up well by describing the tensions that developed between the early church and its alien pagan environment. He observed: "To understand the complexity of this situation, we must recall the continuing tensions between the church and the world of that time. The origin of these tensions is given, once for all, in the crucifixion of Jesus by the political and religious authorities of his day."[78] The crucifixion of Jesus brought to the front the extreme nature of the tension that was developing between the disciples of Jesus and the Jewish and Roman world. Looking at the events of the cross from a sociological perspective, one glimpses clearly the extent to which the Jewish and Roman mind would go in order to maintain their delicate political balance.

It is difficult today for Christians living in a Western world that stands securely within a history of several centuries of Christian culture to visualize a situation in which Christians faced such open hostility. Perhaps the recent experience of Christian missionaries facing Muslim opposition in regions where Islam is the predominant religion helps us understand the dilemma faced by the early church. Western Christians today, whether in a postmodern, secular society or not, are accustomed to living in communities in which the Christian faith forms the majority culture. Christians are surrounded by the objects of their faith; large centralized cathedrals and places of Christian worship in almost every community. For example, in my home town in South Africa, the main street is called Church Street, and a secondary main street is Chapel Street. Likewise, large church squares dominate the center of most European and Latin American cities, and even in a society that has struggled for seventy years under communistic atheism, the Russian culture is still dominated by Russian Orthodox cathedrals and monasteries which have been central to the Russian psyche for over a thousand years.

In contrast to this, first-century Christianity was looked upon as a minority subgroup or "aberrant" community that was marginal to the mainstream of society. In some situations Christians were accused of the vilest crimes and incest due to the intense fellowship expressed in the Christian love feasts. It is vital to our understanding of the *raison d'être* of Revelation that we grasp that Christianity sprang to life and spread in an environment of community hostility and political mistrust which often rapidly declined into open opposition and persecution. Without this clear understanding one is unable to grasp the intensity of the call for radical discipleship and an uncompromising faith found in the New Testament, and specifically in Revelation. The crises encountered by the New Testament church, and hence the origin of much of its literature, lay in the nexus of severe social, political, and religious rejection which led in many instances to open conflict. This environment shaped the crisis confronting the first-century church as it struggled under Roman provincial rule, rejection by the Synagogue, and a pagan culture in which Christianity was looked upon with both suspicion and distaste.

Yarbro Collins makes much of this point. In her doctoral dissertation, later published under the title, *Combat Mythology in the Book of Revelation,* she discusses at length the significance of the crisis encountered by the church of the first century. Yarbro Collins supports the traditional view that Revelation was "written in response to the second major Roman persecution of Christians which was initiated by Domitian." However, in developing her point that the opposition encountered by the church at the close of the first century was not a formalized Roman legal persecution, she argues that the crisis was more sociological than political. Although not ruling out altogether the reality of a Roman persecution, Yarbro Collins suggests several other elements of crisis at the close of the first century that could be added to the cause for the writing of Revelation. She lists as examples of these elements the continuing conflict with the Jews (citing 2:9 and 3:9), the antipathy of the neighboring Gentiles, the conflict over wealth, and the general condition of social unrest in Asia and its precarious relations with Rome. Yarbro Collins thus finds ample reason for several crises behind the writing of Revelation, especially the severe social conflicts and trauma of Christians living in a hostile pagan society.[79]

This may be a reasonable appraisal of the situation in Asia, but John, seer or prophet, without overlooking these very real sociological factors, saw beyond the immediate traumas encountered by the church. He was privy to visions which spoke to him of a burgeoning official Roman opposition and persecution that was to become formalized in the next century. The language and tenor of Revelation indicate a crisis much deeper and more serious than mere social estrangement. The crises already experienced by the church in the first century were a prelude to what John saw breaking in and developing in the immediate future, hence the urgent call to faithfulness.

Within these fragile and threatening contexts, it was natural that John, in keeping with his Jewish tradition and mindset, would choose to set his message in the accepted genre of his day, an apocalyptic drama.

The Nature of John's Apocalyptic Genre

Traces of this apocalyptic expression can be found in Israel as early as the sixth century B. C. in Isaiah and Jeremiah. Subsequent to these great prophetic works a whole library of literature flowed out of the nexus of Jewish suffering and persecution into an apocalyptic and pseudepigraphical corpus or "library." The early Christian church, familiar with this corpus of apocalyptic literature, and facing similar sociological and political crises, naturally adopted this same form of apocalyptic expression to pour out their frustration and hope of a divine intervention. Much of the early Jewish apocalyptic literary can be found in the writings identified by modern scholarship as the Apocrypha and Pseudepigrapha.[80] George Nickelsburg's excellent study, *Jewish Literature Between the Bible and the Mishna* (2d ed., 2005) presents an historical survey of this literature, drawing attention to the apocalyptic strain in this library of Jewish and Christian deutero-canonical literature.

Although what we know of this unique phenomenon is found mostly in specific literary forms it is helpful to understand this concept as a specific mindset or worldview which was expressed in a literary form. Thus it is important to understand this form of expression as a mindset or worldview that took form in a literature of oppression and persecution. As a mindset and worldview it was extremely pessimistic about human effort and history, but ultimately optimistic concerning God's divine intervention in redeeming and vindicating his people.

Much scholarly research and discussion has in recent years been devoted to the roots of apocalyptic expression and its impact on modern culture. Apocalyptic works can be traced to ancient Greece and Rome, Persia (Babylon), Egypt, and Judaism.[81] Some have appropriately suggested that the Christian form of apocalyptic had its roots solely within the narrow world of prophetic Judaism.[82] Scholars now recognize, however, that apocalyptic was a readily recognized genre in an ancient world far wider than prophetic

Judaism, and that it is encountered in a variety of forms and categories. It is widely recognized today that Jewish apocalyptic traditions were in fact shaped by these Egyptian, Babylonian, and Greek traditions. Although apocalyptic had a broad ethnic heritage (as indicated above, Greek, Babylonian, Egyptian, Roman, etc.) it is now understood that Christian forms of apocalyptic drew most heavily on their Jewish roots, and that prophetic Judaism as well as the apocryphal and pseudepigraphical traditions had a profound impact on the apocalyptic tradition of the New Testament church.

Several characteristics are common within most Jewish and Christian apocalyptic works.[83] These characteristics include dramatic cosmic otherworldly visions, rich symbolism, worldly upheavals, fearsome beasts, angels, primordial events, an eschatological apocalyptic view of history, judgments, the triumph and wrath of God, pessimism as to the role of history, some form of prophetic futuristic reference, a sense of determinism, an adoption of some forms of Canaanite mythology, and in most cases, pseudonymity. Mystical experiences of "chariot" journeys into heaven and the throne room of God are common occurrence of the seer responsible for the apocalypse. An interesting view of dualism also runs throughout most apocalyptic thought. This dualism is not of an eternal dualism of two gods eternally opposed to one another, but of the admission of an evil demonic opposition to the will of God.

An additional word must be said regarding Jewish and Christian apocalyptic attitudes toward history. To put it simply, the apocalyptist was generally pessimistic about history and the human role in history. Solutions to sociological and political crises do not in the apocalyptist's mind lie within man's potential and the role of history. In some general apocalyptic works one encounters history rewritten to suit the situation. In the case of Jewish and Christian apocalyptic perspectives of history, we find a keen sense of human impotence and God's ultimate control of history. Although it seemed to some persecuted believers that their immediate world was under the control of Satan, the apocalyptic view of reality recognized the power of satanic forces but denied them any sense of ultimacy. For the apocalyptist the solution to the crises being encountered lay ultimately in God's hands, not in human effort, or the role in history. This divine solution, therefore, lies outside of history and beyond human control, hence the predilection for cosmic visions that exemplify the apocalyptic mindset. It is because of this that apocalyptic adopts a figurative, symbolic, mythological posture toward time and history.

Although apocalyptists were extremely pessimistic concerning the solution to their crises taking place in the normal development of history, they were, however, absolutely optimistic in regard to God's predetermined plan for history and the world, and his divine intervention in history. They were confident that God is in control of history; that God will use history for his purpose, and in the end judge history. Hence the apocalyptist has a keen sense of *Heilsgeschichte* (here simply understood as God's saving plan for and in history). The apocalyptist encouraged his hearers or readers to maintain their faith in God's plan, not to compromise their faith with the world, but to see the big picture of God's eternal plan rather than the immediate context of world history.

It is noteworthy that although apocalyptic effort is always located within a specific historical situation or crisis, apocalyptic does not express its solution to the crisis in historical constructs or historical narrative form. The genre of apocalyptic is not in the historical narrative tradition, but rather in the mythological legend or mystical tradition. The "story" of apocalyptic, therefore, is most often told in transcendent cosmic visions. To seek the interpretation of apocalyptic story in historical constructs will inevitably lead to confusion. To ask apocalyptic "when" questions is, therefore, to ask the wrong kind of question, for the solution to the crisis lies not in the "when" of history but in the "what" of God's transcendental power and activity. At the same time, to remove the crisis from a real historical context, and not to see the crisis in that historical context, would fail to do justice to the apocalyptic solution.

The "story" or heart of Jewish-Christian apocalyptic is that God will break into history transcendentally from beyond history to redeem history. This is uniquely exemplified in God's divine intervention in the birth, ministry, death, and resurrection of Jesus. The solution to the crisis is, therefore, not an historical solution, but of a divine intervention. In fact, the solution may not lie in this world or in history at all. This "unhistorical" dynamic is another way of illustrating the apocalyptist's pessimism toward history, or man's efforts in history. The non-historical dimension of apocalyptic stresses the absolute confidence the apocalyptist has that the solution can be found only in God's eschatological, transcendent plan for history.

With regard to history, time, and the dating of events, the apocalyptist either rewrites history to suit his transcendent special interests or seeks its solutions in the cosmic world which are removed from time. Apocalyptic is fundamentally unconcerned with fixing or dating historical events. Apocalyptic's interest is to project one's thinking from ones temporal horizons into transcendent images. Attempts to date the symbolic events described in apocalyptic constructs, or to determine future dates based on such, lies beyond the genius of apocalyptic. This is an extremely significant point when dealing with the apocalyptic genre, and one to which most futurist and dispensationalist interpretations give insufficient attention. It is imperative that one understand the character of apocalyptic "time" and "history" if one is to interpret it accurately.

A useful analogy in understanding this "history/time" or "when" element in apocalyptic and Revelation is to refer to a simple well known story such as the one which follows. "Once upon a time there was a little girl who dressed in a red raincoat and whose grandmother lived in a forest. This little girl went to visit her grandmother, but unfortunately there was also an evil wolf living in that forest. The wolf ate the grandmother. When the little girl got to grandmother's house, the wolf dressed as grandmother was in grandmother's bed. . . ."[84] We all know the story well. Its literary genre is a fairy tale. Several things point to this. First, it begins with "Once upon a time," one of the classic literary characteristics of a fairy tale. Second, wolves do not eat grandmothers and then dress up as grandmothers. We know from experience that fairy tales tell their story by drawing on symbolism, not through the form of historical narrative. No one asks "When did Little Red Riding Hood happen?" The "when" of Little Red Riding Hood is inconsequential. We know that to ask "when" questions would miss the point of the fairy tale. The correct question should be "What does the fairy tale mean?" My point in this simple illustration is not to claim that apocalyptic or Revelation are a fairy tale, but to demonstrate that different literary types (genre) bear within them their own characteristics and procedural questions. The wrong questions will result in the wrong answers which do an injustice to the literary genre. The correct approach to apocalyptic is to learn its literary genre, and therefore to understand its characteristics and procedural questions, especially in regard to time and history. Only when we have done this are we prepared to ask the correct kind of questions.

In his excellent work, *The Apocalyptic Imagination*, John Collins expresses the nature and characteristic of apocalyptic in broad terms, recognizing that there are a wide variety of types of apocalyptic within the genre. The serious student of Revelation will do well to read this fine definitive work. At the risk of simplifying this vast subject we include here a few observations by Collins that will be helpful in understanding comments that will be made in the commentary section of this book. Collins observes:

> The form of the apocalypse involves a narrative framework that describes the manner of revelation. The main means of revelation are visions and other-worldly journeys, supplemented by discourse or dialogue and occasionally by a heavenly book. The constant element is the presence of an angel who interprets the vision or serves as a guide on the otherworldly journey. This figure indicates that the revelation is not intelligible without supernatural aid. *It is out of this world*. In all the Jewish apocalypses the human recipient is a venerable figure from the distant past, whose name is used pseudonymously. This device adds to the remoteness and mystery of the revelation. The disposition of the seer before the revelation and his reaction to it typically emphasize the human helplessness in the face of the supernatural.
>
> The content of the apocalypse, as noted, involves both a temporal and a spatial dimension. . . . It would seem that there are two standards of Jewish apocalypses, one of which is characterized by visions, with an interest in the development of history, while the other is marked by otherworldly journeys with a stronger interest in cosmological speculation.[85]

Collins and his apocalyptic study group have developed the following working definition of apocalyptic. An apocalypse is

> a genre of revelatory literature with a narrative framework, in which a revelation is mediated by an otherworldly being to a human recipient, disclosing a transcendent reality which is both temporal, insofar as it envisages eschatological salvation, and spatial insofar as it involves another, supernatural world.[86]

The Theology of Apocalyptic

In one sense both apocalyptic and Revelation are theodicies, that is, a defense of the righteousness of God in the presence of the problem of evil. Furthermore, their theology intends to encourage their followers to seek the solution to their crises beyond history and human resolution, and to find it in the powerful eschatological intervention of God. Both the apocalyptist and the author of Revelation are deeply committed to the fact that God is in control of the universe, that he can and does use evil situations to achieve his purpose, and that in the end he will overcome, judge, and condemn evil. Apocalyptic and Revelation are, therefore, a response to the cry of crises, an encouragement against compromise with the world, and a call to keep faith. It is easy for the student of apocalyptic and Revelation to become so engrossed in and fascinated by the characteristics of apocalyptic and Revelation that one misses the powerful theology of apocalyptic and Revelation. It is precisely because of the theology of apocalyptic that John deliberately chose this genre as the vehicle for achieving his purpose of encouraging the saints of Asia to resist compromise and to keep faith in the God who is above and over history. The theology of Revelation can therefore be condensed into one small statement, "victory in Christ".

The Impact of Apocalyptic Thinking on Modern Culture

Although the apocalyptic genre we have been considering arose and was relevant within historical circumstances of the first century of the Christian era, apocalyptic has impacted both Christian and Western culture in a number of intriguing ways since the first century. On a number of occasions groups experiencing frustration with secular or religious cultures have taken consolation in the apocalyptic mindset and a search for a new world, or new heaven and new earth. Huguenots fleeing religious persecution in Europe in the sixteenth century sought a new world in Southern Africa and other regions. Europeans and English settlers immigrating to America in the seventeenth century were moving to new world. Later as they pressed westward in the seventeenth and eighteenth centuries they were again driven by an apocalyptic vision of new frontiers. The conviction that their future was a manifest destiny determined by God drove them on.

Religious Reformers in the decades following the Great Awakening in America in the eighteenth and early nineteenth centuries were motivated by a period of apocalyptic millennial excitement sometimes described as pre- or postmillennial. In the mid 1800s William Miller, founder of Seventh Day Adventism, and Joseph Smith, founder of the Church of Jesus Christ of Latter Day Saints (Mormons) were driven by apocalyptic hopes of a new world that would be separate from "corrupt" or "failed" mainstream Christianity in America. This hope caused them to press on to new frontiers of religious expression. Millerites adopted a premillennial stance, selling their possessions as they anticipated the arrival of the millennium in 1843. The Mormons under Joseph Smith sought their new world in Utah.

In more recent years several radical forms of millennial faith have been tragically driven by apocalyptic visions of new worlds. First, Jim Jones and his group of followers sought their new world in a mass suicide in Guyana, and then David Koresh led his Branch Davidians into a clash with government authorities and a tragic loss of life in Waco, Texas. One cannot escape noting the mistaken identification made by the Branch Davidians with the first-century Christians struggles with the beast, the political power of Rome.[87]

In his challenging book, *Reviving the Ancient Faith: The Story of Churches of Christ in America*,[88] Richard Hughes has argued that among Churches of Christ Barton W. Stone's apocalyptic focus on the kingdom offered an alternative to Alexander Campbell's postmillennial focus on the church in the nineteenth century, which difference, Hughes believes, contributed to two separate dynamics within what is known in some church circles as the Restoration Movement. These differences led ultimately in the 1930s and later to bitter clashes over pacifism and premillennialism. Hughes argues that David Lipscomb's political pacifism in the early twentieth century was motivated by an apocalyptic mindset in which Christians were encouraged to turn away from political "this world" concerns. Hughes also maintains that it was the fundamental difference between an "apocalyptic" and "rationalist" mindset that led to bitter attacks against premillennialism, David Lipscomb College, and Harding College in the early years of the twentieth century.

Although functioning with a different focus, and from within a different context than experienced in the first-century church in Asia, the apocalyptic mindset is still alive in certain levels of the contemporary American psyche. It is often manifest in a rejection of what it sees as extreme political intervention in religious life, or the failure of contemporary life to provide meaningful peace. The apocalyptist's other worldly focus stands in sharp contrast to the rationalist progressive mindset which is a comfortable house-guest of the concept of historical and human progress often found in the American culture. One finds this in some postmodern thinking which eschews the rationalism of modernity and manifests similar apocalyptic leanings. Nevertheless, it is apparent that those dissatisfied with their present situation and who are driven by a longing for a new world in which to find meaning are driven by some form of apocalyptic passion.

Eschatology[89] and Eschatological Language

We turn now to eschatology, a theological "cousin" to apocalyptic. We begin with the observation that whereas apocalyptic is a mindset regarding history, eschatology is a mindset regarding time. Whereas apocalyptic is negative regarding history, eschatology examines time according to a different mindset that does not define time chronologically.[90]

The following is a brief discussion of five aspects of eschatological thought. First, eschatology reflects a particular mindset, primarily Jewish,[91] regarding time. It emphasizes that time is linear, under the control of a sovereign God, has a beginning and an end, that God alone is responsible for both the beginning and the end, and at the end God will judge the world in righteousness. Eschatology focuses attention on the end time. For the Jewish Old Testament mindset at the end (the *eschaton*) God will judge the world in righteousness and restore his kingdom under his appointed Messiah. Eschatology understood in this manner sees time as the "place" where God has been working his divine plan for man, and that God's saving activity takes place in this time. Scholars call this awareness of God's saving activity in time *Heilsgeschichte*. The Christian understanding of eschatology fits into the Jewish mindset but focuses the end in the Christian age, understanding the Christian age to be the end of God's *Heilsgeschichte*. In this Christian view, God has established his kingdom (an inaugurated eschatology) under his Messiah and the end of the age, the *eschaton*, has broken into history in the person of the Messiah, Jesus.[92]

Second, eschatology reflects on matters involving the last days or the end of the world not as a point in time or the end of a space-time continuum, but as the climax of God's saving activity in time. The Jewish perspective identified the end or eschaton with the coming of a Messiah or the establishment of God's kingdom under His Messianic king. N. T. Wright correctly observes that "there is virtually no evidence that Jews were expecting the end of the space-time universe . . . they believed that *the present world order* would come to an end—the world order in which pagans held power, and Jews, the covenant people of god (*sic*), did not."[93] Wright argues persuasively that the Jews, including Jesus, Paul, and John used end of the world language as a metaphor indicating the severity of the action of God when judging Israel's and the church's enemies, or in Wright's terminology, the pagan world. Wright stresses that eschatology thus understood as a metaphor speaks of "the climax of Israel's history, involving events for which end-of-the-world language is the only set of metaphors to express the significance of what will happen, but resulting in a new and quite different phase within space-time history."[94] In this context the Christian perspective defines the end or eschaton as having begun (broken in, been inaugurated) with the coming of the Messiah and ending with the second coming (parousia) of the Messiah. Hence, the Christian perspective speaks of the end as an eschatological age rather than a point in time. In Jewish eschatological expectation the belief was that the Messiah would redeem Israel, set up his kingdom, and judge the wicked nations. This did not involve an end to time as we understand it, but rather a climax of God's redemptive purpose. The Christian understanding of inaugurated eschatology is that this process has already begun with the coming of the Messiah. He has brought redemption to Israel, set up his kingdom, and is already judging evil nations. The difference between futurist, premillennial, and dispensational eschatology and inaugurated eschatology is that futurists believe the Messiah has only brought redemption in the present, but will in the future set up his Messianic kingdom on earth and judge the evil nations. Inaugurated eschatology holds that the end, including the Messianic kingdom, has already broken into human history in the person of Jesus.

Third, although eschatology has reference to end of the world matters, eschatological language can be used in other contexts to imply that a specific event has end of the world implications or significance even far in advance of the final end. The implication is that a current or present event has end of the world or final climactic consequences. I will refer to this as a proleptic eschatological event or expectation.

Fourth, Christian eschatology interpreted the coming of the Messiah as the inauguration of the eschatological kingdom and salvation. Rejection of the Messiah carried in it end of the world climactic significance and consequences. Christians thus speak of an inaugurated eschatology in which the eschatological kingdom was inaugurated with the coming of the Messiah, with the church age being the inauguration of the kingdom age. The end (eschatological age) began with the coming of Jesus and will reach a climax when he returns (his *parousia*, second coming) at the final end of this age. With this in mind Peter could speak of the events of the day of Pentecost as occurring in the "last days" (Acts 2:17, Joel 2:28), and the writer of Hebrews can write of God speaking to us "in these last days through his Son" (Heb. 1:2).

Fifth, in Revelation, John draws heavily on this eschatological dynamic and language by stating that Jesus would come soon[95] on both the churches in Asia and Rome bringing imminent judgment. To demonstrate that this coming soon would have end time significance John describes such imminent comings of Jesus in eschatological or end of the world language. When John does this he is not speaking of the final end of the world judgment, but an imminent judgment in the life of the first century church and first century Rome that would have end of the world significance and consequences. This fits into the mindset of a proleptic eschatological mindset.[96]

In conclusion to this discussion, it is imperative that the reader of Revelation understands John's use of proleptic eschatological language, and that John and apocalyptists speak of the end of the age as a metaphor, not a point in time. A failure to do so results in forced futurist interpretations.

THE LITERARY AND COMPOSITIONAL STYLE OF REVELATION

The parabolic and mythological nature of the visions and scenes of Revelation obviously should not therefore be taken literally as one would in an historical narrative. The following is a broad description of the literary style of Revelation.

Dramatic

Many scholars have noted that Revelation is in the form of a drama set in two major Acts, Revelation 1–11, and Revelation 12–22.[97] The dramatic nature of Revelation with its many visions and scenes adds to this effect. Since, as we shall note in a later stage of this study, Revelation was intended to be *read aloud* to the congregation, John's dramatic style would add to the power of its impact on the audience.[98] Listening to Revelation read aloud leaves one with little doubt regarding its dramatic impact on those hearing this powerful message from God.[99] Several commentators have been so drawn to the dramatic element of Revelation that they have framed their commentaries around a dramatic composition. Among them the works of Michael Wilcock, *I Saw Heaven Opened*, and Calvin Miller, *The Finale*, in *The Singer Trilogy* are noteworthy.[100] I also find interesting parallels between Revelation and John D. W. Watts' commentary on Isaiah. Watts sees Isaiah in a visionary dramatic structure.[101]

Impressionistic

The dramatic impact of the many visions described by John is startling. Beasts coming out of the sea, dragons with seven heads, women riding on strange beasts, bottomless pits, and rivers turned to blood; all of these remarkable scenes were intended by John to create vivid impressions on a cosmic scale. Impressionistic art is intended to be viewed from a distance without detailed attention to the finer brush strokes. When one comes too close to impressionistic art it loses its impact. So it is with Revelation. It was intended to be read aloud and heard so that the visions could create dramatic scenes, and for the full impact of the story being told to strike the listener vividly and to sink into the mind. Although at times we will be drawn into the details, we should resist the temptation to read more into the visions than the impact they were intended to create on the listener.

Symbolic

The obvious symbolism of Revelation should encourage one to see it symbolically rather than as a literal historical narrative. Unfortunately, some commentators of a futurist or dispensational persuasion[102] tend to overlook this aspect of the book, and take the visions and scenes literally, attempting to project from the symbolism of numbers in Revelation a timetable for the future. All of the visions and numbers in Revelation are intended to be understood symbolically as metaphors to conjure up visions of what can be through faith in Jesus.

Figurative

One overlooks the figurative dynamic of Revelation with disastrous results. Much of the study of Revelation will hinge around understanding the origin and meaning of the many figures adopted by John in writing this great book. We have already noticed the importance of the Old Testament and the apocalyptic tradition for interpreting Revelation. The extra-biblical library of writings forms a wonderful resource for understanding how John uses the many figurative images of his resources in Revelation.

Summary

It is absolutely imperative that we stress the importance of understanding the dramatic, symbolic, figurative and impressionistic character of Revelation. Attempts to interpret Revelation literally will of necessity result in a distorted interpretation.

THE AUTHOR AND DATE OF WRITING

Some consensus has resulted concerning the date, and in most cases the conclusion regarding the author is that he was a respected Christian leader in Asia whose name was John. Few contemporary scholars are in agreement with the ancient church that the author was the Apostle John. However, Grant Osborne writes: "The problems of the authorship of Revelation are indeed formidable, for the author makes no explicit identification of himself with John the apostle . . . . . Yet there are good reasons for upholding the viability of Revelation as penned by the apostle John and for downplaying the differences between it and the Fourth Gospel. "[103] I must mention, however, that neither the conclusion concerning the precise date of writing nor that relating to the authorship is vital to understanding the message of Revelation.

The Dating of Revelation

Three dates are traditionally suggested for the writing of Revelation.[104] Discussion of these dates can be found in most Introductions to the New Testament, Bible dictionaries, and commentaries. We will not devote much space here to discussing these in detail, other than to mention them as matters of interest. Whichever date is favored, all three fall within the space of about forty-five years during the Roman reign over the Mediterranean world. The first date, that of Nero, does involve some disturbing implications for biblical interpretation, and is consequently not favored by modern scholarship for sound reasons.[105]

Nero

A past generation was of the opinion that the Roman and Jewish contexts of Revelation are best explained by a Neronean date (54–68), hence a date of approximately 59 was proposed for the writing of Revelation. Arguments for this early date include the rough literary and Greek style of Revelation, the view that the Temple in Jerusalem was still standing (11), the women sitting on the beast is identified as Jerusalem and Jewish opposition of Christianity, and some evidence claimed to be from the Syriac (*Peshitta*) version of Revelation. At one time it was believed that the *Peshitta* was an early Syriac version dating from approximately 125. The Peshitta states in its superscription that John was banished to Patmos by Nero. However, the Peshitta is now known to be a late 5th century revision of the Old Syriac Version. In fact, the Old Syriac Version did not even contain the book of Revelation since the Syrian churches at this early date did not accept the canonicity of Revelation.

One additional argument for the Neronean date surrounds the legendary Nero *redivivus* myth which will be discussed in due course in the commentary on the text. Suffice it for now to say that this myth held that Nero would return again to persecute the saints. The fact that a Nero *redivivus* myth circulated among the early church is assumed by some to be an argument in favor of the Neronean date. J W Roberts[106] who rejected the Neronean date observes regarding the Nero *redivivus* myth:"Actually the facts should be taken in just the opposite order. There is no proof that this legend, current after the death of Nero, was current during his life and during the time when he was persecuting the churches. Hence the theory actually supports the later date."[107] Roberts, who at one time favored the later Domitian date because it agreed more favorably with the historical circumstances faced by the churches in Asia under Roman persecution,[108] observed regarding the Jewish implications of the Neronean date: "The earlier dating is generally connected with the interpretation that the visions of Revelation, in part at least, picture the persecution of the church by the Jews and foretell the destruction of Jerusalem and the consequent downfall of the Jewish state."[109]

A Jewish persecution and identifying Babylon in Revelation as Jerusalem obviously has significant implications for interpreting Revelation. Shifting the enemy from Rome to Jerusalem and the Jews provides a significantly different sociological and religious flavor to Revelation. It is noteworthy, however, that the early church set the interpretation of Revelation in the later Roman context as opposed to the earlier Jerusalem setting.

Finally, identifying Babylon as Jerusalem because the Temple is measured in chapter 11 overlooks the fact that the Temple in Jerusalem was measured in Ezekiel even after

Jerusalem had fallen in Ezekiel's day. This tendency overlooks the symbolic nature of Revelation and interprets the text literally rather than figuratively.

Few contemporary scholars hold to the Neronean/Jerusalem view today since most of the arguments in favor of the Neronian date have been disputed or shown to be in error.

Vespasian

Working from an interpretation of 17:8–14, there are those who would date John's experience of the visions during the reign of Vespasian (69–79). The argument is that in this pericope we have internal evidence for the dating of the visionary experience. We will explore this in greater detail below in the commentary on this text. Suffice it to say at this point that the evidence is not as firm as some would have us believe, and that this view relies on speculation in regard to the emperors involved. In addition, this type of interpretation forces the exegetic and hermeneutic method beyond the apocalyptic literary genre of the text, and beyond the non-historical characteristics of Revelation, and toward viewing this pericope as a form of historical narrative.

In order to have Revelation written during the reign of Vespasian, one has to make several arbitrary decisions regarding the identification of the seven kings John refers to in 17:8 The first is that one has to decide that Augustus was the first Emperor, arbitrarily choosing Augustus over Julius Caesar contrary to several Roman historians such as Suetonius, Dio Chrysostom, and Josephus. Then one has to drop Galba, Otho, and Vitellius from the normal list of Emperors since they ruled for only a short time. Some have suggested that the visions were received during Vespasian's reign and only written down during the reign of Domitian. Others have proposed that they were written down during the reign of Vespasian and received by the church in Ephesus as per Irenaeus during the reign of Domitian.[110]

Caird raises serious questions in regard to this view, suggesting that by attempting to identify the specific number of emperors mentioned in 17:8 "we are looking for the wrong sort of solution."[111] John's choice of seven throughout the book has been symbolic or stylistic, not literal, not historical. Why in this case would John shift to a literal use of seven in favor of his characteristic symbolic application? Caird suggests that to attempt to date the visions from this text is to force the text beyond its purpose. Too many questions remain in regard to attempts to determine dates from this text, not withstanding that the nature of apocalyptic tends to deny historical precision. We are reminded that apocalyptic tends either to rewrite history or to use it symbolically.

Yarbro Collins and Elisabeth Schüssler Fiorenza conclude that theories of dating based of the seven kings of 17:8–14 are faced with insurmountable difficulties[112] and are capable of a number of different conclusions. Those interested in a more comprehensive examination of the problems encountered in this theory are encouraged to refer to Yarbro Collins' study of the proposed solutions to this conjecture. Fiorenza is in agreement with Yarbro Collins and observes, "scholars have not yet succeeded in decoding this information. They do not agree whether or not to begin with Caesar, Augustus, Caligula, or Nero."[113]

As noted above, some[114] have reasoned that possibly John saw the visions while on the Isle of Patmos. He then subsequently wrote the visions into his final work, Revelation, which work was received by the churches in Asia during the reign of Domitian. While this possibility cannot be denied it is felt that this approach is an attempt to satisfy the historical interests of some interpreters while flying in the face of the exegetical problems of interpreting apocalyptic genre in historical constructs.

Domitian

The traditional view for dating the writing of Revelation has been to favor a time during the reign of Domitian (89–96). Both internal and external evidence favor this date. Although some question the accuracy of Irenaeus's statements regarding the date, there is considerable support from second century writers in support of Irenaeus. Eusebius notes that Irenaeus (ca.150) observed that the "vision [the apocalypse] was seen not very long since, but almost in our day, toward the end of Domitian's reign" (*Adv. Haer.* 5. 30. 3). Clement of Rome (ca.95), Origen (ca.225), Victorinus (ca.303) and Eusebius (ca.300) are in agreement with Irenaeus regarding the Domitian date. The circumstances depicted in Revelation seem to fit best with those sociologic and religious crises that can be identified from historical sources describing the reign of Domitian. Yarbro Collins discusses this view in considerable detail and concludes:

> The strongest external evidence for the date of Revelation is the testimony of Irenaeus. He says that the Apocalypse was seen at the end of Domitian's reign. This comment refers to a date of 95 or 96 C.E. . . . Since there is no positive evidence for a later date, it seems best to consider Irenaeus' remark to support a date of 95 or 96 C.E.
> . . . No compelling reason exists to reject Irenaeus' testimony to the date. Ambiguous passages with relevance for the date can be interpreted plausibly against the background of Domitian's reign. That background provides a credible context for the book's content and function.[115]

This commentary is written under the conviction that Irenaeus was correct and that the best circumstances and date for interpreting Revelation are the reign of Domitian, 95–96.

Authorship

Setting the date for Revelation normally involves some discussion of the authorship of Revelation. The text of Revelation identifies the author as God's "servant John" (1:1), or simply, "I John, your brother. . . " (1:9). Several suggestions as to the identity of this person, John, have been made since the fourth century with no clear-cut argument being conclusive. In this commentary we will reserve the discussion of the authorship of Revelation until the comments on 1:1,4, where the text refers to the author simply as John. Whether Revelation was written by the Apostle John or another John who was prominent in the life of the church in Asia at the close of the first century matters little to the authority and power of Revelation. That Revelation was accepted into the canon as "apostolic," together with the character and importance of its Christian message, are sufficient arguments at this stage for discussion regarding the authority and power of Revelation without defining with precision the actual authorship.

INTERPRETING REVELATION[116]

Numerous approaches to Revelation have been adopted down through the centuries of biblical interpretation in attempts to unravel its "mysteries." Each of the approaches tends to shape or direct the theological context and purpose of Revelation, and eventually the interpretation of the text.[117]

For the sake of convenience these various methods will be surveyed under the following descriptive categories: chiliast, Montanist, Alexandrian, recapitulation, eschatological, continuous historical, futurist, millennial (including premillennial, postmillennial, and dispensational), preterist, philosophy of history, moderate preterist (or exegetical), and amillennial. Although this categorization serves the purposes of only a brief survey it should be pointed out that the categories chosen, although somewhat arbitrary, clearly cover much of the field of interpretive method in regard to Revelation studies. Considerable overlapping of methods is evident, and several scholars adopt some form of eclecticism.[118] Some methods of interpretation have been challenged and disappear for a while, and like Gog and Magog of chapter 20, they resurface again with remarkable resilience, but usually in some modified form. It is possible to consider some commentators on Revelation under several of the categories mentioned above, since they share common methodological characteristics. The following summary, then, is merely an attempt to identify various approaches to interpreting Revelation. We should bear in mind however that these categories also cut across denominational or church lines and that one can find several models of interpretation or persuasion within any one religious movement.

Chiliast Models

The term chiliast derives from the Greek *chilias* meaning "thousand." It is a term best reserved in Revelation studies for ancient second and third century views relating to the 1000 years of chapter 20. Justin Martyr (ca. 150), Irenaeus (ca. 180), Tertullian (ca. 200), and Melito of Sardis (ca. 180) were early proponents of chiliasm. Simply stated, chiliasm holds that Jesus will return to earth at the end of the age and establish his kingdom of a thousand years. Most, but not all chiliasts view this thousand-year reign as a literal reign on earth. There is some question as to whether the thousand years should be interpreted literally or symbolically, or whether it must be on earth or not. Since the prevailing biblical hermeneutic in the early years of Christian interpretation was overwhelmingly literalist in its method, chiliasm reflected this literalist approach to Scripture. Suffice it to say that even today literalist views of Scripture generally accept the church age as a form of the spiritual kingdom of Jesus on earth, albeit in an imperfect stage, but that the fulfilled kingdom age is yet future. Chiliast's held that Christ had overcome Satan on the cross, but it would only be after his *parousia* (return, or second coming) that Satan would be finally destroyed and the kingdom on earth fully established. The point to notice at this stage is that the chiliast often equated the church age with a form of the kingdom and reign of Christ, albeit one not yet the fulfilled kingdom on earth.

The historical context of most chiliast interpretations was one of the church struggling under persecution. Under these circumstances it can be understood why the chiliast believed that Christ was already reigning in his kingdom but not yet fully in an earthly kingdom. It was apparent that although Christ was reigning in his *spiritual* kingdom, many on earth do not acknowledge his sovereignty. It would therefore be necessary according to the chiliast view for Christ to return to earth to fully and finally establish his sovereignty and literally reign over all the earth.[119] (Cf. the diagram of chiliasm in the glossary.)

I conclude with the observation that the chiliast model is a form of futurist premillennial view in that it holds that Christ must return to earth before he can literally and fully establish his thousand-year reign and kingdom. We should, however, not be hasty as are some premillennialists (George Eldon Ladd for instance) to identify chiliasm with premillennialism, calling modern premillennialism historic premillennialism, indicating that premillennialism was the historic view of the second-century church.[120] There are similarities between chiliasm and premillennialism, but also notable differences. The major failure of the chiliast and all pre-millennial futurist views is their excessive literalist interpretation of Scripture in which all texts are treated on the same level, thus ignoring the nature of symbolism and allegory in the various literary forms of Scripture.

Montanist Interpretation

The Montanists were a "heretical" charismatic movement of the second century under the teaching of their founder, Montanus (ca. 150). Montanus claimed that the Holy Spirit empowered him to utter inspired oracles in the name of God. The Montanists taught that the heavenly Jerusalem would descend on the village of Pepuza in Phrygia (Turkey) within the lifetime of Montanus, establishing a literal thousand-year kingdom on earth. Montanists anticipated the inauguration of the millennial kingdom within their own lifetime. The Montanist view of the millennium was different from Chiliasm in that it predicted an imminent establishment of the kingdom in Phrygia rather than a future kingdom to be established in Jerusalem. Montanism was a major threat to mainstream Christianity and was strenuously opposed by the early church. Because the Montanists' radical millennial views were based in Revelation and were communicated through personal charismatic revelations and not through the normal apostolic tradition, mainstream orthodox churches not only rejected Montanism, but initially also the Montanists' primary millennial text, Revelation. The Montanist movement was so persuasive that even the great second century church leader and teacher, Irenaeus, became a devotee of Montanism. [121]

Alexandrian Allegoricalism

The ancient Chiliast model of interpretation was seriously challenged and in some sense negated by an early form of Alexandrian allegorical exegesis. The Christian application of this method seemingly originated in the Alexandrian church in Egypt in the late second and early third centuries. Origen (ca. 220), an aggressive opponent of Chiliasm, adapted a symbolic spiritualizing model of biblical interpretation rather than the literal method of some early Christian hermeneutics. He formulated his model of exegesis into a threefold hermeneutic in which he identified three levels of meaning in a text; the literal, the moral, and the spiritual. Origen held that since Scripture came by the inspiration of the Holy Spirit it held a deeper meaning than the superficial literal meaning. This model immediately posed a serious challenge to the literalist Chiliast model of interpretation. As a result of the erudition of Origen and the impact of the Alexandrian allegorical method the Chiliast millennial interpretation faded from the scene for a considerable time, only to resurface at certain points of church history when literalist models of interpretation returned to favor. The cycle of the literalist-allegorical (spiritualizing) tension continues to this day in the Dispensationalist-Amillennial debate.[122]

The fourth century Donatist leader and biblical interpreter, Tyconius, and the renowned church father, Augustine of Hippo, although opponents in the debate over church or ecclesiastical purity, both adopted a similar allegorizing "Origenistic" Alexandrian or "spiritualizing" model of biblical hermeneutic.[123] Athanasius, the bishop of Alexandria (ca. 350) also fell in line with this model of interpreting Scripture in his debates over the Arian views of the Trinity in which the Arians denied the eternal nature of the Son and Trinity. This Alexandrian mind-set raised serious questions for the literalist chiliast interpretation of Revelation leading to the temporary demise of this "premillennial" chiliast, literalist interpretation of Revelation.

Recapitulationist Models

Irenaeus in the early second century had used the term *recapitulatio* on several occasions in reference to certain literary features of Scripture. Irenaeus thus became the originator of a model of exegesis to be known in later years as the recapitulation theory. In regard to Revelation, however, it is the Donatist exegete Tyconius (ca. 370–390) to whom the honor was attributed of being the first to identify recapitulation as a characteristic of John's literary style.[124] Recapitulation has as a result through the centuries been recognized as a fundamental ingredient of John's literary structure and therefore a hermeneutic key to understanding Revelation. Recapitulation has reference to the fact that certain themes recur throughout Revelation in an unusual pattern. Tyconius, Victorinus of Pettau (ca. 340), and Augustine of Hippo (ca. 400) concluded from this recapitulation phenomenon the important realization that the visions of Revelation are not consecutive or sequential accounts of events, but are a repetitive description of similar facts or events in different forms and visions, hence the seven seals, seven trumpets, and seven bowls are held to recapitulate or repeat similar messages.

All serious structural theories since Tyconius have had to deal with this recapitulation characteristic. In more modern times William Hendriksen[125] and Austin Farrer[126] have included the recapitulation characteristic in their interpretations or structural outlines of Revelation. Yarbro Collins and others who identify in Revelation either a chiastic structure[127] or at least a repetitive theme for Revelation include some form of recapitulation in their structural analysis of Revelation.

The salient contribution of Recapitulation theories is the proposal that the series of visions in Revelation should not be considered sequentially, but are theological or incremental emphases of certain recurring themes within Revelation.

Eschatological Models

Strictly speaking the Chiliast school was the first truly eschatological model[128] of interpretation applied to Revelation. By eschatological models we mean forms of interpretation that shift the message of Revelation from the first century to end of the world or to futurist concerns. The first full eschatological interpretation of Revelation dates from the sixteenth century when Jesuits responded to the anti-Catholic exegesis of Protestant Reformers who identified the Pope and Rome with the Beasts of chapter 13. In an attempt to remove themselves, that is, the Roman Catholic Church and the Pope, as far as possible from the sixteenth century attacks of the Protestants, the Jesuits moved the interpretation of Revelation to eschatological (end of the world) judgment concerns. The Spanish Jesuit Franciscus Ribeira[129] was the most notable proponent of this model of exegesis. Ribeira by adopting this model, moved the meaning of Revelation from the Roman-Protestant debate to the far distant future, whenever that may be. Modern adaptations of an eschatological model will be considered below under the Futurist and Dispensationalist schools of interpretation.

We should note, however, that the message of Revelation is impressively couched in eschatological language.[130] How this eschatological language is to be understood becomes a vital component in understanding the style and message of Revelation. Considerable space will be devoted in the textual commentary that follows this introduction to discussion of the use of the eschatological language in Revelation.

Continuous Historical Models[131]

Sometimes called the chronological method, this model was introduced by Hentenius of Louvain in 1547.[132] Hentenius divided the prophetic sections of Revelation into two parts; chs. 6–11 and 12–19. Although later exegetes have recognized a possible division or shift in thought at chapter 11, Hentenius incorporated a subjective identification of Muhammed and Islam into his interpretation. In succeeding years, scholars adopting this model of interpretation have "discovered" other contemporary historical events and "sinister" characters in Revelation, thus making this model a highly subjective, fluid, or speculative model. In its final form this model has developed into a theological survey of church history from some point in the history of the church in which the interpreter is working, moving toward a final consummation. The end product results most often in a survey of Western or European church history. Some recent scholars have adopted a form of Continuous History in their structure of Revelation. Ernst Renan (1871), Albert Barnes (1852), Sir William Ramsey (1904), and P. Touilleux (1935) are among those who incorporate some form of historical approach in their program.[133] In many cases where Revelation has been interpreted by well meaning church ministers and leaders who do not have well developed tools of biblical study and interpretation, this model has been favored. Its appeal is that it makes Revelation relevant to those who are familiar with the events, circumstances, and sinister characters being read into Revelation.

Continuous historical models of interpretation are always suspect in regard to their subjective contemporaneous interpretation and viewpoint. There appears to be no adequate controls in the selection of the characters infused into their history. Furthermore, as other somewhat "odious" characters appear in church history, Muhammed, Hitler, Mussolini, Stalin, the Ayatolla Khomeni, Sadam Hussein, the continuous historical model has to be revised and updated. In certain situations, mostly extremely conservative, anti higher education Protestant mind-sets, approaches to Revelation have fallen into this model of interpretation. The tendency in these cases is to identify the Roman Pope or other political or religious figures as the "antichrist" or beast of Revelation.

Major weaknesses in this interpretive model are the over speculative, subjective, unbiblical,[134] and strident orthodoxy which adjusts the focus of history to benefit its own stance in history. In most cases the interpretation favors an overt Western slant to history.[135]

Futurist Models[136]

I have separated the eschatological model from the futurist for the sake of differentiating between the older eschatological views and more modern approaches. We have also included the Dispensational views of Revelation under a separate category from the Futurist, although they too consider Revelation to be involved almost exclusively with the future final days of history. Although similar in their futuristic and eschatological perspectives each of these three models, the eschatological, the futurist, and the dispensationalist have unique characteristics that lend to separate categorization.

Ernst Lohmeyer (1926) would be typical of a modern eschatological or futurist interpretation, but one would not include him under the dispensational category. Lohmeyer considers 4–21 to be a strictly eschatological or non-historical, non-temporal concept of salvation; a timeless eschatology. Abraham Kuyper (1953), Merrell C. Tenney (1957), and William Barclay (1959) would fall under this grouping in that they place much stress on the final victory of Christ over Satan "in the last days." Mathias Rissi (1966) also considers most of Revelation to be a discussion of the final days of history. He nevertheless holds that the writing of Revelation should maintained in the context of the church at the time of John's writing. G. R. Beasley-Murray, likewise finds much relating to the final days of history in his interpretation. G. K. Beale, although claiming to be eclectic, and one who sets Revelation firmly in the context of the church in Asia at the close of the first century (as a moderate preterist would), is somewhat biased in favor of an eschatological futurist view.[137] Grant R. Osborne appropriately criticizes Beale, Mounce, Ladd, Beasley-Murray, and Michaels for the centrality they give to the futurist interpretation.[138] I agree with Osborne's evaluation of these scholars.

I have several problems with futurist approaches to Revelation. The first problem is that it gives little comfort to the church in the first century for which it was written, and has little relevance for the church in the present time since it pushes everything in these great chapters down to the last days, leaving Revelation with little significance for those to whom it was originally addressed, or to the contemporary reader facing crises other than those relating to the final judgment.[139] A second, and perhaps more serious objection I have to this model is that it has a poor understanding of the apocalyptic eschatological language of Revelation.[140] By this I infer that these views tend to interpret all apocalyptic eschatological language as reference to the future final days of history. We will notice later in this study that this approach is in my opinion not a felicitous understanding of John's use of proleptic eschatological style in which he describes present or imminent events and their significance in eschatological end of the world language and constructs, stressing that the present events bear end of the world significance and consequences.[141] I am also persuaded by Wolfhart Pannenberg's observation that the present is the arrival of the future. [142]

Millennial Models[143]

Several models fall under the nomenclature of Millennialism or Millenarianism. All reflect in some measure an eschatological or futurist interpretation, each with their own peculiar characteristics and nuances. All millennial views are an attempt to explain the fascinating and challenging use of a thousand years in chapter 20 ("millennial" deriving from the Latin *mille*, 1000). The first two to be considered, premillennialism and dispensationalism, are characterized by an extreme literal interpretation, particularly of Old Testament prophecy, and a futurist inclination. The third group, postmillennialism shares with premillennialism and dispensationalism only the fact that it is a form of millennial interpretation, albeit significantly different from the previous two. Both premillennialism and dispensationalism consider 4–21 to deal exclusively with the final days of history. They are in that sense fully eschatological interpretations. We will look finally at Amillennialism, which although it shares with the above three views the term "millennialism," differs in that it does not break history into millennial dispensations, nor does it take a thousand years literally as a reference to time. I will present a diagrammatic overview of the various millennial positions in the glossary of this book.

Premillennialism

In some senses, premillennialism is very similar to chiliasm. George Eldon Ladd argues his case for historic premillennialism (another way of defining modern premillennialism) from chiliasm, maintaining that historical (modern) premillennialism, with its roots in chiliasm, is in fact the oldest known form of Revelation hermeneutic.[144] Modern premillennialism, however, differs from ancient chiliasm in that it separates the church age from the kingdom age, and places significant emphasis on the final "signs of the times" which are anticipated immediately prior to the final eschatological end of the world. Most modern premillennial views understand the church age to be a form of "spiritual" kingdom which has yet to be fulfilled. The fulfillment of the messianic kingdom will come only after the return of Jesus. Modern premillennial interpretations vary considerably, manifesting a wide range of interests. A major claim of this group is that certain national prophecies made to Israel were not fulfilled, either in Israel or the church. These prophecies therefore remain to be fulfilled in a future kingdom of God to be established under Jesus on earth. Most premillennial views identifying Jerusalem as the place of that fulfillment. In some premillennial programs the return of Jesus to establish his kingdom will be "triggered" by the rediscovery of the ark of the covenant. A major weakness of this method of interpretation is its literalist interpretation Scripture. In addition to George Eldon Ladd, one of the more competent, yet moderate premillennial interpreters in recent years has been G. R. Beasley-Murray (1974).[145] (See the chart on premillennialism in the glossary.)

Dispensationalism[146]

Dispensationalism is an extreme form of premillennialism. The origins of dispensationalism can be traced to John Nelson Darby (1850), one of the founders of the Plymouth Brethren movement in Ireland. Darby was a well educated lawyer. Dissatisfied with his Church of England roots he separated from them over problems relating to allegiance to the King and State. Darby argued that the prophecies to Israel regarding the kingdom had not been fulfilled in the church and remained yet to be fulfilled. In fact, Darby argued, the Old Testament is silent regarding the church. Darby's views eventually found their way to the United States.

An American business man and successful real estate investor, William E. Blackstone (1908) was impressed with Darby's literalist interpretation of Scripture and became a proponent of this view. Darby's dispensational views were also adopted by C. I. Schofield (of *The Schofield Reference Bible* fame, 1909). Schofield became a Presbyterian minister in Dallas, Texas. John Walvoord (1959) subsequently came under the influence of Schofield's dispensational leanings. Through his teaching and writing, Walvoord became mentor to Hal Lindsey, who then popularized a dispensational model through his best selling work, *The Late Great Planet Earth* (1970). Dispensational views cut across most denominational lines and can be found in the Seventh Day Adventist Church (William Miller of the 1840's being a pioneer of this movement), The Church of Jesus Christ of Latter Day Saints (Joseph Smith, 1830, was the founder of this restoration and millennial movement), the Jehovah's Witnesses (founder, Charles Taze Russell, 1870), and the World Wide Church of God (founder Herbert W. Armstrong, 1933). The Dallas Theological Seminary has been a primary source of dispensational theology since its inception. The founder and first president of the seminary was Dr. Lewis Sperry Chafer, 1924. Dr. John Walvoord was the second president and professor, 1950's. A popular contemporary pop-theology writer, Tim F. Lahaye, co-writer of the *Left Behind* series, reflects dispensational views.

Basic dispensational views (and there are a variety of dispensational interpretations) hold that God had *intended* to establish his kingdom under Jesus, but when the

Jews rejected Jesus, God postponed his kingdom, stopping the prophetic clock. Daniel 9 is a key passage for all dispensational interpretation. At some time in the future, indicated to man by the "signs of the times," God would restart the clock and the final "week" of Daniel 9 would begin. The final week will be marked by seven years of tribulation, a rapture, and Jesus' second coming to establish his delayed kingdom on earth in Jerusalem. A "realized Jewish kingdom" and the Jewish system will be reestablished with the rebuilding of the Temple in Jerusalem.

Clarence B. Bass, *Backgrounds to Dispensationalism*, while tracing the origins of Dispensationalism back to Darby, summarizes the basic tenets of this model of interpreting Revelation and the Bible as follows:

> What, then, are the distinguishing features of dispensationalism? They are: its view of the nature and purpose of a dispensation; a rigid applied literalism in the interpretation of Scripture; a dichotomy between Israel and the church; a restricted view of the church; a Jewish concept of the kingdom; a postponement of the kingdom; a distinction between law and grace that creates a multiple basis for God's dealing with man; its view of the purpose of the great tribulation; its view of the nature of the millennial reign of Christ; its view of the eternal state, and its view of the apostate nature of Christendom.[147]

Bass, himself originally a dispensationalist, mounted a successful argument against dispensationalism in his doctoral studies and dissertation which resulted in his "conversion" or persuasion against dispensationalism. His research was published in his book *Backgrounds to Dispensationalism*.

The major objection I have to this system is its radical literal interpretation of Scripture, the restoration of the Jewish Temple and sacrificial cultus, and the radical speculation and timetable of history triggered by every war or uprising in the Middle-East. Furthermore, this system like other futurist eschatological models removes the message of Revelation from those for whom the book was originally written and who urgently needed comfort and encouragement. There is little encouragement held out for the persecuted first century church in the Dispensational hermeneutic of Revelation.[148] (See the chart on dispensationalism in the glossary.)

Postmillennialism[149]

Postmillennialism was initially popularized by Daniel Whitby (1638–1726), a Unitarian minister in England. As Postmillennialism has developed since Whitby, the basic proposition of postmillennial thinking is that the thousand years is not necessarily a literal time period but is symbolic of an age of great religious optimism and awakening in which the kingdom of God is extended in the world through the preaching of the gospel and the saving work of the Holy Spirit. It holds that the world is getting better and will eventually be "Christianized." The return of Christ will follow the Christianization of the world. The Christianized period is therefore referred to as the millennium. The view is highly optimistic to say the least, and is fundamentally more sociologically motivated than biblically grounded.

Postmillennialism became popular in America in the late eighteenth and early nineteenth centuries and flourished under the burgeoning influence of the progressive rationalism of the age. The optimism of the age, however, was dealt a serious blow by the American Civil War which could hardly be considered as a harbinger of the spread of the gospel of peace. Such was the optimism and confidence of postmillennialists in the nineteenth century that the movement was not unduly set back by these events.

Alexander Campbell, a prominent leader of the Restoration Movement and Churches of Christ in America in the nineteenth century was a staunch supporter and proponent of postmillennialism. Campbell had read a book by Elias Smith on postmillennialism and fully accepted Smith's view. Campbell developed and popularized his postmillennial thoughts through his religious journal *The Millennial Harbinger*. In later years Moses Lard and T. W. Brents of the same Restoration Movement turned away from Campbell's postmillennialism and introduced a form of chiliast pre-millennialism. Brents had learned of chiliasm from reading John Albrecht Bengel, *Gnomon Novi Testamenti* (1752), in which Bengel revived a form of ancient chiliasm.

Other nineteenth century American postmillennialists were Charles Hodge, David Brown, and B. B. Warfield. More recent postmillennialists are Loraine Boettner and Marcellus Kik.

The major problems encountered in postmillennialism are first, the doctrine is simply not biblically supported, and second, postmillennialism is plainly sociologically naive. Postmillennialism would not fit comfortably in a postmodern culture.

Preterist Models[150]

The English word preterist, or preterit, as a grammatical term has primary reference to the past tense. The preterist model proposes that everything in Revelation, with the exception of the second coming of Jesus and the final judgment, has already been fulfilled, or at least is related to the circumstances of the first-century Christians. This group is divided into two basic schools of thought: radical preterist and moderate preterist. The radical group suggests that John wrote the events of 4–21 to predict historical catastrophes expected during his life and immediately preceding the destruction of Rome, hence from the modern interpreter's stance, the radical preterist holds that 4–21 speaks to the very early and historically past context of the church. The radical preterist believes that the prophecies of 4–21 have already all been fulfilled. This first group is typical and more representative of a generation of learned scholars at the close of the nineteenth and the early twentieth centuries, among them R. H. Charles and James Moffatt.

The second preterist group, the moderate preterists, holds that the visions and prophecies of 4–21 are set in the context of the churches in Asia in the first century and promise the martyrs of John's day encouragement in the face of the social and religious crises they were about to face under Roman opposition and persecution. The sense of the past context of the church in Asia provides the preterist definition to the moderate preterist.

However, the moderate preterist finds reference in Revelation to a future final judgment and home in heaven, the new Jerusalem. The moderate preterist sees Revelation in the same light as one would view the Corinthian correspondence, a document written to the church in first-century Achaia facing religious problems in its own context. The theological principles highlighted in Corinthians would be applicable to all ages. Likewise, in Revelation the theological principles surfaced would have relevance to the church in all ages. This group maintains that historical, sociological, and literary criticism are the appropriate disciplines for interpreting Revelation. They hold that John's genius, under the guidance of the Holy Spirit has produced a highly symbolic work leaning heavily on the apocalyptic genre, but set in the historical context of the church in first-century Asia. As an apocalyptic drama, Revelation explained how God had already judged Rome and the satanic power behind Rome with eschatological judgment. There are, however, significant allusions to a final judgment in Revelation that are included to bring the theodicy of Revelation to closure. The final judgment scenes are not the major purpose of Revelation, but in the theodicy of Revelation that evil must in the end be judged.

A difference between the radical preterist and the moderate preterist is in some ways narrow; however, the radical fulfillment mind-set manifest in some radical preterist hermeneutic supposes that everything predicted in 4–21 has already been fulfilled and that this text does not discuss any form of second coming or final judgment. The more moderate hermeneutic proposes that everything in 4–21 leads up to the judgment of Rome and Satan, but that the theodicy of Revelation and final verdict on evil is not complete until the power behind Rome and all other persecuting powers, namely Satan, is finally and fully judged and destroyed at the final judgment still to come. Moderate preterists maintain that although Revelation is fundamentally set in the context of the first century (the past, hence preterist), a small section of Rev. 20:11–15 describes this final judgment of Satan, and the final chapters of the book speak in highly symbolic terms of the future heavenly glory of the church following the final judgment. This moderate preterist view also holds that Revelation defines certain great religious principles that hold true under all circumstances of crisis similar to those discussed in Revelation.

Most amillennial interpretations of Revelation fall under some form of preterist model. Some identify their "soft" preterist approach as a philosophy of history (see below) or dramatic approach. This commentary is written under a moderate preterist and amillennial hermeneutic with an idealist, philosophy of history, theological approach to its dynamic. Beale and Osborne speak appropriately of an eclectic approach to Revelation that incorporates a moderate preterist approach, an idealist (philosophy of history), a poetic dramatic approach, and some form of futurist concern. Other than what I believe to be an excessive futurist interest in Beale, my approach could be considered as a similar eclectic model to Beale's. Typical of the model espoused in this commentary would also be Albertus Pieters, H. B. Swete, Yarbro Collins, G. B. Caird, G. K. Beale,[151] David Aune, Eugene Boring, and Grant R. Osborne.

Philosophy of History or Idealist Model[152]

The philosophy of history model of interpretation leans heavily on the dramatic style of Revelation and the literary character of the work. In some definitions this view is identified as the idealist view. This method of hermeneutic holds that Revelation is a timeless drama, reflecting a crisis between the forces of evil and good. There is much to be said for this model, and when combined with a moderate preterist hermeneutic, it provides a meaningful vehicle of interpretation. William Milligan, Henry Alford, R. C. H. Lenski, Leon Morris, Ray Summers, and Michael Wilcock could be included in some way as representative of this group. In some measure Yarbro Collins could also be included under this school of thought, as could most moderate preterist and amillennial thinkers. The strength of this view is that its stress on the theological core of Revelation keeps the theology of Revelation relevant to every age.

Amillennial Models[153]

I prefer to discuss the amillennial model at this point rather than earlier in the context of other millennial theories. Amillennial scholars draw heavily on both the moderate preterist and philosophy of history schools of thought. They do not see in the thousand years a literal reference to a time period. Amillennialism is thus opposed to a millennial interpretation that fixates on a period of time. Hence, it is amillennial, or not-millennial.

The amillennial approach to Revelation is sensitive to historical, sociological, literary, and reader-response concerns that recognize that Revelation is a highly theological, symbolic work with a unique apocalyptic and eschatological mindset. Amillennial thinkers are also sensitive to the heightened dramatic element in Revelation. Most amillennial scholars can, therefore, be subsumed under either the moderate preterist or philosophy of history group.

The amillennial school, because of its responsive mindset to the full range of biblical hermeneutics, is "allergic" to literalist approaches to Revelation. Reluctant to interpret the high symbolism and apocalypticism of Revelation literally, the amillennialist sees in the numerical symbolism of Revelation theological rather than literal or temporal references. Amillennialism perceives the thousand-year reign of the saints with Christ to be symbolic, not of temporal concerns, but of a condition relating to the extent and completeness of the reign of martyrs who have died for their witness to Christ. Amillennialists do not understand the millennium to be a *period* of time, but find in it a set of conditions symbolically depicted by a thousand years.

Amillennialists consider Revelation to be set in the context of the first-century church struggling to be faithful to God and Christ in a pagan world that does not understand its Christian commitment. Amillennialists consider the theology of Revelation to confirm that death (martyrdom) for Christ is not defeat, but a sacrifice that results in a resounding personal victory in Christ. Those who die for (and with) Christ as martyrs reign with him completely (symbolized by a thousand years, one thousand symbolizing completeness).

This commentary assumes a moderate preterist model combined with a philosophy of history sensitivity that results in an amillennial perspective. Amillennialist commentators lean heavily on a literary critical analysis of Revelation.

STRUCTURE AND OUTLINE

Attempts at determining some form of structure for Revelation have been a prominent concern of interpreters throughout the centuries. A survey of commentaries in recent years indicates that there is no consensus of structure among scholars. Nevertheless, all find some form of structure in either the syntactical, grammatical composition of Revelation, certain thematic phrases, the repetition of John's numerical symbolism, or other seeming structural keys. What complicates structural attempts is John's remarkably tightly knit composition. Elisabeth Schüssler Fiorenza has correctly argued, however, that without some understanding of structure no commentator would be able to understand how John has blended his sources into a theological whole. She demonstrates how form (structure) and content (sources) fuse into meaning, and argues that in Revelation "the form is not a container for the content but the patterning and arrangement of it. Fiorenza observes that the exegete must not only adopt the disciplines of "form and tradition-criticism, redaction criticism, compositional analysis, and genre criticism, but also structural or architectural analysis."[154]

Beale observes that the history of attempts at determining a structural outline for Revelation are as confusing as is the history of interpretive models. "The diverse proposals are a maze of interpretive confusion."[155] While I agree with Beale regarding the difficulty of arriving at a satisfactory structural outline for Revelation, I concur with Schüssler Fiorenza that some form of structure is essential to interpretation.

Bauckham has observed regarding structure that "the book of Revelation is an extraordinarily complex literary composition." He adds, "it is important to realize that the essential structure of the book, without recognition of which it would be incomprehensible, must have been intended to be perceptible in oral performance."[156] However, Bauckham appropriately notices a comment by D. L. Barr that "whereas our concern is to divide the book, John's concern was to bind together."[157] Regarding our attempts to separate the units of the composition into a structural form, he warns that "John has taken considerable care to integrate the various parts of his work into a literary whole."[158] Reinforcing his concern for structure without destroying the unity of Revelation, he states, "the more Revelation is studied in detail, the more clear it becomes that it is not simply a literary unit, but actually one of the most unified works in the New Testament."[159]

Several issues must be considered when examining a possible structure to Revelation. These are the well-known fact of recapitulation, the intricate "hooking," or interlinking devices John uses to tie his various visions together, the centuries-long observation that there is an obvious break following Revelation 11, John's predilection for listing visions in series of septets, and the obvious prologue and epilogue. Several additional literary characteristics have been proposed as essential to the structure of Revelation,[160] but when one works through all of these, one still arrives at only a tentative resolution to the structural issues. While I agree with Beale and others in regard to the various problems encountered in most structural analyses, I find his resolution to the problem no more satisfying, and possibly more complicated than others.

In spite of the confusing possibilities presented by scholars, I agree with Schüssler Fiorenza that some concept of structure is necessary to understanding the theological message of the book.

Recapitulation[161]

One of the oldest devices identified as part of John's "architectural" palette is a phenomenon already discussed above under models of interpretation, namely, recapitulation. Recapitulation refers to the literary device of stylistically repeating words or themes at strategic places in a text. Victorinus of Pettau (ca. 275–300), the first known author of a commentary on Revelation, noticed that Revelation incorporates several examples of recapitulation. All critical commentators have had to deal with recapitulation in some form. Although challenged by Johannes Weiss and R. H. Charles, the recapitulation theory was revived and established as an acceptable hypothesis by Günter Bornkamm in 1937. All serious scholars today working out of a critical model of biblical interpretation, especially literary criticism, recognize recapitulation to some degree as a literary component of structure. For some, for example Yarbro Collins,[162] this device is a fundamental characteristic of an interpretive program.

Examples of recapitulation can be seen in the repetition of themes and phrases in the prologue (1:1–8) and epilogue (22:6–21), in the repetition of the 144,000 in 7 and 14, and in a significant manner in the themes repeated in the series of septets; the seven seals, the seven trumpets, the seven unnumbered visions, the seven bowls of wrath, and the second series of seven unnumbered visions. The thematic recapitulation found in these septets becomes the central core to Yarbro Collins's interpretation of Revelation. Collins identifies the following three themes repeated in the septets; persecution, punishment of the nations, and the triumph of God, the Lamb, and the faithful.

Bornkamm proposes a significant recapitulation of themes in 4–20.[163] He identifies two great cycles in this block of material, the midpoint being found at the end of 11. The first cycle tells the story in an indirect, veiled, generic manner, while the second is more specific. Bornkamm was not the first to identify this twofold dramatic narrative structure, but it was his expression that gave it credibility in the modern period.

A significant key provided by recapitulation is that it shows that the visions of Revelation are not chronologically sequential with one series of visions following the pervious in a continuous historical narrative, but that the visions are most often repetitive, linked together by John in an impressive manner. Recapitulation suggests the possibility that the visions are "kaleidoscopic" with the later series of recapitulations repeating the earlier, but in greater detail or explanation. Often at the first appearance of an image John does not describe it in detail, but later he returns to the same image and recapitulates or fleshes out the detail with greater meaning. Perhaps the best example can be seen in the repetition of "those who overcome (conquer)" in the seven letters in 2 and

3, and the 144,000 in 7 and 14 in which John clarifies in 14 with greater specificity who the 144,000 represent.

Austin Farrer in his study of Revelation, *A Rebirth of Images*, describes the phenomenon of recapitulation as a rebirth of images previously introduced.[164] John introduces an image that he intends to develop at a later stage and then at the appropriate point returns to that image and gives it greater explanation, hence, the rebirth of that image. The phenomena of recapitulation and rebirth provide the narrative with a sense of progression, with the progression being thematic rather than simply chronologically sequential. William Hendriksen in his commentary, *More than Conquerors*, adopted the recapitulation model and twofold division of Revelation in a scheme of "progressive parallelism"[165] in which each of seven cycles repeats the previous and develops the theme more fully toward the final judgment and eternity. Although interesting, and in its own time significant, Hendriksen's model does not do full justice to recapitulation and the structural analysis of Revelation. Recapitulation as a rebirth of images will be incorporated into the structural outline of this study and will become a key hermeneutic principle for interpreting and understanding Revelation.

Two-Section Structure

The twofold structure of Revelation adopted by Bornkamm has been developed more fully in recent years. Yarbro Collins observes that this apparent characteristic has become pivotal to recent structural analyses of Revelation.[166] Clearly, this feature should be taken seriously when analyzing John's structural design. A simplified two-section structure to Revelation would be as follows:[167]

1. God and Christ versus the World of Evil (1–11)
     A. Prologue (1)
     B. Seven Letters (2–3)
     C. Heavenly Vision (4)
     D. Seven Seals (5–7)
     E. Seven Trumpets (8–11)

2. The Church Verses the Beast and Satan (12–22)
     A. Seven Unnumbered Visions (12–14)
     B. Heavenly Vision Repeated (15)
     C. Seven Bowls (16–18)
     D. Seven Unnumbered Visions (19–21)
     E. Epilogue (22)

The Septets and Chiasm

One cannot study Revelation and escape the obvious use John makes of presenting visions and proclamations in groups of seven. In some form all studies of Revelation take considerable note of this unique characteristic of Revelation. Scholars are divided as to whether there are five, six, or seven groups of seven pronouncements. Austin Farrer identified five septets; Yarbro Collins at different times has proposed both six and seven. As already emphasized, the septets form part of John's rebirth of images style.

In 1940 William Hendriksen recognized the relationship of recapitulation and the grouping of the visions of Revelation into septets and built this into his concept of progressive parallelism. He proposed a structure of eschatological progression as a solution to combining both recapitulation and the septets. Hendriksen divided the book into seven sections of visions progressing toward the ultimate eschatological consummation of all things.[168]

The combination of progressive parallelism and septets led several scholars to propose a chiastic structure to Revelation. The phenomenon of chiasm was a well developed literary device in antiquity and was adapted as a common means of developing theological emphases in the New Testament. (Cf. the chart and brief definition of chiasm in the glossary). Ronald E. Mann comments regarding chiasm (sometimes called chiasmus) that it may be defined as "a stylistic literary figure which consists of a series of two or more elements followed by a presentation of corresponding elements in reverse order." He further observes that "the individual elements may consist of single words, phrases, sentences, paragraphs, or even longer sections of material."[169] Charles H. Talbert describes chiasm as adopting a particular symmetric design that was common to Semitic, Greek, and Latin cultures. It was out of this Semitic background that chiasm became part of the literary style of the Old Testament and ultimately of the New Testament as well.

Johann Albrecht Bengel (ca. 1740), the great German textual critic and New Testament theologian, was one of the first critical scholars to identify chiasm as a legitimate biblical literary device. Bengel incorporated it into his exegetical model described in his *Gnomon of the New Testament*. Only in 1942, however, did chiasm become of real interest to American New Testament scholarship. In that year Nils Wilhelm Lund drew attention in a systematic manner to the value of chiasm in biblical interpretation.[170] Following Lund's pivotal work, J. Jeremias in 1958 developed the concept of chiasm in the Pauline literature in a significant journal article.[171]

In 1977 Jacques Ellul proposed a grouping of what he identified as five septets into a chiastic structure, introducing the concept of a chiasmus into the model of recapitulation in Revelation studies.[172] Ellul's arrangement was a major improvement over Hendriksen's progressive parallelism.

Since Ellul's work, several scholars have proposed different chiastic structures to the septets and the book as a whole. Yarbro Collins (1976), Schüssler Fiorenza (1977), and more recently Charles Homer Giblin (1994) have refined the concept of chiasm in Revelation and developed their structural analyses around this device.[173]

This study of Revelation proposes a thematic chiastic structure, which will be outlined in detail below. The goal of this structure is to incorporate the literary and theological themes of recapitulation, the grouping of septets, and the apparent progression of a theological message into a meaningful dramatic cosmic narrative. This narrative progresses from the historical context of imminent persecution in the first century in

Asia to the climactic reality of Christ's victory on the cross. It concludes with the ultimate judgment of Rome and of Satan and the future reward of the saints in the new Jerusalem, heaven. This structure also progressively develops the theme of God's vindication of the martyred saints.

In this thematic chiastic structure, the prologue (1:1–20) and the epilogue (22:6–21) serve in the place of the traditional A, A[1] introduction and conclusion (*conclusio*) of a chiasm and are understood to be in a parallel form. The seven letters of the church in imperfection (2, 3) and the seven unnumbered descriptions of the church in perfection (21–22:5) are in parallel form and comprise the B, B[1] form of the chiasm. Following this arrangement, the chiastic structure leads to the seven unnumbered figures of 12:1–14:20, which form the apex of the chiasm, and thus the focal point of the chiasm, emphasizing that it is Christ, the Lamb, that is God's answer to the problem of evil and suffering, and the high point of Revelation.

In this thematic chiastic structure John has developed his theodicy (defense of the righteousness of God) in such a way as to demonstrate that God is aware of the situation of the church in Asia (he describes the present and future state of the church), that God has a plan (*Heilsgeschichte*) for resolving the problem of evil (the scroll with seven seals), and that this plan reached its climax or fulfillment in the crucified Christ, the Lamb of God.

Prologue (1:1–20)
    I. The Church in Imperfection (2:1–3:22)—Seven Letters to the Seven Churches
        II. The Authority of God over Evil Explained (4:1–8:6)—Seven Seals on theScroll
            III. The Warning Judgments (8:1–11:19)—Seven Trumpets
                IV. The Lamb—God's Answer to Evil. (12:1–14:20)—Seven Unnumbered Figures[174]
            V. The Consummated Judgments (15:1–16:21)—Seven Bowls of Wrath
        VI. The Authority of God over Evil Exercised (17:1–20:15)—Seven Unnumbered Descriptions of God's Judgments
    VII. The Church in Perfection (21:1–22:5) - Seven Unnumbered Descriptions of the Church in Perfection
Epilogue (22:6–21)

This chiastic structure is broken down into the following, more workable outline of Revelation, which will be the outline around which this commentary will be structured.

Prologue 1:1–20
    A. The Source and Urgency of the Revelation (1:1–3)
    B. The Salutation (1:4–8)
    C. The Vision of the Son of Man (1:9–20)

I. The Church in Imperfection (2:1–3:22)—The Seven Letters to the Seven Churches
    A. Ephesus (2:1–7)

B. Smyrna (2:8–11)

C. Pergamum (2:12–17)

D. Thyatira (2:18–29)

E. Sardis (3:1–6)

F. Philadelphia (3:7–13)

G. Laodicea (3:14–22)

II. The Authority of God over Evil Explained (4:1–8:6)

    A. The Heavenly Worship (4:1–11)

    B. The Scroll and the Seven Seals (5:1–14)

    C. The Seven Seals (6:1–8:6)

        1. War (6:1-2)

        2. Rebellion (6:3–4)

        3. Famine (6:5–6)

        4. Death (6:7–8)

        5. Martyrdom (6:9–11)

        6. Cosmic Signs of Judgment (6:12–17)

           Interlude 7:1–17

              a. Sealing the 144,000 (7:1–8)

              b. The Great Multitude (7:9–17)

        7. Seven Trumpets Introduced (8:1–6)

III. The Warning Judgments 8:1–11:19—The Seven Trumpets (Warning Judgments)

    A. Introduction—The Seventh Seal (8:1–6)

    B. Seven Trumpets (8:7–11:19)

        1. Hail, Fire, and Blood (8:7)

        2. The Sea of Blood (8:8–9)

        3. The Falling Star (8:10–11)

        4. The Darkening of the Sun, Moon, and Stars (8:12–13)

        5. Opening the Bottomless Pit, the First Woe (9:1–12)

        6. Four Angels Released, the Second Woe (9:13–21)

           Interlude (10:1–11)

              a. John Eats the Little Scroll (10:1–11)

              b. The Temple Measured and Two Witnesses (11:1–14)

        7. The Consummating Judgment, the Third Woe (11:15–19)

IV. The Lamb—God's Answer to Evil (12:1–14:20)—The Seven Unnumbered Figures

    A. The Woman with Child (12:1–2)

    B. The Dragon (12:3–4)

    C. The Male Child (12:5–6)

    D. The Angel Michael (12:7–17)

    E. The Beast from the Sea (13:1–10)

    F. The Beast from the Land (13:11–18)

G. The Lamb on Mount Zion (14:1–5)
   Interlude—Seven Angelic Messages (14:6–20)
   1. Good News Preached (14:6–7)
   2. Babylon is Fallen (4:8)
   3. God's Wrath on Those Worshiping the Beast (4:9–12)
   4. Pronouncement of Blessing (14:13)
   5. The Earth Is Ripe for Harvest—Judgment (14:14–16)
   6. The Harvesting Angel Is Ready (14:17)
   7. The Judgment of Evil (14:18–20)

V. The Consummated Judgments (15:1–16:21)—The Seven Bowls of Wrath
   A. The Vision of Heaven (15:1–8)
   B. The Seven Bowls (5:5–16:21)
   1. Sores in Men (16:2)
   2. Sea Becomes Blood (16:3)
   3. Rivers and Fountains Become Blood (16:4–7)
   4. Fierce Heat of the Sun (16:8–9)
   5. Darkness (16:10–11)
   6. Foul Spirits and Armageddon (6:12–16)
   7. The Earthquake (16:17–21)

VI. The Authority of God over Evil Exercises (17:1–20:15)— Seven Unnumbered Descriptions of God's Wrath
   A. The Harlot and the Beast Identified (17:1–18)
   B. The Doom of Babylon Announced (18:1–18:20)
   C. The Doom of Babylon Described (8:21–24)
   D. The Marriage Supper of the Lamb (19:1–10)
   E. The Defeat of the Beast and the False Prophet (19:11–21)
   F. The Binding and Limitation of Satan (20:1–10)
   G. The Final Judgment (20:11–15)

VII. The Church in Perfection (21:1–22:5)— Seven Unnumbered Descriptions of the Church in Perfection
   A. The New Heaven and the New Earth (21:1)
   B. The New Jerusalem—the Dwelling of God (21:2–8)
   C. The Glory of the Holy City, Jerusalem (21:9–14)
   D. The Measurements of the City (21:15–18)
   E. The Foundations of the City (21:19–21)
   F. The Light of the City (21:22–27)
   G. The Sustenance of the City (22:1–5)

Epilogue 22:6–21
   A. Testimony to the Truth of the Revelation (22:6–9)
   B. The Time Is Near (22:10–15)

C. The Invitation Given (22:16–20)

D. Benediction (22:21)

THE THEOLOGY AND RELEVANCE OF REVELATION[175]

One reason Christians have difficulty making sense of Revelation and its mysterious visions and images is that they do not understand how this strange book written over 1900 years ago can have meaning today. One's ability to find contemporary relevance in Revelation will determine how seriously one takes this magnificent book and how often one returns to it for encouragement and comfort. It is unlikely that Christians living in the twenty-first century in western nations dominated by a Christian mindset will have to endure the kind of radical persecution endured in the first three centuries of Christianity. Therefore, much of the message of Revelation, shrouded in its strange otherworldly apocalyptic genre, will seem remote to many Christians. On the other hand, it is certain that Christians will face social trauma, terminal illness, and personal suffering.[176] The question is, therefore, "What does Revelation say to Christians living in a twenty first-century, postmodern society, and how does it convey its message?"

The search for contemporary relevance for Revelation is compounded further by premillennial and dispensational theories which tend to shift the meaning of Revelation away from contemporary trauma and suffering to the end of the world and final judgment. Once this shift has been accomplished contemporary concerns over the "signs of the times," the second coming of Jesus, and the end of the world have been substituted for the indispensable historical and socio-religious context of the oppression and persecution of the seven churches in Asia and Revelation, and the underlying theological message of this great book.

It is easy for the serious student of Revelation to get caught up in the euphoria of apocalyptic study, combat mythology, and the literary genius of John, and lose sight of John's primary concern, namely, that Christians should not succumb to the pressures of their often pagan culture, and compromise their faith with their secular world. There is always the temptation to approach a book such as Revelation from an academic standpoint. We become so fascinated with the strange visions and otherworldly images that our curiosity drives us deeper into the fields of literary and historical criticism in our quest to understand this unusual and fascinating book. The challenge to "master" the mysteries can cloud our vision and obscure the real meaning and purpose of the book. Rudolf Bultmann and Karl Barth warned in the early twentieth century against an obsession to master the text rather than being mastered by the message of the text. This warning is surely appropriate in the case of Revelation.

There will be times when Christians will feel powerless before illness, suffering, personal problems, and death. Revelation speaks as clearly in such contexts today as it did to Christians facing persecution in the first century. John's message encouraged Christians to lift their eyes from their oppressive present and to elevate their horizons from the persecutions of culture and the power of Rome. It encouraged Christians to see their hope, not in the powers of this world, but in the heavenly (or cosmic) world of God's divine power. It encouraged them to see beyond their present suffering and to take courage in God's sovereign power over the schemes of Satan, which sovereign power and victory God had already proven and established in Jesus' death and resurrection.

Revelation challenges Christians today to have confidence in God's power to provide a secure future for them. The message of Revelation is that in Christ God has provided an effectual victory over suffering and despair and a pathway into a loving fellowship with the one who sits on the heavenly throne. Revelation draws attention to a Trinitarian God whose loving concern is to nurture the lonely, the hurting, the disenfranchised, and those without hope. The same God who lovingly gave his own son to die for the world and who through his Holy Spirit was able to raise that Son to a triumphant victory over Satan is also able to transform present Christian oppression and suffering into a glorious victory over suffering, death, and the power of Satan.

The primary message is that Christians can achieve a magnificent victory in Christ over the power of Satan and this world. Christians facing extreme trauma are encouraged to keep their faith in the God in whom they have put their trust, never to compromise that faith, and to know that in Christ "we are more than conquerors through him who loved us" (Rom 8:37).

A secondary message was that the seven churches should examine their faith before serious crises break in on them. Times of crisis are not the occasion for building faith. In such times faith needs to break through the crisis and sustain the believer. Christians are encouraged to build their faith before crises strike so that faith may be ready to sustain them in times of tragedy.

Furthermore, Revelation encourages Christians to contemplate the holiness, sovereignty, and righteousness of God while things are going reasonably well. Before catastrophe strikes, Christians need to have their faith fully informed about the God in whom they believe. When Christians understand the sovereignty of God, that He is in control of the universe, not Satan, they are better prepared to withstand Satan and his wiles. When Christians understand the holiness of God, that He is wholly different from everything sinful and weak, then Christians too can strive to be different (holy) from the world and their secular culture. When Christians understand the righteousness of God, that He never makes a mistake,[177] then they are able to see life from a different perspective and to work through the troubling times and disturbing questions that surface in the trials of life, understanding that God is greater than the trials that surround them. Revelation does not attempt to deny the reality of persecution and oppression, but encourages Christians to see beyond these to a God who has been, and who continues to be, able to transcend all human suffering. This God is the Almighty Lord of Hosts who is, who was, and who is to come.

An equally important lesson to be learned from Revelation is that this God has eternally been concerned for his saints. He began planning in eternity for their needs well in advance of any future necessity, and he has been working that plan in history throughout the ages. This is seen in the breaking open the sealed scroll of chapter 5. This leads through a series of septets in a dramatic progression toward the revelation of Jesus, the triumphant Lamb in 12:10, 11 who has already conquered Satan and his power. This scroll and series of seals assures the saints that God has an eternal plan for his creation and that he has been working that plan.[178] This plan reaches its apex in the death and resurrection of Jesus. Christians are thus assured in Revelation of the abiding presence of this triumphant Jesus in the everyday events and struggles of life, for this Jesus walks constantly in the presence of his churches (lampstands, 2:1).

The theology of Revelation, therefore, is that God is the loving sovereign of the universe. Although he hates sin and evil, he temporarily tolerates it in his love for man but will eventually destroy evil and those associated with evil. Revelation admits that God understands his creation will suffer under the evil workings of Satan, but affirms that he has already provided an escape from Satan and the power of evil through the death and resurrection of Jesus. Revelation affirms that God will in the end reach into the affairs of this world and judge and destroy Satan and those who follow him. In the meantime, those who endure faithfully are guaranteed that they will reign with Christ in his kingdom. Perhaps the climax of Revelation is found in 12:10–11: "Now the salvation [victory] and the power and the kingdom [reign]of our God and the authority of his Christ have come, for the accuser of our brethren has been thrown down, who accuses them day and night before our God. And they have conquered him by the blood of the Lamb and by the word of their testimony, for they loved not their lives even unto death."

In the title to his commentary, *More Than Conquerors*, William Hendriksen caught the meaning and theology of Revelation. He drew on that great passage in Romans 8:37: "who shall separate us from the love of Christ? Shall tribulation, or distress, or persecution, or famine, or nakedness, or peril, or sword? No, in all these things we are more than conquerors through him who loved us."

Chapter 1

The Prologue

1:1–20

THE STRUCTURE OF REVELATION

In order to facilitate the reading of Revelation within the structure of the narrative, we must keep the chiastic structure of Revelation in mind. We begin by noticing the relationship of the prologue to the remainder of the book and notably to the epilogue.

Prologue 1:1–20
    I. The Church in Imperfection (2:1–3:22)
      Seven Letters to the Seven Churches
        II. The Authority of God over Evil Explained (4:1–8:6)
          Seven Seals on the Scroll
            III. The Warning Judgments (8:1–11:19)
              Seven Trumpets
                IV. The Lamb—God's Answer to Evil (12:1–14:20)
                  Seven Unnumbered Figures
              V. The Consummated Judgments (15:1–16:21)
              Seven Bowls of Wrath
          VI. The Authority of God over Evil Exercised (17:1–20:15)
            Seven Unnumbered Descriptions of God's Judgments
      VII. The Church in Perfection (21:1–22:5)
        Seven Unnumbered Descriptions of the Church in Perfection
Epilogue 22:6–21

The prologue of Revelation includes three major sections: The source of the revelation (1:1–3), the salutation (1:4–8), and the vision of the triumphant Jesus (1:9–20). The careful student will notice that some of the language and terminology of the prologue and epilogue are similar (cf. 1:1, 22:6; 1:3, 22:10; 1:3, 22:18,19), a common characteristic of a chiasm. Both sections focus attention on the urgency of the crises to which Revelation is addressed. The prologue stresses the urgency and authority of the revelatory message and the royal dignity and majesty of the Christ. The epilogue stresses the urgency and trustworthiness of the message. Both the prologue and the epilogue accent the imminence of the impending crisis and Jesus' intervention on behalf of the saints.

THE SOURCE OF THE REVELATION (1:1–3)

The Text[1]

The revelation of Jesus Christ, which God gave him to show his servants what must soon take place. He made it known by sending his angel to his servant John, [2]who testifies to everything he saw—that is, the word of God and the testimony of Jesus Christ. [3]Blessed is the one who reads the words of this prophecy, and blessed are those who hear it and take to heart what is written in it, because the time is near.

1:1. *The revelation of Jesus Christ*. The word "revelation" indicates the origin of the title of the book as well as the content of the book. It refers to the revealing of a message from Jesus to John and the seven churches. The Greek word in 1:1 for revelation is *apokalypsis* (an uncovering or revealing of some message or instruction). In this instance, however, it has no reference to the name of the literary genre that gives Revelation its unique flavor and that scholars have called apocalyptic.[2] Here revelation simply refers to the fact that God had a message that he wanted John to *reveal* to his people. This message is not a revelation about or concerning Jesus, as one might expect in the Gospels, but a revelation from Jesus,[3] or a revelation of which Jesus is the source. In this case we are looking at a subjective genitive *tou christou, from Jesus Christ*, and not an objective genitive.[4] This is a message that **God gave him** (Jesus) **to show to his servants**. Hence the message comes from both God and Jesus Christ, emphasizing the importance of the message.[5] Furthermore, it is a revelation concerning **what must soon take place**. This expression is key to determining the context and nature of the crisis faced by the churches in Asia and the message of Revelation. The phrase is repeated in the epilogue (22:6).

Some have interpreted **what must soon take place** as a reference to the rapidity in which the end of the world will take place once the end of the world begins, understanding the Greek *en tachei* as "quickly" rather than "soon". This interpretation is based on the fact that the Greek *en tachei* can in addition to "soon" also be translated as "quickly, speedily, with haste, at once, or without delay." However, a cursory examination of the major translations will reveal that most, if not all, agree with the King James Version (1611), "to shew unto his servants things which must shortly come to pass." Because of the eschatological context of Revelation and the nature of the apocalyptic literary genre adopted by John, all major translations render *en tachei* here as "shortly" or "soon."[6]

Beckwith translates this as "things which must shortly come to pass," and observes that the phrase defines the contents of the revelation.[7] Timothy Friberg, Barbara Friberg, and Neva Miller observe that adverbially *en tachei* means without delay, at once, speedily.[8]

Some understand this discussion in the context of an imminent expectation of the end of the world. However, Caird appropriately observes that in the social context of the first-century church this expression is a reference to the crisis the church in Asia is about to face rather than a reference to the end of the world, either an imminent expectation or future expectation of the final end. He observes:

> What then was it that John expected to happen **soon**? There is a general agreement that he expected persecution of the church by the Roman Empire. But like the other apocalyptic writers he has set this threat against a background of world history, and his prophecy carries us from a vision of God the Creator at one extreme to a vision of the Last Judgment and the eternal city of God at the other. We cannot, however, do justice to this very plain opening statement . . . by saying that he foresaw a long series of events covering centuries, which could be described as imminent because they were to *begin* shortly. Whatever earthly realities correspond to John's symbols, he expected them to be accomplished quickly *in their entirety*. We must choose between two answers to our question. The one answer, which would have the support of a majority of modern scholars, is that John expected the End, the final crisis of world history, the return of Christ in victory and judgment; and that everything else in his vision are only premonitory signs heralding the great day of God. The other answer, which I believe to be the true one, is that John's coming **crisis** was simply the persecution of the church, and that all the varied imagery of his book has no other purpose than this, to disclose to the martyrs the real nature of their suffering and its place in the eternal purpose of God.[9]

I concur with Caird that the best interpretation of *soon* is a reference to the impending crises about to break in on the church, implying that this will come to pass in the days of John, and not a statement concerning the final eschatological end and *parousia*.

There is a striking parallel in language here in 1:1 in the statement "to show . . . what must soon take place" with Daniel 2:28–30, 45–47: "what must come to pass." Caird expresses this well:

> **What is bound to happen** is an echo of Daniel ii:28, and John clearly expected his readers to know their Old Testament well enough to pick up his frequent allusions to it. Sometimes, no doubt, he uses biblical phrases, much as the Puritans did, simply because the language of the Bible came naturally to mind and was the natural vehicle for self expression. But here something more seems to be involved. For this phrase comes from Daniel's prediction of the end of the four tyrannical world empires and the establishment of a new empire under the sovereignty of God, and this prophecy is to play a substantive part in John's

later visions. Thus by this allusion John is indicating that his prophecy gathers up all the threads of Old Testament hope; the crisis is sure to come, not for any merely political reason, but because it has been written by God in the scroll of the world's destiny and prefigured in Scriptures.[10]

I agree in part with Beale's observations regarding this striking parallel reference to Daniel:

> John's substitution of *en tachei* implies his expectation that the final tribulation, defeat of evil, and establishment of the kingdom, which Daniel expected to occur instantly "in the latter days," would begin in his own generation, and indeed, that it had already begun to happen."[11]

Contrary to Beale, I do not see this expression as indicating that John expected "the final tribulation" and "the establishment of the kingdom."[12] As already noted, Caird argued persuasively that what was soon to take place was not the final end, but an imminent social and religious crisis about to impact the churches in Asia in the first century. In keeping with a proleptic inaugurated eschatological understanding of Revelation, I may be able to see in this expression the inauguration of the eschatological age, but not the final tribulation or end. However, along with Caird and Beale, I hold that the expression *en tachei* is a specific reference to an imminent crisis (tribulation). I detect also an expression of God's sovereign reign over the crisis and the subtle evil associated with the impending tyrannical reign of Rome as an evil world empire.

Furthermore, in keeping with Dan. 2 I find in this expression an imminent divine judgment on Rome and those who choose to be associated with Rome, which judgment had already begun to happen (to use Beale's expression) in John's "own generation." This "prophetic fulfillment" is one of analogical or typological fulfillment and not one of a temporal historical fulfillment.[13] As expressed by Caird, John draws into this "analogical fulfillment" all of the images and messages inherent in Daniel's "prophecy."

We need to realize that 1:1, ***what must soon take place***, is the opening thought of a *conclusio* in the pericope of 1:1-3 and should be kept in parallel context with the closing thought of the pericope, ***because the time is near.***

Excursus on Beale's Final Tribulation Comment

Beale's approach to Revelation is mostly excellent, but in view of his observations regarding the similarity of 1:1 with Daniel 2:28, and his tendency on occasion to a futurist leaning of eschatological language, especially in his comment "John's substitution of *en tachei* implies his expectation that the *final tribulation* (italics mine, IAF), defeat of evil and establishment of the kingdom . . . had already begun to begin", I find it necessary to digress somewhat at this point and enlarge on my (and Caird's) understanding of proleptic inaugurated eschatology. I do not believe that Beale and I are far apart in our understanding of inaugurated eschatology. However, Beale's comment that the *final* tribulation, defeat of evil, etc, had already begun, raises some concern on my part. On the point that the establishment of the kingdom had already begun I have no argument with Beale. However, I do question his comment that the *final* tribulation and judgment of evil had also already begun. On the surface, a minor point, but in the big picture of Revelation one that raises some concern.

The *crises* indicated by *en tachei*, **soon**, and the promises of eschatological judgment that follow are not a reference to the *final* judgment of the world and evil or a beginning of that final judgment, but a discussion of the imminent judgment God would bring on the enemies of the church. The central focus of Revelation is on the first century crisis faced by the church in Asia and God's promise to judge their enemies with imminent severe judgment, so severe that it can be described in end-of-the-world terms. As mentioned in the introduction, the relevance of Revelation for today lies in the theological principles located in the historical circumstances of the book, and the application of these theological principles to current circumstances. One such theological principle is that God judges the enemies of the church in the present time with the severity of his final judgment of evil, hence his present judgment is expressed in eschatological language.

As previoiusly noted in the introduction, apocalyptic, although set in an historical context, does not express its theology in historical constructs. Furthermore, the use of time references in prophecy and especially apocalyptic eschatology are most often symbolic. As Mounce notes, "Time as a chronological sequence is of secondary concern to prophecy."[14] When prophetic expression is set in an apocalyptic eschatology, its reference is not to temporal fulfillment, but to analogical or typological fulfillment. We are reminded of Roberts' study of the use of eschatology in Revelation.[15] I agree with the views introduced by Roberts and Cullmann and their understanding of eschatological time references.[16] Cullmann spoke of "inaugurated eschatology," according to which, the eschatological kingdom or reign of God began breaking into human experience with the incarnation of Christ. Accordingly, we are now living in the eschatological age, or "the last days." (Cf. Acts 2:17 and Peter's sermon in which he claimed that what they were experiencing was the fulfillment of Joel's prophecy concerning "the last days," and Heb. 1:2, where the writer claims that God has "in these last days. . . spoken to us by a Son").[17] In other words, the last days have already begun, and we are now already living in the eschatological age.

The genius of John's eschatology in Revelation and its apocalyptic style is that crises of extreme urgency with end-of-the-world implications are thus described in eschatological language. To those not sensitive to this idiom, the use of eschatological language can be confusing, leading them to read into any eschatological statement an expression of an end-of-the-world event rather than recognizing that the intended reference is to a present event involving or having end-of-the-world implications.[18] The intention of the use of eschatological language at this point is to dramatize the urgency involved in the situation. It also demonstrates dramatically the seriousness and certainty of God's action in that the implied crisis has already been considered and judged by God with end-of-the-world finality.

The Apostle Paul, perhaps not overtly an apocalyptist, was familiar and comfortable with the apocalyptic style.[19] In Rom. 1:18–32, where Paul describes the decline of human morality, he clearly states in apocalyptic style, "For the wrath of God is revealed from heaven against all ungodliness and wickedness of men who by their wickedness suppress the truth." A more precise translation is "For the wrath of God is already being revealed." In Paul's apocalyptic mind set, God's end-of-the-world judgment" is already being pronounced on present-day situations, reinforcing the use of apocalyptic and eschatological language to describe the seriousness and divine judgment of present-day events.[20]

One must keep in mind the poetic symbolism of the apocalyptic genre. To take poetic symbolism literally is to lose the genius of the poetic style. Caird observes:

> I intend to argue that Biblical eschatology is a characteristic product of the Semitic mind, which only Gentiles or pedants would dream of taking literally; that its primary concern is not with the future but with the present; and that it is in fact a figurative way of interpreting current history. . . .
>
> If, however, we recognize the poetic nature of apocalyptic eschatology, have we any business to introduce quite different standards of interpretation in dealing with the wildly proliferating concreteness of apocalyptic writings. . . . I should want to argue that they [the authors of Daniel and Revelation] were no more concerned with the end of the age and no less concerned with the historic crisis of their own day than any of the prophets before them.[21]

Caird continues to explain that in apocalyptic eschatology the present crisis and future end coalesce in one poetic structure:

> When the prophets looked forward to the future, they did so in two ways. . . . On the one hand they predicted an historic crisis which was to happen within the time series. . . . On the other hand they looked forward to the absolute crisis of divine judgment. . . . The two crises, therefore, always tended to coalesce, and the one inevitably called up the other by association. The two pictures lay, paratactically, side by side, in his mind. It was as though they were in twin lenses of a stereoscope which could be focused so as to merge into one symbolic vision.[22]

Caird argues that the two perspectives of the apocalyptist, the present historical and the future final eschatological judgment, coalesce in such a manner that the apocalyptist can define the present crisis in poetic form in eschatological language. Because of the poetic symbolic nature of the apocalyptic genre, especially biblical apocalyptic, it is incorrect to take apocalyptic eschatology literally and to press the language consistently toward the future end.

Regarding John's eschatological style Beale does however observe that the verses that follow 1:1 show "that the beginning of fulfillment and not the final fulfillment is the focus. . . . The references to the imminent eschatological period . . . point strongly to this focus."[23] More will be said on the imminence of the message of Revelation under the comments on 1:3.

In contrast to interpretations that consider *what must soon take place* as a reference to an imminent expectation of the end of the world or an imminent *parousia* (the second coming of Christ), or as a reference to the final events as a sudden happening whenever they begin (premillennial or futurist interpretations), John is discussing a present first-century crisis that has either already in his day begun or is on the point of beginning. John stresses that God has already pronounced unconditional judgment on Rome and the church's enemies and has described this as having end-of-the-world implications. In view of the fact that John will on several occasions refer to events happening *soon* (e. g. "I am coming soon," 22:7, 20), this stylistic use of eschatological language in Revelation will have profound implications for interpretation of the book. In the context of Revelation, *what must soon take place* must be considered along with the similar expressions *for the time is near* (1:3) and *what is to take place hereafter* (1:19) as reference to imminent crises (pagan and Jewish opposition and Roman persecution) that were about to break into their lives.[24] Caird observes:

> I put forward the hypothesis that the only event which John expected to happen in the near future was a general persecution of the Church by the Roman government, and that the whole intention of the rich and varied imagery of his heavenly drama was to nerve Christians for the coming ordeal by helping them to see the indispensable contribution that their martyrdom would make to the grand strategy of God's war against the forces of the Abyss.[25]

Because of the seriousness and nature of these imminent and urgent crises, God considered it imperative that he send to his church the message of Revelation, a critical and urgent message with immediate implications.

He made it known by sending his angel to his servant John. In true apocalyptic style an angel communicates an urgent divine message to a human being responsible for a community of believers. Aune makes much of John's style that incorporates an *angelus interpres* (angelic interpreter)[26] feature in biblical and extrabiblical Jewish apocalyptic literature. Angels spoke to Abraham and Lot (Gen. 18, 19), mediated the law to Moses (Acts 7:53; Gal. 3:19; Heb. 2:1), appeared to Joseph and Mary on the occasion of the conception of Jesus (Matt. 1:20; Luke 1:26), and ministered to Jesus in the wilderness after his temptation (Matt. 4:11). The ministry of angels to John while receiving his revelation validates the divine authority and urgency of the message. Besides this point of urgency, John was emphasizing that he was merely a servant of God, pointing again to God as the divine source of the Revelation.

1:2. *Who testifies to everything he saw—that is, the word of God and the* **testimony** *of Jesus Christ.* In Greek *who testifies* is in the aorist tense, possibly implying that what John saw and that to which he was testifying was an experience in the past, namely, the visions he received while on Patmos. The aorist is also a tense of certainty. John's comment regarding testifying is, therefore, a signature device intended to confirm the trustworthiness of the revelation he is about to record. The epilogue (22:6) has a similar confirmatory statement: "These words are trustworthy and true." The expression *he saw—that is, the word of God* signifies that the content of John's testimony, namely, the visions he is about to describe, actually were a message from God, the *revelation*. Caird translates *the word of God* as "the purpose declared by God." *Logos*, here translated "word" has a broad range of meanings whose interpretation should favor the context in which it stands. *Logos* can mean "a spoken word," "an assertion," "a statement," "a speech," "a message," or "a reason." Caird thus renders it "the purpose declared," implying that the content of John's revelation contained a message regarding the purpose of God.

The expression *the testimony of Jesus Christ* suggests several possibilities.[27] It could refer to the content of the message Jesus was passing on to John, that is, the content of the book of Revelation,[28] or it could refer to the testimony (witness) Jesus had made in his own life, that is, Jesus' faithfulness to God resulting in his crucifixion and martyrdom.[29] Thirdly, it could refer to the message concerning Jesus Christ (an objective genitive), Jesus is Lord.

Mounce believes *the testimony of Jesus* refers to the content of Revelation, that is, the purpose or message of God. Used in this manner, it reinforces the view that the message of the book of Revelation is precisely that which Jesus passed on[30].

Caird's proposal also bears merit, that the testimony of Jesus was his own martyrdom. If this is the case, the testimony of the Christians, namely their martyrdom, is the same as, and draws strength from, Jesus' martyrdom.

I prefer the sense that this message, the testimony of Jesus, is one concerning Jesus (an objective genitive), that is, the message which came from God to John concerning the lordship of Jesus. Thus the *word of God* simply referred to the content of Revelation, the revelation itself, concerned Jesus' lordship.[31] As Revelation unfolds we will learn that God's message was that Jesus is Lord; Caesar is not! The saints should be true to the Lordship of Jesus.

The phrase *to everything he saw* strengthens John's argument for the completeness of his revelation. John is revealing exactly what was revealed to him on Patmos. This expression reinforces John's claim that this revelation bears the full weight and source of divine authority. The epilogue (22:18,19) is similar: the stress is on the authenticity and authority of the revelation. *I warn everyone who hears the words of the prophecy of this book: If anyone adds anything to them, God will add to him the plagues described in this book. And if anyone takes words away from this book of prophecy, God will take away from him his share in the tree of life and in the holy city, which are described in this book.*

1:3. Blessed is the one who reads the words of this prophecy, and blessed are those who hear it and take to heart what is written in it, because the time is near. John stresses the urgency of his message by pronouncing a blessing on those who read, hear, and keep the message. The RSV translates *reads* as "reads aloud" (Greek, *anaginōskō*, "read," "read aloud in public"; cf. 1 Tim. 4:13, "public reading of Scripture," and Col. 4:16 and

1 Thess. 5:27, which imply that letters were read in the churches,[32] The members of the early churches, especially those in Asia, did not have individual copies of either the Scriptures or this revelation. The nature and urgency of the epistle, written to the seven named churches, implies an early copying of the letter for immediate and repeated use in the individual congregation. Someone in the assembly read the letter to the congregation. Following the tradition of the Synagogue liturgy in which a major component of the assembly was reading aloud from the Torah, early Christian worship featured public reading of Scripture.[33] The exhortation to read the revelation aloud in public has caused some, with justification, to identify Revelation as incorporating both epistolary and liturgical elements.[34] In this compelling exhortation to the churches, John encourages the repeated reading of the revelation. All of the participles in this sentence "read aloud," "hear," and "take to heart," are in the present tense, implying repeated action. The nature of Christian assemblies in the first century suggest that this reading most likely took place in the weekly assembly. The urgency of the crisis and the need of the churches to strengthen their faith and commitment to Jesus would justify the steady and repeated reading of the revelation.

The Greek *makarios* (blessing) in both the Septuagint and New Testament implies something far deeper than mere happiness, for it would be strange for those undergoing severe persecution and suffering to find happiness in the trials they face. The word implies a spiritual richness as in the beatitudes of Matthew 5. Blessings as in the beatitudes formed a rich part of John's literary and theological style in Revelation. In keeping with his predilection for septets, there are seven blessings in Revelation (1:3; 14:13; 16:15; 19:9; 20:6; 22:7). Aune finds an apocalyptic use of the beatitude, implying that this genre also was prominent in times of persecution and suffering.[35]

The final clause of this exhortation is one of the most intense and compelling expressions in the book and one of the most important in setting the theological context for Revelation. John's use of the phrase *because the time is near* heightens the urgency of the message. The seriousness of the situation faced by the church in Asia is impacted by this, perhaps the most loaded and densely packed eschatological phrase in the book. The phrase *ho gar kairos eggus*, in an eschatological context loses all sense of time in stressing the imminence or certainty of the occasion.[36] Possibly the best translation of this expression in its eschatological context is that "the crisis is certain."

Greek has two terms for *time*. The one, *chronos* implies time that passes. The other *kairos*, used in this expression, stresses urgent time, even crisis time.[37] In the expression *because the time is near*, John uses the word *kairos*, that is, "urgent, significant, crisis time." Osborne observes regarding *kairos* at 11:19 that the verse "is introduced by *ho kairos* ... which occurs five times in the book (1:3; 11:18; 12:12,14; 22:10) and refers not to chronological time but to eschatological time, a period filled with the sense of God's judgment on those who do evil and his salvation for those who live for righteousness."[38]

John urges immediate concern for deepening spiritual strength in view of imminent *crises* that were about to break in on the church.[39] Aune states that *hō kairos* "is an important technical term ... which refers to the impending crisis that will overtake the world and that involves a traditional program of eschatological events."[40] Beale describes the words *hō gar kairos eggus* as "an exaggerated expression of imminence that includes a notion of present time." Schüssler Fiorenza observes: "Instead of a divine plan of historical events the author of Rev. introduces the imminent expectation. . . John does not intend to show as in Dan 2:28 (LXX) what must occur at the last day (*ep eschaton ton emeron*) but what must happen soon (*ha dei genesthai en tachei*; Rev. 1:1; 22:6). All the visions and images of Revelation—are determined by such an imminent expectation."[41]

Summary of Revelation 1:1–3

The meaning and implications of the first paragraph of the prologue are vital to understanding the historical setting and meaning of the message of Revelation, and to stressing the urgency of the "word" that God was revealing to his church through Jesus. It sets the message in the first century life of the church in Asia and demonstrates that God recognizes the difficulties his church faces, in particular the plight of the churches in the Roman Province of Asia. Revelation urges Christians to hear God's call to faithfulness, for a severe crisis was about to break in upon the church. The divine source of the revelation stresses the authority and urgency of the message. The call to faithfulness in Jesus, who had himself proven faithful, demonstrates that God is not asking his people to do anything that Jesus himself has not already done. The exaggerated imminence of 1:1, 3, **what must soon take place** and **for the crisis time is certain**, fixes the remainder of the message of Revelation firmly within the context of the first-century church, not on the far distant future of the end of the world. Imminent situations to be faced by the church will be explained in eschatological language to stress the urgency of the situation and the eschatological implications of the church's reaction to them. This is in keeping with John's predilection for using proleptic eschatological expression to explain that imminent situations and the church's reaction to them have eschatological significance.

THE SALUTATION—1:4–8

The Text

John, To the seven churches in the province of Asia: Grace and peace to you from him who is, and who was, and who is to come, and from the seven spirits before his throne, ⁵and from Jesus Christ, who is the faithful witness, the firstborn from the dead, and the ruler of the kings of the earth. To him who loves us and has freed us from our sins by his blood, ⁶and has made us to be a kingdom and priests to serve his God and Father—to him be glory and power for ever and ever. Amen. ⁷ "Look, he is coming with the clouds, and every eye will see him, even those who pierced him; and all the peoples of the earth will mourn because of him. So shall it be. Amen. ⁸"I am the Alpha and the Omega," says the Lord God, "who is, and who was, and who is to come, the Almighty."

John has purposely adapted the standard Christian epistolary form to personalize his message to the churches in Asia.[42] This reinforces the intimate nature of the communication, emphasizing John's pastoral concern for these churches.

1:4. *John, To the seven churches*. Since the second century people have debated the authorship of Revelation. First, the text itself does not identify which John wrote it. Second, apocalyptic literature traditionally is predominantly pseudonymous. Third, the early church for at least a hundred years was comfortable with Irenaeus's observation (ca. 150) that the author was John the apostle. Finally, as early as the mid third century the apostolic authorship was seriously questioned by Dionysius of Alexandria and subsequently by others. That it was written towards the close of the first century is almost universally accepted today (see the introduction for other views). Thus whoever wrote the book must have been well known to the churches in Asia at the close of the first century.

However, the position of the early church was relatively firm that the author was the apostle John. As indicated above, one of the first to identify the author as the apostle John was Irenaeus. In *Against Heresies* (normally identified by its Latin name *Adv. Haer.*), Irenaeus frequently identified the writer as "John the disciple of the Lord" (*Adv. Haer.*, iv. 14.1; v. 26.1). Justin Martyr (ca. 100), likewise, is recorded by Eusebius as attributing the work to the Apostle John (*Eccl. Hist.* iv. 18). Eusebius, however, did not accept apostolic authorship. Clement of Alexandria (ca. 200, *Paed*. Ii:119; *Quis. Div. Salv.* 42; *Strom.* vi. 106) and Tertullian of Carthage (ca. 200, *Adv. Marc.* iii. 14, 24) were also of the opinion that the author was the apostle John.

The first serious challenge to the apostolic authorship of Revelation came from Dionysius of Alexandria, a student of Origen (ca. 260). Eusebius records that Dionysius questioned apostolic authorship on the grounds that the Greek of Revelation was far inferior to that of the Gospel of John. This indicated to Dionysius that Revelation and the Gospel of John could not have been written by the same author, namely, the apostle John (*Eccl. Hist.* vii. 25). One may question Dionysius's motivation for this challenge to apostolic authorship, for apparently his opposition can be traced to his need to challenge the apostolic authority of Revelation in his arguments against the adoption of excessive chiliasm among his parishioners.[43]

Much modern scholarship has tended to follow Dionysius's argument that Revelation and the Gospel of John could not have been written by the same author. J W Roberts observes, however, that the differences in the Greek between the Gospel and Revelation have been exaggerated:

> Revelation is the poorer Greek when contrasted with the Gospel of John. It is not necessary, however, to resort to a theory of language improvement to explain the situation. The most common explanation is that New Testament writers often made use of scribes or literary assistants in writing. . . . It would be quite likely that if John had used help in composing his other books he would not have had such when in exile on Patmos. It has been pointed out that in some sections of Revelation John writes good Greek. Most of the solecisms

are in sections which seem consciously modeled on the language of the Old Testament. Hence the style may be intentional.[44]

Although the discussion of the quality of the Greek in Revelation does little to settle the identity of the author, modern scholarship does not always agree with Dionysius regarding the poor quality of the Greek in Revelation. Dionysius had maintained that the writer of the Greek of Revelation is "not accurate, but that he employs barbarous idioms, in some places committing downright solecisms" (*Eccl. Hist.* VII. xxv. 27). Caird sets the discussion of the quality of John's Greek in a different light, voicing what has become a reasonable consensus among scholars today.

> R. H. Charles has written most persuasively that John's Greek, for all its idio-syncrasy, is not ungrammatical, but has a grammar of its own, unparalleled in any other ancient writing, but none the less real and consistent, the hybrid grammar of a man thinking in Hebrew while he wrote in Greek. But because a man writes in Hebraic Greek, it does not inevitably follow that this is the only Greek he is capable of writing. He may have adopted this style quite deliber-ately for reasons of his own, as Luke appears to have imitated the style of the Septuagint in his nativity stories. . . . John's Greek may be all his own, but it is not the product of incompetence, for he handles it with brilliant lucidity and compelling power, so that he cannot be held accountable for any of our difficulties of comprehension.[45]

Caird's and Charles's views do not settle the question of the authorship of Revelation, but they do demonstrate that Dionysius's arguments are not persuasive.

The integrity of Revelation does not reside in identifying the person referred to in Revelation as John, or the fact that he was, or was not an apostle. The canonicity of Revelation, the fact that Revelation eventually became widely accepted by the early church as authentic, that its message was in keeping with other known Scripture, and that this message was certainly "apostolic," all sustain the place of Revelation in the Church's understanding of Scripture.

Yarbro Collins discusses convincingly the concerns expressed by some regarding Irenaeus's precision in matters relating to authorship:

> Although we must admit that we cannot identify the author of Revelation with any historical person otherwise known, we can infer a great deal about his social identity. He played the role of prophet; that is, his function was to medi-ate an intelligible message to his fellow Christians, a message that he claimed derived ultimately from God. He was clearly influenced by the written records and oral traditions about the classical prophets of Israel, but at the same time he should be seen as part of the phenomenon of early Christian prophecy. . . . He knew one or more Semitic languages, as well as Greek. Two aspects of his social identity are very important for understanding the origin and meaning

of his book. One is his affinity with the Jewish sibylline tradition. The other is his role as an itinerant prophet.[46]

In view of the ongoing discussion on the authorship of Revelation, Mounce's conclusion is worthy of consideration, although not definitive:

> . . . the unusually strong and early evidence supporting apostolic authorship should cause us to hesitate before accepting a conclusion based on subjective appraisal of internal considerations. Since internal evidence is not entirely unfavorable to apostolic authorship and since external evidence is unanimous in its support, the wisest course of action is either to leave the question open or to accept in a tentative way that the Apocalypse was written by John the apostle, the son of Zebedee and disciple of Jesus.[47]

We can be sure that Revelation is not pseudonymous. Charles has argued convincingly against claims that since most apocalyptic works are pseudonymous Revelation should be considered as such. He concludes that there is "not a shred of evidence" or "the shadow of a probability for such a hypothesis."[48]

To the seven churches in the province of Asia. The selection of seven churches in the proconsular district of Asia is the first indication in Revelation of John's stylistic use of the symbolism of seven (commonly identified in scholarly works on Revelation as septets). There were other churches in Asia beyond the seven named by John; there was a church in Colossae (Col. 1:2) one in Hierapolis (Col. 1:13), and another in Troas (Acts 20:5; Troas was approximately 75 miles from Pergamum). John's selection of only seven in the context of Revelation must surely have been intentional and symbolic. In fact, John resorts to the use of seven fifty-four times in Revelation. Beale draws attention to the fact that seven was a number common in both the Old Testament and the apocalyptic tradition.[49] Most commentators suggest that the number seven is symbolic of completeness, and as such plays a large role in the symbolism of Revelation.[50] Aune, citing Yarbro Collins, raises questions regarding the symbol of completeness or fullness, suggesting that seven was also a favored number for the origin of divine authority. The choice of the expression "seven churches" then may point to the divine authority of the message of John and to the divine character of the churches. I find this proposal intriguing, but in the context of 1:4 and the seven churches, not perhaps the most felicitous suggestion in that the message would be relevant to all of the churches in Asia at this time, thus suggesting completeness.[51]

Suggestions have also been made that the seven churches were chosen because they were "on the great circular road that bound the most populous, wealthy, and influential part of the Province."[52] Hemer, while not denying Ramsey's argument, proposes that the seven churches were most probably already recognized as a group and formed a center of communication for Christians scattered throughout the region.[53] Mounce suggests that these seven were selected because these cities were involved in some special sense with emperor worship.[54] This certainly seems to be a problem some of these churches faced to some degree.

Although we have no definitive solution to the selection of the seven cities, underlying the choice of seven lay more than merely geographic interests or the problems these churches faced with the emperor cult, for one must take into consideration John's stylistic grouping of visions and messages throughout Revelation into septets. Since seven was apparently the symbol of completeness and played such a significant role in Revelation, most likely John had in mind a divine authoritative message for the whole church in the Roman province of Asia. Furthermore, his choice of well-known cities would give the message a sense of realism and historical relevance.

Grace and peace to you. John adopts the traditional "Pauline" greeting, which by the end of the first century had become the standard Christian epistolary greeting.[55] *Grace* (Greek *charis*) is an adaptation of the traditional Greek *chairein*, which simply meant "greeting." In Christian circles Paul had apparently transformed the customary greeting into "grace," from the Greek *charis*, meaning "favor." The similarity of *chairein* and *charis* is not accidental, for both are related to the same Greek root. Grace in the Christian tradition signifies "divine favor," or as it is implied in the context of the theology of the Epistle to the Romans, "unmerited favor." This seems to be good reason to believe that in Paul's and John's mind this Christian greeting was associated with the Hebrew greeting, *shalom*, implying a "state of spiritual peace and prosperity." The Christian formulation becomes more than a casual greeting. It invokes a prayer on behalf of the recipients bestowing "grace, mercy, peace, and spiritual well-being."[56]

From him who is, and who was, and who is to come. The first part of John's salutation begins in majestic manner, for this greeting comes not simply from John, but from the eternal God. John will at 1:4b and 5a also include God's Holy Spirit and Jesus, God's Son, in his salutation. With John's adoption of this Old Testament and Jewish favorite expression *him who is, and who was, and who is to come*, he brings a serious theological opening to the Revelation. Richard Bauckham observes that the "theology of Revelation is highly theocentric. This, along with its distinctive doctrine of God, is its greatest contribution to New Testament theology." This trifold reference to God sets the scene for John's high theology. Under the heading "The Divine Trinity" Bauckham adds, "Among early Christian letter-openings, John's is unique in giving the standard form of salutation a 'trinitarian' character." In fact, Bauckham expresses this as a "deliberately 'trinitarian'" quality. That the divine formula of 1:4 occurs with some variation five times in Revelation leads Bauckham to conclude that this unique formula is a conscious attempt to focus attention on the eternal nature of God. Bauckham suggests that the formula is an interpretation of the divine name YHWH, which in later Judaism was an expression of the divine eternity.[57]

Bauckham's theological observations bring into clear focus how important knowing the real nature of the divine, in its full trinitarian form, is to the theology of Revelation. This stresses how important understanding the absolute holiness, sovereignty, and righteousness of the divine Trinity is to discerning the theodicy John will develop in Revelation.

John's adaptation of God's name from Exodus 3:14 (LXX) is interesting.[58] "God said to Moses, 'I AM WHO I AM.' This is what you are to say to the Israelites: 'I AM has sent me to you.'" The LXX reads "He who is" (Greek, *ho ōn*) in place of "I am who I am." This expression is one of the solecisms (grammatical inconsistencies or errors) in Revelation that some following Dionysius of Alexandria have referred to as rough or barbarian Greek. The problem for those interested in the sometimes confusing formalities or niceties of Greek grammar is that in Greek the preposition *apo* (*from*) should be followed by a noun in the genitive case; for instance in this case it should read *apo tou ontos*. But in 1:4 *apo* is followed by a nominative noun *ho ōn*. John is deliberately preserving the LXX reading of Exod. 3:14 (*egō eimi ho ōn*), where *ho ōn* is correctly in the nominative case. By preserving the nominative case of Exod. 3:14 in 1:4 rather than using the genitive case following *apo*, John intentionally and stylistically "abused" the Greek.[59] John's use of "who is" (*ho ōn*) at 1:8, where he correctly preserved the nominative, indicates that he clearly understood the intricacies of Greek grammar. This is an early example of John's stylistic adaptation or use of the Old Testament in Revelation.

John has thus adapted the "name" for God as translated in the LXX into a title, stressing that the revelation comes directly from the eternal God. He (God) always was in the past, he is constantly in the present, and he is coming in the future. He is Lord of eternity. The Christians in Asia, facing an uncertain future, needed to be reminded that God has always been the Sovereign Lord of history, is presently the powerful Sovereign Lord of the universe, and always will be Sovereign Lord of all creation. Caird adds: "John keeps the divine title in the nominative, always the subject, he always holds the initiative, and things happen because he chooses, not because men force his hand and so put him into the accusative."[60] In view of the rising crisis, the Christians needed to be reminded that Caesar and Rome were not in charge of either the universe or the Christians' destiny.

And from the seven spirits before his throne. Caird proposes that the seven spirits represent the completeness of God's Holy Spirit in the fullness of divine activity, basing his view on Zech. 4:1–6, where the seven lampstands seem to represent the Spirit of God, and Isa. 11:2, which seems to imply a sevenfold spirit of God. Beale agrees with Caird and observes that this may be a "figurative designation of the effective working of the Holy spirit."[61] Mounce, however, contends that this may be inserting a later Trinitarian theology into the text from beyond the text. Boring agrees with Mounce,[62] who goes on to state that this Trinitarian interpretation can be traced back to Victorinus of Pettau (ca. 300).

The interpretation is complicated by the fact that this expression is found only in Revelation and only in three other places, 3:1, 4:5, and 5:6. In 3:1 it is associated with Jesus, *who holds the seven spirits of God and the seven stars*. The seven stars, Jesus explains in 1:19, are *the angels of the seven churches*. In 4:5 John writes *Before the throne, seven lamps were blazing. These are the seven spirits of God*, associating the seven spirits of God with the seven lampstands, which Jesus explains in 1:19 are the seven churches.

In 5:6 John adds that the Lamb had *seven horns and seven eyes, which are the seven spirits of God sent out into all the earth*, now associating the seven spirits of God with the Lamb having seven horns and seven eyes. Consequently, no clear definition is given anywhere in Revelation that determines the meaning of this interesting reference to the seven spirits. Boring suggests tentatively, and Aune more affirmatively, that the seven spirits may be the seven angels of the churches in 2, 3.[63] Mounce proposes that "Although only a conjecture, it would seem that they (the seven spirits of God) are perhaps part of a heavenly entourage that has a special ministry in connection with the Lamb."

Caird's and Beale's proposal that the seven spirits of God could be a reference to the Holy Spirit is not farfetched, for contrary to Mounce, a Trinitarian formula was already fairly common in Christian circles at the time of writing Revelation. Beasley-Murray is possibly more to the point, agreeing with Caird that the expression possibly has roots in Zechariah and other similar traditions. Beasley-Murray concludes, "The seven spirits of God represent the Holy Spirit in his fullness of life and blessing. . . . The complex origin of the symbol is matched by its complex application in John's vision, but he and his readers were happy to have it so."[64] A Trinitarian formulation including the Holy Spirit should not be difficult to accept. The context of the expression is couched in a greeting from God and Jesus. To include the Holy Spirit in this greeting would be most appropriate.

This use of Old Testament references to the spirit and other traditions is typical of John's style of using the Old Testament throughout the book. This expression relates to the fullness of the presence of the Holy Spirit "must certainly be taken as a symbolic or allegorical way of expressing the full range of exercise of the Divine power in the seven churches."[65]

1:5a. *And from Jesus Christ, who is the faithful witness, the firstborn from the dead, and the ruler of the kings of the earth.* Not only God the Father and the Holy Spirit are concerned for the saints in Asia. Jesus is also dynamically involved and concerned. The addition of the term Christ (Messiah, a term involving the anointed king) to the name of Jesus and the greeting add solemnity to the message. John introduces Jesus with a trifold description that is especially relevant to the crisis about to descend on the saints and to the content of the message he is about to unfold. Jesus is *the faithful witness.* John must demonstrate that Jesus, whom the disciples are encouraged to emulate and worship, was not only a *faithful witness*, but the epitome of faithful witnesses.[66] The Greek word group for "witness" (*marturia, martus, marturion,* and *martureō*) has in English in religio-political contexts become a technical term, martyr, speaking of those who die for their faith and commitment. Although it might be questionable whether the Greek term had by the first century become a technical term, throughout Revelation the context of the word implies a witnessing to one's faith with one's life with a special emphasis on dying for one's faith in God. It is most certainly the context and theology of Revelation that contributed to the development of the terms martyr and martyrdom in the English-speaking Christian tradition. Mounce observes that the Christological term "faithful witness" refers to the "larger purpose of his life as the one who bore witness to the truth from God . . . with special emphasis on his death that followed as a result."[67] Witness does not simply imply verbal testimony. It is a life-giving witness:

> I know where you live—where Satan has his throne. Yet you remain true to my name. You did not renounce your faith in me, even in the days of Antipas, my faithful witness, who was put to death in your city where Satan lives. (2:13)
>
> I saw that the woman was drunk with the blood of the saints, the blood of those who bore testimony to Jesus. (17:6. The RSV translates the final phrase as *"the martyrs of Jesus."* The RSV in 17:6 reads closer to the Greek of *tōn marturiōn Iesou*.)

Christian martyrs join Jesus in "faithful witness" by dying for their faith just as Jesus had died, faithful to God and to the purpose of God. One should not overlook the sense of faithful to the purpose of God. The death of the saints serves the divine purpose of God, just as Jesus' death had served the divine purpose of God, even though this may not be fully clear to saints at the time. Their death becomes a sacrifice to God, for God and his purpose are worthy of such sacrifice. This idea is illustrated dramatically in chapter 4 in the heavenly throne scene where the twenty-four elders cast their crowns at the feet of God. Martyrdom thus becomes a priestly service to and for God (1:6).

The firstborn from the dead. This additional qualifying statement regarding Jesus had become by the close of the first century a technical term describing Jesus' preeminence and all sufficiency. In Col. 1:18 Jesus is referred to as "the firstborn from among the dead." This Christian messianic emphasis seems to have been influenced by Ps. 89:26, 27: "He will call out to me, 'You are my Father, my God, the Rock my Savior. I will also appoint him my firstborn, the most exalted of the kings of the earth.'"

In the Septuagint, the firstborn, *ho prōtotokos*, does not literally mean "the one born first." The term is a Semitism that means the one who bears the privileges and benefits of the firstborn of the family. In Gen. 27:18-40 Esau sold his birthright to Jacob, his younger twin brother. In this action of "despising" his birthright, he lost the right to be the firstborn son. Jacob thus became the "firstborn" son to Isaac and Rebekah.

In Col 1:15–20, Paul speaks of Jesus as the "firstborn over all creation," not implying that Jesus was the first person born among all creation, although some heretical religions have held to this doctrine. Paul uses this familiar Septuagintal term to stress that of all creation Jesus was preeminent and over all, for,

> by him all things were created: things in heaven and on earth, visible and invisible, whether thrones or powers or rulers or authorities; all things were created by him and for him. He is before all things, and in him all things hold together. And he is the head of the body, the church; he is the beginning and the firstborn from among the dead, so that in everything he might have the supremacy. For God was pleased to have all his fullness dwell in him, and through him to

reconcile to himself all things, whether things on earth or things in heaven, by making peace through his blood, shed on the cross. (Col. 1:16–20).

By referring to Jesus as the *firstborn from the dead* John is implying that of all those who have been raised from the dead Jesus is the preeminent one, or the one upon whom all resurrections have been, and will be, based. A minor textual variant in this clause results in the reading "firstborn of the dead" (as in the RSV and the NRSV) in which case the meaning would be that of all the dead, Jesus is the preeminent one.[68] There is little change in the meaning of the text in either case. Of all those who have been raised from the dead, Jesus as the preeminent one is the one who makes all resurrections possible.[69] The phrase is included by John as a reminder to the saints facing death that martyrdom does not imply failure to fulfill God's purpose, since in Jesus' case martyrdom led to the situation in which Jesus was exalted to the position of "firstborn," for

> *. . . God exalted him to the highest place*
> *and gave him the name that is above every name,*
> *that at the name of Jesus every knee should bow,*
> *in heaven and on earth and under the earth,*
> *and every tongue confess that Jesus Christ is Lord,*
> *to the glory of God the Father.* **(Phil 2:9–11)**

We are introduced at this point to a theological principle that John will progressively develop throughout Revelation.[70] The message to those dying for their faith in Jesus is that those who share in his death share also in Christ's resurrection and messianic reign in God's kingdom. Jesus reigns from "Mount Zion" because he died on the cross as a martyr to God. Through dying without compromising their faith in God and Christ, the martyrs will share in the messianic reign of Christ. That is the major underlying message and theme of Revelation.

The ruler of the kings of the earth. The final clause of John's threefold Christological title should not be separated from the previous two. If indeed the background to this title is Ps.. 89:27, then the connection to "firstborn" is not accidental. John draws on and develops the Davidic Messianic promise to Jesus: "I will also appoint him my **firstborn**, the most exalted of the kings of the earth" (Ps. 89:27).

The themes of faithful witness and resurrection from the dead are connected to his being king of kings, for it was in his death and resurrection that Jesus was vindicated by God and exalted to be acknowledged as the supreme ruler of nations (Phil. 2:10, 11). In Revelation a prominent theme is that Jesus reigns through faithfully dying on the cross. He is king because of his faithful witness (martyrdom) and subsequent resurrection from the dead by the power of God (cf. 17:14; 19:16). This God who raised Jesus from the dead to reign on his throne will also raise the martyr from the dead to reign with Christ from Mount Zion. The saints' victorious resurrection from the dead is described in Revelation as a vindication of their sacrifice and of their commitment to God and Christ, just as Jesus' resurrection vindicated his life and purpose. God's vindication of the martyrs, based on his vindication of Jesus, plays a significant role in the unfolding story line of Revelation (cf. 11:9–13).

The threefold Christological title of Jesus serves a major purpose in John's theological scheme: It pulls martyrdom, resurrection, and reigning together into a powerful theological argument. Through this theological emphasis John encourages Christians to endure persecution and martyrdom in the firm assurance that God will raise the martyr to share the throne and reign of Jesus in Jesus' eternal kingdom (3:21, 20:4–6). John encourages the Christians by reminding them that Jesus has already endured such suffering and death, and that he, John, is also already sharing with them in this crisis (1:9). The theme of dying for their faith in Jesus and being raised to reign with Jesus is certainly the major theme of Revelation. Dying as a martyr as Jesus had died assures the saints facing persecution that through resurrection the martyr will gain victory over Satan and Rome. Dying in Revelation is not disgrace or defeat; it is to conquer with Jesus. (Note the RSV translation "*conquering*" in 2:7; 11; 17; 26; 3:5; 12; 21. The NIV translation of *nikaō* as "overcoming" is unfortunate. The RSV *conquer* is better.[71]).

1:5b, 6. *To him who loves us and has freed us from our sins by his blood,* [6]*and has made us to be a kingdom and priests to serve his God and Father—to him be glory and power for ever and ever. Amen.* Jesus is the one who loves us, has freed us, and has made us a kingdom where saints reign with him. The beleaguered saints are also reminded of the abiding love of God and Jesus. God is after all "*He who loves forever*" (Lam. 3:22, 23, 24; Ps. 136), and "who can separate us from the love of Christ," for "we are more than conquerors through him who loved us" (Rom 8:31–39). The present tense of the participle "loves" reinforces the constant abiding presence and love of Christ. The aorist tense of the participle "freed" expresses the certainty of his action; he has already freed us from our sins.[72] In that action we have been redeemed and now belong to Christ. Through the saving action of his death, Jesus has made us *a kingdom and priests*. Christians have been brought into the reign (*basileia*, kingship) of Christ. They reign with him in his kingdom. In addition, Christians serve God in a priestly role by offering their own lives as a sacrifice to God (cf. Rom 12:1, 2). The RSV and NRSV translation of "has made us a kingdom, priests to his God" is preferred, although ultimately there is little difference in meaning between a "kingdom and priests," a "kingdom of priests," or a "kingdom, priests to his God." John must have had in mind Exod. 19:6: "'you will be for me a kingdom of priests and a holy nation.' These are the words you are to speak to the Israelites."

Like Israel the church is a kingdom of priests. Boring stresses that the sense is not that Christ made a kingdom for the Christians, but that he made them into a kingdom.[73] Caird is more to the point:

> They (Israel) were a kingdom because they belonged to God the King; and they were priests because they had been set apart out of all nations for a special vocation of holiness, just as within Israel the tribe of Levi was chosen to offer to God a representative holiness. But John is not necessarily bound by the limitations of the Old Testament. He believed that those who Christ had

released from their sins were called to be **a royal house**, not merely because he reigned over them as King, but because they were to share his regal authority over the nations (cf .ii.26; iii.21; v.10; xx.6). Ought we not therefore to expect that they are to share his priestly office also, and be a body through which he can exercise his redemptive as well as his regal power?[74]

The Christian martyrs' lives would not be wasted, for in dying as martyrs they would be offering their lives to God as priests in the kingdom of Christ. The saints in Asia needed strong assurance. Although we may not be facing suffering to the degree that the saints in Asia were facing at the close of the first century, the message to them is relevant today. God will in Christ give us victory over Satan and we will also share with him in his kingdom through our faithful commitment to Jesus.

To him be glory and power for ever and ever. Amen. This doxological statement is the first of many in Revelation in which both God and Jesus are worshipped (cf. 4:11; 5:9, 12–13; 7:10; et al.). Since Revelation was to be read in the assembly, such praise of God and Jesus would strengthen the liturgical life of the church. In spite of his cruel death in disgrace as a criminal on a Roman cross, all glory and power belong to Christ. He is God's sovereign ruler over all nations and deserves all praise and glory.

The irony of the Christian faith is in every sense one of the paradoxes of life. One dies in shame yet is vindicated in glory. The martyrs will share in Jesus' glory and power as they too are martyred and vindicated by God in glory. Although in Revelation John will depict Jesus as a savior who has sacrificed his life for God, he is never portrayed as an impotent king. Later in Revelation he is pictured as the sovereign conquering Lord of lords and King of kings (1:12–18; 19:11–16). Even though he is referred to as the Lamb, it is through his voluntary sacrificial death that he reigns victoriously as God's sovereign ruler over all rebellious nations as the Lion of the tribe of Judah (5:5). As the Lamb in Revelation, he reigns as God's sovereign king, for he is the Lamb who stands on Mount Zion,[75] victorious over death and sovereign ruler over God's kingdom. In 5:5 Jesus is portrayed in messianic terms as the Lion of the Tribe of Judah because he became the Lamb of God, a veiled allusion to a kingdom of priests who reign through self sacrifice to God.

The "*amen*" at the end of the doxology stands as an exclamation mark, confirming the truth of the praise. Two magnificent doxological passages in 5:9, 10 and 12 are fuller developments of this doxological theme:

[9] **And they sang a new song:**
"You are worthy to take the scroll and to open its seals,
because you were slain,
and with your blood you purchased men for God from every tribe and language and people and nation.
[10]**You have made them to be a kingdom and priests to serve our God,**
and they will reign on the earth. "
[12] **In a loud voice they sang:**

"Worthy is the Lamb, who was slain,
to receive power and wealth and wisdom and strength
and honor and glory and praise. "

1:7. *Look, he is coming with the clouds, and every eye will see him, even those who pierced him; and all the peoples of the earth will mourn because of him. So shall it be. Amen.* The demonstrative particle *idou* (here *look*) is a marker emphasizing what follows. The translation "behold (RSV), although somewhat archaic, is preferred. *Behold* (*idou*) is found twenty six times in Revelation at strategic points in the drama.[76] This has caused some to conclude that in 1:7 John is drawing attention to a major point, or motto, in the theological drama he is about to reveal.[77]

In this collage of terms and ideas,[78] John has obviously cast his mind back to Dan. 7:13 and associated it with Zech. 12:10. This is typical of John's "Old Testament" literary style. Boring and others observe that John nowhere quotes directly from the Old Testament, but takes ideas, images, and dramatic concepts and, like a master painter, dips his pen into this Old Testament palette as he conjures up powerful new ideas and visions. Boring observes:

> The use of sources and traditional materials is not incompatible with authentic visionary experience. What sources and traditions did John actually use? First and foremost, his Bible: Revelation is saturated with allusions to the Old Testament, showing that the author's mind was itself steeped in Scripture, the words and images which were available to provide raw material for his visions, and literary means by which to later express them. . . . [T]here are approximately five hundred allusions to the Scriptures. Yet, though John uses the words and images of Scripture in almost every line of his letter, he never once formally cites an Old Testament passage. The text becomes in his hand the vehicle for communicating the present word of the risen Lord.[79]

Daniel 7:13 provides John with the first image of one like a son of man coming in the clouds to receive authority, glory, sovereign power, everlasting dominion, and a kingdom that shall never be destroyed.[80] In Hebrew idiom, the coming with clouds is often associated with divine presence and judgment (Exod. 13:21; 16:10; Isa. 19:1; Ezek. 30:1–3. 32:7). The frequency of this type of phraseology in the New Testament and other sources (Mark 13:26; 14:62; Matt. 24:30; 26:64; Acts 1:9; Rev. 14:14–16; 4 Ezra 13:3) suggests that the coming with clouds may have become in the Christian tradition a favored eschatological and apocalyptic expression.[81] John fuses this Danielic reference of Jesus' coming with the clouds with Zechariah 12:8–14, in which God promises to come in judgment on the nations, but in grace on Jerusalem. All nations of the earth will mourn God's coming, for it speaks of his coming in salvation of Jerusalem, God's people, but also a coming in judgment on the nations. The same combination of Daniel 7 and Zechariah 12 occurs in Matthew 24:30, suggesting that both John and Matthew were drawing on a common Christian eschatological tradition in which these two passages were already joined in reference to Jesus' coming in judgment on those who oppose him. Mounce suggests that this language, "extends to all those of every age whose careless indifference to Jesus is typified in the act of piercing. . . . The mourning of Zechariah 12:10–12 was that of repentance, but the mourning of Revelation is the remorse accompanying the disclosure of divine judgment at the coming of Christ (16:9, 11, 21)."[82]

The intriguing question is whether this reference to the coming of Jesus with clouds is to his parousia at the end of time or whether in Revelation and other apocalyptic passages Jesus is constantly coming to the church in vindication of their martyrdom, or coming to the church and the church's enemies in judgment of specific situations. John's use of eschatological language in Revelation adopts as I have suggested a proleptic eschatological expectation. As an example, in 2:5, Jesus promises to come in judgment on the church in Ephesus, unless they repent. Similarly, in 2:16, he promises to come in judgment on the church in Pergamum, unless they repent. It is obvious, based on the statement, unless they repent, that these comings in judgment are conditional promises. The same language is repeated in other of the seven letters, and in each case it is obvious that this is not a reference to the *parousia*, but a proleptic judgment on the church that has eschatological implications. The same language and proleptic eschatological judgment is adopted in describing the judgment of Jerusalem in Matt. 24.

Beale observes that although an allusion to the final *parousia* is included in this juxtapositioning of Dan. 7 and Zech. 12, the primary reference must be to the present situation of the seven churches and the crisis they are about to experience.

> since the Son of man allusion in Rev 1:13 has present application . . . as do the Old Testament references in 1:5–6 and 1:14–20 . . . the same citation from Dan 7:13 in Mark 13:26 and 14:62 refers not to the final coming of Christ, but to the Son of man's coming in Judgment of Jerusalem in A. D. 70, and the identical combination of Dan 7:13 with Zech 12:10 in Matt 24:30 is susceptible of the same meaning, although the final parousia could be in mind. . . . These references in the Synoptics could have prepared John's readers for another application of the Son of man prophecy to a time preceding, as well as including, his final coming at the climax of history. . . . Furthermore, Christ's "coming" in the letters of chs. 2 and 3 appears to be his conditional visitation in judgment of the churches, though an allusion to the second coming could be included. . . . This points to a close conceptual link between the comings in the letters and in the conclusion of the book. Therefore, Christ's "coming" in 1:7 and elsewhere in the Apocalypse is understood better as a process occurring throughout history; the so-called "second coming" is actually a final coming concluding the whole process of comings.[83]

The language of proleptic eschatological expectation strengthens the certainty of the coming of Jesus in judgment on Rome and in vindication of the saints for their martyrdom. His coming on the churches and on Rome will assuredly occur before the eschatological end. Thus in 1:7 this eschatological end-of-the-world language is used to describe the certainty and finality of Jesus' and God's judgment on the churches that do not repent (2–3), and on Rome. The expression *So shall it be. Amen* serves both as a doxological conclusion to the salutation of the "epistle" and an affirmation of the fact stressed throughout Revelation that God and Jesus will judge the oppressors.

1:8. *"I am the Alpha and the Omega", says the Lord God, "who is, and who was, and who is to come, the Almighty".* John opened the salutation of the letter to the seven churches (1:4) with the comment that the letter was coming directly from the eternal godhead, *"the one who is, who was, and who is to come."* He closes the salutation in similar fashion, reminding the reader of the divine source and authority of the revelation and message: *"I am the Alpha and the Omega . . . who is, and who was, and who is to come, the Almighty."* Later, in the epilogue (21:6), God will bring closure to the whole revelation by repeating the expression *I am the Alpha and the Omega* (the first and last letters of the Greek alphabet). However, in the epilogue God adds an expression of finality: *It is done. I am the Alpha and the Omega, the Beginning and the End.* Again in 22:13 he applies this formula to himself, *I am the Alpha and the Omega, the First and the Last, the Beginning and the End.* Finally, in closing the salutation (1:8), God adds the additional statement that he is *the Almighty*. The term *Almighty* (*ho pantokratōr*) is used extensively throughout the LXX, and is found nine times in Revelation (1:8; 4:8; 11:17; 15:3; 16:7, 14; 19:6, 15; and 21:22). *Ho pantokratōr*, is "one of several ways the LXX translates the Hebrew phrase 'Yahweh of Sebaoth', the powerful, avenging, conquering Lord of 'hosts'."[84] The context of combat mythology[85] in Revelation makes this statement all the more meaningful. God is not only the eternal God; he is also the all powerful eternal supreme ruler and sovereign of the universe. He is the eternal God, the "captain" of the victorious angelic hosts. Caesar was not the almighty or sovereign power over the world; God is. This high point of God's eternal sovereignty is an appropriate conclusion to John's salutation to the seven churches of Asia who stand intimidated by the awesome power of Rome. It adds solemnity, power, and ultimate authority to the revelation that is to follow.

Summary to the Salutation

The salutation of Revelation draws attention immediately to the fact that the whole godhead is concerned for the churches in Asia. Not only the eternal God, but also his ever-present Spirit and Jesus Christ, the loving Redeemer, care for the church. Furthermore, the saints have been called by Jesus to share in his kingdom (reign) in which they will serve God as priests; their lives being the sacrifice they offer to God in awe of his sovereign power and dominion. The resurrection of the martyrs is assured since Jesus is the preeminent one of all the dead whose own resurrection has become the firstfruits and assurance of many resurrections to follow. The Spirit who raised Jesus from the dead will also raise them (Rom 8:11). Jesus will come in a proleptic eschatological judgment on the churches and their oppressive enemy, the nation Rome, for its persecution of God's saints. The promise of victory and vindication is secured by the eternal nature and sovereign power of God.

THE VISION OF THE TRIUMPHANT JESUS—1:9–20
The Text

I John, your brother and companion in the suffering and kingdom and patient endurance that are ours in Jesus, was on the island of Patmos because of the word of God and the testimony of Jesus. ¹⁰On the Lord's Day I was in the Spirit, and I heard behind me a loud voice like a trumpet,¹¹which said: "Write on a scroll what you see and send it to the seven churches: to Ephesus, Smyrna, Pergamum, Thyatira, Sardis, Philadelphia and Laodicea."

¹²I turned around to see the voice that was speaking to me. And when I turned I saw seven golden lampstands, ¹³and among the lampstands was someone "like a son of man," dressed in a robe reaching down to his feet and with a golden sash around his chest. ¹⁴His head and hair were white like wool, as white as snow, and his eyes were like blazing fire. ¹⁵His feet were like bronze glowing in a furnace, and his voice was like the sound of rushing waters. ¹⁶In his right hand he held seven stars, and out of his mouth came a sharp double-edged sword. His face was like the sun shining in all its brilliance.

¹⁷When I saw him, I fell at his feet as though dead. Then he placed his right hand on me and said: "Do not be afraid. I am the First and the Last. ¹⁸I am the Living One; I was dead, and behold I am alive for ever and ever. And I hold the keys of death and Hades.

¹⁹"Write, therefore, what you have seen, what is now and what will take place later. ²⁰The mystery of the seven stars that you saw in my right hand and of the seven golden lampstands is this: The seven stars are the angels of the seven churches, and the seven lampstands are the seven churches.

1:9. I, John, your brother and companion in the suffering and kingdom and patient endurance that are ours in Jesus, was on the island of Patmos because of the word of God and the testimony of Jesus. John reminds the churches that he was already encountering what they all were about to experience; suffering, faithfulness, and sharing in the reign of Jesus. There is considerable debate among scholars as to exactly what Roman decree or law it was under which John was in exile on Patmos. There were possibly at least two types of exile that may have applied to John; one, a severe deportation that could only be pronounced by the emperor; the other could be pronounced by a provincial governor. The only information we have regarding John's exile is an early third-century report by Tertullian (ca. 200). Tertullian, a lawyer, recorded that John was on Patmos for the lesser crime pronounced by the provincial governor (*De Praescript. Haer.* 36). In any case, John must have run contrary to Roman pleasure by his message concerning the messianic sovereign nature of Christ, and John's steadfast refusal to honor any other being, even a Caesar, as Lord. Whatever the exact legal situation may have been, John's explanation **because of the word of God and the testimony of Jesus** is all we really know as to why

John was on Patmos.[86] Apparently, the Roman authorities had determined that John's preaching was disturbing the peace and had banished him to the island forty-two miles southwest of Ephesus. Patmos was a Roman penal colony in a group of islands called the Sporades. Primarily, the island was used for the banishment of political offenders.

At 1:2 *the testimony of Jesus* in all probability referred to the *message that came from God concerning Jesus*. This message included the fact that Jesus, not Caesar, was Lord and Sovereign. Likewise in this case *the testimony of Jesus* at 1:9 would mean John's preaching concerning Jesus (an objective genitive) as sovereign Lord of all.[87]

John refers to himself as *your brother and companion in the suffering and kingdom and patient endurance that are ours in Jesus*. The phrase *your brother* indicates that John was well known to the churches in Asia Minor. He shares with them the problems the church has with the Roman authorities because of their preaching and faith in Jesus. He juxtaposes three key concepts, suffering, endurance, and kingdom, which become part of the fabric of his theology. Caird renders *suffering* here aptly as "ordeal." This trifold expression of John's is another case in which John is laying a theological foundation for the message of Revelation. He makes the point that sharing in the kingdom, or reign[88] of Jesus comes through faithfully enduring suffering (the ordeal) and persecution. Caird translates *kingdom* here as "sovereignty," which is appropriate and fits well into the context of the theology of Revelation.[89] The reward for dying as a martyr (conqueror) in Revelation is that the martyr receives a crown of life and reigns with Christ in his kingdom. Beale observes, "This is a formula for kingship: faithful endurance through tribulation is the means by which one reigns in the present with Jesus."[90] John progressively develops this theme in the discussion of the seven letters of 2–3.

1:10. *On the Lord's Day I was in the Spirit, and I heard behind me a loud voice like a trumpet,* [11]*which said* . . . This is the first reference to *the Lord's Day* in Christian literature. It was common practice among pagan religions to designate a special day in honor of one of the gods or the emperor. It is quite natural that Christians should designate the day on which their savior was raised and on which they gathered to celebrate the Eucharist as *the Lord's Day* in opposition to any day in honor of the emperor.[91] John states that he *was in the Spirit* (*en pneumati*) on this occasion. Normally, the expression refers to a deep state of spiritual experience, or ecstasy. Peter (Acts 10:10; 11:5) and Paul (Acts 22:17; cf. 2 Cor 12:1-4) experienced similar encounters with the Spirit, but Luke uses the term *en ecstasei* (ecstasy) to describe their experience. John uses the same expression *in the Spirit* at 4:2 to describe his experience of being under the influence of the Spirit, with another possible reference in 17:3. Many reasons could be suggested as to why John was open to such an experience, but the simplest is that it was the Lord's Day and John was deep in spiritual meditation. In this "ecstatic" experience John came under the empowering influence of the Holy Spirit. Caird and Mounce[92] suggest that this spiritual condition may have been some form of spiritual "trance." Aune likewise suggests that John was in a prophetic trance.[93]

1:11. *Write on a scroll what you see and send it to the seven churches: to Ephesus, Smyrna, Pergamum, Thyatira, Sardis, Philadelphia and Laodicea.* John is instructed by the *loud voice like a trumpet* (a reference to the importance of Jesus' instruction) to write the visions he had seen in a *scroll* (RSV book[94]) and to send it to the seven churches in Asia Minor. At Daniel 12:4, 9, Daniel was told to seal the book he was writing, for the message was for a later date. In contrast to Daniel, here in the prologue of 1:11, John was told to write his message in a scroll. In the epilogue of 22:10, he is told not to seal up his message, *for the time is near.* In contrast to Daniel, there is a sense of urgency to the message that John is told to write to the seven churches.

Regarding the choice of seven churches much has been said of the route along a major road connecting the cities on which these seven churches are located,[95] and this may be somewhat relevant,[96] but the symbolism of John's use of septets in Revelation points more to a theological than a geographic implication, and the "reverse" paralleling of his message to that of Daniel adds a sense of theological urgency to his message. The important point to note here is that Daniel was told to seal up his book for the message was for a later time. Here John is told to wrote the message down and send it to the seven churches, reinforcing the urgency of the message and the imminence of the crises to by faced by the seven churches.

1:12. *I turned around to see the voice that was speaking to me.* The voice John turns to see is the voice of 1:10, which he will again hear in 4:1, he describes this voice as the one that spoke to him like a trumpet. Mounce sums up the opinion of most that "the One who speaks is none other than the exalted Christ."[97] Whether the voice should be understood in light of Old Testament and Jewish use of the expression "the voice" in reference to God, or an hypostatic heavenly creature, or an angel is not clear, but from the context of 1:12-16, it seems clear that the reference is to the Christ, and in view of similar Old Testament uses, the exalted Christ is pictured in "his superhuman glory."[98]

1:12b, 13. *And when I turned I saw seven golden lampstands.* [13]*And among the lampstands was someone "like a son of man."* This is no impotent and dying Jesus that John sees; this is a magnificent, conquering, and sovereign Christ who appears. Christians, whenever they suffer hardship and oppression, need to see this sovereign Christ; the one who holds the destiny of the world, in particular their destiny, in his hand.

The first vision John has is of *seven golden lampstands* and in the midst of them one *like a son of man.* The seven lampstands have as their source Zech. 4, featured on several occasions in Revelation. In the early chapters of Zechariah are a number of other visions relating to the rebuilding of the temple that are also featured in Revelation: the four horsemen, the four horns, the measuring of the city, and the lampstands and olive trees. In Zech. 4 the candelabrum in the temple represented the word of the Lord and the light of the world. In the Christian tradition Christians or the church are to be the light of the world (Matt. 5:14; Phil. 2:15). The seven lampstands following immediately after the mention of the seven churches leads one to conclude that the best interpretation here of the seven lampstands is that they represent the seven churches who are God's light in the gentile world. Revelation 1:20, however, solidifies this thought and defines the lampstands as the churches. Beale adds that the lampstands in the temple represented the presence of God; therefore, since the lampstands in Revelation represent the churches, then the imagery of the lampstands speaks of God's presence with and in his churches.[99] Furthermore, this imagery of the presence of God among his churches is enhanced by Jesus constantly walking around among the seven lampstands, or churches (2:1).

There is some speculation as to whether *one like a son of man* has reference to one in the form of a human being (which would be in keeping with normal Hebrew idiom) or whether this is a reference to Jesus' personal preference for the title Son of Man over Messiah in the synoptic tradition. The debate on whether the term in the Gospels is in the Danielic tradition or whether it follows that of the Ezekiel tradition has raged for decades.[100] However, the striking influence of Daniel 7 and 10 on Revelation most likely implies a link with the Danielic tradition. Charles suggests that *like a son of man* could be understood in the apocalyptic genre as a reference to an angel.[101] This seems unlikely in the context of 1:11. The coming of a transcendent son of man to vindicate the saints in Daniel 7 provides much of the imagery of Revelation.[102]

Whatever the case, this son of man, clothed in impressive regalia, has died and come to life again. He is the risen Christ (see 1:18). Beale observes that most commentators agree that the significance of this *son of man* language is "that Christ is portrayed as a kingly and priestly figure, since the two Daniel texts have the same features." Beale adds that this reference "also evokes his role as the latter day, divine judge."[103] The point is threefold; first, this son of man speaks with divine authority and is worthy of worship; second, he is present in the midst of the churches; and third, he is the supernatural judge of nations. Christ is not an absentee king, but one who is involved in the life of his church. This will be developed in great detail in the seven letters of 2–3.

1:14–16. The one like the son of man is *dressed in a robe reaching down to his feet and with a golden sash around his chest.* [14]*His head and hair were white like wool, as white as snow, and his eyes were like blazing fire.* [15]*His feet were like bronze glowing in a furnace, and his voice was like the sound of rushing waters.* [16]*In his right hand he held seven stars, and out of his mouth came a sharp double-edged sword. His face was like the sun shining in all its brilliance.* Caird appropriately cautions against over interpretation of this pericope. The description of Jesus, the risen Lord, should not to be taken in too great detail, but is symbolic. In keeping with the striking kaleidoscopic symbolism of Revelation and its intended purpose to be read aloud in the assembly, the description of Jesus in such impressionistic imagery has dramatic effect. Again, Daniel 7 and 10 apparently form the source of much of John's imagery in this pericope. The robe reaching down to his feet and the girdle are the regalia of the high priest (Exod. 28:4; 29:29) and emphasize the high priestly role of Christ. The white hair is symbolic of the Ancient of Days (Dan. 7:9), emphasizing his divine stature alongside God the Father. Whatever the full symbolism of this vision might be, the visual (to John) and audible (to the churches) impact was strikingly similar to that of Daniel as expressed in Daniel 10:4–9. Caird is right:

> The description of the Son of Man is full of Old Testament phrases, which we
> may track down to their various sources. . . . But to compile such a catalogue
> is to unweave the rainbow. John uses his allusions not as a code in which each
> symbol requires separate and exact translation, but rather for their evocative
> and emotive power. This is not photographic art. His aim is to set the echoes
> of memory and association ringing.[104]

John's literary style is artistic. The scenes keep moving, sometimes ever so slightly, at
other times dramatically. The scenes are not chronologically sequential as in a movie,
but are scenes repeated in broad strokes as when a kaleidoscope is turned and the images
adjusted. To examine the images under a microscopic lens is to lose the powerful impact
of the images. One should "stand back" and see and hear the total impact rather than
the individual brush strokes. As Caird has observed, when one "unweaves the rainbow"
one destroys it.[105]

In his right hand he held seven stars. There is no apparent agreement as to the origin
of the seven stars. Suggestions have been made in regard to astrological images and
the existence of seven stars in constellations familiar at the time of John's writing.[106]
Revelation 1:20, however, explains that the seven stars represent the seven angels of the
seven churches. At 2, 3 each church is represented by an angel, so suggestion has been
made that the seven stars are the heavenly representatives of the church. There is no need
to go beyond the context of seven churches into astrological symbolism for the meaning
of the seven stars. The symbolism of seven stars, seven angels, and seven churches apparently means that Jesus holds the destiny of all the churches in Asia in his right hand.
It is not Rome, the Roman governor, or emperor who holds the destiny of the church.
It is Jesus who as sovereign over the whole world controls the destiny of the church.[107]

Out of his mouth came a sharp double-edged sword. This is the only indication of any
weapon possessed by the triumphant Christ. His weapon in reality is his message. By
his word he creates, delivers, saves, judges, and brings everything to finality and closure!
The letter to Pergamum (2:12, 16) has similar wording. The sharp-two edged Roman
sword was a symbol of proconsular power over life. In this vision it is Jesus, not Rome,
who holds the executive power over life and death, and this right is expressed as a sword
proceeding out of his mouth, namely, his final word of judgment. It is Jesus' word and
message, not the word of the Caesar, that will judge the nations. This symbolism is particularly relevant in the case of the church in Pergamum (cf. 2:12.) The imagery of God's
word as a sharp two-edged sword by which he will judge the nations has roots in Old
Testament and Jewish tradition (Isa. 11:4; 49:2; 4 Ezra 13:4, 10; Wis. 18:15) as well as in
the New Testament (Heb. 4:12). John returns to this image of the sword of judgment at
19:15, where he describes Jesus' judgment of the nations, specifically the beast and the
false prophet, that is Rome in its dual role of civil and religious power. That Jesus has this
sharp two-edged sword reinforces the fact that it is he who is the divine eschatological
judge, not the emperor of Rome, a view already established in Dan. 7.[108]

1:17, 18. *When I saw him, I fell at his feet as though dead. Then he placed his right hand on me and said: "Do not be afraid. I am the First and the Last.* [18]*I am the Living One; I was dead, and behold I am alive for ever and ever. And I hold the keys of death and Hades.* Such was the impact of the vision on John that he was overwhelmed with overpowering awe. Similar experiences are found (e.g., in Josh. 5:14; Isa. 6:3-5; Ezek. 1:28; Dan. 8:17) indicating the response of those struck by the awesome majesty of divinity. Jesus encouraged John not to be afraid. He then identified himself in terms previously used of God, implying that he, Jesus, bears the full dignity of divinity, and consonant divine power and authority. Like the eternal God, Jesus is *the First and the Last.* Jesus again at 22:13 refers to himself in this manner. As the divine creative power of the universe, Jesus spoke it into being (John 1:1–3; Heb. 1:2) and, as the divine eschatological, judge he will speak the word that brings the world to final judgment (Acts 17:31). There can be no question that this vision is of Jesus, for he adds *I am the Living One; I was dead, and behold I am alive for ever and ever.* This reference to Jesus' death and resurrection is vital to the message of Revelation. That the resurrected Jesus is alive forevermore forms the basis of John's call to the churches to be faithful unto death.

Finally, Jesus explains to John that it is he, Jesus, who holds *the keys of death and Hades.* Jesus holds the authority (*keys*) and power over death and the place of the dead. This statement is obviously to reassure John and the churches that their ultimate destiny lay not with Rome and the Caesar, but with Jesus, the one who had overcome death by the power of his resurrection. Furthermore, at the command of Jesus at the final judgment, death and Hades will give up their dead for judgment (20:13).

1:19. *Write, therefore, what you have seen, what is now and what will take place later.* As with 1:1, 3, this text is densely packed and pivotal to the interpretation of Revelation. The syntax of the text requires careful attention to the grammatical possibilities within the text. Beale is correct in observing "The meaning of v 19 is crucial since it is usually understood to be paradigmatic for the structure and content of the whole book".[109] The command *Write* holds little mystery, for Jesus once again instructs John (see 1:11) to write a message to the churches about the visions he has seen. To some, there appears to be a trifold construction in the words *what you saw, what is now, and what will take place later.* Charles and Swete accept the trifold formula with reluctance, stating that it is a rough construction.[110] Beasley-Murray observes that this trifold division of the statement has led to "frequent misunderstanding,"[111] while Caird is more to the point by commenting that the trifold construction in some interpretations is "a grotesque over-simplification."[112] Beale and Aune appropriately reject the trifold interpretation; Aune suggests that John has modified a Hellenistic tripartite formula to refer only to two aspects, the present and the future.[113]

John writes *write . . . what you saw, what is now, and what will take place later* (*grapson oun ha eides kai ha eisin kai ha mellei genesthai meta tauta*). A literal translation would be "*write therefore what you saw and what is and what is about to be after these things*". The Greek construction has the initial clause *grapson oun ha eides,* **write therefore what** *you saw*, followed by two clauses each introduced by the conjunction *kai*, which could be translated by the coordinating conjunction "and." However, the grammatical construction suggests that the first *kai* is emphatic and should be read as an epexegetical *kai*, in which case it should be translated "indeed."[114] The second *kai* would then be coordinating, explaining the two things following define first epexegetical *kai*. As Beckwith, Caird, Mounce, Boring, Beale, and Aune[115] have suggested, John is being told by Jesus to "*write what you saw in a scroll, that is, what is now happening and is about to break into the life of the churches.* I am intrigued by Kiddle's appropriate translation of 1:19, "Write down your vision of what is and what is to be hereafter."[116] Mounce is correct in observing that the initial clause, "write therefore what you saw," is parallel to 1:11, in which Jesus instructs John to "write what you see in a book." He concludes that "write what you saw" and "write what you see" are proleptic relative clauses that "have as their referents the vision to be unfolded in the coming chapters."[117]

This verse holds one more important, if not vital, key to the appropriate translation of this text. The Greek reads *ha mellei genesthai meta tauta*. *Genesthai* is an aorist infinitive verb form of *ginomai*, which can mean "to become," "to be," or "to happen." When *mellō* (or *mellei* as it is found in the text of 1:19) is used with the aorist infinitive, it becomes "*on the point of happening*."[118] The things John is to write are "on the point of happening." This construction is therefore not a trifold construction, but a twofold construction. ***Write what you see, indeed what is** (happening), **and what is on the point of happening.*** Commenting on the nature of the third part of the formula, ***what will take place later**, Beale finds parallels to Daniel 2 and observes that "In fact, it likely has inaugurated end-time meaning in the light of the context in ch. 1."[119]

Revelation 1:19 is pivotal to understanding the content of Revelation and an appropriate interpretation of the book. The statement of 1:19, ***write**, must be translated both within the unique grammatical syntax (construction) of the sentence, and the sociohistorical context of the book. The instruction to John to "*Write . . . things that are about to happen*" draws attention to the urgency of God's and Jesus' message to the churches living in the shadow of the Roman empire in the first century of Christianity. Beal is thus correct, stating, "The meaning of v 19 is crucial since it is usually understood to be paradigmatic for the structure and content of the whole book".[120]

1:20. *The mystery of the seven stars that you saw in my right hand and of the seven golden lampstands is this: The seven stars are the angels of the seven churches, and the seven lampstands are the seven churches.* The RSV and the NRSV both begin this sentence with ***as for***, indicating a break between 1:19 and 20. This suggests that 1:20 serves as a connective between the command of Jesus to write and the seven letters that follow, a device typical of John's literary linking style, connecting one block of material to the next with "hook" words or ideas. Aune, following Kraft, suggests that this verse could be a gloss (later insertion) by John "in order to link the commission of 1:9–20 to the proclamations to the seven churches in 2–3."[121] Aune's view that the verse may be a gloss is questionable, but he is correct in seeing in this verse a connective between the two blocks of material. The KJV and ASV translators attempted to emphasize the connective style of 1:20 between 1:19 and 2:1 by breaking the 1:20 into two sentences, apparently applying the first half of 1:20 to verse 19, the second half to 2:1. The punctuation of the ASV and the KJV breaks 1:20 thereby tying the last sentence of 1:20 as a link or connective to the next chapter and the seven letters.:

> *Write therefore the things which thou sawest, and the things which are, and the things which shall come to pass hereafter;* [20]*the mystery of the seven stars which thou sawest in my right hand, and the seven golden candlesticks. The seven stars are the angels of the seven churches: and the seven candlesticks are seven churches.*

However, based on the grammatical awkwardness of the initial clause[122] of the verse, commentators have differed in regard to their application. Commentators drawing on the RSV, NRSV, and NIV have preferred these translations and have followed the suggested punctuation of the Nestle and Aland Greek texts. By maintaining the unity of 1:20, the RSV, NRSV, and NIV indicate that the mystery that Jesus is about to reveal (1:20) relates to the seven stars and seven lampstands that are in fact the church. The **mystery of the seven stars** *(mustērion)*, referring to something formerly unknown but now revealed, becomes apparent once John reveals the message of Jesus in the letters that follow. Jesus explains that the seven stars, seven angels, and seven lampstands are simply symbols of the seven churches. The number seven represents the completeness of God's action or plan. Thus the Revelation, although addressed to seven specific churches, is intended to proclaim a divine message to all of the churches in Asia.

The meaning of the angels in relation to the seven churches has given rise to considerable discussion[123]. One theory is that the angel represents the bishop of the church, another is that the angel is the guardian angel of the church, a third is that the angel is equal to the church itself, or its personified life.[124] Some have equated the angel with the preacher or minister of the church since the word angel simply means "a messenger."[125] Caird, Beasley-Murray, Boring, and Mounce correctly conclude that the angels are heavenly beings, possibly guardian angels, who represent the churches.[126] Beale considers the angels to be the corporate heavenly representatives of the church,[127] while Aune adds that they are "supernatural beings serving as the messengers of God."[128] They are responsible for the welfare of the churches. Caird concludes the "The Jews had long since become accustomed to the idea that each nation had its own angelic representatives in heaven who presided over its fortunes and was held accountable for its misdeeds, and John is simply adapting this familiar notion to a new situation."[129] Since the word angel or angels appears some seventy-seven times in Revelation (NIV) in the context of heavenly beings, we should understand them as such, namely, "heavenly beings that serve God and his purpose." In Revelation we encounter angels of the water, angels of the wind, angels of the trees, angels of the bottomless pit, mighty angels, among many other kinds of angels. Furthermore, angels as heavenly beings signifying divine intervention in all apocalyptic and biblical literature.

Summary of The Vision of the Triumphant Jesus, Rev. 1:9–20

Two points of considerable import to the theology of Revelation are developed in this section.

1) John explains to his audience that they are not alone in their distress, for he too is experiencing persecution and exile on account of his faith in Jesus, and message regarding Jesus. John fuses three concepts together that he will develop progressively at various stages in the unfolding of this revelation from God. Reigning with Christ in his kingdom is the reward for patiently enduring the persecution and trials that result from professing faith in Christ without compromise.

2) The One who speaks God's message is the victorious and powerful Christ, the one who died but who is now alive and who ultimately controls life, death, and Hades. This magnificent vision of Christ features prominently in each of the seven letters to the churches in Asia Minor (2 and 3) and also in the "worthiness" of Christ to open the seals of the scroll of 5, 6. Christ, not the emperor, not Rome, not Satan, holds the destiny of the church in his hand. It is only the risen Christ who is worthy and able to reveal the message of the scroll that we will later learn is in the Almighty's hand.

Summary of the Prologue

The prologue to Revelation sets the visions John has experienced in the context of the church in the first century. The visions experienced by John reveal a crisis that is about to break in on the church in Asia Minor *(what must soon take place. . . for the 'crisis' time is near)*. God is warning his church, encouraging them to examine their faith in view of the impending crisis.

The prologue stresses that the revelation comes from the full godhead, but especially from the God who is the Almighty Sovereign of the universe. In the prologue John promises that Jesus will certainly come in judgment on their situation to judge the oppressors with eschatological consequences. In so doing, he will also vindicate his church.

John introduces a fundamental principle of Revelation that victory and reigning with Christ come through patient endurance of crises. The patient endurance must be without compromise of faith.

The vision of the risen, living, sovereign Christ in all his divine majesty is intended to show that it is the Christ (not Rome or Satan) who holds in his hand the destiny of the church and who has authority over death and Hades. This powerful Christ moves constantly in the presence of his church, fully aware of its trials and ready to judge the church's oppressors.

The prologue sets the scene for the seven letters to the seven churches that follow and to the revelation, meaning, and message of God's divine purpose (*Heilsgeschichte*).

Without this vision of the victorious sovereign Christ, the call to faithfulness in the face of certain martyrdom would be impotent and meaningless.

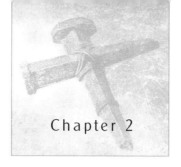

Chapter 2

The Church in Imperfection

The Seven Letters

Part 1

Ephesus, Smyrna, and Pergamum

2:1–2:17

INTRODUCTION:

Following the prologue, the first block of material in the narrative, level I, is the church in imperfection. In the chiastic structure this is parallel to level VII, the church in perfection.

Prologue. 1:1–20
    I. The Church in Imperfection (2:1–3:22)
    Seven Letters to the Seven Churches
        II. The Authority of God over Evil Explained (4:1–8:6)
        Seven Seals of the Scroll
            III. The Warning Judgments (8:1–11:19)
            Seven Trumpets
                IV. The Lamb—God's Answer to Evil (12:1–14:20)
                Seven Unnumbered Figures
            V. The Consummated Judgments (15:1–16:21)
            Seven Bowls of Wrath
        VI. The Authority of God over Evil Exercised (17:1–20:15)
        Seven Unnumbered Descriptions of God's Judgments
    VII. The Church in Perfection (21:1–22:5)
    Seven Unnumbered Descriptions of the Church in Perfection
Epilogue. 22:6–21

The church in imperfection records Jesus' letters to the seven churches of Asia. These are real churches that symbolically represent all of the churches in Asia. Archaeological discoveries and reconstruction in western Turkey have brought these seven cities to life. In this section Jesus addresses the seven churches in a strikingly personal manner. Five of them, Ephesus, Pergamum, Thyatira, Sardis, and Laodicea, he calls to repentance, having discerned faith problems within the congregations. Two of them, Smyrna and Philadelphia he commends for their faithfulness. Jesus encourages the saints to become believers who overcome, better translated "those who conquer" and understood as martyrdom. The theme of Revelation is outlined in these seven letters: those who conquer Satan through their faith in Jesus and martyrdom will be rewarded with spiritual food that gives life, by a victor's crown, and with the promise of reigning with Christ in his kingdom.

The theme of sitting on thrones with Christ and reigning fully with him (symbolically for a thousand years) is laid out clearly in these seven letters and becomes a major theological theme in Revelation. This section is paralleled by section 7, the church in perfection in heaven.

INTRODUCTION

Introduced by seven letters to seven churches in Asia, Revelation is in one sense a letter written by Jesus to all his churches throughout the ages. In another sense it contains a religious drama set on a cosmic stage in which God, Satan, the church, and Rome are the lead characters. The seven letters personify the mysterious message; they bring the message of Revelation into the life of all churches. The cosmic stage demonstrates that the church in all ages is in a battle with Satan, who through various agents seeks to get the church to compromise its faith in Jesus. In the case of the seven churches, the agent of Satan is primarily the provincial governors and the civil and religious power of Rome, aided by the Jews who sought to distance themselves from the burgeoning church in Asia. The church found itself challenged also by its neighbors to compromise its faith with pagan culture and practices. Churches and Christians have always been challenged by various forces to conform and find a middle ground between their commitment to Jesus and their secular culture. In these seven churches Jesus calls on his people to hold an uncompromising faith even in the face of the severest challenge: martyrdom. The rewards for faithfulness are described as eating the tree of life and living forever, receiving crowns of victory for conquering, and reigning with Christ as he reigns with God on his throne. John is laying the foundation in these letters for the major theme of Revelation: by dying faithfully to Jesus, Christians conquer Satan and are raised to sit with Jesus as he reigns in his kingdom.

The seven letters to the seven churches form the heart of the book of Revelation, namely, God's concern for his church. The letters are stimulated by the crisis God predicted the churches would face in their imminent future. In the seven letters each church is encouraged to see itself as God sees it, in its immaturity and imperfection. These churches are basically faithful to God and Christ, but five in particular, Ephesus, Pergamum, Thyatira, Sardis, and Laodicea, manifest serious weaknesses. Jesus warns each of these five to address their imperfection, to repent, and to focus their faith on him. Jesus encourages the two faithful churches, Smyrna and Philadelphia, to maintain their faith and not to surrender or compromise that faith in any manner.

Map of Asia and the Seven Churches

The Seven Letters

The specific content of the letters suggests that Revelation is addressed to seven real churches. They are stylistically selected from among other churches in Asia in that they are representative of all the Asian churches in their strengths and weaknesses. Jesus reminds them that to withstand the crises they are about to encounter they need to repent and refocus their faith on God's divine activity and on Jesus as the sovereign king of God's kingdom. They are to turn away from all worldly or pagan compromises. In view of the impending crises that God foresaw on the horizon of the churches in Asia, each church must be resolute in its commitment to God and Jesus. Failure to be resolute or to repent will result in certain imminent rejection or judgment by Jesus.

In the impending crises those Christians who remain resolute and do not compromise their faith with pagan and secular influences may have to die as martyrs for this commitment, but God will raise them from martyrdom and seeming defeat and transform such defeat into a resounding victory over their oppressors. Their reward, eternal life in God and Christ's kingdom, as one who overcomes (NIV) or as a conqueror (RSV). Conquering is John's term explaining that martyrdom for Christ is victory over Satan and his agents, would be secured by the Almighty and Holy God's sovereign power. Martyrs will reign completely with Jesus in his kingdom as their reward and vindication.

The seven letters form a precursor to chapter 20, the symbolic thousand-year reign of the saints with Christ. Failure to repent will result in imminent judgment by Jesus ("I am coming soon, and I will come to you and remove your lampstand from its place"). The underlying reason for these letters was the impending crises faced by the church in Asia and the awesome challenges these would bring for faith in Jesus. Faith needed to be established and secured before crises broke in on the church. Jesus urged each church to examine its faith and commitment with this in mind. Even great churches such as Ephesus needed to be aware of possible weaknesses in their faith. Perhaps the most striking point of the letters is that faith must be centered on God and Jesus, not on church, church works, or human endeavor. In this chapter we will explore the faith issues and challenges facing three churches, Ephesus (2:1–7), Smyrna (2:8–11), and Pergamum (2:12–17).[1]

There is a symmetry to all seven letters: each is addressed to the angel of a church; each identifies the sender of the message as Jesus and describes him in terms of the vision seen by John of the risen and victorious Jesus; each reminds the church that Jesus has a personal knowledge of the church—its strengths, weaknesses, needs; each contains a warning or encouragement from Jesus; five include a call to repentance; and finally each concludes with a formula statement promising a reward for faithfulness and conquering. John demonstrates his genius by drawing on a symbolism rich in meaning and from a fertile heritage of Jewish and early Christian literature and traditions as he addresses each church. Although couched in this rich symbolism, the letters are authentic messages to historical churches, touching on real socio-religious problems present in the life of the church.

The Letters in the Structure of Revelation

In the chiastic structure of Revelation, the seven letters depicting the church in imperfection are structurally balanced by the seven unnumbered visions or descriptions of the church in perfection in the new heaven and new earth scenes of 21:1–22:5. The focus of these letters in the structure of Revelation is on the spiritual condition of churches and their need for divine strength. Demonstrating an awareness of the imperfections and strengths of each church, each letter includes a commendation, a call for self examination and repentance (in the case of two churches, Smyrna and Philadelphia there is no call to repentance), a warning, a promise of reward for conquering, and a call to listen carefully to the message that comes not only from Jesus, but also from the Holy Spirit.[2]

THE MESSAGE TO THE CHURCH IN EPHESUS. (2:1–7)

The Text

[1]*To the angel of the church in Ephesus write: These are the words of him who holds the seven stars in his right hand and walks among the seven golden lampstands:* [2]*I know your deeds,*

your hard work and your perseverance. I know that you cannot tolerate wicked men, that you have tested those who claim to be apostles but are not, and have found them false. ³You have persevered and have endured hardships for my name, and have not grown weary. ⁴Yet I hold this against you: You have forsaken your first love. ⁵Remember the height from which you have fallen. Repent and do the things you did at first. If you do not repent, I will come to you and remove your lampstand from its place. ⁶But you have this in your favor: You hate the practices of the Nicolaitans, which I also hate. ⁷He who has an ear, let him hear what the Spirit says to the churches. To him who overcomes, I will give the right to eat from the tree of life, which is in the paradise of God.

2:1. *To the angel of the church in Ephesus write:* Each of the seven "letters" begins in the same manner. The letter is addressed to the angel of each church. Because of this unique address, some have questioned whether these are real letters or merely "symbolic messages" to churches in general. Whether authentic letters or merely "symbolic messages" makes little difference, for each letter is couched in an epistolary form and contains powerful messages for each church. The angels are most likely references to the "guardian angels," or spiritual beings, responsible for, or representative of, each church.[3] Beckwith suggests that although the meaning of the term angel may be uncertain, "the 'angel' is completely identified with his church."[4] We should then understand each angel to be in some relationship with the spiritual character of each church. Beale adds that the angels are "corporate representatives" of the churches. He observes that this corporate representation by angels is common in the Jewish and Christian traditions.[5] Although such views may be difficult for some, angels are a phenomenon testified to in Scripture as being as real as the Holy Spirit and God. Although little is revealed about angels regarding their origin, it is apparent from Scripture that they were created by God to be his special servants in specific ministries to his created world, in this case, they were special servants to each church. Angels are featured prominently in Revelation as God's special servants.[6]

Ephesus is mentioned first in the order of the seven churches because it was the most prominent church and city in Asia. It was not the imperial capital of the province (that lot fell to Pergamum), but it flourished as a most important seaport and commercial center, with three great trade routes converging there. Ephesus was one of the three most prominent cities of Asia at the time of the writing of Revelation (Ephesus, Smyrna, and Pergamum). Ephesus, situated at the mouth of the Cayster river on the Aegean Sea, was a serious commercial and cultural rival to Smyrna, another important seaport to Asia.

Culturally and religiously Ephesus was dominated by the striking temple to Artemis (the Anatolian fertility goddess). An imposing avenue lined with marble columns ran from the harbor to the city center. A large *agora* (market place), a magnificent amphitheater, architecturally striking temples, and marble buildings made Ephesus an impressive city. Estimates of the population of Ephesus at the close of the first century reach as high as 250,000.[7] The imperial cult was featured prominently in Ephesus with several temples built in honor of the emperors. One of the most impressive temples to the emperors was that in honor of Domitian which dated from the last decade of the first century (the time of the writing of Revelation). This temple contained an enormous statue of Domitian, part of which can be seen today in the museum at Ephesus (modern Selcuk). The city was a free city, having been granted by Rome the right to self-government.

The church in Ephesus at the time of Revelation had been in existence for at least forty to fifty years, having been ministered to by the Apostle Paul, Timothy, and the Apostle John.[8] Although a synagogue is mentioned in Ephesus in Acts 18:36, no archaeological remains of a synagogue have been located. Josephus in his *Antiquities* speaks of a large community of Jews having been in Ephesus during the third century B.C.[9]

Koester proposes that there were at least four varieties of Christians in Ephesus at the beginning of the second century: 1) the church established by Paul, 2) a Jewish-Christian "school," 3) a heretical sect called the Nicolaitans, and 4) a Jewish-Christian group led by John of Patmos.[10] If Koester is correct, this would account for John's warning regarding false teachers, false apostles, and the Nicolaitans in Ephesus (2:2, 6). That Christianity continued to flourish in Ephesus although Ephesus itself was in decline is seen in the large sixth century Church, or Basilica, of St. John, the archeological remains of which even today are impressive. A "grave," or epitaph and inscription, claiming to be the burial site of the Apostle John[11] is located within the ruins of the church.

These are the words of him who holds the seven stars in his right hand and walks among the seven golden lampstands: The two participial verb forms of this statement (*holds* and *walks*) are in the present tense, indicating Jesus is the one who is constantly holding the destiny of the church and is constantly walking in the midst of his church. Furthermore, the verb here translated *holds*, *krateō*, is a verb of strong action implying "to take into one's possession, to grasp, to seize forcibly, to hold fast."Jesus wanted the church to know that its destiny was firmly in his control and that he was constantly in its presence. Caird suggests that this expression assures that Jesus "keeps all the churches in his active care."[12] Caird draws attention to coins from the reign of Domitian that portray Domitian's heir, an infant son who died in childhood, as Zeus playing with the stars and holding them in his hand, implying the cosmic dominion of Domitian over the whole world. The description of Jesus holding *the seven stars in his right hand*, Caird suggests, is a direct challenge to the divinized myth of the imperial cult and Domitian.[13]

2:2. *I know your deeds, your hard work.* I prefer here the translation of the RSV, *I know your works* rather than *I know your deeds.* (The Greek *ta ergon sou* can be translated either as your works, your deeds, or your actions). In fact, I prefer the translation *I know your actions* because *works* or *actions* fits in better with the statement that Jesus made following this expression. The juxtapositioning of *deeds* and *hard work* in Jesus' expression here is both interesting and emphatic. Jesus was so aware of the church that he knew every aspect of church life. This is perhaps one of the most sobering thoughts of the Bible, and certainly of Revelation. God and Jesus know all about the church, all of the church's actions. Yet this is also one of the most encouraging thoughts in that Jesus and God also know all about the church's struggles and needs. It is obvious that Jesus intended both meanings, for these letters both reassure the church of his careful concern and admonish the church to remedy those spiritual weaknesses that Jesus identifies in their faith. This formulaic expression occurs in five of the seven letters in Revelation, with only a minor variation in two (Smyrna and Pergamum), where Jesus remarks, "I know your tribulation" and "I know where you dwell." The primary point is that Jesus knows the exact condition of every church, their strengths, their weaknesses, their triumphs, and their defeats.

Jesus acknowledged that the church in Ephesus was an active, hard working church. He was fully aware of their **deeds**, **actions**, or *lifestyle,* which included hard work, perseverance, and faithful concern for sound doctrine. Here again is an indication of John's familiarity with the niceties of Greek syntax, for he ties several statements together, namely their **deeds**, their **hard work**, and their **patient endurance**, with a string of coordinating conjunctions (*kai,* often understood simply as *and* [*oida ta erga sou kai ton kopon kai ten hupomonēn sou kai hoti ou dunē bastasai kakous, kai epeirasas tous legontas heautous apostolous kai ouk eisin kai heures autous pseudeis,* ³*kai; hupomonēn echeis kai ebastasas dia to onoma mou kai ou kekopiakes*]). The force is lost in the English translation. To emphasize the impact of this text, the following is my free translation of 2:2. The first *kai* following **I know . . . you have accomplished** is *epexegetical,* implying "*that is,*" or "*namely,*" while the remaining uses of *kai* describe the nature of the deeds that Jesus knows and of which he approves. More precisely, Jesus said, *I really know* (*really* know expresses the force of the Greek verb *oida* in contrast to the normal Greek *ginōskō, I know*) *about your deeds or works you have accomplished, namely, your hard work and patience endurance, that you could not bear evil men, and that you have tested those who falsely called themselves apostles.*[14]

This was a church that had for at least forty to fifty years been steadfast. Both the apostle Paul and his disciple Timothy had worked there for several years. Paul had written two epistles to Timothy while Timothy was in Ephesus. In the years just prior to John's writing Revelation, tradition has it that the Apostle John had ministered for several years in and around Ephesus. While there he had presumably written the Gospel of John[15] and 1, 2, and 3 John. This was a great church with a great heritage, and most likely at the time of writing the largest and most prominent church in Christendom. The church was the center of much mission work in Asia. (See Acts 19:10, "so that all the Jews and Greeks who lived in the province of Asia heard the word of the Lord.") Not only had the church in Ephesus labored hard and long for the Lord; they had persevered through many hardships and trials.[16]

2:2b. Ephesus was not only an active church, but also one that was deeply concerned over the purity of the Gospel message, for Jesus observes: **I know that you cannot tolerate wicked men, that you have tested those who claim to be apostles but are not, and have found them false.** One would expect this strident concern for doctrine from a church in which the Apostle Paul had labored for many years and to which so much had been written regarding the true faith, false teachers, and those (the antichrist) who denied that

Jesus was the Christ (1 John 2:18-25). In a parting message to the elders of the church in Ephesus, while at Miletus, Paul had admonished them:

> Keep watch over yourselves and all the flock of which the Holy Spirit has made you overseers. Be shepherds of the church of God, which he bought with his own blood. I know that after I leave, savage wolves will come in among you and will not spare the flock. Even from your own number men will arise and distort the truth in order to draw away disciples after them. So be on your guard. Remember that for three years I never stopped warning each of you night and day with tears (Acts 20:28–31).

The presence of false teachers in Ephesus is confirmed by Koester's comments regarding the various forms of Christianity that had developed in Asia by the end of the first century and the syncretistic nature of religion in the region.[17] The presence of a Nicolaitan group in Ephesus highlights Jesus' and the Ephesian church's concern over false apostles. Furthermore, both Pauline letters to Timothy (who was located in Ephesus at the time the Pastorals were written) are replete with warnings against false teachers and false doctrine (1 Tim. 3:1–7; 2 Tim. 3,4). Timothy was instructed to test both doctrine and teachers against that which was apostolic and widely recognized and practiced in the early church (cf. also 1 Thess. 5:21; 1 Cor. 14:29; 1 John 4:1; *Didache* 11:8). The church in Ephesus had taken these warnings seriously and had become a "pillar of the truth." Those who falsely claimed to be apostles had been tested and rejected, indicating the real presence of false apostles in the early church and the background for Jesus' commendation to Ephesus (cf. also 2 Cor. 1:13; 12:12).

2:3. Jesus commends them for this; *You have persevered and have endured hardships for my name, and have not grown weary.* Perseverance, hardship, and faithful endurance are key words in John's theology (cf. 1:9 and the comments at that place).

2:4. By most standards the church in Ephesus was a strong church, but it appears that they were motivated by a misplaced driving force. The church in Ephesus teaches us that it is possible to do the right thing but for the wrong reason, for Jesus follows his fine commendation with a stern warning, *Yet I hold this against you: You have forsaken your first love.* For some reason, due possibly to the passing of time and the extreme warnings against false teachers (Acts 20:28–30; 1 Tim. 1:3; 2 Tim. 1:13; 2:14–3:9; 4:3, 4; 1 John 4:1), the church at Ephesus at the close of the first century was driven by determining form and orthodoxy rather than by being shaped by love and their relationship with Christ. The passing of the centuries since the writing of this letter has not changed the church much, for in every generation churches have tended to become more concerned with formal religion that becomes fixated on orthodoxy rather than on orthopraxy as the appropriate response to faith in Jesus.

The church in Ephesus had apparently not maintained a faith and practice grounded in love and in their relationship with Jesus. They obviously were driven more by a formal religion of an orthodox nature than by their *first love*, which they had apparently *forsaken.* Jesus reminded them of the *height from which* (they had) *fallen* and called for their repentance. His admonition was for the Ephesian church to return to the kind of works motivated by love that had characterized them in their beginning. Jesus' reminder regarding the original love of the Ephesian Christians must surely be a reference to the fact that the Ephesian Christians should be motivated and controlled by their love for Jesus rather than merely by the formality of their religion.[18]

There is a question in the mind of some as to whether the love referred to here is love for Jesus, for the brethren, or for humankind in general. All three are involved and should not be separated. The Epistle of 1 John states that it is impossible to love God and not love one's "brother" (1 John 4:20, 21). Likewise to say that one loved Jesus and not one's brother is equally impossible. Furthermore, Jesus loved the lost world and was willing to die for the lost. In the true sense of Christian faith, love for Jesus must result in love for one another and love for the lost. In a church such as the Ephesian church, where faith was characterized by a commitment to a formalized religion of hard work and an excessive stress on correct doctrine, the danger was that both love for Christ and love for brethren were displaced as the center of faith by a strict formal orthodoxy. Often the shift is so gentle that it is not noticed, but when orthodoxy becomes the driving force in Christian faith, and correct ecclesiology the measure of the true church, then love for Christ and brethren, although given token acknowledgment, is often moved to the periphery of faith and seldom emphasized in excessive orthodoxy as marks of the true church.

If the problems indicated in the Johannine Epistles have any message, it is that an overzealous orthodoxy needs the corrective focus of love. Apparently, John's admonition that God is love and that his children should live by love had not yet become part of the Ephesian community to where it provided a balance between extreme orthodoxy and orthopraxy. Thus Jesus' sharp rebuke in 2:4–5 was most appropriate. Roberts stresses that "The loyal spirit of defense of the truth had bred an attitude of intolerance and spite toward those in error."[19] Roberts observes that the Ephesian church had in their zeal for truth forgotten that the goal of sound doctrine "is love, which comes from a pure heart and a good conscience and a sincere faith" (1 Tim. 1:5). Caird expresses this problem well:

> The one charge against the Ephesians is that their intolerance of imposture, their unflagging loyalty, and hatred of heresy had bred an inquisitorial spirit which left no room for love. They had set out to be defenders of the faith, arming themselves with the heroic virtues of truth and courage, only to discover that in the battle they had lost the one quality without which all others are worthless . . . but he [Jesus] recognizes the appalling danger of a religion prompted more by hate than by love. The only legitimate hatred is a revulsion against all that thwarts the operation of love; and how easily that hatred can turn into something less innocent.[20]

In regard to the relationship between love for God and for fellow Christians, Mounce observes:

Good works and our doctrine are not adequate substitutes for that rich relationship of mutual love shared by persons who have just experienced the redemptive love of God. The Ephesian church had lost its first love. The expression includes both love of God and love of mankind at large, but seems to refer mainly to their love for one another. [21]

Furthermore, Mounce adds, "It seems probable that the desire for sound teaching and the resulting forthright action taken to exclude all imposters had created a climate of suspicion in which brotherly love could no longer exist."[22] He cites Barclay, who "conjectured that 'the eagerness to root out all mistaken men had ended in a sour and rigid orthodoxy.'"[23] It seems that the church in Ephesus had forgotten the vital principle that love lies at the very foundation of God's attitude toward mankind and at the very foundation of the Christian faith and appeal.

2:5. *Remember the height from which you have fallen. Repent and do the things you did at first. Remember* (*mnēmoneue*, from *mnēmoneuō* in the Greek is in the present tense, emphasizing a *continuous action of calling to mind*; a habitual action, which stands out against the aorist imperative, *repent*, *metanoēson*, which derives from *metanoeō* and implies a dramatic, certain action, or decisive break, a distinct change in lifestyle). *Remembering* in the present tense, implying a continuous calling to mind, is a constant daily reference to the foundation of one's faith and practice. The implication is that remembering as the root of continued faith should be a regular practice in Christian life. Aune, citing A. J. Malherbe, observes that "remembering is a recurring topos in the moral paranesis that emphasizes that paranesis supposedly contains nothing new or original."[24] In other words, what Jesus is calling for in practice was something they had known and practiced from the beginning.

The command to *repent* is a call for a radical change of heart and lifestyle. To repent is not merely to regret and change one's mind, but involves a radical change that reorients life in a full practical sense, a decisive break in lifestyle. What the Ephesians had lost, they needed to reacquire immediately, and the need was so radical that Jesus attaches the compelling concept of *repent*. The perfect tense *have fallen* adds a fatal sense of completeness. It is not that they were in the process of falling; they have fallen. Because of the completeness of this fall, Jesus encouraged an active process of remembering and a decisive step of repentance in which they must turn from their failed way of life and do the first works of love.[25] The aorist imperative *poiēson* translated *do* the things you did at first likewise stresses the decisiveness of the action called for. Jesus was calling for a radical reformation of faith and practice in the life of the Ephesian church. The church must return to the works of love that had characterized it in the early stages of its Christian life. Jesus' admonition to the church is therefore to repent immediately, for *if you do not repent, I will come to you and remove your lampstand from its place.* The Greek reads *erchomai*, "but if not, I am coming." Although in the present tense, *erchomai* can read as a future tense, as it has been rendered in most translations *I will come to you and I will remove your lampstand.*" However, this may not be the best rendering of *erchomai.* The sense of the future here should not be "coming sometime in the future, but I am already coming," or "I am in the process of coming."

There are two conditional statements in Jesus' stern challenge to the church in Ephesus: 1) if you do not repent, *I will come*, and 2) if you do no repent, *I will remove your lampstand*.[26] The removal of the lampstand refers to the removal of their right to be a church.[27] Regarding Jesus' "threat," Aune observes, "This is nothing less than a threat to obliterate the Ephesian congregation as an empirical Christian community."[28] The present tense of I am coming and the context requiring immediate repentance remove this as a reference to Jesus' end-of-the-world *parousia* and add urgency and imminence to Jesus' warning. There are some who would argue that the first threat regarding Jesus' coming is not part of the conditional statement of Jesus and therefore refers to the *parousia,* but that the second part of the statement, will remove, is conditional and refers to Jesus' imminent removal of the church from his community. Beale appropriately argues that both are conditional and, citing Caird in particular, states that the majority of commentators hold the same position. Beale correctly concludes that both conditional statements, or threats, refer to Jesus' action before the final *parousia.*[29] Beasley-Murray, in agreement with the interpretation of an imminent coming of Jesus in judgment on the Ephesian church, summarizes the opinion of several:

> The bluntness of the words must be allowed full force. Christ will come to the Ephesian church for judgment, as one day he will come to the world in judgment to sweep away its evil. (This is more natural to the context than to interpret the words as a threat of judgment upon the Ephesian church at the parousia of Christ.)[30]

This conditional argument regarding Jesus' coming *soon* on the church at Ephesus is significant. Repeatedly in Revelation John refers to Jesus' coming *soon* in judgment either on the church or on those who dwell on earth, that is, on those who worship the beast and oppose God's *Heilsgeschichtlichen*[31] purpose in Jesus. This use of proleptic eschatological style heightens the seriousness of the immediate situation. Jesus will judge the Ephesian church in the immediate futuristic present[32] with end-of-the-world finality unless she repents. Mounce adds that "The reference is not so much to the parousia as it is to an immediate visitation for preliminary judgment."[33]

Caird summarizes Jesus' coming on the churches in Asia:

> The threatened coming of Christ would not, in fact, be a worldwide crisis, but a crisis private to the churches concerned. . . . If we take this view, we shall take the conditional threats to Ephesus, Pergamum, and Sardis as evidence that an imminent Parousia was not one of the events which John believed were "bound to happen soon" (i. 1), and that even in the apocalyptic visions his immediate concern is with martyrdom rather than the End.[34]

As I have argued above, the significance of Jesus' statement *I will come* as a conditional "threat" pointing to imminent action and not the final *parousia* cannot be overstressed.

Jesus is not only there to comfort but also to hold his churches responsible in the immedi-ate future for their faith. Those who deny Jesus and who will not honor his word will not only be judged for this at the end of the world, but they are already judged by Jesus in the present with eschatological judgment and all of its implications unless they repent. In this same proleptic eschatological style John can argue that those who presently believe in Jesus already have eternal life (1 John 5:13).

2:6. *But you have this in your favor: You hate the practices of the Nicolaitans, which I also hate.* Little is known about the Nicolaitans beyond what is said here in 2:9 and 15. Although several early writers (Irenaeus, Hippolytus, and Clement of Alexandria) men-tion the Nicolaitans as a heretical group, Caird observes that it is likely that they knew little of the Nicolaitans beyond what they read in Revelation.[35] Eusebius mentions that the sect lasted only "a very short time" (*Eccl. Hist.* 3. 29. 1). Some connect the Nicolaitans here and in 2:15 (Pergamum) with a group of gnostic-type heretics who were antino-mian (no law binds Christians) and licentious. By some strange process of thought, not altogether absent in contemporary times, they believed they had license under grace to commit all kinds of sexual sins since the flesh is not in fact the real person.[36] Mounce observes that "Broadly speaking, they had worked out a compromise with the pagan society in which they lived."[37] The language of Jesus, *which I also hate*, indicates the intensity of the Nicolaitan problem and the serious stance Jesus took against them. At least, and to their credit, the Ephesians shared this strong dislike and rejection with Jesus.

2:7. *He who has an ear, let him hear what the Spirit says to the churches. To him who overcomes, I will give the right to eat from the tree of life, which is in the paradise of God.* The Semitic idiom "he who has an ear" (or a variation of this) introduces a formulaic statement that recurs in each of the seven letters. (See the similar formula in Matt. 11:15; 13:9; 43; Mark 4:23)[38] In this case it is not Jesus alone who is speaking to the church, but also the Spirit. The combination of Jesus, the Spirit, and an imperative form of the verb add intensity to the message from Jesus. Furthermore, the plural "churches" indicates that this message and the other six messages to the churches in Asia have universal significance for all churches. *To him who overcomes* in the NIV is not the most felicitous translation of the Greek participle *to nikonti*, the one who conquers or overcomes. The context of combat mythology or a war scroll,[39] or simply a war between God and Satan, Christ and Rome, indicates that in Revelation the military concept of the one who con-quers, as in the RSV and the NRSV, is a more appropriate rendition of the noun form of the participle. Aune suggests that the term *nikan* [or *nikaō*; "to conquer, be victorious") can be either a military or an athletic metaphor, though in Revelation it is probably drawn from military language since it often involves the possibility of death."[40] This formulaic theme of conquering is a primary motif in the theology of Revelation and one that appears in each of the seven letters. As the term appears progressively in Revelation, John develops it along the lines of Austin Farrer's notion of the "rebirth of images." John initially inserts the concept of conquering into the Ephesian letter without much discussion or explanation. However, as the scenes of Revelation progress, the theme of conquering is advanced until in 12:11 John unfolds the full statement that the saints "have conquered"[41] Satan "by the blood of the Lamb and by the word of their testimony; they did not love their lives so much as to shrink from death."

John uses *nikaō* (to conquer) in various forms. It appears sixteen (16) times in Revelation. In the RSV translation it is translated eight times as "conquers," four times as "conquered," and four times as "conquer." In John's use, *nikaō* becomes an important theological term stressing the victorious nature of Christian martyrdom. The martyrs from the perspective of "those who live on this world" (another theological expression progressively developed by John to describe those who oppose and persecute Christians) die in ignominy or shame, their lives wasted for a deluded cause. However, through the eyes of faith, the martyrs are assured that their death is not in vain, that they will be vindicated by God, raised in victory over Satan and Rome, to reign fully with Christ. John wraps all of this victorious theology into the developing understanding of *nikaō*. To translate *nikaō* as "overcome" is therefore to diminish or denude the term *nikaō* of its major theological thrust in Revelation, especially in the context of combat mythology.[42]

Nikaō appears in each of the seven letters involving a promise or reward to those (soon-to–be-martyrs) who remain faithful to Jesus, even in the face of death. It appears also in conjunction with several metaphors for eternal life, such as in the Ephesian letter (2:7): *To him who conquers I will grant to eat of the tree of life, which is in the paradise of God.* Similar expressions of eternal life as the reward of the martyr can be seen in 2:11: *He who conquers shall not be hurt by the second death*; 2:17: *To him who conquers I will give some of the hidden manna*; and 3:11: *He who conquers, I will grant him to sit with me on my throne, as I myself conquered and sat down with my Father on his throne.* In the theology of Revelation, the martyrs, or those who conquer, are assured of a victory over Satan and Rome, of eternal life, and a reward, which in the case of chapter 20 will be expressed as reigning fully (figuratively for a thousand years) with Christ in his kingdom. Conquering in Revelation therefore becomes a powerful synonym for martyrdom expressing its eternal value over its immediate threat.[43]

Jesus concludes his call for immediate and radical repentance with the promise of eternal life for those who respond in faith: *To him who overcomes* [conquers], *I will give the right to eat from the tree of life, which is in the paradise of God.* Several sources for the metaphor of the tree of life have been proposed, but fundamental to this metaphor is the coalescing of Jewish apocalyptic and rabbinic traditions around Gen. 3:22.[44] Drawing on these Jewish traditions, Jesus promised that the martyr will be raised from the dead to enjoy eternal life. In the Christian faith, death, even the vilest death, is not the end of life, but merely a transition to eternal life in heaven with God and Christ. However, in Johannine terms eternal life means real spiritual life (cf. John 3:15, 16, 36; 1 John 2:25; 5:13). For John, eternal life is enjoyed now in part but comes fully after the resurrection. In the case of the conqueror, eternal life is the assurance of a reward for faithful service and martyrdom. The reward of the martyr is the pledge of divine power that creates and sustains all real life. Eating the tree of life is another metaphor used by Jesus to remind the church in Asia that God has the power to create and sustain eternal life, which life is the crowning reward of martyrdom.

The word *life* occurs eighteen times in Revelation, variously as the tree of life, the crown of life, the breath of life, the book of life, the water of life, or simply come to life. Beckwith, Beale, Aune, and others concur that the concept of life was one favored by both the Jewish and Christian traditions, both in the canonical and extra-canonical literature. The Gospel of John is replete with references to life, as is the First Epistle of John. On numerous occasions in the Johannine tradition, the concept is associated with the word "eternal." Although eternal life does not occur in Revelation, it is clear that when John refers to life in Revelation, he has in ind the concept of eternal life.

Questions arise regarding the meaning of life, or eternal life, as it is found in the Johannine tradition and its significance to the promises by God and Jesus to the saints facing persecution and martyrdom in Asia. Smalley observes:

"Eternal life" is a spiritual quality of life, which God gives every believer through Jesus his Son (cf. John 3:16; 17:2–3). It is not thought of as life prolonged to infinity, but as a sharing of living fellowship with the Father, in which "the category of time recedes before that of moral quality."

Raymond E. Brown observes that this eternal life is that quality of life that not even death can destroy. He adds "duration . . . is not the primary issue; it is life from another eon . . . or sphere. Indeed it is the life of God Himself." The life giving propensity of the tree of life in the paradise of God must be seen in the light of martyrdom and death facing the church in Asia. The life that God and Jesus promise these saints is one that not even death can destroy, for it is the very quality of the life of God that they will enjoy with God in heaven.

Two texts are informative: the first 1 Cor 15: 54, 55, "Death has been swallowed up in victory. " "Where, O death, is your victory? Where, O death, is your sting?" The second is 21:4, "Now the dwelling of God is with men, and he will live with them. They will be his people, and God himself will be with them and be their God. 4 He will wipe every tear from their eyes. There will be no more death or mourning or crying or pain, for the old order of things has passed away. "

The tree of life appears again in 22:2ff as the life sustaining power of God's presence. Similar life promising metaphors are repeated in each of the remaining six letters. To the church at Smyrna Jesus promises the crown of life. To the church at Pergamum, he promises the hidden manna and an invitation to the eschatological banquet. Paradise derives from a Persian or Iranian term for a garden or place of blessedness. The concept of a garden of blessedness was combined in the Jewish apocalyptic and later rabbinic traditions with the garden of Eden in Gen 2, 3 to represent a "place" or condition of heavenly blessedness.

THE MESSAGE TO THE CHURCH IN SMYRNA. (2:8–11)

The Text

[8]*To the angel of the church in Smyrna write: These are the words of him who is the First and the Last, who died and came to life again.* [9]*I know your afflictions and your poverty—yet you are rich. I know the slander of those who say they are Jews and are not, but are a synagogue of Satan.* [10]*Do not be afraid of what you are about to suffer. I tell you, the devil will put some of you in prison to test you, and you will suffer persecution for ten days. Be faithful, even to the point of death, and I will give you the crown of life.* [11]*He who has an ear, let him hear what the Spirit says to the churches. He who overcomes will not be hurt at all by the second death.*

The church in Smyrna. An ancient Greek fortress city that stood on the site of the Smyrna of John's day had been destroyed by the Lydians in 600 B.C. Rebuilt in 290 B.C., Smyrna was proclaimed by many to be the most beautiful city in Asia. Hemer observes that it was known among the cities of Asia as "a paradise of municipal vanity."[45] Among its many claims to fame was that it was the birthplace of the great epic poet Homer and the place where Galen, the "father of medicine and the study of anatomy," studied as a young man. Smyrna (modern Izmir) was one of the oldest cities of the Mediterranean world and has been of almost continuous historical importance during the last five thousand years. Excavations indicate settlement contemporary with that of the first city of Troy, dating from the third millennium B.C.[46] Undoubtedly its location at the foot of Mount Pagus and along the seashore had much to do with its natural beauty, but most of the praise had to do with the symmetry and beauty of its architecture.

In John's day, Smyrna, with a population of between a hundred thousand[47] and two hundred thousand[48] and a large and powerful Jewish community, was surpassed in size in Asia only by Ephesus. With a famous agora, stadium, acropolis, library, and theatre, Smyrna was a city of considerable culture and pride. Early in its history Smyrna had aligned itself with Rome during Rome's struggles with the Carthaginian empire, and therefore sustained a special standing with Rome. Smyrna was the first city in the ancient world to build a temple in honor of the Roman goddess Roma.[49] The city as a seaport seriously challenged Ephesus for importance and prominence in commercial interests in Asia.

The history of the church in Smyrna is best identified with such notables as the elderly bishop Polycarp, commonly known as the "twelfth martyr of Smyrna,"[50] and Ignatius, Bishop of Antioch (c. 117), who wrote one of his famous martyr epistles to Smyrna. One can hardly do justice to Smyrna without citing Polycarp's famous confession when the governor addressed Polycarp with these words: "Take the oath (to Caesar) and I will let you go, revile Christ." Polycarp answered with these now famous words, "For eighty and six years have I been his servant, and he has done me no wrong, and how can I blaspheme my King who saved me?" When the governor persisted, "Swear by the genius of Caesar," Polycarp said, "If you vainly suppose I will swear by the genius of Caesar, as you say, and pretend that you are ignorant who I am, listen plainly: I am a Christian"[51] Although this exchange took place sixty years after John penned Revelation, one can gain some understanding of the crisis foreseen by John and the impact of Jesus' letter on the church in Smyrna.

Izmir, the modern city on the site of Smyrna, with a population of well over 2.5 million, is today a thriving seaport and the third city of Turkey after the modern capital, Ankara, and Istanbul. Unfortunately, few archaeological remains are to be found in the city that has grown up, over, and around the original site of Smyrna.

It is noteworthy that the church in Smyrna is one of only two in Revelation, the other being the church in Philadelphia, that received no condemnation from Jesus. They were also the two churches among the seven who experienced severe opposition from the synagogue.

2:8. The expression *These are the words of him who is the First and the Last, who died and came to life again* draws from John's majestic image of Jesus in 1:12-20. With this expression Jesus placed himself on an equally divine level with the eternal nature of God (cf. Phil 2:6). By using the phrase *the First and the Last*, synonymous with *the Alpha and the Omega*, which was used in reference to the Lord God the Almighty in 1:8, Jesus aligned himself with the Almighty God, thereby stressing the power and authority of his message to Smyrna. This phrase is used three times in Revelation: 1:17; 2:8; 22:13, and always of Jesus as an allusion to the divine name of Isaiah 41:4; 44:6; and 48:12, "I, the Lord, the first, and the last; I am He," and "I am the first and I am the last."

The statement that he was the one *who died and came to life again* would certainly resonate with the church and remind them that Jesus had himself died as a martyr and had been raised from the dead by the power of God. Aune points out that the usual words for the resurrection, *egeirein* and *anhistēmi* do not occur in Revelation. Here John uses the word *edzēsen* ("*came to life*") in place of *resurrection*.[52] Jesus had personally experienced what he was calling on the saints to endure. The assurance that God had raised him from the dead, that he was now alive, would remind the saints of God's faithfulness and power to grant life to those who loved him and who were faithful to him and his purpose. This must have been particularly encouraging to the church at Smyrna, as it would be to all the churches in Asia, and must have contributed to the remarkable spiritual strength of Polycarp just sixty years later.

2:9. Jesus' words *I know your afflictions and your poverty—yet you are rich* informed the church that he was well aware of their plight. The word John used here to describe the poverty of the church in Smyrna, *ptōchos*, implies abject poverty, "possessing nothing at all." The juxtapositioning of afflictions (*thlipsis*) and poverty may imply that their poverty was associated with the crisis they were encountering. Certainly, much of their problem lay in the social pressures they were facing because of their confession of Jesus as Lord.[53] Confessing Christ in the first century often brought with it economic hardship. Beale notes that the church in Smyrna was facing an emerging Jewish opposition that surfaced later in the saga of Polycarp's martyrdom.[54] Furthermore, Smyrna was particularly loyal to Rome and the imperial cult.[55] The comment by Jesus, *yet you are rich*, stresses that the physical poverty experienced by the saints in Smyrna faded into oblivion when compared to their surpassing spiritual richness in Christ. (Cf. similar thoughts in Paul, Phil 3:8, "What is more, I consider everything a loss compared to the surpassing greatness of knowing Christ Jesus my Lord, for whose sake I have lost all things", and 2 Cor 4:116-18, "Therefore we do not lose heart. Though outwardly we are wasting away, yet inwardly we are being renewed day by day. [17] For our light and momentary troubles are achieving for us an eternal glory that far outweighs them all. [18] So we fix our eyes not on what is seen, but on what is unseen. For what is seen is temporary, but what is unseen is eternal.")

I know the slander of those who say they are Jews and are not, but are a synagogue of Satan. From Eusebius' comments regarding the church in Smyrna's experience with the Jews, it seems that this harsh statement was in reference to the severe opposition encountered by the church at the hands of the Jewish community in Smyrna, or at least instigated by the Jewish community.[56] Jesus was very clear that those Jews who denied him were not God's people and their synagogue was in reality not a synagogue (gathering or meeting place) of God's people but of Satan's people.[57] This stinging rebuke and rejection of the synagogue community was in small measure a vindication of the Christian community and their faithfulness.[58]

2:10. *Do not be afraid of what you are about to suffer. I tell you, the devil will put some of you in prison to test you, and you will suffer persecution for ten days.* Being tested in prison *for ten days* may refer to the completeness of the persecution they would endure (see Summers and Mounce[59]),or it may refer to a short period of persecution, or a limited period of persecution (Kiddle and Caird).[60] Perhaps the best solution is that it draws on Daniel 1:8–16, where Daniel offered to be tested for ten days as a sign of the faithfulness of his God (Beale).[61] The symbolic reference to a brief period of acute testing in which God would not fail his servants seems to fit the context of Revelation better than other possibilities.

Be faithful, even to the point of death, and I will give you the crown of life. Jesus promises that those who die for their faith will be rewarded with eternal life. The expression *even to the point of death* (*ginou pistis achri thanatou*) or *be faithful unto death* (RSV), or *until death* (NASV, NRSV) does not mean "until you die," but carries the meaning "even if faithfulness leads to death,"[62] or as the NIV appropriately translates it, *Be faithful even to the point of death*. The Greek preposition *achri* can mean "until," "to," "as far as," "until the time when." In Acts 22:4 Luke records Paul's defense and statement that he persecuted the Way to the death (*ediōxsa achri thanatou*). The death demonstrates the limitation of the persecution. Likewise, here in 2:8 *achri* points to or provides the limitation of the faithfulness, resulting in the translation "even if faithfulness leads to death." *The crown of life* refers, not to a royal crown (*diadēma*), but to the *laurel wreath* (*stephanos*) awarded to victors in the Roman or Greek games.[63] The genitive qualifying expression *of life* (Gk. *tēs zōēs, of life*) is an appositive or epexegetical genitive construction describing the nature of the victory laurel or reward, namely, *life*. Aune translates this as "I will give you the wreath of life."[64] The crown of life thus becomes a metaphor for eternal life.[65] The emphasis on eternal life, therefore, is not in reference to the duration of life, but expresses the quality of life to be enjoyed by the believer. Eternal life is the victory laurel wreath or reward given to those who die for their faith.

2:11. *He who has an ear, let him hear what the Spirit says to the churches.* Jesus again draws on the familiar Jewish Hebraism favored by the earthly Jesus in his teaching ministry, yet here with the Holy Spirit included, to emphasize the urgency and importance of his message. The expression stresses that those looking martyrdom squarely in the face need to give serious attention to the message from Jesus. *He who overcomes will not be hurt at all by the second death.* Here, Jesus promises that those who conquer, who die as martyrs, need have no fear of the second death since they will already have the crown (reward) of eternal life. The first death, in one sense a judgment, has struck each martyr. They now need not fear the second death. The expression *the second death* is a rabbinic term for the judgment (death) of the wicked at the end of the age.[66] John refers *to the second death* again in 20:14, when he discusses the final judgment, *then death and Hades were thrown into the lake of fire. The lake of fire is the second death.* The second death as the final judgment will have no power over those who have not compromised their faith and who have died as martyrs. They have achieved the final level of eternal life and reign victoriously with Christ.

The Message to the Church in Pergamum. (2:12–17)

The Text

[12] *To the angel of the church in Pergamum write: These are the words of him who has the sharp, double-edged sword.* [13] *I know where you live—where Satan has his throne. Yet you remain true to my name. You did not renounce your faith in me, even in the days of Antipas, my faithful witness, who was put to death in your city—where Satan lives.* [14] *Nevertheless, I have a few things against you: You have people there who hold to the teaching of Balaam, who taught Balak to entice the Israelites to sin by eating food sacrificed to idols and by committing sexual immorality.* [15] *Likewise you also have those who hold to the teaching of the Nicolaitans.* [16] *Repent therefore. Otherwise, I will soon come to you and will fight against them with the sword of my mouth.* [17] *He who has an ear, let him hear what the Spirit says to the churches. To him who overcomes, I will give some of the hidden manna. I will also give him a white stone with a new name written on it, known only to him who receives it.*

2:12. *To the angel of the church in Pergamum write:* The city of Pergamum was, and its ruins still are, one of the spectacular wonders of Asia Minor, or modern Turkey. Set high on an acropolis (a city fortress on a mountain or high hill), a thousand feet above the Caicus valley, Pergamum commanded a magnificent view of its surroundings. The name of the city means "a citadel."[67] As the capital city of the Roman Province of Asia, it was only about ten miles inland from the Aegean Sea. As early as the second century B.C., the city was recognized as one of the finest achievements of Hellenic civilization. In the second century, Pliny described Pergamum as the most distinguished city of Asia. The most impressive part of Pergamum was the upper terrace. With several sacred temples to pagan divinities (Zeus, Athena, Dionysius, and Asclepius), several temples in honor of the imperial cult, and a "royal" governor's palace, Pergamum was in every sense a magnificent capital city. The views from this upper terrace overlook an impressive and steeply terraced theater with the temple of Asklepios below. The shrine of Asclepius was located at the foot of the citadel or hill. It housed one of the most famous hospitals of its time. The renowned physician Galen worked in the hospital associated with the temple of Asclepius. The Asclepion attracted wealthy and influential patients from all over the world. As the Roman capital of Asia, Pergamum was the official center for the imperial cult in Asia. This made the city with its broad pagan culture and imperial cultus a dangerous threat to the Christians living in that area who refused to honor the emperor as the divine lord over their lives.[68] The valley to the west of Pergamum, two thousand years after the glorious age of Pergamum, is still strikingly beautiful.[69]

The city housed one of the finest libraries of ancient times with over 200,000 books. An interesting legend recounts the history of a significant development in the production and preservation of books and writing materials. In the second century B.C., Eumenes II, ruler of the Greek kingdom of Pergamum, tried to hire the librarian of the world-famous library in Alexandria, Egypt. The Egyptian king, Ptolemy VI, consequently banned the export of papyrus in reprisal for Eumenes' plans to build a great library in Pergamum. Papyrus was the material on which most scrolls were written at that time. In response, Eumenes' librarians developed a new writing material that became known as parchment, or vellum (Greek for parchment, *pergamene*, named after the city of Pergamum). This material was made by stretching and refining animal skins. Parchment could be written on both sides and sewn together in the form of a book. This form of "book" became known as a *codex* (Lat. "writing tablet"). The results of the discovery of vellum had a significant impact on the preservation of biblical manuscripts and the transmission of materials from ancient times.

The expression ***these are the words of him who has the sharp, double-edged sword*** most likely is a reference to the fact that the Roman proconsul wielded the sword of Roman power and judgment from the city of Pergamum, the seat of Roman proconsular government over Asia. The sword described here is a large cutting sword, not a short dagger. This expression is also found in the description of Jesus in 1:16 and again in 19:15, 21. In both these references the sword is coming out of Jesus' mouth, referring to the power of his word. The power of life and death lay in Jesus' word of salvation (approval) or his final word of judgment. Jesus reminded the Christians that it is he, not the Roman proconsul, who holds the sovereign power over life. This statement stressed the fact that the power of life and death ultimately belonged to Jesus, not to the Roman proconsul. Beale observes that the double-edged sword in the case of Pergamum represents "Christ standing over the church as a threatening judge of the church's sin" and that this "is the thought pervading the entire epistle to Pergamum." He adds, "The judicial power of Christ's sword is not only intended to judge apostates in the church (cf 2:16), but also stands as a polemical image against the satanic center of Roman justice in Pergamum."[70]

2:13. *I know where you live—where Satan has his throne.* As in the case of Ephesus, Jesus knew all about the Christians and their situation in Pergamum. Aune observes that Roman opposition to Christianity was particularly malevolent in Pergamum.[71] Jesus knew that the Christians lived constantly under the threat of Roman power, but he wanted to assure them that the proconsul's power, contrary to the claims of the imperial cult, was merely a satanic power, not a divine power. Much speculation has taken place in regard to the exact identification of this satanic throne. Some have suggested the famous altar of Zeus, others the temple of Asklepios. The reference seems best understood, however, in regard to Pergamum as the seat of Roman power and the imperial cult.[72] The imperial cult, supported by the power of Rome, could easily be mistakenly identified by some as the seat of a divine power. Jesus sharply rejected any such claims and described Pergamum as the seat, not of a divine authority, but of a satanic power.[73]

Jesus' statement *yet you remain true to my name. You did not renounce your faith in me*, indicates again that Jesus was fully aware of the trials faced by the Christians in Pergamum. *Name* in biblical use, both Old and New Testaments, draws on a Hebraism in which the name represents all that the person is, or stands for. To do something in someone's name is to do it as though the person himself or herself had done it (cf. Col. 3:17). *Name* in this text stands for the person of Jesus. The Christians in Pergamum had simply remained faithful to Jesus. They had not denied Jesus. What follows with the mention of Antipas is a clear historical reference to persecution in Pergamum. *Even in the days of Antipas, my faithful witness, who was put to death in your city—where Satan lives.* Little is known of Antipas or the circumstances of his martyrdom, although an interesting legend survives regarding his death. The legend records that Antipas was slowly roasted inside a bull during the reign of Domitian.[74] Whatever the cause of his death, Jesus singles Antipas out as **my** *faithful witness.* The Greek term for witness here is *martus*, thus giving rise to the translation of this term as *martyr* by Charles and Bruce.[75] Aune traces an interesting development of the term *martus* from that of witness to that of martyr.[76] Ferguson, citing Ignatius, Clement of Alexandria, Origen, and others, observes that in the early centuries of the church it was common to define those who died in witness to Christ as *martyrs*. Origen, in his *Commentary on John* (2:34[=28].210) wrote:

> But it has become the custom of the brotherhood, struck with amazement at the condition of those who struggled until death on behalf of truth or courage, properly to give the name "martyrs" only to those who by pouring out of their own blood have borne witness to the mystery of godliness, although the Savior names martyrs all who testify to things proclaimed concerning him [Acts 1:8].[77]

Bruce considered this reference to martyr in 2:13 to be possibly the earliest use of *martus* as a technical term for martyr. In keeping with this understanding, the term *marturia* in 17:6 is translated as "martyrs" in the RSV, whereas the NIV translates it simply *as those who bore testimony to Jesus.*

Jesus reminds the church that Antipas was *put to death* (martyred) *in your city— where Satan lives*. The reminder of this tragic event, tied to the comment *where Satan lives*, possibly supports the suggestion that Antipas' death was related in some manner to the threat of the imperial cult.[78] It is known that Domitian at this time required to be addressed as *dominus et deus* (Lord and God),[79] possibly indicating the presence of a strong imperial cult in Pergamum supported by its religious demands at the time that John is writing Revelation. The expression *where Satan lives* is a reference to Pergamum as home to the agent of Satan, the Roman proconsul.[80]

2:14, 15. *Nevertheless, I have a few things against you.* Aune translates this as "But I hold a minor matter against you," translating the Greek *oligos* as a minor matter in favor of a few things.[81] While this is possible, how can the reference to Balaam's compromise and the Nicolaitans be a minor matter, especially in view of Jesus "hatred" of the Nicolaitans as expressed in the letter to the Ephesians (2:6). Unlike the gentle remarks to the church in Smyrna, this letter immediately challenges the church in Pergamum to look deeply into the genuineness and practicality of its faith. *You have people there who hold to the teaching of Balaam, who taught Balak to entice the Israelites to sin by eating food sacrificed to idols and by committing sexual immorality.* [15] *Likewise you also have those who hold to the teaching of the Nicolaitans.* From the nature of the concerns listed by Jesus, it is apparent that these concerns involved both spiritual and ethical problems. The mention of Balaam immediately conjures up memories of Num. 24:10-25, 25:1-5 and 31:15–16. Caird notes that the "Balaam saga" had developed in the Jewish midrash into a cautionary tale, warning against the mercenary spirit found in Balaam, the encouragement to compromise faith, and the tendency to look lightly on fornication.[82] Mounce cites Blaiklock, who saw Balaam's seduction of Israel as a means of breaking down their resolve to be the unique people of God. Blaiklock states, "Pagan food and pagan women were his (Balaam's) powerful tools against the rigidity of the Mosaic Law."[83] Aune notes that in the rabbinic tradition, Balaam is contrasted in a derogatory manner with Abraham, the father of faith.[84]

Caird and Mounce consider the incidents mentioned here to be descriptive of one, not two, Christian groups that manifested both the tendencies, compromise and lascivious, rather than two groups. "Both describe an antinomian group which had accommodated itself to the religious and social requirements of the pagan society in which they lived."[85] Aune agrees with the combination of the two emphases of Balaam and the Nicolaitans, observing that "the teaching of Balaam" is the same as "the teaching of the Nicolaitans"[86] since the Greek *houtos* ("*so, thus, in this way*") coordinates the two phrases.[87] Furthermore, Aune adds that the comparison of persons or parties in one place with disreputable persons in another place was a familiar technical and pejorative tool of denouncing a group.[88]

Mounce summarizes these views, "Thus Balaam became a prototype of all corrupt teachers who betrayed believers into fatal compromise with worldly ideologies."[89] Caird suggests that this Pergamum group believed it possible to maintain peaceful co-existence with Rome without disloyalty to one's Christian faith. This compromise by some in the church in Pergamum with Rome and its paganism was apparently tolerated in the remainder of the church. Caird at this point is not clear that sexual fornication is what Jesus had in mind since the term *porneia* can be used metaphorically for spiritual fornication rising out of compromise.[90] However, pagan religious practices of the day often involved physical sexual fornication with temple prostitutes; thus the compromise practiced by the Balaam-Nicolaitans most likely involved a compromise with the pagan cults and sexual fornication. Aune observes that "A close association is assumed by Judaism to exist between idolatry and sexual immorality.[91] The NIV translates *porneuō* here as **committing sexual fornication**, while the RSV simply translates it as to **practice immorality**. Both however imply sexual promiscuity. *Porneuō* can therefore be precisely understood here as to prostitute, practice prostitution or sexual immorality.[92]

2:16. *Repent therefore. Otherwise, I will soon come to you and will fight against them with the sword of my mouth.* Jesus finds this practice of *porneuō* reprehensible, calling on those who hold this view to **repent** immediately or face his stern judgment. As in 2:5, an aorist imperative for **repent** calls for drastic change. The change called for in the word *metanoeō* is a radical change in life style. *I will soon come* implies that this judgment will not wait until the final day of judgment, but has imminent implications. Both Aune and Beale agree with Caird[93] that this is not a reference to the *parousia* but a reference to the imminent coming of Jesus in judgment on the church in Pergamum, *unless they repent.* As in 2:5, the imminent coming in judgment is *conditional* and based on their response to Jesus' call for repentance. As in 2:5, this is one of those unique "proleptic eschatological expressions" in which John's eschatology and apocalyptic understanding cause him to view present or imminent incidents as having end-time implications. Jesus will *soon come* (in the imminent future) to the church in Pergamum and judge it with final end-of-the-world consequences, unless they repent.

With the sword of my mouth refers as in 2:12 to the judging word of Jesus. That message came from **him who has the sharp, double-edged sword.** Likewise at 1:16 there is a similar reference to Jesus' sovereign power, **and out of his mouth came a sharp double-edged sword.** Mounce observes that "the sword in these vignettes symbolizes the irresistible power of divine judgment."[94] In addition, the contrast of **a sharp double-edged sword** in Jesus' mouth with the Roman sword as a symbol of power and sovereignty emphasizes that it is Jesus not Rome who holds in his word absolute power as the eschatological judge over the nations.[95]

2:17. *He who has an ear, let him hear what the Spirit says to the churches.* The urgency of Jesus' admonition is brought home again by his repeated use of this interesting Hebrew formula calling on his hearers to pay careful attention to his words, and to the inclusion of the Holy Spirit in the message. **To him who overcomes, I will give some of the hidden manna.** Once again, Jesus offers a promise to those who conquer, that is, to those who die as martyrs for maintaining the purity of their faith without compromise. They will be given *some of the hidden manna*. Manna was the food supplied to Israel by God as he sustained her through her wilderness wanderings (Exod. 16:31). There was always something supernatural about this food, reminding Israel that it came directly from the loving concern of their God.

A rabbinic tradition held that some of the supernatural manna had been preserved in a golden jar that was hidden by Jeremiah or an angel at the destruction of the temple. This *hidden manna* would reappear at the beginning of the messianic age as spiritual food, sustaining the saints. Several texts illustrate this tradition of spiritual food, among them 2 Maccabees 2:4, 2 Baruch 29.8, and Sibylline Oracles 7:149.[96] Some think that the reference here to this spiritual food is to be seen in contrast to *the teaching of Balaam, who taught Balak to entice the Israelites to sin by eating food sacrificed to idols*.[97] A parallel to this contrast between spiritual and pagan, or idolatrous, food may be seen in Paul's admonition in 1 Corinthians 10: 14–22.

The point made by Paul in 1 Corinthians and Jesus here is that it is not acceptable or even possible to eat the food of idols, that is, compromise one's faith by participating in pagan practices, and benefit at the same time from the spiritual food promised by Jesus. Some connection with Jesus' teaching that he is the bread of life and those who eat of his body (believe in him) will have eternal life (John 6:22–48) seems apparent in Jesus' promise to the church in Pergamum. Those who refuse to compromise their faith may die for that faith, but Jesus promises they will participate in this eschatological banquet in advance of the final eschatological banquet through their martyrdom. The reference to eating the hidden manna in this text is certainly John's way of connecting the reward of martyrdom to the Jewish tradition of an eschatological banquet to be shared by God's people after the final end. In the Christian tradition there is also a clear connection between the Eucharistic Communion, or Lord's Supper, celebrated each Lord's day, and participating in the eschatological messianic banquet. The Christians at Pergamum are warned not to forfeit the blessed experience of participating in the final great eschatological banquet by compromising their faith with pagan idolatry, and in particular with the imperial cult.

The connection to the eschatological banquet is reinforced by the statement that follows: *I will also give him a white stone with a new name written on it, known only to him who receives it.* Considerable speculation has surfaced over the interpretation of this little white stone. Pieces of marble were common in ancient times as forms of communication and expression. They served as lots in ballots, as rewards given to gladiators when inscribed in some fashion, and as tokens given as invitations and entrance "invitations" to special banquets. In the context of the hidden manna, it seems most likely that the last option may possibly be the meaning of the white stone. With a new name, possibly conqueror, written on the little white stone, the bearers would be assured of their reward, namely, the invitation to the eschatological banquet.[98] There is the possibility that the name inscribed on the stone may derive from the gladiatorial victors whose names were often written on awards of white marble or stone.

SUMMARY OF THE LETTERS TO THE CHURCHES IN EPHESUS, SMYRNA, AND PERGAMUM.

The seven letters to the seven churches reflect several profound lessons to which all churches and Christians need to be sensitive:

1. That Jesus knows all about his church. He knows its strengths and its weaknesses.
2. That Jesus is deeply concerned for the spiritual wellbeing of his church. He warns the church of faith crises and to be prepared for trials that challenge faith.
3. That churches need to look deeply into their faith to determine whether that faith is focused in the right place, which is Jesus Christ, rather than in church organization or some form of extreme doctrinal orthodoxy.
4. That churches should beware of compromise with their "pagan," or worldly, secular neighbors.
5. That often churches, unaware of faith and identity drifts, conform more to their social environment than is healthy.

In the case of **Ephesus,** the church was so heavily involved with the superficial aspects of their religion that they had lost their original love for and commitment to Jesus. Ephesus was orthodox, religious, and hard working, but lacking in love. They needed to be aware that an overly formal ecclesiological (church) approach to religion must not supplant their Christological focus. There is the danger that groups stressing orthodoxy tend to be more concerned with the organization or doctrinal structure of the church than they are with the church's inner commitment to Jesus. The church as an organized body is always important, but only because it is defined as the body of Christ, which he loved and for which he died. The church should never become the center of faith when doctrinal formality and orthodoxy rise to the surface, for the true center of the Christian faith is Jesus Christ, not the church, and the true identity of the disciple of Christ is one who is in an appropriate relationship with him rather than with the correct structure or formal doctrine of church. It is love and commitment to Jesus and love for one another (John 13:35) that identifies the true church and true Christian, not simply knowledge of the correct church form. Jesus does not denigrate the Ephesian passion for doctrinal fidelity he commends it, as should we. Neither does he disparage hard work and commitment to the church. But when these become the center of faith and defining characteristics of the church in place of love, Jesus demands repentance and a refocus of faith. As in the case of the Ephesian church, all churches and Christians need desperately to examine their faith, especially in times of crisis. Faith focused alone on orthodoxy will not sustain Christians in times of crisis. In fact, when faith is focused primarily on orthodoxy or doctrine, division within the body of Christ occurs. Only a faith focused on Jesus in love and commitment has the necessary sustaining power of unity. Under such conditions of trial, Jesus promised his ever abiding presence and support. However, in Revelation

John goes on to explain that a radical call to faith focused on the love of Jesus as Lord above all other commitments will inevitably bring suffering, even martyrdom. The cost of faithfulness to Jesus is often high. If martyrdom be the case, Jesus has promised ultimate vindication and victory to those who die for their faith, for they would be the real conquerors who share in his messianic kingdom. Christians today may not have to die as martyrs, but the temptation to compromise faith and substitute religion in place of a life and love commitment to Jesus and one another is an ever present reality. The danger of orthodoxy has often been a loss of concern and passion for people, especially the fellow Christian who does not march according to the perceived standards of orthodoxy. A passion for orthodoxy must never be at the expense of a passion for orthopraxy or love for one another. Church history warns that an over emphasis on orthodoxy leads to legalism, harshness, and sectarianism. Ephesus stood at the head of that historical line, and Jesus called it to repentance.

Smyrna, was one of the two churches that were not reprimanded by Jesus in his letters to the seven churches. We could characterize the church in Smyrna (along with Philadelphia, the other church receiving no condemnation from Jesus) as *faithful unto death*. They had already tasted the results of a refusal to compromise their faith. They endured poverty because of their faith, but for that faith they had received an inner spiritual richness. They had experienced the rejection of their religious neighbors, especially the Jewish community, but were assured by Jesus that their reward was secure. Faced with certain death because of their faith, they were promised life in return for death. They experienced the judgment and rejection of their neighbors, but were assured of Jesus' support and acceptance. In Jesus' mind they had already been vindicated, and would at the eschatological end be rewarded by the supreme judge. Christians today need to be reassured that rejection by their secular community is not to be compared with acceptance by the supreme judge, for the richness of the Christian reward far surpasses the riches of this world.

Pergamum. This church, surrounded by pagan culture and the panoply of Roman power and the imperial cult, was faithful. However, they tended to tolerate those who compromised with their pagan cultural surroundings. Like all Christians, they needed to be encouraged never to weaken their commitment by conciliation with their secular culture. Rather than eating food offered to idols, they were offered by Jesus a real spiritual food and an invitation to share with Jesus at the richness of his eschatological table. The lure of the richness of worldly life will always draw Christians to worldly compromise, but Christians should be reminded by Paul's encouragement not to be conformed to this world (Rom 12:2), but rather to offer their lives as a living sacrifice to God, for this is a good, acceptable, and mature response to God's loving grace.

Chapter 3

The Church in Imperfection

The Seven Letters

Part 2

Thyatira, Sardis, Philadelphia, and Laodicea

2:18–3:22

THE MESSAGE TO THE CHURCH IN THYATIRA. (2:18–29)

The Text

[18] To the angel of the church in Thyatira write: These are the words of the Son of God, whose eyes are like blazing fire and whose feet are like burnished bronze. [19] I know your deeds, your love and faith, your service and perseverance, and that you are now doing more than you did at first. [20] Nevertheless, I have this against you: You tolerate that woman Jezebel, who calls herself a prophetess. By her teaching she misleads my servants into sexual immorality and the eating of food sacrificed to idols. [21] I have given her time to repent of her immorality, but she is unwilling. [22] So I will cast her on a bed of suffering, and I will make those who commit adultery with her suffer intensely, unless they repent of her ways. [23] I will strike her children dead. Then all the churches will know that I am he who searches hearts and minds, and I will repay each of you according to your deeds. [24] Now I say to the rest of you in Thyatira, to you who do not hold to her teaching and have not learned Satan's so-called deep secrets (I will not impose any other burden on you):[25] Only hold on to what you have until I come. [26] To him who overcomes and does my will to the end, I will give authority over the nations—[27] 'He will rule them with an iron scepter; he will dash them to pieces like pottery' [Ps. 2:9]—just as I have received authority from my Father. [28] I will also give him the morning star. [29] He who has an ear, let him hear what the Spirit says to the churches.

2:18. *To the angel of the church in Thyatira.* The letter to Thyatira is the longest of the seven letters, which is surprising since the church at Thyatira was not one of the major churches in Asia. Thyatira had originally been founded as a military outpost, but had developed into a thriving and prosperous manufacturing and marketing center. Many trade guilds were located in the city. Lydia, a trader of purple, lived in Thyatira (Acts 16:14). Among the guilds there were those promoting metal working, wool production, leather works, pottery manufacturing, linen weaving, and apparently also bronze-smiths. By the first century the wealth and fame of Thyatira had spread as far as Greece and Macedonia across the Aegean Sea. Membership in the trade guilds involved certain religious practices that would present faith challenges to Christians. It is almost certain that these religious practices included homage to the imperial cult as well as veneration of the local deity, Tyrimnos (or Apollo Tyrimnaeus), a personification of the Greek sun-god Apollo.[1]

Apparently, the severity of the challenges presented by the trade and metal-smith guilds and especially their allegiance to the imperial cult were the focus of Jesus' concern. With this in mind Jesus identified himself by adapting his self-description to the interests of the Thyatirans: ***These are the words of the Son of God, whose eyes are like blazing fire and whose feet are like burnished bronze.*** Jesus drew attention to the fact that it is he, the Son of God, who alone is worthy of Christian worship. The reference to ***eyes like blazing fire*** *and feet like burnished bronze* focuses specific attention on what may have been the center of the problem faced by the Christians in Thyatira, namely, membership in the trade guilds and the worship of Tyrimnos.[2]

2:19. The congregation at Thyatira was in some fashion a faithful one since Jesus addressed them kindly, ***I know your deeds, your love and faith, your service and perseverance, and that you are now doing more than you did at first.*** The fact that they had matured and continued to grow in their faithful service and yet received a stern reprimand (cf. v. 20) stresses the need for Christians to continually re-asses their faith and to address those areas needing attention. Contrary to the church at Ephesus, this church was characterized by its love that worked with its faith to produce commendable Christian service and perseverance.

2:20. In spite of this commendation, a serious problem in Thyatira needed immediate attention. Jesus continues, in spite of the good he saw in Thyatira, with a stern rebuke. [20] ***You tolerate that woman Jezebel, who calls herself a prophetess. By her teaching she misleads my servants into sexual immorality and the eating of food sacrificed to idols.*** The best understanding of this expression is to see in it an analogous reference to Jezebel, the evil wife of king Ahab of 1 Kings 16:29–34 and 2 Kings 9:30–37, and not a literal reference to a woman whose name was Jezebel.[3] There is some discussion among commentators as to whether this reference was to a specific woman, to a woman who was a prominent leader in the Thyatiran church, or to the church itself, which tolerated a mood of compromise.[4] Whoever this person was or whatever this trend represented, Jesus dramatically drew attention to the problem at hand by charging that the church was being corrupted by a compromising attitude toward sexual immorality. ***By her teaching she misleads my servants into sexual immorality and the eating of food sacrificed to idols***. The statement that this woman called herself a prophetess and that she was active in teaching possibly supports the view that this woman represented a tendency toward tolerant compromise rather than to an individual person. Furthermore, the association of Jezebel with the Nicolaitans in these letters could support the view that this Jezebel represents a mood rather than a specific person. Thus Jezebel was a convenient metaphor for the mood of compromise.

The correlation of sexual immorality (*porneuō, porneia*, to practice prostitution, fornication, or pure sexual immorality) and eating food offered to idols should not be surprising in a pagan culture where sexual immorality and eating sacrificial foods in pagan temples was common. Both were familiar practices associated with pagan worship ceremonies.[5] Boring observes that John uses three "persons," each with similar characteristics, to describe the problem of pagan idolatry and cultural assimilation faced by the church in Asia, seemingly a problem faced by all churches in every place and time.

> Since these [the Nicolaitans, Balaam, and Jezebel] are described in identical terms, they are probably all designations of the same group or movement. "Balaam" and "Jezebel" are obviously John's own symbolic designations drawn from the story of the opponents and seducers of God's people in the Old Testament story and Jewish tradition (Num 22–25; 31:16; I Kings 16:31; 18:1–19; 19:1–2; cf. II Peter 2:15; Jude11). . . . The "Nicolaitans," "Balaam," and "Jezebel" promoted the "progressive" doctrine of accommodation to the culture around them. The question of the manner and degree of the Christians' participation in the ordinary business of the world in which they lived, especially as it dealt with the issues of whether they could attend pagan festival meals and eat meat "contaminated" by its association with the sacrificial cult of some pagan deity, had troubled Christians in other times and places. . . . John saw the issue in either/or terms: To participate in such activities was to take part in the false worship of pagan religion.[6]

One might differ with Boring in identifying these three as representatives of the same group or movement, but they certainly represent the same mood, cultural assimilation and compromise, especially in regard to pagan festivals and sacrifices. Boring, however, fails to note that a major aspect of the problem with pagan religious sacrifices and festivals was the sexual immorality often practiced in the name of fertility and other cults. Caird prefers to identify the problem of fornication with religious infidelity.[7] Beasley-Murray, along with Mounce, Beale, and Aune more correctly recognize that fornication may be more than religious infidelity, identifying this more specifically as sexual immorality associated with pagan festivals. Beasley-Murray refers to Jezebel's "paramours,"[8] while Mounce adds, "Since the eating of 'food sacrificed to idols' is undoubtedly intended in a literal sense, it is best to take "sexual immorality" in the same way. Pagan feasts often led to sexual promiscuity."[9]

2:21–23. In a long condemnation of this "Jezebel mood of compromise," Jesus pronounces a severe judgment on this tolerant attitude, *I have given her time to repent of her immorality, but she is unwilling. ²² So I will cast her on a bed of suffering, and I will make those who commit adultery with her suffer intensely, unless they repent of her ways. ²³ I will strike her children dead. Then all the churches will know that I am he who searches hearts and minds, and I will repay each of you according to your deeds.* The time for serious repentance in Thyatira is emphasized by the fact that Jesus states that they had already had enough time to manifest a contrite heart and repentance. Whereas in 2:20 John had identified the nature of the sin under discussion as *fornication* (*porneia*) he now refers to this as *adultery* (*moicheia, moicheuō*), which under normal circumstances speaks of a break in a covenant relationships such as marriage. The point made is that sexual immorality (*porneia*) practiced by Christians was a break in covenant relationship with Christ, hence that it can also be spoken of as adultery (*moicheia*). Regardless of the serious nature of the sin, Jesus grants the sinner the opportunity and time to repent. However, in the case of the trend in Thyatira, the problem had persisted too long and Jesus' condemnation is strikingly harsh and immediate. Jesus had *given her time to repent* but to no avail. This emphasizes the seriousness of the problem of widespread tolerated immorality among the Christians in Thyatira. In similar fashion, Paul, in 1 Corinthians 5:1–13, had called for stern measures to be taken when known, tolerated, and unrepented immorality persisted among Corinthians. We are not sure of the nature of Jesus' statement *I will cast her on a bed of suffering*, but the analogy to the bed of fornication or adultery as a euphemism for a somber judgment of fornication seems likely.[10] Likewise, the harsh statement *I will strike her children dead* is difficult but would draw swift and urgent attention to Jesus' uncompromising attitude toward sexual immorality and pagan idolatry. An example of God's abhorrence of sexual adultery can be seen in his harsh judgment of David for his sin of adultery with Bathsheba and the resultant death of their infant son (2 Sam. 12:14–18).[11] Jesus' distaste for pagan sexual immorality expressed here in regard to Thyatira and notably toward the Jezebel mood of sexual compromise is in keeping with traditional Judeo-Christian condemnation of this sin. Mounce suggests that Jesus makes an analogy here between Jezebel's children and the killing of the seventy sons of Ahab in 2 Kings 10:1–11.

> Jezebel's "children" are not the literal offspring of her adulteries or a second generation of heretics, but those who have unreservedly embraced the antinomian doctrines of their spiritual mother that are best described as younger members of her family. The killing of Jezebel's children may reflect the bloody occasion when the rulers of Samaria murdered the seventy sons of Ahab and sent their heads to Jezreel in baskets (2 Kgs 10:1–11). If a distinction is to be drawn between the children of Jezebel and "those who commit adultery with her" (v. 22), the latter would be those who "flirt with her teaching" and the former, "the totally converted." The persuasive logic of the compromisers had confused many in the church at Thyatira, but imminent punishment

would demonstrate that the one who searches "hearts and minds" of people had found them guilty.[12]

Jesus intended the church in Thyatira, and universally in Asia, to know unmistakably that he knows precisely what is going on in the life of the church, even in the secret parts of their lives, for he searches the deep realms of their *hearts and minds*. The term translated "hearts" in the English Bibles is from the Greek *nephros*, which normally means *kidneys*. Here, in keeping with Jewish style, it is translated hearts to signify the inner life or depth of emotional and spiritual commitment. Aune observes that Jesus' statement here is drawn from Jer. 17:10a, where Yahweh says, "I, the Lord, search the mind and try the heart." Aune identifies in this expression an important Christological statement about Jesus: he possesses the same omniscient ability as Yahweh, for he is God. Jesus knows exactly where the true commitment of his churches lies. In the case of those in Thyatira who superficially professed Christian faith, yet who compromised that Christian commitment and ethic with pagan practices, Jesus urges a fresh examination of that commitment and a concomitant radical repentance. If the Christians in Thyatira were willing to compromise their faith with pagan immorality, they surely would not be able to withstand the impending crisis and challenging compromise of faith shortly to break in upon them. A compromised faith is without question unable to stand in the face of serious faith crises.

2:24. Jesus' reference to those who *have not learned Satan's so-called deep secrets* indicates the depth of depravity involved in the religious compromise and fornication practiced by some in Thyatira. John's use of the expression *so called deep secrets* is translated in the RSV and NRSV as "what some call," indicating that there were some in Thyatira who were arrogant enough to make excuse for their behavior. Either way, this expression is used by Jesus to stress his condemnation of such antinomian or licentious attitudes toward sexual immorality. Aune suggests that the expression *Satan's so-called deep secrets* could be seen as a sarcastic contrast to the wisdom or "deep things of God" in 1 Cor. 2:10, and in this case in contrast to knowing the deep secrets of God.[13] The practice of sexual immorality would then be understood as the practice of the deep secrets of Satan rather than the wisdom of God. Mounce, however, suggests, along with Moffatt and others, that the background to this expression may lie in an early form of gnostic Orphite tradition that later surfaced in late second-century Gnosticism as an antinomian teaching that promoted the view that in order to fully appreciate the grace of God one had to know the depths of sin and Satan's realm.[14] This antinomian, grace-oriented, incipient Gnostic ethic suggested that the true spiritual nature of man, which had been redeemed by special esoteric knowledge, should not be held accountable for the physical nature of man and his sensual tendencies. In condemning those who claim to know such false "deep things," Jesus clearly indicates his attitude toward antinomian licentiousness. Such "deep things" were none other than *the deep things of Satan*, rather than "the deep things of God."[15] It is not uncommon even today for those who excuse themselves of sexual licentiousness on the grounds of a grace principle to claim that those who oppose them simply do not understand the real depth and nature of the forgiving grace of God. To this excuse Jesus would respond that beds of deep spiritual sickness await such nonsense.

2:25. To the exhortation [25]*only hold on to what you have until I come,* Jesus adds [26] *to him who overcomes and does my will to the end, I will give authority over the nations.* [27] *'He will rule them with an iron scepter; he will dash them to pieces like pottery' just as I have received authority from my Father.* The statement *until I come* poses some challenges. First, what prompted Jesus to encourage the saints to hold fast to what they had until he came? Was it merely the problem of immorality, or was there possibly the larger faith concern? The context shows that this encouragement was to hold fast to their faith and not to succumb to compromising influences in general. The culture of pagan immorality and fornication would be a problem in itself; but when we add the mood of the pagan culture and of the presence of the demanding imperial cult, it may imply more than a mere concern for immorality. The initial tendency to compromise with the Jezebel movement in regard to sexual immorality associated with pagan sacrifices could create a future inclination to compromise with an even greater, more threatening mood, that is, to compromise with the imperial cult and veneration of the emperor, as in the case of Domitian's claims to be the lord and god (*dominus et deus*).[16] Jesus follows this exhortation to *only hold on to what you have* with the citation from Psalm 2 and the promise to *give* them *authority over the nations* and a *rule . . . with an iron rod,* which sets this warning and promise firmly in one of the major theological themes of Revelation, a refusal to compromise with the imperial cult and the reward and vindication of reigning with Christ.[17]

A second problem posed by Jesus' exhortation to hold fast is his reference to his coming. Is this an allusion to the final *parousia,* or to an imminent coming in judgment on the immorality of those in Thyatira who have corrupted the faith of the church? It is important that we view this expression within the context of similar statements in the seven letters, that is with parallel promises of Jesus to "come soon," to "come to you soon," or "I will come upon you" and "I am coming soon" as in 2:5; 2:16; 3:3; and 3:11 (see my comments on 2:5 and 16).

In each case, in contrast to the judgment on those who might not repent, there would be a reward for those who kept their faith and conquered. In Thyatira there would likewise be a reward for those who kept their faith until he came. Here, as in 2:25, Jesus' statement *until I come* should be understood as a reference to his imminent coming in judgment on those who refuse to repent of their compromise with the Jezebel mood and his vindication of the faithful, as was the case of Ephesus and Pergamum. The saints in Thyatira, who would be full of questions regarding their suffering and what God and Jesus were doing about this, were at the same time being encouraged by Jesus to *hold on to what you have,* or to "keep your uncompromising faith without losing hope" until Jesus came in judgment on the Christians who would not repent. He would come soon in judgment of the oppressive enemies of the faithful and on those who would contaminate their faith with the Jezebel compromise with the imperial cultus, thus assuring the faithful of his concern and retribution on those who were unfaithful. Caird argues that the enjoyment of those in Thyatira in the reward for conquering is not something to be anticipated at the distant future end of the world, but is to be experienced by the martyrs as their reward for faithfulness at their death in keeping with similar promises elsewhere to those who conquer:

> We are compelled therefore to look for the fulfillment of this promise *within the present order*; and since the Christian becomes a **Conqueror** in this world only in the moment of his leaving it, the fulfillment must be the actual death of the martyrs.[18]

The encouragement to hold fast to what they had, that is, their faith until Jesus comes, must also be kept within the context of the discussion at hand, namely his coming in judgment on those in Thyatira who held to the compromising practice of the Jezebel mood. It is possible that Jesus repeats the main thoughts of this expression in the next verse *to him who overcomes and does my will to the end*, indicating that he does not have the final *parousia* in mind, only the perseverance of the saints in light of the coming persecution and martyrdom. Beale refers this discussion to his comments on the conditional aspects of Jesus' coming soon in 1:7, and 2:5 (I would also add, 2:16).[19] Beale considers 2:25 in the same context as other conditional statements regarding Jesus' coming in imminent judgment on the churches and those who oppress them.

2:26, 27. Jesus' promise to Thyatira was *to him who overcomes and does my will to the end, I will give authority over the nations.* [27] *'He will rule them with an iron scepter; he will dash them to pieces like pottery' [Ps. 2:9] just as I have received authority from my Father.* The conqueror (he who overcomes) refers to the martyred saint. To his reference to the conqueror Jesus adds *and does my will to the end*. Surely, this is a definition of a conqueror, one who maintains faith right to the end of life. In the context of the conditional nature of the promises, this clearly does not refer to the *parousia* but to the death of the faithful saints. Beale adds, "Their perseverance 'until the end' is the condition that must be met for them to receive what is promised."[20] To the saints that persevere *to the end*, Jesus promises to give authority over the nations.

The expression *to him who overcomes* (*conquers*, RSV) repeats the formula of encouragement found in all seven letters. Those who remain faithful, that is, who are willing to offer their lives as a sacrifice to God through their martyrdom and thus become a conqueror, will be richly rewarded by God. This reward is not only to be received at the final end of the age or world, but will be received in advance at the conquering. Those who remain faithful, or who do Jesus' will *to the end*, that is, even to the point of dying for him in martyrdom, will receive an immediate reward, *authority over the nations*. Again, we should read this comment through the lens of proleptic eschatological expectation. The Ephesians were promised the *tree of life* (Rev. 2:7), the Smyrnaeans the *crown of life* (2:10), the Pergamenians the *hidden manna* and proleptic access to the eschatological banquet; later we will learn that the faithful in Laodicea were promised by Jesus that they would *sit* with him *on his throne* (3:21). In the case of Thyatira, the precise promise was that Jesus would give them *authority* or power *over the nations*. They would share with him in his sovereign reign.

The expression *I will give authority over the nations* is only the first portion of Jesus' promise, for he adds, '*He will rule them with an iron scepter; he will dash them to pieces like pottery' just as I have received authority from my Father.* This is one of the many striking references in Revelation to Psalm 2, a psalm of kingly ascent. In his commentary on Psalm 2, Craigie refers to this psalm as a coronation psalm".[21] Verse 1 sets the theme, the nations conspiring and plotting against God's anointed king. Verses 8–9 are particularly relevant:

> [8] Ask of me,
>> and I will make the nations your inheritance,
>> the ends of the earth your possession.
> [9] You will rule them with an iron scepter;
>> you will dash them to pieces like pottery. "

The enigmatic expression *You will rule them with an iron scepter; you will dash them to pieces like pottery* derives from an Egyptian practice of a new Pharaoh ascending to his new role as king. He would go into the palace kitchen and break all of the clay vessels in a ritual demonstrating that a new king was now reigning. This symbolic act in time became a Hebraism and part of the Jewish royal Psalmic tradition as seen in Psalm 2, which became a traditional psalm of kingly ascent.[22] Jesus drew on this royal ascent aspect of the psalm to validate his claim that the martyrs would share in his kingly reign. This kingdom theme, announced as early as 1:6, 9, is one that John repeats throughout Revelation, each time expanding on it until 20:4, where John announces that the martyred saints reign fully with Christ in his kingdom. Here in 2:26–27, John continues his expansion of his kingdom theme.

Mounce observes that Psalm 2:8–9 has a long tradition of messianic interpretation that reaches back into the first century B.C. This messianic tradition can be seen in *The Psalms of Solomon*, 17:23–24, (70–40 B.C.), which apply these verses from Ps. 2 to the anticipated coming of a messianic Son of David who would rule over Israel. "It was a regular feature of Jewish eschatology that followers of the Messiah would share in his final rule. This feature carried over into Christian thought (1 Cor. 6:3, Rev. 5:10)."[23]

Jesus and John in Revelation draw on the reigning aspect of Ps. 2 to reinforce their claim that those who follow the Messiah, to the point of death, share also in his messianic reign. Psalm 2:8–9 thus forms one of the major theological emphases in Revelation indicating that the martyrs (conquerors, overcomers) as true disciples of the conquering Messiah will in the same fashion as the Messiah be raised to share in God's reign over the nations.

Caird correctly argues that this participation in the reign of Christ is not something to be anticipated only in the distant future end of the world, but is to be experienced by the martyrs as their reward for faithfulness at their death. This is in keeping with similar promises of imminent reward made to those who conquer, which promises would be enjoyed in the immediate present of their martyrdom[24] (cf. 2:7, "to eat from the tree of life," 2:11 "not be hurt at all by the second death," 2:17 "give some of the hidden manna"). Jesus adds that the authority of the conquerors to rule will be *just as I have received authority from my Father*. By conquering Satan in his death, Jesus was raised to sit on God's throne. Likewise, the martyrs at their death would be raised to sit on thrones with Jesus. Explanations of how the saints will reign with Christ on his throne and share in his judgment of the nations should keep in mind John's awareness of the Jewish concept of corporate personality in which the king represents the nation and the nation represents the king.

2:28. Jesus concludes this encouragement with the promise *I will also give him the morning star*. Although this expression has messianic connotations, there is considerable debate over the meaning of the phrase. Mounce and Hemer conclude that there is no one completely satisfying solution to the several proposals made in regard to the background and use of the expression *the morning star*. The parallel messianic traditions of Psalm 2 and Numbers 24:17 (which couples the coming of a star with a scepter that will crush the forehead of Moab) lead to a possible conclusion of messianic significance for the saying.[25] Beasley-Murray adds that a possible background reference to Venus, the morning star in Roman contexts, as a symbol of victory could mean that "The conqueror is therefore doubly assured of his participation with Christ in the glory of his kingdom."[26] The relationship of this expression to that in 22:16, where Christ is referred to as *the bright Morning Star*, seems to imply that the conqueror is here promised a share in the messianic glory of Christ. This interpretation is in keeping with the observation of Beasley-Murray above that the conqueror is doubly assured of a share in the messianic reign and glory of Christ.

The final exhortation of the letter to the church in Thyatira follows the concluding formula of each of the other letters. [29] *He who has an ear, let him hear what the Spirit says to the churches*. By concluding his letter with these formulaic words, Jesus reminds the church at Thyatira of the importance of his letter and the overall message of Revelation by again observing that his message comes also from the Holy Spirit, thus adding both authentication and urgency to the letter and that it has universal relevance to *the churches*.

THE MESSAGE TO THE CHURCH IN SARDIS. (3:1–6)

The Text

"To the angel of the church in Sardis write: These are the words of him who holds the seven spirits of God and the seven stars. I know your deeds; you have a reputation of being alive, but you are dead. ² Wake up. Strengthen what remains and is about to die, for I have not found your deeds complete in the sight of my God. ³ Remember, therefore, what you have received and heard; obey it, and repent. But if you do not wake up, I will come like a thief, and you will not know at what time I will come to you. ⁴ Yet you have a few people in Sardis who have not soiled

their clothes. They will walk with me, dressed in white, for they are worthy. [5] *He who overcomes will, like them, be dressed in white. I will never blot out his name from the book of life, but will acknowledge his name before my Father and his angels.* [6] *He who has an ear, let him hear what the Spirit says to the churches.*

The description of the church at Sardis in many ways mirrors the city itself. Once one of the powerful cities of Asia, Sardis had been the capital of the mighty and wealthy kingdom of Lydia. Legend has it that under their great king Croesus (from which we derive the expression "wealthy as Croesus") Sardis had been an impregnable fortress. With its power and wealth, Sardis had reigned sovereign over Lydia until its defeat by the Persian army under Cyrus.[27] Overlooking the fertile plain of the Hermus, the city of Sardis lay at the foot of a narrow mountain promontory with steep cliffs rising fifteen hundred feet above the plain below. There were in fact two parts of the city, the lower city where the people lived, and the smaller citadel, or acropolis, on the plateau above, to which the king and his soldiers could retreat in times of trouble. Access from the lower city to the acropolis was extremely difficult due to the steep cliffs, which were comprised of a rock that crumbled at the touch. The topography of the acropolis made it an ideal, almost impregnable fortress. Sardis, however, fell repeatedly through a lack of vigilance.

A legendary account in the writings of Herodotus tells how the Persian king Cyrus besieged the acropolis city of Sardis in 546 B.C. and captured the Lydian king Croesus. Convinced of his safety in the fortress, Croesus and his army were asleep in their unguarded citadel when Persian soldiers found a "chimney" in the cliff face through which they scaled and entered the city, taking Croesus and his army off guard, capturing Croesus while he slept. Shortly after the Croesus-Cyrus debacle, the citadel was again taken during a Lydian revolt as the occupants slept. In 214 B.C. the citadel again fell, this time to Antiochus III through a lack of vigil. In the days of the Roman provincial government and the writing of Revelation, the influence of Sardis had declined so that Smyrna, not Sardis, was chosen for the building of an imperial temple.[28]

Recent discovery of the remains of a large synagogue in Sardis indicate the presence of a strong Jewish population dating possibly from the third century B.C. The size and nature of the synagogue complex, which possibly included some form of gymnasium, indicate the affluence and influence of the Jewish community in Sardis. The presence of Greek inscriptions and the reuse of Lydian religious reliefs in the architecture of the synagogue, indicate a comfortable pagan accommodation within the Jewish cultus of the Sardian synagogue (some Jews claiming to be *Sardianoi*—Sardian citizens). The Jewish community was obviously influential in both civic and political spheres in Sardis, for according to Josephus, approval was given by Caesar for the Jewish practice of taking contributions from the synagogue and sending them to Jerusalem. This apparent ease with Roman and Sardian paganism indicated a lax religious commitment on the part of the synagogue toward their traditional Jewish heritage.[29]

Mirroring the sad history of Sardis and its tradition of careless negligence, the church, like its Jewish neighbors, was untroubled by its pagan culture and seemingly unperturbed by the dangers that threatened it. Although some were "worthy" (indicating in Revelation, faithfulness), little good could be said to commend the church at Sardis. Thinking they were alive, with works that were "unperfected," the church was, in reality, dead, resulting in the most severe reprimand from Jesus of the five condemned churches.

3:1. *These are the words of him who holds the seven spirits of God and the seven stars.* The greeting at1:4 to the seven churches *was from him who is, and who was, and who is to come, and from the seven spirits before his throne, and from Jesus Christ.* . . . Cf. 1:4 for discussion of *the seven spirits.* In itself, the phrase *the seven stars* poses no real difficulty in that Jesus has already informed us that *the seven stars* are the angels of the seven churches. What complicates the text is that Jesus adds *the seven stars* to the expression *the seven spirits of God,* connecting the two expressions with a coordinating conjunction *kai* ("and"). How the two expressions are coordinated poses problems. Mounce[30] observes that the expression *seven spirits of God* is at best enigmatic. Most commentators however observe that this expression is similar to that of 1:4 and that *the seven spirits of God* refers to the Holy Spirit, stressing the divine power of the message. Aune[31] suggests that the *kai* may be understood as an *epexegetical* or emphatic conjunction, thus rendering the text *the words of him who holds the seven spirits of God namely the seven stars,"* or *who holds the seven spirits of God indeed the seven stars.* What the interpretation of Aune would do is make the seven stars an explanation of the seven spirits, implying that the seven spirits represent the seven churches. However, Jesus could have meant that it was he who spoke with the Holy Spirit, who held the destiny of the seven angels/churches. Jesus closed each of the seven letters with the exhortation to *hear what the Spirit says to the churches,* indicating that his message came with the full approval and authority of the Holy Spirit of God. Probably, *the seven spirits of God* is best understood as a reference to the Holy Spirit. Ramsay adds that the expression "must certainly be taken as a symbolic or allegorical way of expressing the full range of exercise of the Divine power in the seven churches."[32] Beasley-Murray, likewise, stresses that the addition the Holy Spirit emphasizes the importance and severity of the message of Jesus to the church at Sardis: "The seven spirits represent the Holy Spirit sent in his fullness to the seven churches."[33] Caird and Osborne add that it is only the life giving power of the Holy Spirit of God in all of its fullness that can bring the dead church at Sardis back to life.[34]

With the stinging rebuke *you have a reputation of being alive, but you are dead,* Jesus gets right to the point: the church at Sardis was in critical condition. Ramsay appropriately titles his chapter on Sardis as "The City of Death."[35] Too often churches wrapped up going through the motions of playing church overlook the fact that God and the local community expect more from a church than going through the motions of playing church or being assimilated into the local culture. The message of discipleship enunciated by Jesus in the Gospel of Matthew (cf. for ex., Matt. 6:7) called for disciples to be radically different from their surrounding culture. The church in Sardis apparently failed miserably in this. Dietrich Bonhöffer protested against the war policies of first Kaiser Wilhelm II and later Adolf Hitler, accusing the church of "playing church," the mainline Protestant churches of Germany chose the easier road of conformity rather than prophetic outcry against social injustice. For this reason, German Neo-orthodox theologians rejected "religion," their terminology for culturally assimilated churches, which they interpreted as playing church, in favor of "faith," which was understood as an honest response to the message of God seen in the person Jesus. There is always the danger that churches choose the easier road of social and cultural conformity rather than the more difficult and socially threatening path of cultural opposition. Churches forget that Jesus called his disciples to be radically different from their neighbors and to be salt and light to the world, recognizing that this would lead to cultural and religious rejection (cf. Matt. 10:16-23).

3:2. In the case of Sardis, apathy or carelessness coupled with a lack of vigilance left the church in the critical condition of being religiously asleep rather than spiritually alert. Jesus' strident rebuke was a sobering challenge to this church, *Wake up. Strengthen what remains and is about to die, for I have not found your deeds complete in the sight of my God.* On the surface the church presented a strong religious front while all the time it was weakened by spiritual lethargy. Jesus knew that the impending crises about to break in on the churches of Asia would strike Sardis with catastrophic results "while it slept" unless repentance became a burning reality. The reference to Christian deeds not being complete in the sight of God indicates that all too often Christian piety can be superficial. The two imperatival warnings *Wake up*[36] and *Strengthen what remains* are the first of a string of five imperatives in Jesus' warning to Sardis: *wake up, strengthen, remember, obey,* and *repent.* Together they stress the gravity of Sardis's condition and the urgency of responding to Jesus' warning.

3:3. If the Christians of Sardis did not grasp the seriousness of the impending crisis and *remember* the message they had *received and heard* and did not *obey it and repent,* Jesus' judgment would be sudden and unexpected. He *will come like a thief, and you will not know at what time I will come to you.* This type of expression, which stresses the suddenness of Jesus' coming in judgment, although found in similar form in other eschatological contexts in reference to the final judgment (Matt. 24:42–44; 1 Thess. 5:2; and 2 Pet. 3:10), is a reference to Jesus' imminent yet conditional coming in judgment of the church in Sardis, should it fail to repent. If Sardis did not repent, and if it became necessary for Jesus to come in judgment on Sardis, his judgment would be sudden, like a thief in the night. Although not a reference to the final judgment, his impending judgment would have end-of-the-world consequences for Sardis, another example of John's use of proleptic eschatological language. The expression "thief at night" would also resonate with Sardis' past defeats due to not being prepared for attacks.

John's use of this loaded eschatological terminology intensifies the seriousness of the situation in Sardis and Jesus imminent coming on them in judgment. Mounce adds "If the church does not wake up to its perilous position, Christ will 'come like a thief' (i.e., unexpectedly) and visit them in judgment". He adds that "in other NT passages where the coming of Christ is said to be like a thief in the night (Matt 24:42-44; 1 Thess 5:2; 2 Pet 3:10) the second advent is in view." Here, however, some historical visitation must be in mind since the eschatological coming is not dependent on repentance in Sardis."[37] Aune agrees and points to 16:15, the only other reference in Revelation to Jesus' coming as a thief. Aune adds that the expression sometimes used of the parousia or second coming "could be applied to Christ's 'coming' in other ways".[38]

3:4. *Yet you have a few people in Sardis who have not soiled their clothes. They will walk with me, dressed in white, for they are worthy*. Elsewhere in Revelation "worthy" is used once of God (4:11) and four times of Jesus (5:2, 4, 9, 12). At ch. 5, no one other than Jesus was found worthy to open the seals on the scroll in the hand of God. The heavenly choir sang "You are worthy to take the scroll and to open its seals, because you were slain," 5:9. The connection between worthiness and martyrdom is clearly seen in this hymn of praise sung by the heavenly choir. Jesus was worthy because he had died as a martyr. The small group of saints in Sardis who were worthy were so because of their faithfulness and willingness to die as martyrs for Jesus. Like Jesus, they too through martyrdom would manifest worthiness. By conquering (martyrdom), saints share in Jesus' worthiness, blessings, richness, and kingdom.

3:4b, 5. The expression *dressed in white*, a concept introduced here for the first time in Revelation, becomes a major theological emphasis as the drama unfolds. [5]*He who overcomes will, like them, be dressed in white*. The one who overcomes or conquers as a martyr receives the white robe. The white robe is often considered a symbol of purity and victory, but in Revelation it also refers to conquering through martyrdom,[39] "the conqueror will appear in garments of holiness, and he will be vindicated in the judgment".[40] The symbol of being dressed in white robes is found also in 3:18; 4:4; 6:11; 7:9; and 7:13,14. In each case the ones wearing these robes are those who have conquered, wear crowns of gold, who are crying out from the altar having been slain because of the word, and who have come out of the great tribulation. Those who receive such white robes have offered themselves as martyrs for their faith. Jesus' promise that the few in Sardis who have not compromised their faith *will walk with me, dressed in white, for they are worthy* has both a sweet and bitter essence to it. For example, at 10:5 John is told to take a scroll and eat it, symbolizing that he still has more to prophesy: "I took the little scroll from the angels hand and ate it. It tasted as sweet as honey in my mouth, but when I had eaten it, my stomach turned sour. Jesus' bitter message of "faithfulness unto death" implies that the saints will in all probability die for their faith, but the sweet message[41] of reward is life eternal in the presence of God and sharing in the reign of his Son, the Messiah. To the faithful in Sardis, Jesus acknowledges their worthiness, but warns that this will cost them dearly. The message of Christ is both sweet and bitter for it contains both reward and suffering!

Jesus adds a final word of encouragement for those who are worthy: *I will never blot out his name from the book of life, but will acknowledge his name before my Father and his angels*. Cities in ancient times maintained a citizens roll, metaphorically referred to here in regard to those who are faithful unto death being enrolled in the book of life. Having one's name written in the citizens book involved several citizen benefits. Having one's name erased from a citizens roll implied denial of benefits. Beale points out that in the Old Testament there are various kinds of books mentioned, but emphasizes that the meaning of the book of life here must be determined from John's use of the expression throughout the Apocalypse."[42] He adds that this expression should be seen in contrast to the book of sins, and in this case this *book of life* should be understood as the book of salvation.[43] There is also here possibly a pagan (Athenian) background that involved the names of criminals being erased from the citizens roll.[44] Within the context of Revelation and Christians condemned to die as martyrs, there might be a similar criminal concept involved in Jesus use of this expression. The saints who were condemned as criminals (martyrs) and whose names would be erased from the city citizens roll would in contrast have their names written in the Lambs book of life from which their names would not be erased. Furthermore, the martyrs names would be confessed by Jesus before his Father as conquerors (see also 13:8; 17:8; 20:12, 15; 21:27).

There is some discussion here among commentators who believe in either a concept of predestinary salvation, preservation of the saints, once saved always saved, and conditional predestination in regard to the concept of having ones name erased from the book of life. Questions arise as to whether this should only be taken symbolically, whether it falls within the foreknowledge of God, or whether the book of life refers to something altogether different! Without wishing to enter the theological debate surrounding these issues, Mounce appropriately suggests that one should interpret the expression within the context of Revelation and not within the broader theological perspective of predestination.[45]

3:6. The letter to Sardis closes with the same urgent formulaic message from Jesus and the Holy Spirit as found in the other letters, stressing the urgency of the message of Jesus to the church. The plural *churches* again indicates the universal nature of this warning to all the churches in Asia. *⁶He who has an ear, let him hear what the Spirit says to the churches.*

THE MESSAGE TO THE CHURCH IN PHILADELPHIA. (3:7–13)

The Text

"To the angel of the church in Philadelphia write: These are the words of him who is holy and true, who holds the key of David. What he opens no one can shut, and what he shuts no one can open. ⁸ I know your deeds. See, I have placed before you an open door that no one can shut. I know that you have little strength, yet you have kept my word and have not denied my name. ⁹ I will make those who are of the synagogue of Satan, who claim to be Jews though they are not, but are liars—I will make them come and fall down at your feet and acknowledge that I have loved you. ¹⁰ Since you have kept my command to endure patiently, I will also keep you from the hour of trial that is going to come upon the whole world to test those who live on the earth. ¹¹ I am coming soon. Hold on to what you have, so that no one will take your crown. ¹² Him who overcomes I will make a pillar in the temple of my God. Never again will he leave it. I will write on him the name of my God and the name of the

city of my God, the new Jerusalem, which is coming down out of heaven from my God; and I will also write on him my new name. [13] *He who has an ear, let him hear what the Spirit says to the churches.*

Philadelphia, founded sometime between 189 and 138 B.C., is the youngest of the seven cities represented in Revelation. Now completely encompassed and covered up by the modern city of Alashehir, Philadelphia lay at the eastern head of a broad fertile valley that ran through Sardis and Smyrna before reaching the Aegean Sea. An important agricultural area, astride major trade roads that led to Mysia, Lydia, and Phrygia, Philadelphia was a strategically situated city of commercial and agricultural importance. Scholarly opinion varies on the founding of Philadelphia, but most agree that the naming of the city Philadelphia (Greek *Philadelphia* from *philadelphos*—*"loving one's brother or sister,"* a feminine noun but not related specifically to gender) commemorated the devotion of two brothers, Attalus II and Eumenes II, one the king of Pergamum. There is some debate as to which of the two brothers was king at the time since both reigned while the other was alive.[46]

The cross-road topography of Philadelphia, with major trade routes running through the city, and certain comments of Jesus in the letter to the Philadelphians have led some commentators to propose a "missionary" potential for the church in Philadelphia.[47] There may be a connection between Philadelphia and the rise of the heretical group, Montanism, and W. M. Calder proposed such a connection. His argument was that the Montanists claimed a certain prophetess and resident of Philadelphia, Ammia, as one of the forerunners of their ecstatic experiences.[48] Eusebius provides some indication of this connection from the writings of Apolinarius who spoke out scathingly against the ecstatic claims of the Montanists.[49] Hemer suggests that there is some merit in Calder's connection of the rise of Montanism and the prophetic heritage of Philadelphia.[50] The crossroads nature of Philadelphia, and the easy access from Philadelphia to the hotbed of Montanism, Phrygia, support the claims[51] for the "missionary" potential of the church of Philadelphia, even if only in a negative manner, although Hemer warns against too strong an argument in this regard.[52]

The rich volcanic soil of the region contributed to the growth of a thriving wine industry in the plain surrounding Philadelphia, so much so that a "bitterly unpopular" edict by Domitian in 92 which charged that half of the vineyards in the area were to be destroyed led to considerable local dissatisfaction with Domitian.[53] Because of the thriving wine trade, the pagan cult of Dionysius was the principle religion of Philadelphia.

A violent earthquake in the region of Philadelphia in 17 A.D. and records of imperial assistance in rebuilding the cities of Sardis and Philadelphia gave rise to inscriptions recalling the favor showered on the region by the Emperor Vespasian (69–79). The great honor granted the city the use of the imperial designation "Flavia," bound the city closely to the imperial cultus. The rebuilt city was honored by adding the term *Neocaesareia* (temple of the Caesars) to its name. Later in 214 under Emperor Cara-calla the city was honored with the name *Nekoros* ("temple warden for the Imperial cult").[54] In spite of the city's displeasure with Domitian, the imperial cult flourished in Philadelphia.

3:7. The designation of Jesus as the one who is *holy and true* emphasizes his divine authority, for in the Jewish tradition the designation the Holy One is reserved for God (Isa. 40:25; Hab. 3:3; John 6:69). The Greek here is stronger than the English translation and should read *the* holy one, *the* true one (*ho hagios, ho alēthinos*). Jesus is the Holy One and the True (genuine) One.[55] Thus Jesus speaks to the Philadelphian church with absolute authority, for he is truly and genuinely divine, on an equal standing with the Almighty God.

Jesus identified himself also as the one *who holds the key of David* and added *what he opens no one can shut, and what he shuts no one can open.* The reference to the key of David connects this letter to the image of Jesus in 1:18. Jewish tradition stemming from Isaiah 22:22, especially the Isaiah *Targum*, taught that the future messiah would hold the key of David.[56] By applying this appellation to himself, Jesus claimed that he is the one who controls the royal house of the messianic kingdom.

Philadelphia, with its ready access to Phrygia and the West may thus be reasonably considered a "missionary" city. Consequently, some have suggested that the *open door* Jesus sets before the Philadelphian church is an open door to Christian missions (Cf. 1Cor. 6:9 and 2 Cor. 2:12), indicating a possible conversion of the Jews.[57] This possibility does not necessarily follow. The expression *the key of David*, drawing most likely from Isaiah 22:15–25, seems not to be in an evangelistic context, but rather a messianic one. Mounce is correct in observing that "The language of Isaiah is used to present Christ as the Davidic Messiah with absolute power to control entrance to the heavenly kingdom."[58] In Isaiah the expression is used of Eliakim, Hezekiah's steward, who was given authority in the king's royal house. In the context of Revelation, those who remained faithful would be given free access to, and participation in, the messianic kingdom by Jesus, the messianic King. Thus *the key of David* and the *open door* statement that follows indicate God's progressive promises that those who conquer (die as martyrs) will share fully in the messianic reign of Jesus (cf. 20:4-6). This concept is strengthened by the expression that follows, *see, I have placed before you an open door that no one can shut.* It may have seemed to the Christians in Philadelphia that the Jews and others had unlimited power to oppress them, possibly even having closed the door of the synagogue to them. But it is Jesus who ultimately controls their destiny and holds the key to their sharing in the messianic reign.[59]

3:8, 9. Jesus follows this observation regarding access into his messianic kingdom by stating the grounds for his setting an open door to his kingdom before the Philadelphians. *I know your deeds.* Jesus was very aware of their situation and their faithfulness. Like the letter to Smyrna, this letter contains no condemnation or rebuke. Jesus knew the true character of this church, and added, *I know that you have little strength, yet you have kept my word and have not denied my name.* Whatever the *little strength* may refer to, this church had persevered. In the light of Jesus' positive statements about the church in Philadelphia, it is unlikely that this statement is a reflection on their faith, indicating poverty of faith and spirituality as in Sardis, especially in view of the statement that follows indicating that they have not denied Jesus' name or person. More likely, this is a reference to the size of the congregation or possibly the influence of the congregation in civil affairs in Philadelphia.[60] Apparently, the Christians in Philadelphia had not compromised their faith by confessing Caesar as Lord. The *name* of Jesus is a Hebraism for his person. By confessing Caesar as Lord they would deny Jesus' lordship and messianic person. This they had not done. Since they had kept their confession regarding Jesus firm, he would certainly keep his word in their behalf. This thought is developed further in verse 10, *Since you have kept my command to endure patiently*.

In **3:9** Jesus passes a scathing condemnation on the Jews of the synagogue. *I will make those who are of the synagogue of Satan, who claim to be Jews though they are not, but are liars—I will make them come and fall down at your feet and acknowledge that I have loved you*. This possibly should be seen as a parenthetical statement to Jesus' positive commendation of the church in Philadelphia. Hemer finds no external evidence at the time of writing Revelation of a Jewish community or synagogue in Philadelphia, but does recognize a considerable Jewish influence in the letter to Philadelphia.[61] Beale, however, refers to Ignatius, *Philad*. 6:1, as a possible early second-century external reference to problems between the church in Philadelphia and the synagogue.[62] Radical statements such as *I will make those who are of the synagogue of Satan, who claim to be Jews though they are not, but are liars* indicate the presence of an active Jewish-Christian antagonism in Philadelphia. A similar statement is found at 2:9. The early apostolic church believed the Jews had abdicated their right to be called the people of God by rejecting the messiah of God, namely, Jesus the son of Joseph (cf. Rom. 2:17–29 and 9–11). In Paul's mind, being an ethnic Jew did not equate with being a Jew defined as a person of God. In the case of a seemingly strong Jewish presence and synagogues in both Smyrna and Philadelphia, and their rejection of Jesus as the messiah, Jesus charged that the claims of the synagogue to be the people of God amounted to nothing less than a lie. The statement, *I will make them come and fall down at your feet and acknowledge that I have loved you* refers to Jesus' vindication of the saints in Philadelphia. In his letter to Sardis, Jesus promised to acknowledge the faithful saints before God. Now in God's *Heilsgeschichte* even the Jews would eventually have to acknowledge that the saints they had persecuted were God's people, and that Jesus, the Messiah, loved the ones they opposed and betrayed to the Romans.[63] The image of the Jew falling down to acknowledge the saints draws on passages such as Isaiah 45:14; 49:23; 60:14, and is a reverse "collective allusion" to the Gentiles bowing before Israel and Israel's God in the last days. Caird observes that in this context the Jewish eschatological hopes had been turned upside down.[64]

3:10. Returning to the faithfulness of the Philadelphian saints in 3:8, Jesus adds, *Since you have kept my command to endure patiently, I will also keep you from the hour of trial that is going to come upon the whole world to test those who live on the earth*. Jesus refers to his message regarding faithfulness here not as a request or warning, but as *my command*. This should leave little doubt as to the urgency of Revelation. God and Jesus intend their church to be faithful since there was an hour of trial that was *soon to come* (3:10) upon those *who live on earth*. (The RSV translates this as *those who dwell on earth*)). This expression emphasizes the true nature of those referred to. It does not refer to the locality of their residence, but their spiritual condition. This is the first of seven times the expression those who dwell on earth or those *who live on the earth* will be featured in Revelation (3:10; 6:10; 8:13; 11:10 [twice]; 13:14; 14:6). In this, the first occasion, John does not elaborate on precisely who it is that will be tested, but progressively through the Revelation he builds on this theme.

The expression *those who live on earth* has become a major challenge to interpreters of Revelation in view of the many diverse premillennial and dispensational persuasions to be found in contemporary popular theology. Aune identifies the theological issues encountered in this text:

> This verse has been a *crux* for the modern argument between the Pretribulation and Posttribulation views on when Christ will return. . . . Unfortunately, both sides of the debate have ignored the fact that the promise made here pertains to Philadelphian Christians *only* and cannot be generalized to include Christians in other churches in Asia, much less Christians in all places and times. Furthermore, to be "preserved from the hour of tribulation" means not that they will be physically absent but rather that they will not be touched by that which touches others.[65]

Among the challenges in this text, two are pertinent to the context and theology of Revelation as a whole.[66] The first the *trial which is coming on the whole world*, the second is *those who dwell upon the earth*. The context of Revelation as well as Jewish and apocalyptic tradition suggest that they should be interpreted symbolically.[67] Aune proposes that they form a rough attempt at poetic parallelism, implying that they should be considered as referring to the same concept. The expression "*those who dwell upon the earth*" as we have already pointed out, is found seven times in Revelation (3:10; 6:10; 8:13; 11:10; 13:14; 14:6). This is "a technical term throughout Revelation for unbelieving idolaters, who suffer under various forms of retributive tribulation."[68] The phrase appears "always in a negative sense of non-Christian persecutors of Christians."[69] Where the phrase occurs "the enemies of the church are always in mind."[70] Roberts notes:

> Who are the dwellers upon the earth? The term . . . is more generally a technical term for the Roman Empire. John's own usage of the term . . . shows that he means the enemies of the Christian community. This term occurs seven times elsewhere in Revelation. In 6:10 it designates the persecutors against whom the souls under the altar cry; in 8:13 they are the recipients of the triple woe; in 11:10 they rejoice over the death of the two witnesses; in 13:8, 14 they worship the beast from the sea . . . in 17:8 they marvel at the beast. Clearly they are the Roman followers of the beast opposed to the Christians.[71]

In the context of Revelation, *those who live on the earth* are those who persecute the Christians, who align themselves with Rome and the beast, and who will along with the beast, the false prophet, and Satan be judged by Jesus. They will finally be thrown into the lake of fire, which is the second death (19:20, 20:11–15). Those in Philadelphia who have proven themselves faithful to God have no need to fear this *hour of trial*, or retributive judgment, that is to come on their persecutors.[72]

3:11, 12. For Jesus' promise that he is *coming soon*, see 1:1, 2:5, 2:16. The church in Philadelphia is encouraged to remain faithful so that no one can *seize their crown*. This crown (*stephanos*) is the same victory wreath already promised to the church in Smyrna (2:10). Jesus will make those who *overcome* (*conquer*) *a pillar in the temple of my God*. Citizens in Asia, and all over the ancient world were familiar with temples, especially temples dedicated to specific "gods". The names of the community's god was inscribed on the temples, ensuring divine gifts to the worshippers at the temple and divine ownership of the temple. The widespread presence of magnificent temples in Asia, with the names of gods inscribed on them, was a meaningful metaphor to use of those faithful to the Christian's divine beings, Jesus the Messiah and his Almighty Father. The metaphor of being a pillar in the temple of God was also a familiar one among Jewish and Christian circles (1 Kgs. 7:21; Gal. 2:9; 1 Tim. 3:15; *1 Enoch* 90:28, 29). Pillars implied stability and permanence. The conquering martyrs were promised that they would be a vital part in the temple of the living God rather than an insignificant part in the temple of a lifeless pagan god. Jesus promised to write on the martyr-pillars of the temple of God *the name of my God* (signifying God's ownership, identity, and intimate presence), *the name of the city of my God the new Jerusalem* (God's own dwelling place that the martyrs would share), and also Jesus' *own new name* (Lord of lords and King of kings). This is the first of three references in Revelation (3:12; 21:2; 21:10) to Jerusalem, the new Jerusalem, or the holy city Jerusalem. Each implies the holy presence of God in the place of his own dwelling, that is, heaven, a theme John will develop.

3:13. Jesus concludes his message to Philadelphia with his familiar formula *He who has an ear, let him hear what the Spirit says to the churches*, emphasizing once more the urgency and authority of the message of Revelation.

The Message to the Church in Laodicea. (3:14–22)
The Text
[14] *"To the angel of the church in Laodicea write: These are the words of the Amen, the faithful and true witness, the ruler of God's creation.* [15] *I know your deeds, that you are neither cold nor hot. I wish you were either one or the other.* [16] *So, because you are lukewarm—neither hot nor cold—I am about to spit you out of my mouth.* [17] *You say, 'I am rich; I have acquired wealth and do not need a thing. But you do not realize that you are wretched, pitiful, poor, blind and naked.* [18] *I counsel you to buy from me gold refined in the fire, so you can become rich; and white clothes to wear, so you can cover your shameful nakedness; and salve to put on your eyes, so you can see.* [19] *Those whom I love I rebuke and discipline. So be earnest, and repent.* [20] *Here I am. I stand at the door and knock. If anyone hears my voice and opens the door, I will come in and eat with him, and he with me.* [21] *To him who overcomes, I will give the right to sit with me on*

my throne, just as I overcame and sat down with my Father on his throne. [22] *He who has an ear, let him hear what the Spirit says to the churches"*

Laodicea was one of three cities located in the beautiful Lycus Valley. There were churches at the time of writing Revelation in all three of the cities, Laodicea, Colossae, and Hierapolis. Possibly Jesus' purpose in sending the message to Laodicea was that the church in that city represented the mood of the region. In the sevenfold nature of Revelation, the number of cities addressed is seven, thus excluding the churches in Colossae and Hierapolis. The Lycus Valley was a broad fertile valley of alluvial soil deposits. The river was one of the main rivers in the region of western Asia. Laodicea was located on the eastern side of the Lycus Valley, about six miles across the valley from Hierapolis, and not far from Colossae. The magnificent calcareous cliff-like deposits of modern Pamukkale (ancient Hierapolis) could be clearly seen across the valley from Laodicea. The city was located at the crossroads running from Ephesus to the east, the other from Pergamum through Thyatira, Sardis, and Philadelphia to the south.[73] Situated on the great "highway" that stretched from Rome and Corinth through Ephesus to Phrygia ("The Gateway to Phrygia") and the east, Laodicea, under Roman rule, was a vibrant manufacturing and commercial city.[74] At one time Laodicea had been the greatest and wealthiest city of the Lycus Valley. Laodicea had been founded by Antiochus II (261–246 B.C.) on a former city foundation previously known as Diospolis. Antiochus II named it after his wife, Laodice. A major medical school is known to have existed in Laodicea, possibly making the city famous for its eye salve. The water supply in the valley was plentiful, but known for its calcareous deposits and poor taste. The ruins of Laodicea are not as well restored as at Ephesus and Pergamum, but several interesting structures have been identified. Perhaps the most famous is a large tower that had supported a water aqueduct running from the hills to the east into the city. Several clay pipes are still openly visible, all lined with the characteristic calcareous deposits typical of the region. Two fairly large amphitheaters and a large hippodrome are indicative of a wealthy and strong Roman presence at one time.[75]

There was possibly a large community of Jews in Laodicea. Some have considered that this Jewish population may have been as large as 7,550 adult freemen. The Jewish population may have contributed to the lax attitude and comfort in riches found in the Laodicean church.[76] The church was obviously influenced by its opulent surroundings (3:17). The presence of a wealthy banking system in Laodicea also contributed to the materialistic comfort of the community and church.

3:14. *To the angel of the church in Laodicea write: These are the words of the Amen, the faithful and true witness, the ruler of God's creation.* Jesus' opening statement to the church in Laodicea called them back to a more reliable and lasting foundation than the corruptible one with which they were obviously more comfortable. Jesus emphasized to the Laodiceans that the words of this letter were *the words of the Amen* (the one who is genuine and true) who *is the faithful and true witness, the ruler of God's creation.* Jesus, the sovereign ruler of God's creation, was calling them away from the false security of riches and self-reliance. The trifold self-description of Jesus, the only sure and firm foundation of church life, in 3:14, *the Amen, the faithful and true witness, the ruler of God's creation*, forms an important Christological formula for Jesus, establishing him on equal terms with the Almighty God.

The term *the Amen* appears only here in Revelation in the New Testament in regard to Jesus.[77] It most likely draws on the statement in Isaiah 65:16, where it is used of *Yahweh* (YHWH). The expression *the faithful and true witness* has already been used of Jesus at 1:5, driving home Jesus' role in the trifold greeting of Revelation as coming from the eternal God, from Jesus the faithful witness, and from the Holy Spirit who sees everything. That Jesus is *the ruler of God's creation* is doubtless associated with the pervasive Christian claim that Jesus was the creative power behind God's creation. We are reminded of the Johannine observation that Jesus, the Word, was the one who made everything that was made or created (John 1:3), and of Paul's claims that Jesus was the source (*archē*) and *firstborn* (*prōtotokos*, the one bearing the blessings of being born first, but not necessarily the one born first) of all creation (Col. 1:15, 18)[78]. These expressions at 3:14 draw on the view that Jesus is the privileged son of God through whom all things were created (Col. 1:16 and 1 Cor. 8:6), and whose testament is genuine. The writer of the Epistle to the Hebrews also claimed that it was through Jesus, the Son, that God had created the world (Heb. 1:3). Aune states, "Christologically this title is significant since it attributes to Christ a title associated only with God".[79]

3:15. As in the other letters, Jesus lets the church in Laodicea know that he was fully aware of their strengths and weaknesses, *I know your deeds.* The statement *you are neither cold nor hot* refers to the spiritual condition of the church. However, the background to this expression has posed challenging questions. The consensus is that it draws its imagery from the poor water condition in Laodicea and that part of the Lycus Valley. The water coming in through the aqueduct and clay pipe system is estimated by some to have been in the range of ninety degrees F., a tepid temperature for water. Whatever the case, the water was distasteful. The lime deposits and encrustation of the clay pipe delivery system must also have contributed to the poor quality of the local water. The unfortunate characteristic of lukewarm water is that it is neither hot nor cold and thus repugnant. Jesus observed that the works of the Laodiceans, like the water, were offensive, being neither hot nor cold. He expressed the wish that they were either one or the other. The danger of lukewarm Christians is that they do not recognize that they are tending toward the cold.[80]

3:16. Jesus' harsh statement is that he will *spit* (RSV, "spew") the Laodiceans out of his mouth because they are lukewarm emphasizes the extreme seriousness of their condition. The word *spit* is better understood as "vomit you out of my mouth" (*emeō*, vomit, spew, spit out as distasteful).

3:17, 18. The symbolism and metaphors used by Jesus in 3:17, 18 reinforce the conclusion that this church had its faith focused on the wrong place, that is, on their own ability and wealth. The crisis about to come upon the churches in Asia would eliminate the false sense of security in wealth upon which the church in Laodicea obviously relied. Jesus charged, *You say, 'I am rich; I have acquired wealth and do not need a thing.* The tragedy was that they did not recognize the seriousness of their situation, *you do not realize that you are wretched, pitiful, poor, blind and naked.* Too often self-satisfaction can be confused with strength, resulting in a real spiritual blindness.

Blaiklock, perceives a considerable "sustained irony" encountered in 3:17, 18 in which the materialistic self-satisfaction of the Laodiceans is contrasted with their deep spiritual lethargy and shallowness.[81] The Laodiceans saw themselves as rich, yet they were poor, wretched, pitiable and blind. It is possible that their false sense of material "health" lay in the fact that Laodicea was blessed by both a healthy economy environment and the presence of a prominent hospital in the community that manufactured an eye salve that was exported as a "Phrygian powder."[82] Material health too often obscures spiritual disease and poverty and leads to a false sense of spiritual security.

The only solution to the crisis about to fall on Laodicea was urgent repentance and return to faithfulness focused in Jesus. Wealth alone would not sustain the church through the crisis. The metaphor of nakedness relates to spiritual shame. The church standing on its own financial strength is wretched, pitiful, poor, blind, and naked. Consequently, Jesus counseled the church in Laodicea to *buy from me gold refined in the fire, so you can become rich; and white clothes to wear, so you can cover your shameful nakedness; and salve to put on your eyes, so you can see.* Gold refined by fire is an analogy to a genuine faith in Jesus that would be tested in the crucible of extreme trial. Persecution from pagan neighbors and martyrdom would be the true testing of their faith.

3:18b, 19. The attire, *white clothes to wear, so you can cover your shameful nakedness*, represents the worthiness of those who are prepared to face tribulation and persecution and die for their faith. Jesus had promised the faithful (*worthy*) saints in Sardis who were willing to die for their faith in Jesus that they would walk with him in *white robes* (3:5). White robes or clothes in Revelation represent faithfulness and worthiness. He stressed that his harsh rebuke stemmed not simply from anger but from his sincere concern and deep love for them. His words, *Those whom I love I rebuke and discipline. So be earnest, and repent*, warned them that repentance and not a superficial faith was required from the church in Laodicea in view of the impending crisis.

3:20. The sharp contrast between the harsh words of 3:17, 18 and the "softer, kinder" words of 3:20, 21 is interesting. *Here I am. I stand at the door and knock. If anyone hears my voice and opens the door, I will come in and eat with him, and he with me.* [21] *To him who overcomes, I will give the right to sit with me on my throne, just as I overcame and sat down with my Father on his throne.* [22] *He who has an ear, let him hear what the Spirit says to the churches.* This contrast motivated Ramsey to lift 3:20-21 from the context of the Laodicean letter and view them as an epilogue to all seven letters.[83] Others correctly reject Ramsey's proposal, stating that there is no compelling reason for lifting these verses from within the message to the Laodiceans.[84] Beasley-Murray sees this verse in harmony with the previous urgent call to repentance.[85]

This softer and kinder comment of Jesus has suggested several possibilities. The major questions again relate to whether this "visit" refers to Jesus' *parousia* at the final end or his conditional coming on the churches in their immediate context, whether the meal referred to is the eschatological banquet of Jewish/Christian expectation, perhaps the Eucharistic meal celebrated on the Lord's day, or merely a fellowship meal common to eastern cultures. Questions also relate to whether Jesus is the host of the eschatological meal or whether he is the guest who wants to enter the lives of the Laodiceans but cannot do so without their opening the door of their hearts. Most recognize the invitation to the meal contains deep fellowship overtones. Beale points out that this invitation to open the door "provides a motivation for the call for repentance given here." Caird observes that this statement could hardly fail to bring to mind Jesus' last meal of fellowship with the disciples on the night of the Passover.[86]

In keeping with the other promises made by Jesus in the other six letters, this should also be seen as a conditional promise of imminent blessing in a personal relationship with Jesus. He is the one who constantly walks around in the midst of the lampstands or churches. Certainly the concept of an invitation to the eschatological banquet is included, but the proleptic nature of eschatological expectation is present everywhere in Revelation. Jesus' communing in the present with the Laodiceans is a proleptic experience of the eschatological communion. Jesus at the door of the Laodiceans must therefore be an immediate request for entrance and communing. In one sense, the regular experience of the Eucharist is a constant reminder of Jesus' presence and continued blessing of his church since the Eucharist is a proleptic experience of the eschatological banquet at the end of time.

3:21. The remainder of Jesus' promise to the Laodicean conquerors is in keeping with the promises to the conquerors in the other six letters. *To him who overcomes, I will give the right to sit with me on my throne, just as I overcame and sat down with my Father on his throne.* The promised reward of sitting with Jesus on his throne is vital to understanding the central message of Revelation, especially of chapter 20. Alongside Jesus' promise to the church at Thyatira, where the reward was that conquerors would have authority over the nations and would rule with a rod of iron, Jesus now promises that he will give the conqueror (martyr) the right to sit with him on his throne, just as he overcame (conquered) and sat down with his Father on his throne. This reward of sitting with Jesus on his throne is a sustained development of the major theme of reigning in Revelation introduced initially at 1:9. The message was that through being willing to die for faithfulness to Jesus, the martyr would share fully in the kingdom (reign) of God and Christ. The martyrs may not share in the blessings of the Roman kingdom, but they certainly will share the blessings of the kingdom of God. Chapter 20 will reveal that they will reign completely (for one thousand years) with Jesus in his kingdom.

With these emphases of faithfulness through persecution and of sitting on thrones and reigning with Jesus, John is building a major theological theme in these first three chapters that he will progressively develop throughout Revelation, demonstrating that persecution, suffering faithfully, and reigning with Christ are the theological core of Revelation that culminates in 20:4 with the martyred saints, who reign with Christ for one thousand years.

3:22. In keeping with each of the other six letters, Jesus concludes with his urgent formulaic call to the church at Laodicea to pay careful attention to the urgent message that comes with the authority of the full godhead: *He who has an ear, let him hear what the Spirit says to the churches.*

Summary of the letters to the churches in Thyatira, Sardis, Philadelphia, and Laodicea:

The seven letters to the seven churches reflect several profound lessons to which all churches and Christians need to be sensitive:

1. That Jesus knows all about his church. He knows its strengths and its weaknesses.
2. That Jesus is deeply concerned for the spiritual wellbeing of his church. He warns the church in advance of faith crises to be prepared for trials that challenge faith.
3. That churches need to look deeply into their faith to determine whether that faith is focused in the right place, which is Jesus Christ, rather than in church organization, some form of church orthodoxy, or financial security.
4. That churches should beware of compromise with their "pagan," or secular neighbors.
5. That churches, unaware of faith and identity drifts, often conform more to their social environment than is healthy.

The church in **Thyatira** received one of the harshest condemnations of all seven churches. The chief problem was a person or group, metaphorically identified as the Old Testament woman Jezebel. The issue Jesus took up with the church was not only that this "woman" was leading Christians to compromise their faith by engaging in sexual immorality and eating food sacrificed to idols, but that the church was tolerating this mood. Jesus warned that as the one who searched the inner corners of their hearts and lives, he would come soon in judgment on this group and those who were led astray by their compromise. To those who remained faithful right through martyrdom (conquering) Jesus would grant power over the nations and a share in his reign over their enemies. The first major lesson churches in the twenty-first century can learn from this letter is that Jesus will not tolerate the practice of sexual immorality, especially among his people, and neither will he look lightly on those who tolerate any compromise with the world in these and similar matters. The second major lesson is that suffering for Jesus is not defeat, for in conquering temptation through the strength we gain from our faith in Jesus, we become the victors over Satan and share in Jesus' kingdom reign.

Sardis presented a depressing picture of a church spiritually dead with a faith that had not matured. On the outside they looked alive, but spiritually they were asleep and not alert to the trials and temptations they faced. Nevertheless, there were some who had kept their faith intact and who refused to compromise with their pagan culture. Jesus promised not to remove them from the roster of the faithful, the book of life. Contemporary churches need to recognize clearly the dangers of secular popularity, spiritual compromise, lethargy, and immaturity. Faith must never become satisfied with a false sense of security, but must continue to grow and mature in Christ.

The church in **Philadelphia** was one of two churches in Asia, the other Smyrna, that received no condemnation but only encouragement from Jesus. Apparently small, and in the view of their neighbors weak, the church was encouraged to see that they were the true house, or temple, of God, in spite of fierce opposition from the Jewish synagogue. The church was encouraged to realize that they were the people of God and therefore were protected by God. The reference to the synagogue of Satan encouraged the faithful to know they were the true pillars in God's temple. The synagogue was no longer the house, or gathering place, of the people of God. Jesus promised to come soon in judgment of those who persecuted the saints. Christians today should see that their strength lies not in their physical size and material wealth, but in God's support.

If there is one church among the seven churches of Asia that speaks clearly to churches in twenty-first century America and the Western world, it is **Laodicea**. This church epitomizes the wealthy self-satisfied mindset of its community. Wealthy and laboring under the false premise that wealth equated with strength, the church did not realize its poverty, weakness, and spiritual nakedness. It is often difficult for churches and Christians living in comfortable circumstances to realize they have drifted away from the true nature and purpose of their mission. Thinking they are alive because of the perceived promises of their religion, they become lukewarm toward real commitment. To Jesus this condition is distasteful and deserving only of the harshest rebuke. Too many churches and Christians have lost sight of the radical nature of discipleship and live only a small step away from their worldly neighbors. The danger modern churches face lies in the assumption that their wealth and security equates with spiritual strength. Too often Jesus is outside the perimeter of faith and practice, longing to be admitted into the life of the church. Churches through the ages have struggled with the reality of Jesus' radical call to discipleship. Jesus calls us to be different, but we are often afraid of being too different.

The Heavenly Throne Room

God Is in Control of the Universe

4:1–11

INTRODUCTION

Having completed the second major section, level I in the chiastic structure, we begin level II, which parallels level VI.

Prologue. 1:1–20
> I. The Church in Imperfection (2:1–3:22)
> Seven Letters to the Seven Churches
>> **II. The Authority of God over Evil Explained (4:1–8:6)**
>> **Seven Seals on the Scroll**
>>> III. The Warning Judgments (8:1–11:19)
>>> Seven Trumpets
>>>> IV. The Lamb—God's Answer to Evil (12:1–14:20)
>>>> Seven Unnumbered Figures
>>> V. The Consummated Judgments (15:1–16:21)
>>> Seven Bowls of Wrath
>> **VI. The Authority of God over Evil Exercised (17:1–20:15)**
>> **Seven Unnumbered Descriptions of God's Judgments**
> VII. The Church in Perfection (21:1–22:5)
> Seven Unnumbered Descriptions of the Church in Perfection
Epilogue. (22:6–21)

In this heavenly throne room scene, John sets the tone for the narrative drama that he begins to unfold. God is seated on his heavenly throne surrounded by four living creatures, twenty-four elders, and the heavenly host, all singing praises to God's power and glory. In what some scholars (cf. Aune, 1.276-77) liken to a Merkabah chariot encounter described in Jewish mysticism, John is carried into heaven to experience the presence of God in a powerful manner. The experience is similar to that of Isaiah and Ezekiel, which set their prophetic ministry in context. The powerful mystical experience was necessary for both John and his readers in that they needed assurance that the message to follow came directly from the throne of God. In many ways this scene sets the tone for the remainder of the message of Revelation.

Caird suggests that with chapter 4 we have come to the apocalypse proper[1]. This raises the significant question of how the great throne room scenes of 4 and 5 relate to the seven letters of 2 and 3 and the remainder of Revelation. For those who prefer a tripartite division of 1:19 (which I and others reject as poor exegesis of the text), the scene in 4 begins the discussion of events relating to the end of the world. Beale observes that futurists take 4:1 "as one of the most obvious indicators of their position."[2] He adds that most commentators "see 4:1 as an introduction to a new section in the book, and the majority of these view it as introducing all the remaining visions."[3] Beale devotes 19 pages to explaining the meaning and significance of 1:19 to the interpretation of Revelation[4]. A cursory study of commentaries indicates how important understanding 1:19 becomes for the study of Revelation, especially the role of the remainder of the book (4–22), and how 4 fits into this sequence. Beasley-Murray considers 4 and 5 to be "the pivot of the structure which holds the book together".[5] This then underscores the importance of how the heavenly throne room relates to the seven letters (2, 3) as well as to 1:19 and 5–22. The visions of the great throne room (4, 5) tie the visions that follow back to the seven letters by introducing the imminent crises for which Jesus is preparing the churches in the seven letters. These chapters explain the "what is and what is to take place in the immediate future" as described in 1:19.

The mystical heavenly throne room scene of 4 then elaborates on what Jesus meant by "namely," or "that is" when he told John to write "what you see, *namely, what is and what is already breaking in.*" Chapter 4 serves as a connective to the crises facing the churches described in 2 and 3 and the imminent circumstances described in the remainder of Revelation. It sets what was already breaking into the experience of the churches in the context of God's sovereign power, a message the church urgently needed to hear. What better way to describe the awful experience of martyrdom than to set it in the context of God's sovereign glory.

Caird observes the role of chapter 4 and the seven letters to the churches in Asia:

Structurally the first three chapters are a covering letter to accompany and introduce the account of John's apocalyptic visions, which begins here in chapter iv. But John intended his readers to come to the visions with their minds prepared by what they had read in the letters. From the warnings, from the

scrutiny of their strengths and weaknesses, and above all from the promises
to the Conqueror, they now knew that the church faced an imminent ordeal;
and they could expect the apocalypse would disclose to them the nature of
this coming conflict.[6]

Mounce adds that the great heavenly throne room visions of 4 and 5 remind the readers
that they are living in the shadow of an impending persecution, and that the Almighty
God sitting on his heavenly throne is still in control. He observes:

> . . . that an omnipotent and omniscient God was still in control. This vision,
> it should be emphasized, must be understood as in close relationship to the
> preceding letters to the churches, offering encouragement for their present
> and future struggle with the Empire, but also reminding them that they, too,
> are under his sovereignty.[7]

Beale stresses that Revelation speaks in an inaugurated eschatological genre in which
events in the immediate future are described in an inaugurated eschatological style that
emphasizes that the impending events will be judged by Jesus in the immediate future
with end-of-world judgment. Revelation 4–22 is an account of events that have already
been inaugurated in the life of the Asian churches rather than in some distant end-of-
the-world future as predicted by futurists.[8]

Revelation 4–22 must be seen as describing in highly symbolic and apocalyptic
eschatological language the crises that the church in Asia is already beginning to experience (*inaugurated eschatology*) and will be facing in their immediate future. It is in view
of these imminent crises that the churches in Asia must maintain resolute faith in Jesus
as the King of kings, and Lord of lords. John was to write *what he saw* (the visions that
began on the Isle of Patmos), *namely, what was already happening* and was *at the point of
taking place in the near future* in an even more aggressive manner (1:19).

Chapter 4 contains the first pure visionary scene of Revelation, and the first urgent
eschatological apocalyptic message of Revelation. The heavenly vision sets the tone
for the remainder of the visions and plays a significant role in the unfolding plan of
Revelation, for it connects the visions that follow to the socio-religious context of the
seven churches in Asia. John sets this magnificent vision in scenes reminiscent of his
roots in Jewish mysticism.[9] John saw an open door into heaven, and through that door he
was transported in the Spirit into the very throne room of heaven. What John describes
in the chapters that follow is built on the majesty of this heavenly scene. The visions
that follow describe an urgent message regarding the imminent crises that were about
to break in on the churches of Asia.

The use of the expression *kai eidon* at 5:1 connects chapter 4 to what is to be revealed
in chapter 5 in the sense that what is described in 5 also takes place in the heavenly throne
room where the eternal God is seated on his throne. John thus stylistically moves from
the throne room in 4 to the vision of the scroll in 5 by using what becomes for him in
Revelation a dynamic connector, namely the expression *kai eidon* (and I saw). John uses

kai eidon as a simple yet dynamic connector thirty-two times in Revelation as he moves from one vision to the next, not implying a chronological sequence, but merely a visionary sequence. In addition, he uses the expression *meta tauta eidon* (and I looked) four times (4:1; 7:9; 15:5; 18:1) and *meta touto eidon* (and I saw) once (7:1). In all five instances this expression simply implies that what follows is another vision that appeared to John after the previous one. Beale notes at 7:9: "As in 4:1a, *Meta tauta* ('after these things') does not mean that the events of this vision occur in history after those of 7:1–8 but only that this vision itself came after the preceding one."[10]

The use of *meta tauta eidon* in 4:1 connects 4:1, the heavenly throne room to the seven letters in 2 and 3, implying that the message of 4–22 explains the urgent need for the churches in Asia to focus their faith resolutely on Jesus in view of the crises John is about to unfold and address. The use of *kai eidon* in 5:1 reinforces the fact that what we have in 4 and 5 is one literary unit (as is 4–22) in which *kai eidon* provides a connection between 4 and 5.

Revelation 4 and 5 repeat fourteen elements of Daniel 7 in the same order as recorded in Daniel[11]. The dependence of 4 and 5 on Daniel 7 is one not of historical fulfillment, but of typological or theological fulfillment in which John is drawing an analogy regarding the circumstances in Asia at the time of writing Revelation to the circumstances described in Daniel 7. Daniel 7 becomes a primary theological statement to which John will return repeatedly throughout Revelation.

In recent years considerable attention has been devoted to traditional Jewish and Jewish mystical antecedents to the throne room vision. Prigent has drawn attention to synagogue liturgical structures. Aune and others have noted Jewish rabbinic *hekhalot* literary relationships as well as strains of *merkavah* mysticism. Orlov has reopened the discussion of the Enoch-Metatron Tradition and the concept of Enochian chariot mysticism and its impact on New Testament studies and relevance to the heavenly throne room. Bucur and Orlov have stressed the importance of "angelomorphic pneumatology" and the celestial choirmaster for the angelic and heavenly throne room scenes in Revelation.[12] Each of these contributions to the heavenly throne room scene drives home the importance of this vision with its introduction of heavenly creatures (angels, archangels, seraphim and cherubim) to the understanding of 4 and the pivotal role it plays in Revelation.[13]

THE HEAVENLY THRONE ROOM. (4:1–11)

The Text

[1] *After this I looked, and there before me was a door standing open in heaven. And the voice I had first heard speaking to me like a trumpet said, "Come up here, and I will show you what must take place after this."* [2] *At once I was in the Spirit, and there before me was a throne in heaven with someone sitting on it.* [3] *And the one who sat there had the appearance of jasper and carnelian. A rainbow, resembling an emerald, encircled the throne.* [4] *Surrounding the throne were twenty-four other thrones, and seated on them were twenty-four elders. They were dressed in white and had crowns of gold on their heads.* [5] *From the throne came flashes of lightning,*

rumblings and peals of thunder. Before the throne, seven lamps were blazing. These are the seven spirits of God. [6] *Also before the throne there was what looked like a sea of glass, clear as crystal. In the center, around the throne, were four living creatures, and they were covered with eyes, in front and in back.* [7] *The first living creature was like a lion, the second was like an ox, the third had a face like a man, the fourth was like a flying eagle.* [8] *Each of the four living creatures had six wings and was covered with eyes all around, even under his wings. Day and night they never stop saying: "Holy, holy, holy is the Lord God Almighty, who was, and is, and is to come."* [9] *Whenever the living creatures give glory, honor and thanks to him who sits on the throne and who lives for ever and ever,* [10] *the twenty-four elders fall down before him who sits on the throne, and worship him who lives for ever and ever. They lay their crowns before the throne and say:* [11] *"You are worthy, our Lord and God, to receive glory and honor and power, for you created all things, and by your will they were created and have their being."*

The scene opens with a vision of the eternal God seated on his heavenly throne. He is surrounded by four awesome living creatures and twenty-four elders. The four living creatures and twenty-four elders all sing God's praises and proclaim his holiness.

Caird describes this scene as God's heavenly war control room from which he conducts his battle with Satan. This is in keeping with the combat mythology concept later proposed by Yarbro Collins.[14] Caird's description is dramatic:

> John, believing that the church faces an immediate life-and-death battle, which is not theirs alone but God's, is summoned to the control room at Supreme Headquarters. Imagine a room lined with maps, in which someone has placed clusters of little flags. . . . It is wartime, and the flags represent units of a military command.[15]

Caird and Collins[16] stress that at the beginning of the series of visions John will describe there is a war taking place both in heaven and on earth. This understanding provides an important ingredient to both the theological and literary setting and style of the book of Revelation.

One cannot escape the striking liturgical nature of this scene: God is on his throne; his presence is like precious jewels of jasper and carnelian; there are a magnificent rainbow, angels, awesome living creatures, and all of heaven worshipping the almighty God. Twenty-four elders cast their victory crowns down before His throne; the words Holy, Holy, Holy are chorused; and God's sovereign worthiness is praised. The scene is overwhelming in its beauty and power. Only after such a vision and by being mystically carried into the magnificent heavenly throne room could John be prepared to reveal the awesome mysteries he is about to see.

4:1. *After this I looked, and there before me was a door standing open in heaven. And the voice I had first heard speaking to me like a trumpet said, "Come up here, and I will show you what must take place after this."* John's use of the expression *meta tauta* (*after this*) connects the visions about to be revealed to the preceding seven letters to the seven churches[17].

As Beale stated, futurists prefer to see the chapters that follow as the beginning of a new series of visions relating to the distant future, while the seven letters are seen to relate to the church in the first century. Beale, Caird, and others appropriately see the visions that follow as an explanation of the crises to be experienced by the church in the immediate future.[18] This is important in understanding the structure of Revelation. The visions that follow in 4–22 are not visions of the far distant future, but relate to events to be faced by the churches in Asia (*soon*, 1:1; *the crisis time is at hand*, 1:3). Certainly, the visions are described in eschatological language, but this stresses that the immediate circumstances of the churches in Asia involve end-of-the-world significance.[19] John's literary style links new pericopes or visions about to be discussed back to previous revelations or visions by the use of "hook words". *Meta tauta eidon* (*after this*) and *kai eidon* (*and I saw*) are forms of such hookwords.

John writes, "*before me was a door standing open in heaven.*" This is similar to Ezekiel, where *the heavens were opened* (Ezek. 1:1). Likewise, Isaiah had been granted a vision of God on his heavenly throne surrounded by seraphim (Isa. 6:1-9). Emphasizing his prophetic office, John begins his visionary journey by being granted extraordinary visionary access to the heavenly throne room. There is clearly Jewish mysticism behind the concept of an open door through which seers are transported in a condition of ecstasy into heaven.[20]

4:1b. *And the voice I had first heard speaking to me like a trumpet said, "Come up here, and I will show you what must take place after this."* The voice John had previously heard speaking (1:10) was now speaking again, but this time speaking *like a trumpet*. We assume that this was the voice of Jesus (1:10). Although many commentators[21] are comfortable identifying this voice with that of Jesus in 1:10, Aune argues that the voice in 1:10 is an *angelus interpres* (interpreting angel). Some, however, prefer to leave the voice unidentified.[22] However, those who have problems with identifying this voice and that of 1:10 with the risen Jesus do so because they "approach the Apocalypse without a sympathetic imagination."[23] The voice of Jesus ties this vision to 1:10, 19, where Jesus instructed John to write letters to the seven churches, linking this chapter of visionary experiences to the message of the seven letters. Beale observes that the eschatological style of these verses relates to the "latter days" interest of Revelation which reveals an eschatology that is both realized and unrealized,[24] an eschatology of the "now" and "not yet" or "times" that are set in motion but "not yet" consummated. In other words, this style of inaugurated eschatology, and even a proleptic eschatology, speak of "events" that include the eschatological present as well as the eschatological future. The visions that follow in 5–22:5 flow dynamically out of the vision of 4 and reveal scenes (the scroll of 5) that emphasize the "already-and-not yet" nature of the eschatological visions that follow.[25] The links between 2–3 (the seven letters), 4 (the heavenly throne room), and the events to be described in the scroll of 5 demonstrate how the crises faced by the churches in Asia are the beginnings (the now) of an inaugurated eschatological story (the not yet) that has final end-time implications.

The voice of Jesus invited John to enter the throne room where he would be shown *what must take place after this.* The Greek *dei* ("is necessary") strengthens the view that what is about to come upon the churches in Asia is certain and inevitable. Jesus had often warned his disciples that persecution would follow discipleship (Matt. 10:16-33). Beale has convincingly demonstrated that the use of *meta tauta* in 4:1 does not imply that the visions to be revealed relate to the distant future, but in keeping with John's unique inaugurated eschatological style, relate to the immediate realized/unrealized present/future.

4:2 At once I was in the Spirit, and there before me was a throne in heaven with someone sitting on it. ³And the one who sat there had the appearance of jasper and carnelian. A rainbow, resembling an emerald, encircled the throne."

For a second time John explains that he is in a state of spiritual ecstasy (cf. 1:10). Although John does not describe in detail the one seated on the throne, this is the Almighty God, *the one who is and who was and who is to come* (1:8). Similar visionary experiences of a throne in heaven with one (God) seated on the throne are found in Isa. 6:1, Ezek. 1:26–28, Dan. 7:10. Furthermore, this type of mystical "Ezekiel chariot" experience of one being transported into heaven to experience the Almighty God is also reflected in the Jewish merkavah or kabalistic genre. Recent studies in Jewish mysticism have drawn attention to the concept of the "chariot throne" and merkavah tradition in the literature of the Dead Sea Covenanters (or The Priests of Zadok Covenanters) or early Second Temple Judaism. John must have been aware of this tradition as he described the mystical and dramatic scene of 4. [26] The throne of 4 is a symbol of God's sovereign power over all creation. The precious jewels and rainbow are intended to emphasize the glory of the Almighty seated on the throne. Caird, however, suggests that the rainbow reflects God's merciful covenant to Noah that he would not destroy the earth again by flood (Gen. 8:8-22), implying that "his mercy is as great as his majesty (Eccles 2.18)." In the context of Revelation and the misery to be experienced by the churches, Caird sees in the connection between God's sovereignty on his throne and his mercy depicted in the rainbow no awkward contradiction. He suggests that this "tells us that there is to be no triumph for God's sovereignty at the expense of his mercy, and it warns us not to interpret the visions of disaster that follow as though God had forgotten his promise to Noah."[27] Beasley-Murray observes "The throne, symbol of the Creator's omnipotence, is surrounded with the sign of his divine mercy."[28]

4:4 Surrounding the throne were twenty-four other thrones, and seated on them were twenty-four elders. They were dressed in white and had crowns of gold on their heads. Suggestions as to who the elders may be include a council of angels, the twelve patriarchs and twelve apostles, the twenty-four star gods of the Babylonian pantheon, or the twenty-four courses of priests.[29] Beale seems more comfortable with the view that the twenty-four elders corporately represent the Old and New Testament saints.[30] I am inclined to agree, with the further understanding that they cumulatively represent martyred saints from all ages. In any case, whether we agree with the view that they corporately and figuratively represent twelve Old Testament saints (12 Tribes) and twelve

New Testament saints (12 Apostles), they obviously have died and now sit on thrones before the throne of God. John later connects the twelve tribes of Israel and the twelve apostles (7:1–8; 21:12–14). Whoever these twenty four-elders are, they are clad in white robes and have golden crowns (*stephanoi*). Likewise, in 3:5 conquerors were promised white robes. These themes are repeated throughout Revelation as part of John's literary device in a "rebirth of images" (cf 4:10; 6:2; 9:7; 12:1; 14:4, et al.). Such references seem to indicate that the twenty-four elders corporately represent martyred saints of God's people throughout the ages who are now seen in the robes of conquerors. These twenty-four elders have conquered and are seated on thrones before the Almighty God.

This vision, with previous references in the seven letters regarding conquerors reigning with Christ (2:16; 3:21), will have pivotal significance to John's later emphasis in 20 to martyred saints, who reign with Christ. The martyrs sit on *thrones* with God in his throne room. At 4:10 the twenty-four elders fall down at God's feet and cast their crowns down before Him, indicating that God is fully worthy of martyrdom. They sing, "You are worthy, our Lord and God, to receive glory and honor and power, for you created all things and by your will they were created and have their being." There is no complaint from the twenty-four elders regarding to their martyrdom. In contrast to the glory, holiness, and sovereignty of God, all evil, suffering, and even martyrdom fade from the picture.

4:5. Emphasizing the sovereignty and holiness of God and his throne room, John observes that *from the throne came flashes of lightning, rumblings and peals of thunder. Before the throne, seven lamps were blazing. These are the seven spirits of God.* The image of the seven lamps (Greek *seven lamps of fire*) is apparently drawn from Zechariah 4:2-6, where the lamps are associated with faithful witness for God. In both Zechariah 4 and here the lamps are also associated with the Holy Spirit of God. Parallels to the seven branched menorah of Judaism (Exod. 25:31-40; 27:20–21; Lev. 24:1–2) are obvious. John clearly associates the lampstands with the presence of the Holy Spirit of God, or the seven spirits of God (cf. 1:4 and 5:6). John develops the ministry of the seven spirits of God, or the Holy Spirit, at 5:6.[31] What is important at this point is that in the heavenly throne room present are the Almighty God, the Holy Spirit, the Lamb (see the Lamb in 5), the four living creatures (4:6–7), the twenty-four elders (the conquerors), and a host of angels (5:11). The scene in both chapters 4 and 5 is one of worship and adoration of the Almighty God and the Lamb, Jesus, and the acknowledgement that the faithful martyrs who have conquered are represented in the throne room worshipping the Almighty. The image of the lamps as flaming fire and the flashes of lightning and peals of thunder emphasize the awesome power, majesty, and holiness of the Almighty God and the solemnity of the occasion. The flashes of lightning and rumblings of thunder are repeated at 8:5; 11:19; and 16:18, and draw on Exodus 19:16-25, emphasizing the Sinai experience of divine presence and glory.[32]

4:6a. At this juncture John introduces another enigmatic image, the *sea of glass*. *Also before the throne there was what looked like a sea of glass, clear as crystal.* Caird concludes that the most likely solution to this difficult expression is that the sea represents "a reservoir of evil out of which arises the monster."[33] Beale notes that the sea in Jewish mythology was a sinister place in which evil monsters swam.[34] (cf. Ps. 74:13; Isa. 27:1). Possible roots for this concept lay in Babylonian mythology, for in the Mesopotamian creation epic *Enuma Elish*, Tiamat, the sea monster, created an army of monstrous creatures. The sea monster is also depicted in Babylonian mythology as a huge bloated dragon that swam around in an ocean that personified chaos.[35] Apparently the sea in Revelation represents one of the sources of evil reflected in Canaanite and Jewish mythology. In this heavenly scene (4:6), in the presence of the Almighty God, the sea as a source of evil lies calm (NIV *a sea of glass, clear as crystal*; Greek, *hōs thalassa hualinēn homoia krustallō, as if a sea, glasslike like crystal*). This could mean that the sea as a source of evil in the presence of God has been purified like crystal or that in the presence of God it is glasslike, calm, not turbulent. Beale says "John sees the chaotic powers of the sea as calmed by divine sovereignty," associated with the power of the cross over the power of evil.[36] The contrast between the power, majesty, and glory of the Almighty God, and the impotence of evil in his presence is dramatic.

There is a progression of thought in John's use of the sea in Revelation. In this text (4:6) the sea is glasslike in the presence of God, indicating that in the presence of the holiness of God the sea loses its threatening power. In 13 an evil persecuting beast rises out of the sea. In 15:2 the sea is mixed with the purifying power of fire. Finally, according to 21:1, after God judges Satan and evil, the sea is no more.

4:6b, 7. *In the center, around the throne*, were four living creatures. The Greek text *kai en mesō tou thronou* poses a slight problem for translation. The NIV reads *in the center of the throne*, which "geographically" does not make sense since God is seated on the throne. The RSV and NASV translate this as "and around the throne"; the NRSV "and in front of the throne," while the ASV "and in the midst of the throne." *Mesō* literally means "in the middle," "among." Since the expression is most likely drawn from Isaiah 6:2 (LXX) we should understand it as in the Septuagintal Isaiah, which reads "And seraphim stood around him," where *kuklō* (around) is used in LXX Isa. 6:2 rather than *mesō* in 4:6. Thus the RSV translation, and around the throne is preferred. A possible translation could be as in the RSV of Isa. 6:2, "Above him stood the seraphim," which would reinforce the image of the seraphim, or four living creatures, proclaiming and defending the holiness of God.

This statement introduces *four living creatures . . . covered with eyes, in front and in back*, with each creature also having *six wings*. In 4 and 5 these four living creatures function prominently in revealing God's plan for dealing with the problem of evil. The imagery for these four living creatures is obviously drawn from Ezekiel 1:4-21 and Isaiah 6:2-4 (cf. 1 Sam. 4:4; 2 Sam. 6:2; Ps. 80:1; and 99:1 for other references to four living creatures, cherubim, or seraphim, the terms being used interchangeably). The four living creatures, cherubim, or seraphim in the Old Testament and the Jewish literary tradition are associated with the holiness of God. These creatures either proclaim or defend the holiness of God.[37] When Uzzah reached out to steady the ark of the covenant, on which images of the living creatures were cast (Exod. 25:18–19), he was struck dead (2 Sam. 6:6ff). In Ezek. 10:1-19 when the holiness of God left Jerusalem and the temple, the living creatures were seen flying away from the temple. In the new temple to be rebuilt, images of the cherubim were to be carved into the wood panels, indicating the return of the holiness of God to the temple (Ezek. 41:15-20.). McNicol adds that the cherubim-like figures are "symbolic of the all pervasive seeing and knowing that comes from God's throne" and adds that "ancient Israelites believed the cherubim, fierce creatures that were part human and part beast, lived in the heavenly realm. John reuses the Old Testament imagery for his own purposes. . . . The total scene is one of awesome power".[38] One simply does not challenge the holiness of God. Whenever one does, the four living creatures spring into action, for they represent and proclaim the awesome power of God and protect his holiness.

4:8–11. This pericope describes the magnificent heavenly worship scene of the throne room of God. This heavenly worship scene forms a pivotal link between the seven letters and the scene of the Almighty God sitting on his throne. Osborne points out that such unending praise in the context of heavenly "visits" is not uncommon in the Jewish apocalyptic genre (see *1 Enoch* 39:12; 40:2; 71:7; *2 Enoch* 19:6; 21:1; *2 Baruch* 51:11; *Testament of Levi* 3:8).[39] It is appropriate that in the face of the serious impending challenges to the faith of believers that God be pictured in the fullness of his power as the absolute sovereign ruler and creator of all existence, both heavenly and earthly. The impending challenge from the Roman political power and Domitian needed to be set in the appropriate perspective. Domitian, contrary to his opinion, did not rule the universe. God does! McNicol observes that, facing the crisis of Emperor worship, the church needed to be assured of the ultimate impotence of the Roman emperors and the absolute sovereignty of the Almighty God. Regarding the statement that Jesus holds the seven stars of the cosmos in his hand (cf. 1:16) "John is saying that it is not the Roman emperor that rules the cosmos but Christ."[40]

The trifold singing of God's holiness stresses his "wholly otherness" from all creation. The fact that he is the Almighty God and exists from and to eternity emphasizes his right to judge all creation. Osborne emphasizes that there are not only theological implications in this scene of heavenly worship, but also political implications. It is not the Caesar who is almighty and who judges the world; it is not Caesar Domitian who is *dominus et deus noster*, but God who is the ultimate ruler of everything, the cosmos, and all mankind. The absolute sovereignty of the Almighty God is the primary emphasis. Furthermore, in the latter part of the worship scene, God is not simply the creator of all; he and his divine will preexisted creation itself. "Behind creation is divine providence; his 'will' is the basis for every aspect of creation."[41] Thus John emphasizes the eternal nature and power of God's will and purpose, setting the scene for the revelations, rewards, and judgments that follow in 5–22.

4:8. The four living creatures praise God's holiness, singing, *Holy, holy, holy is the Lord God Almighty, who was, and is, and is to come.* This hymn, drawn from Isaiah 6:2–3, is intended to demonstrate the prophetic kinship between John and Isaiah and to remind John and his audience that God was, is, and always will be the Almighty Sovereign creator of everything. In commissioning Isaiah for his "impossible" ministry, it was necessary for Isaiah to see and understand fully and the holiness of God. He was given a glimpse into the heavenly presence of God, where the four living creatures proclaimed "Holy, holy, holy is the LORD Almighty; the whole earth is full of his glory." The impact of this awareness was a life transforming experience for Isaiah. Likewise, John, about to embark on his difficult mission of informing the churches that they may have to die for their faith, needed to experience the holiness and sovereignty of God, as did the readers or hearers of the message of Revelation. His heavenly transport and awesome experience also clearly established John as a prophet of God and, in the tradition of Isa. 6, became his "badge of prophetic office."

The words of the hymn, *"Holy, holy, holy is the Lord God Almighty, who was, and is, and is to come"* are drawn from Isaiah 6, Daniel 7, and Ezekiel 1. The linking of 4 and Isaiah 6 and the setting of both in the heavenly throne room demonstrate the divine mission of John.[42] The threefold title of God as the Holy One, the Almighty One, and the One who was and is and is to come" expresses the divine infinity and sovereignty" of God over history.[43]

Such praise, "'day and night without ceasing'... in continuous adoration is a common feature in apocalyptic descriptions of heaven" (cf. *1 Enoch* 39:12; *2 Enoch* 21:1; and *Test. of Levi* 3:8).[44] Beale adds that "the hymns make explicit the main point of the vision and of the whole chapter; God is to be glorified because of his holiness and sovereignty."[45]

When the four living creatures began this song in praise for God's holiness, the twenty-four elders joined in with a chorus of their own, in spite of the suffering they had experienced in conquering. They sang that God was worthy of all praise, for he was, is, and always will be the Almighty sovereign creator of everything and ruler of the universe.

An interesting note is appended at the close of this hymn, 4:11, *"You are worthy, our Lord and God, to receive glory and honor and power, for you created all things, and by your will they were created and have their being."* The purpose of every Christian is to live and die, to serve and bring honor and glory to God. It was for this purpose that we were created. Paul stresses that the Christian's sole purpose is to live for the praise of his glory (Eph. 4:12). That the twenty-four elder-conquerors joined in this hymn of praise to God indicated that they understood the significance and vital role their martyrdom played in God's overall plan for the ages.

4:9–11. The final verses of 4 return again to the twenty-four elders. Without complaint they join in the heavenly chorus, proclaiming the holiness and worthiness of God for his sovereignty and creative power. *Whenever the living creatures give glory, honor and thanks to him who sits on the throne and who lives for ever and ever,*[10] *the twenty-four elders fall down before him who sits on the throne, and worship him who lives for ever* *and ever. They lay their crowns before the throne and say:* [11] *"You are worthy, our Lord and God, to receive glory and honor and power, for you created all things, and by your will they were created and have their being."* Here it is the Lord God who is worthy to be praised; in 5 it is the Lamb who is worthy to be praised. In this pericope thanks are given to the Almighty God, for he is the creator of all things and it was by his will that all things exist (4:11). Not even martyrdom detracts from the praise given God by all of heaven, including the twenty-four martyred elders. All of the heavenly creation sings of the Almighty God's praise and worthiness. In 5 thanks and divine praise are given to the Lamb, for he has ransomed men from every nation and made them a kingdom and priests to God. Not only is the Almighty God worthy of praise and glory, but the Lamb is set at the same high exalted position as the Almighty God. He too is divine and he has played a vital role in God's plan of creation and *Heilsgeschichte.*[46]

They lay their crowns before the throne as translated in the NIV is not the most felicitous translation of what the twenty-four elders did. They prostrated themselves before the throne, worshipping him who lives forever and ever, and then they *cast* (*balousin* from *ballō* is better understood as *cast* or *throw*, rather than *lay* as in the NIV) their crowns before the throne. Before the elders cast their crowns at the foot of the throne, they *fall down before him who sits on the throne.* There is some debate regarding the meaning of *fall down,* but Osborne[47] correctly points out that in the liturgical context of this pericope there is little difference between fall down and prostrate themselves. The imagery is of worship, not of vassalage.[48] The act of prostrating oneself before a king was an act of reverence and respect that was common among peoples of the East.[49] Opinion as to the significance of casting their crowns down before or at the feet of the Almighty are also varied. Certainly it was an act of respect for the sovereignty of God and an admission that any authority they had was subordinated to God. However, if these elders are representative of martyrs of all ages (they have golden crowns signifying victory and are clothed in white robes, both symbolic of victory and conquering as seen in the seven letters to the seven churches), then these elders as representative conquering martyrs are acknowledging that their death was nothing short of a worthy act of sacrifice to God and that their crowns and victory belong to God.

The final words of the heavenly hymns, *"You are worthy, our Lord and God, to receive glory and honor and power, for you created all things, and by your will they were created and have their being,"* draw attention that all of creation was created for the will and purpose of God and reflect his glory and power. All of creation, even evil, suffering, and martyrdom, are to be subsumed under the divine sovereign purpose of God. Certainly trust in the Almighty God and his divine purpose are essential, but how is this to work out in the end? Beale answers: "Through Christ's death and resurrection and that Spirit which God gives to his followers."[50] Chapter 5 shows the sovereign power of God over all creation, good and evil, carried out symbolically, notably in the mission of the four horsemen and the remaining three seals to the great scroll.

This heavenly worship scene reinforces the point that it is the eternal God alone who is worthy of worship and that it stands as "a warning to compromisers not to worship pagan gods and kings who arrogate to themselves titles that belong only to the true God. God's eternal reign supersedes the temporary reign of evil, pseudo-divine kings who ultimately will be judged."[51]

Summary of the Heavenly Throne Room Scene

This scene depicts God in his heavenly war room seated on his throne, with his holiness and sovereignty proclaimed and defended by the four living creatures and the twenty-four elder conquerors ceaselessly singing his praise. The Almighty God is worthy of all praise, for he is the creator of all things, and all things fall under his sovereignty. The sea of cosmic evil is pictured as conquered and submissive in the presence of the holiness of God.

John will take up the theological problem of evil (a *theodicy*) in chapters 5 and 6. The scroll of 5 will contain John's revelation regarding the problem of evil (the sea), how God can use evil to bring about his purpose and cause evil men to repent, and how God will in the end judge both evil and Satan. The revelation and high point in God's plan of redemption centers in 5 in the worthiness of Jesus, "for he was slain and by his blood had ransomed men for God from every tribe, tongue, people and nation."

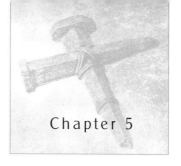

Chapter 5

The Scroll

God's Plan for Handling the Problem of Evil Is Revealed in and by Christ

5:1–14

That God has a plan for dealing with evil is key to the theology and theodicy of Revelation. The great scroll in God's hand with seven seals, which seals only Jesus is worthy to reveal, contains God's plan for dealing with evil. In powerful apocalyptic genre filled with Old Testament and Jewish extra-canonical references, John describes the scroll and the worshipping praise of those surrounding God's throne in heaven, including the four living creatures, the twenty-four elders, and the heavenly host of angelic beings.

INTRODUCTION

The introductory words of 5:1, "and I saw" (*kai eidon*) indicate that the visions of 5:1-22:5 are a continuation of the heavenly throne room scene of 4:1–11. Chapter 5 continues the throne room scene and reveals God with a scroll sealed with seven seals in his hand. Beale had argued impressively at 4:1 that the *Meta tauta eidon, After this I looked* should link directly back to the seven letters and to 1:19 indicating that what was to be revealed referred to what was to occur in the imminent future of the seven churches, and not a new series of events relating to the far distant future. Chapter 6 will begin the revelation of a series of visions that describe the contents of the scroll as they relate to the seven churches and the crises they are already beginning to experience. Chapter 7 includes the first of two interludes intended to slow the "anticipation" and "excitement" building up in the narrative. Chapter 8:1 prepares the reader for the crescendo of events to be revealed at the opening of the seventh seal. The seventh seal, in John's use of the sevens (heptets) in Revelation, should be the completion of the scroll's message, or the final revelation of the scroll, but we will see that the seventh seal introduces us to seven trumpets, and the "story" continues!

The thoughts of chapter 5 coalesce around the theme of God's plan demonstrating his ultimate victory over evil in the death, burial, and resurrection of Christ. Both ends of the *eschaton* appear in this chapter. Osborne observes that "the atmosphere in this chapter is probably that of the eschaton (depending on one's view of the scroll). . . . imminent events will usher in the final events of history and the consummation of God's plan. There is a breathless sense of anticipation."[1] Osborne adds that this chapter contains some of the most magnificent Christological expressions encountered in the New Testament. "The reader is overwhelmed by the sheer power of the picture of Christ as it unfolds. He adds that the "Only the Lamb has the power to open the seals . . . The Lamb has purchased the people of God with his blood sacrifice (v.9) and thereby rendered himself 'worthy' to lead also in judgment (6:1-2) . . . The cross forms the basis of both the divine love (redemption) and justice (judgment) of God."[2] Thus by holding the present crises facing the church in dynamic tension with God's ultimate judgment of evil, John begins to develop his theme that Jesus and his death and resurrection form the central theme, or theology, of the message of Revelation (cf. 12:10–11).

Aune suggests that the *kai eidon* here could be translated "then I saw", reinforcing the coordinating function of the *kai* and that "and I saw" can be used in three ways in Revelation: 1) to introduce a new vision narrative, 2) to introduce a major scene within a continuing vision narrative, or 3) to focus on a new or significant figure or action that occurs within a continuing narrative. He suggests that it is in either the second or third options, or perhaps a combination of both, that the *kai eidon* functions in 5:1: to introduce the scroll scene of 5:1-14 within the continuing vision and heavenly worship narrative of 4:1–11 or to focus on a new or significant figure, thus introducing the Lamb as the new and central figure in the continuing heavenly throne scene.[3]

Several proposals have been made regarding the setting for the scroll in 5. Some identify 5 as the enthronement of the Lamb, others as the commission of the Lamb in the heavenly court, or the investiture of the Lamb, each highlighting a nuance of this significant scene.[4] I prefer to see the heavenly scroll scene as one that praises both the Eternal God and his Son for the triumphant role they play in creation and the redemption of creation from the grasp of Satan and his evil agents or forces. The heavenly throne room scene of 4 demonstrates the sovereignty and holiness of God; the heavenly scroll scene demonstrates that the Eternal God and his Son (described as the Lion of the tribe of Judah and the Lamb) have a plan in their divine providence for dealing with evil and redeeming creation from evil.

SCROLLS

Scrolls, or "books" (translated from the same Greek family of words, *biblos* or *biblion*, which can be translated *book, sacred book, venerable book,* or simply *scroll*),[5] appear in several key texts in the Old Testament and apocalyptic tradition. In the Old Testament "scroll" is found in approximately sixty-one verses, In most cases the term is translated "scroll," in some places "book." Scrolls were a popular medium for writing significant narratives and documents.

In all probability the chief background behind John's use of scroll (*biblion*) was Daniel 12:4 and Ezekiel 2:9, 10. McNicol observes that "Revelation recycles images and even quotations from Daniel, Isaiah, Ezekiel, and elsewhere, all the while creating something entirely new."[6] (other uses of *biblos* or scroll in the Old Testament: Exod. 17:4; Ps. 139:16; Isa. 29:11, 12. References in Jewish extrabiblical literature include *1 Enoch* 93:1–15; *2 Esdras* 2; and *Odes Sol* 22 and 23.) The concept of "*scrolls*" and the role they play in God's system were well known to people of John's time familiar with the Judeo-Christian tradition.[7]

What role does the scroll play in John's Revelation? Caird, Beckwith, Beale, Osborne, and Aune (along with most commentators)[8] discuss several proposals regarding the meaning of the scroll in 5. It is the conclusion of both Caird and Beale, and I concur with this decision, that the scroll in 5 has reference to a redemptive plan (*heilsgeschichte*) God has had in mind from eternity. Caird observes, "The scroll, then, contains the world's destiny, foreordained by the gracious purpose of God."[9] Beale adds, "The 'book' is best understood as containing God's plan of judgment and redemption, which has been set in motion by Christ's death and resurrection but has not yet been completed."[10] Aune provides and extensive list of approaches to the meaning or content of the scroll, one of which is in keeping with the direction proposed by Caird and Beale. He suggests that the scroll "is a 'book of destiny, consisting of God's predetermined plan for human beings and the world...or the foreordained eschatological plan of God, which cannot be known until the period of fulfillment, a biblical tradition reflected in Ezek 2:9-10; Dan 8:26; 12:9; Jub 32:20-22; I Enoch 81:2-3."[11]

In evangelical circles one speaks of salvation and redemption on a personal level, referring to the redemption or salvation of the individual; the apocalyptist views redemption on a cosmic scale. He thinks of the redemption of the whole cosmic system struggling under the power of sin (cf. Rom. 8:18–25). Furthermore, the apocalyptist looks for the final redemption of God's people from the evil powers, including the judgment of evil and the vindication of God's people. The scroll declares that God has a plan of redemption, a plan for redeeming the whole of creation from the grasp of evil, a plan he has been working from the foundation of the earth. This plan explains, most often in dramatic cosmic symbolism, how God can and will handle the problem of evil. The apocalyptic concept of redemption revealed in the scroll is best defined especially here in Revelation by what theologians call *Heilsgeschichte*, God's sovereign and eternal redemptive plan for the universe. These apocalyptic scrolls "contain the secrets of the future, and the opening of the books signifies the fulfillment of hidden things."[12]

The scroll of 5, therefore, includes information, possibly even in "secret," or "mystical" terms relating to God's plan for taking care of evil and for rewarding those who suffer at the hands of evil: God does not cause evil, but he uses evil to get the attention of evil men and offer them an opportunity to repent. He also uses evil to judge and destroy evil nations. The main point of the scroll is to explain that God has a plan, that the world is not out of control, and that God is still in control of the universe. Central to the theology of the scroll, and of Revelation, is that it is in the death and resurrection of Jesus that God's plan is fulfilled and evil is judged, defeated, and destroyed, and the saints are vindicated and redeemed. Jesus takes the central place in the revelation of the scroll in 5, as well as in the book of Revelation as a whole.

The Heavenly Scroll

The Text

Then I saw in the right hand of him who sat on the throne a scroll with writing on both sides and sealed with seven seals. [2] And I saw a mighty angel proclaiming in a loud voice, "Who is worthy to break the seals and open the scroll?" [3] But no one in heaven or on earth or under the earth could open the scroll or even look inside it. [4] I wept and wept because no one was found who was worthy to open the scroll or look inside. [5] Then one of the elders said to me, "Do not weep. See, the Lion of the tribe of Judah, the Root of David, has triumphed. He is able to open the scroll and its seven seals. "

[6] Then I saw a Lamb, looking as if it had been slain, standing in the center of the throne, encircled by the four living creatures and the elders. He had seven horns and seven eyes, which are the seven spirits of God sent out into all the earth. [7] He came and took the scroll from the right hand of him who sat on the throne. [8] And when he had taken it, the four living creatures and the twenty-four elders fell down before the Lamb. Each one had a harp and they were holding golden bowls full of incense, which are the prayers of the saints. [9] And they sang a new song:

> *"You are worthy to take the scroll*
> > *and to open its seals,*
> *because you were slain,*
> > *and with your blood you purchased men for God*
> > *from every tribe and language and people and nation.*
> *[10] You have made them to be a kingdom and priests to serve our God,*
> > *and they will reign on the earth."*

[11] Then I looked and heard the voice of many angels, numbering thousands upon thousands, and ten thousand times ten thousand. They encircled the throne and the living creatures and the elders. [12] In a loud voice they sang:

> *"Worthy is the Lamb, who was slain,*
> *to receive power and wealth and wisdom and strength*
> *and honor and glory and praise."*

[13] Then I heard every creature in heaven and on earth and under the earth and on the sea, and all that is in them, singing:

> *"To him who sits on the throne and to the Lamb*
> *be praise and honor and glory and power,*
> *for ever and ever."*

[14] *The four living creatures said, "Amen," and the elders fell down and worshiped.*

5:1. As observed above, the *kai eidon* **then I saw** connects the message of the scroll about to be revealed to the heavenly throne room and back to the seven letters to the seven churches (2, 3). The message of the scroll, therefore, comes directly from the Eternal and Almighty God seated on his throne in his command post. *Kai eidon* plays a pivotal role in the literary and theological structure of Revelation.[13] This expression is found four times in chapter 5 (1, 2, 6, 11) and divides the chapter into separate scenes.[14] The expression is found thirty-nine times in Revelation. While it is not a key factor in determining structure, it is significant to the literary style of Revelation.[15] In this case the *kai eidon* emphasizes the key role that the Lamb plays in unfolding the eschatological plan in the mind of the Eternal God in his heavenly throne room and is directly connected to the message of the seven letters.

John saw **in the right hand of him who sat on the throne a scroll with writing on both sides and sealed with seven seals**. That the scroll is in the right hand of God implies its divine royal authority, and adds a sense of urgency to the message of the scroll. John's description of the scroll is shaped by the language and message of Ezekiel, for in Ezekiel 2:10: "On both sides of it were written words of lament and mourning and woe." The scroll of 5 has writing on both sides. John's message, like that of Ezekiel, comes during a time of extreme crisis, and like Ezekiel's scroll contains," words of lament, mourning, and woe."

Some compare the sealed scroll of 5 with that of Isaiah 29:11, in which case the people complained because they could not read the message:[16] "For you this whole vision is nothing but words sealed in a scroll. And if you give the scroll to someone who can read, and say to him, 'Read this, please,' he will answer, 'I can't; it is sealed'[12] Or if you give the scroll to someone who cannot read, and say, 'Read this, please,' he will answer, 'I don't know how to read'" (Isa. 29:11). The connection may, however, be no more than that a divine scroll sealed by God cannot be read and understood unless it is God himself who reveals or permits it to be read and understood.

In Daniel's case (Dan. 12:4) the words of his book (scroll) were sealed for a revelation at a later time. In John's case, however, although the scroll is also sealed, it is about to be opened, implying both the imminence and urgency of the message of the scroll in 5. It is intended to be read and understood in the present context of the seven letters. Some see this as a historic or linear prophetic fulfillment of Daniel 12. While there is a "fulfillment" element in the parallel scrolls of Daniel 12 and Revelation 5, the question is whether the text is referring to a historical fulfillment or one of analogous or typological fulfillment.[17] An appropriate use of Daniel by John is to see the fulfillment as an *analogous* application. John knows that Daniel's scroll was sealed and that Daniel's message was not for Daniel's time. John also knows that the sealed scroll in the hand of the Almighty has a message and that this message is about to be revealed with the breaking of the seals. The message of the scroll about to be reveled is for John's time, not for a time much later as was the case of Daniels' sealed scroll. The breaking or opening the seals of 5 implies the revealing of a message that is both imminent and urgent to John's audience.

The scroll is *sealed with seven seals*. The number "seven" appears fifty-five times in thirty-one verses in Revelation. It is the consensus of scholars[18] that seven primarily symbolizes completeness, fulfillment, or perfection. The number seven in the sealing of the scroll is well attested in the Jewish tradition, indicating the impossibility for an unauthorized person to gain access to the message sealed by God.[19] That the scroll is sealed with seven seals implies that it is completely sealed; that without divine authority or power its message remains unrevealed to man. However, with the opening of the seals, God's message and eternal plan is about to be fully revealed. God proffers the scroll in his right hand and a strong angel asks who could open the seals of the scroll, indicating God's wish that the scroll be opened and the message revealed.[20]

5:2. *A mighty angel* asks a question in *a loud voice* regarding the scroll, implying that the answer must be significant. The question *"Who is worthy to break the seals and open the scroll?"* implies that no one present was worthy to open the seals, for John writes, *"no one in heaven or on earth or under the earth could open the scroll or even look inside it."* Five of the six occurrences of *axios, worthy,* found in Revelation occur in this chapter. [21] Certainly God is worthy, but in this case it is he who is proffering the scroll and its message, indicating that someone else who is worthy needs to open it and reveal its message. As we will learn, it is only Jesus who was worthy to break the seals and reveal the divine message of the scroll. Worthiness in Revelation does not simply mean to be able, but carries the sense of one qualified by having faced the ultimate test (cf. the letter to Sardis). In Revelation *axios* (worthiness) refers to those who are worthy because they are willing to die for their faith. In the case of Jesus, the four living creatures and the twenty-four elders acknowledge this and praise Jesus for his worthiness *"because you were slain, and with your blood you purchased men for God from every tribe and language and people and nation."*

Beale is correct in observing that the scroll in 5 concerns "a predestined plan that is eschatological in nature, since its contents are revealed in 6–22 and are summarized in 4:1 as 'what must take place after these things.'" In contrast to Beale's translation *"after these things"* a better translation is that of the RSV and NIV, *"I will show you what must take place after this,"* implying the immediate eschatological future of the churches in Asia is in mind, not in the far distant future of the final eschaton.[22] The events described in 6–22 are therefore presented in an inaugurated eschatological genre relating to the immediate future of the seven churches, but involving final judgment issues.[23] Beal adds the scroll contains a "covenantal promise of an inheritance." He finds parallels with the *Odes of Solomon* 23, which, although possibly later than Revelation (the *Odes* possibly dating ca. 100), refer to a people "who want to 'take and read' a 'sealed letter . . . written by the finger of God.'"[24] "The judicial nature of the book, although redemptive elements are also present,"[25] emphasizes not only the covenantal nature of the book and Christ's redeeming activity, but also his sovereign judgment over history, which involves not only the present circumstances of the churches in Asia, but also the final eschatological future of the church. [26]

5:3–5. When no one in heaven or on earth is worthy to open the scroll, bringing John to tears of frustration and concern, *one of the elders* announces, *Do not weep. See, the Lion of the tribe of Judah, the Root of David, has triumphed*. The verb *has triumphed* (*enikēsen*) is the perfect tense of *nikaō* (to conquer). It emphasizes the certainty of Jesus' victory; Jesus *has already conquered*. Therefore *he is able to open the scroll and its seven seals*. The word order in the Greek places "he has conquered" at the head of the sentence for emphasis: "Do not weep; behold he has conquered, the Lion of the Tribe of Judah, the root of David." John draws attention to *the conquering role* of Jesus in the war between Satan and God's people.

The Lion of the tribe of Judah and *the Root of David*, both strong Messianic terms drawing from Old Testament imagery, emphasize the kingly messianic role of Jesus. *The Root of David* portrays Jesus as the militant Messiah.[27] As God's victorious king, he is now qualified to open the seals by having conquered Satan. The verb *has conquered* is used without an object that would limit the action. Jesus' conquering victory is unlimited and absolute.[28] "This also means that the great victory over Satan has already occurred: the cross is the central point of history."[29] In 12:11, the martyrs, because of Jesus' victory, have also already conquered Satan by the blood of the lamb and their faithful testimony.

5:6. *Then I saw a Lamb, looking as if it had been slain*. When John sees the Lion of the tribe of Judah and the Root of David, what he sees is not a lion, but a lamb who has been slain. Osborne adds "This is one of the most beautiful mixed metaphors in all the Bible—the lion (5:5) is a lamb. The direction of the transformation is very important; the final stage is the lamb, not the lion."[30]

The juxtaposition of these two concepts of lion and lamb is vital to John's message. Jesus reigns as the messianic lion because he has died as a lamb. Martyrdom is interpreted as a sacrifice worthy of God that assures one of the kingdom and reigning with Christ. The saints as martyrs become conquerors, receive crowns, and reign with Jesus.[31]

Regarding John's use of the metaphors of Jesus as the Lion of the Tribe of Judah and the Lamb of God, Caird observes:

> By this one stroke of brilliant artistry John has given us the key to all his use of the Old Testament. He constantly echoes the Old Testament writings (without ever actually quoting them), partly because of the powerful emotive effect of familiar associations, and partly no doubt because his vision had actually taken its form, though not its content, from the permanent furniture of his well-stocked mind. But to all this we must add that he believed the Old Testament Scriptures to be the oracles of God, and that the same God who had spoken in partial and shadowy ways through the prophets had now spoken fully in his Son. The Old Testament was indispensable to the understanding of the character and purpose of God, but it must be read in the light of the fuller illumination of Christ.[32]

The movement of *the Lion* (sovereign) into *the Lamb* (sacrifice) in this text is an excellent example of John's literary and theological genius. The striking connection of dying and reigning reinforces this major theological key to understanding Revelation. This theological theme reinforces the promise to the saints in Asia (and all saints) that should they die as martyrs for their faith in God and Jesus, although humiliated in the eyes of their pagan neighbors, they are vindicated by God, become conquers (2–3), and reign victoriously with Christ in his and God's eternal kingdom.

M. Carrez contends that the Lamb is the central figure of Revelation and points to the cross as the climax in the theodicy of Revelation.[33] Others identify the paschal lamb imagery of Isaiah 53:7 which is another proposed focus on the lamb as an atoning symbol. Some have identified suffering servant images from Isaiah 53. Although Osborne suggests that the best possible interpretation is that John combines images of the paschal lamb and the suffering servant lamb,[34] John's literary style enables him to pull into his images a comprehensive messianic view in which Jesus fulfills a "welter of Old Testament images." Caird contends that whenever we encounter the Lamb in Revelation we are to think of the Lion, and vice versa, and that "wherever the Old Testament speaks of the victory of the Messiah or the overthrow of the enemies of God, we are to remember that the gospel recognizes no other way of achieving these ends than the way of the Cross."[35]

The NIV describes the Lamb as "standing *in the center* of the throne, encircled by the four living creatures and the elders." This unfortunate translation creates a problem since in this scene it is the Eternal and Almighty God who is on the throne, not Jesus. The RSV translates this more appropriately as "*between* the throne and the four living creatures." The Greek *en mesō* can be translated as *in the middle, between, among, through.* The RSV translation "between" is more accurate translation and more in keeping with the context of the passage than that of the NIV.[36]

5:6. John remarks that he saw the Lamb *looking as if it had been slain*, standing between the throne and the four living creatures. The Greek (*Kai eidon en mesō tou thronou kai tōn tessarōn zōōn kai en mesō tōn presbuterōn arnion estēkos hōs esphagmenon*) translates more accurately as "And I saw between the throne and the four living creatures, indeed in the midst of the elders, a lamb standing as though it had been slaughtered." Again the translation of the RSV is more in keeping with the Greek. The Greek *esphagmenon* (a perfect participle of *sphadzō*) means "slaughter" or "murder." John's imagery again concentrates all the sacrificial images into one; Jesus was not just killed, but slaughtered as a sacrificial lamb.[37] Mounce traces the source of this image to Isaiah 53:7, "He was oppressed and afflicted, yet he did not open his mouth; he was led like a lamb to the slaughter." However, Jesus is not lying dead as a slaughtered lamb; he is standing in the presence of God in the heavenly throne room. Images of the resurrection as well as of victory and vindication are clear. The Greek *estēkos* (a perfect participle of *histēmi*) implies that although he looked as though he had been slaughtered, he is actually *standing firmly* as one who lives.

The Lamb *has seven horns and seven eyes, which are the seven spirits of God.* The composite image of the Lamb brings together important images of God, thus emphasizing the divine nature of the Lamb. The seven horns draws from the Jewish and apocalyptic traditions of military power (Deut. 33:17; 1 Kgs. 22:11; Ps. 89:17; Dan. 7:7; *1 Enoch* 90:6–12, 37). There is also a burgeoning messianic tradition that saw the messiah with horns as a conquering messiah (*1 Enoch* 90; Test. *Jos.* 19). The seven eyes point back to Zechariah 3 and 4, in which the seven lamps and seven eyes represent God's all seeing and knowing Spirit. John adds to these two images of the horns and eyes the third one of the seven spirits, which dramatizes the presence of divine wisdom and insight in the Lamb (see comments at 1:4–5 for the probability the seven spirits represent the fullness of the Holy Spirit).[38] The blending of the three images of seven horns, seven eyes, and seven spirits of God into a composite image of the Lamb focuses attention on the divine power and knowledge of the Lamb as God's sovereign Messiah in God's plan.[39]

Rev. 5:7–9a. *He came and took the scroll from the right hand of him who sat on the throne.* When the Lamb took the scroll from the hand of the Almighty, *the four living creatures and the twenty-four elders fell down before the Lamb. Each one had a harp and they were holding golden bowls full of incense, which are the prayers of the saints.* [9] *And they sang a new song.* Previously, when the four living creatures and the twenty-four elders sang a hymn, it was in praise of the Eternal God (4:8-11). Now they sing a new song of praise, but this time in honor of the Lamb. We are reminded that it was the duty of the four living creatures to proclaim and protect the holiness of God. When the Lamb receives the scroll from the right hand of God, John introduces the transfer of sovereignty from the Eternal God to the Lamb, who now becomes the central theme of Revelation. Osborne comments regarding this subtle shift of emphasis,

> More precisely, he exercises the Father's reign which has now been handed over to him . . . Due to his sacrifice on the cross, only the Lamb is "worthy" to take the scroll. The Emphasis is on the shift from God to the Lamb, who will now execute the divinely mandated plan. Opening the scroll means the judgment of the world and the vindication of the saints.[40]

Beale identifies a "continued adherence to the pattern of Daniel 7:9ff." when the Lamb takes the scroll and receives the praise of the four living creatures.[41] God, by passing the scroll on to Jesus, is acknowledging Jesus' complete reign and full authority over his eternal kingdom. Beale sees similar references to the Lamb on the throne in 3:21; 7:17; and 22:1.[42]

Of the four living creatures and twenty-four elders, John writes that *each one had a harp.* As early as David, the harp (technically a kithara or lyre with ten or twelve strings) was the favored instrument for singing psalms celebrating occasions of festive joy and thanksgiving and to accompany temple choirs. [43] The full implication of the singing with harps is emphasized in the nature of the new song and the association of this song with the golden censors and prayers of the saints. The praise of God and Jesus is associated with the suffering of the saints. John will develop this theme. At this point the suffering of the saints is introduced as a sacrifice to God and something to be celebrated with joy. In John's theodicy the suffering of the saints in comparison to the glory and holiness of God and Jesus is seen as a minor factor.

5:8b. *Each one had a harp and they were holding golden bowls full of incense, which are the prayers of the saints.* In this worship scene John introduces a new theme that speaks of *golden bowls of incense, which are the prayers of the saints.* John does not tell us here what the prayers are, but merely introduces the image. He will progressively[44] come back to the prayers of the saints as he connects the suffering of the saints to God's plan of redemption (see:10, 10:6). The imagery of the golden bowls full of incense, the playing of harps, and of angels acting as prayer intercessors for God's people is drawn from a rich Jewish apocalyptic tradition (Tobit 12:15; 3 Baruch 11). The "angels function throughout the book as priests in the heavenly temple performing cultic duties,"[45] and the twenty-four elders act as the intercessors.[46]

The term translated bowls here is *phialē*, usually used in temple cultic contexts of bowls containing offerings that may be associated with prayers. Whereas some form of sacred incense was normally used in such cultic offerings, here the "incense" of the bowls is the prayers of the saints.[47] John's use of the prayers of the saints in place of cultic incense is metaphorical in that incense was often associated in the Jewish tradition with prayers and sacrificial offerings.[48] (See 6:10 and 10:6 for the significance of these prayers, their connection with the sacrificial offering, and the role they play in the theodicy of Revelation.)

John describes the song of the four living creatures and twenty-four elders *as a new song*. The thought of a new song is possibly drawn from Psalm 98, in which the psalmist encourages the congregation to sing a new song of praise to God for his righteous judgments.

Thus John intentionally draws on the Old Testament Psalmic tradition of associating new songs with songs of praise to God for his deliverance and judgments. Furthermore, in some Jewish traditions new songs are associated with the coming of the Messiah or messianic age.[49] The intention of the new song of praise sung to Jesus here draws attention to his role as sovereign redeemer and eschatological judge. Jesus alone can reveal the contents of God's plan and bring God's judgments on the enemies of God and his people. The new song heightens the worthiness of the Lamb to receive all power and glory because of his redeeming sacrifice.

5:9–10. *You are worthy to take the scroll and to open its seals, because you were slain.* In Revelation worthiness is associated with willingness to suffer for one's faith rather than moral rectitude. There were those in the church at Sardis who were worthy because they had not soiled their garments by compromise (3:4) and who obviously were willing to suffer for their faith. As a role model for all Christians, Jesus was worthy because he had given his life as a sacrifice to God in order to ransom men from bondage to sin and Satan. *Because you were slain* is clearly the reason for Jesus' worthiness to open the scroll. With his *blood* he *purchased men for God from every tribe and language and people and nation.* The RSV in its translation of *egorasas* (aorist tense of *agoradzō*) as *ransomed* men for God is better than the NIV rendering of *purchased* since this seems more in agreement with the biblical doctrine of redemption and fits in better with the Roman and ancient culture of slavery.

The expression *from every tribe and language and people and nation* has generated some discussion among commentators in regard to its universality. This Danielic formula (from Dan. 7:9 *passim*) is repeated in several places in Revelation (7:9; 10:11; 11:9; 13:7; 17:15) with minor variation and is regarded by scholars as a stylistic literary formula of John. Most recognize John's use of this formula as a reference to the universality of the church; the church is drawn from all nations.[50]

Jesus has also in his atoning death *made them to be a kingdom and priests to serve our God.*[51] In his messianic kingdom the saints serve as priests of God, honoring God in this "cultic" service of Psalmic praise. In addition to being made a kingdom of priests, they *will reign on earth* (again connecting martyrdom, a priestly service to God, and reigning in the messianic kingdom). Jesus' atoning death makes it possible for one to become a priest who serves in the kingdom. John had introduced the theme of a *kingdom of priests* in 1:6. This motif of becoming a kingdom of priests is mentioned three times in Revelation (1:6; 5:10; 20:6). It may have been drawn from an early Christian or primitive hymn.[52] Caird observes, "To be a Christian is to be both king and priest, but with a sovereignty and priesthood derived from Christ."[53] The background of 1:6 and 5:10 is obviously Exodus 19:6, reshaped by John for his purpose of emphasizing that the saints reign as priests in Jesus' kingdom because they offer their lives in sacrifice to God.[54] This priestly reign of the saints, however, is not brought about solely by their suffering and martyrdom. Its efficacy is found only in association with Jesus' atoning death (see 12:10–11).

Martyrdom, no matter how worthily it may be conceived, when removed from Jesus' atoning death and resurrection may be commendable, but apart from the cross it is powerless. Repeatedly, John explains that martyrdom for God and Christ, empowered by the cross, is to be understood as a transforming sacrifice in which the martyred saints are resurrected with Christ and become conquerors who are exalted to sit with Christ on his messianic throne. This theme, introduced in 2:26-28, will reach a crescendo in 20:4.

John's comment that the saints *will reign on the earth* should not be interpreted as some premillennialists or futurists have attempted concerning a future reign with Christ on earth. The argument in favor of a future reign of the martyrs in the kingdom rather than a present reign is based on the UBS and Nestle Greek texts that favor the future tense of *basileusousin* (*will reign*) over the present tense of *basileuousin* (*reign*). The textual evidence, however, in favor of either *basileusousin* or *basileuousin* is equal and inconclusive.[55] Caird, Beale, and Aune argue in favor of the present tense since a present reign of the conquering martyrs in the kingdom with Christ has already been clearly established in Revelation.[56]

Since John has already mentioned that, through Christ's atoning sacrifice, the saints have already been made priests and kings, they must surely be serving as priests in the service of God and reigning with Christ in the kingdom of God and Christ. John and his readers are well aware of the concept of corporate personality, which maintains that all in a corporate relationship with the king reign with the king. This has been the center of Jesus' promises to the saints in the seven letters of chapters 2 and 3. As Jesus is now the sovereign king who reigns over all the earth, including the Roman Empire, so too the saints reign with him over the earth in a corporate sense.

5:11–14. *Then I looked and heard the voice of many angels, numbering thousands upon thousands, and ten thousand times ten thousand* circling the throne of God and the elders and the four living creatures. *In a loud voice* this angelic chorus now sang a hymn of praise to Jesus, the Lamb. The song of the Lamb's seven-fold worthiness is expressed in keeping with John's literary and theological style: *"Worthy is the Lamb, who was slain, to receive power and wealth and wisdom and strength and honor and glory and praise."* This is similar to the divine praise that had been sung to the eternal God on his heavenly throne (4:11). Now this same language is used of Jesus, emphasizing again the transfer of authority and power to Jesus as God's sovereign ruler. This heavenly chorus was joined in John's cosmic style by *every creature in heaven and on earth and under the earth and on the sea, and all that is in them.* All of God's creation now adds their song of praise, honoring the one who was the primary creative Word (John 1:1–4), through whom God created all things (Heb. 1:2) and through whom he will judge the world in righteousness (Acts 17:30–31). The creator *Word* of John 1:1–3 has now become the messianic redeemer of all creation (the apocalyptic genre does not see only the redemption of the individual through faith, but the redemption of all creation as a part of God's eternal purpose; cf. Rom. 8:18–25). Their song places the Lamb on equal footing with the Eternal God: *"To him who sits on the throne and to the Lamb be praise and honor and glory and power, for ever and ever."* Were such words blasphemous, the four living creatures would have immediately sprung into decisive judgment on the blasphemers, but instead of judgment the defenders of God's holy being sang *"Amen"* and fell at his feet in worship, and the elders around the heavenly throne fall down and worship the Eternal God and the Lamb.

The transfer of attention has been successfully shifted temporarily from the throne of God to the Lamb of God, who reigns over God's kingdom. The addition of *numbering thousands upon thousands, and ten thousand times ten thousand* merely stresses the magnitude and glory of the angels' hymn of praise to the Lamb. The exact number is not the point. What is being emphasized here is the extent and significance of the praise.[57]

The scene now has been set for the introduction of a new vision in 6:1 which opens with John's stylistic repeated use of *kai eidon*, and introduces a new scene in the continuing narrative of the heavenly throne room and the presentation of the seven-sealed scroll. The seals are about to be broken, each seal revealing a specific vision of how God uses events for his eternal purpose.

Chapter 6

The Seven Seals

Christ Reveals God's Plan for Dealing with Evil

6:1–8:6

This section examines the seven seals of the great scroll in which God reveals his plan for dealing with the problem of evil. God explains that he uses evil men and evil forces to make those who oppose his purposes repent. A major theme of this section is the prayers of the martyred saints for vindication. God promises vindication and reward for the saints but encourages them to wait faithfully while he carries out his purpose. Surprisingly, the seventh seal becomes seven warning trumpets of 8:1–11:19. At strategic points, when anticipation reaches almost a climax, John inserts two interludes (7 and 10) in which he encourages the saints to remain faithful while God carries out his plan.

INTRODUCTION

The scenes about to be revealed at the opening of the scroll of Revelation 6 are a continuation of the heavenly throne room scene of chapters 4 and 5 and are therefore connected to the seven letters to the seven churches of Asia of chapters 2 and 3. Chapter 6 begins the revelation of a series of visions that describe the contents of the scroll as they relate to the seven churches and the crises they are already beginning to experience. Chapter 7 introduces an interlude that slows down the "anticipation" and "excitement" building in the narrative. Revelation 8:1 prepares the reader for the crescendo of the opening of the seventh seal. The seventh seal, in John's use of the sevens (septets) in Revelation, should complete the scroll's message, or the final revelation of the scroll, but the seventh seal introduces seven trumpets and the "story" continues.

It is obvious that the breaking of the seven seals and revealing their message by Jesus is a sign of Jesus' absolute sovereignty over all of creation. Jesus is *the ruler of the kings of the earth,* (17:14); *he is Lord of lords and King of kings,* (19:16). *On his robe and on his thigh he has this name written: KING OF KINGS AND LORD OF LORDS.* John emphasizes Christ's reign over earthly kings, demonstrating that his messianic reign has already begun. Revelation 6:1–8 demonstrates that Christ's reign extends over every situation that the churches in Asia will shortly be facing, including societal opposition, persecution, suffering, and even martyrdom. Beale observes,

> Rev 6:1–8 is intended to show that Christ rules over such an apparently chaotic world and that suffering does not occur indiscriminately or by chance. This section reveals, in fact, that destructive events are brought about by Christ for both redemptive and judicial purposes. . . . The command for each of the four destructive horses and riders originates from the throne room, where Christ opens each seal. . . . Therefore, in connection with ch. 5, Rev 6:1–8 describes the operation of the destructive forces that were unleashed immediately on the world as a result of Christ's victorious suffering at the cross, his resurrection, and his ascent to a position of rule at his Father's right hand. . . . In Christ's exercise of kingship he empowers each horseman through his cherubic servants.[1]

Caird adds that John expresses the common belief of "the whole early church" that Christ was already reigning at the right hand of God over both heaven and earth and that this reign was not something to take place after his *parousia,* but one that was already established. Caird asserts that this view was one that was well attested in Scripture, building on a view expressed in Psalm 110:1 that the Messiah "was destined so to reign until God had put all his enemies under his feet (Ps. cx. 1; cf. Mark xiii. 35–37; Acts ii. 33ff; v. 31; vii. 55ff; Rom. Viii. 34; 1 Cor. Xv. 25; Eph. i. 20; Col. Iii. 1; Heb. i. 3; 13; x. 12f. I Pet iii. 22)." He continues,

> If John has something new to communicate about the reign of Christ, it is because he insists on taking the traditional belief with utmost seriousness. It is not enough for him to assert that Christ's reign is already established in heaven and will ultimately be established on earth also at his Parousia; for heavenly events must have here and now their earthly counterparts. It is not enough for him to hold that the regnant Christ reigns over the hearts of those who love him, that he reigns only in so far as men by obedience and loyalty allow him to reign. He believes that Christ is already the 'ruler of earthly kings' (i. 5.) Unless Christ can be said to reign over the world of hard facts in which Christians must live their lives, he can hardly be said to reign at all.[2]

Osborne argues that the seven seals are preliminary judgments on earth that prepare for the seven trumpets and bowls that follow: "The thematic parallels are striking—war, international strife, famine, death, persecution, earthquakes and cosmic disturbances." Osborne then identifies seven major themes in the three great judgment scenes of Revelation, the seven seals, the seven trumpets, and the seven bowls of wrath:

1. They represent God's judgments on those who dwell on the earth, the saints being protected (sealed) by God.
2. The judgments are God's response to the "imprecatory prayers of the saints for justice" in 5:8; 6:10; 8:3–5; 10:6.
3. The judgments stress the judgments of God throughout Revelation.
4. God does not command evil to do his will but simply allows it to operate.
5. The response of those who dwell on earth proves their total depravity.
6. The outpouring of judgments have a redemptive purpose and offer a final opportunity to repent in 9:20.
7. There is a "progressive dismantling of creation, as the created order is shaken" in the seals and finally judged in the bowls.[3]

Each of these concepts will play a pivotal role in understanding and correctly interpreting the breaking of the seven seals and revealing the message of 6–22.

1. Jesus is the sovereign ruler of all heaven and earth and is already reigning as king of kings over God's eternal kingdom.
2. The messianic kingdom is not something the saints can look forward to after the *parousia*, but is already in effect.
3. The seven seals set the scene for the developing message of Revelation.
4. God does not create evil, but uses it for his redemptive purpose.
5. He will in the immediate future judge those who dwell on earth (those who worship the beast and persecute the saints). This judgment will be described in eschatological language to stress that the judgment has final, end-of-the-world significance.

THE SEVEN SEALS, 6:1–8:6

John first discusses six seals, followed by an interlude. The interlude is intentional in order to slow down the intensity of the message being revealed. Following the interlude he returns to the message of the seals.

THE FIRST SIX SEALS, 6:1–17

The Text

[1]*I watched as the Lamb opened the first of the seven seals. Then I heard one of the four living creatures say in a voice like thunder, "Come." [2] I looked, and there before me was a white horse. Its rider held a bow, and he was given a crown, and he rode out as a conqueror bent on conquest. [3] When the Lamb opened the second seal, I heard the second living creature say, "Come." [4] Then another horse came out, a fiery red one. Its rider was given power to take peace from the earth and to make men slay each other. To him was given a large sword. [5] When the Lamb opened the third seal, I heard the third living creature say, "Come." I looked, and there before me was a black horse. Its rider was holding a pair of scales in his hand. [6] Then I heard what sounded like a voice among the four living creatures, saying, "A quart of wheat for a day's wages, and three quarts of barley for a day's wages, and do not damage the oil and the wine." [7] When the Lamb*

opened the fourth seal, I heard the voice of the fourth living creature say, "Come." [8] *I looked, and there before me was a pale horse. Its rider was named Death, and Hades was following close behind him. They were given power over a fourth of the earth to kill by sword, famine and plague, and by the wild beasts of the earth.* [9] *When he opened the fifth seal, I saw under the altar the souls of those who had been slain because of the word of God and the testimony they had maintained.* [10] *They called out in a loud voice, "How long, Sovereign Lord, holy and true, until you judge the inhabitants of the earth and avenge our blood?"* [11] *Then each of them was given a white robe, and they were told to wait a little longer, until the number of their fellow servants and brothers who were to be killed as they had been was completed.* [12] *I watched as he opened the sixth seal. There was a great earthquake. The sun turned black like sackcloth made of goat hair, the whole moon turned blood red,* [13] *and the stars in the sky fell to earth, as late figs drop from a fig tree when shaken by a strong wind.* [14] *The sky receded like a scroll, rolling up, and every mountain and island was removed from its place.* [15] *Then the kings of the earth, the princes, the generals, the rich, the mighty, and every slave and every free man hid in caves and among the rocks of the mountains.* [16] *They called to the mountains and the rocks, "Fall on us and hide us from the face of him who sits on the throne and from the wrath of the Lamb.* [17] *For the great day of their wrath has come, and who can stand?"*

General Comments on the Four Horsemen

First, we should view Revelation as a theodicy, a defense of the righteousness of God in the context of evil. Why does a loving and almighty God do nothing to stop evil and the cruel suffering of the saints? Revelation answers this question by demonstrating that the Almighty God has already acted against evil in the person of Jesus and the cross, that he has already defeated evil, that he will judge all evil, and that he will finally destroy evil and its source. Revelation as a theodicy explains that God has used and will use evil for redemptive purposes. The solution to the problem of evil in Revelation is primarily located in the cross and the role Jesus has already played in the defeat of Satan. The solution is also seen in the role the saints play in the defeat of Satan through martyrdom for their faith in Jesus. Finally, the explanation is that God has a redemptive plan that he has been working since before the beginning of creation and the saints in Asia are at one point in that plan.

Second, the first four seals reveal four horsemen, commonly known as the four horsemen of the apocalypse. It might be more appropriate to identify them as the four horsemen of Zechariah, for it is from Zechariah 1:8–20; 6:1–8 that John draws his images. These horsemen patrol the earth for God as his watchmen on earth. Each of the horsemen is sent out by one of the four living creatures, indicating that what they do falls within the parameters of the holiness of God.

Third, the first four seals, revealing the four horsemen, lead into a final three seals. All seven progressively narrate God's *Heilsgeschichte,* which will finally reveal his ultimate judgment over the forces of evil and his vindication of the saints. God's plan may involve suffering, but the suffering will have a redemptive and purifying role. Furthermore, God's holiness and glory are magnified through the suffering of his people (cf. the throne room scene of chapter 4). The key to the solution of the problem of evil is to see the whole picture of God's plan form beginning to end!

Fourth, the dramatic description of the events related to the four horsemen refer to recent events that the church and Rome in the first century had already experienced. Included are the defeat of the Romans by the Parthian army in 62, earthquakes reported to have taken place in 60, the four-year horror of the Jewish war of rebellion leading up to the destruction of Jerusalem in 66–70, the consequent famine that ravaged Judea, the Neronian persecution of 68, and finally, the eruption of Mount Vesuvius in 79. Whether these concepts are necessary to understanding Revelation is immaterial, for the saints in Asia would surely have known of these events and may have made some connection to them as occasions of suffering.[4]

THE FIRST SEAL—FIRST HORSEMAN OF THE APOCALYPSE

6:1, 2. *I watched as the Lamb opened the first of the seven seals. Then I heard one of the four living creatures say in a voice like thunder, "Come." [2] I looked, and there before me was a white horse. Its rider held a bow, and he was given a crown, and he rode out as a conqueror bent on conquest.* The first horseman on a **white horse** is commanded by one of the four living creatures to go do God's business. The passive imperative verb *erchou* (translated in the NIV, the RSV, and the NRSV as *"come"*) has the force of a command to "go and do your thing." When coupled with the statement that the first horseman "was given a crown," the command *to go* is even stronger, implying God's blessings on his service. The passive imperative construction *edothē* (*he was given*) is considered by scholars to imply *divine permission* granted by God. Beale, Aune, Osborne, and others draw attention to this use of the divine passive in Revelation.[5] In place of *come* one could and possibly should translate it as "go." "

There are some textual variants regarding "come," implying that this is an invitation to the seer, John, calling him to come and see rather than a command to the horseman to go. However, the reading *erchou* as a command to the horseman is stronger than the variant reading *erchou kai eidon*. I agree with Beale regarding the divine imperative *erchou* and divine passive *edothē*:

> The unloosing of the first seal by Christ represents a decree from the throne room carried out by one of the throne attendants. . . . That this command originates from the throne room is emphasized by the description of the command "as a voice of thunder," which echoes 4:5, where the "voices (sounds) and thunders" arising "from the throne" are found in direct association with the four cherubim (cf. 4:6). In this light, the thunderous voices in 4:5 may be understood as the decree of God (or Christ) concerning tribulation now being carried out by the cherubim or anticipating their work.[6]

While many commentators believe the white horse represents war, there is disagreement over whether the white horse represents Christ since he is elsewhere in Revelation seen as riding in judgment and victory on a white horse (19:11–16).[7] Again, several see in the four horsemen, in particular this first horseman, "satanic forces attempting to defeat and oppress believers spiritually through deception, persecution, or both.[8] This figure has been interpreted both positively (Christ and the gospel), and negatively (military conquest, the Antichrist, the sun god Mithras, the Parthians, and Apollo), but it certainly represents human lust for war in general, and its consequences.[9]

The rider of the white horse has a bow, was given a crown, and rides out as a conqueror. A cavalry rider with a bow certainly would be reminiscent of Parthian warriors, not Roman infantry. *Crowns* (*stephanoi*) have already been used symbolically as rewards for *victory* (2:10), and *conquering* (*nikaō, conquer, vanquish, overcome*) is a major theme for John's message. That this rider is a victorious conqueror holds several implications for the saints in Asia. First, they would know that the Romans could be defeated, as in the case of the Parthians; second, that God could use a conquering army for his purpose; and third, that there would be no permanent peace under Roman rule. God had the power to send and use victorious armies for his purpose.[10]

THE SECOND SEAL—THE SECOND HORSEMAN

6:3–4. *When the Lamb opened the second seal, I heard the second living creature say, "Come.* [4] *Then another horse came out, a fiery red one. Its rider was given power to take peace from the earth and to make men slay each other. To him was given a large sword.* Most commentators agree that the second, third, and fourth horsemen are a continuation of the narrative begun with the first horseman. They represent evil forces that God can use for his purpose.[11] This second rider was given power (divine permission) to take peace from the earth, symbolizing civil war, rebellion, and internecine warfare. Civil war and internal insecurity were part of the Roman scene. The history of the period of Seleucid and Antiochian rule over Israel in the era just prior to the Roman occupation of Israel and then the constant rebellion of Israel against Roman suzerainship would certainly remind the saints that this world would never be without some civil war, some form of political unrest. In the life of the first-century church, there would never be an ideal peaceful citizenship. God can use rebellion and civil unrest to bring about his purpose and remind depraved humanity that they do not have the answer to lasting peace. The large sword in Revelation typically represents authority. This horseman has God's authority to keep humanity off balance.

THE THIRD SEAL—THE THIRD HORSEMAN

6:5–6. *When the Lamb opened the third seal, I heard the third living creature say, "Come." I looked, and there before me was a black horse. Its rider was holding a pair of scales in his hand.* [6] *Then I heard what sounded like a voice among the four living creatures, saying, "A quart of wheat for a day's wages, and three quarts of barley for a day's wages, and do not damage the oil and the wine."* The third and fourth seals follow the same pattern as the first two. A horseman is given divine authority to come forth and bring suffering on the earth. This rider represents famine, a natural corollary of war. The scale in ancient time represented honest justice. A quart of wheat was barely enough to feed one person for one day, and three quarts of barley were barely enough to feed a small family for one day. A day's wages were barely enough to purchase a quart of wheat and three quarts of barley.[12] The price was nothing short of enormous.[13] The oil and wine relate to the theme of famine.[14] The point is that God has the power to both permit and control famine.

THE FOURTH SEAL—THE FOURTH HORSEMAN

6:7–8. When the Lamb opened the fourth seal, I heard the voice of the fourth living creature say, "Come."[8] *I looked, and there before me was a pale horse. Its rider was named Death, and Hades was following close behind him. They were given power over a fourth of the earth to kill by sword, famine and plague, and by the wild beasts of the earth.* The translation "pale horse" comes up a little short of the Greek *hippos chlōros*. The Greek *chlōros* means *a yellowish green*, but can be used of a person *"pale as the color in sickness as contrasted with his appearance in health."*[15] This horseman represents a deathly image. In fact, the rider's name is Death. *Hadēs* does not mean hell. It refers to *the underworld as the place of the dead*. Death follows this horseman wherever he rides.

Metzger notes that the four scenes are like a cameo, small vignettes of God's judgments being worked out in history. He observes that one of John's distinguishing features is his attempt to show how the exercise of power fits into the divine scheme of things. God is the absolute ruler of the world who has given to humans the power of free will. When they abuse this gift, suffering and disaster result. Abuse of this freedom brings divine justice. The disasters are the working out of God's righteous laws for the universe. God does not approve of famine and suffering, but they must follow when men persist in opposing God's rule. The woes of the four horsemen are the result of not taking God seriously.[16] God does not arbitrarily decree these disasters and sufferings, but they are nevertheless the result of his divine judgments on evil. The salient point in Revelation is that God can and does use tragedies and suffering to bring about his eternal purpose of redemption. The narratives of the Old Testament prophets clearly show that God's plan for the universe includes both judgment and redemption.

In spite of God's judgments on evil men for their refusal to repent he still continues to offer opportunities for repentance as illustrated in the text cited above. God's plan for the universe includes both judgment and redemption. This is clearly seen in the narratives of the Old Testament prophets.

We will notice shortly when John discusses the plagues brought on men in 9:20, 21 that *the rest of mankind that were not killed by these plagues still did not repent of the work of their hands; they did not stop worshiping demons, and idols of gold, silver, bronze, stone and wood—idols that cannot see or hear or walk.*[21] *Nor did they repent of their murders, their magic arts, their sexual immorality or their thefts.*

When the next seal is opened, a cry comes from the suffering saints for justice and vindication. This cry or prayer becomes a central theme in John's working out of God's plan as revealed in Revelation. Although the saints are suffering, God has a plan to resolve this and reward his saints for their anguish.

THE FIFTH SEAL—THE MARTYR'S CRY FOR JUSTICE AND VINDICATION

6:9–11. *When he opened the fifth seal, I saw under the altar the souls of those who had been slain because of the word of God and the testimony they had maintained.* [10] *They called out in a loud voice, "How long, Sovereign Lord, holy and true, until you judge the inhabitants of the earth and avenge our blood?"* [11] *Then each of them was given a white robe, and they were told to wait a little longer, until the number of their fellow servants and brothers who were to be killed as they had been was completed.* By inserting this prayer as one of the seals of the scroll, John drives home that the saint's suffering and prayers for justice are central to the theodicy of Revelation. John sees an altar and beneath it the souls of those *who had been slain* for the word of God. At 5:9 the term *slain*, referring to the lamb, had sacrificial implications. Here it is the souls of those who had been slain, presumably the souls of the martyred saints, that John has in mind.[17] The Greek term *esphagmenōn* is often associated with slaughtering a lamb on an altar.[18] The word group carries the idea of violent death including that of a sacrificial nature. The Christian understanding was that Jesus' cruel death was in fact a sacrifice of love for man. This would give some meaning to the cruel death of the martyrs as a sacrifice of love to God. The souls that John describes are *under the altar*. The connection to Jesus' sacrificial death is obvious. The association of their death with an altar implies two possibilities, either the altar of sacrifice or the altar of incense and prayer. Both are implied.[19] John blends two significant possibilities into one powerful message.

John clarifies the reason for the saints having been slain. It was *because of the word of God and the testimony they had maintained.* I prefer the reading of the RSV, *those who had been slain for the word of God and for the witness they had borne.* This specifies more clearly the meaning of the imperfect verb *eichon, referring to the testimony they had made.*[20] The imperfect verb emphasizes their continual action in the past, or faithfulness regarding their testimony. Two meanings are possible: They were slaughtered *because of the word of God*, or they were slaughtered *because of the testimony they had made*. John introduces the two phrases with the preposition *dia*, coupled with accusative nouns *ton logon* and *tēn maturian. Dia* with the accusative noun can be "causal, to indicate a reason, *on account of, because of, for the sake of.*"[21] These two phrases state the reason for the saints having been slain: because of, or on account of the message of God revealed in Revelation that they had faithfully held or made regarding Jesus. They had been slain because of the message from God and because of their faithful adherence to Jesus as Lord, not Caesar.

The expression *because of the word of God* could be a subjective genitive, translated as *because of the word that comes from God*, that is *the revelation from God*, or it could be an objective genitive, *because of the word that belongs to God*. Both translations would be possible within the context. In agreement with 1:2 and 1:9 I prefer **the word of God** to be a subjective genitive, the message that *came from God*, that is, the message of revelation.

Commentators have identified a formulaic statement that draws on similar texts in Revelation such as 1:2, 9; 6:9.[22] This formulaic expression at 6:9, *for the word of God and for the witness they had borne* is similar to that of 1:2, *who bore witness to the word of God and the testimony of Jesus Christ*. Different and somewhat confusing conclusions regarding the genitive construction of these two statements reflect diverse opinions!

Osborne observes that the statements of 6:9 could be "based on a formula that occurs four times in the book (1:2, 9; 6:9; 20:4), with 12:7 and 14:12 paraphrasing the formula."[23] He indicates that in the case of these four formulaic statements the expression *of God* could be considered either subjective or objective genitives, but prefers seeing it as an objective genitive *concerning or for God*. A subjective genitive *from God* would refer to the message of Revelation. An objective genitive would read *they were slain because of the word concerning God*. He is firm in his view that the statements relating to the testimony Jesus had made at 1:9 and consequently that of 6:9 must be objective genitives, hence *of God* should also be an objective genitive meaning *referring to or concerning God*.[24] Aune does not agree with Osborne, and Beale prefers a general genitive, which is in his opinion an "intentional ambivalence."[25]

Within the formula concept, parallels can be recognized between *the testimony of Jesus* (1:2, 9) and *the testimony they had borne* (6:9). If *the testimony of Jesus* is a subjective genitive, which is what some commentators find, then should not the *testimony they had borne* also possibly correspond to a subjective genitive indicating a testimony from the saints? Beckwith and Charles who find a subjective genitive in all four texts concerning Jesus; hence they consider *the testimony they had borne* to be parallel to 1:2, *the testimony of Jesus* (*of Jesus* being a subjective genitive, cf. comments at1:2) and to refer therefore to the testimony *they had made about Jesus*.[26] However, the problem is further compounded by the fact that John joins the two phrases with the coordinating conjunction *kai*, which in this case could serve as an *epexegetical kai*. In this construction the second phrase, *the testimony they had borne* is a phrase that further defines the first phrase, *the word of God*. Reading 6:9 this way would mean the saints were slain "*because of the message of God, that is, the testimony they had borne concerning Jesus*."

Beale bypasses the "road block of opinion" by defining the two genitives as general genitives, preferring the resulting ambiguity, which he believes is intentional. Beckwith, Charles, and Aune, however, prefer a consistent subjective meaning throughout while recognizing some alternate possibilities.[27] There is always some ambivalence in genitive constructions, and one should be sensitive to both alternatives, and not succumb to the simplest solution.

Although Osborne's view is a minority one, perhaps we should not exclude it from all consideration. There may be some value in determining whether in the context of 6:9 his alternative voice has some meaning. We should concede that John is not rigid in his use of images in Revelation and varies them to suit his purpose.

Perhaps we should not hold John to our strict views of formulaic parallelism and grant him the freedom to move form subjective to objective genitive as suits his context and purpose!

John makes a similar comment at 12:17, where he speaks of the rest of the woman's offspring (the church as the messianic community of faith) bearing *testimony to Jesus* (RSV and Beale).[28] Surely in the context of Revelation, the slaughtered saints' testimony concerned Jesus, that he alone is Lord of Lords and King of Kings. In the face of the Roman imperial cult and the testimony that Caesar Domitian was Lord, the Christian testimony would have led to persecution and death. If Osborne's view has value, then the combined expressions may refer to "those who obey God's commandments, referring in this case to their testimony concerning Jesus."[29] The two expressions might mean that the saints were martyred because of their adherence to the message and commands of God, which resulted in their testimony concerning the lordship of Jesus.

6:10. The souls of the martyred saints cried out in a loud voice for justice and vindication, *How long, Sovereign Lord, holy and true, until you judge the inhabitants of the earth and avenge our blood?* In spite of their suffering and martyrdom, they recognize God as the Sovereign Lord. *Ho despotēs* (*Sovereign Lord*) is an unusual address for God and is found only here in Revelation in the New Testament in reference to God. It means *master, owner, lord*. The expression is used seventeen times of God in the LXX and frequently in early Jewish literature. Here it refers not to Jesus, but to the almighty God.[30] Furthermore, the saints in spite of their suffering and martyrdom recognize God as sovereign, powerful, holy, and true. The reference to the holy and true affirms that God is a genuine God who is wholly different from all other beings. This address is an affirmation of the majesty of God and refers to the absolute authority of God.[31] The cry for justice, vindication, and vengeance, although questioned by some (Charles and Kiddle), is in keeping with the pattern of imprecatory psalms and prayers in the Old Testament (cf. Ps. 6:3; 74:10; 79:5; 80:4) and should be interpreted in the context of the deep anguish of the saints, yet also in their confidence that God will judge their oppressors righteously. The expression *inhabitants of the earth* refers to those who worship the beast and who persecute the saints.

6:11. *Then each of them was given a white robe, and they were told to wait a little longer, until the number of their fellow servants and brothers who were to be killed as they had been was completed.* The RSV is a better translation: *Then they were each given a white robe and told to rest* (anapauō, *rest, take rest, refresh*) *a little longer, until the number of their fellow servants and their brethren should be complete, who were to be killed as they themselves had been.* At 3:4–5 white garments or robes were given to those who were worthy or who had conquered and died as martyrs. Here again, as in chapter 3, John assures the saints that martyrdom is interpreted by God as conquering and victory. The saints were *told to rest a little longer*, implying that God had heard their prayers but there was still work that needed to be completed in his ultimate plan. This little phrase becomes a minor key to the message of Revelation, for in 10:6 God responds that *there* *should be no more delay,* [7] *but that in the days of the trumpet call to be sounded by the seventh angel, the mystery of God, as he announced to his servants the prophets, should be fulfilled.* God has heard their cry and will respond in due course as he carries out his plan. He is working that plan in spite of seemingly contrary circumstances. The unusual comment *until the number of their fellow servants and their brethren should be complete* has caused considerable discussion. The Greek *heōs plerōthōsin* is translated here *until the number . . . should be complete.* To the western mind, this implies that God has a fixed number of people that must die before he will act to save his people. However, this comment should not be interpreted literally.[32] In addition to 6:11, similar references to this expression appear elsewhere in the New Testament (see Rom. 11:12, 25). Citing texts such as 1 Enoch 47:1–4, 4 Ezra 4:35–37, and 2 Baruch 23:4–5, most commentators see in this terminology an emphasis on a divine plan. While God is working, others unfortunately will also have to suffer and die as martyrs. This is not God's will, but is the consequence of the working of Satan, the evil enemy of God. In 9:20 God's plan incorporates an opportunity for even the evil persecutors to repent; he has an eternal gospel to preach to them (14:6). The story of Revelation demonstrates that those who have died from martyrdom recognize this; hence, as told at 4:10 they throw their crowns before God at his feet and worship him. Because of the faithfulness of the saints to God and his purpose, suffering and martyrdom in an evil world is inevitable (13:9–10; cf. Eph. 1:3–11). The strange expression to the Western mind simply means that God is still working his plan and unfortunately others will have to die before God completes his plan which includes offering many others, even their tormentors, the chance to repent.

Bauckham observes that although the apocalyptic references cited above have minor differences, they all seem to draw on a common apocalyptic tradition, and that John was obviously aware of this.[33] The closing clause of this fifth seal, *who were to be killed as they themselves had been,* informs the martyred saints that Satan still is active and that others will die (*apoktennēsthai,* "die," "be put to death") as martyrs for their faith as God works his plan, just as they had died for their faith in God's plan.

THE SIXTH SEAL—APOCALYPTIC UPHEAVALS

6:12–17. *I watched as he opened the sixth seal. There was a great earthquake. The sun turned black like sackcloth made of goat hair, the whole moon turned blood red,* [13] *and the stars in the sky fell to earth, as late figs drop from a fig tree when shaken by a strong wind.* [14] *The sky receded like a scroll, rolling up, and every mountain and island was removed from its place.* [15] *Then the kings of the earth, the princes, the generals, the rich, the mighty, and every slave and every free man hid in caves and among the rocks of the mountains.* [16] *They called to the mountains and the rocks, "Fall on us and hide us from the face of him who sits on the throne and from the wrath of the Lamb.* [17] *For the great day of their wrath has come, and who can stand?"* In this pericope John draws on a prominent apocalyptic theme with special meaning for his message. Speaking of a great earthquake, John is drawing on one of the most regular features of Jewish apocalyptic.[34] There is a rich Old Testament background behind the apocalyptic earthquake; it is a sign of God's righteous judgment upon nations for their disobedience and evil.[35]

In this pericope John not only pulls together Old Testament and traditional Jewish apocalyptic images of earthquakes, but combines these with several other traditional apocalyptic images, all of which draw attention to God's judgment on evil nations that oppose his divine will and plan. Figuratively, the sun, the moon, the stars, the sky, and the mountains are all affected by the opening of this dramatic sixth seal. Each of these images, along with reference to earthquakes, powerfully shapes the traditional apocalyptic genre as signs of God's impending judgment. In Exodus 10:22, the plague of darkness on Egypt must have featured in the apocalyptic mindset of God's judgment on persecuting nations. The images of 6:12–13 are vital to understanding this piece of apocalyptic genre:

1. A great earthquake occurred.
2. The sun turned to darkness (turned black like sackcloth made of goat hair).
3. The moon turned to blood.
4. The stars fell from the sky.
5. The sky rolled up like a scroll.
6. The mountains and islands were removed from their place.

Even a cursory reading of the above list would reveal that it is only the Almighty God, the creator and ruler of heaven and earth that can bring these things about.

An examination of the contexts in which these dramatic expressions appear in the Old Testament, the New Testament, and the apocalyptic tradition reveal a common thread throughout.

Text	Contents	Judged
Isa. 13:10–13	Earth, stars, sun, moon	Babylon
Isa. 24:1–6, 19–23	Earth desolate, suffering, moon, sun	All mankind for sin
Isa. 34:4	Mountains, heaven, sky rolled up	The nations
Jer. 4:23–28	Earth, heavens, mountains, heavens black	Judah, Jerusalem
Ezek. 32:6–8	Mountains, heavens, stars, sun, moon	Pharaoh and Egypt
Joel 2:10	Earthquake, heavens, sun, moon, stars	Zion, Judah, Jerusalem
Joel 2:30–31	Heavens, earth, blood, fire, smoke, sun, moon	Jerusalem
Joel 3:15–16	Sun, moon, stars, heavens, earthquake	Zion, Jerusalem
Amos 8:8–10	Land tremble, sun, earth	Israel
Matt. 24:29	Sun, moon, stars, heaven	Jerusalem
Mark 13:24–25	Sun, moon, stars, heaven	Jerusalem

Test. Moses 10:3–6	Earth, mountains, sun, moon, stars, sea	Syria (Antiochus IV), Rome
4 Ezra 5:4–8	Earth confused, sun, moon, blood, chaos, fire	Rome
Summary	Earthquakes, heavens, sun, moon, stars	Nations are judged.

A common thread runs through each of these "apocalyptic" texts. In each case the context is the judgment of nations for their disobedience and opposition to God's plans. The nations are judged, and chaos results.

Thus in the sixth seal a nation is being judged! The context of Revelation at the close of the first century points specifically to the Roman Empire. The prayers of the martyred saints in the fifth seal which requested vindication and judgment on their oppressors for their faithful death are being answered. The sixth seal reveals that God will judge Rome for its disobedience and oppression of God's people.

Highlighting the confusion encountered in interpreting this complex pericope, Beale observes, that "all commentators agree that the cosmic phenomena of 6:12–14 connote judgment as in all the OT and NT contexts, but they disagree whether this is merely a temporal tribulation before the actual, final judgment and the end of the cosmos or whether it is the last judgment itself and the very end of the world."[36] He concludes that these dramatic scenes depict the "inauguration of the last judgment," not trials preceding that judgment. Furthermore, he argues that 6:12–14 is "a figurative sketch" of the final judgment.[37] He is aware that some commentators dispute whether the language of 6:2–14 speaks of the final judgment or possibly of earlier judgments, but is firm in his opinion that these scenes do just that. Osborne, likewise, although he observes that the language of 6:12–14 is frequently used of judgment scenes, agrees that in this case it refers to the final apocalyptic judgment at the end of the world.[38]

A survey of the more comprehensive commentaries on Revelation (Swete, Beckwith, Charles, Caird, Kiddle, Mounce, Beale, Aune, Osborne) reveals that this pericope, 6:1–12 (or even verses 1–17) has given rise to considerable speculation and difference of opinion regarding John's use of highly symbolic apocalyptic judgment language. Many recognize that John did not expect these catastrophic events to take place literally and that he was drawing on a well-known and often repeated apocalyptic tradition. Although some recognize this apocalyptic tradition and the figurative nature of the expressions, they distance their interpretation from the apocalyptic tradition in its historical heritage of judging nations and see them as predictions of the final end of the world. Unfortunately, some are not sensitive to the nature of the inaugurated and proleptic eschatology adopted by John in Revelation.

Beasley-Murray at this point speaks of John's "intelligence and artistic sense."[39] In this pericope we have John at his literary and theological best. Drawing on an apocalyptic tradition going back well into Old Testament prophetic history, he answers the cry of the souls under the altar, "How long before you judge the world and avenge our blood?" The saints under the altar were told to "rest a little longer" while God carried out his plan of redemption. Later at 10:6 they will be told that "there should be no more delay."" It seems strange in light of the context of these apocalyptic expressions that John would answer them with a prediction that God would avenge their blood at the end of the world. Such an interpretation is unnecessary in light of the proleptic eschatology John has developed in Revelation.

The dramatic apocalyptic language in this pericope should not be taken literally, and should be seen within its own tradition as a judgment on evil nations in the past, and now on Rome. Adopting his inaugurated and proleptic eschatological style, John pronounces God's certain imminent judgment on Rome in end-of-the-world terminology. This judgment will finally be fulfilled at the end of time, but is already being inaugurated in history. God's judgment on Rome is described for dramatic effect in end-of-the-world language without implying that John has the end of the world in mind at this point.

Several contextual considerations are vital to understanding this pericope:

1. The environment of the seven churches in Asia facing severe crises and Roman persecution
2. John's unique literary and theological eschatological style
3. The context of 6:12–17 within the flow of thought revealed in the seven seals
4. The prayer of the saints under the altar for vindication and judgment on their oppressors

Thus these apocalyptic predictions should be kept within God's answer to the cry of the saints for vindication, their Roman persecution and martyrdom, and the interlude that follows before the opening of the seventh seal.

The closing comment at the breaking of the sixth seal is "Who can stand before the wrath of the Lamb?" The interlude that follows at 7:1–8 discloses that those who have been marked by the seal of God are able to stand before the wrath of the Lamb. Later (14) it is the saints (the one hundred forty-four thousand) who have conquered who bear the seal of God. Those faithful servants sealed by God have no fear of the wrath of the Lamb that was revealed in the above apocalyptic visions. This wrath is to be poured out on those who oppress God's people and who refuse to obey his will, not on the saints under the altar.

God's judgment of rebellious nations is derived from the highly figurative terminology of the Old Testament apocalyptic tradition, and John has adapted this to answer the saints prayer and speak dramatically of his imminent eschatological judgment on Rome. These judgments in their original context referred not to the end-of-the-world judgment but to God's imminent judgment on nations that opposed his will. God's apocalyptic judgments in the Old Testament texts were all poured out in history and are not awaiting end-of-the-world fulfillment. God has already judged Rome with end-of-the-world consequences!

6:15–17. *Then the kings of the earth, the princes, the generals, the rich, the mighty, and every slave and every free man hid in caves and among the rocks of the mountains.* [16]

*They called to the mountains and the rocks, "Fall on us and hide us from the face of him
who sits on the throne and from the wrath of the Lamb.* [17] *For the great day of their wrath
has come, and who can stand?"* John is given to hyperbole! Revelation 6:15–17 is a good
example of his impressionistic style. He is obviously drawing on the imagery of Isaiah
2:10–19, in which Isaiah speaks of God's judgment on Jerusalem and Judea.

Osborne observes in regard to 6:14 that we have in this verse the final apocalyptic
event, the removal of the mountains and islands. "This image would be very powerful due to the place of mountains in the religious life of the people." Unfortunately,
Osborne projects this language to the end of history, the final judgment of the world.
He fails to see the proleptic eschatology in John's reference to the judgment of the
Lamb on those who have persecuted the saints.[40] However, he is correct in seeing this
as a judgment of those who dwell on earth and who "have 'invaded' and plundered
the people of God."[41] He is correct in assigning this judgment scene to the Roman
Empire and its vassal kings. My problem with Osborne lies in his identifying this as
the final judgment in which God and the Lamb will judge Rome. John's point here,
however, is that God and the Lamb have already judged Rome with final end-of-the-
world judgment implications and severity. The saints needed to be assured that God
and the Lamb have already acted in their behalf. Osborne's discussion is in some ways
apropos, so I quote it here.

> The sevenfold list of people groups in 6:15 is quite similar to the list of those
> in 19:18 whose flesh the carrion birds are invited to eat after the battle of
> Armageddon. Therefore, there is probably a connection between these two
> events. The judgment envisaged will take place in 19:17-18, 21. . . . the picture
> of hiding in caves from an irresistible force is frequent in the OT. Lot and his
> daughters lived in a cave in fear after the destruction of Sodom and Gomorrah
> (Gen 19:30); five Amorite kings hid in a cave after Joshua had destroyed
> their armies (Josh. 10:16); and David hid in a cave from the wrath of Saul (1
> Sam. 22:1). In Sam 13:6 the armies of Israel hid in caves and rocks from the
> Philistines. In particular, the passage probably alludes to Isa 2:10, 19, 21.[42]

John is referring to the judgment of the Lamb on those who have persecuted the saints.
This as a judgment of those who dwell on earth and who "have 'invaded' and plundered
the people of God." The strange apocalyptic pericope assures the saints that God and the
Lamb have already acted in their behalf. So severe is the judgment of God and the Lamb
upon these "invaders" of God's people that they, in similar vein to Isaiah's prediction
regarding Jerusalem and Judea, will figuratively attempt to hide in mountains and caves
from the wrath of the Lamb.

John's words in 6:17, *For the great day of their wrath has come, and who can stand*
do not say that the day of their wrath will come at the final end of the world, but that
it *has come*. First, the word order of the Greek (*hoti ēlthen hē hēmera hē megalētēs orgēs
autōn, kai tis dunatai stathēnai*) is literally "for it has come the day of the great wrath of
theirs, indeed who is able to stand?" The Greek writer normally places thoughts to be

emphasized either at the beginning of a phrase or at the end. Emphasis is provided by word order. Second, *ēlthen* is an aorist indicative third person singular of *erchomai* (to *come, show up*) and as an aorist should be translated "it has already come" which our translators recognize. There is no futurity in this use of this aorist tense. The great day of God's judgment has come; Rome has already in God's plan been judged. The rhetorical question, **who can stand**, is answered by John in the interlude that follows in 7:1-17: those who have been sealed with the seal of God need have no fear of this awesome wrath of God and the Lamb.

The Interlude 7:1–17
The Text
After this I saw four angels standing at the four corners of the earth, holding back the four winds of the earth to prevent any wind from blowing on the land or on the sea or on any tree. [2] Then I saw another angel coming up from the east, having the seal of the living God. He called out in a loud voice to the four angels who had been given power to harm the land and the sea: [3] "Do not harm the land or the sea or the trees until we put a seal on the foreheads of the servants of our God." [4] Then I heard the number of those who were sealed: 144,000 from all the tribes of Israel. [5] From the tribe of Judah 12,000 were sealed, from the tribe of Reuben 12,000, from the tribe of Gad 12,000, [6] from the tribe of Asher 12,000, from the tribe of Naphtali 12,000, from the tribe of Manasseh 12,000, [7] from the tribe of Simeon 12,000, from the tribe of Levi 12,000, from the tribe of Issachar 12,000, [8] from the tribe of Zebulun 12,000, from the tribe of Joseph 12,000, from the tribe of Benjamin 12,000. [9] After this I looked and there before me was a great multitude that no one could count, from every nation, tribe, people and language, standing before the throne and in front of the Lamb. They were wearing white robes and were holding palm branches in their hands. [10] And they cried out in a loud voice: "Salvation belongs to our God, who sits on the throne, and to the Lamb." [11] All the angels were standing around the throne and around the elders and the four living creatures. They fell down on their faces before the throne and worshiped God, [12] saying: "Amen. Praise and glory and wisdom and thanks and honor and power and strength be to our God for ever and ever. Amen." [13] Then one of the elders asked me, "These in white robes—who are they, and where did they come from?" [14] I answered, "Sir, you know." And he said, "These are they who have come out of the great tribulation; they have washed their robes and made them white in the blood of the Lamb. [15] Therefore, "they are before the throne of God and serve him day and night in his temple; and he who sits on the throne will spread his tent over them. [16] Never again will they hunger; never again will they thirst. The sun will not beat upon them, nor any scorching heat. [17] For the Lamb at the center of the throne will be their shepherd; he will lead them to springs of living water and God will wipe away every tear from their eyes."

The Sealing of the One Hundred Forty-Four Thousand—7:1–8.
After this I saw four angels standing at the four corners of the earth, holding back the four winds of the earth to prevent any wind from blowing on the land or on the sea or on any tree. [2] Then I saw another angel coming up from the east, having the seal of the

living God. He called out in a loud voice to the four angels who had been given power to harm the land and the sea:[3] *"Do not harm the land or the sea or the trees until we put a seal on the foreheads of the servants of our God."*[4] *Then I heard the number of those who were sealed: 144,000 from all the tribes of Israel.* [5] *From the tribe of Judah 12,000 were sealed, from the tribe of Reuben 12,000, from the tribe of Gad 12,000,* [6] *from the tribe of Asher 12,000, from the tribe of Naphtali 12,000, from the tribe of Manasseh 12,000,* [7] *from the tribe of Simeon 12,000, from the tribe of Levi 12,000, from the tribe of Issachar 12,000,* [8] *from the tribe of Zebulun 12,000, from the tribe of Joseph 12,000, from the tribe of Benjamin 12,000.*

In this enigmatic listing of those who are sealed by God, John is fully aware of the figurative and theological use of his listing of the twelve tribes of Israel.

7:1. *After this I saw four angels standing at the four corners of the earth, holding back the four winds of the earth to prevent any wind from blowing on the land or on the sea or on any tree.* As in 4:1, *meta tauta eidon* (*after this I saw*) does not imply a chronological sequence following the previous visionary scene as in the sixth seal, but merely introduces another scene of vision that builds on or explains the previous vision in 6:17. This vision is intended to slow the anticipation of the seventh judgment seal by explaining who have no need to fear the wrath of God and the Lamb. John sees *four angels standing at the four corners of the earth, holding back the four winds of the earth to prevent any wind from blowing on the land or on the sea or on any tree.* The four angels at the four corners of the earth are parallel to the four horsemen, who are God's ministering servants who patrol the earth (6:1-8).[43] That there are four horsemen, four winds, and four corners of the earth is no surprise since along with the numbers three, seven, ten, twelve, twenty-four, and multiples of these numbers, four is one of the holy numbers of Jewish mysticism and apocalyptic (Isa. 11:12; Ezek. 7:2; Rev. 20:8; 2 Bar. 6:4–7:2; Test. Asher 7:1–7; 3 Enoch 48:10).

These four winds represent divine judgment against those who dwell on earth and persecute the saints.[44] The four angels' mission is to restrain the destructive winds of judgment. The limitation of the judgments to land, sea, and trees indicates that these judgments are a warnings anticipating a later complete judgment on the dwellers on earth. John will address this later. These different visions or scenes of judgment are not in an evolutionary time sequence; they are rather layers of warnings and partial judgments. That the visions of Revelation are not necessarily sequential but "overlapping" developments of God's warnings and eventual judgments can be seen from the fact that the seventh seal in fact turns into the seven trumpets of 8:1-11:19 and that in 9:20 John observes that the six trumpets of plagues poured out on the earth have not caused evil men (the dwellers on earth, the persecutors of the saints) to repent.

The seventh trumpet at 11:15 reveals God's judgment and triumph over the dwellers on earth. The seventh trumpet is the final trumpet of God's judgment on Rome and those who follow the Roman imperial and civil cult. Now this judgment at 7:2, 3 on the earth, land, sea, and trees is a judgment on the physical earth and serves as the first warning trumpet leading up eventually to God's decisive judgment of Rome at 11:15. In the apocalyptic tradition the physical earth is included in the corruption and suffering caused by man's sin (cf. Rom 8:18-25, in which Paul in apocalyptic style personifies the physical creation.) Furthermore, in 8:1-11:19 the trumpets are blown and judgment is poured out *on the earth*. However, the judgments are under God's restraint and control, and they are not poured out on the saints who are to be sealed with the seal of the living God.

7:2,3. Then I saw another angel coming up from the east, having the seal of the living God. He called out in a loud voice to the four angels who had been given power to harm the land and the sea: [3] *"Do not harm the land or the sea or the trees until we put a seal on the foreheads of the servants of our God."*

These two verses are somewhat repetitious of verse 1; a new angel appears on the scene with the seal of God, and this angel has the power to command the four angels of the winds not to blow until he has completed his sealing of the saints. Who this angel is and why he comes from the east has given cause for considerable debate among commentators.[45] The angel comes from the east, possibly suggesting the region of threatening Parthian warriors, Persia, the perennial threat to the hegemony of Rome. Perhaps this threatening judgment of God against Rome may be what John has in mind.[46]

People being sealed played a significant role in ancient times, especially among many Graeco-Roman cults, as well as in the Jewish tradition. Being sealed was a sign of ownership; slaves were sealed with the seal of their owner.[47] Sealing, however, also connoted protection by the owner. The most significant image of sealing was the seal of blood that was placed in the lintel of a doorpost in Egypt during the original Passover, indicating that the occupants of that house were protected by God.

Both the Old and New Testaments are replete with images of souls being sealed as a sign of God's ownership and protection. Possibly the foundation to John's image of sealing can be traced to Ezekiel 9:4–6. God commanded that the faithful be sealed to protect them from his coming judgment on Jerusalem and Judah.

Similar references to sealing God's people appear in the New Testament. In keeping with the reference in 7:2–3, sealing is normally used in a figurative sense (cf., for example, Eph. 1:13–14;Eph. 4:30; and 2 Cor. 1:22). In the sixth scroll seal of chapter 6, God had warned of his imminent judgment on those who had persecuted the saints. This sealing of chapter 7 is in answer to the cries of the souls who were beneath the altar of sacrifice who had been slain for their faithfulness to Jesus, God promised judgment on their persecutors. God would avenge their blood and vindicate them. However, so threatening was the description of the wrath of God in the sixth seal that men cried "Who can stand in the presence of the day of God's wrath?" Revelation 7:2–3 and the sealing of the saints introduces an interlude that explains that they need not fear the day of imminent wrath, for they are protected by God's life-saving seal. In 13:16 the sealing of the saints here in 7:2–3 stands in stark contrast to those who received the mark of the beast for worshipping the beast (the emperor). In 14:1 John will explain that the one hundred forty-four thousand who are standing with the Lamb on Mount Zion (where God's king, the Lamb reigns) have the "seal" of God's name written on their foreheads. The theme of sealing the saints here in 7, with the numbering of the one hundred forty-four thousand, binds chapters 7 and 14 together.

The One Hundred Forty-Four Thousand

Beale observes, "The identification of the group is debated."[48] Osborne adds, "The list of the twelve tribes is problematic, for no list in the OT has this exact order."[49] Although some difficulty surrounds the identification of the group "numbered" and "sealed" here, together with 7:9–17 and 14:11–5, they play a pivotal role in the message of Revelation.

Rev. 7:4–8. *Then I heard the number of those who were sealed: 144,000 from all the tribes of Israel.* John proceeds by explaining who it is that are sealed, but in doing so challenges the imagination of the reader. Careful reading of the text reveals that John is not speaking literally but theologically or metaphorically. First, he describes the number of those sealed in an unusual manner, twelve thousand from each of the twelve tribes of Israel. Most commentators see 144,000 as a symbol representing completeness (12 by 12 and multiples of 1000 symbolizing completeness). Therefore, initially John sets the tone for a figurative numbering of people to imply some form of numerical completeness. Second, most recognize that the listing of the tribes is not in keeping with the normal Jewish tradition. For instance, normally one would have Reuben listed first (Gen. 35:23–25; Num. 34:19–29; Josh. 21:4–7; 1 Chron. 12:23-39). Here in 7:5 Judah is listed first. Third, in the chapter 7 listing, Dan is omitted. Most agree that this omission is intentional due to Dan's unfaithfulness and fall into idolatry (Judg. 18).[50] Fourth, in an unusual combination of the twelve tribes, John includes Manasseh, and in place of Ephraim (Manasseh's brother) he includes Joseph their father.[51] Furthermore, there is some disparity in the listing of Levi, for instance normally when Joseph is mentioned Levi is not and Ephraim and Manasseh are mentioned. (cf. Num. 1:1-15, Deut. 27:12, 13.) Whichever way one looks at this text, it is difficult to see it as a literal listing of the twelve tribes of Israel. One can safely conclude, therefore, that John is making a figurative theological point rather than doing "literal mathematics"[52] or making a point based in a literal understanding of the twelve tribes.[53]

This discussion, however, raises an additional question: What theological point is John making, and to whom do the one hundred forty-four thousand refer? Some conclude that the number refers to all of God's people. Others see this as referring to the whole church. Or they may represent the believing and saved remnant of Israel. Others conclude that these are literally ethnic Jews or Jewish Christians. Again, some see this as a fulfillment of Romans 11 ("all Israel will be saved")[54] although others reject this view.[55] Perhaps this is another instance of John's creative intertextual[56] use of his sources and Old Testament images.

Three proposals for the number stand out. The first is that it refers to the whole church.[57] This view has some merit, but in light of the context of chapters 7 and 14 is somewhat incomplete in regard to the full implications of the sealing. The second is that the number should refer to martyrs.[58] This too has some merit, but likewise is lacking in light of the relationship of this group with chapter 14. The third is that it refers to the faithful saints who face certain martyrdom and who are concerned over their future and the wrath of the Lamb.[59] This understanding answers more satisfactorily the question of who can stand in the presence of the wrath of the Lamb and the later development of this theme in chapter 14. We will see that chapter 14 is in a military context leading some to conclude that the number 144,000 here in 7 refers to the church or saints militant.

The Church Militant and the Church Victorious

First, I draw the reader's attention to the literary style of recapitulation of images used by John throughout Revelation in which he introduces a concept and then develops it as his narrative matures. Second, Yarbro Collins and Richard Bauckham[60] have focused attention on the context of Revelation as a combat theme. Although at first glance one may not identify the numbering of the twelve tribes as a military theme, in Israel such numbering was a preliminary feature of military conflict (Num. 1:3, 18, 20; 26:2, 4; 1 Chron. 27:23; 2 Sam. 24:1–9). However, in 14:1–5 the imagery projected by John is decidedly military. In 14:4 the hundred forty-four thousand "*are those who did not defile themselves with women, for they kept themselves pure. They follow the Lamb wherever he goes.*" The imagery here, drawn from the Old Testament (1 Sam. 21:4–5; Deut. 20; 23:9–10) obviously has reference to the dedication of an army for military action. With these images, several have concluded that the numbering of the twelve tribes has clear references to military census, military action, and conflict.[61] In this regard, Boring refers to the two groups in 7:4–8 and 14:1–5 as the church militant and the church triumphant.[62] Bauckham describes this group as the messianic army.[63]

Having set 6 and 7, the sealing of the saints and the sixth seal of the scroll, in the proper military context we observe the following:

1. At 6:12–14, great apocalyptic images are presented that imply that God is describing the extent and severity of his judgment on the nations that are opposing his purpose and persecuting his people.
2. At 6:15–17, so threatening is the wrath of God and the Lamb that is about to be poured out on the nations that they try to hide in caves in the mountains from the Lamb's wrath.
3. At 6:17, they cry out "who can stand before the Lamb's wrath?" The saints need assurance that they are safe from the awful threat of the Lamb's wrath.
4. At 7:1–3, the process of the pouring out of the Lamb's wrath is "halted" while the saints are sealed.
5. At 7:4–8, the saints to be sealed are numbered in a military census, as a church militant prepared for battle. They are protected, not from death and martyrdom, but from the wrath of the Lamb.

6. At 7:9–17 (see below), the saints are depicted as ultimately victorious, standing before the throne with the Lamb. They have been sealed and protected from the wrath of the Lamb.

The Interlude Continued
7:9–17, The Great Multitude Robed in White

7:9–10. Dramatically, John shifts attention to another scene, *a great multitude*. When John shifts to another cosmic scene, he is not progressing chronologically, but is renewing and enlarging on the previous scene. In this instance, the scene of the great multitude standing before the lamb is a development of the previous scene. This great multitude is merely another scene describing the hundred forty-four thousand, not necessarily another group of saints. Notice Beale's observation in this regard:[64]

> A number of commentators, including those holding to a literal view of the 144,000, argue that this segment introduces a new group, different from the group in 7:3-8, because that group was precisely numbered, whereas the multitude in 7:9 is without number. Furthermore, the first group is identified as a remnant of Israelites and the second as people from throughout the earth. Others make a distinction along different lines, seeing the 144,000 as martyrs and the second group as all believers, including martyrs. Some see both groups only as martyrs.
>
> However, as others have observed, the likelihood is that there is only one group, portrayed from different perspectives. The first pictures the church as the restored remnant of true Israel, whose salvific security has been guaranteed.... The second picture in 7:9-17 understands the same host from the viewpoint of their vast number.... 7:9-17 describes the heavenly reward of those who have been sealed and able to persevere through their tribulation. . . .

In the rebirth of imagery John describes the first group in new concepts no longer merely the church militant, but now the church victorious. This scene of the great multitude takes John's narrative one step further as he explains the security of the saints from the wrath of the Lamb. In 7:4–8 the hundred forty-four thousand are described as the church militant about to go into battle. In this scene (7:9–17) they are described along with a host of other conquerors standing with the Lamb, victorious, and ready to worship God at his throne of judgment. John will describe them again in 14:1-5 with the Lamb standing on Mount Zion. In 14:1 Mount Zion represents the heavenly "place" from where God's king reigns.

John sees the hundred forty-four thousand now through a different shift of his kaleidoscope as being a great multitude *from every nation, tribe, people and language, standing before the throne and in front of the Lamb*. It seems best to understand this scene as John being granted a preview of heaven with the martyred saints who as the church militant had been sealed (7:3–8) now standing before the throne of God and the Lamb.[65] We are taken back to chapter 4 in a mystical "temple chariot"[66] experience to the throne room of God. The Lamb is now also present. The fact that *they were wearing white robes and were holding palm branches in their hands . . . and crying out in a loud voice: "Salvation belongs to our God, who sits on the throne, and to the Lamb"* reinforces the view that they represent the church victorious who have conquered the enemy, Satan and Rome. The white robes were promised by Jesus to saints that conquered (3:5). Palm branches were associated with celebration and victory processions.[67] In the context of combat mythology, it is better to translate *sotēria* as "victory."[68] The conquering martyrs do not attribute the victory to their work but to God who sits on his throne and to the Lamb. John will develop this further in 12:10–11, when he notes that the victory is the result of the blood of the Lamb (the cross) and the faithfulness of the saints who *loved not their lives even unto death* (RSV).

Most commentators observe that there are at least three grammatical incongruities in 7:9 that relate to the order of the Greek words. Bauckham states,

> For this reason, the order in which John's standard four-part expression (*ethnē kai phulai kai laoi kai glōssai*) here occurs may not be arbitrary; . . . the placing of *ethnous* first, with grammatical awkwardness (not parallel in other instances of the expression in Revelation) which sets *pantos ethnous* apart from the other three plural members, enables 7:9 . . . to echo the promise to the patriarchs (Gen. 17:4 LXX)[69]

Such grammatical incongruities may be intentional to echo Old Testament promises to the patriarchs (as in Gen. 17:5). Beale and others propose that in keeping with John's stylistic use of his resources, these may be "stylistic signposts further hinting that an OT allusion is to be recognized."[70]

7:11–12. Referring to the *Merkavah*-like throne room scene (4), John notes, *All the angels were standing around the throne and around the elders and the four living creatures. They fell down on their faces before the throne and worshiped God,* [12] *saying: "Amen. Praise and glory and wisdom and thanks and honor and power and strength be to our God for ever and ever. Amen."* In chapter 4 the twenty-four elders threw their crowns down before him who was seated on the throne, joining in with the living creatures and the angels in singing God's worthiness and praise. Here all fall down before God, repeating the sevenfold praise song similar to that of the Lamb in 5:12. God is worthy of all praise and glory. There is no mention of grieving here over their suffering and death, only praise. When suffering for God is set in the correct context, it matures into praise of God.

7:13. *Then one of the elders asked me, "These in white robes—who are they, and where did they come from?"* [14] *I answered, "Sir, you know."* The RSV translates the first words of 7:13 as "Then one of the elders *addressed* me, saying, . . . " This slight difference introduces another of John's stylistic uses of the Old Testament or Hebrew idiom. The Greek word translated here as either "asked" or "addressed" is *apekrithē*, which means "answered." Osborne observes that "this is a Semitic idiom that leads into an explanation of the preceding utterance; in other words, it presupposes John's unasked question,"[71] "who are these in the great multitude that I am seeing in this vision?" In answer to this rhetorical question by the elder, John replies *"Sir, you know,"* implying that he did not know but that the elder did. The term "Sir" (*kurie,* "sir," "lord," "master") implies respect and submission. *These clad in white robes* is a reference to martyrs who have conquered (3:5). The remainder of the question, *where did they come from?* is revealed at 7:14b, *"These are they who have come out of the great tribulation; they have washed their robes and made them white in the blood of the Lamb."*

7:14. *"These are they who have come out of the great tribulation; they have washed their robes and made them white in the blood of the Lamb.* Osborne argues that "there is no evidence in the book that this is a title for this final period" and that in all probability it refers to a tribulation already being experienced by the churches in Asia.[72] Beale draws attention to John's fondness for finding in Daniel 12 a source for his imagery. In Daniel 12:1 the idea of a great tribulation was introduced, referring to "the eschatological opponent" who "persecutes the saints because of their covenant loyalty to God." The same idea is involved in the tribulation in 7:14 "Therefore, the tribulation consists of pressures to compromise faith, these pressures coming from both within the church community through seductive teaching and from without through overt persecution. . . . Whatever its nature, tribulation always comes because of believer's faithfulness to Jesus.[73] *Thlipseōs* is the genitive form of the noun *thlipsis,* which can mean pressure, suffering, oppression, or persecution, depending on context. Since the context of Revelation is combat mythology, oppression, or persecution, *thlipseōs* here is best understood as oppression and suffering rather than tribulation.

Clearly, the elder has identified the great multitude as saints who have come through persecution and martyrdom, in other words, the conquerors of chapters 2 and 3 who are now included among the great saints in heaven. That *they have washed their robes and made them white in the blood of the Lamb* is again an instance of John's rebirth of images, for in 12:10–11 he describes the martyrs as those who have conquered Satan by the blood of the Lamb. It is not simply martyrdom that brings victory, but martyrdom for the cause and cross of Christ that makes the difference.

7:15. Because of their faithful testimony for Jesus, *"they are before the throne of God and serve him day and night in his temple; and he who sits on the throne will spread his tent over them. [16] Never again will they hunger; never again will they thirst. The sun will not beat upon them, nor any scorching heat. [17] For the Lamb at the center of the throne will be their shepherd; he will lead them to springs of living water. And God will wipe away every tear from their eyes."* As in chapter 4, the conquering saints are in the very presence of the throne of God. Where the NIV translates *kai ho kathēmenos epi tou thronou skēnōsei ep autous* as **he who sits on the throne will spread his tent over them,** the RSV has *"he who sits upon the throne will shelter them with his presence."* The verb *skēnōsei* (a future indicative form of the verb of *skēnoō*) means "to live," or "dwell," or take up residence." However, *skēnoō* derives from the noun *skēnē*, which can be translated "tent," "booth," "lodging," or "dwelling." *Skēnoō* stands within a cherished Jewish tradition of God's presence in the wilderness tabernacle and later the holy of holies in the temple, which represented the very presence of God with his people. In contrast to the omnipotent, Holy God dwelling among his people in the tent of dwelling, here the saints dwell with the omnipotent Holy God who sits on his throne in heaven and spreads his protection over them. Beale observes that the image of God sitting on his throne and spreading his tent over them conjures up "a fantastic image that brings together several key biblical themes. It is the omnipotent God . . . who will 'tabernacle' over them." These images signify "the glory of God dwelling among his people for guidance and protection." Beale adds that in the intertestamental period of Judaism the concept of "'Shekinah' became a major concept for the working of God among his people."[74] Aune adds that, during a later rabbinic period, Rabbi Akiba interpreted the expression to mean "under the protection of My cloud . . . implying God's protective presence."[75] Therefore, I prefer the RSV translation "he who sits upon the throne will shelter them with his presence" since it brings out more clearly the fact that the great multitude who have come out of great tribulation now sit in the very presence of the omnipotent God, who spreads his protection over them.

7:16–17. *Never again will they hunger; never again will they thirst. The sun will not beat upon them, nor any scorching heat.* [17] *For the Lamb at the center of the throne will be their shepherd; he will lead them to springs of living water. And God will wipe away every tear from their eyes.* In contrast to their struggles, God will in his infinite love and protection wipe away every tear from their eyes. The background to John's imagery here is obviously Isaiah 49:9–10. Osborne observes that John is apparently making a "midrashic expansion" of God's promise of restoration to Israel in Isaiah 40:10:"They will feed beside the roads and find pasture on every barren hill. [10] They will neither hunger nor thirst, nor will the desert heat or the sun beat upon them. He who has compassion on them will guide them and lead them beside springs of water." The concept of *living water* as *eternal life* certainly draws on the Johannine and Old Testament tradition, notably reflected in Jesus' discussion with the Samaritan woman at the well in Sychar (John 4:10–14).It is also reflected in Jesus' discussion on the bread of life in John 6:35 and Old Testament shepherd images such as Psalm 23:2. Furthermore, John is probably making another midrashic application, this time from Ezekiel 34:11–16, in which God promises to bring his people out from among the nations and to protect them.

The image that *God will wipe away every tear from their eyes* will be developed further in 22:3–4, where in the new Jerusalem, namely, the final home of the saints in heaven, John writes, *"Now the dwelling of God is with men, and he will live with them. They will be his people, and God himself will be with them and be their God.* [4] *He will wipe every tear from their eyes. There will be no more death or mourning or crying or pain, for the old order of things has passed away."* What John is describing in 7:17 is another of his *proleptic eschatological* descriptions of what the final reward of all saints will be. The great multitude who have come out of the great tribulation of suffering under the

Roman system and who as victorious conquering martyrs have received white robes are now pictured as enjoying in advance of the final victory of God, the full rewards of being in the presence of God.

Summary of the Interlude of Revelation 7

The interlude of is strategically placed between the sixth and seventh seals of the scroll of chapter [5].

The seven sealed scroll informed the saints in the seven churches of Asia that their world was not one of complete chaos; that although they were about to encounter suffering and oppression almost beyond comprehension, God was still in control, working his eternal plan of redemption; and that he used evil in his strategy for judging and defeating evil men.

The fifth seal revealed saints beneath a sacrificial altar crying out to God for relief and vindication. They were told to wait patiently while God worked his plan.

The sixth seal revealed God's terrifying judgment against evil nations for their opposition to his plan and oppression of his people. This judgment was so fierce that men would seek to hide from God's wrath. A cry was heard, "Who can stand before the wrath of the Lamb?"

Before the seventh and final seal to God's plan is opened, John deliberately slows the action to explain that the faithful saints need not fear the wrath of the Lamb, for God would "seal them," protecting them from his wrath. They would suffer, but not from the wrath of the Lamb. Demonstrating that the church was in a war with evil, John sees the saints numbered as for a military campaign, the hundred forty-four thousand sealed saints representing the church militant.

John is again taken into the throne room, where he sees a great multitude proclaiming that victory belonged to God who sits on the throne, and to the Lamb. God and the Lamb had triumphed over evil. With God were those who had come out of the great tribulation God had warned that the saints would suffer for their faithfulness, but there were no complaints coming from the saints, for they were now in the protecting presence of the Almighty God.

John is ready to move on to the opening of the seventh and final seal, bringing down the curtain on the first act of the apocalyptic drama of Revelation. God is about to reveal the extent of his terrifying judgment of evil men.

This final seal introduces seven trumpets that reveal the nature and extent of God's judgment on those who dwell on the earth, that is, on those who oppress and persecute God's people. Those who dwell on earth are those who worship the beast (Rome) and who oppose God's purpose by oppressing and persecuting the saints.

THE SEVENTH SEAL INTRODUCING THE SEVEN TRUMPETS—8:1–6

The Text

When he opened the seventh seal, there was silence in heaven for about half an hour. [2] *And I saw the seven angels who stand before God, and to them were given seven trumpets.* [3] *Another angel, who had a golden censer, came and stood at the altar. He was given much incense to offer, with the prayers of all the saints, on the golden altar before the throne.* [4] *The smoke of the incense, together with the prayers of the saints, went up before God from the angel's hand.* [5] *Then the angel took the censer, filled it with fire from the altar, and hurled it on the earth; and there came peals of thunder, rumblings, flashes of lightning and an earthquake.* [6] *Then the seven angels who had the seven trumpets prepared to sound them.*

In this deft linking move John extends the narrative of the wrath of the Lamb against those who dwell on the earth into seven trumpets of God's judgment. By doing this John explains in greater detail God's answer to the saints who had cried out for vindication. They were to wait patiently while God completed his redemptive work. In this series of seven trumpets describing God's judgments, John will introduce the reason for the apparent delay. There is a divine purpose in God's delay, and the saints play a patient role in God's plan.

8:1. When he opened the seventh seal, there was silence in heaven for about half an hour. So important and dramatic is the opening of the seventh seal that all of heaven comes to an expectant standstill. But there is obviously more to the silence than merely the expectation of the seventh seal. Most commentators correctly identify at least six or seven possible backgrounds for John's mention of silence at this point in his narrative, depending on how they are grouped. The following possibilities may lie behind John's "silence."[76]

1. Since there is no real content to the seventh seal, as in the other seals, other than the seven trumpets and bowls that follow, then the seven trumpets and bowls are the contents of the seventh seal. But why this would lead to silence in heaven is not clear.

2. Some see a cessation of God's revelation or divine rest in the silence of heaven.

3. Others identify this silence with the primeval silence before creation and following the final judgment.

4. The possibility of a liturgical silence is seen here, indicating silence in the presence of the Holy.

5. The silence in heaven may be a silence so the prayers of the saints may be heard.

6. So dramatic are the judgments that follow that silence and awe are the natural attitude of all, even those in heaven.

7. Others seemingly see this silence as that of the condemned as they await their judgment.
8. A more probable reason may be the silence of expectation as all heaven awaits God's divine intervention in the affairs of history.

Beale and Osborne observe that the above reasons for the silence are not mutually exclusive and may all be grounded in both the Old Testament and Jewish traditions speaking of God's omnipotence and holiness. Beale finds three possible reasons explaining the "silence," while Osborne summarizes them in two possible sources.[77] Beale writes "In the light of the overall discussion, the 'silence' of Rev. 8:1 can be taken as a metaphor with multifaceted meanings and associations, . . . all of which revolve around the notion of judgment."[78] He identifies these as follows: (1) silence as an indication that God has heard the prayers of the saints, (2) silence as an indication of a revelatory announcement by God, (3) silence in relation to the temple liturgy. Osborne identifies the following two prime reasons for the dramatic silence: (1) the hushed expectancy for the judgment of God that is about to unfold, (2) the liturgical silence in heaven relating to the incense and the prayers of the saints.

John was fully aware of the dramatic implications surrounding his use of the metaphor silence in heaven. The silence served to dramatize the expectancy surrounding God's judgment as an answer to the prayers of the saints, an expectancy that would encourage traumatized saints and assure them of God's vindication of their suffering.

8:2. *And I saw the seven angels who stand before God, and to them were given seven trumpets.* It is a common view of commentators from as early as Beckwith (1919) and Charles (1920) that the seven angels represent the seven archangels of the Presence who among other duties stand before God and express the prayers of troubled saints (see *Tob.* 12:15; *Test. of Levi* 8:2; 1 *Enoch* 90:21; 3 *Enoch* 17:1, and *passim* in the Jewish apocalyptic, rabbinic, and mystical traditions).[79] There may be some connection with the seven angels of the seven churches of 1:20. These seven angels (or archangels) are given seven trumpets, which symbolize seven judgments of God. The connection of the seven trumpets to the sixth seal, the awesome terror of the coming wrath of the Lamb, and the seven bowls of wrath (15 and 16) cannot be missed. Osborne notes:

> The content of the scroll is now unveiled in the trumpets and bowls. The trumpet judgments form the middle of the three septets but are more closely related in style and substance to the bowls of judgments. The seals are preliminary judgments that explore the depravity of humankind and demonstrate the necessity of judgment. The saints are sealed from the wrath of God and the judgments themselves but face the wrath of the earth-dwellers. The silence in heaven is an expectant hush awaiting the action of God, but that is not to be just an outpouring of wrath but God's answer to the imprecatory prayers of the saints (6:9–11 recapitulated in 8:3–4). Thus there is worship (the golden censer with incense) behind the justice.[80]

8:3, 4. *Another angel, who had a golden censer, came and stood at the altar. He was given much incense to offer, with the prayers of all the saints, on the golden altar before the throne.* [4] *The smoke of the incense, together with the prayers of the saints, went up before God from the angel's hand.* John introduces *another angel*, different from the seven archangels, who brings with him the imprecatory prayers of the saints (6:9–11) to present them to God. John intends the reader to understand the connection of the trumpets of judgment about to be sounded with the prayers of the saints. These judgments are not only to be seen as judgments against the dwellers on earth (the oppressors and persecutors of the saints), but also as God's answer to the prayers of the saints and of their vindication. This "other angel" has been identified as Christ in his intercessory role but this does not seem to be in keeping with the flow of thought of the priestly function of angels in Revelation.[81] J. Ramsey Michaels observes that the one referred to here to as *another angel* has become "a kind of high priest ministering in behalf of a larger priesthood, the people of God."[82] However, the larger group of priests this angel represents is the saints under the altar who have cried out to God for vindication. Caird, however, draws attention to *the prayers of all the saints* rather than merely those martyred and addressed in 6:10.[83] This may be true, but in the context of Revelation, this does not detract from the trumpets' being in response to the cry for vindication since these judgments are only on those who dwell on earth, namely, those who worship the beast and oppress the saints. Osborne is correct in observing "The major thrust is that the fiery judgments . . . are God's response to cries of his people and his vindication of his followers for all they have suffered."[84]

The liturgical combination of prayer, altar of sacrifice, incense, and fire has clear Old Testament roots (Lev. 16:11–13, Exod. 29:18, 25, and Ps. 141:1–2). John's combination of the altar of prayer and the altar of sacrifice in 6:10, where he pictures the *prayers* of the saints beneath the altar with their having offered their lives as a *sacrifice* to God, echoes concepts associated with the offering of Aaron at the mercy seat of God on the Day of Atonement (Exod. 29:18, 25; Lev. 16:11–13; Ps. 141:1–2).

8:5, 6. *Then the angel took the censer, filled it with fire from the altar, and hurled it on the earth; and there came peals of thunder, rumblings, flashes of lightning and an earthquake.* [6] *Then the seven angels who had the seven trumpets prepared to sound them.* John continues to tie the theology he has been developing to the prayers of the saints for vindication (6:10):

> God's formal acknowledgement of the angel's presentation of the saints' prayers and his positive response is the unmentioned link between vv. 4 and 5. This is evident as we recognize v. 5 as a clear divine answer to the petition in 6:10. The verse formally interprets the scenes of woe in 6:12–17 and 8:1 as the answer to the prayer of 6:10. . . . In response to the saints' prayer God sends judgment on the earth. The angel is the angel who executes the judgment.[85]

The altar, the place associated with the mercy of God, has in this scene become the source of divine judgment. In the Jewish tradition mercy and judgment, love and wrath, are inseparable characteristics of God's nature.[86] When the angel throws the censor filled with fire, representing the prayers of the saints, on the earth, signifying that this censor of prayer has now become the censor of divine judgment, *there came peals of thunder, rumblings, flashes of lightning and an earthquake*. Each of these phenomena is common to the Old Testament and Jewish apocalyptic tradition and is usually associated with divine theophanies and judgments. Bauckham has argued that earthquakes in the Old Testament "accompanied the expected coming of God as King and Judge." He observes that "earthquakes in the Apocalypse of John play no part in the preliminary judgments. Their role . . . is the more traditional Old Testament one of heralding the coming of God in judgment."[87] In 4:5 John records that *from the throne came flashes of lightning, rumblings and peals of thunder*. In 11:19, regarding the seventh and final trumpet of judgment, John writes, *Then God's temple in heaven was opened, and within his temple was seen the ark of his covenant. And there came flashes of lightning, rumblings, peals of thunder, an earthquake and a great hailstorm*. Revelation 8:6 and 11:19 form an *inclusio* emphasizing that the trumpets of this section speak to the extent of God's wrath and judgments on those who dwell on the earth, namely, those who worship the Beast (13:14, 15) and who oppress the saints and oppose God's purpose. In keeping with this concept, Bauckham suggests that the "theophany formula in 8:5 encompasses the whole series of trumpet judgments up to its recurrence in 11:19."[88]

8:6. John now announces that *the seven angels who had the seven trumpets prepared to sound them*. The sounding of trumpets draws on several Old Testament events and provides a transition from the seventh seal to the outpouring of God's judgments on those who dwell on the earth, that is Rome and those who oppress the saints. The mention of trumpets in 8:6 is in keeping with John's use of Old Testament images to impress on his readers the significance of his visions.

Trumpets were sounded in the Old Testament and the Jewish apocalyptic and other traditions for a number of reasons, most of which were connected with the holiness and sovereignty of God:

1. They announce a holy war against Israel's enemies or against Israel as the enemy of God (Judg. 7:16–22; Jer. 4:5–21; 42:14; 51:27; Ezek. 7:14; Hos. 8:1)
2. They blow at the enthronement of a king (1 Kgs. 1:34, 39; 2 Kgs. 9:13)
3. They are associated with the kingship of God (Ps. 47:5; 98:6; Num. 23:21; Zech. 9:14)
4. They gather God's people for some form of convocation or ceremonial procession; three of which mention seven trumpets (Josh. 6:1; 1 Chron. 15:24; Neh. 12:41).
5. They signal the arrival of the Day of the Lord (Zech. 9:14; Zeph. 1:14–16; *Apoc. of Abraham* 31:1, 4; *4 Ezra* 6:23; *Sib. Or.* 4:124; *Greek Apoc. of Ezra* 4:36)
6. They are associated with all feasts, on the first day of each month, and for the daily sacrifices (Num. 10:10; *29:1-6*)

7. The sound as an alarm signal, calling Israel to repentance in the face of immi-
    nent divine judgment (Jer. 4:5; 6:1, 17; Ezek. 33:3-6; Isa. 58:1; Joel 2:1, 15).[89]

In 8:6, they are connected to many of the above occasions but specifically in this case
the seven trumpets remind the reader to the plagues poured out in judgment on Egypt
(Exod. 7). Osborne observes regarding 8:7 that "The purpose is to prove the sovereignty
of God and to give a last chance for repentance. . . . The trumpet judgments intensify the
seals, affecting a third of the earth, and are intensified in turn by the bowls that affect
the whole earth."[90]

The connection of the seven trumpets of judgment, six of which are warning trumpets, with the seventh being the trumpet of judgment reminiscent of the seven trumpets
blown at the fall of Jericho (Josh. 6) is unmistakable since the seven trumpets at Jericho
were blown by seven priests (Josh. 6). Now seven angels (8–9) who are priestly figures
blow seven trumpets (8:5–6).[91]

The message of 5:1-8:6, has centered on the great seven-sealed scroll presented to
Jesus from God's hand. The prayers of the saints for vindication in 6:10 have formed a
pivotal point around which much of this section has hinged. The martyred saints have
called for vindication, and God has promised immediate judgment on the persecutors.
But something new is about to be revealed. The sovereign God of the universe is also
the loving God of redemption. Before he pronounces eschatological judgment on those
who dwell on earth, who worship the beast, and who persecute his people, God extends
repentance and an eternal gospel (9:20 and 14:6-7) to them. The trumpets of 8:6 are not
final judgments on the earth, but warning judgments on the dwellers on earth, calling
them to repent and worship God, not man (the Roman emperor). The purpose of these
seven trumpets "is to work repentance"[92]

The parallel with 2 Peter 3:3–13 is clear. God pronounces judgment on scoffers and
those opposed to his will, but before he brings this judgment down on them, he provides
"occasion" for repentance.

Summary of the Interlude of Revelation 7 and the Seventh Seal Revealing Seven Trumpets

The crescendo of theological thought leading up to the announcement of the
seventh seal and its seven trumpets was slowed down by the introduction of
an interlude to reassure the saints that God excluded them from the judgments
about to be revealed. As the hundred forty-four thousand of God's church militant, they are sealed against his wrath. Once more, however, God demonstrates
his patience even with those who oppose him and persecute his servants. The
seven trumpets of judgment are warnings to those who dwell on earth (who persecute the saints and worship the beast, 13:8,14), calling them to repent (9:20, 21).

Chapter 7

The Seven Trumpets

The Second Interlude
8:7–11:19

In keeping with God's love for his creation, and in spite of humanity's rejection, God's grace causes him to give even the rebellious nations an opportunity to repent. The seventh seal of Revelation 8 now turns into seven warning trumpets by which God calls on evil men to repent. Following the sixth warning trumpet of 9:19-20, in which men refuse to repent, God prepares to move toward the consummation of his warning judgments (cf. level V in the chiastic structure below). However, as in chapter 7, John inserts two interludes, one in chapter 10, in which he promises that there will be no more delay in his vindication of the saints and judgment of their enemies, and the other in chapter 11, in which he demonstrates that, even if killed as faithful witnesses and martyrs, they will be raised to be with God in heaven. The purpose of these interludes is to reassure the saints that, since they have been faithful to God, they need not fear his wrath.

In the chiastic structure of Revelation, level III parallels level V. In level III are warning judgments. In level V the judgments are no longer warning, but consummated.

Prologue 1:1–20
      I. The Church in Imperfection (2:1–3:22)
      Seven Letters to the Seven Churches
        II. The Authority of God over Evil Explained (4:1–8:6)
        Seven Seals on the Scroll
          III. The Warning Judgments (8:1–11:19)
          Seven Trumpets

IV. The Lamb—God's Answer to Evil (12:1–14:20)
Seven Unnumbered Figures
V. The Consummated Judgments (15:1–16:21)
Seven Bowls of Wrath
VI. The Authority of God over Evil Exercised (17:1–20:15)
Seven Unnumbered Descriptions of God's Judgments
VII. The Church in Perfection (21:1–22:5)
Seven Unnumbered Descriptions of the Church in Perfection
Epilogue 22:6–21

INTRODUCTION

The previous chapter closed with the linking pericope revealing the opening of the seventh seal and an introduction to the seven trumpets. It is a matter of stylistic choice whether to include 8:1–6 in the previous chapter or to place it here. I have placed it in the previous chapter since it serves as a link between the interlude of chapter 7 and the dramatic blowing of the seven trumpets of warning judgments that are about to be introduced.[1]

The purpose of these seven trumpets is to warn the unbelievers, those who dwell on earth, that they face the wrath of God for their persecution of the saints unless they repent. They also demonstrate the absolute sovereignty of God, who provides them with an eternal gospel and calls them to repentance.[2] These trumpets warn of impending danger.[3] The background to these warnings is the ten plagues against Egypt (Exod. 4–12), where the first nine plagues were a warning, calling on the Pharaoh to repent and release Israel from slavery.

These trumpets do not refer to the final trumpet that will be blown at the final judgment, but are proleptic eschatological judgments pronounced on the enemies of the church in the first century context of Rome, that is, on those who dwell on the earth, who worship the beast, and who persecute the saints. God is warning them that he will judge them soon, with final eschatological judgment, unless they repent. The trumpets purpose is not simply retribution but a call to repentance.[4]

The prayers of the saints in 8:3–5 play a significant role in both the interpretation of this section and of Revelation as a whole. The seven trumpets are blown at the behest of an angel who stood with a golden censor beside the altar and who mixed incense with the prayers of the saints.[5] John is apparently referring to 6:10, where the saints' prayer cried out from beneath the altar, asking God when he would avenge their blood on those who had shed it. John intends these trumpets to be related to God's answer.[6]

The seven trumpets in this section are rich in Jewish imagery and fall into three groupings:

1.   four natural plagues: hail, fire, and blood; the sea becoming blood; the falling star; the darkening of sun, moon, and stars
2.   two demonic plagues: the bottomless pit and four violent angels released

3. a heavenly vision: the kingdom reign of God

This chapter includes discussion of the first six warning trumpets (8:7–21), the little scroll interlude (10:1–11), the two witnesses interlude (11:1–14), and the final warning trumpet (11:15–19).

THE SEVEN TRUMPETS, INCLUDING THE SECOND INTERLUDE
The Text

When he opened the seventh seal, there was silence in heaven for about half an hour.
² And I saw the seven angels who stand before God, and to them were given seven trumpets.

³ Another angel, who had a golden censer, came and stood at the altar. He was given much incense to offer, with the prayers of all the saints, on the golden altar before the throne. ⁴ The smoke of the incense, together with the prayers of the saints, went up before God from the angel's hand. ⁵ Then the angel took the censer, filled it with fire from the altar, and hurled it on the earth; and there came peals of thunder, rumblings, flashes of lightning and an earthquake. ⁶ Then the seven angels who had the seven trumpets prepared to sound them. ⁷ The first angel sounded his trumpet, and there came hail and fire mixed with blood, and it was hurled down upon the earth. A third of the earth was burned up, a third of the trees were burned up, and all the green grass was burned up. ⁸ The second angel sounded his trumpet, and something like a huge mountain, all ablaze, was thrown into the sea. A third of the sea turned into blood,⁹ a third of the living creatures in the sea died, and a third of the ships were destroyed. ¹⁰ The third angel sounded his trumpet, and a great star, blazing like a torch, fell from the sky on a third of the rivers and on the springs of water—¹¹ the name of the star is Wormwood. A third of the waters turned bitter, and many people died from the waters that had become bitter. ¹² The fourth angel sounded his trumpet, and a third of the sun was struck, a third of the moon, and a third of the stars, so that a third of them turned dark. A third of the day was without light, and also a third of the night. ¹³ As I watched, I heard an eagle that was flying in midair call out in a loud voice: "Woe. Woe. Woe to the inhabitants of the earth, because of the trumpet blasts about to be sounded by the other three angels." ⁹ The fifth angel sounded his trumpet, and I saw a star that had fallen from the sky to the earth. The star was given the key to the shaft of the Abyss. ² When he opened the Abyss, smoke rose from it like the smoke from a gigantic furnace. The sun and sky were darkened by the smoke from the Abyss. ³ And out of the smoke locusts came down upon the earth and were given power like that of scorpions of the earth. ⁴ They were told not to harm the grass of the earth or any plant or tree, but only those people who did not have the seal of God on their foreheads. ⁵ They were not given power to kill them, but only to torture them for five months. And the agony they suffered was like that of the sting of a scorpion when it strikes a man. ⁶ During those days men will seek death, but will not find it; they will long to die, but death will elude them.

⁷ The locusts looked like horses prepared for battle. On their heads they wore something like crowns of gold, and their faces resembled human faces. ⁸ Their hair was like women's hair, and their teeth were like lions' teeth. ⁹ They had breastplates like breastplates of iron, and the

sound of their wings was like the thundering of many horses and chariots rushing into battle.
[10] They had tails and stings like scorpions, and in their tails they had power to torment people for five months. [11] They had as king over them the angel of the Abyss, whose name in Hebrew is Abaddon, and in Greek, Apollyon.

[12] The first woe is past; two other woes are yet to come. [13] The sixth angel sounded his trumpet, and I heard a voice coming from the horns of the golden altar that is before God. [14] It said to the sixth angel who had the trumpet, "Release the four angels who are bound at the great river Euphrates." [15] And the four angels who had been kept ready for this very hour and day and month and year were released to kill a third of mankind. [16] The number of the mounted troops was two hundred million. I heard their number. [17] The horses and riders I saw in my vision looked like this: Their breastplates were fiery red, dark blue, and yellow as sulfur. The heads of the horses resembled the heads of lions, and out of their mouths came fire, smoke and sulfur. [18] A third of mankind was killed by the three plagues of fire, smoke and sulfur that came out of their mouths. [19] The power of the horses was in their mouths and in their tails; for their tails were like snakes, having heads with which they inflict injury. [20] The rest of mankind that were not killed by these plagues still did not repent of the work of their hands; they did not stop worshiping demons, and idols of gold, silver, bronze, stone and wood—idols that cannot see or hear or walk. [21] Nor did they repent of their murders, their magic arts, their sexual immorality or their thefts.

[10] Then I saw another mighty angel coming down from heaven. He was robed in a cloud, with a rainbow above his head; his face was like the sun, and his legs were like fiery pillars. [2] He was holding a little scroll, which lay open in his hand. He planted his right foot on the sea and his left foot on the land, [3] and he gave a loud shout like the roar of a lion. When he shouted, the voices of the seven thunders spoke. [4] And when the seven thunders spoke, I was about to write; but I heard a voice from heaven say, "Seal up what the seven thunders have said and do not write it down." [5] Then the angel I had seen standing on the sea and on the land raised his right hand to heaven. [6] And he swore by him who lives for ever and ever, who created the heavens and all that is in them, the earth and all that is in it, and the sea and all that is in it, and said, "There will be no more delay. [7] But in the days when the seventh angel is about to sound his trumpet, the mystery of God will be accomplished, just as he announced to his servants the prophets." [8] Then the voice that I had heard from heaven spoke to me once more: "Go, take the scroll that lies open in the hand of the angel who is standing on the sea and on the land." [9] So I went to the angel and asked him to give me the little scroll. He said to me, "Take it and eat it. It will turn your stomach sour, but in your mouth it will be as sweet as honey." [10] I took the little scroll from the angel's hand and ate it. It tasted as sweet as honey in my mouth, but when I had eaten it, my stomach turned sour. [11] Then I was told, "You must prophesy again about many peoples, nations, languages and kings."

[11] I was given a reed like a measuring rod and was told, "Go and measure the temple of God and the altar, and count the worshipers there. [2] But exclude the outer court; do not measure it, because it has been given to the Gentiles. They will trample on the holy city for 42 months. [3] And I will give power to my two witnesses, and they will prophesy for 1,260 days, clothed in sackcloth." [4] These are the two olive trees and the two lampstands that stand before the Lord of the earth. [5] If anyone tries to harm them, fire comes from their mouths and devours their enemies.

This is how anyone who wants to harm them must die. [6] *These men have power to shut up the sky so that it will not rain during the time they are prophesying; and they have power to turn the waters into blood and to strike the earth with every kind of plague as often as they want.* [7] *Now when they have finished their testimony, the beast that comes up from the Abyss will attack them, and overpower and kill them.* [8] *Their bodies will lie in the street of the great city, which is figuratively called Sodom and Egypt, where also their Lord was crucified.* [9] *For three and a half days men from every people, tribe, language and nation will gaze on their bodies and refuse them burial.* [10] *The inhabitants of the earth will gloat over them and will celebrate by sending each other gifts, because these two prophets had tormented those who live on the earth.* [11] *But after the three and a half days a breath of life from God entered them, and they stood on their feet, and terror struck those who saw them.* [12] *Then they heard a loud voice from heaven saying to them, "Come up here." And they went up to heaven in a cloud, while their enemies looked on.* [13] *At that very hour there was a severe earthquake and a tenth of the city collapsed. Seven thousand people were killed in the earthquake, and the survivors were terrified and gave glory to the God of heaven.* [14] *The second woe has passed; the third woe is coming soon.*

[15] *The seventh angel sounded his trumpet, and there were loud voices in heaven, which said: "The kingdom of the world has become the kingdom of our Lord and of his Christ, and he will reign for ever and ever."* [16] *And the twenty-four elders, who were seated on their thrones before God, fell on their faces and worshiped God,* [17] *saying: "We give thanks to you, Lord God Almighty, the One who is and who was, because you have taken your great power and have begun to reign.* [18] *The nations were angry; and your wrath has come. The time has come for judging the dead, and for rewarding your servants the prophets and your saints and those who reverence your name, both small and great— and for destroying those who destroy the earth."* [19] *Then God's temple in heaven was opened, and within his temple was seen the ark of his covenant. And there came flashes of lightning, rumblings, peals of thunder, an earthquake and a great hailstorm.*

THE FIRST WARNING TRUMPET

8:7. *The first angel sounded his trumpet, and there came hail and fire mixed with blood, and it was hurled down upon the earth. A third of the earth was burned up, a third of the trees were burned up, and all the green grass was burned up.* The seven trumpets are intended to be partial judgments, not the final judgment. In each instance of the first six trumpets, only one third of the earth or physical creation experiences the judgment. 9:20–21 reveals that the rest of mankind not killed by these plagues still did not give up worshiping demons and idols, nor did they repent of their murders, magic arts, sexual immorality, or thefts. The seven trumpets, therefore, are not the final judgment but like the ten plagues on Egypt are intended to demonstrate the sovereignty of God and his merciful call to repentance. Act One of the narrative drama of Revelation ends with the blowing of the seventh trumpet (11:15–19). But the narrative continues through Act Two of the drama until in the end Satan, the beast, and those who had been deceived by Satan and the beast, that is, those who bear the mark of the beast, are all thrown into the lake of fire and judged with end-of-the-world judgment (20:10–15). The proleptic eschatological judgments of this section never lose sight of the final eschatological judgment which will close out John's theodicy.

The first angel[7] brought a plague of ***hail and fire, mixed with blood*** upon the earth and ***one third of the trees were burnt up.*** The imagery of hail and fire, mixed with blood draws heavily from the Jewish apocalyptic tradition, notably Joel 2:30 and the Egyptian plagues. Great hailstones were a common symbol of divine judgment (Josh. 10:11; Job 38:22–23; Ps. 78:47). Blood and fire were also frequent symbols of judgment (Isa. 9:5; Ezek. 21:32; 38:22; *Sib. Or.* 5:365). These were not only traditional Jewish symbols, for they can also be found in secular literature (cf. Cicero, *De div.* 1.43.98; Pliny, *Hist. nat.* 2.57.147).[8] Osborne and Aune, however, do not rule out the desert wilderness community's experience of bloody rain caused by rain being mixed with red desert sand as possible background.[9] My own past experience living in Lubbock, Texas, confirms this, with mud balls raining during dust storms. Commentators speculate regarding the trees as to whether they refer to fruit trees, trees in general, or plant life in general,[10] but such speculation is unnecessary. The warning is severe enough as it stands. The "burning up" of one third of the trees alone is a stark statement of this severity.

THE SECOND WARNING TRUMPET

8:8–9. *The second angel sounded his trumpet, and something like a huge mountain, all ablaze, was thrown into the sea. A third of the sea turned into blood,* [9] *a third of the living creatures in the sea died, and a third of the ships were destroyed.* John introduces an enigmatic symbol into the Egyptian typology of the sea, or waters, turning to blood: a huge mountain ablaze with fire. The image of the mountain may be drawn from [1] *Enoch* 18:13, where the mountain is actually seven stars that represent seven angels, or more likely from the *Sibylline Oracles* 5:158–159, where a great star will fall from heaven into the sea, pointing to the destruction of Rome. However, the most likely source for the idea of a great mountain's being cast into the sea is Jeremiah 51:24–25 and 42–43, where the reference is to God's judgment on Babylon.

Another proposal is that this may be a reference to the eruption of Mount Vesuvius that buried Pompeii, the Roman resort, in 79. Aune draws attention to the *Sibylline Oracles* 4:130–134, in which the reference apparently is to God's judgment of Rome.[11] One cannot escape the allusions to Babylon and Pompeii, both symbols of oppressive and Roman power facing imminent judgment from God. All options speak to the same thought: Rome as an enemy of God and oppressor of the saints will be judged with severe judgment.[12] As in the first trumpet, the judgment is only partial, one third of the sea is turned to blood, and one third of the living creatures in the sea die, and one third of the ships sink. God intended this trumpet to be a wake-up call to Rome.

THE THIRD WARNING TRUMPET

8:10–11. *The third angel sounded his trumpet, and a great star, blazing like a torch, fell from the sky on a third of the rivers and on the springs of water—*[11] *the name of the star is Wormwood. A third of the waters turned bitter, and many people died from the waters* *that had become bitter.* A great star falling would not surprise readers familiar with the Old Testament, in particular Isaiah 14:12–20, where the great star represents Babylon. Babylon in Revelation becomes a metaphor for Rome.[13] Repeatedly, John returns to the Babylon metaphor to predict God's displeasure with Rome and his decisive judgment of Rome and its oppressive powers (specifically by name, six times, in addition to oblique metaphorical references such as those seen in the second trumpet (cf. 14:8; 16:19; 17:5; 18:2, 10, 21). The identification of the great falling star has produced several possibilities in addition to Isaiah 14:12–22. Some make reference to Persian eschatological sources in which a falling star, Gurzihar, falls as a sign of a final catastrophe.[14] Beale states, "The identification of the star as Babylon's representative angel becomes more convincing if v10 is understood as alluding to Isa 14:12–15."[15] Caird refers to "an ancient myth in which Heylel, the morning star (Venus) tried to climb the walls of a city of the gods to make himself king of heaven, only to be driven from the sky by the rising sun." He claims that in Isaiah 14:12–20 "this myth is given historical application." Caird concludes, "It cannot be accidental that John has used in such quick succession echoes of two Old Testament prophecies which have to do with the fall of ancient Babylon."[16] This reference to the great star that fell burning from heaven is to Rome. Rome's influence among the nations was bitter and poisonous; hence the great star is called "Wormwood" (*ho apsinthos*), which derives from the bitter herb absinthe, a bitter dark green oil with alcoholic potential. In the Old Testament *apsinthos* is a symbol of bitter sorrow (Prov. 5:4; Deut. 29:18) and of God's bitter judgment (Jer. 9. 15; 23:15; Lam. 3:15, 19). The water becoming bitter from *apsinthos* is a reflection of the waters of Egypt being turned to blood. Again, the warning judgment is not intended to be a reference to the final judgment since only a third of the waters turn bitter.

THE FOURTH WARNING TRUMPET

8:12. *The fourth angel sounded his trumpet, and a third of the sun was struck, a third of the moon, and a third of the stars, so that a third of them turned dark. A third of the day was without light, and also a third of the night.* Although this trumpet calls to mind the ninth plague on Egypt, when darkness covered Egypt for three days (Exod. 10:21-23), the literary style is patently apocalyptic. John draws on traditional Jewish apocalyptic symbols to drive home his point that God is judging a nation for its evil opposition to his purposes (see 6:12, 13). Here again John's reference is to God's judgment on Rome, at this point a warning judgment that will be consummated later in the final judgment (cf. 20:1–14).

THE FIFTH WARNING JUDGMENT AND FIRST WOE

8:13–9:12. *As I watched, I heard an eagle that was flying in midair call out in a loud voice: "Woe. Woe. Woe to the inhabitants of the earth, because of the trumpet blasts about to be sounded by the other three angels."* 9:1 *The fifth angel sounded his trumpet, and I saw a star that had fallen from the sky to the earth. The star was given the key to the shaft of the Abyss.* [2] *When he opened the Abyss, smoke rose from it like the smoke from a gigantic furnace. The sun and sky were darkened by the smoke from the Abyss.* [3] *And out of the smoke locusts came down upon the earth and were given power like that of scorpions of the earth.* [4] *They were told not to harm the grass of the earth or any plant or tree, but only those people who did not have the seal of God on their foreheads.* [5] *They were not given power to kill them, but only to torture them for five months. And the agony they suffered was like that of the sting of a scorpion when it strikes a man.* [6] *During those days men will seek death, but will not find it; they will long to die, but death will elude them.* [7] *The locusts looked like horses prepared for battle. On their heads they wore something like crowns of gold, and their faces resembled human faces.* [8] *Their hair was like women's hair, and their teeth were like lions' teeth.* [9] *They had breastplates like breastplates of iron, and the sound of their wings was like the thundering of many horses and chariots rushing into battle.* [10] *They had tails and stings like scorpions, and in their tails they had power to torment people for five months.* [11] *They had as king over them the angel of the Abyss, whose name in Hebrew is Abaddon, and in Greek, Apollyon.*

[12] *The first woe is past; two other woes are yet to come.*

8:13. This is a transitional verse that introduces the final three warning trumpets. The eagle flying in midair (RSV midheaven) has intrigued commentators, with some viewing the eagle as a reference to the Roman ensign. However, the word translated eagle is *ho aetos*, can be translated as eagle or vulture since it actually has reference to a bird of carrion. In the Old Testament and related Jewish literature the eagle/vulture was an unclean bird (Lev. 11:13; Deut. 14:12), which in apocalyptic contexts conveyed messages mostly of doom and judgment (2 *Baruch* 77:17–26) and where it later became a symbol of the Roman Empire (2 *Esdras* [4 Ezra] 11:1–12:30; *Assumption of Moses* 10:8).[17] Here the eagle/vulture announces three warning woes of doom.

These three woe/trumpets continue the first four trumpets with woes and warning judgments against Rome. Something had died and the vultures were gathering for the feast. The term *woe* in the Jewish apocalyptic tradition was associated with pronouncements of doom and judgment. In keeping with this tradition, Matthew gathered Jesus' pronouncements of judgments against the Scribes and Pharisees in Matthew 23 into seven woes introducing what has become known, especially in regard to Mark 13, as the little apocalypse. The appearance of an eagle/vulture in 8:13 "forebodes climactic trials" which are "worse than the initial" four trumpets.[18] The background to these three woes is almost certainly the "woe oracles" of the Old Testament that "depict the anger and guarantee of the judgment of God against those who have forsaken him (e.g., Isa. 5:8–9; Amos 6:1–2; Hab 2:9–10)."[19]

The fifth and sixth trumpets do not refer to the final judgment, but Beale proposes that the seventh does.[20] However, I do not agree that this seventh trumpet necessarily refers to the final end-of-the-world judgment, only to God's final expression of judgment against Rome. Habakkuk 1:8 and Jeremiah 4:13 are particularly relevant since they include the expression "woe to us" and "a three-fold sounding of a trumpet . . . as an announcement of judgment."[21] The seventh trumpet and third woe should signal the end or finality of

God's patience with Rome, but in 11:15 (the seventh trumpet and third woe) the scene is radically different. It celebrates that God has taken his great power and exercised his reign. Osborne observes that unlike the seals and bowls which have a 4+3 arrangement, the trumpets have a 4+2+1 arrangement indicating that the seventh trumpet is different from the first six. He adds that whereas the fifth and sixth trumpets are warning trumpets of judgments, the seventh symbolizes the eschaton.[22] (What he means by the eschaton is not at this point immediately apparent.) However, the seventh trumpet is different, rather than a pronouncement of doom, this one depicts a scene of heavenly adulation.[23] The seventh trumpet is a jubilant fanfare, proclaiming the enthronement of the King of kings.[24] Beasley-Murray proposes yet another possibility regarding the seventh trumpet or third woe, "The world has become the sphere of the visible reign of God in Christ."[25]

Before proposing a solution to this enigmatic seventh trumpet, we note the statement in 8:13 that these three woes are pronounced on those *who dwell on the earth* (RSV). Osborne observes that this is the third time out of ten occasions that this expression has been used in Revelation, indicating that the expression is significant to the message of Revelation. It refers to "those who follow the beast (13:8; 17:8) and both oppose and kill the saints (6:10; 11:10)," and it is "the antithesis of 'those who dwell in heaven' (12:12; 13:6)." It is natural that they should be the object of the wrath of God."[26]

These woes are not poured out on every human being as at the end of the world; they are poured out on "those who dwell on the earth," namely, those who oppose God and persecute his people, the saints in Asia. Even the oppressive persecutors of the church, *those who dwell on the earth*, will have to bow to God's sovereign king and accept his reign. The message is a vindication of Christ and the saints.

9:1. Considerable discussion has also been given to the phrase ***a star that had fallen from the sky to the earth. The star was given the key to the shaft of the Abyss***, indicating conflicting views in regard to the identity of the star and the authority exercised by the star (cf. 1:20; cf. also Judg. 5:20; Job 8:7; Dan. 8:10; *1 Enoch* 86:3; 88:1; *Test. Sol.* 8:2–11). The discussion centers not on whether this star represents an angel, but on whether this angel is a good angel or "demonic" angel (cf. Osborne[27] and Beale[28]). Conclusions regarding this angel range from its being demonic, Satan himself, or a good angel carrying out God's purpose. Suggestions range from the archangel Uriel, who was over "Tartarus," to Saraqael, who was over the spirits who have sinned and fallen from God's favor. Most of these proposals are supported by references to the Jewish and apocalyptic traditions found in the Pseudepigrapha.[29] This angel may represent the corporate nature of the Roman Empire or the lives of men in revolt against God's purpose[30] or one of many angels that appear in Revelation with a divine commission.[31]

The complexity of identifying the angel is compounded by the fact that the term "that fell" or "had fallen" is a perfect tense verb, *peptōkota (*from *piptō*) and can mean "fall down," "descend," or "be cast down" (cf. Beale[32], Osborne,[33] S. Thompson,[34] and Mounce, J. Ramsey Michaels, and Aune[35]). Although the references to this star, in view of the possible *inclusio* of the pericope, could be to a fallen angel, I agree with Osborne that we should simply consider this star to be one of many angelic messengers in Revelation who carry out God's purposes.

This angel/star *was given* (*edothē*) *the key to the shaft of the Abyss.* (See the discussion of the *divine permission* implications of the Greek *edothē* at 6:2). This angelic messenger has the authority from God to open the Abyss, indicating God's sovereign control even over the Abyss and whatever the opening of the shaft into the Abyss may involve.[36] John will again refer to the key to the Abyss in 20:1, where the angel "seized the dragon, that ancient serpent, who is the Devil and Satan" (RSV) and threw him into the Abyss for a thousand years." This parallel reference indicates that this angel is not Satan or a demonic angel. *The key to the shaft of the Abyss* describes the key to the entrance of the underworld, the place of demonic spirits and all kinds of evil. The Greek term translated *Abyss* (*abyssou*) means "bottomless pit" (as in the RSV, "place without depth"). *Abyssou* is the genitive form of the noun *abyssos,* which is derived from the Greek *buthos* (*depth*) with the *alpha privative* resulting in *without depth, fathomless,* or *bottomless.* The term *abussos* has a rich background in the Jewish, Latin, and Hellenistic traditions, implying the place of the dead, the place of evil spirits, and demonic beings. Osborne observes that in Revelation it refers to a closed prison.[37] From the context of this text and 20:1, I also understand this angel to have come from God who has ultimate control of the Abyss and has sent the angel to carry out his bidding.

9:2. *When he opened the Abyss, smoke rose from it like the smoke from a gigantic furnace. The sun and sky were darkened by the smoke from the Abyss.* Although smoke is often a symbol of a theophany in the Old Testament (Exod. 19:18; Ps. 104:32; 144:5) or a symbol of divine wrath (Gen. 19:28; 2 Sam. 22:9; Ps. 18:8; Job 41:20), most likely in this case it is the smoke of the fire of hell, Gehenna, that forms the background to this scene (Matt. 18:9, the hell [Gehenna] of fire). John will refer later in Revelation to the lake of fire as a metaphor of hell (19:20; 20:10, 14–15). The darkening of the sun, however, is typical of Jewish apocalyptic metaphors for divine judgment (Joel 2:31; Isa. 13:10; Ezek. 32:7), which drives home the point that in this fifth trumpet we have not left the scenes of divine judgment.

9:3. *And out of the smoke locusts came down upon the earth and were given power like that of scorpions of the earth.* Calling on passages such as Joel 1–2 and Exodus 10:1–20, John describes God's judgment as a plague of locusts. The locust plague is obviously demonic since it rises out of the bottomless pit. John's purpose here is to intimidate those who dwell on earth and who oppress God's people, and calling on their knowledge of Joel's locust judgment, to encourage the saints.[38]

9:4–7. *They were told not to harm the grass of the earth or any plant or tree, but only those people who did not have the seal of God on their foreheads. [5] They were not given power to kill them, but only to torture them for five months. And the agony they suffered was like that of the sting of a scorpion when it strikes a man. [6] During those days men will seek death, but will not find it; they will long to die, but death will elude them.* Contrary to the first four trumpet plagues, which were pronounced on the earth, waters, trees and plant life, this plague and the one that follows have their effect on men, but only on those men who were not sealed with the seal of God. John draws on 7:3, where the servants of God were sealed with the seal of God on their foreheads as a sign of God's ownership and protection. The sealing of men plays a significant role in Revelation; God's faithful servants are sealed with the seal of God. Those who worship the beast and the image of the beast will receive the seal or mark of the beast (13:16–18). Although not specifically identified in 9:4 as those who receive the mark of the beast, they are the ones who John has in mind who will be tortured by these scorpions/locusts to bring them to repentance (9: 20). That this judgment is not final is indicated by the fact that these scorpions as locusts do not have power to kill but only to torture, and this only for five months. First, note the reciprocal nature of the torture to be endured by those who oppress the saints with the torture they have inflicted on the saints. Second, what does John mean by five months? Most commentators observe that the five-month limitation of the activity is in keeping with God's limitation of the remaining trumpet plagues and that the number is symbolic. Most also refer to the normal life span of the locust and the summer period in which locusts swarmed. Some indicate that normally locusts moved on to another "field" within a short time, much shorter than five months, indicating the severity of a five-month plague. No firm conclusion is reached other than that the plague is limited by divine decree.[39]

9:7–11. *The locusts looked like horses prepared for battle. On their heads they wore something like crowns of gold, and their faces resembled human faces. [8] Their hair was like women's hair, and their teeth were like lions' teeth. [9] They had breastplates like breastplates of iron, and the sound of their wings was like the thundering of many horses and chariots rushing into battle. [10] They had tails and stings like scorpions, and in their tails they had power to torment people for five months. [11] They had as king over them the angel of the Abyss, whose name in Hebrew is Abaddon, and in Greek, Apollyon.* Beckwith astutely observes that the "Apocalyptist in vv. 7-11 adds a more detailed description of the form of the monsters, their terrible array, and their manner of torture."[40] Mounce observes that "the total impact is one of unnatural and awesome cruelty."[41] Comparisons to fierce armies faced by Rome in their past are referenced by most commentators, notably Osborne who gives a detailed description of the nature of these locust warriors and their warhorses. Osborne mentions the Parthian army who had twice defeated the Romans. [42] Again, John mentions that these fierce and awesome warriors were limited, or had limited power. They operate for five months. Abaddon is derived from the Hebrew *abaddon* and means to destroy, with the proper noun meaning of Destroyer. Apollyon is from the Greek *Apolluōn* which is almost a synonym for Abaddon in that it also means destroyer. The double reference to The Destroyer leads some to identify two demonic beings or forces in this text. Beale proposes that The Destroyer is either the devil himself or some demonic representative of the Satan.[43] Some, however, see in The Destroyer an allusion to Domitian (or possibly Nero) who liked to identify himself as the Greek god Apollo (Apollo also being derived from the Greek *Apolluōn*, destroyer, or the verb form *apollumi*, to destroy).[44] I find this strange that Domitian is considered since it is on the dwellers on earth (Rome) that this judgment is expressed. Rather than seeing Domitian in this reference I prefer Bauckham's view "that 'Abaddon' refers to the 'angel of death' (2 *Bar.* 21.23) to whom God has assigned the underworld . . ."[45]

9:12. *The first woe is past; two other woes are yet to come.* Indicating the seriousness of this first woe, John has devoted twelve verses to the description of the fifth trumpet (the first woe) while giving only twelve verses to all of the first four trumpets.

THE SIXTH WARNING TRUMPET AND SECOND WOE

9:13–19. *The sixth angel sounded his trumpet, and I heard a voice coming from the horns of the golden altar that is before God.* [14] *It said to the sixth angel who had the trumpet, "Release the four angels who are bound at the great river Euphrates." * [15] *And the four angels who had been kept ready for this very hour and day and month and year were released to kill a third of mankind.* [16] *The number of the mounted troops was two hundred million. I heard their number.* [17] *The horses and riders I saw in my vision looked like this: Their breastplates were fiery red, dark blue, and yellow as sulfur. The heads of the horses resembled the heads of lions, and out of their mouths came fire, smoke and sulfur.* [18] *A third of mankind was killed by the three plagues of fire, smoke and sulfur that came out of their mouths.* [19] *The power of the horses was in their mouths and in their tails; for their tails were like snakes, having heads with which they inflict injury.* Removing any doubt as to the origin of these woes, when the sixth angel blew his trumpet a voice spoke from the horns of the golden altar commanding that the four angels be released who were bound at the Euphrates river, yet ready to do God's bidding. That the voice came from the horns of the golden altar that is before God is significant to John's message and this woe. The RSV and NRSV include four horns while the NIV omits four. There is a textual variant at this point and some discussion as to whether the word *tessarōn*, four, is a scribal omission or scribal addition. Since the altar had four horns, it may be that the word four is intended, but the omission or addition does not make much difference to the meaning of the text.[46] This is the third time Revelation speaks of the golden altar (6:9 and 8:3) and the only time that it speaks of the horns of the golden altar. What the horns (*keratōn*) represent is unclear other than that horns can represent power, indicating the presence of the power of God. In 1 Kings 1:50–51 and 2:28, Adonijah and Joab, fearing Solomon, "caught hold of the horns of the altar" in the tabernacle as a place of refuge from Solomon. Possibly the mention of the horns is a reminder of refuge in God's presence. Although several suggestions are made regarding the voice that spoke from the golden altar, it is best to connect this with a response to the prayers from beneath the golden altar of 6:9 and of the saints at 8:39.[47] This voice and the woe to be announced are divine retribution for the suffering of the saints.[48] This voice pronounces the terrible judgment as God's response to the prayers of the saints in 6:10 for vengeance and retribution.[49] Whoever it is that speaks from the golden altar, the voice speaks for God.[50]

These divinely commissioned angels are to release God's wrath against the dwellers on earth for their ungodly persecution of the saints. The terrifying description of these troops and their readiness at the river Euphrates seem once more (cf. 9:7–10) to indicate a reference to the fearful Parthian army. That the troops are mounted cavalry seems to solidify their identity as Parthian warriors, whom the Romans feared. God is reminding the saints that Rome is not invincible, and Rome that he will bring fierce retribution against them unless they repent. As in the previous woe, the saints are spared while the warning judgment is poured out on the enemy. The power of the "Parthian" warriors is however limited since only one third of mankind is killed.[51]

9:20–21. *The rest of mankind that were not killed by these plagues still did not repent of the work of their hands; they did not stop worshiping demons, and idols of gold, silver, bronze, stone and wood—idols that cannot see or hear or walk.* [21] *Nor did they repent of their murders, their magic arts, their sexual immorality or their thefts.* These are warning trumpets whose intention, like the first nine Egyptian plagues, was to bring those dwellers on earth to repentance. At 14:6 John will again note that God does not arbitrarily condemn people, but gives even his enemies every opportunity to repent. That text tells of an angel flying in midheaven proclaiming an eternal gospel, calling on those who dwell on earth and all people to "Fear God and give him glory, because the hour of his judgment has come. Worship him who made the heavens, the earth, the sea and the springs of water. "Notice the emphasis at 14:6 that the hour of judgment on those who dwell on earth has already come. In the words of 2 Pet 3:9 God is not willing that any should perish but that all should come to repentance, including those who dwell on earth, namely, who persecute his people and worship the beast. The litany of sin that John mentions is in keeping with the pagan idolatry of a world that has little respect for God.[52]

As was the case after the ninth Egyptian plague, one anticipates the arrival of the final plague or at least the seventh warning trumpet and last of the three woes announced by the eagle/vulture flying in mid heaven. Once more the drama is building in intensity, but before the final woe John needed to bring a word of encouragement and explanation of how the drama was unfolding, so we encounter a second major interlude in 10, 11.

THE SECOND INTERLUDE - 10:1–11:14

The Text

Then I saw another mighty angel coming down from heaven. He was robed in a cloud, with a rainbow above his head; his face was like the sun, and his legs were like fiery pillars. [2] *He was holding a little scroll, which lay open in his hand. He planted his right foot on the sea and his left foot on the land,*[3] *and he gave a loud shout like the roar of a lion. When he shouted, the voices of the seven thunders spoke.* [4] *And when the seven thunders spoke, I was about to write; but I heard a voice from heaven say, "Seal up what the seven thunders have said and do not write it down."*[5] *Then the angel I had seen standing on the sea and on the land raised his right hand to heaven.* [6] *And he swore by him who lives for ever and ever, who created the heavens and all that is in them, the earth and all that is in it, and the sea and all that is in it, and said, "There will be no more delay. ⁷ But in the days when the seventh angel is about to sound his trumpet, the mystery of God will be accomplished, just as he announced to his servants the prophets." ⁸ Then the voice that I had heard from heaven spoke to me once more: "Go, take the scroll that lies open in the hand of the angel who is standing on the sea and on the land." ⁹ So I went to the angel and asked him to give me the little scroll. He said to me, "Take it and eat it. It will turn your stomach sour, but in your mouth it will be as sweet as honey." ¹⁰ I took the little scroll from the angel's hand and ate it. It tasted as sweet as honey in my mouth, but when I had eaten it, my stomach turned sour. ¹¹ Then I was told, "You must prophesy again about many peoples, nations, languages and kings." 11:1 I was given a reed like a measuring rod and was told, "Go and measure the temple of God and the altar, and count the worshipers there. ² But exclude the outer court; do not measure it, because it has been given to the Gentiles. They will trample on the holy city for ⁴² months. ³ And I will give power to my two witnesses, and they will prophesy for 1,260 days, clothed in sackcloth." ⁴ These are the two olive trees and the two lampstands that stand before the Lord of the earth. ⁵ If anyone tries to harm them, fire comes from their mouths and devours their enemies. This is how anyone who wants to harm them must die. ⁶ These men have power to shut up the sky so that it will not rain during the time they are prophesying; and they have power to turn the waters into blood and to strike the earth with every kind of plague as often as they want. ⁷ Now when they have finished their testimony, the beast that comes up from the Abyss will attack them, and overpower and kill them. ⁸ Their bodies will lie in the street of the great city, which is figuratively called Sodom and Egypt, where also their Lord was crucified. ⁹ For three and a half days men from every people, tribe, language and nation will gaze on their bodies and refuse them burial. ¹⁰ The inhabitants of the earth will gloat over them and will celebrate by sending each other gifts, because these two prophets had tormented those who live on the earth. ¹¹ But after the three and a half days a breath of life from God entered them, and they stood on their feet, and terror struck those who saw them. ¹² Then they heard a loud voice from heaven saying to them, "Come up here." And they went up to heaven in a cloud, while their enemies looked on. ¹³ At that very hour there was a severe earthquake and a tenth of the city collapsed. Seven thousand people were killed in the earthquake, and the survivors were terrified and gave glory to the God of heaven.*

¹⁴ The second woe has passed; the third woe is coming soon.

THE LITTLE SCROLL

10:1–11. Drawing on images from Ezek 3:3 ff, Dan 12 ff, and Ezek 37:4 John is told by God to take the little scroll offered by the angel and to eat it. In this section, as in Rev 1:3, John explains the prophetic nature of his ministry (10:7, 11; 11:3, 6, 10).[53] Osborne adds that John's prophetic commission is renewed and that it is God himself who is involving John in his revelatory activity.[54] This interlude reemphasizes that God is aware of the suffering and faithfulness of the saints and will vindicate their suffering by judging their oppressors. Bauckham argues that this section of Revelation develops a major theme, the conversion of the nations. I am not convinced that it plays a central role even though it is always included in God's purpose and is an important ingredient to the message of the book.[55] If nothing else, Bauckham's observation illustrates the importance of this pericope to the message of Revelation.

10:1. *Then I saw another mighty angel coming down from heaven. He was robed in a cloud, with a rainbow above his head; his face was like the sun, and his legs were like fiery pillars.* In Revelation and the Jewish tradition mighty angels announce mighty messages, or messages of great significance! This angel's message is significant because it takes one back to 6:10 where we read of the prayers of the saints calling out to God for vindication. It connects the narrative of Revelation to the cry of the slaughtered saints for retribution. This angelic message attaches to the prayer of the saints and explains that what is to follow, notably in the third woe and seventh trumpet, answers those prayers. This mighty angel appears at three strategic points in the book, 5:2 at the opening of the major scroll of Revelation; 10:1 at a crucial turning point in Revelation; and 18:21 at the destruction of "Babylon." Some connect the angel with Gabriel (Charles, Sweet, Kraft, Beasley-Murray); some with Christ (Moffatt, Sweet, Beale), some with an "angelo-morphic Christology" (Gundry), and some simply to the central important message of Revelation (Bauckham, Aune, Fair).[56] He is associated with clouds and a rainbow, indicating the divine nature and origin of his message. On several occasions God "appeared" in clouds as a sign of his glory; especially in the wilderness the pillar of cloud was a symbol of God's presence (Exod. 13: 21–22; 16:10; Lev. 16:2; 2 Chron. 5:14–15; 6:1; 1 Kgs 8:10; Ezek. 10:4). In Daniel 7:13 the "son of man" is revealed as appearing in clouds before the Ancient of Days to receive a kingdom, and in Matthew 24:30 Jesus predicted that "the son of man" would come in clouds from heaven in judgment on Jerusalem. In 4:3 in the heavenly throne room a rainbow surrounded the throne of God as a sign of God's mercy. At Ezekiel 1:28 Ezekiel saw what looked like a man, with a "brilliant light" surrounding him. Here the mighty angel has legs like fiery pillars, possibly recalling the fiery pillar of God's presence (Exod. 31:20), which led and protected Israel in the wilderness.[57] The special attributes of the angel "serve to give him the appearance of heavenly glory. They do not however furnish ground for identifying him with Christ.[58]

10:2–3. *He was holding a little scroll, which lay open in his hand. He planted his right foot on the sea and his left foot on the land,* [3] *and he gave a loud shout like the roar of a lion. When he shouted, the voices of the seven thunders spoke.* Adding to the striking appearance of this mighty angel is the description of his stance with his right foot on the sea and his left foot on the land. John may be reflecting on the Colossus of Rhodes, one of the seven wonders of the ancient world, which was still standing during his time.[59] However, standing on land and sea may simply be another illustration of God's sovereign control of creation.[60]

The *little scroll* has generated considerable discussion among commentators. The fact that the little scroll was open in the angel's hand adds to the fact that the message of the scroll is to be readily available. The Greek *biblaridion* ("little scroll") is a diminutive of *biblion*, which is in turn a diminutive of *biblos* ("scroll" or "book"). *Biblaridion* is not found elsewhere in the New Testament and has caused some to question whether it is in fact a diminutive.[61] The major debate relates to whether the little scroll of 10:2 is part of the large scroll of 5:1 or possibly a new, different scroll. Commentators differ on the meaning of the little scroll (see Beckwith,[62] Caird,[63] Morris,[64] Mounce,[65] Beasley-Murray,[66] Beale,[67] and Osborne[68]).

It should be apparent that the little scroll of chapter 10 is part of the overall message of the large scroll of chapter 5. The little scroll is a reemphasis of John's prophetic commission. When the angel spoke *he gave a loud shout like the roar of a lion* signifying the importance of his message. The background to this metaphor is obviously Amos 3:7–8 (see also Hos. 11:10; Ezra 11:37; 12:31 for examples of the LORD roaring like a lion). The message the angel announces comes with the authority and sovereignty of God. Most agree that the voice of the angel with its divine sovereign message refers to Psalm 29 which speaks of the sovereign power of God over creation.[69] When the angel *shouted, the voices of the seven thunders spoke*. The introduction of *thunders* introduces a new concept. Thunders in the plural appears only twice in Revelation (10:3, 4), while thunder appears seven times (4:5; 6:1; 8:5; 11:19; 14:2; 19:6) and all in association with messages that have divine sanction and power. The implication of the mighty angel's shout accompanied by *the roar of a lion* and *seven thunders* is that his message carries within it the sovereign authority and assurance of God.

10:4. *And when the seven thunders spoke, I was about to write; but I heard a voice from heaven say, "Seal up what the seven thunders have said and do not write it down.* Commentators disagree over this verse. If the little scroll relates to part of the message of the large scroll of chapter 5, the message of which was that God had an eternal plan for dealing with evil and suffering and the redemption of his creation, then we should keep the message of the little scroll and the angel of seven thunders within this greater message of God's sovereign *Heilsgeschichte*. The real issue, however, lies in the command not to write this message down and to seal up the message. Three texts and contexts seem to relate to this conundrum: Daniel 12:4; Revelation 6:10, and 22:10.

Daniel 12:4 must play a major role here. Daniel was told *"But you, Daniel, close up and seal the words of the scroll until the time of the end.* In Daniel's message God would take care of the oppressors in his good time, *at the end.* Daniel was to write the message down and close or seal his book for later readers. John draws somewhat of a reverse analogy from this in regard to the message of the little scroll. He is told to close the book, for its message is so urgent that it is not even to be written down. His message is for the immediate context, the now of the saints.

As stated in the prologue of Revelation, the message had to do with things *soon* or shortly to take place in the life of the church, for *the time is near*. At 6:10 the saints under the altar cried out to God for vengeance and vindication; they were told to wait a while for God's purpose to run its course when the number of their fellow servants would be complete. The saints were to patiently rely on God's sovereign power and purpose. At 10:6 the saints will be told that there would be *no more delay* (RSV). God was about to answer their prayers and cry for vindication. Thus the message of 10:4 that was to be sealed up and not written down must relate to the saints' prayers for vindication. There was to be no need to write it down for later times, for the message was "for now." In the epilogue of (22:10) John will repeat the language of the prologue, *"for the time is near"* (RSV) indicating the imminence of the trials facing the saints, the imminence of their vindication, and the urgency of the message. In the context of the imminence of the crises, John is instructed at 22:10, **"*Do not seal up the words of the prophecy of this book.*"** In contrast to Daniels instruction to seal up his message for the message was for a later time, John is instructed not to seal up his message for it pertained to the present crises being faced by the church.

The seventh trumpet was about to be blown announcing the third woe to be pronounced. God was about to pronounce judgment on those who dwell on the earth, who worship the beast, and who oppress his people. When viewed with Daniel 12:4 and 22:10, although this directive may be confusing to us, however, the saints to whom John wrote would have understood it as an urgent message intended to reassure them of God's concern for their imminent trials.

10:5–7. *Then the angel I had seen standing on the sea and on the land raised his right hand to heaven.* ⁶ *And he swore by him who lives for ever and ever, who created the heavens and all that is in them, the earth and all that is in it, and the sea and all that is in it, and said, "There will be no more delay.* ⁷ *But in the days when the seventh angel is about to sound his trumpet, the mystery of God will be accomplished, just as he announced to his servants the prophets."* The raising of the right hand was a common action for taking a solemn oath and a commitment to carrying out that oath (Deut. 32:40).[70] That God swore oaths is well attested in the Old Testament (Exod. 6:8; Ezek. 20:5, 15). That the oath was sworn in the name of the eternal creator God adds to the serious nature of the oath. Images of the oath can be traced back to Numbers 14:21; Judges 8:19; and Daniel 12:7. The content of the oath, however, in one sense is more striking than the oath itself. *There will be no more delay*.

The meaning of the angel's solemn oath that "***There will be no more delay***" has been understood by commentators is a surprising number of ways. First, however, the translation of the phrase itself has led to some varied discussion. The Greek reads *hoti chronos ouketi estai*. The *hoti* is untranslatable as it merely introduces a direct statement as in the NIV and NRSV. Most translations however follow the KJV without rendering the *hoti* as a sign introducing direct speech to follow. We note here the various translations of this phrase in which indirect speech is preferred; the KJV renders this "*that there should be time no longer*", the ASV "*that there shall be delay no longer*", the NASV "*that there will be delay no longer*", the RSV "*that there should be no more delay*". The more appropriate direct speech translations are as follows, the NIV "*There will be no more delay*", and the NRSV "*There will be no more delay*". The KJV maintains an early third century translation of *chronos* as in Andreas of Caesarea, *Apoc.* 10.6, which seems to have been followed by subsequent church fathers.[71] Most other translations prefer to understand *chronos* as some form of *delay*.

Working with this variant understanding of *chronos*, Aune argues for a translation of the text that is different from the major translations, rendering the phrase as "*There will be no more time interval,*" stating that "delay is an inappropriate translation of *chronos.*" However, it appears that Aune is more concerned with the theological meaning of the phrase and the statements that follow, for his *translation* is not that much different from that of the NIV, RSV, or NRSV! That *there will be no more time interval* means the same as *there will be no more delay!*[72]

Timothy Friberg, Barbara Friberg, and Neva F. Miller suggest two interesting possibilities for understanding *chronos,* "as marking an event *point of time* . . . as time available for something *opportunity, occasion* . . . time taken or allowed for something *respite, delay, opportunity* (Rev 2.21; 10.6)"[73].

Aune's reason for translating the text as he does leads into a discussion of how the events described by the angel are to be understood. Interpretations of the text that follow are as many as there are commentators, indicating the enigmatic and complex nature of the statement "***the mystery of God will be accomplished***". If this text is inserted into a futurist interpretation of Revelation, as is the case with many, notably Mounce and Beale, then it can either refer to the eschatological end of the world or God's redemptive plan which culminates with the final end. I have already argued that the futurist view transfers the context, theology, and message of Revelation away from the historical, sociological, and theological context of first century Christianity in Asia, and therefore *does not do justice to the message of encouragement God and Jesus intended the suffering saints to receive.* The message of Revelation must be kept in the strict context of the imminent struggles of the first century church in Asia and not forced to address twenty-first century interests. This does not mean that there are not powerful themes and theological principles for contemporary readers, but hermeneutic must follow exegesis and not vice versa! The point of my argument is that the ***mystery*** that is to be ***accomplished*** must be relevant to the context of the saints who have cried out for vindication.

Several scholars have commented regarding the similarity of 6:10 and 10:6 to Daniel 12:6–7 and to the fulfillment of Daniel's prophecy.[74] Caird draws an *analogous* relationship between Daniel's situation and John's in Asia in that the context of Daniel should be understood as the persecution of Israel by Antiochus Epiphanes:[75] "The persecutor was Antiochus Epiphanes, and the three and a half times were years, whether literal or symbolic, during which the author of Daniel expected the persecution to last."[76] John's situation of persecution in Asia under a new Antiochus Epiphanes, Rome and Domitian, was *analogous* to Daniel's situation. Therefore, John is using Daniel 12:6–7 in a symbolic or *analogous*[77] sense of fulfillment for his own situation of persecution in Asia. Caird states, "John believed that the prophecy of Daniel, along with other Old Testament prophecies, was about to have a new and richer fulfillment."[78]

This text must be kept within the framework of the first-century church in Asia, the imminent oppression that was about to break in on the church under a new Babylon, or "Antiochus Epiphanes," namely Rome and Domitian. This means that the cry of the martyrs, "O Sovereign Lord, holy and true, how long before thou wilt judge and avenge our blood on those who dwell upon the earth," and the statement of the mighty angel, "*There will be no more delay,*" must be seen in the context of the saints' prayer for vindication (6:10). The angel's statement was therefore in response to the cry of the saints under the altar, not in any temporal fulfillment to Daniel's prophetic statement at Daniel 12.[79] Mounce is correct in stating, "The announcement of no further delay would come as welcome news. The martyrs under the altar (6:9–12) had been told to rest a while until the full number of their fellow servants and brothers and sisters should be put to death. The seven thunders would have involved yet another delay had they not been cancelled."[80]

Set in the context of the first century church in Asia, the drama that John is presenting regarding faithfulness under severe persecution, often resulting in martyrdom, and the saints' cry for vindication, this scene of the little scroll and the solemn oath of the angel, "*There will be no more delay,*" must be seen in response to the saints' cry for vindication, not a reference to the final eschatological age and fulfillment of God's scheme of redemption. The significance of this statement regarding *no more delay* is that God was about to answer the prayer of the saints under the altar. Beale correctly identifies the connection between 6:10 and 10:6–7, stating that there is a "conceptual link between 6:11 and 10:6b–7" which can be seen in "their verbal similarity."[81]

Sensitivity to the role played by the saints' cry to God for vindication and the solemn statement of this mighty angel is central to the flow of thought John has been developing as the seals are opened and the trumpets blown. Much of what has transpired so far in the opening of the scroll and the blowing of the six trumpets has been dynamically connected to the saints' fundamental cry, "How long before you do something to vindicate us?" They had been told to wait a while as God carried out his plan of redemption. In anticipation of the sounding of the seventh and final warning trumpet and third woe, the drama moves toward a climax, and the solemn oath that *there will be no more delay*. This oath comes as a powerful word of encouragement and relief to the saints. God is about to act in their behalf.

We should not see in this significant statement an historical timetable relating to the beginning of the eschaton. Time schedules in the apocalyptic genre are not the focus. Time references, as are all numerical references in Revelation, such as four, seven, ten, and twelve, are symbols of some theological consequence. Seven churches does not limit the number churches in Asia to seven but indicates that the message of Revelation is intended for all the churches belonging to God in Asia. Seven is a symbolic number for completeness and holiness. Historical schedules or time reference are not the point in Revelation; the theological symbols and statements couched in the "temporal symbols," such as ten days' testing in 2:10, are the concern. That the historical context of the first-century church in Asia sets the historical scene for understanding the message of Revelation does nothing more that set the narrative drama in an historical context, namely the crises about to be faced by the first-century churches of Asia. The dynamic of the apocalyptic genre is not to be found in any temporal or historical symbols, but in the theological message implied. Revelation is set in the apocalyptic genre and does not ask *when* questions. The import of the temporal symbols is *what* they mean. The theological meaning of the symbols is the intent. The oath, *there will be no more delay*, is a theological statement, not a temporal commitment. The language similarity in this text to Daniel 12 does not indicate a fulfillment of the eschaton prophesied in Daniel. The connection to Daniel 12 is a *typological* or *analogical* fulfillment, not a temporal or historical fulfillment. At Daniel 12:5–9, Daniel asks, *"How long will it be before these astonishing things are fulfilled?"* He is told to go his way for the answer to his question is not for him to know; it is to be revealed later. He is to trust in God's purpose. As Osborne however succinctly suggests, "The answer there is 'Only God who knows,'" The language and nuances of Dan 12 are however so rich and pregnant in meaning that John draws on them from his literary and theological palate and paints a new analogous picture for his readers from Daniel's images. In contrast to Daniel's context, the saints in Revelation are told under solemn oath, *there will be no more delay.* The reader of Revelation has already been informed that the "events" to be revealed by John will *soon* take place, in contrast to Daniel's *later.* In the seventh trumpet God is going to symbolically yet powerfully answer their cry. He will act decisively in their behalf and vindicate them.

The primary purpose of the theological drama presented by John in Revelation was to assure the saints that God would act in their behalf. Nevertheless, they needed to realize that God would act in his own sovereign time according to his own sovereign plan. But that he will act in their behalf and that they will be vindicated is certain. ***In the days when the seventh angel is about to sound his trumpet, the mystery of God will be accomplished, just as he announced to his servants the prophets.*** When the seventh trumpet is blown in this theological drama, the saints would learn how God was about to answer their cry. The ***mystery*** of God's plan for vindicating the saints would be revealed.

In regard to the ***accomplishment of the mystery*** of God, Caird again draws an analogy from Daniel and observes, "The persecution of the church is thus the secret weapon by which God intends to win his victory over the church's persecutors and to achieve his purpose of redemption."[82] This would be a rewarding and encouraging vindication of the saints and answer to their prayer. God is going to use their suffering and martyrdom to bring about his defeat of the enemy, those who dwell on the earth, an action that would be in keeping with God's previous similar statements to the prophets.

The statement ***just as he announced to his servants the prophets*** reinforces that God has previously predicted his divine purpose through the prophets and that he has a plan for handling the problem of evil, oppression, suffering, and persecution.

The comment regarding prophetic involvement leads directly into the next pericope, which stresses John's prophetic office, ministry, and message. The difficult yet urgent message that John brings places him among God's prophets. The verb **announced** (*euēggelisen*) can also be understood to mean "evangelized," indicating that the revelation of the mystery, or message, held good news. Osborne observes, "This is both the culmination of all 'gospel' messages and the most important 'good news' ever given."[83] It is "the completion of the 'mystery,' . . . the conclusion of God's plan that was initiated before the foundation of the world and is now "finally" to be realized in its fullness."[84] I am somewhat unenthusiastic regarding Osborne's use of the word finally in that it tends toward a futurist interpretation.

Surprisingly at 11:15, the seventh trumpet does not resonate with strident judgment against those who dwell on the earth, but sounds more like an encouraging and triumphant kingdom announcement to the suffering saints. God has taken up his reign over the earth through his Son Jesus Christ. This sovereign reign of God through Jesus Christ is the content of the **mystery**. Nevertheless, although the seventh trumpet is a triumphant statement of Christ's reign over all the earth in vindication of the saints, it is also a threatening judgment on those who dwell on the earth and have rejected God's kingdom and the sovereign reign of his Son, and a statement that God has judged their enemies. That Jesus will reign as sovereign over all creation and is in fact already reigning as such, is both a sobering thought and the climax of all gospel good news. The realization that Jesus is reigning over all the earth as the ultimate sovereign of creation is in fact a threatening judgment for those who dwell on the earth. N. T. Wright considers the kingdom or reign of Christ to be the center of the gospel message proclaimed by Jesus and his disciples, and the focal point of New Testament theology.[85] Wright observes that the kingdom and reign of God is the message of Old Testament prophecy as interpreted by Jesus. Here it is the **mystery**, or climax, of God's plan to judge those who dwell on earth and Rome.

10:8–11. *Then the voice that I had heard from heaven spoke to me once more: "Go, take the scroll that lies open in the hand of the angel who is standing on the sea and on the land."* [9] *So I went to the angel and asked him to give me the little scroll. He said to me, "Take it and eat it. It will turn your stomach sour, but in your mouth it will be as sweet as honey."* [10] *I took the little scroll from the angel's hand and ate it. It tasted as sweet as honey in my mouth, but when I had eaten it, my stomach turned sour.* [11] *Then I was told, "You must prophesy again about many peoples, nations, languages and kings."* John returns to the little scroll that was open (cf. also 10:2) in the hand of the mighty angel. That this scroll was open and not sealed indicates that its message was ready to be revealed and "presently" relevant to the churches in Asia. It was, however, intended for both John and the church in Asia. John needed to know the urgent nature of his message. The saints needed to hear the present relevance of the message. The message was not for later days, as in the case of Daniel (Dan 12:4), but related to things *soon to take place*.[86] There are two emphases in this vision of the little scroll, one relates to John's commission as a prophet, and the other contains the message that he is to prophesy again to the saints.[87] The instruction to eat the little scroll (Ezek. 2:9–3:4), as in the case of Ezekiel, serves the dual role of a prophetic commission and reference to an urgent message.

As was the case with Ezekiel, who needed prophetic commission (cf. also the case of Isaiah in Isa. 6:1-5), John needed divine confirmation and commission. Because of the dramatic nature of John's message, the churches of Asia and John himself needed to be reassured of the divine nature of John's prophetic office and message.[88]

The instruction to eat the scroll indicates that John is to internalize and personalize the message before proclaiming it due to its urgent, serious, and terrifying implications. Ezekiel's message was to be "sweet," for it spoke to Israel, a rebellious people, to let them know that the God who had turned away from them was willing to return to them if they repented and turned back to him. In contrast to John's message, there is no mention of "bitterness" in Ezekiel's message, yet Ezekiel's message was one of judgment on a rebellious people who would refuse to hear Ezekiel's message. Ezekiel's message was to warn Israel of impending doom should they not repent and return to God. There is a similar situation in John's message. He is warning the churches in Asia of impending doom both from their enemies and from God if they did not repent and return to him (as in the case of five of the churches). The addition of bitterness in John's message emphasizes the serious nature of the situation faced by the church in Asia. The "veiled" theme in John's message for the churches in Asia was that God would not desert them if they remained faithful to him. However John's message was different in one sense from that of Ezekiel; it contained a bitter component in addition to the sweet.[89] Beale suggests that it is sweet because it involves God's word.[90] Aune[91] refers to the pseudepigraphical text *Joseph and Aseneth* in which Aseneth is given a honeycomb and told to eat it. The sweetness in *Joseph and Aseneth* relates to the supernatural origin of the benefits of the honeycomb (*Joseph and Aseneth* 16:15–16).

Caird adds that the sweetness of John's message refers to the word of grace about to be announced by the prophet emphasizing that "the way of victory is the way of the Cross.[92] Osborne observes that consuming the word of God occurs often in the Old Testament[93] (Ps. 119:103; Jer. 15:16). However, this message involves the whole church in Asia, not simply John, and in the context of Revelation was intended to encourage the suffering saints in the churches in Asia. In this context it is best to see the message of the scroll, both bitter and sweet, being addressed to the saints in Asia proclaiming both bad days and victory over their enemies. The message is bitter in that the circumstances of the church in Asia determine that it is inevitable that the saints will suffer persecution from their pagan neighbors, possibly even martyrdom. It is sweet in that it contains a word of grace from God who will raise and vindicate them and set them on thrones with Christ from which they will judge the nations. The message is one of victory in Christ through dying faithfully to him.[94] The order of the expression sour–sweet (10:9) is reversed in (10:10) as sweet-sour for emphasis, assuring the saints that although the message is bitter, it is ultimately sweet.

10:11. After "eating" the scroll and "digesting" its message, John is told *"You must prophesy again about many peoples, nations, languages and kings."* The instruction to prophesy *again*, strengthens the emphasis on John's prophetic commission. He has been prophesying already, but he must now do so *again*, this time with the emphasis on *many peoples, nations, languages and kings*. That the instruction to prophesy again is connected to the message of the little scroll is seen in the opening words of 10:11 in the Greek, *kai legousin moi, Dei se palin prophēteusai*, "*and they said to me, 'you must again prophesy.'"* The initial *kai* ("and") of 10:11 is a coordinating conjunction that can be translated "and" or "but," or in certain circumstances as an epexegetical *kai* ("indeed," "therefore," "on this basis," "in this regard") This initial *kai* of 10:11 follows a string of "*kai's*" in 10:10 and ties the message to John to prophesy again to the previous discussion of 10:10 relating to the little scroll. Revelation 10:11 could then open with the statement "*in this regard* you must again prophesy." The difficult exegetical point of the plural *legousin* ("they said") has been sidestepped in the major English translations that translate this as *Then I was told* (NIV), and "*And I was told*" (RSV). Aune, observing that "the plural form of the verb is problematic," makes three suggestions and observes that the most likely is that the indefinite plural may be a substitute for the passive voice, which occurs in Hebrew and Aramaic.[95] A more likely solution, suggested by Beale, is that the *they* may refer to the mighty angel and the seven thunders of 10:4.[96]

The translation of the Greek preposition *epi* in the phrase *epilaois* **about many peoples** is critical to understanding the nature of John's recommission to prophesy *again* to many peoples.[97] When *epi*, is used with a noun in the dative case, as is this instance with *laois* ("people"), *epi* can be translated in several ways (KJV "before," ASV "over," NASV "concerning," RSV, NRSV, NIV "about). The translation may imply a positive message or a negative message. In John's chiastic structure of Revelation, Act Two repeats the message of Act One in more specific terms.

There is some question regarding who the angel had in mind in the reference to *many peoples, nations, languages and kings*. Bauckham suggests that the fourfold listing of peoples, nations, languages, and kings refers to the universal nature of John's message.[98] Bauckham refers to the use of similar language in Daniel 7:14, in which context the emphasis was on the transfer of sovereignty over all people and nations from world empires to the sovereignty and dominion of "one like a son of man" and the people of God.[99] In view of the message of the seventh trumpet about to be sounded proclaiming the sovereignty of Jesus over all creation Bauckham's observation is worthy of note.

In the introduction to this study I suggested that Revelation was written in the literary style of a drama structured in a chiasm with chapters 1–11 forming Act One of the drama and the first level of chiastic thematic presentation. Act Two in the drama is chapters 12–22, which forms the second level of the message. I observed that several scholars had noticed that 12 seems to be a turning point in the composition and theology. The instruction to John that he must *prophesy again* leads into the next section of the chiasm of Revelation (12:1–14:5) which forms the "apex" of the chiastic structure and high point of Revelation, and the beginning of the Act Two of the book. In Act

One the focus had been on the large scroll, which explained to the saints that God had a plan for dealing with the problem of evil. It focused on the prayers of the saints who cried from under the altar to God for vindication and were told to wait for a while as God worked his plan. In the progressive blowing of the seven warning trumpets, just before the seventh trumpet, the anticipation is so high that John has introduced another interlude (10–11). Act Two draws its dynamic from the little scroll of chapter 10 and the repeated prophesying in the expression ***prophesy again***. In this interlude John has again been commissioned to prophesy, but this time regarding a broader range of message. His message must be about many peoples, nations, languages, and kings. These peoples are specifically those who worship the emperor, who receive the mark of the beast, and whom John will increasingly identify as those who dwell on the earth. Whereas Act One emphasized faithfulness through persecution and suffering and the reward of faithfulness, Act Two emphasizes God's powerful and dramatic judgment on those who dwell on the earth.

Before engaging Act Two, we must address the remainder of this enigmatic second interlude, 11:1–14 and the final warning judgment of the seventh trumpet.

The Measuring of the Temple

Perhaps no text in Revelation has created more difficulty for commentators than 11:1–13. Commenting on one aspect of the difficulty, Bauckham states, "This passage has never been fully understood because its character as an interpretation of Daniel has not been recognized" (Bauckham, *The Climax of Prophecy*, 267) Although there are difficulties and possibilities in the understanding of this text, there is a common thread that runs through all, or most, of the possibilities suggested by commentators: God protects and preserves his saints through grave difficulties, even martyrdom for Jesus.

11:1–2. *I was given a reed like a measuring rod and was told, "Go and measure the temple of God and the altar, and count the worshipers there.* [2] *But exclude the outer court; do not measure it, because it has been given to the Gentiles. They will trample on the holy city for* [42] *months."* One major debate among scholars is identifying which temple is being measured, a literal temple or a spiritualized temple.[100] It is apparent that John drew heavily on Ezekiel 40–42 and Zechariah 2:1–5 for the image of the measuring of the temple. In both instances the temple in Jerusalem was no longer standing, and the idealized temple that was measured was looking forward to a new temple or city that was to be restored.[101] Bauckham observes, "It is highly unlikely that in Revelation 11:1–2 John intends to speak literally of a temple which had been destroyed in 70. . . . He understands the temple and the city as symbols of the people of God."[102] Beale observes that "it is the eschatological temple of Ezekiel 40–48 that is John's focus."[103] He notes that

"The Qumran community also spiritualized Ezekiel's temple. Its members declared the Jerusalem temple apostate."[104] Thus the measuring of the temple in Ezekiel, Zechariah, and Revelation is symbolic of something more than merely the temple itself.

The next question to be addressed relates to the meaning of the measuring of the temple. The metaphor of measuring is similar to sealing the saints in that it indicates the ownership and protection of the temple or people by God. This measuring does not mean that the temple or saints will not be harmed physically, but that they are spiritually protected by God.[105] Aune succinctly summarizes the many arguments regarding the measuring of the temple and concludes "Thus the worshippers in the temple of God . . . are analogous to the 144,000 whom God has sealed (7:3–8), for they too are divinely protected against the divine punitive plagues as well as the murderous intention of the enemies of God."[106]

Another question that has initiated considerable debate is the identifying of the *temple*, the **altar**, the **worshippers**, which are measured, and **the *outer court***, which is not to be measured. Most agree that the temple, altar, and worshippers are metaphors that symbolize the church, the saints, or the Christian communities who worship God.[107] The real question however relates to the outer court, which is not measured, indicating that it is not protected by God. John surely would have been clearly aware of the sacrilegious profaning of the temple by Antiochus Epiphanes IV in 167 b.c., and the destruction of Jerusalem and the temple by Rome in 70. The view that the unrepentant Jews are the focus of the outer court, which is given over to the Gentiles, had been proposed by Andreas (Andrew), Bishop of Caesarea in the fifth century, who is accredited with having written one of the first commentaries on Revelation.[108] However, in spite of the fact that Jesus was extremely severe in his condemnation of the synagogue and Jews in Revelation and that the Jews were part of the oppression encountered by the church in Asia, this view has not been popular among modern scholars,[109] mostly because it does not fit well into the overall structure of Revelation, especially regarding the beast that is about to rise from the sea, whom many believe to represent the new Babylon, the civil power of the Roman Empire. I agree with Bauckham that John is reinterpreting Jewish concepts to explain the church's struggle with the new Babylon, Rome.[110]

What is interesting in this discussion is the location of the outer court. It obviously is part of the temple and therefore should represent some aspect of the people of God who would gather there. It must then be some symbol relating to the people of God, explaining something of their relationship with God. In John's description of the outer court, it is not measured; therefore, it is not protected. There must be some aspect of the people of God, the church in Revelation, that is protected and some aspect that is not protected. One major purpose of Revelation was to explain that those who remain faithful to God are *sealed* by God as a sign that God "owns" them and protects them. Now as a similar sign they are *measured* by God. However, this relates to their spiritual life, not their physical life. They will die as martyrs at the hands of the pagan enemies of God. I am, therefore, inclined to agree with Beale: "The significance of the measuring means that their salvation is secured, despite physical harm that they must suffer."[111] The trampling of the outer court "is equivalent to the great martyrdom."[112]

It is possible that the outer court, part of the temple, that is not measure or protected represents the unfaithful Christians who compromise their faith with Rome.

In summary of 11:1–2, the measuring of the temple is a metaphor symbolizing God's "ownership" and protection of the spiritual life of the saints in keeping with 7:34. The outer court that is not measured and protected is a metaphor symbolizing either the physical life of the saints that is not protected, or those Christians who compromise their faith with Rome. It could imply that many will sacrifice their lives to God in martyrdom at the hands of the Gentiles who trample over the city for forty-two months. The sweetness of the scroll in 10:8–10 represents 11:1, the measuring of the temple, and the bitterness of the scroll could represent 11:2, the trampling of the saints under the feet of the Gentiles.[113]

John closes this enigmatic pericope with the statement *they will trample on the holy city for 42 months*, which leads into 11:3 and the two faithful witnesses who are killed by those who make war on the saints. In order to grasp the meaning of the symbol of *42 months*, one must keep it in context. It symbolizes the trampling of the outer court by the Gentiles. The question is what does the figure of forty-two months symbolize? That Daniel 7:25; 12:7; and 12:11–12 come into play seems the best solution to the puzzle. The forty-two months are a symbol of a condition, not a literal period of time. Forty-two months is the same as three and a half years (times) and 1260 days. John carries these symbols through the narrative of Revelation at 11:2–3; 12:14; and 13:5–6. These symbols represent a period of persecution, even martyrdom, in which the saints are called on to remain faithful to their calling (cf. Beale,[114] Osborne,[115] and Caird[116]). Certainly, this condition, or "period" of suffering, is one under God's sovereign control.[117] He permits it to take place and will bring it to an end and judge those who persecute and trample his people under foot.

11:3. *And I will give power to my two witnesses, and they will prophesy for 1,260 days, clothed in sackcloth.* That the period of persecution referred to in the 42 months is under divine control, John records that God will give his two witnesses power to prophecy, and this for 1260 days or during the period of persecution. Normally, the imperfect tense *edothē* ("was given") indicates divine approval and control, as in 6:2, 4, but here John uses the more emphatic future tense *dōsō* ("I will give"). The divine permission is even more pronounced. Throughout the "period" of persecution (42 months, 1260 days), God's faithful witnesses will continue to prophesy. They will be killed but their faithful testimony will continue. That the witnesses are clothed in sackcloth is a symbol of their prophetic office as in Elijah (2 Kgs 1:8) and John the Baptist (Mark 1:6).

The identification of the two faithful witnesses has occupied the attention of commentators throughout the centuries.[118] That John identifies them as *two olive trees and two lampstands* does not simplify the matter. These two witnesses who are faithful now appear as two olive trees 11:4.

11:4–5. *These are the two olive trees and the two lampstands that stand before the Lord of the earth.* ⁵ *If anyone tries to harm them, fire comes from their mouths and devours their enemies. This is how anyone who wants to harm them must die.* In the theme of 11:1–2 and the measuring and protection of the saints, those who would harm the two witnesses will die. Possibly the fire coming from their mouth represents the faithful testimony they give. To develop his point John draws on Zechariah 4:3 for his image of the two olive trees and lampstands as faithful witnesses. The message of Zechariah was that God was in control of rebuilding the temple and his Spirit would overcome their opponents.[119] John uses his sources with considerable freedom as he weaves his story.[120] The image of the two olive branches and lampstands is an example. Most agree that the two witnesses of Zechariah are Joshua the high priest and Zerubbabel the governor. The temple would be rebuilt according to God's plan for he was in control. All Zechariah had to do was prophesy faithfully. Who specifically John had in mind as the two faithful witnesses has also generated considerable discussion, with some calling for two literal persons who could be identified out of Old Testament or Christian history. Aune lists such proposals,[121] but in the context the two witnesses are corporately the church, or possibly the faithful martyrs who by giving their lives witness powerfully for God.[122] Since John has already recorded that the churches in Asia are symbolically seven lampstands, this seems to be the most reliable symbolism of the two witnesses who are also two lampstands.

Why are two witnesses described as olive trees and lampstands when John has already observed that the seven churches are lampstand witnesses? Why not seven lampstands here as well? John was drawing on a Jewish principle that two witnesses are required in judging an offense against the law (Num. 35:30; Deut. 17:6; 19:15; Matt. 18:16). At the word of two witnesses, truth is established. Beale observes that "God sometimes sends two angels to announce judgment, to execute judgment, or to validate the truth of a divine communication (e.g. *2 Macc.* 3:26, 33; *3 Macc.* 6:18; *2 Enoch* 1:4; . . . Acts 1:10–11)."[123]

The two faithful witnesses are the church, in particular the churches in Asia, and the saints who die as martyrs for their faithful testimony regarding Jesus. In chapter 11 these witnesses are persecuted and die for their witness, but God does not fail them. They are vindicated and raised to glory with God and Jesus.

11:6–12. 6 *These men have power to shut up the sky so that it will not rain during the time they are prophesying; and they have power to turn the waters into blood and to strike the earth with every kind of plague as often as they want.* **7** *Now when they have finished their testimony, the beast that comes up from the Abyss will attack them, and overpower and kill them.* **8** *Their bodies will lie in the street of the great city, which is figuratively called Sodom and Egypt, where also their Lord was crucified.* **9** *For three and a half days men from every people, tribe, language and nation will gaze on their bodies and refuse them burial.* **10** *The inhabitants of the earth will gloat over them and will celebrate by sending each other gifts, because these two prophets had tormented those who live on the earth.* **11** *But after the three and a half days a breath of life from God entered them, and they stood on their feet, and terror struck those who saw them.* **12** *Then they heard a loud voice from heaven saying to them, "Come up here."* **And they went up to heaven in a cloud, while their enemies looked on.** Beale observes that 11:6 "is laden with layers of OT background."[124] Aune states that "the narrative is extremely abbreviated and enigmatical," nothing being "specifically said" regarding the details of these events.[125] Their meaning and relevance are taken for granted. Elijah, Moses, Sodom, Egypt and Jerusalem serve as rich metaphors in this masterpiece of symbolism. John is conjuring up images of significant events to drive home the point that even though the prophets of old faced severe adversity, they triumphed over their adversaries through their uncompromising faithfulness. First he draws on Elijah's power to shut up the sky so that it will not rain during the time of his battle with the prophets of Baal (1 Kgs 17:1); then John turns to Moses, for Moses had power to turn the waters into blood and to strike the earth with every kind of plague as often as necessary (Exod. 7:14-7).

11:7. Now, for the first time John introduces *the beast that comes up from the Abyss*. This beast *will attack them, and overpower and kill them*. This introduction of the beast from the Abyss becomes a central theme in Act Two as he begins to focus attention on Rome as an evil, oppressive civil power. The background for this beast is Daniel's dream of four great beasts, one of which was "waging war against the saints and defeating them" (Dan. 7:21). Many believe that these four great beasts of Daniel represent four great political powers (Babylon, Medo-Persia, Greece, and Rome) culminating in either Rome or Antiochus Epiphanes IV (167 B.C.), depending on the dating of Daniel.[126] Beginning at 13:1, John will return on twenty-nine different occasions to this beast as a metaphor for Rome as an evil persecuting pagan power. In an unusual turn of events, God allows the forces of evil to triumph for a time. The reader, however, already knows from chapters 2 and 3 that in "conquering" the saints, the evil powers are themselves "conquered" by the faithful martyrs, who in turn become the conquerors.

11:8. The bodies of the slain saints will *lie in the street of the great city* in disgrace and as objects of derision. John then elaborates on the evil of the great city by identifying it with three other great evil cities, adding that the great city *is figuratively called Sodom and Egypt, where also their Lord was crucified*. To identify the sinister nature of Rome and the inevitable consequence of its war on the saints, John symbolically[127] refers this city and its plight to the doom of Sodom and Gomorrah, Egypt of the Exodus, and Jerusalem, which by the time of John's writing had been destroyed for its rebellion against God and his Messiah. The reference to *the great city which is figuratively called Sodom and Egypt, where also their Lord was crucified* is intended metaphorically. The syntax of this expression leads to some differing opinions regarding identifying *the great city* and *the city where their Lord was crucified*. Consequently, conflicting opinions regarding identifying the great city are found in several commentators. Some[128] argue in favor of Jerusalem, but recognize that, in all the other references to the great city in Revelation, Rome is intended. The confusion lies in the fact that the two other cities referred to in this text, *Sodom and Egypt*, are not separated by a comma, but *the city where their Lord was crucified* is separated from the Sodom and Egypt in the Greek text and some translations by a comma. *Sodoma kai Aiguptōs, hopou kai ho kurios autōn estaurōthē.* However, the punctuation is provided by scholars in their reading of the text and was not part of the original. In my reading of Revelation it is Rome that is the problem and which is

allegorically or *figuratively* referred to as *the great city*, not Jerusalem, which has been
in ruins for almost thirty years at the time of John's writing, and Jerusalem was not an
issue for Christians suffering in the seven cities of Asia; Rome was. Although Jesus was
severe in his condemnation of the evils of the synagogue in Smyrna and Philadelphia, it
is a "long stretch" from these synagogues to Jerusalem. The great city "is heir to the vice
of *Sodom*, the tyranny of Pharaoh's *Egypt*, and the blind disobedience of Jerusalem, but
it is not literally to be identified with any of them."[129] Beale observes that "all the other
uses of 'the great city' in the Apocalypse refer to 'Babylon the Great,' not Jerusalem"[130]
Although Jerusalem literally was the place of Jesus' crucifixion, Rome shared symbolically in the guilt of Jesus' crucifixion. The *great city*, Rome, a symbol of the beast that
would make war on the saints and kill them, would like Sodom, Egypt, and Jerusalem
feel the terrible wrath and judgment of God.[131] Therefore, I am inclined to identify the
great city as Rome, not Jerusalem, realizing that Rome as the great city incorporated all
of the rebellion and evil found in Sodom, Egypt, and Jerusalem where Jesus was crucified.

One reason for the hostility of the beast was that *these two prophets had tormented
those who live (dwell) on the earth. Those who live on the earth* are they who have opposed
the saints, persecuted them, worshipped the beast, and who will receive the mark of the
beast as a sign of their ownership by the beast (13:1–18). It was the resolute refusal of
the saints to honor the beast that tormented those who dwell on the earth.

11:9–11. *For three and a half days men from every people, tribe, language and nation
will gaze on their bodies and refuse them burial.* [10] *The inhabitants of the earth will gloat
over them and will celebrate by sending each other gifts, because these two prophets had
tormented those who live on the earth.* [11] *But after the three and a half days a breath
of life from God entered them, and they stood on their feet, and terror struck those who
saw them.* Understanding the mention of 3½ days involves figurative use of time in
Revelation. Conflicting scholarly opinions are reflected here! Previously John has spoken
of 42 months and 1260 days (11:2, 3). He was obviously drawing on Daniel's symbolism
of "time, two times, and half a time" (Dan 7:25; 12:7), which I understand to mean 3½
years and to symbolically represent a period of severe persecution. Beckwith considered
that 3½, whether it be times, days, or years at 11:9 "is used in its symbolic sense, denoting calamity, as always in the book."[132] Beckwith had previously drawn attention[133] to the
number 3½ interpreted in Talmudic times as an eschatological number, indicating that
in the Jewish tradition the number had traditionally been understood symbolically. Most
commentators follow the line of thought that the number must be seen in Revelation in
this symbolic sense. 3½ has consequently symbolically been identified variously, with
Daniel's period of tribulation and persecution[134], with Jesus' time in the tomb before his
resurrection[135], or with Jesus' personal ministry[136]. Aune suggests;

> The reference to 3½ days (repeated in v 11) corresponds numerically to the
> 1260 days, or 3½ years, during which the two witnesses were active (11:3). This
> number, which is used for the stereotypical period of distress in apocalyptic lit-
> erature (Dan 7:25; 12:7. . .), corresponds to the length of famine during the time

of Elijah according to the tradition found in Luke 4:25, Jas 4:17, and a few rabbinic sources . . . . In rabbinic sources the number "three and one-half" occurs
frequently, with the apparent meaning of "an extended period of time".[137]

Commenting on the disgraceful abuse of the slain saints Osborne notes, "Like Jesus,
they [the slain saints] are insulted and maltreated to the greatest possible extent."[138]
Reinforcing the symbolic nature of this pericope, Osborne cites both Aune and Beale[139]
as finding in Psalm 79 a pattern for interpreting Revelation and notably this pericope.

John is simply saying that these two faithful witnesses who have been slain (the
martyred saints) will be left in the streets of the great city (Rome or wherever the civil
power of Rome is experienced) in disgrace and humiliation for all who pass by (those
who have persecuted them) to mock in them in derision.

**11:10. *The inhabitants of the earth will gloat over them and will celebrate by sending
each other gifts, because these two prophets had tormented those who live on the earth.***
The pagan world had not been able to coerce the faithful saints into denying Jesus. Their
recalcitrant refusal to submit even to the power of Rome was a torment to those who
dwell on the earth. Although death seemingly "cut off" their witness for a short period,
the torment of the oppressors continued even beyond the saints' deaths. The celebration of the oppressors, however, was short lived, for by the power of God, the martyrs'
testimony refused to go away.

**11:11. *After the three and a half days a breath of life from God entered them, and they
stood on their feet, and terror struck those who saw them.*** The time of their celebration
"is cut short, as is common in apocalyptic literature, to demonstrate the sovereignty of
God over all forces of evil."[140] Drawing again on his Old Testament pallet of symbols,
John goes to Elijah's dry bones (Ezek. 37) to reinforce that by the power of God the life
of the martyrs is not over; neither is their testimony. Like Jesus' "captivity" in death,
the experience of the martyrs is comparatively fleeting. In keeping with Ezekiel's mystical story, the dead martyrs came alive and stood on their feet. There is an allusion to
the resurrection in this statement, which John will later develop regarding the reign of
the saints with Jesus (20:4–6). Those who conquer, eat of the tree of life, experience a
resurrection to glory, receive the crown of life, and sit with Jesus on his throne (2–3).
John now begins to develop this theme of resurrection in more specific detail. Life does
not end in martyrdom, for resurrection by the power of God and his life-giving Spirit (a
breath of life from God) ushers in a new existence in the presence of Jesus and God. A
similar expression of the life-giving power of the Holy Spirit in resurrection is found in
Romans 8:11. Ezekiel's story reached a high point with his observation at Ezekiel 37:10,
"So I prophesied as he commanded me, and breath entered them; they came to life and
stood up on their feet—a vast army." That the saints stood on their feet would recall the
striking conclusion to Ezekiel's story of a vast army and remind the saints of the image
of the church militant at 7:1–8, coupled with the church victorious at 14:1–4. The realization of the invincible power of God and his awesome forces would cause even the evil
forces of humanity to cringe in terror.

11:12. *Then they heard a loud voice from heaven saying to them, "Come up here." And they went up to heaven in a cloud, while their enemies looked on.* Loud voices with commanding messages are heard twenty-four times in Revelation but only twice is it recorded that the loud voice came specifically from heaven. There is some speculation as to whether this is the voice of Christ, the same voice that summoned John into heaven in chapter 4 and that sounded like a trumpet at 1:10. The major point, however, is that this voice summoned the raised saints into heaven with the divine invitation to "Come up here." The question is whether this reference to a resurrection into heaven is a pre-figure of the reference to the first resurrection at 20:5 (which is in itself an enigmatic phrase) or to the resurrection of the church (all Christians) as a whole, or to some concept of rapture. Beale, Osborne, and Aune discuss various views of this call into heaven.[141] Mention is made concerning a rapture. The concept of rapture here would be simply speaking of rapture as a technical term for the experience of being called up into the presence of God. Some find in this a reference to the Dispensational doctrine of the Rapture, but I doubt that this calling up into heaven of the martyred saints is a proleptic experience of some Dispensational view of Rapture. To read a "Dispensational Rapture" into Revelation is both a forced exegesis and theologically unnecessary. The most likely reference of this supposed "rapture" must be to the vindication of the martyred saints in the presence of their enemies.[142] Although Caird sees in the earthquake divine judgment on "an idolatrous and ungodly political order," he introduces an interesting thought: "the death and vindication of the martyrs is itself the earthquake shock by which the great city is overthrown."[143] We who look at this drama have two thousand years of res-urrection theology behind us. These saints facing imminent death were in serious need of assurance that there would be life after death; hence the rewards of martyrdom are repeatedly couched in terms of heavenly existence, reigning with Christ, and resurrec-tion. Consequently, I see in this invitation to *Come up here* a proleptic reference to the resurrection of the martyrs as "the first resurrection" of 20:5.

11:13–14. *At that very hour there was a severe earthquake and a tenth of the city col-lapsed. Seven thousand people were killed in the earthquake, and the survivors were terrified and gave glory to the God of heaven.* [14] *The second woe has passed; the third woe is coming soon.* John now prepares to lead the reader into the seventh trumpet and third woe. We are reminded that the sixth trumpet and second woe took place at 9:13–21 and closed with the statement *The rest of mankind that were not killed by these plagues still did not repent of the work of their hands; they did not stop worshiping demons, and idols of gold, silver, bronze, stone and wood—idols that cannot see or hear or walk.* [21] *Nor did they repent of their murders, their magic arts, their sexual immorality or their thefts.* This solemn condemnation was followed by the interlude of the little scroll in 10, indicating that John's prophetic message spoke of both suffering and victory. The measuring of the temple in 11 reassured the saints that they were protected by God. Now the final trumpet was ready to sound to emphasize God's judgment on their oppressors and again reassure the saints who had cried for vindication from beneath the altar (8:3–4) that God would respond to their suffering. John now introduces this terrifying image of an earthquake in which seven thousand (a combination of seven and one thousand) people are killed. We should remember the doom of Pompeii due to the eruption of Mount Vesuvius and that Asia in particular was familiar with the devastating impact of earthquakes. Although this earthquake should have inculcated serious consideration of God's power and glory, it did not initiate repentance among the ungodly persecutors of the saints. The earthquake now introduced the final woe on the saints' ungodly enemies, indicating that the seventh and final trumpet was about to blow. In preparation for this final woe, *at that very hour there was a severe earthquake and a tenth of the city collapsed.* The great earthquake accompanying the dramatic events portrayed by John in this scene is not unusual in the apocalyptic tradition, for earthquakes are often associated with divine activity in Scripture (17 times, 5 times in Revelation: 6:12; 8:5; 11:13; 11:19; 12:18). The reference to seven thousand people killed raises questions as to the precise meaning of seven thousand. In keeping with the numerical tradition of Revelation, one should see the seven thousand as a symbol of completeness. A possible analogy to this number can be found in 1 Kings 19:18, where God has a remnant of seven thousand faithful people who have not bowed the knee to Baal. The figure is obviously intended symbolically, referring to the fact that God had many faithful witnesses during Elijah's days of suffering and prophesying. Here the emphasis may be on the fact that although the judgment was only partial (one tenth of the city fell), the tenth nevertheless represented a large number. However, that not all the city was killed suggests to some that there was real repentance on the part of many in the city who saw in the vindication of the saints the power of God.

John concludes this scene with the comment that *the survivors were terrified and gave glory to the God of heaven.* The question is raised by some whether this constitutes real repentance on the part of the survivors of the earthquake or whether this constituted "forced homage of a defeated foe, as in Phil 2:11."[144] Contrary to the view that this constituted real repentance, Osborne cites Hendriksen, Kiddle, Mounce, Beale and Giesen who draw a parallel to the Egyptian magicians who confessed that the plagues were from the finger of God but did not repent.[145] I am inclined to agree with this view.

The possibility of significant repentance before judgment is finally pronounced is typical of God's unending grace, for repeatedly God has offered such opportunity to the idolatrous enemies of the church. At 14:6–7, John describes a vision of an angel, proclaiming an eternal gospel to those who dwell on the earth, offering them a final opportunity to repent. **Then I saw another angel flying in midair, and he had the eternal gospel to proclaim to those who live on the earth—to every nation, tribe, language and people. [7] He said in a loud voice, "Fear God and give him glory, because the hour of his judgment has come. Worship him who made the heavens, the earth, the sea and the springs of water.** That a call to repentance was intended in this message of imminent judgment is obvious. Even those who betray and murder God's servants are included in his eternal plan of salvation. The call to repentance of the sixth seal (9:20–21), coming before the final woe was announced and the seventh trumpet blown, indicates that in the plan of God there is always time for the idolatrous to repent. However, as mentioned above, I do not see in this call a concept of universal salvation. It is obvious, however, that God intends all men to come to repentance should they so choose (2 Pet. 3:9; Acts 17:30). Nevertheless, there is no indication in Revelation that any of the evil humankind that heard the eternal gospel actually repented. The significant point is that within John's theodicy, God's *Heilsgeschichte,* and God's eternal love for his creation, God always holds out opportunities to idolatrous nations to repent.

11:14. With the statement **The second woe has passed; the third woe is coming soon,** John prepares for the climactic announcement of the third woe and final trumpet. One would think that in keeping with other similar situations in Revelation a mighty angel would pronounce a final judgment on those who dwell on the earth, on those who oppose his will and who persecute his people. At the announcement of the sixth seal, right before the revealing of the seventh seal, which rolled over into the seven trumpets, the enemies of God's people sought to hide in caves and escape the wrath of God and the Lamb (6:12–17). A severe judgment here at the blowing of the seventh trumpet introducing great suffering would have been in keeping with the third woe since those who adamantly continued "worshiping demons and idols," namely those who worshipped the beast, refused to repent of their evil deeds.

However, the seventh trumpet and the third woe reveal a surprising situation. John's expression *the third woe is coming soon* is in line with the theme of imminent action. The Greek of this text reads *hē ousai hē tritē erchetai tachu.* It is the last two words that are of interest to the interpretation of this text, *erchetai tachu.* At 2:16; 3:11, *erchetai tachu,* **coming soon** has a temporal reference stressing the imminence of Jesus' coming in judgment.[146] The expression is used six times in Revelation, all in a similar context of imminence. At 2:16 and 3:11 the coming of Jesus in judgment on the churches in Asia was conditional, therefore not a reference to the final eschatological judgment. Surprisingly, the third woe does not specifically present a judgment vision, but draws attention to Jesus' and God's sovereign reign over the world. It is Jesus who reigns, not Rome and the emperor.

THE SEVENTH WARNING TRUMPET AND THIRD WOE

11:15–19. *The seventh angel sounded his trumpet, and there were loud voices in heaven, which said: "The kingdom of the world has become the kingdom of our Lord and of his Christ, and he will reign for ever and ever."* [16] *And the twenty-four elders, who were seated on their thrones before God, fell on their faces and worshiped God,* [17] *saying: "We give thanks to you, Lord God Almighty, the One who is and who was, because you have taken your great power and have begun to reign.* [18] *The nations were angry; and your wrath has come. The time has come for judging the dead, and for rewarding your servants the prophets and your saints and those who reverence your name, both small and great—and for destroying those who destroy the earth."* [19] *Then God's temple in heaven was opened, and within his temple was seen the ark of his covenant. And there came flashes of lightning, rumblings, peals of thunder, an earthquake and a great hailstorm.* Loud voices refer to a significant announcements. In regard to the seven warning trumpets, which were intended to call Rome and those who dwell on earth to repent, the "tenth plague"[147] of Revelation, the seventh trumpet, pronounces God's and Jesus' judgment on those who dwell on earth and Rome, the power behind them. It is an advanced proleptic judgment reaching far beyond the simple judgment of Rome. It reaches far forward into the future and pronounces God's ultimate judgment on the whole world. God's judgment of Rome is predicated on his final judgment, so here the proleptic eschatological judgment of Rome melds into the final eschatological judgment. In particular I like Caird's observation, "Now futurity is caught up in the eternal present".[148] Jesus has taken his sovereign power, condemned the raging nations (Ps. 2), demonstrated his sovereign power over Rome, and the final judgment of the whole world is introduced. Rome is judged and the saints are ultimately vindicated. The image of Daniel 7 is obvious.

Osborne draws attention to the difficulties faced when interpreting this pericope. "This is another difficult passage, for it announces the 'third woe'; yet instead of judgment, we have a heavenly celebration of the coming of "the kingdom of our Lord' (v. 15)."[149] Osborne then introduces five possible approaches to unraveling this triumphant text. He is correct in observing that this section concludes the major section (4:1–11:19) of the book. It brings Act One to conclusion, and following the command to John to again prophesy to many peoples and tongues and kings, sets the reader up for Act Two, (12–22). Osborne and others point to the *inclusio* of the twenty-four elders (4:4 and 11:16) in support of this conclusion.[150]

Some have thought that the events following in 12–14 are the description of the third woe and seventh trumpet. Others find 12–21 to be the description of the seventh trumpet. The brief hymn of 11:15–19 is considered by some to be an anticipation of what will happen in chapter 20. However, Beale is correct in seeing in this hymn an exultant explanation of the consummation of history rather than a description of that final judgment.[151] In other words, 11:15–19 does not describe in detail the third woe, leaving this to be fleshed out in the remaining chapters. These verses rather praise God for his sovereign power and reign in the language of the magnificent scene of the throne room of chapter 4.

Osborne notes that "The most significant element, however, is the transformation of the threefold title from 1:4, 8; and 4:8, with its variations on the theme of the God who controls past, present, and future—'who is, who was, and who is to come.' . . . The God who was sovereign in the past will also control the future (the very message of this book)."[152]

Revelation is a literary drama played out in cosmic scenes, not a chronological history or plan of events leading up to the final act of God. The seventh trumpet and woe are the closing scene of Act One, and this trumpet projects the mind forward beyond the immediate into the narrative of Act Two. At 10:11 John had been told to prophesy again against nations and kings. The prayer of the saints will be answered and God will judge their enemy, Rome. This will be more specifically described in vivid dramatic imagery in Act Two. The hymn of the twenty-four elders that follows at 11:16 repeats the heavenly throne room theme of chapter 4 as the twenty-four elders praise God for his sovereign reign over all creation.

11:15–16. *"The kingdom of the world has become the kingdom of our Lord and of his Christ, and he will reign for ever and ever."* The cosmic hymn of praise of chapter 4 is captured here as it sets the awesome scenes that are shortly to be revealed in Act 2. God is sovereign and exercises his sovereign reign through Jesus, who in the language of Daniel 7 reigns for ever and ever.

11:17. *"We give thanks to you, Lord God Almighty, the One who is and who was, because you have taken your great power and have begun to reign."* The eternal God has exercised his great power and begun to reign. It is not that God exercises his reign only after the final judgment. He already exercises this reign through his Son, Jesus, who is already sitting on his throne next to God. This has been a constant theme throughout Revelation. Even the martyred saints sit on thrones with Jesus, reigning and judging the nations. *Eilēphas* ("you have taken") is a perfect indicative active verb, which implies that God has already taken and continues to take his great power. Aune points out that the Greek *ebasileusas* ("begun to reign") is an ingressive aorist that implies that he has begun to reign.[153] The point is not that God will one day take his great power and begin to reign; he has already taken this great power and reigns over all creation and history.

11:18. *The nations were angry; and your wrath has come* is intended to remind the reader of Psalm 2, the psalm of kingly ascent and reign, which has already featured prominently in Revelation. The nations (Rome) have been angry but God's wrath has come. *The time has come for judging the dead, and for rewarding your servants the prophets and your saints and those who reverence your name, both small and great—and for destroying those who destroy the earth.* Osborne points out that the remainder of the hymn is set out in a chiastic structure that contrasts the judgment of God (A and A1) with the rewards of God (B and B1).

> A   *The time has come for judging the dead*
>   B   *And for rewarding your servants the prophets*
>   B1   *And your saints and those who reverence your name, small and great*
> A1   *And for destroying those who destroy the earth.*[154]

John uses the word *kairos* for time, signifying not chronological time, but significant eschatological time. This he couples with the aorist *ēlthen* ("has come") signifying that *the* eschatological time has come for judging and rewarding. Osborne concludes that "three aorist infinitives follow the idea of the God-appointed 'time.' It is time for judging, for rewarding, and for destroying.[155]

11:19. This verse brings Act One to dramatic closure. Apocalyptic and Old Testament images and concepts are melded together in terms somewhat reminiscent of chapter 4 and the cosmic throne room scene. The terms are different, but the message is the same. God is in control, and from his heavenly throne-room he has acted in decisive manner. *Then God's temple in heaven was opened, and within his temple was seen the ark of his covenant. And there came flashes of lightning, rumblings, peals of thunder,* *an earthquake and a great hailstorm.* The ark of the covenant signified God's firm covenant with his people, the presence of God with his people, and God's acts of mercy in behalf of his people.

Summary of 8:7–11:19: The Seventh Trumpet and Second Interlude

So climactic was the announcement of the seventh trumpet that there was silence in heaven for about thirty minutes. The seven seals of the great scroll of chapter 5 had expanded into seven warning trumpets of God's judgments against those who dwell on earth, those who persecute the saints. At the opening of the sixth seal, the saints had cried out for vindication and for judgment on those who had caused their death, or more precisely, slaughtered them. They were told to wait while God worked out his purpose. The seventh seal became seven trumpets, leading the reader to work through the first six warning trumpets in expectation of the final warning trumpet. In the interim at chapter 10, John introduced his second great interlude, which again was intended to calm the crescendo of expectation. He was told to eat a little scroll, which would be bitter and sweet—bitter in that it predicted more suffering, but sweet in the promise of salvation and vindication that lay ahead. Then before he revealed the final, seventh trumpet, chapter 11 opened with the measuring of the temple as a promise that God knew his people and would protect them. The magnificent narrative of the two witnesses promised that, although they would die for their faithful witness, they would share in his resurrection. Finally, the seventh warning trumpet had morphed into a magnificent scene of praise to God for his having taken his great power and begun to exercise his sovereign reign over the world. John never actually narrates the coming of the third woe. In place of the third woe, "A loud hymn of praise bursts forth from heavenly voices celebrating the incoming of the kingdom of God, as if already present. The hymn is one of the author's anticipatory outbursts of praise uttered from the beginning of a movement from the standpoint of the final issue

The mystique of the morphing of the seventh trumpet and third woe into a triumphant hymn of praise announcing the sovereign reign of God over all of creation is best seen as another of John's eschatological views in which the past, present, and future are collapsed into the present in a dramatic statement of God's sovereign power. In Act Two, John will explain that Rome is none other than an agent of Satan and his demonic power. What is prefigured here in this hymn praising God's sovereign reign will be seen in its completion in the final judgment scenes. Act Two will reveal the war of God against the demonic powers of Satan. John will describe God's ultimate victory over Satan and his agents, the final judgment, which is prefigured here (11:15–19) in the morphed third woe, and ultimate vindication of the saints for their faithfulness also prefigured in the resurrection of the two faithful witnesses of chapter 11:11-12.

Chapter 8

The Seven Mystic Figures

The High Point of Revelation

12:1–14:20

Chapter 12 is the theological high point. John begins by demonstrating that Satan has already been defeated by Michael in a cosmic war. In this cosmic drama Satan has descended to earth and attempted to defeat God's messianic purpose and plan. He tried to destroy the Messiah but was again defeated at the cross and resurrection of Christ. Satan continues to make war on the church (the messianic woman who symbolically flees into the wilderness and is protected by God). The saints, through their faith in the death, burial, and resurrection of Jesus, and refusal to compromise their faith in Jesus, can conquer Satan and share in his defeat. Revelation 12:10–11 resounds with victory, "And I heard a loud voice in heaven, saying, 'Now the salvation and the power and the kingdom of our God and the authority of his Christ have come, for the accuser of our brethren has been thrown down, who accuses them day and night before our God. And they have conquered him by the blood of the Lamb and by the word of their testimony, for they loved not their lives even unto death'" (RSV).

In chapter 13 John portrays the enemy more specifically as two beasts, a sea beast and a land beast. The enemy is identified as a major political power with religious implications. As the narrative unfolds, the enemy is Rome and the imperial cult. Chapter 14 closes with seven angelic messages, culminating with an announcement of divine wrath and judgment on Rome, now symbolically identified as Babylon the Great.

W e have now reached the apex of the chiastic structure of Revelation, indicating that we have reached the high point in the theology and theodicy of the narrative drama. Mounce identifies the scenes that follow in 12:1–14:20 as the opening of a pageant,[1] reinforcing that what we have in Revelation is a powerful drama set on a cosmic stage. Only when we understand the literary genre of Revelation are we in a position to unravel it's amazing, spectacular scenes and visions.

Prologue 1:1–20

      I. The Church in Imperfection (2:1–3:22)

          Seven Letters to the Seven Churches

      II. The Authority of God over Evil Explained (4:1–8:6)

          Seven Seals on the Scroll

        III. The Warning Judgments (8:1–11:19)

          Seven Trumpets

          IV. The Lamb—God's Answer to Evil (12:1–14:20)

             Seven Unnumbered Figures

        V. The Consummated Judgments (15:1–16:21)

          Seven Bowls of Wrath

      VI. The Authority of God over Evil Exercised (17:1–20:15)

          Seven Unnumbered Descriptions of God's Judgments

     VII. The Church in Perfection (21:1–22:5)

          Seven Unnumbered Descriptions of the Church in Perfection

Epilogue 22:6–21

INTRODUCTION

A glance at the major commentaries reveals that most consider this section to be central to the narrative of the drama. It is common to see 1–11 as Act One in the theological drama John is presenting. In 12 – 20 John unfolds Act Two, which focuses on the challenges to faith about to be encountered by the Christians in Asia at the close of the first century.[2] In 12:1–14:20 John speaks of the ongoing battle between Satan, the dragon, and God, in which Satan, realizing his defeat at the hands of God and Christ, moves on to make war on the church. First his battle is against the Jewish messianic community (the woman), then the male child (Jesus), then the church as the new messianic community (the woman again).[3] Beale observes that thematically this new section retells the story of Act One, only in more detail and specificity, describing the battle by going into in "deeper dimension of the spiritual conflict between the church and the world, which has been developed progressively in chs. 1–11."[4] John explains that although the immediate enemies seem to be Rome, the synagogue, and the pagan culture in which the churches live in Asia, the real power is that of Satan, the Deceiver. John makes the climactic claim that although Satan has great power and uses all of the worldly and demonic powers at his disposal, he has already been defeated by God and Christ. Furthermore, the saints can share in this defeat by their faithful witness in martyrdom, drawing on the power and victory of the death and resurrection of Jesus (12:10–11).

    Structurally this section has presented several possibilities ranging from John's use of the familiar rhetorical expression *kai eidon*, "and I saw,"[5] to identifying seven dramatic figures (the woman, the dragon, the male child, the angel Michael, the beast from the sea, the beast from the land, and the lamb).[6]

Most commentators have drawn attention to the similarity of the battle of the woman with Satan with ancient pagan myths (Greek, Persian, Babylonian, Egyptian, and Roman).[7] The recipients of Revelation in Asia would certainly have been familiar with these mythic battles between the gods and men. Caird observes that John has rewritten the old pagan myths deliberately to contradict the current perceptions and Roman propaganda for imperial authority.[8] Beasley-Murray observes that Jews, with a knowledge of Old Testament messianic expectation, would have experienced little difficulty identifying John's mythical presentation with messianic hope.[9] The gist of this narrative is that God's people, the saints in Asia, would shortly be engaged in a titanic battle with Satan and his agent, the powers of Rome, but that as in other Jewish "mythological" battles in which Michael the archangel is engaged, Satan would be defeated.

THE WOMAN WITH CHILD – 12:1, 2

The Text

12:1–2. *A great and wondrous sign appeared in heaven: a woman clothed with the sun, with the moon under her feet and a crown of twelve stars on her head. ² She was pregnant and cried out in pain as she was about to give birth.*

12:1. *A great and wondrous sign appeared in heaven* describes the setting of this scene. This is the same location as the visions of 11:19 and the other scenes of Revelation, the cosmic heaven. John intend that the reader be struck by the significance of this scene, for he describes it as *a great and wondrous sign*. A radiant *woman clothed with the sun with the moon under her feet is seen*, but the meaning focuses more on the radiance of her nature than simply on her attire. John apparently has drawn his description from the beauty of the bride in the Song of Solomon (Song of Solomon, 6:4, 10). This imagery is often used in Jewish literature of Jerusalem.[10] Isaiah 60:19–20 also describes restored Israel in similar terms to Song of Solomon 6:10 when describing her as the bride of Jehovah. The woman clothed with the sun connotes majesty, while the moon signifies beauty and glory (Song of Solomon, 6:10). *The crown of twelve stars on her head* has given rise to several interpretations. Osborne[11] lists the possibilities as follows: either they refer to the signs of the Zodiac (Charles[12], Beckwith[13], Beasley-Murray[14], Aune[15]), the twelve tribes of Israel (Kraft, Prigent, Roloff, Thomas, Beale[16]), or the twelve apostles (Sweet, Mounce[17]). Osborne observes that at 1:20 the seven stars represent the angels of the churches, leading him to suggest that the twelve stars might refer to "the whole people of God."[18] It is difficult to say precisely what John had in mind in this reference to the twelve stars, but whatever it may have been, it speaks of the beauty and majesty of the woman and may infer her role as "mother Zion," the mother of God's people. This reference draws on Old Testament imagery of "Mother Zion bringing forth children for the messianic age" (cf. Isa. 66:7, the believing remnant of Israel; Isa. 26:16–27; *Qumran Thanksgiving Hymn* E).[19] The heavenly imagery of the woman's brightness "connotes the heavenly identity and heavenly protection of the people of God, as well as their purity, which safeguards their ultimate spiritual invincibility against persecution and corruption by temptation, deception, or any vice."[20]

Interpretations of the identity of the woman include Mary the mother of Jesus, Israel, the Jewish messianic community, the church, the faithful remnant of Israel, and the persecuted people of God.[21] It is possible that several concepts are included in the reference to the woman. That she is the "mother" of the Messiah is fairly obvious.[22] However, the possibility of her being literally Mary the mother of Jesus is remote.[23] I see in this woman a reference to the messianic community both before the birth of the Messiah and after the death of the Messiah. If this is the case, then Yarbro Collins is correct in seeing the woman as "the persecuted people of God from whom comes the Messiah."[24] The woman therefore refers to the faithful remnant of Israel and later on to the church; the faithful messianic community persecuted by Satan and his agents. The woman who *was pregnant and cried out in pain as she was about to give birth* is first symbolically the messianic community awaiting the birth of the Messiah and then, in 12:6, the church as the messianic community pursued by Satan and his agents.

THE DRAGON, THE CHILD, THE FLEEING WOMAN, AND THE WILDERNESS – 12:3–6

The Text

12:3–6. *Then another sign appeared in heaven: an enormous red dragon with seven heads and ten horns and seven crowns on his heads. [4] His tail swept a third of the stars out of the sky and flung them to the earth. The dragon stood in front of the woman who was about to give birth, so that he might devour her child the moment it was born. [5] She gave birth to a son, a male child, who will rule all the nations with an iron scepter. And her child was snatched up to God and to his throne. [6] The woman fled into the desert to a place prepared for her by God, where she might be taken care of for 1,260 days.*

12:3. The second sign in heaven is *an enormous red dragon with seven heads and ten horns and seven crowns on his heads*. At this point John does not identify the dragon, but later in 12:9 he states that *the dragon is the Devil and Satan, the deceiver of the whole world*. Initially, John draws on Canaanite and other ancient Near Eastern mythology regarding a dragon (possibly the sea dragon Leviathan) who is the enemy of the people and Israel's enemy. At Psalm 74:14 he is Leviathan or Egypt. At Ezekiel 29:3 he is the Pharaoh, "the great monster lying among streams." At Job 40:18 he is Behemoth a great beast. In Isa 27:1 he is Assyria and Babylon.[25] That he has *seven heads and seven crowns* symbolizes great power. The crowns are *diadems* (Greek *diadema*), not *crowns* as in *stephanos* (2:10; 3:11; 4:4, 10; 6:2; 14:14). The seven heads and diadems represent false claims to universal sovereignty.[26] *Ten horns* draws on the beast of Daniel 7:7, 24, with the ten horns representing ten kings coming from the fourth empire, and speaks of awesome power.[27] This image of the dragon suggests "crowns of arrogated authority" and presumptions of royal power.[28] John will later, in a rebirth of images at 13:1 refer to the beast from the sea as having *seven heads* and *ten diadems*, and again in 17:12, in the context of the eighth king, of ten horns as ten kings. These later references are intended to show that the beast and eighth king of 17: 11 are the servants of the Dragon, Satan.

12:4. The tail of the dragon sweeping away a third of the stars of the sky to the earth speaks of the great, yet limited power of the dragon.[29] There is considerable discussion as to what or whom the stars represent. *His tail swept a third of the stars out of the sky and flung them to the earth*. Some argue, based on Daniel 8:10, that the stars refer to the angels who joined Satan in his original revolt against God,[30] while others argue that they foretell of his power to persecute the saints.[31] The dragon appears standing *in front of the woman who was about to give birth, so that he might devour her child the moment it was born.* In this cosmic drama the scene of the pageant moves from the heavens to the earth, revealing the plan of the dragon now to defeat the purpose of God on earth. Beale comments on the ease of John's moving from the pre-messianic persecution of the saints through the birth of the Messiah to the post-messianic persecution of the church as possibly due to John's telescoping style rather than his temporal concerns, which could include "aspects of the OT age and the intertestamental period leading up to the time of Christ.[32]

The scene of the dragon seeking to kill the unborn child of the woman was not new to the world of the churches in Asia. John draws on ancient Near Eastern mythology relating to similar legends, rewriting them to suit his purpose (cf. Caird[33]).

12:5. The details of the Messiah's life, ministry, death, and resurrection, although important to the Gospel narrative, are not the high point in John's drama, and he assumes that the reader knows the gospel narrative well. Therefore, he abbreviates and telescopes events that were well known to the readers.[34] The woman *gave birth to a son, a male child, who will rule all the nations with an iron scepter. And her child was snatched up to God and to his throne.* That John intends the reader to associate this son with the Messiah is established by the statement that this child *will rule all the nations with an iron scepter.* The reader would immediately recognize this expression from Psalm 2, the psalm of kingly ascent, which John has already used at 2:26 and to which he repeatedly returns to make the connection with Jesus (cf. 19:15, where he records that Christ will "strike down the nations. 'He will rule them with an iron scepter'). Since it is the messianic community (faithful Israel) that gives birth to this child and the faithful messianic community (the church) that flees into the desert, under the circumstances most Christians, already familiar with the Gospel birth narratives, would make an immediate connection to the male child as Jesus.[35] John intends to encourage those children of the new persecuted messianic community, the church, to see a connection in the Gospel narrative of Jesus' being opposed by Herod as Satan's agent, dying on the cross, and being *snatched up to God to his throne.*

Some commentators[36] see a connection here to the faithful disciples in Jerusalem fleeing into the desert in A.D. 66 when God used the Roman armies to destroy Jerusalem. Early accounts of disciples fleeing to Pella (Eusebius, *Eccl. Hist.* 3:5) might be one of the colors of John's palette to his drama. Aune considers the flight into the wilderness to be problematic since there appears to be a number of possible mythical images in this reference and flights into the wilderness appear to be common in apocalyptic contexts (cf. Matt. 24:15–22, which speaks of the flight of faithful disciples from Jerusalem in A.D. 66).[37] What Aune possibly misses is John's impressionistic style in which he picks up images from various sources and blends them into a new representation. We should not define John's source narrowly since he is accustomed to combining sources in a montage of ideas.

12:6. *The woman fled into the desert to a place prepared for her by God, where she might be taken care of for 1,260 days.* The woman, now the church as the messianic community, *fled into the desert to a place prepared for her by God.* The exodus connection is clear. The safety of the desert was not an easy time, but through faithfulness to God Israel could, and many did prevail. The implication is that, although Satan pursues the church, God has a place of safety for them that they access through faithfulness to his purpose. The messianic community would in all probability face continuing hardship, but they too through faithfulness would prevail. That *she might be taken care of for 1,260 days* returns to Daniel 7:25 and 12:7 (already at 11:3). In fact, John makes use of this symbolic image of twelve hundred sixty days five times (11:2, 3; 12:6, 14; 13:5). At 11:2 that the numbers represent a period of severe persecution during which God would protect his people through their faith and by his power. At 12:6 "that day of evil is short, temporary, and strictly controlled by God." This symbolic time reference relates to a severe time of persecution during which God is still in control and during which he will preserve the saints. They may have to die for their faith, but they will be the ultimate conqueror of Satan.[38] In victorious terms he states, *"Now have come the salvation and the power and the kingdom of our God, and the authority of his Christ. For the accuser of our brothers, who accuses them before our God day and night, has been hurled down. They overcame him by the blood of the Lamb and by the word of their testimony; they did not love their lives so much as to shrink from death."*

THE WAR IN HEAVEN – 12:7–12
The Text
12:7–12. *And there was war in heaven. Michael and his angels fought against the dragon, and the dragon and his angels fought back.* [8] *But he was not strong enough, and they lost their place in heaven.* [9] *The great dragon was hurled down—that ancient serpent called the devil, or Satan, who leads the whole world astray. He was hurled to the earth, and his angels with him.* [10] *Then I heard a loud voice in heaven say: "Now have come the salvation and the power and the kingdom of our God, and the authority of his Christ. For the accuser of our brothers, who accuses them before our God day and night, has been hurled down.* [11] *They overcame him by the blood of the Lamb and by the word of their testimony; they did not love their lives so much as to shrink from death.* [12] *Therefore rejoice, you heavens and you who dwell in them. But woe to the earth and the sea, because the devil has gone down to you. He is filled with fury, because he knows that his time is short."*

Most commentators observe that the concept of a messianic war plays a major role in the theology and symbolism of Revelation. Yarbro Collins argues that any interpretation of Revelation must be defined by the imagery of conflict and combat.[39] Bauckham likewise stresses the role of the relationship of a cosmic war and the theology of Revelation[40] and adds that a Holy War played a major role in Jewish Messianic expectation.[41] Without question, John draws richly from passages such as Isaiah 14 and Daniel 10. John's view also has precedents "in later apocalyptic literature (1 *Enoch, 4 Ezra, 2 Baruch, 1QM.*"[42] Not to be overlooked in this brief summary of the concept of cosmic wars in the Jewish tradition is the War Scroll of the Dead Sea Covenanters. Charlesworth draws attention to the connection between cosmic conflict and Michael (12:7) when speaking of the major differences between Jesus and the Dead Sea Covenanters, or Essenes. "Jesus never mentioned Michael, Gabriel, Raphael, and Sariel. The Essenes, however, developed an extensive angelology; and these names appear, for example, in the War Scroll" (*1QM* 9:15–16). Charlesworth notes, however, that these ideas Jesus shared with many other Jews, so it is unwise to seek to discern some influence from the Essenes.[43]

Any tendency to limit this cosmic war to an historical time, either primordial or at some point in history, fails to understand the message conveyed in cosmic war symbolism. The apocalyptic genre stresses a continuing battle between the forces of evil (Satan and his angels) and the forces of good (Michael as the representative of God, and his angels). There probably is a primordial element in this battle, which Aune also describes as protological,[44] reflecting and explaining the original fall of Satan and his angels, as well as a Christological element relating to the defeat of Satan at the cross and resurrection of Jesus. John wants his readers to understand that persecution and oppression is the work of Satan and his agents (in Revelation, the pagan world and Rome) and that Michael and Jesus have already fought and won this battle. Satan, however, refuses to concede and continues to make war against the saints, a war that he cannot win but that can possibly cause the saints to compromise their faith (with the Roman imperial cult). As the narrative continues, the saints will join Jesus in his victory and conquer Satan through their life-giving confession of faith.

Mythology does not refer to stories that are not true, but to events that can only be described in extra-human or extra-terrestrial terms. Stories about origins and the gods and demon powers are most often recounted in mythological form. Myths are culturally and religiously grounded in the sociology of peoples. John is presenting in dramatic style an age-old battle between Satan and God. How else could he do this than to draw on mythological language? The question is not when or where this war took place, but what it means, for the apocalyptic mindset is not interested in historical questions, but explores theological concerns. Satan has already been defeated and will in every other conflict likewise be defeated. In point of fact, John will argue at 12:10–11 that Satan has already been "thrown down" and "they have already conquered him by the blood of the Lamb" and their "faithful testimony" in martyrdom for Jesus.

Revelation 12:7–11 is divided into two parts: (1) the cosmic battle between the dragon and the forces of God with Michael as the prince and leader of the heavenly host (12:7–9) and (2) the contextualization of the battle on earth between the dragon and the saints, and the victory of the saints over the dragon through their uncompromising faith and the power of the death and resurrection of Jesus (12:10–11). The language of Daniel 10:13. and 12:7–9 is similar. In Daniel 10 Michael, one of the chief princes, intervened between Daniel and the prince of Persia. Beale points out that the parallels between Michael and Jesus are also notable. Michael is "closely associated with the Son of Man, and both are set forth as heavenly representatives of Israel." Michael helps the Son of man fight against the forces of evil.[45] Likewise in chapter 12 Michael and Christ are associated in the ongoing defeat of Satan.

12:7–9. *And there was war in heaven. Michael and his angels fought against the dragon, and the dragon and his angels fought back.* [8] *But he was not strong enough, and they lost their place in heaven.* [9] *The great dragon was hurled down—that ancient serpent called the devil, or Satan, who leads the whole world astray. He was hurled to the earth, and his angels with him.* Jewish thought saw Michael as the prince of angels and a military leader of the heavenly hosts (Cf. Duane F. Watson's summary of the role Michael played in Jewish and early Christian thought[46]).

   In the cosmic conflict with Michael, Satan and his angels were *not strong enough, and they lost their place in heaven.* Consequently Satan and his angels were hurled down out of heaven to the earth where they continue their war through their agent (Rome) against the saints (Rev. 13). John is explicit as to the nature of Satan. He is *that ancient serpent called the devil, or Satan, who leads the whole world astray.* It was he who tempted Adam and Eve (Gen. 3:1-7). John describes him as *the devil,* a term familiar to Christians. *Devil, diabolos,* was a common term in both the Septuagint and New Testament as a translation of the Hebrew, which is a judicial term referring to an "accuser," "slanderer," "calumniator," or "adversary" in a court of law (cf. Ps. 109:6). The New Testament also uses the transliteration *satanos,* which is synonymous with *diabolos* (cf. 12:9). *Diabolos* is rare outside the LXX and the New Testament in the Jewish and Christian literary tradition (it is found in *Wis.* 2:23–24, which identifies the serpent of Gen. 3 with the devil).[47] The expression *the great dragon was hurled down . . . to the earth* is not literal; it is a dramatic statement of Satan's fall from divine favor and community, and limitation of his power. In John's mythological drama, the fall was primordial, at the cross, and on the occasion of the martyrdom of every saint. The concept regarding the limitation of Satan's power through his fall and the power of God comes into clearer focus in the discussion of the saints in Asia and the Roman imperial power at chapter 20, where Satan is bound with a great chain for a thousand years.

12:10–11. *Then I heard a loud voice in heaven say: "Now have come the salvation and the power and the kingdom of our God, and the authority of his Christ. For the accuser of our brothers, who accuses them before our God day and night, has been hurled down.* [11] *They overcame him by the blood of the Lamb and by the word of their testimony; they did not love their lives so much as to shrink from death."* These two verses are the high point in the chiastic structure and theology of Revelation. Several have pointed out the hymnic nature of 12:10–11.[48] Osborne observes that hymns function "like a Greek chorus in a play, not only celebrating but also interpreting the significance of the narrative.

Thus, the hymn here interprets the significance of 12:7–9 for the people of God." There are three parts to this celebrative hymn:[49] (1) the celebration of God's deliverance in the defeat of Satan by Michael (12:10), (2) the expansion of that victory to include the conquering of Satan by the saints (12:11), and (3) the implication of the victory over Satan for heaven and earth (12:12).

Now have come the salvation and the power and the kingdom of our God, and the authority of his Christ. Although the major English translations render the word *sōtēria* here as "salvation," it is more appropriate and in keeping with the combat myth of cosmic war to translate it here and in 7:10 as victory.[50] The statement regarding the coming of the victory and power and the kingdom is introduced by the temporal adverb *arti* ("now"), which when combined with the aorist verb *egeneto* (from *ginomai*, "come"), results in a perfected sense of "have come." Thus John's celebrative hymn proclaims that the victory of Christ over Satan and the whole world has already begun. The reason for this victory is that *the accuser of our brothers, who accuses them before our God day and night, has been hurled down.* Although the decisive aspect of the victory was realized in the cross, John fixes its roots in the primordial and protological victory over Satan. Now comes the resounding crescendo. The saints (John refers to them in a sense of communion as *brothers*, NIV, RSV reads *brethren*) *overcome him by the blood of the Lamb and by the word of their testimony; they did not love their lives so much as to shrink from death.* The RSV renders it more precisely: *and they have conquered him by the blood of the Lamb and by the word of their testimony, for they loved not their lives even unto death.* Again we encounter the use of an aorist verb, in this case *enikēsen* (from *nikaō*, "to overcome," "), to emphasize the already nature, or perfective sense, of their conquering Satan. In keeping with the combat context of Revelation, the RSV translation is preferred (see Arndt and Gingrich[51]). The saints' victory over Satan lay in two realities: (1) *the blood of the Lamb* and (2) *the word of their testimony*. A third clause clarifies the nature of their testimony, *they loved not their lives even unto death*. The Greek *achri thanatou* "until death" is precise. *Achri* as an improper preposition which with a genitive of time (*thanatou*) could mean "until the end" or with a genitive of place (as can be read in this construction) "until death," or "even up to the point" of death. A similar use of this preposition at 2:10 supports this conclusion (see also this use in Acts 22:4, where Paul "persecuted the followers of this Way to their death").[52] These saints were faithful even to the cost of their lives.

In these five verses, 12:7–11, we have the climax of the theology of Revelation. Satan, through his agents (soon to be revealed as the civil and religious power of Rome), carries on his persistent war against the forces of God, in this case the church, and relives the defeat he has been doomed to experience ever since his primordial defeat at the hands of Michael. By the word of their testimony regarding Jesus as their Lord, not Caesar, and drawing on the power of the cross and Jesus' resurrection, the saints share in a real sense Jesus' victory over Satan. Paraphrasing the words of Paul at Romans 8:37, "in all these things (they) are more than conquerors through him who loved us."

The "victory" of Satan over the saints is earthly and temporal, but the saints' "victory" over Satan is final and eternal.[53] Summarizing this pericope, Osborne remarks, "whenever Satan takes the life of one of the faithful, he participates in his own defeat." Osborne refers to the death of Jesus on the cross at the hands of Satan as the greatest military victory in history.[54]

12:12. The final statement in this hymn *therefore rejoice, you heavens and you who dwell in them. But woe to the earth and the sea, because the devil has gone down to you. He is filled with fury, because he knows that his time is short"* carries the celebration of this victory into heaven itself, but it also includes a warning to those still living on earth. In his fury Satan lashes out against the messianic community, or woman. John contextualizes the continuation of this mythological cosmic war on earth in the chapters that follow (especially 13), in which the dragon (Satan) "calls" up a fierce beast out of the sea with the commission to wage war on the saints and to conquer them.

The Struggle Carried down to Earth – 12:13–17

The Text

12:13–17. *When the dragon saw that he had been hurled to the earth, he pursued the woman who had given birth to the male child.* [14] *The woman was given the two wings of a great eagle, so that she might fly to the place prepared for her in the desert, where she would be taken care of for a time, times and half a time, out of the serpent's reach.* [15] *Then from his mouth the serpent spewed water like a river, to overtake the woman and sweep her away with the torrent.* [16] *But the earth helped the woman by opening its mouth and swallowing the river that the dragon had spewed out of his mouth.* [17] *Then the dragon was enraged at the woman and went off to make war against the rest of her offspring—those who obey God's commandments and hold to the testimony of Jesus.*

12:13, 14. When the dragon saw that he had been hurled to the earth, he pursued the woman who had given birth to the male child. Revelation 12:13 picks up the narrative from 12:6, where John recorded that the woman fled into the wilderness where she had a place of protection that had been prepared by God for her during persecution. The passage relating to twelve hundred sixty days and persecution draws its symbolism from Daniel. In John's narrative the defeated and enraged dragon now pursued God's people of the messianic community to make war on them, but the woman is to be protected by God. John's drama is not set out in a simple chronological manner, but repeated visions build on previous visions in a kaleidoscopic overlaying manner: **The woman was given the two wings of a great eagle, so that she might fly to the place prepared for her in the desert, where she would be taken care of for a time, times and half a time, out of the serpent's reach.** The symbolism of the **two wings of the great eagle** (drawn from Exod. 19:4) is sharpened by the tradition of God's continued protection of his people as in Deut. 32:10–12 and Moses' song of deliverance and protection at the close of his life,

In a desert land he found him,
in a barren and howling waste.
He shielded him and cared for him;

he guarded him as the apple of his eye,
like an eagle that stirs up its nest
and hovers over its young,
that spreads its wings to catch them
and carries them on its pinions.
The LORD alone led him;
no foreign god was with him.[55]

John is careful to emphasize that the messianic community would be taken care of by God and be *out of the serpent's reach*. This does not imply that the dragon or serpent would have no power over the saints to hurt them. It stresses the theme that, although the saints would be persecuted by the dragon, they would be ultimately protected by God.

12:15–16. John continues the symbolism of Egypt and the wilderness exodus in the statement *Then from his mouth the serpent spewed water like a river, to overtake the woman and sweep her away with the torrent.* [16] *But the earth helped the woman by opening its mouth and swallowing the river that the dragon had spewed out of his mouth.* This recalling of Israel's crossing the Red Sea on dry land reminds the saints that God has used, and can still use, his creation to save his people. It also reminds the saints that the dragon, Satan, uses political powers (Egypt) to achieve his purpose. In chapter 13, John draws on Daniel (beasts represent political powers) and other Old Testament symbols (such as Leviathan) to demonstrate that Satan will use political power, notably the beast from the sea who represents the imperial power of Rome, to achieve his purpose of opposing God's people and purpose.

12:17. *Then the dragon was enraged at the woman and went off to make war against the rest of her offspring—those who obey God's commandments and hold to the testimony of Jesus.* Now the cosmic war is moved down to earth and into a human context. John will return to the concept of demonic-messianic war five more times after 12:7, 17 (13:4; 7; 17:14; 19:11; and 19:19). He now defines more precisely who it is that the dragon opposes; it is *those who obey God's commandments and hold to the testimony of Jesus.* Those who hold to the testimony of Jesus are offering themselves in a sacrificial obedience to God's commandments rather than to the edicts of Roman law.

12:17/13:1a. We encounter an interesting textual variant in 12.17 and 13:1. The NIV considers the statement *and the dragon stood on the shore of the sea* as being in the same paragraph as 12:13-17, including 13:1a in 12:17. The NIV then has 13:1b starting a new paragraph. The RSV has this statement as a continuation of 12:17. The Aland, Matthew Black, *et al The Greek New Testament* text of 2001[56] identifies this clause as 12:18 while the NIV and RSV have no verse 12:18! The RSV includes 12:18 in vs. 17! Osborne states that "early tradition saw 12:18 with 13:1. . . . Most certainly John wrote this to serve as a transition from chapter 12 to chapter 13."[57] The major difference raised by the placement of this transitional verse is how one is to understand the textual variant found in the Greek *estathē* ("he stood"). The textual variant reads *estathēn* ("I stood"). The best manuscripts support *estathē*, implying that the dragon stood on the sand of the sea and called the beast of 13:1 out of the sea, rather than John standing on the sand of the sea and calling to the beast. Aune argues that this variant is important to the structure of Revelation.[58] He supports the reading of the RSV.[59] John develops his narrative by linking the dragon's war on the woman's offspring (12:17) with the beast from the sea (13:1), demonstrating that the beast comes out of the sea in response to the calling of the dragon, who stands on the sand of the sea.

THE BEAST FROM THE SEA – 13:1–10

The Text

And I saw a beast coming out of the sea. He had ten horns and seven heads, with ten crowns on his horns, and on each head a blasphemous name. [2] The beast I saw resembled a leopard, but had feet like those of a bear and a mouth like that of a lion. The dragon gave the beast his power and his throne and great authority. [3] One of the heads of the beast seemed to have had a fatal wound, but the fatal wound had been healed. The whole world was astonished and followed the beast. [4] Men worshiped the dragon because he had given authority to the beast, and they also worshiped the beast and asked, "Who is like the beast? Who can make war against him?" [5] The beast was given a mouth to utter proud words and blasphemies and to exercise his authority for forty-two months. [6] He opened his mouth to blaspheme God, and to slander his name and his dwelling place and those who live in heaven. [7] He was given power to make war against the saints and to conquer them. And he was given authority over every tribe, people, language and nation. [8] All inhabitants of the earth will worship the beast—all whose names have not been written in the book of life belonging to the Lamb that was slain from the creation of the world. [9] He who has an ear, let him hear.

> [10] *If anyone is to go into captivity,*
> *into captivity he will go*
> *If anyone is to be killed with the sword,*
> *with the sword he will be killed.*
> *This calls for patient endurance and faithfulness on the part of the saints.*

13:1. *And I saw a beast coming out of the sea. He had ten horns and seven heads, with ten crowns on his horns, and on each head a blasphemous name*. Linking 13:1 to the previous paragraph, John saw the results of the dragon standing on the sands of the sea: a terrifying, awesome beast came up out of the sea in response to the call of the dragon. The connection of the beast to the dragon is obvious. The beast (Rome) is the agent of the dragon, Satan (13:2), who will carry out the dragon's war (13:7) against the saints. That this beast rises *out of the sea* is significant. In Revelation, as in ancient Canaanite and Hebrew mythology, the sea was one of the sources of evil.[60] The other is the abyss or bottomless pit (9:1, 2, 11; 11:7; 17:8; and 20:1). Beale observes that the sea is synonymous with the "abyss," which is "the spiritual storehouse of evil, where wicked spirits are confined under God's sovereignty."[61] The tradition of a sea monster called Leviathan was familiar to both Christians and Jews, for it occurs six times in the Old Testament (Job 3:8; 41:1; Ps. 74:14; Isa. 27:1). Those familiar with their Old Testament heritage would have understood the nature of this beast arising out of the sea:

> On the assumption that the beginning of history must be recapitulated at the end of history, Judaism crystallized the implicit expectation of Job. Rev. 12:1–11 also echoes the Jewish tradition. The tradition held that on the fifth day of creation God created Leviathan to be in the sea and Behemoth to dwell on land (*1 En.* 60:7–10; *4 Ezra* 6:49–52; *2 Bar.* 29:4; *b. Baba Bathra* 74b–75a; *Pesikta de Rab Kahana*, supplement 2:4). These two beasts were symbolic of the powers of evil and were to be destroyed at the final judgment.[62]

Daniel 7:3 and the four beasts that rose out of the sea must have played a part in John's imagery. John's beast *had ten horns and seven heads, with ten crowns on his horns*. John had previously described the dragon, Satan, in similar terms. However, here he reverses the order of the dragon who has *seven heads and ten horns* (12:3). John clearly intends to identify this beast with the dragon. That John's beast had *ten horns* as did Daniel's fourth beast implies that, like Daniel's beast, John's beast represents a great nation with enormous imperial civil power. As the vision develops, this beast is representative of the enormous civil power of Rome, which as in Daniel's case made war on God's people. In Daniel 7 the four beasts and ten kings represent nations who attack and persecute Israel. This is the image of the beast John desires to conjure up.[63] That the *ten crowns* referred to here were in fact diadems (Greek *diadēma, royal crowns*), not the laurel wreaths of victory (Greek *stephanos, laurel wreaths of victory*) used by John in regard to the martyred saints, reinforces the view that these horns with ten crowns represented royal, or imperial, power. The strong inference of imperial power in the first century in Asia would immediately be construed in reference to Rome.[64]

This beast also has *seven heads,* which may draw on a Near Eastern tradition of a sea monster with seven heads or may represent the composite heads of the four beasts in Daniel 7.[65] On *each head* was written *a blasphemous name*. Although early Roman emperors did not personally claim divine rights, such divine designations were pronounced on them at their death and in the imperial temples built in their memory and honor. Domitian, the emperor at the time of Revelation, however, "changed the rules and demanded such titles for himself, even calling for sacrifices to himself in Rome."[66] Daniel had observed that the little horn, which arose among the ten horns "will speak against the Most High and oppress his saints." In keeping with his analogous parallel references to Daniel, John describes the claims of the imperial power (notably Domitian) to divinity as blasphemy.[67] Osborne observes that John's purpose was "to present a beast that is incredibly hideous and completely horrifying, for it is the embodiment of all evil."[68] John progressively identifies the real nature of the Roman imperial cult as a blasphemous demonic power. Some discussion takes place among commentators as to whether John is describing the imperial cult or an individual emperor, but such differentiation is unnecessary since John drives home his purpose of identifying the evil nature of Satan's agents and of the church's enemy. Later in 17:8–14 John will return to this description of the beast with seven heads who comes out of the abyss and affirm that the seven heads are seven mountains (kingdoms) and seven kings, all of whom are destined to destruction.

13:2–3. *The beast I saw resembled a leopard, but had feet like those of a bear and a mouth like that of a lion. The dragon gave the beast his power and his throne and great authority.* [3] *One of the heads of the beast seemed to have had a fatal wound, but the fatal wound had been healed. The whole world was astonished and followed the beast.* Driving home his identification of the beast as an imperial civil power in line with Daniel 7, John states that the dragon *gave* his *power* and *throne* and *great authority* to the beast. Osborne sees in this an intentional parody on the divine right and power of God and Christ.[69] Satan presumes to exercise the same supreme power. Key to this view is John's frequent use of the divine passive aorist tense *edothē* ("was given, cf. 6:2, 4, 8, 11; 7:2; 8:2, 3; 9:1). Here, however, John uses the aorist indicative *edōken* ("gave"). This play on words is intended to highlight Satan's usurpation of divine authority,[70] stressing that in this pericope is a version of the struggle between the forces of God and those of Satan.

13:3. *One of the heads of the beast seemed to have had a fatal wound, but the fatal wound had been healed. The whole world was astonished and followed the beast.* In this caricature of Christ's death and resurrection, John drew on the Nero redivivus myth, which caused considerable concern among early Christians and the Jewish communities of the first and second centuries. This redivivus myth held that Nero, who had been censured by the Roman Senate on June 8, 68 and had subsequently committee suicide, was not in fact dead, but lurking in Parthia (Persia) waiting an opportunity to return to Rome and seize power. The thought of a recurrence of Nero's brutal reign raised great concern among not only the Christians and Jews, but also Romans. The realization that this beast was depicted as Nero would cause great astonishment and concern. John fashions the vision of this beast after the Nero redivivus myth for the purpose of stressing the terrifying power and nature of the beast that rises out of the sea.[71]

13:4. *Men worshiped the dragon because he had given authority to the beast, and they also worshiped the beast and asked, "Who is like the beast? Who can make war against him?"* John begins a theme that will become a signature tune for the remainder of Revelation: the worship of the dragon and the beast as opposed to the worship of God and Christ. At 13:15–18 John will clarify the significance of both worshipping the beast and refusing to worship the beast. Those who worship the beast will receive the mark of the beast on their forehead and hand. Those who are deceived and who worship the beast are described as those who dwell on the earth (NIV, *the inhabitants of the earth*). Those who refuse to worship the beast are slain by the beast (13:15). The two cries, *"Who is like the beast? Who can make war against him?"* are the cries of those who are astonished at the power of the beast, but also recall the apocalyptic cry of the saints, "Who can defeat the beast?" In answer of the apocalyptist and seer, John, has already been answered, "Michael can." The details will shortly be unfolded in greater detail and specificity, "Christ can."

13:5–7 *The beast was given a mouth to utter proud words and blasphemies and to exercise his authority for forty-two months.* [6] *He opened his mouth to blaspheme God, and to slander his name and his dwelling place and those who live in heaven.* [7] *He was given power to make war against the saints and to conquer them. And he was given authority over every tribe, people, language and nation.* In another caricature of Christ's authority, the beast *was given* permission (*edothē*, the divine passive) by the dragon to utter blasphemous words *and to exercise his authority for forty-two months* (cf. 11:1–2 for discussion of the significance of these numbers). The subliminal message in this satire is that although the dragon gave power to the beast for forty-two months, this power had already been limited by God (11:1–4), during which period of persecution God would protect his saints. While "the beast's authority appeared to come from Satan; in reality, God was the true source, permitting him to do his work. However, God allows that authority to be exercised only for a limited time, namely forty-two months."[72] The expression *those who live in heaven* (RSV, *those who dwell in heaven*) is interesting since it is the obverse to the expression *the inhabitants of the earth* (NIV 13:8, 12, 14) or *those who dwell on earth* (RSV 13:8, 12, 14) which John uses in reference to those who worship the beast (13:15).[73] The implication is that the beast will slander those who worship God's name. In doing this he will slander God's dwelling place, that is, those who dwell in his holy dwelling place. The Greek does not include the coordinating conjunction *kai* ("and") between God's *dwelling place* (*skēnē*, "tabernacle") and *those who live in heaven.* The force of the Greek is that *those who live in heaven* are the *tabernacle* of God. At 21:3 a heavenly voice proclaims, *Now the dwelling of God is with men, and he will live with them.* The implication is that God's dwelling, or tabernacle, is not a place, but his people.[74] Although the beast *was given power* by the dragon *to make war against the saints and to conquer them,* this power was permitted and limited by God. To those who dwell on the earth, that is, those who worship the beast, it would seem that the beast would conquer the saints, but the irony is that in conquering them the beast would in turn be conquered by the blood of the lamb. It would seem to those who dwell on the earth that the power of the beast was recognized as universal, and this would be the natural assumption of those awed by the power of imperial Rome.

13:8. *All inhabitants of the earth will worship the beast—all whose names have not been written in the book of life belonging to the Lamb that was slain from the creation of the world.* Those who *inhabit the earth* in Revelation does not refer to all those who live on earth. It is a unique Johannine expression used to define those who worship the beast and who persecute the saints as opposed to those who worship God. Those who *inhabit the earth*, namely those who worship the beast, do not have their names *written in the book of life belonging to the Lamb*. The implication is that their citizenship is Roman, earthly, demonic, and not divine. The Jewish literary tradition is replete with references to a citizenship roll, or book. This was also the case in the Graeco-Roman world (cf. Exod. 32:32–33; Ps. 9:5; 69:28; 87:6; Isa. 4:3; and Dan. 12:1).[75] The saints are reassured that the Lamb also has a *book of life* in which the names of those who worship the beast will not be written[76] (cf. Exod. 32:32–33).

It is unclear is whether the expression *from the creation of the world* refers to the writing of names in the book of life or the slaying of the Lamb. Some modern translations prefer *written before the foundation of the world,* or something similar (RSV, NRSV, NASV, ESV). Others (KJV, NEB, and NIV) render this *slain from the creation of the world,* or something akin to that. Commentators are likewise divided. Although the word order of the text and possibly the syntax support *slain from the foundation of the world,* a major reason for *written from or before the foundation of the world* is 17:8 which reads *the inhabitants of the earth whose names have not been written in the book of life from the creation of the world.* It is argued that John should be permitted to stray from uniformity and express freedom in writing 13:8 differently from 17:8. To insist "that John must be absolutely consistent in his literary expression is questionable."[77] Beale concludes that "believers have assurance that their souls can weather any Satanic storm because of the safety accorded by the Lamb's book. This safety is the precreation identification of God's people with the Lamb's death."[78] Additional support for the translation *slain before the foundation of the world* might lie in 1 Peter 1:19–20, and Ephesians 1:4. It seemingly was also a Jewish tradition that Moses was prepared by God for his ministry *"before the foundation of the world"* (*Assumption of Moses,* 1:14).

13:9–10. John reinforces his contention that persecution is inevitable under Satan and Rome with the enigmatic saying: *Let anyone who has an ear listen:*

> [10] *If you are to be taken captive,*
> > *into captivity you go;*
> *if you kill with the sword,*
> > *with the sword you must be killed.*
> *Here is a call for the endurance and faith of the saints.*

The poetic structure serves as a striking summary of the sea-beast and land-beast pericopes and the corresponding call for faithfulness in spite of suffering and persecution. John's words *Let anyone who has an ear listen* is a typical Hebraism calling for careful attention. Similar expressions at the conclusion of Jesus' messages to the seven churches *"He who has an ear, let him hear what the Spirit says to the churches"* highlight the importance of the closing words of this pericope regarding the dragon, the sea-beast, and his war on the saints. Some of John's audience possibly would not be willing to receive his warning kindly, but others would take it to heart. John couched this call for serious ears in a hymnic collage of thoughts drawn from Isa 33:1; Jeremiah 15:2, and 43:11. The thrust of this hymnic message is that some things in life are inevitable. Evil, persecution, and suffering are certain to come. In the present circumstances in which the churches lived in Asia, John warned that faithfulness to Jesus and rejection of an imperial cult would inevitably bring persecution and suffering. In this hymnic warning, John also conveys a subtle *call for the endurance and faith of the saints.*

The message of Revelation throughout has been that through faithful endurance and persecution the saints would ultimately conquer evil and reign with Christ. The cosmic war in heaven had now come close to home. But all is not yet over in this terrifying image of the fearsome sea-beast, for yet another beast is about to appear, one who draws on the power of the first beast and his demonic master, Satan. He is the land beast of 13:11. But John's message will proclaim that all is not lost. For finally these two beasts are followed by another great symbol, a Lamb who was slain and is now standing sovereign on Mount Zion. The saints must be aware that Satan will use all of his powers to make life difficult for the church, but the saints must look beyond the two beasts to the Lamb standing on Mount Zion.

THE BEAST FROM THE LAND – 13:11–18
The Text
13:11–18. *Then I saw another beast that rose out of the earth; it had two horns like a lamb and it spoke like a dragon. [12] It exercises all the authority of the first beast on its behalf, and it makes the earth and its inhabitants worship the first beast, whose mortal wound had been healed. [13] It performs great signs, even making fire come down from heaven to earth in the sight of all; [14] and by the signs that it is allowed to perform on behalf of the beast, it deceives the inhabitants of earth, telling them to make an image for the beast that had been wounded by the sword and yet lived; [15] and it was allowed to give breath to the image of the beast so that the image of the beast could even speak and cause those who would not worship the image of the beast to be killed. [16] Also it causes all, both small and great, both rich and poor, both free and slave, to be marked on the right hand or the forehead, [17] so that no one can buy or sell who does not have the mark, that is, the name of the beast or the number of its name. [18] This calls for wisdom: let anyone with understanding calculate the number of the beast, for it is the number of a person. Its number is six hundred sixty-six.*

The mythological tradition of two primeval monsters was widely known in Near Eastern cultures of the first century, notably in the Jewish pseudepigraphical and apocalyptic traditions. The first beast of 13, the sea beast, Leviathan, has already appeared. First, 1 Enoch 60:1–7 records that the female feature of this belief, Leviathan, "lived in the abyss of the ocean." The second beast, a male figure, Behemoth, is located in the "waste wilderness of Duidain" (cf. 1 *Enoch* 60:7–9). Similar references occur in 4 *Ezra* 6:49–52 and 2 *Baruch* 29:4. In the Biblical tradition Job 40:15 and 41:1 speak of Leviathan and Behemoth.

In the Jewish tradition and Ancient Near Eastern mythology, both monsters are powerful, evil, and to be feared. In Revelation the sea beast, Leviathan, is in the tradition of Daniel, a great nation or political power. As the drama of Revelation proceeds, the intended villain is Rome. The earth beast, Behemoth, is a deceiving false prophet, a religious power that John will characterize as the Roman imperial cult.

13:11. *Then I saw another beast that rose out of the earth; it had two horns like a lamb and it spoke like a dragon.* In contrast to the sea beast, this beast is modeled after a lamb, a religious symbol, and not Daniel's beasts, which are national political symbols. The imagery is again a parody of Christ, the Lamb of God, but in contrast to Christ, who speaks for God, this beast speaks for the dragon. That he is a religious figure or influence is clear, but the question is raised as to who he actually represents. Beale observes that "this beast from the land has been variously identified as Satan, Antichrist, the Roman imperial priesthood, the Catholic Church (so the Reformers), and false teachers."[79] Unfortunately, as indicated by Beale, many commentaries speak here of the Antichrist or an Antichrist. I am uncomfortable with the Antichrist terminology in the context of Revelation. First, I am concerned since the term antichrist is not found in Revelation. It is found in the New Testament only four times and only in 1 and 2 John (1 John 2:18; 22; 4:3; 2 John 7). Whether the noun *antichristos* is anarthrous or articular (with the identifying article *the*, or the qualifying *an*) makes little difference in the case of Revelation. In the Johannine Epistles the antichrist "spirit" or person is one who denies that Christ came in the flesh, namely, Gnostic false teachers. In 1 John 2:18 John observes that many antichrists have already come but that others will surface, denying Christ (cf. 1 John 2:22; 2 John 7). The issue in Revelation is not a Gnostic denial that Christ came in the flesh, but one of denying the absolute sovereignty of Jesus and worshipping a human being in the place of God and Christ, a point that will be clarified in detail at 13:18: and the number of the beast, namely, 666.

13:12. *It exercises all the authority of the first beast on its behalf, and it makes the earth and its inhabitants worship the first beast, whose mortal wound had been healed.* This beast works in close association with the sea beast, the civil political power of Rome, and serves the purpose of making *the earth and its inhabitants*, that is, people, worship the sea beast or political power of Rome. The earth beast "has primarily a religious role since it is later repeatedly called 'the false prophet' (16:13; 19:20; 20:10)."[80] John clearly indicates that the role of this beast is to make the earth worship the first beast. The priestly role of the earth beast identifies it clearly as a religious power. "In John's day the reference would be either to the local priests of the imperial cult or to the provincial council responsible for enforcing emperor worship throughout Asia."[81] Several commentators discuss the role of the Asian "communes" (or "*commune Asaie*" or *Asiarchs* [Acts 19:31]) who "were members of the commune and probably local priests of the imperial cult."[82] Charles observes that "from Victorinus downwards a number of notable scholars have identified the beast with the heathen priesthood, but it is best with Holtzmann, Pfleiderer, Bousset, J. Weis to understand it in relation to the imperial priesthood of the provinces."[83] Although identifying the beast is problematic, it seems that John "has in mind a specific contemporary individual or institution that promotes the imperial cult."[84] Attempts to identify the beast with more contemporary "false prophets" or movements such as the Catholic Church (the Protestant Reformers point of view) Muhammad, Hitler, Stalin, and other opponents of the Judaeo-Christian faith fail in that they remove the beast from its first-century Asian context. I prefer to see in the land beast the Roman Imperial cult, either in the form of the cult priests, the Asian communes, or Domitian, although I find identifying the beast as the Emperor Domitian to be somewhat of a "stretch." This is not meant to imply that Domitian did not promote worship of himself as *Dominus et Deus noster*, "our Lord and God."[85]

13:13–15. *It performs great signs, even making fire come down from heaven to earth in the sight of all;* [14] *and by the signs that it is allowed to perform on behalf of the beast, it deceives the inhabitants of earth, telling them to make an image for the beast that had been wounded by the sword and yet lived;* [15] *and it was allowed to give breath to the image of the beast so that the image of the beast could even speak and cause those who would not worship the image of the beast to be killed.* That the beast as a false prophet could perform great signs would not be unfamiliar to those living in ancient times, for priests functioned as magicians from as early as Moses' experience in Egypt with Pharaoh's priestly magicians (Exod. 7:9–13).

The repeated warnings against false teachers in both the Old and New Testaments and the Jewish pseudepigrapha and apocalyptic traditions (Deut. 13:1–2; 2 Thess. 2:9–10; 2 Pet. 2:1–3; *Sib. Or.* 3:63; *Apoc. of Elijah* 3:1, 5; *Ascen. of Isa.* 4:10) highlight the real problem of false prophets who could perform impressive signs in efforts to confirm their message and confuse the uninformed. By the time of the first century in Asia, there was universal knowledge of the existence of the Oracle at Delphi, dating from [1400] B.C., where priests would enter into the large idol of Apollo and speak prophetic oracles to the people. Perceptive Greeks had in time grown tired of such "impressive" acts of prophetic activity. Images of Deuteronomy 13:1–2 must have flashed through John's and his readers' minds at the mention of such false prophets.

John is explicit that this earth beast works *on behalf of the* first *beast*, promoting its greatness. This role would fit the purpose and function of the Roman imperial cult. This beast promotes the war of the first beast against the saints, causing *those who would not worship the image of the beast to be killed.* Although essentially the synagogue and Roman proconsul in Smyrna were responsible for the martyrdom of Polycarp for his refusal to worship the emperor, one cannot escape the connection of that tragic event in history to this text and the earth beast.[86] Those who worship the beast receive the mark of the beast as a sign of their participation in the imperial cult and were permitted to buy and sell, and have no fear of martyrdom (13:16-17; 14:9). The clearest identification of those who dwell on earth (or inhabit the earth) with those who worship the beast and receive his mark is made in this pericope: "the two motifs of the brand and the worship of the beast are connected not only in vv. 15–16 but also in 14:11; 15:2; 19:20; 20:4."[87]

13:16–18. *Also it causes all, both small and great, both rich and poor, both free and slave, to be marked on the right hand or the forehead,* [17] *so that no one can buy or sell who does not have the mark, that is, the name of the beast or the number of its name.* [18] *This calls for wisdom: let anyone with understanding calculate the number of the beast, for it is the number of a person. Its number is six hundred sixty-six.* In verse 18 John notes that *unraveling this pericope calls for wisdom.* Although decoding the number of the beast is not the critical key to the meaning in this pericope, it does shape much of the discussion of these three verses. Interpreting the number 666 has been one of the most problematical and hotly debated issues in the study of Revelation from earliest times. One can trace a history of the interpretation of Revelation through the history of identifying this number.

Aune and Beale present a complete discussion of the history of interpreting this text, ranging from a discussion of gematria (giving a numerical value to names and concepts) in the Hebrew tradition through the Aramaic and Greek traditions. Perhaps the most common solution to this enigmatic number has been "Nero Caesar".[88] At the heart of the Nero arguments is the possible shift from a Greek gematric process to an Aramaic and Hebrew gematric counting. But 13:18 is in Greek, not Hebrew and Aramaic. Nevertheless, some argument has been made for such a transition from Hebrew/Aramaic symbolism, connecting the number from Greek to a Hebrew symbolic idiom for 666.[89] Aune observes that the concept of gematria can be followed on three levels, 1) an exegetical level, 2) a triangular level, and 3) an apocalyptic level, in which numbers are used symbolically, as in John's use of 7, 12, 1000, 12,000, 144,000. No matter what model of gematria is adopted, the solution to the riddle based on pure gematria remains a mystery!

While I am aware of the numerous impressive arguments relating to identifying 666 (or the textual variant 616), I am not overly impressed by efforts to identify this number with Nero in any form. Caird notes that "Lohmeyer and Farrer have argued that, whatever irrecoverable name may lie behind John's cryptogram, he would not have used Gematria at all unless the number 666 had appealed to him for other symbolic reasons. For 666 is a remarkable number in many ways. It is the number which persistently falls short of the perfect number seven. It is the parody of the number of Jesus, 888."[90]

John is using 666 stylistically in the apocalyptic genre. He intended his readers to know that this number, or "person," was a human being and therefore not worthy of divine worship. An interesting side issue, and one that has greater value than the Nero identification, is that Jesus' number, according to Greek gematria, is given in the *Sibylline Oracles* as 888.[91] When totaled, the number of vowels and consonants in Jesus' name add up to 888. Dating the *Sibylline Oracles* is difficult, and apparently some of the oracles in their present form represent a Christian reworking of earlier Jewish oracles. J. J. Collins has proposed dates ranging from second century B.C. to the seventh century A.D. It seems possible, therefore, that early readers of Revelation were already familiar with the number 888 and its connection to Jesus. The contrast with 666 would have been meaningful.

It is doubtful that one will ever be able to resolve this problem of identifying the number 666 with a specific individual. But John is clear that *the number is a human number* (RSV), or *the number of a man* (NIV). The implication is that by worshiping a beast whose number is 666 one is worshiping a human being!

13:16–17. *Also it causes all, both small and great, both rich and poor, both free and slave, to be marked on the right hand or the forehead, [17] so that no one can buy or sell who does not have the mark, that is, the name of the beast or the number of its name.* The land beast sets a sign of ownership or identification on those who worship the sea beast, or Roman imperial power. Those familiar with the branding of slaves in ancient times would immediately recognize the implication of this marking. However, soldiers in ancient times were also marked as a sign of allegiance to their emperor. Since Revelation is in the context of combat mythology, it is possible that both concepts may have been implicit. The threefold grouping of *small and great, both rich and poor, both free and slave* may represent the social stratification of Roman culture at the time of writing. The intention was that everyone must receive this "certification" as a sign of allegiance to the Roman powers.[92] The Greek *charagma* ("mark," or "an engraved stamp") was a technical term used in conjunction with the imperial seal of office that signified ownership or identification. Not having the imperial brand would indicate a social outcast. However, at 14:9 John clarifies this by adding that it is those who worship the beast who receive the mark of the beast on their forehead and hand who are those he has in mind. These will be judged, not by Roman cultural approval, but by the wrath of God. The contrast with those who receive the seal of God (cf. 7:3–4) which signified membership in the messianic army, and those now receiving the mark of the beast, would be immediate. A key decision had to be made. Whose mark did the saints want to carry? The expression *that is* signified that the mark of the beast represented both *the name of the beast or the number of its name*. The fact that *the name of the beast* could be expressed in a symbolic number representing character was familiar to those in ancient times. Finally, the number of the beast was *a man's number* (NIV) or *a human number* (RSV) or *the number of a person* (NRSV). This beast was not divine, but a very human agent of the beast, even demonic in nature.

THE LAMB ON MOUNT ZION – 14:1–5
The Text
14:1–5. *Then I looked, and there before me was the Lamb, standing on Mount Zion, and with him 144,000 who had his name and his Father's name written on their foreheads.* [2] *And I heard a sound from heaven like the roar of rushing waters and like a loud peal of thunder. The sound I heard was like that of harpists playing their harps.* [3] *And they sang a new song before the throne and before the four living creatures and the elders. No one could learn the song except the 144,000 who had been redeemed from the earth.* [4] *These are those who did not defile themselves with women, for they kept themselves pure. They follow the Lamb wherever he goes. They were purchased from among men and offered as firstfruits to God and the Lamb.* [5] *No lie was found in their mouths; they are blameless.*

John moves from two fierce and threatening beasts to a Lamb. The contrast is immediately obvious. The Lamb is the last of seven mystical figures. This scene of the Lamb is then followed by another interlude that rounds out this major section of Revelation. The seven mystic figures were the woman with child (12:1–2), the dragon (12:3–4), the male child (12:5–6), the angel Michael (12:7–17), the beast from the sea (13:1–10), the land beast (13:11–18), and the Lamb (14:1–5). The third major interlude, which follows (14:6–20), is intended to connect with the previous interlude of the church militant (7) which now is presented as the church victorious. What began as a fearsome scene of the dragon making war on the messianic community reached a climax with the victory hymn of the conquerors (12:10–12). Then in chiastic style the message moves from the two demonic beasts who make war on the saints to the final scene of the conquering saints standing victoriously with the Lamb on Mount Zion. This final mystical figure of the Lamb on Mount Zion is intended to reassure the saints that they are truly victorious and reign with Christ. This final interlude demonstrates that a righteous Sovereign God offers repentance even to Babylon, but will assuredly judge Babylon (a new symbol for Rome) with an outpouring of his righteous wrath against Satan and his agents. This chapter (14) "forms a climax to the visions of the two preceding chapters" (12–13) and "conveys the assurance of vindication for the followers of the Lamb of God and judgment upon the followers of the beast."[93]

This is not the final judgment, but proleptic eschatological announcements of God's judgment on the beast or Rome. This is not a scene literally depicting either earth or heaven, but a symbolic scene drawing on the imagery of Psalm 2 and its messianic implication. Beasley-Murray notes, "Probably it is right not to think of a location, though it is the triumph of the saints in the kingdom of Christ rather than the age which is in view . . . It is not impossible that Psalm 2:6 was in John's mind at this point. The heathen have raged in vain. God's king stands on his holy hill victorious.[94]

14:1. *Then I looked, and there before me was the Lamb, standing on Mount Zion, and with him 144,000 who had his name and his Father's name written on their foreheads.* As indicated above, Mount Zion was the "place" in Jewish and the apocalyptic tradition where the Messiah would defeat his enemies and judge them (2 *Apoc. Bar.* 40:1–3).[95] This was adopted in the Christian tradition as the place where the conquering and victorious Messiah would stand. Mount Zion was the traditional area where first King David and later the kings of Israel/Judah reigned.[96] The scene has moved from the sands of the sea where the dragon stood, from the two ferocious beasts, to Mount Zion where the conquering Lamb stands surrounded by 144,000 saints who belong to the Father and who bear his name and sign of protecting ownership written on their foreheads (cf. 7:3–8). The 144,000 in this scene is a symbolic number representing "conquering martyrs," or the church militant. Chapter 13 closed with those who worship the beast being marked by the sign of the beast. Chapter 14 opens with the saints sealed with the sign, or mark, of God.

14:2–3. *And I heard a sound from heaven like the roar of rushing waters and like a loud peal of thunder. The sound I heard was like that of harpists playing their harps.* [3] *And they sang a new song before the throne and before the four living creatures and the elders. No one could learn the song except the 144,000 who had been redeemed from the earth.* Sounds of rushing water, loud peals of thunder, and of many harpists signify a glorious hymn of praise to God. The *roar of rushing waters and like a loud peal of thunder* draws from Ezekiel 1:24. This would be like the sound of a mighty cataract or the roar of the ocean[97] or the Mediterranean crashing on the shore[98] The image emphasizes the importance of the song sung by the harpists, who sing a celebratory *new song before the* *throne and before the four living creatures and the elders,* indicating that this singing is in heaven, possibly before the heavenly throne (4), where the martyrs throw their victory crowns at the feat of the Almighty and sing a hymn of praise to God. Osborne observes that the coupling of the loudness and such singing (here and 19:6–7) indicates a boisterous song of celebration.[99] The hymn here would be in celebration of the victory of the Lamb and his army over the beasts of 13. Magnificent songs of praise to God and Christ had already been sung at 4:8-11 and 5:9-10. A similar song of praise now is sung to the Almighty God for his victory and sovereignty over all nations at 15:3-4. In this case, 14:3, this new song is meaningful only to the 144,000 who had been redeemed from the earth, echoing the song of 5:9, where the emphasis was on Jesus' victorious death and "ransom of men for God." John's purpose in mentioning that this song could be learned only by the 144,000 is to emphasize the unique nature of their victory through martyrdom which would not be understood by the world.

14:4–,5. *These are those who did not defile themselves with women, for they kept themselves pure. They follow the Lamb wherever he goes. They were purchased from among men and offered as firstfruits to God and the Lamb.* [5] *No lie was found in their mouths; they are blameless.* John now identifies the nature of the 144,000. At 7:3-8 the numbering of the twelve tribes of Israel was John's way of drawing attention to the military nature of this group. At 7:3-8 the 144,000 represented the church militant in a holy war against Satan and his agents, which war is mentioned in specific detail at 13:7. Caird and Bauckham[100] have argued persuasively that in all probability the discussion of the 144,000, not defiling themselves with women and being chaste, is a symbolic reference drawing on the Greek *parthenoi* (*parthenos,* "a virgin or chaste person." *Parthenos*, a noun of both feminine and masculine gender, can be used "of men who have had no intercourse with women; in this case it is masculine gender for *chaste man.*"[101] This expression (Deut. 23:9–10; 1 Sam. 21:5; 2 Sam. 11:8–11; and *1QM* 7:3–6) is in the context of soldiers preparing for holy war who consecrate themselves before God. Part of that consecration was a vow to celibacy during the conflict (Deut. 23:9–10; 1 Sam. 21:5; 2 Sam. 11:8–11). The symbolism of men being chaste for battle corresponds well with the view that this 144,000 represents the church militant and now victorious. It is the consensus of most commentators[102] that the imagery of the holy war best fits the context of the 144,000 being chaste (virgins), but a minority suggestion is that it might also fit the concept of the church as the bride of Christ, which metaphor will be brought to the front at 19:6-8. The church militant follows *the Lamb wherever he goes.* True discipleship in the second century was clearly interpreted as being willing to follow Jesus even to the point of death (Matt. 16:24-26; Luke 9:22-27). To follow the Lamb wherever he goes implies *imitatio Christi.*[103] Developing further the concept that the conquerors should see their martyrdom as a sacrificial offering to God, John adds that the 144,000 *were purchased from among men and offered as firstfruits to God and the Lamb.* In the Old Testament the offering of the sacrifice of firstfruits implied not only the beginning of the harvest, but also an offering of the best of the harvest or animals. The sacrifice was also a plea or guarantee of other fruits to follow (Num. 18:2; Deut. 18:4; Lev. 23:9–14). In the New Testament those converted to Christ were identified as firstfruits to God and Christ (Rom. 16:25; 1 Cor. 16:15; 2 Thess. 2:13). Here the martyrs were to see themselves as a sacrifice worthy of Christ's sacrifice and a guarantee of other fruit (martyrdom) to follow as a sacrifice to God. The expression *No lie was found in their mouths; they are blameless* is interesting in the light of similar expressions at 21:8 and 22:15 regarding liars. In the context of Revelation the lie is the compromised confession that Caesar, not Jesus, is Lord.[104] It is possible that an allusion is made to Isaiah 53:9, where no deceit is found in the Servant Messiah's mouth.

THE THIRD MAJOR INTERLUDE – SEVEN ANGELIC MESSAGES – 14:6–20

The Text

Then I saw another angel flying in midair, and he had the eternal gospel to proclaim to those who live on the earth—to every nation, tribe, language and people. [7] He said in a loud voice, "Fear God and give him glory, because the hour of his judgment has come. Worship him who made the heavens, the earth, the sea and the springs of water."

[8] A second angel followed and said, "Fallen. Fallen is Babylon the Great, which made all the nations drink the maddening wine of her adulteries."

[9] A third angel followed them and said in a loud voice: "If anyone worships the beast and his image and receives his mark on the forehead or on the hand,[10] he, too, will drink of the wine of God's fury, which has been poured full strength into the cup of his wrath. He will be tormented with burning sulfur in the presence of the holy angels and of the Lamb. [11] And the smoke of their torment rises for ever and ever. There is no rest day or night for those who worship the beast and his image, or for anyone who receives the mark of his name."[12] This calls for patient endurance on the part of the saints who obey God's commandments and remain faithful to Jesus.

[13] Then I heard a voice from heaven say, "Write: Blessed are the dead who die in the Lord from now on."

"Yes," says the Spirit, "they will rest from their labor, for their deeds will follow them."

[14] I looked, and there before me was a white cloud, and seated on the cloud was one "like a son of man" with a crown of gold on his head and a sharp sickle in his hand. [15] Then another angel came out of the temple and called in a loud voice to him who was sitting on the cloud, "Take your sickle and reap, because the time to reap has come, for the harvest of the earth is ripe." [16] So he who was seated on the cloud swung his sickle over the earth, and the earth was harvested.

[17] Another angel came out of the temple in heaven, and he too had a sharp sickle. [18] Still another angel, who had charge of the fire, came from the altar and called in a loud voice to him who had the sharp sickle, "Take your sharp sickle and gather the clusters of grapes from the earth's vine, because its grapes are ripe."[19] The angel swung his sickle on the earth, gathered its grapes and threw them into the great winepress of God's wrath. [20] They were trampled in the winepress outside the city, and blood flowed out of the press, rising as high as the horses' bridles for a distance of [1,600] stadia.

The structure of this section is both interesting and challenging, for it contains messages from three angels,[105] five angels,[106] and six angels. At the same time there are six or seven angelic messages. John begins by counting them, *another angel* [vs. 6], possibly the first, *another angel, a second* [vs. 8], *another angel, a third* [vs. 9], but then stops counting, merely stating *another angel*. How one views the number of angelic messages depends on how one counts them. John numbers three, but then continues to speak of "another angel" without numbering them. Is it that John already thinks in sevens and assumes that the reader will follow his thought and number seven angelic messages? The United Bible Society Greek text has seven paragraphs, which is followed in the RSV and the NIV. With this in mind, I will assume, in keeping with John's penchant for septets, that there are seven angelic messages although John does not stipulate that each message is announced by "another angel."

14:6–7. *Then I saw another angel flying in midair, and he had the eternal gospel to proclaim to those who live on the earth—to every nation, tribe, language and people.* ⁷ *He said in a loud voice, "Fear God and give him glory, because the hour of his judgment has come. Worship him who made the heavens, the earth, the sea and the springs of water."* Aune notes that this is the first time in Jewish or Christian literature that an angel is said to be flying. He adds that it was Tertullian (ca. 155–220) who gave the first clear reference to angels with wings.[107] The reference to *flying in midair* (**midheaven** RSV, Greek *mesouranēmati*, something like *at the zenith of the sun*, or *midheaven*[108]) is not the cosmic heaven, but the sky. This angel had **the eternal gospel to proclaim to those who live on the earth**. Perhaps it is better to read this as "an eternal gospel" since this is the simplest way to read the anarthrous construction *kai eidon allon aggelon*. We should understand this in the sense that even those who worship the beast have an opportunity to repent. The message is simple, "Fear God and worship Him; give God the glory, not Caesar, for God is the creator of earth and the sea (the source of both beasts). You had better do this for the hour or time of God's judgment has already come." The expression **has come** is from the *ēlthen*, a second aorist verb, which implies "has already come." Although Rome, the beast, persists in his war on God's people, God has already judged this evil. This is a final, urgent call to the beast, the civil power of Rome, to repent.

14:8. *A second angel followed and said, "Fallen! Fallen is Babylon the Great, which made all the nations drink the maddening wine of her adulteries.* This is the first of six references to **Babylon** or **Babylon the Great** (14:8; 16:19; 17:5; 18:2; 18:10; 18:21). It was common in early Christianity to refer to Rome as Babylon since in Rome was manifest all of the evils of Babylon. Rome had as early as the writing of 1 Peter 5:13 been associated with Babylon.[109] The expression *"Fallen! Fallen is Babylon the Great"* draws not only on the language of Isaiah 21:9, but also on the message couched in Isaiah's cry that Babylon has been judged by God. The repeated **Fallen! Fallen** express the certainty of divine judgment on Rome, the new Babylon. The intriguing aspect of this message is that at the time Isaiah made this prophecy, Babylon was still standing. Likewise, Rome is still standing but incorporates the certainty of God's judgment. **Fallen, Fallen** (*Epesen,*

Epesen) is a doubling of an aorist verb, which functions as a futuristic, or proleptic, aorist signifying the certainty of a future event.[110] The expression **Babylon the Great** draws on Daniel 4:30, in which king Nebuchadnezzar expressed his pride over Babylon, the city he had built, which pride and city would certainly be destroyed by God. John uses it to denigrate the pride of Rome. **The maddening wine of her adulteries** is a theme that John will develop referring to Rome and the imperial cult's seductive power by which "she" seduced the nations into political alliance. Jeremiah 51:7–9 also played a significant role in shaping John's terminology. This characterization of Rome prefigures the image of 17:1–6, where Rome is described as a harlot sitting on a scarlet beast full of blasphemous names, having seven heads and ten horns. The dramatization of God's certain judgment of Rome in the present context is both to call the idolatrous nation to repentance and to warn the saints of the consequences of a compromising alliance with Rome, as expressed in the following message.

14:9–11. *A third angel followed them and said in a loud voice: "If anyone worships the beast and his image and receives his mark on the forehead or on the hand,*[10] *he, too, will drink of the wine of God's fury, which has been poured full strength into the cup of his wrath. He will be tormented with burning sulfur in the presence of the holy angels and of the Lamb.* [11] *And the smoke of their torment rises for ever and ever. There is no rest day or night for those who worship the beast and his image, or for anyone who receives the mark of his name."*

John returns to the imagery of those who worship **the beast and his image and** receive **his mark on the forehead or on the hand.** The eternal gospel certainly offered repentance to an idolatrous people, but the gospel loses all power unless balanced by the consequences of refusal to repent, namely, eternal judgment. Those who refuse God's eternal gospel will receive the wrath of God poured out unmixed against his enemies. John plays with the concept of the intoxicating power of Rome who had made **the nations drink the maddening wine of her adulteries**, speaking of the full power of **the wine of God's fury**. The common practice of social wine drinking in Graeco-Roman society called for wine and water to be mixed equally. One drank wine **full strength** only for the purpose of getting drunk.[111] The imagery John presents here is that God's judgment will be poured out in all of its power on Rome and those who worship the image of the beast from the sea (the emperor) and receive **his mark on the forehead or on the hand.** Those so judged will be tormented with eternal suffering **in the presence of the holy angels and of the Lamb.** There is a strong image in this expression of the Jewish tradition that eternal suffering in hell is witnessed by angels and all of heaven (Dan. 7:9–12; *1 Enoch* 14:19–23; 40:1–10; 48:9; 60:2–6; *4 Ezra* 7:36–38; *2 Baruch* 30:4). This may have been included by John as some form of answer to the prayers of the saints beneath the altar for vindication in 6:10. He dramatizes the seriousness of divine judgment and eternal hell by drawing on a number of Jewish images. The reference to **burning sulfur** and the **smoke of their torment** that **rises for ever and ever** draws on several Old Testament, Jewish pseudepigraphical, and Dead Sea Scrolls sources such as Sodom and Gomorrah

(Gen.19:24; Deut. 29:23; Job 18:15), Judah (Isa. 30:33), and Gog (Ezek. 38:22; 2 Sam 22:9; 3 *Macc.* 2:5; 1 *Enoch* 91:9; 1QS 2:2–18 and 4:12–14). The reference to **the smoke of their torment** that **rises for ever and ever** may be an allusion drawn from the smoke rising from the eruption of Mount Vesuvius that destroyed Pompeii (ca. 79).

14:12–13. This calls for patient endurance on the part of the saints who obey God's commandments and remain faithful to Jesus. [13] **Then I heard a voice from heaven say, "Write: Blessed are the dead who die in the Lord from now on." "Yes," says the Spirit, "they will rest from their labor, for their deeds will follow them."** There are some questions as to where to place these two verses.[112] I will work with the assumption that 14:12 is a conclusion to 14:9–11 and the third angelic message in agreement with the NIV, and view 14:13 as an independent paragraph that constitutes the fourth angelic message.

14:12. The severe threats of eternal judgment and hell of 14:9–11 constitute a serious call *for patient endurance on the part of the saints who obey God's commandments and remain faithful to Jesus.* God's severe judgment and opposition to idolatry of any form calls for faithful endurance even to the point of martyrdom. This call repeats that at 13:10, following John's statement that persecution and death were inevitable. There is some debate as to the correct understanding of *faithful to Jesus.* The Greek *tēn pistin Iēsou* is literally "the faith of Jesus." *Iēsou*, a noun in the genitive case, could mean "the faith of Jesus," "the faith belonging to Jesus," or "the faith in Jesus." Osborne, citing others, summarizes the thrust if the discussion: "Here *Iēsou* is an objective genitive (so also Sweet 1911: 186; Beckwith 1919: 659), and thus the phrase demands that the saints remain firmly 'faithful to Jesus.'"[113]

Obeying **God's commandments** in the context of Revelation must refer to not worshipping the beast and remaining faithful to Jesus. At 19:10 John is about to fall down and worship an angel and is told, **You must not do that. . . . Worship God.** Again, at 12:17, when the dragon went off to make war on the woman and her offspring, the offspring are **those who obey God's commandments and hold to the testimony of Jesus.**[114]

14:13. I will treat this as an independent fourth angelic message relating to the eternal gospel. **Then I heard a voice from heaven say, "Write: Blessed are the dead who die in the Lord from now on." "Yes," says the Spirit, "they will rest from their labor, for their deeds will follow them."** The voice from heaven, although not specifically identified by John as a fourth angelic message, seems in the context of these messages to constitute a fourth angelic message. The command to **write,** builds on the seven letters from Jesus to the churches and stresses that the message that follows comes right from God and Jesus. A question is whether the blessing that follows is restricted to the martyrs (so Beckwith, 659; Caird, 188; Mounce, 276; Aune, vol. 2, 838–39; Michaels, 176) or is intended as a general blessings for all faithful Christians **who die in the Lord** (Osborne, 544; Beale, 767; Beasley-Murray, 227). In keeping with the overall thrust of Revelation, I am inclined to agree that it relates to the martyrs who are about to die or who have died for their faith in Jesus. The phrase **"Yes," says the Spirit** may be read as an affirmation, yes or truly, for *nai* can be translated "yes, yes indeed, certainly, most assuredly." Thus it is possible to read the expression *from now on* in the previous sentence as a statement of certitude if one reads the Greek *ap arti* as one word *aparti*, which means certainly, exactly, or assuredly. This is of course only a possibility. This would change the sentence structure (also a possibility) to read *"Write: Blessed are the dead who die in the Lord." "Assuredly, yes," says the Spirit.*[115] The next clause, introduced by *hina* ("in order that"), introduces or explains the nature or content of the blessing. The RSV renders this *"that they may rest from their labors"* while the NIV renders it as *"they will rest from their labor,"* implying that the *hina* clause continues the statement of the Spirit, explaining the content of the blessings the martyrs will receive. This would result, as in the NIV, in a statement explaining the content of the blessing pronounced on the martyrs, "Certainly indeed, they will rest from their labors." The statement *for their deeds will follow them* explains why they will rest from their labors, the conjunction *gar*, introducing the reason for their rest.[116] In the general sense, in the case of faithful Christians, *labor* (*kopos*) and *deeds* (*ergon*) may be considered synonymous and would refer to their faithful works of Christian service. Here in the case of the martyrs, the expression refers to their faithfulness to Jesus under extreme persecution resulting in martyrdom. The two words appear in similar circumstances in Jesus' letter to the Ephesians at 2:2. The principle of *lex talionis*, or retribution, is common in Roman law, Scripture, and the Jewish tradition, implying that people, good and bad, will be judged according to their deeds (Ps. 62:12; Eccl. 8:14; Jer. 17:10; Matt. 16:27; Rom. 2:6; *1 Enoch* 41:1–2; 2; *Bar.* 14:12).[117]

14:14–16. This paragraph introduces another angel, possibly a reference to the fifth angel (although not numbered by John). *I looked, and there before me was a white cloud, and seated on the cloud was one "like a son of man" with a crown of gold on his head and a sharp sickle in his hand.* [15] *Then another angel came out of the temple and called in a loud voice to him who was sitting on the cloud, "Take your sickle and reap, because the time to reap has come, for the harvest of the earth is ripe."*[16] *So he who was seated on the cloud swung his sickle over the earth, and the earth was harvested.* Clouds are mentioned seven times in Revelation and white cloud once, here at 14:14. At 1:7 Jesus is said to be coming with clouds. Likewise, Acts 1:9–11 refers to Jesus ascending and descending at his parousia in a cloud. The connection of *one "like a son of man"* and clouds draws on Daniel 7:13. That the cloud is a *white cloud* here in 14:14 introduces a new concept to clouds in Revelation. In Revelation white normally reflects purity, or salvation. Here it is associated with judgment, possibly suggesting that the judgment being introduced by this *son of man* (in Revelation this is normally associated with Jesus) is also associated with the vindication of the martyred saints. Identifying this *son of man* at 14:14 has led to considerable debate. The issue is whether this *son of man* refers to Jesus or to an angel.

Osborne favors identifying the *son of man* here with Jesus, stating "Thus the 'white cloud' signifies the glorious victory of Christ as he prepares to harvest the earth."[118] I agree with Osborne that since "The only other places in the book that echo Dan7:13 allude clearly to Christ as the Son of Man (Rev. 1:7, 13)," 14;14 should also refer to Jesus.[119]

That this *son of man* has a *crown of gold on his head* symbolizes Jesus' identification with the martyrs since crowns (*stephanoi*) had been promised the conquerors (2:10) and the twenty-four elders before the throne of the Almighty had cast their golden crowns before his throne (4:4, 10). The *son of man* had a *sharp sickle in his hand*.

Another angel, the fifth angel *called* on the *son of man* to take his sickle and harvest the earth. This angel did not command the *son of man* to take his sickle and harvest the earth, but *called* on him to do so (*kradzōn*, from *kradzō*, "calling out" or "crying out"). Osborne points out that "Both in the parable of growing seed in Mark 4:29 and seven times in Rev. 14-19 the sickle stands for the judgment of God in the final harvest."[120] I question whether this is a reference to the *final* harvest, as Osborne indicates, or whether this is a proleptic judgment on Rome expressed in the terminology of final judgment to emphasize the seriousness of God's and Jesus' judgment on Rome. John must have been aware of the symbolism of sickles and the harvest of judgment in Joel 3:13. The angel stresses that the time to harvest *has come* (Greek *hoti ēlthen hē hōra*, "because the hour has come"). The construction is emphatic and stresses that the eschatological hour of the judgment of the idolatrous beast and worshippers has already arrived and begun. The verb *ēlthen* is an aorist tense and might more appropriately be translated "has arrived."[121] The concept of *harvest* as an eschatological symbol for divine judgment was prominent in the literature of Israel and Christianity (Jer. 51:33; Hos. 6:11; 2 Esdras 4:35; 2 Baruch 70:3; Matt. 13:39; Mark 4:29).

14:17. *Another angel came out of the temple in heaven, and he too had a sharp sickle.* This *another angel* is most likely the sixth angel of the seven angels of 14:6–20. That he also has a sickle implies that he joins with the *son of man* in his harvest. This should not come as a surprise since Jesus had taught that he would send his angels to gather out of his kingdom all causes of sin (Matt. 13:41, the parable of the tares). That this angel *came out of the temple in heaven* strengthens the emphasis on divine and righteous judgment.

14:18–20. *Still another angel, who had charge of the fire, came from the altar and called in a loud voice to him who had the sharp sickle, "Take your sharp sickle and gather the clusters of grapes from the earth's vine, because its grapes are ripe."* [19] *The angel swung his sickle on the earth, gathered its grapes and threw them into the great winepress of God's wrath.* [20] *They were trampled in the winepress outside the city, and blood flowed out of the press, rising as high as the horses' bridles for a distance of* 1,600 *stadia.* This *another angel*, the seventh angel of what we have assumed to be seven angels in this interlude, *had charge of the fire, came from the altar*. The mention of the altar draws us back to the altar of 6:9–10 and the prayers of the saints for vindication. *Fire* appears in Revelation nineteen times, most often associated with judgment (14 times: 1:14; 2:18; 8:7; 9:17, 18; 11:5; 13:13; 14:18; 16:8; 18:8; 19:12; 20:9, 14, 15) but also with purification (3 times: 3:18; 8:5 [possibly]; 15:2). At times it is difficult to separate judgment from purification. It would seem the most appropriate here, therefore, to associate the *fire* in 14:18 in the context of divine judgment as a response to the prayers of the saints coming from beneath the altar (cf. 8:1–5).[122] The expression *gather the clusters of grapes* *from the earth's vine, because its grapes are ripe* is another reference to divine judgment that draws on Joel 3:13 (cf. Ps. 80:8–13; Isa. 5:5; 63:2–3, 6; Jer. 2:21; Ezek. 18:1–8; Lam. 1:15; and Hos. 10:1–2.)[123] That the harvest of the vineyard speaks of God's judgment is reinforced by the statement John adds regarding the grapes being *trampled in the great winepress of God's wrath.*

That the winepress is located *outside the city* poses the question of which city John has in mind. Obviously, since John has already spoken of Jerusalem (11), one could assume that this city is a metaphor for Jerusalem since Jesus was crucified outside the city and all crucifixions of criminals took place outside the city. As a parody of Jesus crucified outside the city, those who persecute his people will also be judged and condemned *outside the city.* However, the city could refer to Babylon/Rome, although this has little significance to the context of judging the beast and those who worship the beast. However, the city could be the heavenly Jerusalem, which John has not yet introduced. It may be that John in his usual recapitulationist style is here introducing this celestial city, which he will later bring into clearer focus. In time John will stress that nothing (no person) unclean will be able to enter this city since it has angels guarding each of the four gates. Outside the city walls are the dogs and everything unclean. The unclean are those who bear the mark of the beast and have persecuted the saints (cf. 21:27).

It might be more appropriate then to see this city, outside of which God and Jesus will bring their eschatological judgment on the beast and his worshippers, as the heavenly city.[124]

The severity of God's judgment is dramatized as *blood flowed out of the press, rising as high as the horses' bridles for a distance of 1,600 stadia.* The whole phrase is intended to be a symbolic and hyperbolic reference to the severity of God's judgment on the beast (1600 stadia, approx. 184 miles, may imply the figure of 40 squared, 40 being a symbol of judgment).[125] Some have suggested that the 1600 stadia approximates the length of Palestine from Tyre in the north to Egypt in the south.[126] The blood flowing as high as a horses bridle draws on the apocalyptic tradition (1 *Enoch* 100:3; 4 *Ezra* 15:35–36; and several Jewish apocalyptic tracts). 1 *Enoch* 100 predates Revelation while the other sections of Enoch fall a little later than Revelation. The point Bauckham makes is that this horse/blood imagery was common in the apocalyptic tradition. He suggests that this image may have become a widely used apocalyptic *topos* (literary device and reworking of traditional material) that suggests the severe slaughter experienced in war.[127]

Summary of the Seven Mystic Figures of Rev. 12:1–14:20

In this climactic section John has presented the heart of Revelation, the victory of the saints in Christ Jesus over Satan and his agent Rome. It began with Satan making war on the saints and seeking to destroy God's Messiah and the messianic community (faithful Israel as the messianic community and the church as the messianic community). John sets the scene in a cosmic holy war in which Satan and his angels are defeated by Michael and his angels. The scene relocates to earth where Satan has moved his battle now to be against the church. The high point in the theology of Revelation is found in 12:10–11, where in spite of heavy losses (martyrdom), the victory cry is heard, "Now the victory and power and authority of the Lamb have come, for the enemy of the saints (Satan) has been defeated by the blood of the Lamb and the faithful testimony of the martyrs. However, Satan will not give in easily and raises a beast from the sea (Rome) to carry out his war on the church. Another beast, the imperial cult, appears. This beast, drawing on the power of the first beast (the civil power of Rome) causes people to worship the first beast, Rome. Those who are seduced by this second beast and who worship the emperor receive the mark of the beast on their fore-head and hand. This mark is a mystical number 666, which John explains is the mark of a human being, not a divine being. The scene moves to Mount Zion, the metaphoric place of the seat of God's kingdom, where the Lamb gathers with his messianic army. A great expectation lies in wait. But in typical Johannine style, he introduces another interlude, seven angelic messages offering repentance and forgiveness to those who will worship God, not the beast. The eternal gospel contains both encouragement and the threat of judgment to all. To those who worship God, there is the promise of eternal rest from suffering and persecution. To those who refuse God's gift of forgiveness, who worship the beast and who are defined as those who live on the earth, there is the fire of eternal hell. God promises to send his reapers, Christ and his angels, to harvest the earth of its wickedness and judge the unclean with severe eternal punishment. The final act of the theological drama John has been weaving through the first 14 chapters is ready; chapter15, in almost a pattern of chapter 4, will complete the final act of the drama.

Chapter 9

The Seven Bowls of Wrath

THE CONSUMMATED JUDGMENTS

15:1–16:21

Revelation 15 and 16 are parallel to 4 and 6 in that they both open with a heavenly scene and proceed to seven angelic messages. With the messages of 16, the wrath of God against the saints' enemies is brought to final expression; he is about to consummate his judgments against Rome, the beast, and the imperial cult, the false prophet. Again John will refer to Rome as Babylon and proclaim that these judgments are in response to the cries of the saints that came from beneath the altar (6:10 and 10:6). The seven bowls of God's wrath are reminiscent of the Exodus plagues on Egypt.

In our chiastic structure we are now in the "return" section in which level V expresses the consummation of level III.

Prologue 1:1–20
    I. The Church in Imperfection (2:1–3:22)
      Seven Letters to the Seven Churches
        II. The Authority of God over Evil Explained (4:1–8:6)
          Seven Seals on the Scroll
            III. The Warning Judgments (8:1–11:19)
            Seven Trumpets
                IV. The Lamb—God's Answer to Evil (12:1–14:20)
                  Seven Unnumbered Figures
            V. The Consummated Judgments (15:1–16:21)
            Seven Bowls of Wrath

VI. The Authority of God over Evil Exercised (17:1–20:15)
    Seven Unnumbered Descriptions of God's Judgments
VII. The Church in Perfection (21:1–22:5)
    Seven Unnumbered Descriptions of the Church in Perfection
Epilogue 22:6–21

INTRODUCTION

A review of the chiastic structure will indicate that we are in the "descending order" of the structure, having reached the climax of the narrative drama at 12:1–14:20, when Christ and the martyrs are declared victorious over the dragon and his two beasts. Immediately prior to the climax were the seven trumpets, which were warning judgments on those who opposed God and persecuted his people. Now in the final Act, God pronounces judgment on those who refused his offer of repentance (9:20). This is a proleptic description of the consummated judgment on the beast, Rome, for its persecution of the saints and opposition to God's eternal purpose. Act Two builds toward the eventual final judgment, for John must bring closure to his theodicy, but the focus must remain on God's judgment of the beast and vindication of the saints. However, for the story to be complete, Satan must also be judged along with all those through the ages he has seduced to follow his self-destructive example of opposing God and his will. In good prophetic form, John reassures the saints by pronouncing in detail God's rejection and judgment of their enemy, the new Babylon. John draws on the certainty of God's prophesy by pointing to Isaiah's prophecy, which all knew God had fulfilled in detail (Isa. 21:9).The final judgment of the dragon, the beast, the false prophet, and those who worship the beast is reserved for 20:11–15.

THE INTRODUCTORY VISION IN HEAVEN TO THE REVEALING OF SEVEN ANGELS WITH SEVEN BOWLS OF GOD'S WRATH—REV. 15:1–8

The structure of this pericope is both interesting and informative for as Osborne correctly observes it is in a chiastic ABA[1] form.

A. **Seven Angels with Seven Plagues of Judgment: 15:1**
    B. **The Song of the Martyrs in Heaven: 15:2–4**
A[1]. **Seven Angels Come from within the Temple with the Judgments of God: 15:5–8**

This pericope parallels the warning judgments of 8:1–11:19 and proclaims that God has taken his judgment beyond the warning stage to the consummation stage. The drama of seven bowls of wrath is set in an Egyptian plague typology. God has sent his warning judgments, which have been ignored, so now he brings his final judgment on the rebellious new Egypt, that is, Rome. The insertion of the song of the Lamb, a typology of the song of Moses (Deut. 32), celebrates the faithfulness of God and his ability to deliver his people and judge their enemies. This reinforces the Egyptian plague typology of the seven new plagues about to be poured out. This pericope serves as an "interlocking" device between the vindication of the saints described in 14 and the consummated judgments about to be announced and poured out on their enemies. Each of the three components of this chiastic structure (15:1, 2, 5) is introduced by the typical Johannine *kai eidon* ("and I saw") or a similar construction and translation.

The Text

15:1–8. *I saw in heaven another great and marvelous sign: seven angels with the seven last plagues—last, because with them God's wrath is completed. [2] And I saw what looked like a sea of glass mixed with fire and, standing beside the sea, those who had been victorious over the beast and his image and over the number of his name. They held harps given them by God [3] and sang the song of Moses the servant of God and the song of the Lamb: "Great and marvelous are your deeds, Lord God Almighty. Just and true are your ways, King of the ages. [4] Who will not fear you, O Lord, and bring glory to your name? For you alone are holy. All nations will come and worship before you, for your righteous acts have been revealed." [5] After this I looked and in heaven the temple, that is, the tabernacle of the Testimony, was opened. [6] Out of the temple came the seven angels with the seven plagues. They were dressed in clean, shining linen and wore golden sashes around their chests. [7] Then one of the four living creatures gave to the seven angels seven golden bowls filled with the wrath of God, who lives for ever and ever. [8] And the temple was filled with smoke from the glory of God and from his power, and no one could enter the temple until the seven plagues of the seven angels were completed.*

15:1. ***I saw in heaven another great and marvelous sign: seven angels with the seven last plagues—last, because with them God's wrath is completed.*** John leaves no mistake regarding these seven plagues. They are not warning plagues as in 8:1–11:19. The NIV misses the point that John begins this pericope with an epexegetical *kai*, which is translated as *then* in the RSV but should more appropriately be rendered as "Indeed I saw." This connects the seven plagues to the closing thoughts of the previous chapter regarding God's serious judgments on those who dwell on earth; the enemies of the saints. Caird's connects 15 and the seven bowls of wrath to the plagues of Egypt, "By a slight shift of the kaleidoscope the ocean of blood through which the martyrs have passed in the great vintage now becomes a heavenly Red Sea, . . . Another Mosaic series of ***seven plagues*** is to be poured out on the city which is figuratively called Egypt, and these, unlike the call to repentance from the seven trumpets, are to be the ***last***."[1]

These are the last plagues to be poured out on the new Egypt, Rome, in which God's wrath is completed. "The time for mercy is over, and God's law must now take its course. The sanctity of the law is emphasized first by the appearance of the angels in the vestments of priesthood, ***robed in linen*** and with ***gold girdles round their breasts***."[2] God has been faithful and patient, but now the time has come for him to pronounce his judgment on Rome for its rebellion and rejection of his eternal gospel. Warnings are over; consummation is imminent. However, in typical style John introduces another brief interlude before he reveals the awesome judgment of God on Rome, namely, the salutary song of the martyrs who sing the song of Moses and the Lamb. The introduction of the seven angels with seven plagues (15) serves as a thematic link to the pouring out of the seven plagues (16).

Most commentators note the difficulty of understanding the role of these seven plagues.[3] Do the seven plagues refer to the last set of judgments recorded by John in his drama in which finally God's wrath is poured out on Rome, or do they refer to the final eschatological judgment at the end of the world? The seven plagues must be kept in the context of the theological drama that John has been developing, which is set in the real experience of the churches of Asia—persecution, martyrdom, the prayers of the saints for vindication, and God's promise to transform their suffering and martyrdom into a triumphant victory. In this context John has repeatedly stressed that those who dwell on earth, that is those who have persecuted the saints and worshipped the beast, would be judged with a devastating judgment of an eschatological nature and significance. The seven trumpets of 8:1–11:19 were warning trumpets proclaiming God's fierce judgment and wrath on those who dwell on earth and who worship the beast. They refused God's eternal gospel and call to repentance. The visions of the warning trumpet judgments closed with the martyrs rejoicing over their vindication, for God had brought his sovereign power and judgment on his enemies.

Revelation 12:1–14:20 introduced a new series of visions that identified the real enemy, Rome, the agent of Satan, and finally the triumphant victory scene of the lamb and the saints. John dramatized the contrast between the two beasts and the lamb, emphasizing that the Christians in Asia must choose whose mark they would bear, either the mark of the beast or the mark of the Lamb. Before moving on to describe the certainty of God's wrath and judgment, John inserted an interlude of seven angels and an eternal gospel (14:6–20), which offered repentance to those who worship the beast, but which also encouraged the saints to faithfulness. This interlude closed with a vivid description of the fearful nature of God's wrath and judgment. Now in this new series of visions of seven terrifying plagues in which John drew heavily on Egyptian typology, he describes the consummation of God's warning trumpet judgments on the new Egypt (cf. 11:8), depicting his judgments as seven final plagues in which God's fearsome wrath is finally poured out on the enemies of the saints, that is, on those who dwell on earth, who worship the beast, and who persecute the saints. Although the language used by John is couched in eschatological terminology, John has in mind the judgment of God on the imperial cult and those who worship the emperor and the civil power of Rome.

The *seven last plagues* and *with them God's wrath is completed* have generated considerable discussion. These bowls do not refer to the final judgment or mean that they historically refer to the final acts of God in judgment. They must be seen in the context of Revelation and God's assurance that he has already judged the two beasts (Rome) and those who worship the Roman system with the full impact of eschatological judgment. In this sense, then, these plagues are the last in regard to those who dwell on earth and who persecute the saints. John is describing God's final judgment on Rome. Admittedly the judgments may be couched in eschatological terms, but they continue John's use of proleptic eschatological judgments. They certainly are final in regard to Rome, but they are not the final judgment. They explain that the wrath of God revealed "in the seals and the trumpets reaches its goal."[4]

Observing that the expression *etelesthē*, **is completed** (from *teleō*, "bring to an end," "finish," "complete") may be used in a metaphorical sense, Beale concludes that "The consequent meaning of the metaphor of 15:1 is that the seven bowls are "last" in that they portray the full-orbed wrath of God in a more intense manner than any of the previous woe visions."[5] John's point in his drama is that God is bringing judgment on Rome with the full force of the final eschatological judgment. The seven bowls, which are the last, demonstrate that God's eschatological wrath is now being brought to completion. That God, in similar fashion, after patiently waiting for all the ungodly to come to repentance, will eventually bring his wrath to completion at the end of the ages against all ungodliness *is another story* (2 Pet. 3:8–10), nevertheless an important one in that it forms the framework of John's proleptic eschatological theology as expressed in Revelation.

15:2–4. *And I saw what looked like a sea of glass mixed with fire and, standing beside the sea, those who had been victorious over the beast and his image and over the number of his name. They held harps given them by God*[3] *and sang the song of Moses the servant of God and the song of the Lamb: "Great and marvelous are your deeds, Lord God Almighty. Just and true are your ways, King of the ages.*[4] *Who will not fear you, O Lord, and bring glory to your name? For you alone are holy. All nations will come and worship before you, for your righteous acts have been revealed."* Chapters 4 and 15 demonstrate the parallel theological themes of a *sea of glass*. Some consider this to be an analogous reference to the Egyptian exodus and the Red Sea since this fits in well with the Egyptian typology adopted by John in the bowls of plagues. However, we need to keep this reference within the greater context of Revelation and John's other references to the sea.[6] First, it will help to clarify the translation *sea of glass*. The Greek *hōs thalassan hualinēn* is translated *looked like a sea of glass*. In actuality, what John saw was not a sea of glass but something like a sea that was glasslike. The Greek conjunction *hōs* (an adverbial form of *hos, hē, ho*) carries the comparative sense of something like, something that looked like a *sea of glass*. The word *hualinēn (hualinos*, "made of glass" or "transparent") is in the accusative case in agreement with *thalassan*. As such *hualinēn* functions as an attributive adjective modifying *sea*, or explaining that the sea was something like glass, glasslike, or transparent. At 4:6 *the sea of glass* was *like crystal*. Here the sea that was glasslike is *mixed with fire*. Next, we need to re-examine the sea in Revelation. Sea appears twenty-six times in Revelation, but in the same context found here we find the sea mentioned at 4:6; 12:17; 13:1; 15:2; 21:1. At 4:6 the sea was glasslike like crystal in the throne room of God. At 4:6 the sea in all probability represented one of the cosmic or mythological sources of evil. At 4:6 it was accepted as part of God's theodicy, but in the context of God's sovereignty was no real threat. At 12:17 and 13:1 Satan stands by the sea and calls the evil beast out of the sea. Obviously, the sea was intended to be understood as a source of evil. At 21:1

after the final judgment and the destruction of Satan, the sea is no more, implying that all sources of evil have been destroyed and removed. We should keep the sea of 15:2 in this same context. The symbolism of *mixed with fire* is best seen in the context of either purification or divine judgment.

15:2b–4. Standing in the heavenly scene beside the sea are *those who had been victorious over the beast and his image and over the number of his name*. As in 4:6 the martyrs have no fear of evil, for they have already conquered Satan and the beast (12:10–11). With *harps of God* the victorious saints now sing the song of Moses and the Lamb (NIV *they held harps given them by God*, or simply *harps of God*, RSV). *Of God* in Greek is the genitive case *tou theou* and in all probability is an objective genitive, "harps concerning God," that is, "harps played for God" or "harps for playing to God." I would translate this as an objective genitive "harps for praising God."[7] The parallelism and poetic structure are worthy of notice:

> *Great and marvelous are your deeds,*
>   *Lord God Almighty.*
> *Just and true are your ways,*
>   *King of the ages.*
>   [4] *Who will not fear you, O Lord,*
>   *and bring glory to your name?*
> *For you alone are holy.*
>   *All nations will come*
>   *and worship before you,*
>   *for your righteous acts have been revealed.*

Compare this hymn with those at 4:11 and 5:9, 19.

The saints sing *the song of Moses the servant of God and the song of the Lamb*. John continues the exodus typology from Exodus 15:1-18, demonstrating that this song, as was the case with Moses and Israel, is one of celebrating deliverance from the sea and pharaoh as a source of evil. The saints have likewise been delivered from the sea (evil) and the new pharaoh, John describes Moses as *the servant of God*, enlarging on the theme of martyrdom as a service of God. However, the expression translated *the servant* is in fact *tou doulou* (*doulos*, "slave"). Moses is often depicted in the Old Testament as the slave of God (Num. 12:7; Deut. 34:5; Josh. 1:1). Like Moses, the saints (Paul in Rom. 1:1) belong to and, in reality are bond servants of God and Christ, having been purchased by the blood of Christ (cf. 5:9 and 14:4). As a slave of God, Moses sang a song of deliverance from bondage to Egypt. As slaves of God, the saints sing a song of deliverance from bondage to Rome.

This song of deliverance is *the song of Moses and the song of the Lamb*. "Of Moses" and "of the Lamb" are both constructions in the genitive case. The interpretation of this expression is complex since the song of Moses is obviously in reference to the song sung by Moses, hence a subjective genitive, that is, a song like the one sung by Moses.

But is this song one sung by the Lamb or like one sung by the Lamb? In the text it is not the Lamb who is singing but the saints, and we know of no song sung by the Lamb as in Exodus [15]. Is this to be a song sung by the saints in favor of the Lamb or concerning the Lamb, which would then have of the Lamb as an objective genitive? The syntax is complicated by the fact that the song of Moses and the song of the Lamb are connected by *kai,* a coordinating conjunction. It could be that this *kai* is an epexegetical *kai* that can mean "indeed," or "which is also" the song concerning the Lamb. There are not two songs sung here, only one, the song of deliverance symbolized by the song of Moses, which is also the song of deliverance sung concerning Jesus.[8] The implication may be "as Moses triumphed over Egypt and the Pharaoh so Jesus triumphed over Satan in the cross and his resurrection."[9]

The song itself is furthermore a composite construction from several passages in the Old Testament. Snatches from Psalms 119:42; 139:16; ; 145:17; Hosea 14:9; Jeremiah 10:7; Isaiah 2:2–4; 66:23 are drawn together in a majestic hymn of praise to God and the Lamb. In the context of martyrdom, this hymn is a powerful celebration of God's awesome power, righteousness, sovereignty, and holiness as well as of the victory and vindication of the saints.

15:5–6. *After this I looked and in heaven the temple, that is, the tabernacle of the Testimony, was opened.* [6] *Out of the temple came the seven angels with the seven plagues. They were dressed in clean, shining linen and wore golden sashes around their chests.* The introductory phrase *After this* indicates the introduction of a new vision, this one of the heavenly temple described as *the tabernacle of the Testimony*. *After this* does not signal a historically chronological sequence of vision, but a stylistic layering of one vision over the previous one. John's stylistic description of the heavenly temple continues Egypt/Moses typology. The tabernacle in the wilderness symbolized the covenant between God and Israel. In the tabernacle was stored the alter containing the ten commandments which testified or witnessed to God's covenant with Israel. The analogy here reminds the saints that those who broke covenant with God in the wilderness were severely punished by God, but those who were faithful were rewarded by a new home in the promised land. Out of this covenant signified by *the tabernacle of the Testimony* the seven angels appear. The expression *the tabernacle of testimony* (*tēs skēnēs tou marturiou*) is either a genitive construction of apposition or an epexegetical genitive describing the temple. The expression can therefore read "the temple of testimony," or "the temple, namely the tent of witness."[10] That the seven angels with the seven plagues came out of the tabernacle of testimony implies that the plagues represent divine judgments pronounced as a result of broken covenants with God. The broken covenants in the context of Revelation are the sinful compromises with the pagan culture and worship of the beast. The impressive robes of the angels imply purity, glory, and royal dignity. A significant textual variant occurs in this text where the choices are between *shining linen* (Greek *linon*), meaning shining linen garments or robes. The textual variant *lithos* ("stone" or "precious jewel") also implies some form of priestly garment. While both variants are possible, Metzger argues that *linon* is preferred over *lithos* in that *lithos* seems to be a transcriptional error.[11] The ***shining linen*** garments possibly point to the priestly garments of the Old Testament,[12] while the ***golden sashes around their chests*** draws on the garments worn by the Son of Man in 1:13 and possibly Daniel 10:5, indicating that these angels were somehow associated with the Son of Man and act as his representatives in carrying out divine judgment.[13]

15:7–8. *Then one of the four living creatures gave to the seven angels seven golden bowls filled with the wrath of God, who lives for ever and ever.* [8] *And the temple was filled with smoke from the glory of God and from his power, and no one could enter the temple until the seven plagues of the seven angels were completed.* John explains that the seven plagues of 15:1 are in fact seven bowls ***filled with the wrath of God***. Again, in keeping with the Egyptian typology, John focuses the plagues of divine judgment on a pagan nation for its oppression of his people and that the seven bowls of divine wrath were given to the seven angels by ***one of the four living creatures***. The appearance of one of the four living creatures recalls chapter 6, where the four living creatures called the four horsemen out in the seven seals of the great scroll of chapter 5. The inclusion of the living creature here is intended to demonstrate that God's judgment on the beast was an implicit part of his sovereign plan for his creation.[14] The function of this living creature was the commissioning of the seven angels.[15] The seven bowls of wrath link to the golden bowls of incense to the prayers of the saints at 5:8; 6:9–11; 8:3–5.[16] Also in 10:6 an angel declared that there would be no more delay, indicating that these judgments are in answer to the prayers of the saints beneath the altar for vindication. The symbolism of the temple filled with smoke from the glory of God "is modeled in part on Ezekiel 9:1–10:6, where seven angelic beings punish all who do not have the protective mark of God on their foreheads."[17] That ***no one could enter the temple until the seven plagues of the seven angels were completed*** indicates God's divine presence (cf. Exod. 40:35; 1 Kgs 8:11) and that his judgment is so awesome that no one could enter the temple until God's purpose had been carried out. God's judgment on Rome is depicted by John as no small event; all of heaven is focused on these judgments. Several possibilities have been proposed as to the full meaning of the temple or heaven being closed during the duration of these seven plagues. Some suggest that during these judgments there is no possibility for intercession, for that time.[18] Some state that God during this period of judgment cannot be approached due to the significance of his actions.[19] Others suggest that God's presence is so awesome that the temple was closed during his presence.[20] However, this scene primarily links to the prayers of the saints at 8:1, where there was silence in heaven for thirty minutes, indicating again that the divine judgments to follow are connected to the prayers of the saints for vindication.[21]

THE SEVEN BOWLS OF GOD'S CONSUMMATED WRATH: REV. 16:1–21.
The Text
16:1–21. *Then I heard a loud voice from the temple saying to the seven angels, "Go, pour out the seven bowls of God's wrath on the earth."* [2] *The first angel went and poured out his*

bowl on the land, and ugly and painful sores broke out on the people who had the mark of the beast and worshiped his image. [3] The second angel poured out his bowl on the sea, and it turned into blood like that of a dead man, and every living thing in the sea died. [4] The third angel poured out his bowl on the rivers and springs of water, and they became blood. [5] Then I heard the angel in charge of the waters say:

> *"You are just in these judgments,*
> *you who are and who were, the Holy One,*
> *because you have so judged;*
> [6]*for they have shed the blood of your saints and prophets,*
> *and you have given them blood to drink as they deserve."*
> [7]*And I heard the altar respond:*
> *"Yes, Lord God Almighty,*
> *true and just are your judgments."*

[8] *The fourth angel poured out his bowl on the sun, and the sun was given power to scorch people with fire. [9] They were seared by the intense heat and they cursed the name of God, who had control over these plagues, but they refused to repent and glorify him.*

[10] *The fifth angel poured out his bowl on the throne of the beast, and his kingdom was plunged into darkness. Men gnawed their tongues in agony [11] and cursed the God of heaven because of their pains and their sores, but they refused to repent of what they had done.*

[12] *The sixth angel poured out his bowl on the great river Euphrates, and its water was dried up to prepare the way for the kings from the East. [13] Then I saw three evil spirits that looked like frogs; they came out of the mouth of the dragon, out of the mouth of the beast and out of the mouth of the false prophet. [14] They are spirits of demons performing miraculous signs, and they go out to the kings of the whole world, to gather them for the battle on the great day of God Almighty.*

[15] *"Behold, I come like a thief. Blessed is he who stays awake and keeps his clothes with him, so that he may not go naked and be shamefully exposed."*

[16] *Then they gathered the kings together to the place that in Hebrew is called Armageddon.*

[17] *The seventh angel poured out his bowl into the air, and out of the temple came a loud voice from the throne, saying, "It is done." [18] Then there came flashes of lightning, rumblings, peals of thunder and a severe earthquake. No earthquake like it has ever occurred since man has been on earth, so tremendous was the quake. [19] The great city split into three parts, and the cities of the nations collapsed. God remembered Babylon the Great and gave her the cup filled with the wine of the fury of his wrath. [20] Every island fled away and the mountains could not be found. [21] From the sky huge hailstones of about a hundred pounds each fell upon men. And they cursed God on account of the plague of hail, because the plague was so terrible.*

We must remember that this judgment is not the final eschatological judgment of the whole creation. John is describing God's imminent divine judgment on the beast (Rome) and those who worship the beast. To emphasize his point regarding the severity of God's judgment on Rome, John sets this in the language of proleptic eschatological judgment, not intending to discuss at this point the final judgment.

The judgments poured out from the seven bowls of wrath are different from the previous judgments described in the seven seals and seven trumpets, for the previous judgments were warning judgments intended to bring the ungodly worshippers of the beast to repentance. Now the warning judgments become consummated judgments. Whereas the previous judgments had been partial, the judgments of the plagues are complete. In these seven bowls of wrath are "the total deconstruction of the empire of the beast . . . . God has done all that can be done to bring the nations to a realization of his sovereign justice, and now the time for their decisive judgment has come. His wrath is complete."[22] What John is describing is the fact that God has *already* judged Rome and the dwellers on earth with final eschatological judgment. The intention of Revelation is to assure the saints that martyrdom is a victory, that they will be vindicated, and that God has already judged their enemies with severe and ferocious judgment.

The structure of these seven bowls is in John's traditional form of a four plus three grouping (cf. the initial four seals representing the four horsemen, and the first four trumpets which, were more earthly than the remaining three). The seven bowls are a progression from four natural disasters to three direct judgments on the throne of the beast. Caird adds that "the three final plagues are the dethronement of the monster."[23]

Rev. 16:1. *Then I heard a loud voice from the temple saying to the seven angels, "Go, pour out the seven bowls of God's wrath on the earth."* On several occasions John refers to *a loud voice* (1:10; 5:2, 12; 6:10; 7:2, 10; 8:13; 10:3; 11:12, 15; 12:10; 14:7, 9, 15, 18; 19:1, 17; 21:3). Although most commentators suggest that this could be the voice of one of the living creatures, of an angel, of Christ, or of God, in this case it should be understood as God himself speaking. John connects to Isaiah 66:6, in which Isaiah cries, "Hear that uproar from the city, hear that noise from the temple. It is the sound of the LORD repaying his enemies all they deserve." I prefer the RSV here since it speaks more directly to the situation confronted by the saints in Revelation, "Hark. . . . The voice of the Lord, rendering recompense to his enemies." Whereas the four living creatures "commissioned" the four horsemen, and an angel initiated the seven trumpets, this time the sovereign God of the universe speaks, dramatizing the severity, completeness, and finality of his judgment of the beast and those who wear his mark. Pouring out bowls containing God's wrath incorporates a cultic image drawn from several Old Testament passages that speak of God's judgment on the nations (Ps. 69:24; 79:6; Jer. 6:11, 12, 7:20; Zeph. 3:8).[24] In the apocalyptic genre God's judgments are often described as poured out on the earth when the recipients of this judgment are actually men. This is borne out by the fact that the first bowl poured out on the earth (16:2) inflicts severe punishment as *painful sores broke out on the people who had the mark of the beast and worshiped his image.*

The First Bowl: Painful Sores on People—Rev. 16:2
The first angel went and poured out his bowl on the land, and ugly and painful sores broke out on the people who had the mark of the beast and worshiped his image. Reminiscent

of the plagues (specifically Exod. 9:8, the boils and sores), the first bowl is poured out on *the people who had the mark of the beast and worshiped his image*. Whereas the previous warning judgments had been partial on the earth, these plagues are focused on the enemies of the saints. The sequence of prayers and responses (16:6–7) indicates that these judgments are in response to the prayers of the saints at Rev. 6:10.

The Second Bowl: The Sea Becomes Blood—Rev. 16:3

Rev. 16:3. *The second angel poured out his bowl on the sea, and it turned into blood like that of a dead man, and every living thing in the sea died.* John continues the plague typology in telling effect. In the previous warning judgments, notably the second trumpet, one third of the sea became blood. Here all of the sea turns to blood and everything living dies.

The Third Bowl: The Rivers and Fountains Become Blood—Rev. 16:4–7

The third angel poured out his bowl on the rivers and springs of water, and they became blood. [5] *Then I heard the angel in charge of the waters say: "You are just in these judgments, you who are and who were, the Holy One, because you have so judged;* [6] *for they have shed the blood of your saints and prophets, and you have given them blood to drink as they deserve."* [7] *And I heard the altar respond: "Yes, Lord God Almighty, true and just are your judgments."* As already noted, John connects this plague to the prayers of the saints beneath the altar (6:10; 10:6).[25] At the third trumpet a third of the waters became poison, resulting in many deaths. Here all the rivers become poisonous, implying that all receive the consequences of their sin. A possible background to this plague may also be Psalm 78:44, which is set in the narrative of the Egyptian plagues. The implication of this bowl, tied to the prayers coming from beneath the altar, is that those who shed the blood of the saints will have to drink the retributive judgment and blood of this plague. The reference to *the angel in charge of the waters* draws on the Jewish and early Christian view that all the elements of God's creation had guardian angels (cf. 7:1; 14:18; *1 Enoch* 60:17, 19, 21; 61:10; *Jub.* 2:2; *Sib. Or.* 7:33–35; *2 Baruch* 6–9). The angel responsible for the safe keeping of the waters recognizes the righteous judgment of God and registers no protest to the turning of the rivers into blood, thus rendering them poisonous. The altar, representing the prayers of the saints, agrees with the angel regarding the righteous judgment and vindication of the saints.

The Fourth Bowl: The Sun Scorches People with Fire—Rev. 16:8, 9

The fourth angel poured out his bowl on the sun, and the sun was given power to scorch people with fire. [9] *They were seared by the intense heat and they cursed the name of God, who had control over these plagues, but they refused to repent and glorify him.* The first three plagues reflect plague typology; the fourth introduces a new theme, possibly apocalyptic in type. At 6:12 and 9:2 the impact on the cosmic sun was set in an apocalyptic genre, and it is likely that this pouring out the plague of God's wrath on the sun is to be understood symbolically as a sign of divine judgment, not a literal burning of people.[26] The sovereign empowering of the sun to scorch people is strengthened by the use of the divine passive (*edothē*, "was given"). The apocalyptic symbolism of people scorched by the massive sun burst (nova) refers to those who steadfastly refuse to repent, obviously implying the same people reflected in 9:20–21, namely, those who dwell on earth and who worship the beast. This does not refer to the conquering saints because they have been sealed and protected by God's presence (7:16). However, these who are burnt by the scorching sun are beyond repentance, for they have refused God's eternal gospel (14:6) and sold themselves to the beast. Their response to God's judgment is to curse his holy name and refuse to give him sole divine glory, for they have glorified the emperor and worshipped the beast. Describing their cursing God's name, John uses the aorist form of the term commonly rendered blaspheme (*eblasphēmēsan*, from *blasphēmeō*), which indicates an action that has roots in the past and has become part of the present. To blaspheme God in this instance is to injure the reputation of, revile, defame, to slander, or curse God. Beyer[27] describes this as "the thought of violation of the power and majesty of God." By denying God his rightful power and sovereignty and assigning this to a human being, even an emperor, is to violate his majesty. The translation curse in the RSV and NIV does not do justice to the full meaning of blaspheme in the sense of denying God his majesty. Aune observes:

> The response of blaspheming or reviling the name of God on the part of people who have been affected by divine retribution occurs only here and in vv 11 and 21 and forms a distinctive motif in Revelation found only in 16:1–21 (though the beast is said to revile God and his dwelling in 13:6). The reviling or blaspheming of the name of God implicitly involves breaking the third commandment, which warns against the wrongful use of the name of God (Exod 20:7 = Deut 5:11) and is a sin punishable by death (Lev 24:16). This response is repeated in varied language as the human reaction to the seventh bowl.[28]

Concerning God's sovereignty, John states that it was God *who had control over these plagues*.

The Fifth Bowl: The Beast's Throne Enveloped in Darkness—Rev. 16:10, 11

The fifth angel poured out his bowl on the throne of the beast, and his kingdom was plunged into darkness. Men gnawed their tongues in agony [11] *and cursed the God of heaven because of their pains and their sores, but they refused to repent of what they had done.* Caird[29] groups the last three plagues under the heading of "political plagues." All seven are in one respect political in that they are directed at the demise of Rome as a political power, and at God's imminent severe and ultimate judgment on Rome. This does not imply the historical demise, which obviously lay ahead in the future, but the proleptic demise of Rome as a political power in that God would remove Rome as a threat. The prophetic yet enigmatic message of the binding of Satan for a thousand years fits into this concept, proclaiming that God would remove Rome as a political and threatening power and limit Satan's ability to use Rome for his attacks on the church. The three "political plagues" introduced by the fifth bowl are political darkness, threats of a Parthian power, and an earthquake in which "Babylon" would be destroyed.

The fifth bowl is poured out *on the throne of the beast* whose *kingdom was plunged into darkness*. Osborne observes, as do most commentators, that this plague is "anchored in 13:2" where the dragon gave to the beast form the sea power to wage war on the saints. The beast we have already on several occasions identified as the political power of Rome. The result of this plague is darkness, but not simply darkness as a literal concept, but darkness as a political threat. Rome's imperial history is replete with instances of political intrigue, internal anarchy, suspicion, and treason. This plague proclaims that God would increase such "darkness" in a symbolic fashion to the three day darkness that spread over Egypt during the ninth Egyptian plague (Ex 10). God would bring political trauma upon Rome, the enemy of the church. Osborne summarizes this well, "The message is clear: the beast has limited authority, and his throne is temporary and soon to be overwhelmed by the act of God. "[30] This aligns well with John's opening remark that the message of Revelation related to things that "must soon take place" (1:1). Several commentators point out that the *Wisdom of Solomon* 17:2 may have lain behind John's use of political darkness in 16 and the fifth bowl: "For when lawless men supposed that they held the holy nation in their power, they themselves lay as captives of darkness and prisoners of long night, shut in under their roofs, exiles from eternal providence." That is, the Egyptian darkness was more severe than Israel's burden of slavery, indicating furthermore that the darkness that awaited the Egyptians was worse than any suffering endured by Israel, for Wisdom explains, "while over those men alone heavy night was spread, an image of the darkness that was destined to receive them; but still heavier than darkness were they to themselves" (*Wis.* 17:20). It is possible that this plaque and its message is intended to imply that the darkness to be brought by God on Rome would be far more severe than the suffering of the saints.

The expression *men gnawed their tongues in agony* stresses the extent of the trauma and suffering about to descend on Rome as the power of their kingdom is reduced to anarchy. The fact that men *cursed the God of heaven because of their pains and their sores, but they refused to repent of what they had done* is an analogy to the Egyptians, who were "intractable in their nonrepentant attitude and finally condemned . . . 'would not be reformed by that correction . . . will feel a judgment worthy of God.'"[31]

The Sixth Bowl: The Final Showdown, Armageddon—Rev. 16:12–16

The sixth angel poured out his bowl on the great river Euphrates, and its water was dried up to prepare the way for the kings from the East. [13] *Then I saw three evil spirits that looked like frogs; they came out of the mouth of the dragon, out of the mouth of the beast and out of the mouth of the false prophet.* [14] *They are spirits of demons performing miraculous signs, and they go out to the kings of the whole world, to gather them for the battle on the great day of God Almighty.* [15] *"Behold, I come like a thief.*

294   CONQUERING WITH CHRIST

Blessed is he who stays awake and keeps his clothes with him, so that he may not go naked and be shamefully exposed." [16] *Then they gathered the kings together to the place that in Hebrew is called Armageddon.* This paragraph, along with 666, the number of the beast, and the thousand-year reign (20:4), is one of the most recognized and often cited in Revelation. The passage is difficult as John presents his message in what Beale describes as a "figurative universalization."[32] The powerful message of this sixth bowl can be lost if one interprets the symbols literally.[33] Israel's experience of Babylonian exile and the promise of their return figure prominently in this pericope and its images. *The great river Euphrates* has already appeared in 9:14. The imagery of the demonic army gathered at the Euphrates was symbolic of the constant threat faced by Rome from its enemies to the east, the Parthians, or Persian army. John returns to this imagery again as he describes the symbolic fall of the new Babylon under God's judgment. The earlier historical Babylon had fallen to the Medes and Persians under Cyrus in 539 B.C. That the waters of the Euphrates would be *dried up to prepare the way for the kings from the East* would not be a new idea to John's readers, for they were familiar with the Jewish traditions surrounding Isaiah 11:15–16, 44:27; 50:2, in which Isaiah prophesies regarding the drying up of the rivers. This prophecy was partially fulfilled "when Cyrus . . . diverted the Euphrates, crossed the river, and captured Babylon" (Isa. 44:28; Jer. 50:38; 51:36). The point John is making is that the new Babylon, Rome, is not impregnable and can fall just as easily as did the Babylon of old. The threat would come from *the kings from the East*, the Parthians, a traditional threat to Rome.

Rev. 16:13–14. The *three evil spirits that looked like frogs* that John saw *came out of the mouth of the dragon, out of the mouth of the beast and out of the mouth of the false prophet.* The implication of three evil spirits is that whatever the dragon, the sea beast, and the land beast utter is a false message. Jews considered frogs unclean (Lev. 11:10, 11, which prohibited eating creatures that lived in the waters and that swarmed, had no fins, and no scales). However, in view of John's setting of the seven bowls in the context of the plagues, in which frogs were a torment to the Egyptians, we should keep the frogs in the context of the plagues. In the Jewish tradition frogs were considered agents of destruction that emitted harsh noises that were painful to the hearers.[34] This false trinity, the three evil spirits, the dragon, sea beast, and land beast, like frogs, uttered destructive misleading messages that were responsible for deceiving the kings of the whole world. Like the land beast of 13:11, they were *performing miraculous signs.* It is also interesting that frogs were one of the two false "miraculous" signs that the pharaoh's magicians were able to produce (Exod. 8:7).

This sixth bowl began with the kings from the east gathered at the great river Euphrates for battle as in the days of the former great Babylon, which fell to Cyrus, the Persian. The expression *the kings of the whole world* is not to be taken literally, but is symbolic of the power of Rome to seduce nations and of the extent of Rome's reach. The same imagery is repeated at 19:9, where *the kings of the earth* who committed fornication with Rome are distressed be the extent of Rome's demise.

John complicates this challenging pericope further by his statement that *the kings of the whole world* will be gathered *for the battle on the great day of God Almighty*. That a great battle might be fought by the Parthians against Rome reminds us that God has often used pagan nations to bring about the defeat of the enemies of his people. For instance, it was the Medo-Persians who broke the back of Babylon, and it was Rome itself whom God used to bring judgment against an unbelieving Jerusalem (A.D. 66, and Matt. 24). Now it is the new symbolic Parthians (*the kings from the East*) who are drawn into John's drama in this symbolic final defeat and downfall of Rome. They are *gathered . . . together to the place that in Hebrew is called Armageddon* where surely Rome will be defeated.

While commentators are divided in regard to the nature of the battle John is describing, they are nevertheless united in understanding this battle is described in symbolic terms in an apocalyptic or cosmic battle between the forces of evil and the forces of the Almighty God. Some understand this to refer to the Persian-Roman battle and a great battle between the forces of evil and the forces of good. It is imperative in Revelation that we understand John's artistry of combining images for emphasis in a manner that "the whole world" must be kept in the context of those "who live on the earth" and "those who worship the beast" (cf. 13:3, 4, 14.)

Beckwith expresses well the thoughts many have subsequently articulated.

> This vision of the sixth bowl combines two distinct traditions, that of the Parthian host coming with the returning Nero to conquer the Roman world (v. 12), and that of the great assault of the united kings of the earth upon God's people in the last days (vv. 13-14; see on 1420. . .). It might be supposed that the Apocalyptist in the first part (v. 12) has in mind solely the destruction of Rome by the Neronic Antichrist and his Parthian allies, an event falling within the period of the bowl-plagues; while the latter event, the final battle with the Messiah described in 19:11ff. But it is doubtful whether he here conceives a historic program for the future so distinctly articulated . . . a distinct is not made between two classes of the Beast's allies. [35]

Speaking of these kings, Osborne observes that "These are the 'kings of the earth' who commit adultery with the great prostitute (17:2) and reign under her rule (17:18). They are the 'ten horns' of 17:12–14 who 'give their power and authority to the beast' (17:13)."[36]

Aune seeks to resolve the tension between what he sees as two wars by arguing that the kings of 16:13–14 "constitute a later interpolation that exhibits the theme of kings hostile to God and his people." He further notes that "the kings of the whole world are often identified with the ten kings of 17:12–14, 16–17 (Beckwith, 683, Bousset [1906] 397, though in my view the battle in 17:14 is an interpolation)."[37] Although I do not agree with Aune regarding a later interpolation, he raises some interesting points regarding the tension between the two groups of kings. He notes that the assembling of hostile nations for a great battle with God is found in many places in the Old Testament and apocalyptic tradition, including the Qumran War Scroll, 1QM.[38]

John, in his artistic genius, is drawing on several well-known apocalyptic, Jewish, and similar (Qumran) traditions to describe the nature of God's great cosmic battle with the beast (Rome) and the demonic powers supporting it. The end according to the traditions is that God always triumphs and the nations suffer total defeat and destruction.

Aune observes regarding this great battle:

> This theme is found in many apocalyptic battles (Ezek 38-39; Zech 12:1-9; 1 *Enoch* 90:13-19; 99:4; *Jub* 232:23). *1QM* 1:10 mentions . . . "the appointed day," for the battle in which the sons of darkness will be destroyed. Jdt 16:17 pronounces woe on the nations that fight Israel and concludes "The Lord Almighty will take vengeance on them in the day of judgment." While it is difficult to determine if this is eschatology or history . . . the phrase "day of judgment" means the day in which God defeats the enemies of his people, presumably in battle. In the eschatological battle anticipated in Ezek 38-39, many nations assemble for the battle against the people of God (38:1-6). [39]

Eschatological battles are never fixed in any historical time period. They are universal in message and import.

In the context of 16:12–16, the apocalyptic battle involving the new Babylon, Rome, is clarified in the next pericope when the great city, Babylon, is split into three parts. John introduced Parthians armies and the river Euphrates as a warning that the great city Babylon, Rome, can just as easily be defeated as had the previous great Babylon (16:12). Now the armies (of Rome and her allies) are gathered for a great battle with God the Almighty (16:14). There is an *inclusio* in the pericope. It opens with a reference to the great Babylon's defeat and closes with a great battle against God Almighty, which can only result in defeat.

John moves this pericope along by stating that the three evil spirits go out to the kings of the whole world *to gather them for the battle on the great day of God Almighty.* The biblical tradition is replete with images of a great cosmic eschatological battle in which the forces of evil will fight against the forces of God and obviously be crushed by the power of the sovereign ruler of the world. This battle is introduced in a variety of settings, including traditional Jewish sources, the apocalyptic tradition, Qumran Dead Sea scrolls such as the War Scroll, and mystical Judaism such as 1 *Enoch*.[40] This battle will be decisive and the victory overwhelming. Although the language describing this battle is eschatological, it is questionable whether the point of the references is a specific day in history. The apocalyptic hope or confidence is that God will defeat all forces that oppose him, and this cosmic battle becomes a symbol of that victory. The apocalyptic hope or confidence is that God will defeat all forces that oppose him and this cosmic battle becomes a symbol of that victory. It is not uncommon today to refer to some force symbolically meeting up with its Waterloo without intending a reference to a specific day in history. Roberts observes:

The great battle is the great battle of God the Almighty. Here is one of the keys to John's expectations. The destruction of Rome is an event of such importance that it can be spoken of in terms of the "day of God (Yahweh)" (cf. also 6:17). Although this term is sometimes used of the eschatological end of the world, it is also applied to events in Israel's history which, though of supreme importance, did not imply the inauguration of the last time. In these cases there was simply a prophecy of a catastrophe or deliverance which would take place in a conceivable time (Lam 1:21). The overthrow of Jerusalem, for example, was such a day (Ezek. 34:12). [41]

A JOHANNINE PARENTHESIS OR MINOR INTERLUDE —REV. 16:15

Before engaging the interpretation of *Armageddon* I must comment on the expression John draws from Jesus' comment at Matthew 24: 43, which John cites as *"Behold, I come like a thief. Blessed is he who stays awake and keeps his clothes with him, so that he may not go naked and be shamefully exposed."* As John has done previously when matters move toward dramatic climaxes, he introduces a parenthesis. As Jesus had called the Christians in Sardis to be spiritually alert and awake (3:2, 18), so John now calls for spiritual alertness in view of the deceptive witness of the false trinity. John's recalling Jesus' expression *"Behold, I come like a thief. Blessed is he who stays awake"* was not new to the Christian tradition, for most Christians would be familiar with Jesus' warning in the Gospel tradition (Matt. 24:37–43). Paul, likewise, had also previously called on this tradition, 1 Thess. 5:2–4. We find it also in Peter at 2 Pet. 3:10. All three previous expressions are couched in typically apocalyptic contexts and must be interpreted in that genre. When false prophecies are made, the saints are called upon to be spiritually alert. The concept of going **naked** and being **shamefully exposed**, as with the call to be alert draws on Jesus' warning to the church in Laodicea (3:18), but also reflects Old Testament images of being judged by God and consequently being disgraced and shamed (Isa. 20:1–4; Ezek. 16:36; 23:10, 29). Twice John had included the expression *this calls for patient endurance* (13:10; 14:12). This parenthesis functions in similar fashion, calling on the saints to be spiritually alert to the false message of the three false spirits and to be faithful to their Lord. A great cosmic war was pending in which the boastful and lying enemies of the church (the three evil spirits and the nations) would come up against the Almighty God. The saints are warned to be alert and not taken in by any false claims of their enemies. Hear John, *this calls for patient endurance.*

ARMAGEDDON: REV. 16:14–15

The setting and context of this enigmatic battle are vital to any interpretation. We are in the sixth bowl of the consummated judgments of God against the enemies of the saints, namely, the sea beast, the land beast, and those who bear the mark of the beast, who dwell on earth, and who have worshipped the beast. Each one of these definitions of the church's enemies is set in figurative language and concepts. The naming of the great river Euphrates and the description of the river being dried up are symbolic and should not be taken literally. The possibility of a Neronic *redivivus* myth and battle with the Parthians is obviously not to be taken literally.[42] As *Babylon* and *Euphrates* must be taken figuratively, in the same manner *Armageddon* should be taken figuratively, not literally.[43] They should be kept in the context of the consummated judgment of God against Rome and the imperial cult. In similar fashion **the battle on the great day of God Almighty** and **the place that in Hebrew is called Armageddon** must be kept in the context of God's consummated judgment on Rome and the imperial cult (the sea beast, symbolic of the civil power of Rome, and the land beast, symbolic of the imperial cult).[44] The three evil spirits (the dragon, the sea beast, and the land beast) call on the kings they have seduced[45] to gather them for this final battle against God and his servants. We should by now be well prepared for the result of such a battle, for previously the dragon and his army had gone to battle with Michael and his army and been defeated (12:7-9) and now the dragon, Satan, had turned his forces in war against the saints to defeat them (13:1-7). The name of the place of this mysterious cosmic battle is ***Armageddon.***

Whole books have been written on the topic of the Battle of Armageddon, and this has become a popular topic in futurist interpretations of the last days. Beasley-Murray suggests that "Armageddon, presents an even more perplexing puzzle than 666"[46]. Osborne states that there have been many interpretations of "the place called in Hebrew, . . . *Harmagedon*, Armageddon," and cites N. Silberman as producing a significant study (1999) of the topic. Osborne observes that Silberman takes Armageddon "geographically to be ancient Megiddo, now the Jezreel Valley."[47] Osborne lists four geographic and four etymological interpretations of the topic and concludes that "any attempt to find a specific meaning for 'Armageddon' whether literal or symbolic" is difficult. He concludes that "it is more likely that a more general reference is intended, building on the OT connection of Megiddo with warfare."[48] Caird concludes "***Armageddon***, which means Mount Megiddo . . . is best understood as a composite image, compounded of many elements. Megiddo was indeed a famous battlefield, the scene of Sisero's defeat, . . . (Jud. v. 19-20), and the scene also of Josiah's ultimate death (2 Kings 23:29)."[49] Beasley-Murray[50] surprisingly does not prefer the connection with a Mount Megiddo, arguing that the plain of Esrdraelon in Israel has no mountain.[51] Beale although in some agreement with Beasley-Murray observes that in spite of the fact that no "mountain" of Megiddo may have existed, that "even in OT times the city of Megiddo would have sat prominently to a tell. Hebrew *har* could refer to a tell since the word was sometimes used of a settlement on hills."[52] I have personally stood on tell Megiddo which is a small hill in the Valley of Esdraelon on which fortifications have been excavated for over 100 years, beginning in 1903/5 when Gottlieb Schumacher conducted the first excavations at the site. The tell or hill is a small "mount"[53] even today named Megiddo. Beasley-Murray appropriately concludes,

> Whatever the origin of the term, we are not to think in terms of a geographical locality in Israel (the Holy Land does not really feature in John's prophecy) . . .

The name stands for an event. Like his number 666, it will have had a history
in the apocalyptic tradition, lost to us but known to the prophet, and to him
it will have been a symbol of the last resistance of anti-god forces prior to the
kingdom of Christ. "[54]

Caird succinctly sums up the discussion on the term Armageddon by stating that whatever sources John may have used, "this much is clear, that, like John's other names, it is
a symbol. He was not expecting a battle in Northern Palestine, but at Rome.[55]Osborne
adds to the discussion of Armageddon and its connection with Israel's history of warfare
reflected in passages such as Judg. 5:119-21; 2Kings 23:29-30; 2 Chron 35:20-25 with this
observation "The force would be that those who stand against God (broadening apostate
Israel to depict all nations, a method often used in the Apocalypse) will mourn as they
face God's judgment. "[56]

The battle of the kings of the whole world gathered together for the great day of
God the Almighty is symbolically said to take place at a historical military area called in
Hebrew Armageddon. It seems that John expects his readers to know what Armageddon
(*Har Megiddo*) means since he ties it simply without further description to something
or some place called in Hebrew, Armageddon. Armageddon then becomes a symbolic
term associated with a futile battle against God Almighty, the results of which are obvious. In the case of our narrative concerning the churches in Asia it is intended to reassure the saints that the kings of the whole world of their day (Rome and her allies),
and whatever evil demonic powers may assemble with them against the church, will be
decisively defeated.

Whatever this battle may refer to it should not be taken out of the context of the
narrative John has been developing in the seven bowls of judgment, namely the defeat
of the great Babylon (cf. 14:19).

The Seventh Bowl: The Judgment of Babylon—16:17–21

Rev. 16:17–21. *The seventh angel poured out his bowl into the air, and out of the temple
came a loud voice from the throne, saying, "It is done."[18] Then there came flashes of lightning, rumblings, peals of thunder and a severe earthquake. No earthquake like it has ever
occurred since man has been on earth, so tremendous was the quake.* [19] *The great city split
into three parts, and the cities of the nations collapsed. God remembered Babylon the
Great and gave her the cup filled with the wine of the fury of his wrath.* [20] *Every island
fled away and the mountains could not be found.* [21] *From the sky huge hailstones of about
a hundred pounds each fell upon men. And they cursed God on account of the plague of
hail, because the plague was so terrible.* Again a loud voice came from the *temple*, in
fact, from the *throne*. That the voice came from the throne is a reminder of chapters
4 and 5, notably 5, when God, seated on the throne held a scroll that contained God's
plan for dealing with the problem of evil. Now comes a description of the consummation of that plan as it related to the beast from the sea, the land beast, and the prayers
of the saints for vindication. In this scene, Rome is described as judged with all the

fury and power of Almighty God. The end of the world and the final judgment of the dragon, Satan, still awaits revealing. The central purpose of Revelation addresses things that *must soon take place* in the churches in Asia. That John will discuss the final eschatological judgment at Rev. 20:11–15 is necessary to the theodicy of Revelation, for the saints need to be assured that God will finally judge and destroy Satan in Hell.

Rev. 16:17–18. *The seventh angel poured out his bowl into the air, and out of the temple came a loud voice from the throne, saying, "It is done."* [18] *Then there came flashes of lightning, rumblings, peals of thunder and a severe earthquake. No earthquake like it has ever occurred since man has been on earth, so tremendous was the quake.* The seventh angel pours his bowl into the air. John is still working in Egyptian plague typology; at Exodus 10:21 Moses stretched out his hand toward the sky and there was darkness. At 9:2 the air was associated with demonic spirits as at Ephesians 2:2, indicating the that the air is one of the realms in which one encounters Satan and his demonic beings (cf. the Gnostic demi-urges or aeons).[57]

The voice coming right out of the temple cries *"It is done!"* The question is, "What is done"? The Greek is interesting and specific, *gegonen, it is done*, is a second perfect, third person singular verb. Osborne appropriately translates this as "It is over." Beale suggests that "this marks the historical realization of the purpose of the seven bowls in 15:1; in them [the bowls] God's wrath is *consummated*."[58] Although Beale argues that this relates to the final judgment, he is correct in that it does refer to the divine purpose of the bowls of wrath, the judgment on Babylon (the beast, Rome, and the Imperial cult. Specifically, *It is done* must be kept in the context of the prayers of the saints at 6:10 and 10;6 for vindication. In contrast to the expression *gegonen, "It is done!"* in our text here at 16:17, at 21:6 (after the final judgment and as John describes the New Heaven and New Earth) we have again in the NIV and the RSV the expression *"It is done!"* However on this occasion the Greek reads *gegonan, "All things are done"*, second perfect third person *plural* verb as against 16:17 *"It is done'*, second perfect third person *singular* verb. The Greek text indicates no textual variant at either place leaving us with the impression that the text is reliable and that John knew what he was writing![59] It is unfortunate that our English translators have preferred to make 21:6 read in accord with 16:17 rather than in accord with the Greek text! The point that I am making is that 16:17 and 21:6 do not have the same reference! 16:17 describes God's judgment of Rome in proleptic eschatological terms in answer to the prayers of the saints for vindication, stating at 16:17, *"It is done"*, that is, the judgment of Rome and the saints vindication is consummated. At 10:6 the saints were instructed to wait a little longer. Now, however, the judgment is consummated and God's vindication of the saints *is done* or consummated. After the final judgment when all heaven and earth have been judged John can proclaim at 21:6, *"All things are done!"* or consummated.

I obviously disagree with Osborne and some who see in Revelation and specifically at 16:17ff a futurist interpretation regarding the final end of history and of world judgment. Osborne observes "I view the seventh bowl as bringing history to a close."[60] This is unfortunate and misleading since it lifts the "political" judgments against Babylon/Rome from the context of the churches in Asia and God's answer to the prayers of the saints for vindication, and places these plagues in the context of the final judgment. That the bowls of plagues incorporate final eschatological *concepts* is without question, but as I have argued on several occasions, in John's proleptic eschatological style he is addressing the present situation of the churches in Asia dealing with the beast and the false prophet (Rome/Babylon), the prayers of the saints for vindication, and the judgment of Rome in eschatological terms for dramatic emphasis. I am in agreement with Beckwith[61] and Caird[62] who apply the statement *It is done* or *It is over* of 16:17 to the pouring out of the seventh plague and the judgment of the political power of Babylon. Beckwith adds:

> The visitation of Babylon (Rome) occupies a central place in the plague; with the fall of the capital city of the world-empire the present order will be closed . . . The significance of Rome's destruction . . . leads the Apocalyptist to present the subject in the powerful picture that follows (chaps. 17-195).[63]

Roberts observes:

> The bowl series had begun with the announcement that these seven bowls would finish the wrath of God. John had seen the forces gathered against Rome. The battle is never shown, but the climax is reached The prophecy of the angel flying in midheaven—"Babylon is fallen" (14:8)—is now complete.[64]

John continues to describe what has happened in typical apocalyptic terms: *Then there came flashes of lightning, rumblings, peals of thunder and a severe earthquake. No earthquake like it has ever occurred since man has been on earth, so tremendous was the quake.* Similar apocalyptic language appears at 6:12-17 where an earthquake introduced dramatic cosmic upheavals involving mountains.[65] The Old Testament background to these phenomena have specific Sinai theophany connections (Exod. 19:16–19). A strong connection to God's final eschatological judgment is seen, for example, in Hosea 2:6 and Zechariah 14:4. stressing that such phenomena indicate final eschatological implications. John, however, in his eschatological outlook, draws on the implications of this judgment tradition to describe the ultimate judgment of Rome. The judgments of the bowls of plagues, couched in traditional apocalyptic constructs, in the context of Revelation are poured out on Rome, described by John in undisguised terms as Babylon and the great harlot (17).[66]

Rev. 16:19–21. *The great city split into three parts, and the cities of the nations collapsed. God remembered Babylon the Great and gave her the cup filled with the wine of the fury of his wrath.* [20] *Every island fled away and the mountains could not be found.* [21] *From the sky huge hailstones of about a hundred pounds each fell upon men. And they cursed God on account of the plague of hail, because the plague was so terrible.* "Rome is repeatedly referred to as the 'great city' (18: 10, 16, 18, 19, 21). The subsequent reference in the same verse to Babylon does not imply yet another different city."[67] So great is the judgment of God that the great city was split into three parts. John recalls the great earthquake of 6:12-16, in which the mountains and islands were removed from their place. Rome, as was the case with Babylon of old, is to receive *the cup filled with the wine of the fury of his wrath.* John will in the next section graphically and dramatically describe the pouring out of God's judgment from the winepress of his wrath. He had previously introduced the winepress of God's wrath at 14:19. I like the way Osborne translates this phrase, "God gave her the cup of wine, namely his furious wrath."[68] At 14:8 John had charged that Babylon the great had "made all nations drink the wine of her impure passion" (RSV). The NIV reads "made all the nations drink the maddening wine of her adulteries."Osborne appropriately translates this as "the wine that leads to passion for immorality."[69] In a form of *lex talionis* God now makes Babylon drink of the wine of the passion of his wrath. Repeating his statement at 14:8, John adds in apocalyptic form that at the earthquake that represented the wrath of God, *every island fled away and the mountains could not be found.* The enormous size of the hailstones that fell from the sky is in keeping with the dramatic style of John's apocalyptic imagery. John obviously has not yet left the plague typology, for he draws on the hailstones of the seventh plague on Egypt (Exod. 9:13-26) with striking effect. At Exodus 9:24 the hailstones were so great that "such had never been in all the land of Egypt since it became a nation." Now each hailstone weighs over a hundred pounds (Greek *talantiaia*, talents). The Roman talent would be the equivalent of approximately one hundred pounds, which stretches the imagination to the extreme. Osborne notes that the largest hailstones recorded in history weighed 2.25 pounds each.[70] The storm of hailstones in Jewish traditions represented both theophanies and divine judgment on the enemies of God's people (Isa. 28:2; Ezek. 13:11; 38:22).[71] The disturbance of islands, mountains, and the sky is a common metaphor of the apocalyptic genre (cf. Isa. 2:10; 13:10–11; 40:4; 45:2; Ezek. 32:7-8 Matt. 24:29-31; *Sib. Or.* 8:232-250; *Test. Moses* 10:4; *1 Enoch* 1:1-7; *2 Esdras* 15:42). Again, as in the fourth bowl (16:9), men *cursed God on account of the plague of hail, because the plague was so terrible.* By referring to the response of people to the seventh plague as men cursing or blaspheming God, John indicates that the situation has moved from the possibility of repentance to a resolute defiance of God.

Summary of the Seven Bowls of Plagues

In this section John has demonstrated the consequences of refusing God's call to repentance presented in the warning trumpets (8–11) and God's gracious offer in the eternal gospel (14:6) by recounting in graphic detail the consummated judgments of God's wrath. Rome has been given an opportunity to repent; the saints have been called to an uncompromising faith; and now the consequences of a recalcitrant heart are proclaimed. To dramatize the seriousness of the occasion, John draws on the imagery of the Egyptian plagues to make his point with striking vividness. God will judge and has in his eternal plan already judged Rome:

"Fallen, Fallen, is Babylon the Great" (14:8). ***It is done!*** (16:17). In the next section, *The Authority of God over Evil Exercised, Rev. 17:1–20:15, Seven Unnumbered Descriptions of God's Judgments,* John will return to the judgments of God and recount in graphic detail how easy it is for God to judge Rome.

Chapter 10

The Authority of God over Evil Exercised

Seven Unnumbered Descriptions of God's Judgments

17:1–20:15

Although theologically this section is not the high point in Revelation, it is one that most readers have anticipated even before commencing this study: the thousand-year-reign of the saints and the binding of Satan for one thousand years. Chapters 17 and 18 describe how simple a matter it is for God to judge and destroy Rome. He can do this on one day, in fact in only one hour. Chapter 19 opens with the joyful marriage feast of the bride (the church) and the Lamb. It then moves on to describe another feast, this one where the birds of carrion will feast on the flesh of those who have worshipped the beast and persecuted the saints. At 19:11 Jesus appears as the sovereign rider of the white horse who defeats the beast and false prophets and throws them into the lake of fire. Chapter 20 describes the limitation of Satan to use Rome (he is bound for one thousand years, only to be released again to deceive other nations). The martyred saints are rewarded by reigning fully with Christ (symbolically for one thousand years). Satan is finally judged and thrown into the lake of fire, hell, which is the second death, where he, the beast, the false prophet, and all who followed Satan are condemned to eternal torment.

In the chiastic structure of Revelation level VI parallels level II and describes the final judgment, including that of Satan. God has fulfilled his promise to vindicate the saints and finally judge Satan, the beast, the false prophet, and all those who have worshipped the beast. Completing the theodicy of Revelation is the judgment of Satan when he is thrown into the lake of fire (hell) where he and those who have followed him will be eternally tormented. At 21:1 the sea, the source of evil, is no more. Evil has been judged and destroyed.

Prologue 1:1–20
   I. The Church in Imperfection (2:1–3:22)
     Seven Letters to the Seven Churches
      II. The Authority of God over Evil Explained (4:1–8:6)
      Seven Seals on the Scroll
        III. The Warning Judgments (8:1–11:19)
        Seven Trumpets
          IV. The Lamb—God's Answer to Evil (12:1–14:20)
          Seven Unnumbered Figures
        V. The Consummated Judgments (15:1–16:21)
        Seven Bowls of Wrath
      VI. The Authority of God over Evil Exercised (17:1–20:15)
      Seven Unnumbered Descriptions of God's Judgments
   VII. The Church in Perfection (21:1–22:5)
     Seven Unnumbered Descriptions of the Church in Perfection
Epilogue 22:6–21

Since this is a difficult and potentially confusing section, an expanded view of the sixth level of the chiasm is helpful:

THE AUTHORITY OF GOD OVER EVIL EXERCISED 17:1–20:15
The Seven Unnumbered Descriptions of God's Wrath

1. The Harlot and the Beast Identified, 17:1–18
2. The Doom of Babylon Announced, 18:1–20
3. The Doom of Babylon Described, 18:21–24
4. The Marriage Supper of the Lamb, 19:1–10
5. The Defeat of the Beast and the False Prophet, 19:11–21
6. The Binding and Limitation of Satan, 20:1–10
7. The Final Judgment, 20:11–15

The time for warning judgments (8:1–11:19) has passed; the seven bowls, which served also as demonstrations of God's continued warnings of impending judgments on Babylon/Rome, have been poured out; and now in terms of William Hendriksen's progressive parallelism,[1] it is time to prophetically describe these judgments more specifically, including a glimpse of the final judgment.

INTRODUCTION

This is usually the most anticipated section of Revelation, for it covers the thousand-year binding of Satan and millennial reign of the saints. However, in contrast to the millennial theories that have been read into chapter 20, the principle reason for this section is to demonstrate how easy it is for God to judge Satan and Rome and negate their power. Furthermore, with the binding of Satan and his ultimate judgment (20:7–15), John brings his theodicy to closure. John picks up the theme just revealed in the seven bowls of plagues and the pouring out of God's wrath unmixed on Rome, and for dramatic impact he characterizes Rome clearly in terms of fallen Babylon. In this section John presents a detailed picture of the magnitude of God's judgment on Rome as a world power. It is not only Rome as a persecuting power, or the imperial cult that God is judging, but also Rome as a seductive economic power. "Thus it is a serious mistake to suppose that John opposes Rome only because of the imperial cult and the persecution of Christians. Rather this issue serves to bring to the surface evils which were deeply rooted in the whole system of Roman power."[2] "Revelation is one of the fiercest attacks on Rome and one of the most effective pieces of political resistance literature from the period of the early empire."[3] It is in view of Rome's hegemony over not only the political and religious scene, but also over the "global" economic scene that John demonstrates God's sovereign power over both Satan and his agent, Rome in all of its evil seductive power. As a seductive Harlot (17) John describes the demise of Rome as a world economic power (18).

In what has been called a hallelujah hymn of praise, chapter 19 expresses rejoicing over the fall of Babylon/Rome and announces the celebration of the marriage supper of the Lamb and his bride, the church. We recall the church at Pergamum (2:12-17) and the promised reward to those who conquer to receive hidden manna and a white stone as an invitation to the final eschatological banquet.

In the figure of the binding of Satan for a thousand years, John pronounces the limitation of the power of Satan to use Rome indefinitely (20:1–3). John moves on to assure the saints of their complete reign (a thousand years) with Christ on his throne (20:4–6).

John brings the curtain down on dramatic theodicy with a brief and powerful description of the final judgment of Satan and of the end of the age (20:11–15). The brevity of the description of the final judgment supports the point that the final end-of-the-world judgment is not the major theme of Revelation. It also strengthens the point that God's final judgment and sovereignty over evil is in God's hands, a simple act of sovereign divine power. In this section the total depravity of Rome and God's sovereign judgment are uppermost in John's thinking.[4]

THE FIRST UNNUMBERED DESCRIPTION OF GOD'S WRATH: THE GREAT HARLOT ON THE SCARLET BEAST IDENTIFIED— REV. 17:1–6

One cannot miss John's intention as he describes Rome as the great harlot. He has in mind the seductive power of the land beast to prostitute both men and nations to Rome.

John links this section to the previous one by stating that it is one of the seven angels who had seven bowls who spoke to him.

THE GREAT HARLOT IDENTIFIED—REV. 17:1–6

The Text

One of the seven angels who had the seven bowls came and said to me, "Come, I will show you the punishment of the great prostitute, who sits on many waters. [2] With her the kings of the earth committed adultery and the inhabitants of the earth were intoxicated with the wine of her adulteries."[3] Then the angel carried me away in the Spirit into a desert. There I saw a woman sitting on a scarlet beast that was covered with blasphemous names and had seven heads and ten horns. [4] The woman was dressed in purple and scarlet, and was glittering with gold, precious stones and pearls. She held a golden cup in her hand, filled with abominable things and the filth of her adulteries. [5] This title was written on her forehead: MYSTERY, BABYLON THE GREAT, THE MOTHER OF PROSTITUTES AND OF THE ABOMINATIONS OF THE EARTH. [6] I saw that the woman was drunk with the blood of the saints, the blood of those who bore testimony to Jesus. When I saw her, I was greatly astonished.

Rev. 17:1. It is intriguing that it is one of the angels of the seven bowls of God's wrath who takes John and shows him the scenes of God's divine judgment on Rome. John is graphically shown God's judgment (*krima*, "judgment," "condemnation," "punishment," "verdict") of the great harlot. The NIV describes this as **the punishment of the great prostitute**. The connection between the bride of the Lamb that follows at 19:7–8 and the great harlot is not accidental.[5] One turn of the kaleidoscope reveals a harlot, the next the bride of the Lamb. The loathsome picture of Rome as the great harlot and the beauty of the bride of Christ is striking. The Old Testament and Jewish tradition are replete with images that depict both immorality and idolatry in terms of fornication. Hosea describes the Northern Kingdom of Israel as an adulterous wife who has committed fornication with paganism. The sin was not only one of a physical nature of fornication at the altars of Baal, but also one of putting their trust in alliances with Assyria and Egypt rather than in God. In Isaiah 1:21 Isaiah laments that Jerusalem, the faithful city "has become a harlot."Jeremiah speaks of Judah's adulteries (Jer. 13:27). Caird[6] points out that "every dalliance with paganism was *fornication*," indicating that what John had in mind was not only the political seduction and prostitution, but also the sexual dalliance associated with pagan idolatry. Some discussion has taken place among scholars over the background behind John's description of this woman sitting on the blasphemous beast as **THE GREAT THE MOTHER OF PROSTITUTES**. Some see Jezebel; another probability could be Valeria Messalina, the wife of Emperor Claudius.[7] Osborne and Aune suggest that it is most likely the goddess Roma whom John had in mind. Coins minted in 71, during the reign of Emperor Vespasian, the father of Domitian, depicted Roma sitting on the seven hills of Rome bearing a sword. The last proposal seems the most likely since John has the Roman Empire and imperial cult in mind. "Either way, the prostitute is clearly Babylon/Rome, depicted in all her alluring depravity."[8]

With the expression *who sits on many waters*, John introduces a new image into his drama. The background to this image seems to be Isaiah 51:13, where God prophesies the destruction of Babylon of old, "You who live by many waters and are rich in treasures, your end has come, the time for you to be cut off." At 17:15 the many waters where the harlot is seated are many peoples, multitudes, nations and tongues, indicating the worldwide seductive power and allure of Rome.

Rev. 17:2. With the great harlot are those she has seduced; *the kings of the earth committed adultery and the inhabitants of the earth were intoxicated with the wine of her adulteries.* The repeated reference to the wine of her adulteries heightens the enormous seductive and intoxicating power of Rome. This expression is found four times in Revelation (14:8, 10; 17:2; 18:3). Twice John refers to "the maddening wine of her intoxication"(cf. Jer. 51:7).This phrase is a subtle reference to both the political and economic seductive power of Rome.[9]

Rev. 17:3. *Then the angel carried me away in the Spirit into a desert. There I saw a woman sitting on a scarlet beast that was covered with blasphemous names and had seven heads and ten horns.* John is apparently drawing on Isaiah 21:1–2, where Isaiah is witness to an oracle from God against Babylon. However, some commentators propose that the desert could be a place of protection, a place of evil spirits, or a place of visionary experiences.[10] Caird favors the view that it is only in the protective concept of the desert as a place of "security and detachment" that it was "possible for John to see the seducer in her true colors."[11] That this experience is one *in the Spirit* should not be surprising since John uses this terminology four times in Revelation (1:10; 4:2; 17:3; 21:10). This is typical of prophetic commission (Ezek. 2:2; 3:12; 43:5) and implies that the prophet is empowered by God's Holy Spirit as a seer to see things others might miss. Although these observations have much to offer, more probable is the Isaiah background of God's oracle against Babylon. The reference to the beast upon which the woman is seated as a scarlet beast may be related to the fact that she is empowered by the great red dragon, Satan, of 12:3, or it may be simply a reference to the fact that the woman is robed in purple and scarlet, that is, royal regalia. The scarlet robe could signify "ostentatious magnificence."[12] The scarlet could be symbolic of the blood of the martyrs or of the terrifying nature of the dragon.[13] This beast was *covered with blasphemous names and had seven heads and ten horns* (cf. 13:1 and Dan. 7). The connection of the beast to the civil and imperial power of Rome as an idolatrous nation is obvious.

Rev. 17:4–5. The woman was dressed in purple and scarlet, and was glittering with gold, precious stones and pearls. She held a golden cup in her hand, filled with abominable things and the filth of her adulteries. [5] **This title was written on her forehead: MYSTERY, BABYLON THE GREAT, THE MOTHER OF PROSTITUTES AND OF THE ABOMINATIONS OF THE EARTH.** The precious stones and pearls speak of the opulent dress exacted by the paramour from her lovers.[14] The jewels in association with the gold cup from which she poured the wine of her impure intoxicating adultery only add to the vision of extreme wealth and depravity seen in the woman. The ***abominable things*** filling her cup speak of the evil of her wealth and power. Continuing the theme of those who worship the beast as having the mark of the beast on their foreheads (13:16–17), this woman is branded on her forehead as the **MOTHER OF PROSTITUTES**. I prefer the translation in the RSV, "a name of mystery, Babylon the Great, mother of harlots and of earth's abominations." There is some debate as to whether the translation in the NIV and KJV with the word MYSTERY as part of the woman's name is preferred or whether the word mystery is in apposition to, or descriptive of, *a name*, as in the RSV and NRSV. Several commentators prefer the rendering of the RSV, "a name of mystery, Babylon the great"[15] Others point to the fact that prostitutes of the Roman era would often wear a headband with their name inscribed on it for "business" purposes.[16] The expression **MOTHER OF PROSTITUTES** indicates that she is the archetype of prostitutes. Osborne suggests that there may be some connection here with "Cybele, the 'Magna Mater' of the gods, who had an orgiastic cult in the ancient world."[17] Not only is Rome the mother of prostitutes (Aune[18] translates this more graphically as mother of whores), she is also the mother, or archetype, of all Earth's abominations.

Rev. 17:6. *I saw that the woman was drunk with the blood of the saints, the blood of those who bore testimony to Jesus. When I saw her, I was greatly astonished.* Rome was intoxicated by her power to make war on the saints and kill them (13:1–7). The Greek has an epexegetical *kai*, normally translated *and*, following "the blood of the saints," indicating that this was indeed the blood of the martyrs who had in their martyrdom borne testimony to Jesus as Lord and King. John *was greatly astonished* when he saw her. His astonishment lay in the impact of the seductive power and mysterious nature of Rome. There is some discussion regarding *I was astonished*, as to whether it is an introductory rhetorical statement relating to the nature of the great harlot or an introduction to the mystery of the seven kings John is about to introduce. In all probability, in keeping with the paragraphing of the Greek text and most translations, verse 6b should be seen as an introduction of verse 7, which opens the mystery of the seven kings, one who was, one who is not, and who is to ascend from the bottomless pit.

THE MYSTERY OF THE HARLOT, THE EIGHT KINGS, AND THE TEN HORNS—REV. 17:6B–18

The Text

When I saw her, I was greatly astonished. [7] *Then the angel said to me: "Why are you astonished? I will explain to you the mystery of the woman and of the beast she rides, which has the seven heads and ten horns.* [8] *The beast, which you saw, once was, now is not, and will come up out of the Abyss and go to his destruction. The inhabitants of the earth whose names have not been written in the book of life from the creation of the world will be astonished when they see the beast, because he once was, now is not, and yet will come.*

[9] *"This calls for a mind with wisdom. The seven heads are seven hills on which the woman sits.* [10] *They are also seven kings. Five have fallen, one is, the other has not yet come; but when*

he does come, he must remain for a little while. [11] *The beast who once was, and now is not, is an eighth king. He belongs to the seven and is going to his destruction.*

[12] *"The ten horns you saw are ten kings who have not yet received a kingdom, but who for one hour will receive authority as kings along with the beast.* [13] *They have one purpose and will give their power and authority to the beast.* [14] *They will make war against the Lamb, but the Lamb will overcome them because he is Lord of lords and King of kings—and with him will be his called, chosen and faithful followers."*

[15] *Then the angel said to me, "The waters you saw, where the prostitute sits, are peoples, multitudes, nations and languages.* [16] *The beast and the ten horns you saw will hate the prostitute. They will bring her to ruin and leave her naked; they will eat her flesh and burn her with fire.* [17] *For God has put it into their hearts to accomplish his purpose by agreeing to give the beast their power to rule, until God's words are fulfilled.* [18] *The woman you saw is the great city that rules over the kings of the earth."*

John is certainly correct in 17: 9: ***This calls for a mind with wisdom.*** The discussion of the expression ***The beast, which you saw, once was, now is not, and will come up out of the Abyss and go to his destruction*** has generated considerable debate among scholars, especially in regard to dating Revelation. The discussion hinges on the identification of the seven kings, the five that have fallen, the one who now is, a seventh who is to come only for a little while, and the eighth one who was and who is not, but who is now one of the seven.

Rev. 17:6b, 7. ***When I saw her, I was greatly astonished***. The Greek actually reads "I was amazed with great amazement" (or as Osborne suggests, I "was awestruck with wonder"[19]). [7] ***Then the angel said to me: "Why are you astonished? I will explain to you the mystery of the woman and of the beast she rides, which has the seven heads and ten horns.*** [8] ***The beast, which you saw, once was, now is not, and will come up out of the Abyss and go to his destruction. The inhabitants of the earth whose names have not been written in the book of life from the creation of the world will be astonished when they see the beast, because he once was, now is not, and yet will come.*** The angel explains that the shocking description of this woman should not surprise John, for he had already encountered her in a different form. Nevertheless, there is something mysterious about this woman, for she is riding on a beast with seven heads and ten horns. The beast of 13:1–10 had seven heads and ten horns, and this beast, Leviathan the sea beast, represented Rome in its imperial power. It was a blasphemous beast who made war on the saints. All who worshipped this beast, otherwise known as ***the inhabitants of the earth*** and whose ***names have not been written in the book of life belonging to the Lamb*** (13:8) had been seduced by the power of the sea beast, Leviathan, and received the mark of the beast, 666. This beast is none other than the imperial power of Rome, from whom the great harlot drew her power to seduce the nations. Emphasizing the enigmatic nature of the mysterious beast and the seven kings at 17:9, John observes that understanding this woman and the beast upon which she is riding and the seven kings that he is about to describe ***calls for a mind with wisdom***. How apt this observation is can be seen from the numerous attempts of scholars to make sense of this scene and to date the book of Revelation from these kings. Osborne points out that this kind of expression calling for wisdom is common in the Apocalyptic tradition, implying that the riddle being explained needs divine explanation, which the angel now provides.[20]

Rev. 17:8. Regarding the *beast, which you saw, once was, now is not, and will come up out of the Abyss and go to his destruction,* Osborne observes that this is the third time that something evil comes up out of the abyss (11:7; 13:1; 17:8.) However, here John clarifies the mystery in some measure by explaining that the beast goes on to his destruction (RSV perdition). This thought is key to the riddle that follows. Whoever this beast represents and however evil he is, he goes on *to his destruction. The inhabitants of the earth whose names have not been written in the book of life from the creation of the world will be astonished when they see the beast, because he once was, now is not, and yet will come.* Assuming this beast to have been divine in that he once was, now is not, and is yet to come again, those who had worshipped the beast are now astonished to find that he goes on to perdition. Several commentators point out that this little thing about having been, not now being, and coming again is a parody on the eternal nature of God and Christ. Earlier (1:4) it had been said of God that he was, is, and is to come. In a satirical manner John observes that those who inhabit the earth are astonished that this beast who seemingly *once was, now is not, and yet will come* is not eternal, for in contrast to the eternal nature of God and Christ, this beast is to go on *to his destruction.* The major reason for his destruction is the story of Revelation: the beast who has set himself up as god is to be destroyed. The RSV using the translation *perdition* brings out the theme of perdition and total ruin. John is again playing on the Nero *redivivus* myth. In popular fear many thought that Nero was out there somewhere, but would reappear in all of his evil. But John emphasizes that even if this were possible, even if he did return, he would still go on to his destruction.

Rev. 17:9–11. *"This calls for a mind with wisdom. The seven heads are seven hills on which the woman sits.* [10] *They are also seven kings. Five have fallen, one is, the other has not yet come; but when he does come, he must remain for a little while.* [11] *The beast who once was, and now is not, is an eighth king. He belongs to the seven and is going to his destruction.* At least seven approaches can be identified regarding these seven or eight kings that John describes. I will not here comment on most of them since the literature is replete with such observation, but refer the reader to Aune, Osborne, Yarbro Collins, Elisabeth Schussler Fiorenza and the considerable literature on this pericope.[21]

   In the introduction of this commentary, I stated that it is primarily from this passage that scholars have attempted to fix the date of writing during the reign of Emperor Vespasian, ca. 78. Caird argues that using this text to date Revelation is "looking for the wrong sort of solution."[22] Adela Yarbro Collins and Elisabeth Schussler Fiorenza argue that theories of dating based of the seven kings of 17:8–14 are faced with insurmountable difficulties.[23] The use of seven is symbolic or stylistic, not literal, not historical. To try to force historical constructs on the symbolism of the apocalyptic genre and Revelation is to miss altogether the meaning of apocalyptic and its message. Understanding this genre should define the parameters to discussion of this unique quasi-historical pericope.

To try to force historical constructs on the symbolism of the apocalyptic genre and Revelation is to miss altogether the meaning of apocalyptic and its unique message. Furthermore, Fiorenza succinctly demonstrates that the choice adopted by some to force these seven or eight kings into a dating system requires an arbitrary choice of which Emperor to begin with. She argues that "scholars have not yet succeeded in decoding this information. They do not agree whether or not to begin with Caesar, Augustus, Caligula, or Nero."[24]

Since the figure seven has been used symbolically throughout Revelation we should adhere to this symbolic use of seven in this text.

First, the angel explains, these seven kings sit on seven hills. The tradition that seven hills referred to Rome was a well-established metaphor for Rome by the time John wrote Revelation. In fact, during the reign of Domitian, Romans celebrated a major festival in honor of Rome, the *Septimontium*, which was clearly identified with the seven hills of Rome.[25]

There is some discussion among scholars as to whether the reference is to kings, emperors, or empires.[26] Regarding the decision as to where to begin counting the "kings" questions are raised as to whether Julius Caesar should be counted since he was an Emperor (*imperator*) under the former Republic of Rome and not of the subsequent Roman Empire. Augustus was the first Emperor of the new Roman Empire. In this regard the Jewish author of the fifth book of the *Sibylline Oracles* counted Julius Caesar as the first Emperor. [27] Suetonius ca. 70 A.D., the well known Roman historian and biographer, began his list with Julius Caesar, as did Dio Chrysostom, ca. 40-122 A.D., the highly regarded Greek orator and historian of the Roman Empire. Likewise, Flavius Josephus, ca. 37-100 A.D., the Jewish apologist and historian of the Jewish Wars under the Roman rule began with Julius Caesar. However, Tiberius Claudius, Roman Emperor, 41-54 A.D., and an acclaimed historian of the Roman Civil Wars, and Tacitus, another Roman historian, 56-117 A.D., began his Annals with Augustus as the first Emperor. The point that I am making is that there is no uniform listing of the Roman Emperors nor consensus as to who was the first Emperor. [28]Osborne lists seven different approaches among scholars to this riddle. [29]

It is interesting that John is less precise than one might have desired for he does not use the usual Greek term *autokratōr* for emperor or the Latin term *imperator*, but speaks of **kings**, the Greek used by John was *basileus*, "king". Aune observes that the Greek *basileus*, "king", was not widely used as a Greek translation of the Latin *imperator*, "emperor", until the second century. [30] Caird sums the discussion up well observing that by attempting to fix a historical time line in this riddle we are looking in the wrong direction and should see in the seven kings a symbolic number in keeping with John's penchant for the number seven. He observes that the seven kings are "representative of the whole series of emperors, and they would remain seven no matter how long the actual list happened to be." He concludes, "The one point John wishes to emphasize is that the imperial line has only a short time to run before the emergence of a new monstrous Nero, *an eighth who is one of the seven.* "[31]

The final telling point of this enigmatic riddle is in verse 11, *The beast who once was, and now is not, is an eighth king. He belongs to the seven and is going to his destruction.* The point of seven and eight kings is not to set a historical context for Revelation but merely to demonstrate that Roman "kings" come and go, new ones arrive, but their reign is transitory. Reasoned observers of the emperors in the Roman line would understand that emperors have come and gone in conditions of uncertainty regarding how long they have reigned, but in John's use of the Nero *redivivus* myth, the one who is to come in the experience of the Christians of Asia is a parody of Christ's resurrection and reign. Unlike Christ, however, he incorporates all of the evil of the previous emperors, and like theirs, his reign will be brief, for he too will go on to perdition. In the context of the first-century Asian churches, this surely would have been clearly understood as a veiled reference to Domitian. But he too is destined for destruction.

Rev. 17:12–14. *"The ten horns you saw are ten kings who have not yet received a kingdom, but who for one hour will receive authority as kings along with the beast.* [13] *They have one purpose and will give their power and authority to the beast.* [14] *They will make war against the Lamb, but the Lamb will overcome them because he is Lord of lords and King of kings—and with him will be his called, chosen and faithful followers."* On four previous occasions (12:3; 13:1, 17:3; 17:7) John has drawn on the ten horns of Daniel 7, where these horns represented empires. Now here at 17:1, 3 he uses the same symbolism to describe the evil beast upon which the harlot rides. The reference to ten kings speaks of the sinister nature of those nations that have adulterated themselves with the seductive power of Rome to form part of the evil system of the beast. These ten horns, or ten kings, represent the client kings of Rome who had either been defeated by Rome or who had sold out their independence to power and wealth of Rome.

These ten kings represent the "client kings" of Rome to whom Rome has given the authority to rule under her power. That they have *not yet received a kingdom* but rule *for one hour* indicates symbolically the limitation of their power. These client kings, having surrendered their independence, make war on the Lamb and the saints (cf. 13:7). The expression *one purpose* had political implications in the context of Revelation, strengthening the view that the ten kings were in political alliance with Rome.[32] These client kings, according to John, are of one purpose in serving the beast in making *war against the Lamb*; but as in the case with Michael and the dragon (12:7–8), the beast and the client kings are *overcome* (RSV conquered), this time by the Lamb himself. In fact, they have already been defeated by the blood of the Lamb, or the death and resurrection of Jesus (12:10–11). The Lamb is described in divine terms as the *Lord of lords* (a term often used of God in the Septuagint; cf. Deut. 10:17, Dan. 2:37; in the intertestamental literature of the Apocrypha and Pseudepigrapha, 2 *Macc.* 13:4; 1 *Enoch* 9:4; 63:4; and in the New Testament, 1 Tim. 6:15) and *King of kings*. Roman emperors had referred to themselves as the king of kings (especially in regard to the client kings), but here it is Jesus who is really the King of kings, the ruler even over the Roman Empire and its transient emperors. Seen with the Lamb in this battle and victory are *his called, chosen and faithful followers*. At 14:1 the *Lamb* was standing in royal position on *Mount Zion* and with him were the 144,000. At 14:4 these 144,000 saints in military formation followed the Lamb wherever he goes, to martyrdom or to victory.

Rev. 17:15–18. *Then the angel said to me, "The waters you saw, where the prostitute sits, are peoples, multitudes, nations and languages.* [16] *The beast and the ten horns you saw will hate the prostitute. They will bring her to ruin and leave her naked; they will eat her flesh and burn her with fire.* [17] *For God has put it into their hearts to accomplish his purpose by agreeing to give the beast their power to rule, until God's words are fulfilled.* [18] *The woman you saw is the great city that rules over the kings of the earth."* Not only was the harlot depicted at 17:3 as seated on a beast; at 17:1 she was described as seated on *many waters*. At 17:15 an angel now explains to John the nature of these *many waters*. In keeping with the idiom of ten client kings, these waters represent *the multitudes* of *peoples*, *nations*, and *languages* under Rome's hegemony. In a strange turn of thought, the beast, Rome, now hates the harlot who represents the seductive power of Rome. The implication is that Rome was never safe from inner anarchy, rebellion, and treachery. Rome had constantly to retain legions at home and in the conquered lands to maintain the *Pax Romana*. Again God uses war, rebellion, and anarchy to keep Rome off balance and demonstrate the fragile nature of human power, no matter how great that power may be (cf. 6:1-8). *For God has put it into their hearts to accomplish his purpose by agreeing to give the beast their power to rule, until God's words are fulfilled*.

With the statement *The woman you saw is the great city that rules over the kings of the earth*, John concludes with the clear identification of the woman seated on the beast—the great evil city Rome. The two descriptions of the woman form an *inclusio* to the message that Rome, for all her seductive and political power, is doomed to perdition.

Summary of Rev. 17 and Rome, the Great Harlot.

In spite of the monstrous nature of Rome's seductive religious power represented as the harlot sitting on the sinister evil beast, Rome's powerful civil and political power, Osborne observes that "God causes the self-destructive nature of evil to come full circle . . . as Babylon the Great is destroyed by the very powers she serves."

The mystery of the seven and eight kings is that the eighth king, the one with whom the church at the close of the first century has to deal, is that it incorporates all of the evil of the previous seven and may be considered to be Nero *redivivus* in the metaphorical sense that Domitian, the eighth, represents all of the evil of Nero incarnate. However, the saints need not fear, for even the eighth king, like the previous seven, will go on to destruction and, in fact, will be weakened by Rome's own internal evil nature.

THE SECOND UNNUMBERED DESCRIPTION OF GOD'S RIGHTEOUS JUDGMENT REGARDING THE DOOM OF BABYLON/ ROME: SHE HAS ALREADY FALLEN—REV. 18:1–20

John at 18 begins to highlight the destruction of Babylon/Rome in symbolic detail, drawing on the prophetic utterances in the Old Testament regarding the fall of ancient Babylon. As God predicted the fall of ancient Babylon well in advance of its actual historical fall, so God pronounces the fall of the new Babylon, Rome, well in advance of its historical demise. The poetic nature and structure of this section highlights the dramatic nature of God's judgment on Rome. To the Christians struggling under the awful power of Rome, the ease with which God judges Rome is impressive. He can do it in one day (18:8), in fact even in one hour (18:10, 17, 19).[33]

The chapter is presented in five parts which cover the second and third unnumbered description of God's judgment on Babylon/Rome:

1. The Doom of Babylon/Rome Announced (18:1–3)
2. The Call to Come out of Babylon/Rome (18:4–8)
3. The Lament of the World over Babylon's Demise (18:9–19)
4. Heaven's Rejoicing over Babylon/Rome's Demise (18:20)
5. Babylon/Rome's Doom Symbolically Described (18:21–24)

Aune appropriately calls this chapter a "prophetic taunt song" bringing together the dramatic decline and demise of Rome and the joyful celebration of the saints.[34] The chapter proclaims the absolute desolation of Babylon/Rome and the adulterous nature of the imperial cult dramatized as the great harlot.

In typical style John draws on the Old Testament as he describes in vivid poetic detail the doom and demise of the new Babylon. In a combination of passages with reference to God's judgment on nations such as Babylon and Tyre John finds expression, cf. Isaiah 13:21, 22; Jeremiah 50:8, 39; 51:9, 49, 63; Ezekiel 26:13, 27:25-36. John announces Rome's doom, composes three laments over her demise, and symbolically describes her future desolation.

John repeatedly uses the expression *meta tauta eidon*, **after these things I saw**, to introduce a new section (cf. 4:1; 7:1, 9; 15:5), not to lay out a chronological history of that demise, but to describe it in overlapping images.[35] Having described the destruction of the empire through the ruin of the eight kings, John now begins a dramatic description of not only the "kings," or rulers, but of the whole Roman system, its political, economic, and worldwide influence.

THE DOOM OF ROME ANNOUNCED - REV. 18:1–3

The Text

After this I saw another angel coming down from heaven. He had great authority, and the earth was illuminated by his splendor. [2] With a mighty voice he shouted: "Fallen. Fallen is Babylon the Great. She has become a home for demons and a haunt for every evil spirit, a haunt for every unclean and detestable bird. [3] *For all the nations have drunk the maddening wine of her adulteries. The kings of the earth committed adultery with her, and the merchants of the earth grew rich from her excessive luxuries."*

The scene opens with another mighty angel with great authority announcing the fall of Rome, *"Fallen. Fallen is Babylon the Great."* In God's prophetic scheme of redemption, Rome has already been judged and has "fallen". Nothing remains of her past glory, only demons and unclean birds and animals of carrion. Calling on the imagery of Jeremiah 25:15, 27–29, in which God's fury was poured out on Jerusalem, Egypt, Philistia, Edom, Moab, and Babylon, John describes God's judgment on the new Babylon, Rome, *for all the nations have drunk the maddening wine of her adulteries.*

THE CALL TO COME OUT OF ROME - REV. 18:4–8
The Text

> Then I heard another voice from heaven say:
> "Come out of her, my people,
>> so that you will not share in her sins,
> so that you will not receive any of her plagues;
> [5] for her sins are piled up to heaven,
>> and God has remembered her crimes.
> [6] Give back to her as she has given;
>> pay her back double for what she has done.
>> Mix her a double portion from her own cup.
> [7] Give her as much torture and grief
>> as the glory and luxury she gave herself.
> In her heart she boasts,
>> 'I sit as queen; I am not a widow,
>> and I will never mourn. '
> [8] Therefore in one day her plagues will overtake her:
>> death, mourning and famine.
> She will be consumed by fire,
> for mighty is the Lord God who judges her.

The *voice* that calls upon the church in assurance and encouragement, in keeping with the general tenor of the seven letters of 2 and 3, now invokes the saints to *Come out of her, my people.* The saints are to have no part of Rome. This call comes right from the throne of God, almost in the exact voice of Isaiah 48:20–21. Building on this call to have no part in Babylon/Rome, John pulls themes from Jeremiah 50; 51; Ezekiel 28:2; Zephaniah 2:15. The pride of Babylon/Rome will be brought to nothing "in one single day." The call is one of exhortation to an uncompromising faith, including encouragement and vindication in answer to the prayers of the saints (6:10).

There is obviously a sense of and exaggerated *lex talionis* (the law of retribution) in this pericope. Under the *lex talionis* principle, the judgment was supposed to equal the crime, "an eye for an eye and a tooth for a tooth" (Exod. 21:24; Deut. 19:21; Matt. 5:38). Here it seems that Rome is being punished under a more serious principle, double punishment. Rome is being judged and fined with the most severe penalty for its crimes against the saints and humanity. Questions arise regarding whether John has gone beyond legal response to vindictiveness in saying that Rome's punishment is a **double** payment for what she has done. Opinion is divided as to whether this double payment is a metaphor for serious judgment[36] or whether John really means double payment.[37] In the imprecatory psalms and literature such as Revelation, compounded retribution is offset by the heinous and violent nature of the crime.[38]

THE LAMENT OF THE WORLD OVER ROME'S DEMISE —REV. 18:9–19

The Text

"When the kings of the earth who committed adultery with her and shared her luxury see the smoke of her burning, they will weep and mourn over her. [10] *Terrified at her torment, they will stand far off and cry:*

> *"'Woe. Woe, O great city,*
> *O Babylon, city of power.*
> *In one hour your doom has come.'*

[11] *"The merchants of the earth will weep and mourn over her because no one buys their cargoes any more—*[12] *cargoes of gold, silver, precious stones and pearls; fine linen, purple, silk and scarlet cloth; every sort of citron wood, and articles of every kind made of ivory, costly wood, bronze, iron and marble;*[13] *cargoes of cinnamon and spice, of incense, myrrh and frankincense, of wine and olive oil, of fine flour and wheat; cattle and sheep; horses and carriages; and bodies and souls of men.*

[14] *"They will say, 'The fruit you longed for is gone from you. All your riches and splendor have vanished, never to be recovered.'*[15] *The merchants who sold these things and gained their wealth from her will stand far off, terrified at her torment. They will weep and mourn*[16] *and cry out:*

> *"'Woe. Woe, O great city,*
> *dressed in fine linen, purple and scarlet,*
> *and glittering with gold, precious stones and pearls.*
[17] *In one hour such great wealth has been brought to ruin.'*

> *"Every sea captain, and all who travel by ship, the sailors, and all who earn their living from the sea, will stand far off.* [18] *When they see the smoke of her burning, they will exclaim, 'Was there ever a city like this great city?'* [19] *They will throw dust on their heads, and with weeping and mourning cry out:*

> *"'Woe. Woe, O great city,*
> *where all who had ships on the sea*
> *became rich through her wealth.*

In one hour she has been brought to ruin.

The lament is framed in two expressions of *"**Woe, woe***" (RSV *"**Alas, alas**"*; Greek *ouai, ouai*). *Ouai* here is the same word found in the three *woes* of 11:13 and can be either a warning cry or an interjection or exclamation denoting pain or displeasure. Here it is expressed in regard to **the kings of the earth who committed adultery with her and shared her luxury,** who lament the fall of Babylon/Rome, that is, the "ten" client kings (17:12) and those who depended on Rome for their wealth, who, seeing the demise and desolation of Rome, cry out in pain and displeasure. Building on the theme of how easy it is for the Sovereign God to judge Rome and bring her to nothing, John explains that in reality it takes God only one hour to humble Rome, judge her, and bring her to ruin.

That God can and will strike at the infrastructure of Rome is seen in the mourning of the merchants over Rome's demise. The source of their economy has been wiped out. The nature of their trade is global. Riches come in from all over the world: gold, ivory, pearls, fine linen, purple, bronze, spices, cattle, sheep, and human slavery. Not only will God strike at the infrastructure of Rome; he will also destroy the mercantile economy of the empire. The whole purpose of this section is to demonstrate how simple a matter it is for God to strike at the very heart of Rome's seductive power and reduce her to a state of pity.

HEAVEN'S REJOICING OVER ROME'S DEMISE—REV. 18:20

"Rejoice over her, O heaven. Rejoice, saints and apostles and prophets. God has judged her for the way she treated you." In contrast to the scenes of mourning and cries of woe, heaven and the saints sing over the pitiful lot of Rome and God's righteous judgment of the great harlot. God has vindicated his saints and pronounced judgment of their enemy. All of God's faithful servants in the church rejoice at this sovereign power and righteous judgment.

THE THIRD UNNUMBERED DESCRIPTION OF GOD'S WRATH: ROME'S DOOM SYMBOLICALLY DESCRIBED—REV. 18:21–24

The Text

Then a mighty angel picked up a boulder the size of a large millstone and threw it into the sea, and said: "With such violence the great city of Babylon will be thrown down, never to be found again.

[22] The music of harpists and musicians, flute players and trumpeters,
will never be heard in you again.
No workman of any trade
will ever be found in you again.
The sound of a millstone
will never be heard in you again.
[23] The light of a lamp
will never shine in you again.

The voice of bridegroom and bride
will never be heard in you again.
Your merchants were the world's great men.
By your magic spell all the nations were led astray.
²⁴ *In her was found the blood of prophets and of the saints,*
and of all who have been killed on the earth."

The poetic parallelism of the pericope is obvious. Once again, John draws on Old Testament prophetic texts to make his point; Isaiah, Jeremiah, and Ezekiel form the threads of his thoughts as he symbolically describes the utter ruin of Rome in the drama. One cannot escape the symbolic reference to the harlotries of Nineveh (Nah 3:4–7). The rapid and complete demise of Babylon/Rome is dramatized by the illustration of a large millstone being cast into the sea. Two sizes of millstones are mentioned in the Gospels (Matt. 24:41; Mark 9:42), one in Matt 24:41 where Jesus refers to two women grinding at a mill implying that the mill was hand operated, and again in Mk 9:42 where in similar fashion to Jeremiah and John, Jesus speaks of a great millstone being tied round the neck of one who causes vulnerable disciples to fall into sin and being thrown into the sea, this great millstone was in all probability driven by a donkey. The background for John's reference in regard to Babylon/Rome is obviously Jeremiah 51:63–64. The final statement of John's poem of doom focuses on the reason for God's judgment on Rome: *In her was found the blood of prophets and of the saints, and of all who have been killed on the earth.*

THE FOURTH UNNUMBERED DESCRIPTION OF GOD'S WRATH: THE MARRIAGE SUPPER OF THE LAMB—REV. 19:1–10

Before actually describing God's wrath, John celebrates God's vindication of the saints in four hallelujah hymns combined into one great celebration. Again, the poetic structure of this section is worthy of notice:

The Text

After this I heard what sounded like the roar of a great multitude in heaven shouting:
    "Hallelujah!
    Salvation and glory and power belong to our God,
    ² *for true and just are his judgments.*
    He has condemned the great prostitute
    who corrupted the earth by her adulteries.
    He has avenged on her the blood of his servants."
    ³ *And again they shouted:*
    "Hallelujah!
    The smoke from her goes up for ever and ever."
    ⁴ *The twenty-four elders and the four living creatures fell down and worshiped God,*
    who was seated on the throne. And they cried:
    "Amen, Hallelujah!"

[5] *Then a voice came from the throne, saying:*
"Praise our God,
all you his servants,
you who fear him,
both small and great."

[6] *Then I heard what sounded like a great multitude, like the roar of rushing waters and like loud peals of thunder, shouting:*
"Hallelujah!
For our Lord God Almighty reigns.
[7] *Let us rejoice and be glad*
and give him glory.
For the wedding of the Lamb has come,
and his bride has made herself ready.
[8] *Fine linen, bright and clean,*
was given her to wear."
(Fine linen stands for the righteous acts of the saints.)

[9] *Then the angel said to me, "Write: 'Blessed are those who are invited to the wedding supper of the Lamb.'" And he added, "These are the true words of God."*
[10] *At this I fell at his feet to worship him. But he said to me, "Do not do it. I am a fellow servant with you and with your brothers who hold to the testimony of Jesus. Worship God. For the testimony of Jesus is the spirit of prophecy."*

The literary structure of 19 has been viewed in a number of different ways. Revelation 19:1–10 forms a transitional hymn that celebrates the judgment of Babylon/Rome (9:1–5) and the reward of the saints (19:7–10). There is a three-part structure with 19:11–21 with the fourth, and next, unnumbered description of God's wrath unfolding and describing the triumphant judgment of the beast and the false prophet (Rome in its civil and religious power) by the Lamb, who is now the King of kings and Lord of lords. This is reminiscent of previous victory hymns in Revelation that have celebrated Christ's victory.

REV. 19:1–5. THE HYMNS PRAISING THE VICTORY OF GOD AND JUDGMENT OF THE HARLOT

The Text

After this I heard what sounded like the roar of a great multitude in heaven shouting:
"Hallelujah.
Salvation and glory and power belong to our God,
[2] *for true and just are his judgments.*
He has condemned the great prostitute
who corrupted the earth by her adulteries.
He has avenged on her the blood of his servants."
[3] *And again they shouted:*

"Hallelujah.
   The smoke from her goes up for ever and ever."
[4] *The twenty-four elders and the four living creatures fell down and worshiped God,*
who was seated on the throne. And they cried:
   "Amen, Hallelujah."

[5] *Then a voice came from the throne, saying:*
   "Praise our God,
      all you his servants,
   you who fear him,
      both small and great."

The three hymns of praise associated with three cries of Hallelujah are sung by a great multitude in heaven that includes the twenty-four elders seated before the throne of God in the heavenly throne room (chapter 4) where a great multitude including the twenty four-elders sung the song, "Salvation belongs to our God, who sits on the throne, and to the Lamb" (cf. chapter 7). As in 7:10, where salvation (*soteria*) is better translated as "victory" in the context of the war mythology,[39] so it should be here in 19:1: the multitude sing the hymn **Salvation** (Victory) **and glory and power belong to our God** for he has judged and defeated the harlot. His judgments are true and just because our God is righteous, true, and holy, and whatever judgment he pours out on the harlot she deserves double. The triumphant cry of the hymn is the answer to the prayers of the saints at 6:10. In jubilation and vindication they now sing, **"He has avenged on her the blood of his servants."** In celebration **again they shouted: "Hallelujah."** Reminiscent of his judgment on Sodom and Gomorrah (Gen. 19:24-29) and Edom (Isa. 34:10), **the smoke from her** (Babylon/Rome) **goes up for ever and ever**. As in the throne room of chapter 4, the celebration leads into the next hymn where **the twenty-four elders and the four living creatures fell down and worshiped God, who was seated on the throne.**

The "third" **hallelujah** is introduced by the traditional liturgical statement, **"amen,"** signifying that the words of the hymn are true. This second hymn may be merely a continuation of the previous one, but in this case it serves to affirm the previous hymnic praise of the sovereignty of God. John makes significant use of the traditional *amēn* expression in a doxological form on five other occasions (1:6, 7; 5:14; 7:12; 22:20–21). The Greek expression for **"amen, hallelujah"** is a *hapax legomenon* (found in the New Testament only here at 19:4). It is, however, found in the Old Testament at Psalm 106:48 where the Hebrew for *hallelujah* is translated in most English versions as *praise the Lord* following the Septuagint reading. *Amēn* here retains its normal Old Testament meaning of "so be it," authenticating the efficacy of the worship and praise of the hymn.[40]

Following the hymnic praise of the great multitude and twenty-four elders, a voice coming from the throne calls on all saints to **"Praise our God, all you his servants, you who fear him, both small and great."** Identifying the voice has created much speculation. Under normal circumstances one would assume it to be the voice of God, but this is hardly the case since the voice calls on God's servants to praise God. Some have proposed that the voice belongs to one of the living creatures, which is a better suggestion. However, a precise identification of the voice is not as important as its message.[41] The call to **praise our God** is full of Old Testament hymnic nuances drawing heavily on the psalms. The Greek *aineite*, **praise**, is an imperative verb of entreaty or exhortation. In this sense it carries a strong liturgical meaning of sing "a song of joyful praise to God in a doxological hymn or prayer."[42] The use of *douloi* (normally slaves, but in the NIV and RSV rendered as servants) is not unusual in Revelation (1:1; 2:20; 7:3; 11:18; 19:2; 22:3, 6). It stresses the sovereign ownership of God over his people and all creation. The message of Revelation is that God as sovereign ruler of the world is to be worshipped in reverence, a view that resonates with his holiness (cf. 14:7 and 11:18). The expression **both small and great** draws on Psalm 115:13, "The LORD . . . will bless those who fear the LORD—small and great alike."

Rev. 19:6–10. The Marriage Super of the Lamb

The Text

Then I heard what sounded like a great multitude, like the roar of rushing waters and like loud peals of thunder, shouting:

> "Hallelujah!
>> For our Lord God Almighty reigns.
> [7] Let us rejoice and be glad
>> and give him glory.
> For the wedding of the Lamb has come,
>> and his bride has made herself ready.
> [8] Fine linen, bright and clean,
>> was given her to wear."

(Fine linen stands for the righteous acts of the saints.)

[9] Then the angel said to me, "Write: 'Blessed are those who are invited to the wedding supper of the Lamb.'" And he added, "These are the true words of God." [10] At this I fell at his feet to worship him. But he said to me, "Do not do it. I am a fellow servant with you and with your brothers who hold to the testimony of Jesus. Worship God. For the testimony of Jesus is the spirit of prophecy."

The celebration of the victory of the Lamb over the beast and the false prophet (Babylon/ Rome and the harlot) continues in what can be considered a new verse of the hymn. His divine judgment is a manifestation of his sovereign reign. With this pericope, John introduces a new element into the hymn, the marriage of the Lamb to his bride. The hymn is replete with both Old and New Testament images of God, the husband, and his people, the bride. John blends with these images visions of the eschatological banquet. The concept of an eschatological banquet as a reward of faithfulness to Jesus has appeared already in three instances in the seven letters to the churches in Asia, the concept of heavenly spiritual food was the reward of faithfulness (2: 7, the tree of life; 2:17, hidden manna; 3:20, Jesus eating with the faithful). In one instance the reward was a little white stone as an invitation to the eschatological banquet (2:17). Jewish and early Christian tradition developed this concept of a heavenly banquet as the ideal reward for faithfulness and the consummation of heavenly reward. Jesus himself had on one occasion used the marriage feast as an occasion for a lesson on faithful preparedness for the kingdom (Matt. 25:1–13). It is not surprising then that at this celebration John would introduce the marriage feast of the Lamb and his faithful saints. The tradition of the church as the bride of Christ already had a rich Christian tradition as can be seen in Paul (2 Cor. 11:2; cf. also Eph. 5:25–27).

The marriage supper of the Lamb is a striking instance of John's proleptic eschatological style. John is not describing the *parousia*, a view of a rapture, or the final judgment of evil in this and the next pericope, but celebrating the victory of the Lamb and the saints over their Roman enemies. The scenes of their rejoicing are over the triumph of the Lamb, the King of kings, and his judgment of Babylon/Rome. There is a sense of futurity in this marriage feast, but it is the same enjoyment of proleptic eschatological futurity as one celebrates at the Eucharist or Lord's Supper. The present anticipation of the Lord's Supper is a present celebration of the future final eschatological banquet. In Revelation the invitees are the martyrs. The whole purpose of Revelation is to reassure the saints that martyrdom does not separate them from the love of God and Christ, but assures them of their place at that final eschatological banquet (cf. Paul's "song" at Rom. 8:37–39).

Revelation is in the form of a theological drama, building on visions God has given through Jesus of what must soon take place in the life of the churches in Asia (1:1). It tells of a crisis about to break in on the churches (1:3). The drama recounts that God has a plan (*Heilsgeschichte*) for handling evil and that he has already been working that plan. The plan climaxes in the death and resurrection of Jesus Christ. However, Satan continues his struggle to defeat God's plan and people and makes war on the saints (the messianic community, the church). His agent in this struggle in the life of the churches in Asia is the civil power of Rome (the beast) and the imperial cult (the false prophet and harlot). As the drama unfolds, John explains that God and the Lamb have already judged Rome (the beast and the harlot) with final eschatological judgment and have already rewarded the saints by inviting them to the eschatological banquet. The two sections of this pericope describe in vivid terms this eschatological banquet (the marriage feast of the Lamb and his bride) and the judgment of the beast and false prophet by the Lamb, who is in fact the King of kings and Lord of lords. The eschatological images heighten the completeness of God's reward of the saints and the extent of his judgment of Rome.

Regarding the story of Revelation and chapter 1:1-3, Caird asks, "What did John think was 'bound to happen soon'? Certainly not the End, which was at least a millennium away. He expected an event so important that it could properly be described in eschatological terms. . . . That event was the persecution, in which he saw God's victory over Babylon, as surely as in the Cross he had seen God's victory over Satan."[43] Caird had previously stated, "We are bound, then, to conclude that John has deliberately used eschatological language and imagery to depict events which possess only qualified finality, events through which in the course of history men are compelled to face the ultimate lessons in life."[44]

The marriage feast of the Lamb and the defeat of the beast and false prophet (19:11–21) are not about the rapture or the *parousia* of the Christ that introduces the final judgment. Revelation is not primarily about the parousia or final judgment. It is primarily about God's vindication of the saints and judgment on Rome. John will in a closing scene of his drama/theodicy discuss the final judgment, almost as an addendum to his drama, important as is the final judgment in the total scheme of God's *Heilsgeschichte*. His theodicy of how God has a plan for dealing with and judging evil must conclude with the final judgment of Satan and all who follow him. John will eventually close his theodicy in grand form with a brief discussion of the final judgment, including the judgment and condemnation of Satan (20:7–15), remembering that Revelation is however not about the end but about a crisis that must soon take place, about God's judgment of Rome, and of God's vindication of the martyred saints.

Rev. 19:6. *Then I heard what sounded like a great multitude, like the roar of rushing waters and like loud peals of thunder, shouting: "Hallelujah!. For our Lord God Almighty reigns."* John adds to the "jubilant sound" of the great multitude the roar of rushing water and loud peals of thunder. The symbolism is obvious since rushing water and loud thunder do not literally speak words. But they do tell a story. John refers to sounds like rushing waters three times in Revelation (1:15; 14:2; 19:6). At 1:15 it is associated with the voice of Jesus standing robed in all his divine glory. At 14:2 it is associated with the voice of the 144,000 saints sealed with the seal of God and standing with the Lamb on Mount Zion. At 14:2 it is also accompanied by a loud peal of thunder. Such phenomena are associated with proclamations or declarations of divine sovereignty. The scene is rich in Old Testament images (cf. Isa. 17:12; Ezek. 1:24; Dan. 10:6) all related to majestic proclamations. Regarding the hallelujah hymn, Osborne observes, "it's incredible volume is in keeping with the stupendous message it provides."[45]

The expression ***For our Lord God Almighty reigns*** is "the supreme title of the book," stressing that it is the Lord God Almighty who reigns, not Satan, not Caesar, nor anyone else. The expression ***The Lord God Almighty*** appears on numerous occasions (1:8; 4:8; 11:17; 15:3; 16:7, 14; 19:15; 21:22). The term *ho pantokratōr* (the almighty) is found in the Septuagint in several situations in the place of *Yahweh Sebaoth*, which carries the meaning of the Lord of Hosts, stressing his military omnipotence (see 1:8). *Ho pantokratōr* occurs repeatedly in Haggai, Zechariah, and Malachi to refer "to God as the one who sovereignly directs his people's history."[46]

The Greek text reverses the order of the words in this text, reading *"because the Lord reigns, our God, the Lord of hosts."* The Greek for ***reign***, *Ebasileusen*, is an aorist verb, which could be construed in numerous ways. It could be a simple constative aorist, which stresses an act in its entirety, similar to the gnomic aorist, which stresses an act fixed in its certainty. It could be an ingressive aorist, which stresses the beginning of an act. It could be a cumulative aorist, which stresses an act from the viewpoint of its existing results. It could also be considered an iterative aorist in a durative or repetitive action.[47] In the case of 19:6, how one determines which kind of aorist one is translating is primarily a subjective decision shaped by one's theological persuasion regarding the context of the pericope. I consider the aorist in 19:6 to be a simple constative or gnomic aorist, which stresses the reality of an act, the reign of God, or an iterative aorist, which stresses the continuing activity of the verb examined as a whole. In this case, the meaning would be that the Almighty God has again taken up his reign, or is again expressing his reign. Our Almighty God is not absent from his creation, but continues to express his sovereign reign over the world and, in this case, is expressing that sovereign reign in his judgment of Babylon/Rome, the beast, and the harlot. The simple statement of fact in the NIV and RSV translations is that our Almighty God reigns as sovereign over all creation for which, in this specific case of his judgment of Rome, not only the saints celebrate, but all of heaven celebrate his victory and judgments as expressions of that reign.[48]

Rev. 19:7–8. *Let us rejoice and be glad and give him glory. For the wedding of the Lamb has come, and his bride has made herself ready.* [8] *Fine linen, bright and clean, was given her to wear." (Fine linen stands for the righteous acts of the saints.)*

The contrast between the great harlot and the bride is obvious. The saints have proven themselves pure and worthy of marriage to the Lamb. Those who have prostituted themselves with the great harlot (Rome in its imperial cult) have become one with the harlot. As already noted, the imagery of God's faithful presented as his bride has deep roots in both Jewish and Christian traditions (cf. Isa. 49:18; 54:5; 61:10; Jer. 2:2; 31:32; Hosea *passim*; Matt. 22:1–14; 25:1–13; 2 Cor. 11:2; Eph. 5:25–26). John demonstrates here that those who have remained faithful to Jesus and have died in martyrdom are not excluded from the wedding of the body of Christ, the church, to the Lamb. Paul had stressed to the young Thessalonian church that Christians should not be concerned regarding those who had fallen asleep (a euphemism for dead) when the trumpet blows at the final end (the *eschaton*), for God will bring with Christ those who had fallen asleep when Christ returns in triumph, and all the faithful, dead and alive, will be joined with Christ at his *parousia* (1 Thess. 4:13). Likewise here in Revelation, there would be concern over dying before Christ's *parousia* and the real value of martyrdom. The saints needed assurance that they would not be left out of the marriage feast as the bride of the Lamb. This point is reinforced in that the clothes of the bride are *fine linen*, which **stands for the righteous acts of the saints**. Osborne observes,[49] "Here alone in the book are the saints described as 'preparing themselves.' They do so by remaining 'faithful' (2:10, 13; 13:10; 14:12; 17:14), maintaining their 'testimony for Jesus' (1:9; 6:9; 12:11, 17; 20:4), enduring hardship (1:9; 2:2–3, 19; 3:10, 13:10; 14:12), and obeying God's commandments (12:17; 14:12)." He adds, "The 'bright and pure' nature of their clothes symbolizes the spiritual purity of her walk with the Lord (cf. the 'white robes' of 3:4; 6:11; 7:9, 13, 14)."

Rev. 19:9–10. *Then the angel said to me, "Write: 'Blessed are those who are invited to the wedding supper of the Lamb.'" And he added, "These are the true words of God."* [10] *At this I fell at his feet to worship him. But he said to me, "Do not do it. I am a fellow servant with you and with your brothers who hold to the testimony of Jesus. Worship God. For the testimony of Jesus is the spirit of prophecy."* John brings us back to 14:13, where the fourth angelic message had proclaimed, *"Write: Blessed are the dead who die in the Lord from now on."* The mighty angel (19:21) now instructs John to record another blessing on those who are invited to the wedding supper of the Lamb. The martyred saints were promised an invitation to the eschatological banquet (2:17). Here that eschatological banquet is set in the language of the wedding feast of the bride and the Lamb. The words of the mighty angel, *These are the true words of God,* reinforce the promise of 2:17. John was so overwhelmed at this announcement that he fell prostate at the feet of the mighty angel, but the angel warned John not to do this, for he, like John and the faithful martyrs *who hold to the testimony of Jesus* is only a servant of the Almighty God. He charged that only God may be worshipped. The point would not be lost on the saints in Asia, "Do not worship the beast, worship only God." This was also the message of the eternal gospel preached to those who dwell on the earth (14:6–7): *"Fear God and give him glory, because the hour of his judgment has come. Worship him who made the heavens, the earth, the sea and the springs of water."* The same message will be repeated almost in identical words at 22:7–9: *Blessed is he who keeps the words of the prophecy in this book."* [8] *I, John, am the one who heard and saw these things. And when I had heard and seen them, I fell down to worship at the feet of the angel who had been showing them to me.* [9] *But he said to me, "Do not do it. I am a fellow servant with you and with your brothers the prophets and of all who keep the words of this book. Worship God."* The point is obvious, "Do not worship anyone other than God, not the beast nor angels regardless of their power. Fear God and worship him alone."

The expression that follows at 19:10, *for the testimony of Jesus is the spirit of prophecy,* poses several translation possibilities. The challenge relates to how one reads the genitive construction *tēs prophēteias* in the Greek *hē gar marturia Iesou estin to pneuma tēs prophēteias* ("for the testimony of Jesus is the spirit of the prophets"). Most commentators[50] on this passage describe the several interpretational possibilities as follows:

1. testifying about Jesus is the essence of prophecy
2. the testimony Jesus gave (presumably his martyrdom) is the essence of prophecy
3. it is the Spirit who gave them prophecy
4. it is the Spirit inspiring prophecy
5. the testimony Jesus bore is the heart of Spirit-inspired prophecy
6. the testimony Jesus bore is the spirit of the prophets
7. the way believers maintaining their testimony as prophetic people.

One should translate this enigmatic passage in the context of Revelation and the pericope under consideration. Since Jesus is the true example of faithful service and consequently martyrdom, and since faithful witness is the heart of the prophets or prophetic utterance, then possibly we should translate this as "the testimony Jesus bore (martyrdom) is the true spirit of the prophets"; thus the application of the phrase is that faithful witness regarding Jesus (martyrdom) in keeping with the testimony Jesus made (martyrdom) is the true spirit of the prophets.

THE FIFTH UNNUMBERED VISION OF GOD'S WRATH: THE DEFEAT OF THE BEAST AND THE FALSE PROPHET—REV. 19:11–21

The Text

I saw heaven standing open and there before me was a white horse, whose rider is called Faithful and True. With justice he judges and makes war. [12] His eyes are like blazing fire, and on his head are many crowns. He has a name written on him that no one knows but he himself. [13] He is dressed in a robe dipped in blood, and his name is the Word of God. [14] The armies of heaven were following him, riding on white horses and dressed in fine linen, white and clean. [15] Out of his mouth comes a sharp sword with which to strike down the nations. "He will rule them with an iron scepter." He treads the winepress of the fury of the wrath of God Almighty. [16] On his robe and on his thigh he has this name written: KING OF KINGS AND LORD OF LORDS. [17] And I saw an angel standing in the sun, who cried in a loud voice to all the birds flying in midair, "Come, gather together for the great supper of God, [18] so that you may eat the flesh of kings, generals, and mighty men, of horses and their riders, and the flesh of all people, free and slave, small and great." [19] Then I saw the beast and the kings of the earth and their armies gathered together to make war against the rider on the horse and his army. [20] But the beast was captured, and with him the false prophet who had performed the miraculous signs on his behalf. With these signs he had deluded those who had received the mark of the beast and worshiped his image. The two of them were thrown alive into the fiery lake of burning sulfur. [21] The rest of them were killed with the sword that came out of the mouth of the rider on the horse, and all the birds gorged themselves on their flesh.

Mounce succinctly observes,

> By now the reader will be accustomed to the sudden and dramatic changes as vision after vision appears to John . . . . Nowhere in Revelation is the victorious Christ portrayed in symbols and language more likely to convince the reader that in spite of Satan's best efforts, God and the Lamb will emerge triumphant in the end. The language of apocalyptic is sufficiently flexible to allow the destruction of the great city in chapter 18 to be followed by a final battle in chapter 19. Chronology must never be allowed to determine how truth can best be expressed. [51]

The vision being described by John incorporates all of the sovereignty of the final eschatological event in so far as the beast and the false prophet are concerned. To focus attention appropriately on this vision, we note that nowhere in the vision under review is Satan judged and thrown into the lake of fire. (Cf. 20:10-15 for this judgment.) This judgment is on the beast and the false prophet and all who worship the beast. The Sovereign Lord who will judge all of creation with final eschatological judgment has already pronounced that judgment on the beast and the false prophet, Rome, in advance of the end, and the following pericope is a dramatic vision of that judgment on Rome.

Rev. 19:11– 16. Once more (as in 4:1; 11:19; 15:5) John is given a vision of heaven opened, stressing that heaven itself is about to act in favor of the saints. *I saw heaven* *standing open and there before me was a white horse, whose rider is called Faithful and True. With justice he judges and makes war.* [12] *His eyes are like blazing fire, and on his head are many crowns. He has a name written on him that no one knows but he himself.* [13] *He is dressed in a robe dipped in blood, and his name is the Word of God.* [14] *The armies of heaven were following him, riding on white horses and dressed in fine linen, white and clean.* [15] *Out of his mouth comes a sharp sword with which to strike down the nations. "He will rule them with an iron scepter." He treads the winepress of the fury of the wrath of God Almighty.* [16] *On his robe and on his thigh he has this name written: KING OF KINGS AND LORD OF LORDS.*

John draws on several of the images of the triumphant Jesus outlined at 1:12–15 to dramatize the nature of the rider on the ***white horse***. The rider is Jesus. The image of a rider on a white horse has a number of parallels to a triumphant Roman army returning home after a magnificent victory. John's scene obviously draws on a well-known tradition of a triumphant military leader riding onto the scene in a victory parade. The white robes here do not represent purity, but a conquering king on a warhorse.[52] The scene depicts and promises the sovereignty and triumph of Jesus over Rome, the beast, and the false prophet, who have committed blasphemy against God and have persecuted his saints (13). The rider, Jesus the Lamb who is now the "lion of the tribe of Judah" (5:5), is identified as the one who is ***Faithful and True***; he has made promises to redeem and reward the martyrs, to answer their prayers, and to judge their oppressors. He brings ***justice*** and ***makes war*** on his enemies (the beast and the false prophets who made war on his people). At 1:14 John described Jesus' eyes as ***a flame of fire***. Now he sees him with eyes of ***blazing fire***. The word used to describe this fire is *phlox*, as in a flaming fire, which can be read as a raging fire welling up and raging in the rider. The scene also depicts the fact that his eyes burn through all their falsehood. On his head ***are many crowns*** (*diademata*, diadems, the crowns of kings), indicating the unlimited range of his sovereignty, for he is truly ***King of kings and Lord of lords***. That he has ***a name written on him that no one knows but he himself*** poses several possibilities. The numerous proposals regarding the secret, or mysterious, character of the name have again led to much debate and speculation.[53] Most commentators note that the new name could be the *tetragrammaton* YHWH, the name of God that is translated LORD in most English Bibles. However, few are convinced that this is the best understanding of the new name.

Most commentators find a connection between the new name here and 2:17, where the conquering saints at Pergamum were promised a little white stone with ***a new name*** written on it that no one other than the recipient would know or understand. The connection to 2:17 and the conqueror seems to be appropriate. Added to this connection to 2:17 is the idea in Hebrew and Christian tradition that the name of a person represents the character or true nature of the person. The name of the person often stood for the person himself as when Christians do something "in the name of the Lord" (Col. 3:17), meaning that one acts as if the Lord himself were present and involved in the action. Beasley-Murray is correct that "throughout the ancient world a name revealed the nature of an individual, who he is and what he is."[54] In the case of the conqueror (2:17) and of

Christ himself (19:12), the world outside the faithful circle would not understand the meaning and power of martyrdom or dying for a cause such as chosen by Christ and the martyrs, as demonstrated in the case of the aged bishop Polycarp, whom the Roman provincial governor of Smyrna could not understand in his choice to die for Jesus rather than live for Caesar. The Romans and Jewish leaders mocked Jesus at his crucifixion; and at 11:8–9, in the context of the allegorical story of Jesus' crucifixion and the death of the two faithful witnesses, John wrote that *"their bodies will lie in the street of the great city, which is figuratively called Sodom and Egypt, where also their Lord was crucified.* [9] *For three and a half days men from every people, tribe, language and nation will gaze on their bodies and refuse them burial.* [10] *The inhabitants of the earth will gloat over them and will celebrate by sending each other gifts, because these two prophets had tormented those who live on the earth."* The whole purpose for which the conquerors and Christ were given a new name was that the mystery of conquering by dying faithfully gave the conqueror a character, or nature, that was not understood by their enemies, hence a *new name* of mystery. That the rider's name is *Faithful and True* adds to the point that the new name is associated with the character of the rider.

That the rider of the white horse *is dressed in a robe dipped in blood, and his name is the Word of God* says that his name and character are associated with his victorious victory on the cross. However, different views regarding the blood in this text are proposed by commentators. Some see this as the blood of the martyrs, others as the blood of his enemies.[55] I agree with Osborne that it is "possible that this is a reference to the true victory over the forces of evil that Christ won on the cross."[56] The connection to the Gospel of John of the robe dipped in blood and now his name being the Word of God seems obvious, but this is the only occasion in Revelation where Jesus is referred to as the Word of God (*ton logon tou theou*, "the word of God," is found on three other occasions, 1:2, 9; 20:4, but in these three instances it is in regard to the message of God, not Jesus). Mounce observes that in the Gospel of John the Word is the preexistent Son of God. Furthermore, in "Hebrew thought a word is not a lifeless sound but an active agent that achieves the intention of the one who speaks."[57] Mounce suggests that this connection may be John's way of saying that Jesus is fulfilling the divine purpose of God. Thus the rider is the one who is faithful and true, who has conquered the powers of evil in his death, and who is also the preexistent Son of God who carries out the divine purpose of God.

The cavalrymen accompanying Jesus, the conquering king, are also *riding on white horses and dressed in fine linen, white and clean.* It is possible that this army is comprised of angels, but in view of 17:14 the army here most likely includes the saints who have conquered through martyrdom.[58] They join with Christ in bringing judgment on the beast and false prophet. At 19:8 the bride of the Lamb was the saints who had conquered and were clothed in fine linen as they were at 3:5 in Sardis. The fine linen represented their faithful deeds. The heavenly army here is possibly comprised of both angels and the conquering saints.[59] That the conquering saints are included is in keeping with promises made in chapters 2 and 3 that the conquerors would sit with Jesus on his throne and wield a rod of iron as they judge the nations. In the next verse John adds that the rider of the white horse, Jesus, will rule their enemies with a rod of iron. The saints as part of the army of heaven join in with Jesus, the King of kings and Lord of lords, in his victory over evil and judgment of the beast and the false prophet. Their prayer for vindication (6:10) is answered as they join with Jesus in his judgment of those who inhabit the earth and who worship the beast and wear his mark.

Rev. 19:15–16. *Out of his mouth comes a sharp sword with which to strike down the nations. "He will rule them with an iron scepter." He treads the winepress of the fury of the wrath of God Almighty.* [16] *On his robe and on his thigh he has this name written: KING OF KINGS AND LORD OF LORDS.*

Skillfully John draws on images of Jesus previously revealed, the sharp (or double–edged) sword of his mouth (1:16; 2:12, 16) being one. The sword is a symbol of his sovereign reign and sure word of judgment. His ruling the nations with a rod of iron, or iron scepter, is in keeping with the psalm of kingly ascent (Ps. 2:9; Rev. 2:27), symbolizing his sovereign reign. The reference to the winepress of the fury of God's wrath connects to the judgment scene described in 14:19–20. In his sovereign role Jesus brings the full sovereign and divine wrath of God on his enemies because *on his robe and on his thigh he has this name written: KING OF KINGS AND LORD OF LORDS.* Caesar and his imperial cult will learn that it is not Caesar who is king of kings and lord of lords, but Jesus who is the sovereign King and Lord of all creation.

The Judgment of the Beast and the False Prophet— Rev.19: 17–21.

The scene changes dramatically. The marriage feast of the faithful saints and the Lamb and the appearance of the conquering sovereign Messiah and his heavenly army comprised of the faithful saints have taken place. Now comes a vision of a feast of an altogether different kind. God has provided a second banquet, but at this banquet it is the vultures that feast on the flesh of the followers of the beast. Those who had shed the blood of the saints now become the "bloody meal" feasted on by the vultures! The irony of the scene is not easy to miss; those who inhabit the earth, who had worshipped the beast, and who had persecuted the saints, who were associated with the great harlot, who had feasted on the blood of the martyrs (17:6) now become the menu of the banquet of birds of carrion. The scene is one of gruesome horror. Beale refers to this feast as a "macabre parody" of the marriage feast of the saints and the Lamb.[60]

The Text

And I saw an angel standing in the sun, who cried in a loud voice to all the birds flying in midair, "Come, gather together for the great supper of God,[18] so that you may eat the flesh of kings, generals, and mighty men, of horses and their riders, and the flesh of all people, free and slave, small and great." [19] Then I saw the beast and the kings of the earth and their armies gathered together to make war against the rider on the horse and his army. [20] But the beast was captured, and with him the false prophet who had performed the miraculous signs on his behalf. With these signs he had deluded those who had received the mark of the beast and worshiped his image. The two of them were thrown alive into the fiery lake of burning sulfur. [21] *The rest of them were killed with the sword that came out of the mouth of the rider on the horse, and all the birds gorged themselves on their flesh.*

Rev. 19:17. That the *angel* [is] *standing in the sun* implies that he speaks with the full authority of God. On several occasions angels have appeared in association with the sun (10:1; 12:1; 18:10) and Christ's face shone like the sun (1:16). This association with the sun draws on the description of God in several Old Testament texts (Ps. 84:11; Isa. 60:19). The implication of Christ and angels associated with the sun reinforces the divine aspect of their relationship with God Almighty.[61] The linking of 18:1 and 19:17 is interesting in that the first angel announces the doom of Rome and the second angel focuses on the beast and false prophet and their associates.

Rev. 19:18. This second angel invites the birds flying in midair (not heaven) to the great banquet provided for them by God. The *flesh of kings, generals, and mighty men, of horses and their riders, and the flesh of all people, free and slave, small and great* represent the client kings who had been seduced by the false prophet to serve the beast (17:12-14 and 18:9-10).

Rev. 19:19. Then in a futile attempt *the kings of the earth and their armies gathered together to make war against the rider on the horse and his army.* Repeatedly John has predicted the defeat of the beast (cf. 16:16). The scenes of Revelation are not sequential or chronological, but repetitive. In Revelation "chronology is ignored for the sake of rhetorical effect."[62] What John had previously predicted is now described in dramatic terms. The beast (Babylon/Rome) and the false prophet (the imperial cult) are captured and *thrown alive into the fiery lake of burning sulphur.* It is interesting that the armies are killed in the battle, but the beast and false prophet are thrown alive into the lake of fire. The sense of being thrown alive into the lake of fire strengthens the severity of their judgment. They are thus fully aware of the severity and nature of their judgment. The symbolism of this battle is seen in the fact that the armies are killed *with the sword that came out of the mouth of the rider on the horse.* Two symbols need some explanation, first, *the fiery lake of burning sulphur,* second the nature of *the sword.*

There is little background in Scripture to the lake of fire, or *the fiery lake.* The concept of a lake of fire (*tēn limnēn tou puros*) occurs in the New Testament only here in 19:20, 20:15, and 21:8, but in the apocalyptic tradition, both of the Old Testament and later Jewish writings there are references to a river of fire that proceeds from God's throne (Dan. 7:9–11) and the little horn of Daniel 7:8 being thrown into fire. Both *2 Enoch* 10:2 and the *Sibylline Oracles* 2:196 speak of a great river of blazing fire. (Dating much of the apocalyptic tradition is difficult, but the evidence of this fiery symbolism was obviously rich in the Judaeo/Christian apocalyptic tradition.) The reference to sulphur draws on the judgment of Sodom and Gomorrah (Gen. 19:24) and the fire and brimstone of God's judgment of Gog, king of Magog (Ezek. 38:22). There may also be allusions to the fires of Gehenna, which referred to the Valley of Hinnom, which lay just outside the south west walls of Jerusalem. Here during the days of the evil kings Ahaz and Manasseh, human sacrifices were offered in cultic worship to the god Molech (2 Chron. 28:3; 33:6). By the time of the New Testament, Gehenna had become a euphemism for the place of final punishment (Matt 10:28; Mark 9:43–45). Similar references to a place of final judgment and punishment can be found in the *Sibylline Oracles* 4:160-211, 2:222-382. John's reference to the lake of fire obviously draws on the apocalyptic symbolism of eternal judgment and punishment. Later at 20:15 and 21:8 John will refer to the devil, Hades, and all who are cowardly and faithless (in Revelation, those who give in and worship the beast), who are cast into this lake of fire that symbolizes the final judgment, the "second death," and eternal punishment.

The sword that proceeds out of the mouth of the rider, Christ, as noted above (19:5) refers to his sovereign word of authority and judgment. What is noteworthy about this battle is its swiftness. One word from the sovereign King of kings and Lord of lords and the battle is over. The heavenly army that followed the King seemingly play no active role in this battle. They witness his victory and are corporately present in this battle, but the word that proceeds out of his mouth is sufficient for victory, a reminder of 18:8, 10, where in one day, even one hour, God brings the new Babylon, Rome, to ruin.

John closes this ghastly scene with the statement that the birds of carrion *gorged* themselves with the flesh of those killed by the sword of Christ. The dramatic parody of the glorious eschatological banquet to which the conquering saints were invited is striking. Some suggest that we have here a form of *lex talionis* in which the law of retribution is played out in this frightful feast. As repulsive was the thought of the harlot drinking the blood of the saints (17:6), equally staggering is the picture of the punishment of those who worship the beast. The Greek word describing this feast, *echortasthēsan*, connotes a gluttonous feasting on the flesh.[63]

THE SIXTH UNNUMBERED DESCRIPTION OF GOD'S WRATH: THE BINDING AND LIMITATION OF SATAN—REV. 20:1–10

Mounce comments that "judging from the amount of attention given by most writers to the first ten verses of chapter 20, one would think they were the single most important segment of the book of Revelation"[64]. Wilcock writes, "We come in this scene to one of the most difficult, or at any rate on of the most disputed, parts of the book. See what your commentator has to say about Revelation 20, and you will get an idea of his approach to the rest."[65] Caird takes a critical approach to the problems encountered in this text, stating "we come now to a passage which, more than any other in the book, has been the paradise of cranks and fanatics on the one hand and literalists on the other. It bristles with questions."[66] Leon Morris briefly introduces the various millennial views and notes that "evangelicals have divided from one another and sometimes have been quite intolerant of views other than those of their group. It is necessary to approach the chapter with humility and charity."[67] Unfortunately, not all have been characterized by the humble and charitable spirit called for by Morris. Osborne correctly observes that "this is easily the best known portion of the book as well as one of the most divisive passages of the Bible. "[68]

In the introduction, I briefly discussed the various millennial views and have included a diagrammatical overview of millennial positions in the Glossary. Perhaps Osborne is correct in observing that "this issue will not be solved until the events take place, and then we will see who is 'right.'"[69] Various millennial views reflect different ways to study and interpret Scripture, and it is here that the most serious issues in millennial thinking lie.

I take a moderate preterist approach in which Revelation is set in the first century of Christianity in Asia, coupled with a philosophy of history approach that seeks theological principles that are relevant for today. I am of an amillennial persuasion in that I perceive the thousand years of Revelation to be symbolic of emphases that center on the sovereign reign and authority of Christ and not simply a period of time, whether a literal thousand years or a symbolic period of time. I espouse a view commonly described as inaugurated eschatology, which holds that the reign of Christ, or the eschatological age, has begun in time in the coming of Christ and his ministry and in the life of the church. I believe that the kingdom of God, or Christ, has been inaugurated in our time and that it will be fully realized at the second coming of Christ, or the *parousia*. I look forward to the full, or realized, reign of Christ at his *parousia* when he exercises his divine authority over all creation at the final eschatological judgment. Until then I pray that the kingdom may be experienced now on earth just as it is in heaven (Matt. 6:9–10).

Roberts, in his opening comments on the millennial views proposed by many, states: "A correct interpretation can be made only by keeping the exegesis within the framework of the Apocalypse and noting John's own readaptation of apocalyptic ideas." He argues that this is what is missing in most literalistic and futuristic views as in the premillennial or dispensational and continuous historical interpretations of this text.[70] After briefly discussing various views of millennial studies, Osborne observes, "Yet the theological debate should not be the primary issue in a study of this passage. Mainly, we must ask how it functions within the book and what it adds theologically to the developing themes of the book. This is part of a much larger section (17:1–20:15)."[71] He further notes that this passage sums up the major themes and several visions in Revelation.[72] *First*, the theology must be kept within the crises faced by the church in Asia in the first century of Christianity. *Second*, it must be kept within the literary style of Revelation, namely, an apocalyptic genre with its striking symbolic figurative and metaphorical tendency. *Third*, the warlike conflict (combat mythology) of Satan and Rome with the church must be understood and constantly kept in the forefront of interpretation.[73] *Fourth*, the most important context must be the cry of the saints beneath the altar for vindication and God's promise to judge Satan, the beast, the false prophet, and those who worship the beast, and to vindicate and reward the faithful saints who conquer Satan and the beast. *Finally*, I have repeatedly stressed how important 1:1–3 is in demonstrating that this book is not about the end of the world but about crises that will soon break in on the churches in Asia. The end of the world and final eschatological judgment is mentioned in chapter 20, but only tangentially as it is necessary to bring the theodicy of Revelation to a close. Evil must finally be destroyed as the final act of God's plan of salvation.

The tendency of many interpreters at this point is to become apologists for a particular view of the millennium."[74] Without denying the significance of this important passage, it should not be elevated above some of the basic themes of the book that I have mentioned above. Although the precise nature and temporal relationship of chapter 20 to chapter 19 is "hotly debated . . . it is important to remember the genre of Revelation in approaching 20:1–6, especially the programmatic nature of 1:1."[75] When interpreting this challenging pericope, we should hold our interpretation within the concerns of the first-century churches in Asia, Roman imperial and societal persecution, martyrdom, and Jesus' promises to vindicate the saints and judge Rome and the great harlot. We should resist the temptation to read into this pericope interests of contemporary popular millennial theology and concerns for the supposed "signs of the times."

There is some discussion as to whether chapter 20 is in chronological sequence to chapter 19. Both Beale and Osborne argue that although there may be some sequence in theme, the sequential or chronological connection cannot be maintained grammatically. Osborne states (contra Mounce [76]) that the recapitulation of the rhetorical expression *and I saw*, *kai eidon*, throughout Revelation (at least 32 times) indicates *a new scene* or vision which sets 20:1 apart from the defeat of the beast and the false prophet in 19:11-21. Consequently 20:1 is not a chronological sequence to 19:11-21 but a new scene of visions expressing the defeat or limitation of Satan and the victory of Christ and the saints. Osborne argues that *and I saw* "begins this section, . . . it is debated whether it is a chronological indicator . . . On the basis of its use throughout the book, I conclude that it is not. There is a narrative sequence . . . but chronological sequence cannot be proven on the basis of *kai eidon*."[77] Beale concurs.[78] I am of the same opinion. This means that we should not see 20 as a temporal continuity of the casting of the beast and the false prophet into the lake of fire and the orgiastic feast of the birds on the flesh of the followers of the beast. Here John begins another vision that returns to and develops his central theme, the limitation of Satan and Rome by the power and authority of God,[79] the reign of the conquering saints with Christ (2:27, 3:21), and the eventual and final judgment of Satan in the lake of fire along with the beast and false prophet.

It might help our understanding of 20:1–10 to consider a possible structural analysis of the text. Most of our translations divide the text into three paragraphs as follows:

1. 20:1–3, the binding of Satan for a thousand years
2. 20:4–6, the reign of the saints for a thousand years
3. 20:7 10, the loosing and judgment of Satan

I view 20:4–6 as a parenthetical paragraph, permitting one to read from the binding of Satan through his loosing and final judgment in one thought, with 20:4–6 inserted into the flow of thought to focus on the theme of the reign of the saints. Schüssler Fiorenza[80] describes this paragraph, or at least 5b,6, as an interlude introduced into the flow of thought of the major section. I have found it easier to teach this text by leaving the reign of the saints (20:4–6) out of the discussion until we have handled the limitation and judgment of Satan. Finally, I insert the reign of the saints as a significant highlight of the passage. I will handle the text below in the normal manner, but will indicate the connection of thought as we progress through the text.

THE BINDING OF SATAN, THE REIGN OF THE SAINTS, AND THE FINAL JUDGMENT—REV. 20:1–15.

The Text

And I saw an angel coming down out of heaven, having the key to the Abyss and holding in his hand a great chain. [2] He seized the dragon, that ancient serpent, who is the devil, or Satan, and bound him for a thousand years. [3] He threw him into the Abyss, and locked and sealed it over him, to keep him from deceiving the nations anymore until the thousand years were ended. After that, he must be set free for a short time.

[4] I saw thrones on which were seated those who had been given authority to judge. And I saw the souls of those who had been beheaded because of their testimony for Jesus and because of the word of God. They had not worshiped the beast or his image and had not received his mark on their foreheads or their hands. They came to life and reigned with Christ a thousand years. [5] (The rest of the dead did not come to life until the thousand years were ended.) This is the first resurrection. [6] Blessed and holy are those who have part in the first resurrection. The second death has no power over them, but they will be priests of God and of Christ and will reign with him for a thousand years.

[7] When the thousand years are over, Satan will be released from his prison [8] and will go out to deceive the nations in the four corners of the earth—Gog and Magog—to gather them for battle. In number they are like the sand on the seashore. [9] They marched across the breadth of the earth and surrounded the camp of God's people, the city he loves. But fire came down from heaven and devoured them. [10] And the devil, who deceived them, was thrown into the lake of burning sulfur, where the beast and the false prophet had been thrown. They will be tormented day and night for ever and ever.

[11] Then I saw a great white throne and him who was seated on it. Earth and sky fled from his presence, and there was no place for them. [12] And I saw the dead, great and small, standing before the throne, and books were opened. Another book was opened, which is the book of life. The dead were judged according to what they had done as recorded in the books. [13] The sea gave up the dead that were in it, and death and Hades gave up the dead that were in them, and each person was judged according to what he had done. [14] Then death and Hades were thrown into the lake of fire. The lake of fire is the second death. [15] If anyone's name was not found written in the book of life, he was thrown into the lake of fire.

THE BINDING OF SATAN—REV. 20:1–3

And I saw an angel coming down out of heaven, having the key to the Abyss and holding in his hand a great chain. [2] He seized the dragon, that ancient serpent, who is the devil, or Satan, and bound him for a thousand years. [3] He threw him into the Abyss, and locked and sealed it over him, to keep him from deceiving the nations anymore until the thousand years were ended. After that, he must be set free for a short time.

This **angel** has divine authority in that he holds the key to the abyss. Aune indicates that this angel may be a "supernatural being" since he has charge of the abyss. He adds that Jewish tradition held that God does not expel or restrain demons himself but assigns that task to an angel.[81] Some feel that since Michael defeated Satan at 12:7-9 that this angel may be Michael.[82] At 9:1 a star fell from heaven to earth and was given the key of the shaft of the abyss or bottomless pit. We understand this star to be an angel, for angels are referred to as stars in Revelation (1:20, seven stars are seven angels of the churches). Whether we should see these two occasions (9:1 and 20:1) as referring to the same angel, or who that angel may be, is immaterial to the point John is making. The point is that this angel has power over the Abyss, which Abyss in Jewish mythology referred to the source of evil, or a place where evil was contained or restrained, or even a reference to the Satanic realm.[83] In addition to the key to the abyss, the angel holds a great chain with which, we will shortly learn, he binds the dragon (Satan) for 1000 years. That he has great authority is seen in his ability to *seize* the dragon, Satan (*ekratēsen*, an aorist verb which stresses the decisive activity of the angel) and bind him with a chain. Osborne observes that the powerlessness of Satan is quite evident in the fact that he puts up no effort to resist the binding.[84]

Little is said in most commentaries regarding the great chain other than the chain could be a reference to the manacles that would bind a prisoner to the wall of a prison ensuring that the prisoner would not escape from behind the locked doors of the prison. The prisoner would be doubly secured.[85] The tradition of evil spirits or fallen angels being cast into prison or kept under security is fairly common in both the Old and New Testaments, but is enriched by the apocalyptic or extra-biblical tradition of the Jewish literature. Beckwith, Roberts, Aune, Beale, Osborne, and Beasley-Murray suggest that Isa 24:21f may lie behind the concept of evil spirits being cast in a pit or prison, possibly a subterranean dark cavern.[86] Beckwith notes that in Jewish angelology Azazel, a leader among the fallen angels and somewhat akin to Satan, was bound and imprisoned in darkness for an unlimited period.[87] There are several ancient pagan traditions of evil spirits and powers being incarcerated in dark realms[88], but one is not certain whether these played any role in John's drama other than for the fact that the Christians in Asia were at one time pagans, familiar with their own ancient traditions. From John's liberal use of the Jewish apocalyptic and pseudepigraphical literature we can assume that his readers were familiar with these traditions, for we find such references in several sources *1 Enoch* 10:1-7; 13:1-10; 19:1,2; *2 Enoch* 7:1,2; *Prayer of Manasseh* vs. 3; et al. 3). The image of angels or spirits being held in prison is also found in the New Testament, notably in apocalyptic type texts, 1 Pet 3:19; 2 Pet 2:4.

The angel *seized the dragon, that ancient serpent, who is the devil, or Satan, and bound him for a thousand years.* The binding of an evil spirit with a chain has no direct background in Biblical literature but is found in other Jewish sources such as *Tobit* and the *Testament of Levi.* An interesting account of an evil spirit being bound can be found in *Tobit* 8:3. Tobias, the son of Tobit a native of Nineveh (ca. 721 B.C.) goes on a journey and is threatened by a large fish. Tobias is accompanied by an angel, Raphael, who appears to Tobias as a friend, Azarias. Raphael tells Tobias to kill the fish and burn its liver as protection against demonic spirits who cannot tolerate the smell of the burning liver. Tobias is also told to marry a lady, Sarah, who is plagued by a demon spirit. The problem is that she has been offered to seven men before Tobias comes onto the scene and all seven men have died as the result of the work of the evil spirit. Tobias is told by Raphael to burn some of the liver in order to drive the evil spirit out of the house. He pursues the evil spirit into the desert and binds him there. The evil spirit can now no longer torment him and cause him problems. The interesting point of this little narrative is that when one binds an evil spirit it cannot bother one anymore.

Similar instances of binding and limiting spirits can be found in the *Testament of Levi* 18:9-12,

> And the lawless shall cease to do evil. And he shall open the gates of paradise, And shall remove the threatening sword against Adam. And he shall give to the saints to eat from the tree of life, And the spirit of holiness shall be on them. And Belial shall be bound by him, And he shall give power to His children to tread upon the evil spirits.[89]

Another instance of evil spirits being bound is found in1 *Enoch* 18:12-16,

> And on top of that pit I saw a place without the heavenly firmament above the earthly foundation under it or the water. There was nothing on it – not even birds-but it was a desolate and terrible place. And I saw there the seven stars (which) were like great, burning mountains. [14] (Then) the angel said(to me), "This place is the (ultimate) end of heaven and earth: this is the prison house for the stars and the powers of heaven. And the stars which roll over upon the fire, they are the ones which have transgressed the commandment of God from the beginning of [16] their rising, because they did not arrive punctually. And he was wroth with them, and bound them until the time of the completion of their sin in the year of mystery."[90]

The *Similitudes of Enoch* (1 *Enoch*) 54:1-6 tell the story of iron chains being made to bind the host of Azazeel (symbolic of evil angels or demonic beings),

> [1] And I looked and turned to another part of the earth, and saw there a deep valley with burning fire. [2] And they brought the kings and the mighty, and began to cast them into this deep valley. [3] And there mine eyes saw how they made these their instruments, iron chains of immeasurable weight. [4] And I asked the angel of peace who went with me, saying: "For whom are these chains being prepared?" [5] And he said unto me: "These are being prepared for the hosts of Azâzêl, so that they may take them and cast them into the abyss of complete condemnation, and they shall cover their jaws with rough stones as

the Lord of Spirits commanded. [6] And Michael, and Gabriel, and Raphael, and Phanuel shall take hold of them on that great day, and cast them on that day into the burning furnace, that the Lord of Spirits may take vengeance on them for their unrighteousness in becoming subject to Satan and leading astray those who dwell on the earth."[91]

Although the concept of the binding of Satan with a great chain may be unfamiliar to modern readers, it was not for John's audience. They understood that the binding of Satan with a great chain meant the severe limitation of Satan's ability to torment his foes. This angel *seized the dragon, that ancient serpent, who is the devil, or Satan, and bound him for a thousand years.* [3] *He threw him into the Abyss, and locked and sealed it over him, to keep him from deceiving the nations anymore until the thousand years were ended.* The sense of *seized* is strong. The verb *ekratēsen* ("seized") is in the aorist tense, stressing the strong decisive action of the seizing. Likewise *ebalen* ("threw") is also an aorist verb, likewise highlighting the decisive action of the angel.

The ***thousand years*** raises several interesting thoughts and questions. To begin, we should remember that in Revelation John is not primarily interested in the end of the world or when the millennial reign begins or how long will last. He assumes that Christ is already reigning, that the martyred saints are also already reigning with him (for so Jesus promised at 2:17, 27), and that God is in control of the world and its events. Furthermore, John uses numbers symbolically. We saw this in the seven cities of Asia, cognizant of the fact that there were more than seven cities in Asia when John wrote Revelation. The 144,000 members of the twelve tribes of Israel (7 and 14) are symbolic of God's church militant and are in fact a large multitude. The $3\frac{1}{2}$ years, 42 months, and 1260 days are symbolic and represent periods of persecution. In keeping with John's style we should then consider the one thousand years to be symbolic. Harold Hazelip[92] has suggested that all the numbers in the Bible and Revelation are symbolic of ideas. Likewise, Summers maintains that the number does not represent a period of time at all but speaks to the extent Satan is bound or restrained. [93] Harrington likewise considers the one thousand years to have no chronological value, but serves only to symbolize the helplessness of Satan.[94]

Beale makes the interesting observation that the one thousand years here in 20:1-3 is the same figure as that in 20:4. Commenting on 20:4 he observes:

> The focus shifts from what takes place in the abyss (vv 1-3) to what happened in heaven as a result of the binding of Satan. V 4 portrays the effects for the community of saints of Satan's fall in vv 1-3. The main point of v 4 is to explain that Satan's fall is a judgment on him that vindicates the saints . . .
>
>   The events of vv 1-3 and vv 4-6 occur during the same period, which is referred to as "1,000 years". That this is not a chronological number is apparent from: (1) the constant use of numbers elsewhere in the book, (2) The figurative nature of much of the immediate context . . . (3) the predominant figurative

nature of the entire book . . . (4) the figurative use of "1,000" in the OT, and
(5) the use in Jewish and early Christian writings of "1,000" years as a figure
for the eternal blessing of the redeemed . . .[95]

Attempts to find a background to John's use of this enigmatic figure have only served to
complicate the matter. Jewish traditional literary, apocalyptic, and rabbinic sources are
so varied that it is apparent that speculation obviously reigned in this regard. Several of
the prominent commentators (Beckwith, Beale, Osborne, Aune, Beasley-Murray, Morris,
Summers, et al[96]) draw attention the varied Jewish traditions regarding the messianic
reign, ranging from 400 years through 7,000 years to 365,000 years. It is apparent that
no consensus can be arrived at regarding the 1000 years from the Jewish, apocalyptic,
and rabbinic sources.

Aune[97] notes that the nature of this 1000 years has been variously interpreted depending on the theological or ecclesiastical background and persuasion of the interpreter. He
cites Augustine, the Roman Catholic church, Reformed theologians, and Presbyterians
as having interpreted the 1000 years to be the church age. Some Lutherans have seen
in the 1000 years a reference to the quality of life lived by the saints and not a length
of time. Literalists such as the early church fathers Justin, Irenaeus, Melito, Tertullian,
Hippolytus, and Methodius saw in this figure a literal "chiliast" 1000 year reign of Christ
on earth. Others such as Clement of Alexandria, Origen, and Augustine spiritualized the
1000 years to refer to the present reign of the saints with Christ, opened the door to an
Amillennial view. I might add that some protestants have dated the beginning of the
1000 year reign from the Protestant Reformation ca. 1517. Some members of the Stone-
Campbell Restoration movement, mostly postmillennial by nature, date the beginning
of the postmillennial age from the time of the great religious awakening in America
and more specifically Thomas Campbell, Barton W. Stone and Alexander Campbell, ca.
1809.[98] The Bible is replete with references to 1,000 or 10,000 used symbolically for a large
number or complete number. Multiples of 10 or 1,000 often represent completeness. At
Ps 50:10 we read that God has cattle on a thousand hills indicating that all animals are
his. At Deut 5:10; 7:9 God shows his love and makes covenants for a thousand generations. At 1 Chron 16:15 and Ps 105:8 God's word lasts for a thousand generations, thus
is permanent. The concept of ten thousand representing a large or complete number is
found 35 times in the Bible, for example at Lev 26:8 five hundred soldiers will put ten
thousand to flight. At Judg 3:29 Ehud struck down ten thousand Moabites. At Judg 4
ten thousand men followed Deborah and Barak. Beale suggest that a thousand is the
intensifying of ten, or the third power of ten, equaling a perfect number or epoch. [99]

In the six occasions in 20 (vs. 2,3,4,5,6,7) where we have one thousand years I understand the thousand years not to represent a literal period of time, nor a period of time
at all. I understand the thousand years to represent an idea, condition, or concept of
completeness. As we will see, at 20:3 Satan in so far as Rome is concerned is limited or
completely restricted from deceiving the nations that follow the beast. However, Satan is
not yet destroyed. He has other nations to deceive. He will come again and deceive Gog

and Magog (nations symbolic of the resilience of evil) but he and they will be defeated. In contrast to this, the saints whom Satan and the beast have killed are reigning completely (one thousand years) with Christ on his throne (20:4).

Osborne offers the interesting observation that as metaphors "the binding and the millennium are best understood as Christ's authority restraining the devil in some manner during the church age."[100] While I might not be comfortable that the millennium refers to the church age, I agree with Osborne that the millennium should be construed as a metaphor. I would see this as a metaphor speaking of the complete (1000) limitation of Satan to deceive Rome and the nations any more. Thus, the one thousand years becomes a metaphor defining the complete limitation of Satan *in regard to Rome* and the nations seduced by Rome. Osborne agrees that the limitation of Satan is not universal but limited. In regard to the binding of Satan in Mark 3:27 and Matt 12:29 he notes that the binding as a restriction of Satan's activities "highlights the fact that Jesus is sovereign over him and his demonic forces."[101] I will address the limitation of Satan and his release further at 20:7-10.

Rev. 20:3. *He threw him into the Abyss, and locked and sealed it over him, to keep him from deceiving the nations anymore until the thousand years were ended. After that, he must be set free for a short time.* This text defines the purpose of seizing Satan and throwing him into the abyss. *First*, it is a demonstration of divine power and demonic weakness. *Second*, it proclaims both Satan's limitation and the negation of his power to deceive the nations. Satan's power to deceive both Rome and the nations is expressed by commentators either as limited or completely taken away. I understand limited here to mean "taken away".[102] Roberts writes "Jewish apocalyptic writers were familiar with the idea of the limitation of Satan's work by binding . . . . The thousands years probably represents . . . the limitation of Satan's power to persecute. "[103] The extent of Satan's limitation is expressed by the fact that the Abyss is locked and sealed over him. He is securely bound and limited.

The purpose of this binding is introduced by a *hina* clause, *hina mē planēsē, in order that he may not deceive.*[104] The *hina* clause introduces *purpose.* The purpose of his binding is *that he may no longer deceive the nations* who follow the beast. This indicates a severe, complete, curtailment of Satan's ability to use Rome to achieve his purpose. One must beware of reading into the expression **until the thousand years were ended** a temporal meaning for we have already noted that the thousand years is not a temporal or chronological reference but addresses a *concept* or *condition.* The one thousand implies a condition of completeness. The addition of the word **until**, *achri*, implies a limitation, the binding is *until* something occurs, that is, his release *from his prison* in 20:7. This is John's way of stating that although Satan is completely bound in regard to Rome, he still has freedom to work in other places, as we will see in 20:7, 8 where he goes out and deceives other nations such as Gog and Magog. The fact that he is *set free for a short time* builds on his limitation, indicating that he is not free for ever to deceive the nations. The way John expresses this, *he must be set free for a short time*, is interesting for he uses the impersonal verb *dei*, *must* or *is necessary*, which can function like a divine imperative. Osborne speaks of a divine "must" meaning that God has determined it necessary for Satan to be freed for "a final brief period" in order for God to achieve his divine purpose. Osborne asks why God would so determine Satan to be set free and concludes that this must have something to do with John's theodicy which requires Satan to be released and finally judged and thrown into the lake of fire.[105]

THE REIGN OF THE SAINTS—REV. 20:4–6

I saw thrones on which were seated those who had been given authority to judge. And I saw the souls of those who had been beheaded because of their testimony for Jesus and because of the word of God. They had not worshiped the beast or his image and had not received his mark on their foreheads or their hands. They came to life and reigned with Christ a thousand years. [5] *(The rest of the dead did not come to life until the thousand years were ended.) This is the first resurrection.* [6] *Blessed and holy are those who have part in the first resurrection. The second death has no power over them, but they will be priests of God and of Christ and will reign with him for a thousand years.*

Beale, sets the tone and direction for interpreting this great text as well as anyone.

> Life and rule are the primary themes of 20:4-6. This means that the primary point of the millennium is to demonstrate the victory of the suffering Christians. Those "whom the beast put to death are those who will truly live . . . and those who contested his right to rule and suffered for it are those who in the end rule as universally as he—and for much longer," not only for a figurative millennium but for eternity (22:5). This is in line with NT teaching elsewhere, such as 2 Tim 2:11-12: "If we die with him, we will live with him; if we hold fast, we will reign with him."[106]

Fixing the locale of the vision, Beale then adds,

> The focus shifts from what has taken place in the abyss (vv 1-3) to what has happened in heaven as a result of the bonding of Satan. V 4 portrays the effects for the community of the saints of Satan's fall in vv 1-3. The main point of v 4 is to explain that Satan's fall is a judgment on him that vindicates the saints. Their vindication is positively demonstrated by their resurrection and their reign on thrones with Christ (assuming for a moment an answer to the question of the identity of those seated on the thrones).[107]

The point that Beale makes so well is that there is a connection between 20:1-3, the binding and limitation of Satan, and 20:4-7, the reign of the saints with Christ. These two images or messages must be kept in dynamic tension emphasizing the victory of the martyred saints over both Rome and Satan.

Rev 20:4. Shifting attention from the binding of Satan John sees a new vision, he sees thrones. From a prison in the abyss to thrones in the throne room of heaven! The contrast is striking and brilliant. The idea of reigning on thrones is not new here to Revelation, for John has already told us that the twenty four elders were seated on thrones surrounding the throne of God (the elders represent all martyrs form all ages), and the conquering saints will be sated with Jesus on his throne (3:21). Furthermore, since the theology of Revelation is significantly about conquering and reigning with Christ, it is to be expected that saints seated on thrones would play a featured role in the closing scenes of Revelation. The primary question to be asked of this text relates to who is seated on these thrones. The surprising answer to this question is that it is those to whom authority has been given to judge. However, this should not take the serious reader by surprise since we have already read that the conquering martyrs were promised authority over the nations and a "rod of iron with which to break pottery" as a symbol of royal power (Ps 2:8, 9; Rev 2:26, 27; 3:21).

Rev 20:4 has been broken into four sentences in the NIV and three in the RSV. The Greek has most of vs. 4 in one long compound sentence. It is surprising that our major English translations of 20:4 do not follow the punctuation of 20:4 suggested by major Greek texts such as the Barbara and Kurt Aland, et. al.[108] For instance both the NIV and the RSV prefer a period following the expression *given authority to judge* rather than a comma as suggested by the Greek texts. Aune is correct in proposing that the *kai, and,* following the words *given authority to judge* should not begin a new sentence but should be understood as an *epexegetical kai* that emphasizes and clarifies the previous statement. The epexegetical kai should therefore read *that is,* or *indeed.* [109] Aune translates the passage *"Then I saw thrones, and people sat upon them, and they were given the authority to judge, that is, the souls of those who had been beheaded. . . ."* Although Aune's translation is better than that of the NIV and RSV, I would translate this as *"And I saw thrones and seated on them were those to whom judgment was given, indeed, I saw the souls of those who had been beheaded for their testimony to Jesus."* The identity of who the souls were is clarified, therefore, by the next clause, they are those who had not worshipped the beast and its image and had not received the mark of the beast on their foreheads and hands. It is *indeed* the conquering martyrs who are seated on thrones, just as Jesus had promised in 2 and 3. Although this is the first time that John has indicated that the martyrs *had been beheaded* (which being in the past tense, a perfect passive form of the verb, is an interesting historical vignette) it is not surprising for decapitation by the sword or axe was a common form of capital punishment under the Roman system. The reference to decapitation indicates Roman civil involvement.[110] Whether John intended the *beheaded* to be taken literally or as another metaphor for martyrdom makes little difference to the meaning of the text. How they died is not an issue. The point is that they had died for the cause of Christ.

Those who had been beheaded *came to life and reigned with Christ a thousand years*. We have noted that Osborne correctly observed that this text gets to the heart of the millennial debate. He is correct since these words regarding a "resurrection" here and in the next verse pose a real exegetical problem. He also adds that how one interprets of, *edzēsan, came to life*, to some extent determines the issue. *Edzēsan* is the same word used of Christ in 2:8 where it is stated that the words spoken to the church at Smyrna we the words of the one *"who died and came to life again"*. Although not the usual word for resurrection it obviously speaks of the coming to life as a resurrection.

Osborne adds that if it means they were raised bodily from the dead then this must refer to the end of history. Failure to see this in keeping with John's proleptic eschatological style is a mistake one faces in trying to interpret this enigmatic expression. The question is whether this resurrection is a physical resurrection, the same one as the general resurrection that takes place at the final end of history, or is a proleptic experience of this general resurrection. We will note, however, that some Amillennial commentators hold that this resurrection at 20:4 refers to a spiritual resurrection after conversion.[111] To have this resurrection refer to the final resurrection or a spiritual resurrection that takes place at baptism places the interpretation or the text outside of the primary concerns of Revelation. This resurrection must have reference to the type of resurrection referred to in Revelation, specifically in the promises of resurrection to the conquering saints as in 2; 3; 11:11, 12 where those who had been left lying dead in the streets of the diabolical city were called up to heaven and ascended in a cloud. 20:5, 6 will refer to an enigmatic first resurrection upon whom a blessing is pronounced in that they will not share in the second death, the final judgment. The context demands that this *coming to life* is the spiritual reward of those who have conquered the beast and the false prophet and have died as martyrs.

Three things stand out from this clause; 1) *they reigned* which continues the theme of the vindication of the martyrs and their reward of sitting on thrones with Christ. This stresses the fulfillment of those promises; 2) *it is they, the martyred saints, who are reigning for a thousand years*, not Christ; He as sovereign ruler reigns eternally, they share corporately in that reign; and 3) *they reign completely for "a thousand years"*.

Although there is a tendency to see the thousand years as a "period" we should see it as a symbol referring not simply to a period of time but to an ideal condition of completeness. Beale again observes appropriately that 1,000 is 10 cubed, or 10 to the power of ten which at least should indicate an ideal epoch or condition.[112] In keeping with 20:1-3 and the binding of Satan for a thousand years we should not see the number 1,000 as a symbol of a temporal period, but as a symbol of completeness, a condition, or an ideal symbol. At 20:2 it was Satan who was completely bound, restricted, or limited in his ability to use Rome as his agent of persecution. Here it is the saints that are reigning fully with Christ, not marginally, but in reality, completely. As opposed to Satan and Rome who "reign" marginally or temporally, the conquering martyr saints will reign completely with Christ as they sit on thrones with him (2:27; 3:21). Beale is correct that we should not see the figure 1,000 as a literal chronological number, but as an ideal symbol.[113]

Will saints who have not, or who will not die as martyrs not also reign with Christ? Without question they will, for this is the story of the New Testament. They are not however, the concern of John in Revelation. He is writing to reassure the saints who are about to die for their faith. They needed to know with certainty that they were secure in Christ.

Rev 20:5. *(The rest of the dead did not come to life until the thousand years were ended.)* *This is the first resurrection.* 20:5 poses a considerable problem for commentators. Who are the rest of the dead, and why are they included here? Appropriately, the NIV places the first sentence of this verse in parentheses. Interestingly, Aune proposes that this sentence was an annotation added later at a final stage of composition.[114] I am in agreement with the NIV that it is best to see this as a parenthetical statement around which we can read regarding the saints who came to life and reigned for a thousand years (20:4) and to the statement that this is the first resurrection. "This" then connects 20:5b directly to the saints who came to life in 20:4. Accordingly, the coming to life of the saints and their reigning must be what John had in mind with *the first resurrection.* The expression, *this is the first resurrection* occurs only twice in Revelation, both in a contiguous context with the saints who reign with Christ.[115] Aune points out that the word *anastasis, resurrection,* is used in Revelation *only* of the saints, whereas the resurrection of Jesus is referred to as his being *the one who died and is now living for ever* (1:18). *Anastasis* strangely is not used of Jesus' resurrection in Revelation. A *second resurrection* is not specifically mentioned in Revelation but Aune sees in 20:12-13 a possible reference to such a resurrection although the term is not used there. "Antithetically, though a *second* death is mentioned four times (2:11; 20:6, 14; 21:8), no mention is made of a first death"[116] In the mind of some, the possible reference to two resurrections poses a serious hermeneutic problem, notably in regard to the discussion of Premillennial and Amillennial interpretations. Revelation only mentions a first resurrection and not a second resurrection, while Premillennialists require two resurrections of the same type, presumably a physical resurrection, the one specifically mentioned here and another at the general resurrection.

Amillennial interpretations of the first resurrection usually interpret this as a spiritual resurrection with Premillennial interpretations requiring a physical resurrection since the final resurrection will be a physical resurrection. One might question whether the general resurrection involves a physical resurrection or speaks rather of a spiritual resurrection, cf. 1 Cor 15. Premillennialists tend to require that both resurrections, that of the saints here and that of all the dead at the final resurrection, be of the same nature. Beale has argued that it is not inconsistent in Scripture and the Jewish literature to speak of a spiritual resurrection in the same context as a physical resurrection (cf. for example Rom 6:4-13 with the spiritual resurrection of the baptized being spoken of on the same context as the physical resurrection of Jesus).[117]

Morris addresses the predilection of Premillennialists to see the first resurrection in the same light as the eschatological final resurrection (which he notes is not described in Revelation as a resurrection). The reference in our present text to the first resurrection, Morris notes, this

> seems to require that it be taken to denote the raising of the martyrs in glory with Christ. It is a strong point in the pre-millennial view that a first resurrection implies a second . . . Other views make the two resurrections of different types, but the pre-millennial view does not. On the other hand John speaks

only of one resurrection. He never speaks of a "second resurrection" to correspond to the first.[118]

Roberts agrees regarding this first resurrection that it should be read in the light of the raising of the martyrs.

> John had seen the resurrection of the two martyred prophets and their rapture to heaven after their martyrdom by the beast (11:11); the raising of the martyrs here is surely the same. Neither is it an earthly bodily resurrection to an earthly millennial reign in Jerusalem with a reincarnated Jesus. It is the resurrection of their cause. John calls it *the first resurrection* to differentiate it from the general resurrection at the end prior to the great judgment day (20:12,13). It is a limited and unique event: *the rest of the dead* (even the saints not martyred for the testimony of the word of God) *lived not until the thousand years were ended.*[119]

Caird, likewise, sees in the first resurrection a reference to the martyrs. He states that John "requires not one but two resurrections: *the first resurrection* restores the martyrs to life for their millennial reign, the second brings all the dead before the great white throne."[120]

Since John does not speak of a second resurrection, I conclude that he is using the first resurrection in a spiritual sense regarding the resurrection of the martyred saints who have been raised to sit with Christ on thrones, symbolically judging those who brought about their martyrdom. The first resurrection is a symbol of their vindication and victory over Satan and the beast. That there will be a general resurrection at the eschatological end and a final judgment John takes for granted, but at this point his concern is for the saints facing martyrdom, reassuring them that they need have no fear, for if they die for Christ they will be raised with him to sit with him on thrones in his kingdom. In our understanding of this challenging text we should not overlook John's use of proleptic eschatological references when referring to events taking place in the context of the first century saints in Asia.

Perhaps Aune is correct in connecting the parenthetical statement regarding *the rest of the dead* with the general resurrection and final judgment of the dead in 20:11-15 rather than with the first resurrection.[121] Opinions range however, regarding the rest of the dead from a reference to all of the saints who die faithfully, to those who die unfaithfully after confessing Caesar as Lord and bear his number, to all of the dead who will be judged for their sins and evil. We will shortly consider this anomaly or parenthetical comment regarding the rest of the dead in our comments on 20:11-15.

Rev 20:6. *Blessed and holy are those who have part in the first resurrection. The second death has no power over them, but they will be priests of God and of Christ and will reign with him for a thousand years.* At 14:13 John had already recorded a blessing on those who die in the Lord. He now recalls that blessing here in conclusion to his discussion of their reigning completely with Christ, reinforcing the view that the first resurrection refers to the "spiritual" resurrection of the martyrs to reign with Christ. We have already encountered reference to the second death (2:11) where Jesus had promised the church at Smyrna that those who conquered need have no fear of the second death. At 2:11 we observed that the second death referred to the final judgment. John repeats that promise here at 20:6 by stating that the second death has no power over the martyrs, *first* since they have already died, but *primarily* because they have experienced the first resurrection and are sitting with Christ on thrones reigning completely (figuratively for a thousand years) with Christ. They, like Christ, are faithful and true. That John combines the priestly and kingly metaphors here should come as no surprise since he has already laid the foundation for this at 1:6; 5:10. In their kingdom role they offer their lives as sacrifices to God and Christ. Christ became king because he died on the cross, so the martyrs share in that royal and priestly role by dying faithfully to Christ.

Summary of Rev. 20:4–6

John saw thrones and seated on them were the martyrs who had been slain because of their testimony regarding Jesus. They had not worshipped the beast and received his number on their foreheads and hands. They came to life in a proleptic spiritual resurrection and were reigning completely with Christ. This spiritual resurrection was a vindication of their suffering. They are blessed in that the second death, the final judgment, has no power over them, for they have offered their lives as priests in the kingdom as a sacrifice to God. The rest of the dead do not share in this blessing, but await the general resurrection and the final judgment. This paragraph should be seen in dynamic tension with the previous one of the binding of Satan for the one thousand years. It demonstrates the vindication of the saints in contrast to the judgment on Satan. Satan is powerless, bound and in prison; the saints are powerful, reigning with Christ.

THE LOOSING AND JUDGMENT OF SATAN—REV. 20:7–10

When the thousand years are over, Satan will be released from his prison [8] *and will go out to deceive the nations in the four corners of the earth—Gog and Magog—to gather them for battle. In number they are like the sand on the seashore.* [9] *They marched across the breadth of the earth and surrounded the camp of God's people, the city he loves. But fire came down from heaven and devoured them.* [10] *And the devil, who deceived them, was thrown into the lake of burning sulfur, where the beast and the false prophet had been thrown. They will be tormented day and night for ever and ever.*

The *when* should not be read as a temporal statement, but as in the apocalyptic tradition we should ask what the *when* means. John is not setting a chronological sequence between 20:1–3 and 7–10. He is emphasizing that the binding and loosing of Satan represent a condition, not a time period. *When* implies that although Satan has been completely limited in his ability to use Rome to deceive the nations, he still has a future, although limited, and other work he will do. When Satan is defeated in one place, for instance, as in heaven under Michael (12:7-9), he moves on to other sinister works and regions, such as earth, attacking the messianic woman and messianic community (12:13-17). He will continue in this, opposing himself to God until he is finally destroyed, which will be described by John in the pericope that follows. The statement that *Satan will be released from his prison* defines the binding of Satan and casting him into prison at 20:2–3 not as total limitation or restriction of Satan's activity, but only a partial one in regard to Rome.

Rev. 20:8. Upon his release from prison, Satan goes *out to deceive the nations in the four corners of the earth—Gog and Magog—to gather them for battle. In number they are like the sand on the seashore.* Signifying that *the nations in the four corners of the earth* is a symbolic reference, John describes the nations as *Gog and Magog*.[122] Although Gog and Magog at one time (cf. Ezek 38-39) represented a real historical nation named Magog, whose king was Gog (Magog means "the land of Gog"[123]), by the late Jewish and apocalyptic period Magog and Gog had become symbols of nations that rebelled against God, or a symbol of the resilience of evil nations who rise up against God. Aune and Osborne point to the fact that Gog and Magog have been variously defined by scholars indication that attempts to specifically identifying the nations in contemporary times has been problematic.[124] Such attempts are unnecessary since John is speaking symbolically. Demonstrating still further that John is using Gog and Magog metaphorically, he speaks as though they were two nations, not one. Several similar options have been proposed ranging from Gog and Magog being demonic forces, the resurrected dead, and all the dead not mentioned previously. Caird speaks meaningfully to John's symbolism in Gog and Magog and the Ezekiel tradition.

> Magog is mentioned among the northern nations in the genealogy of Noah (Gen. x. 2), and Josephus identified them as the Scythians (Ant. 1. 6. 1; cf. Jub. viii. 25). Ezekiel accepts this northern origin, but with him it is more mytho-logical than a geographical north, the source of an archetypal enemy of whom all historic foes from the north were but a shadowy imitation . . . . It is equally immaterial that Ezekiel's 'Gog of the land of Magog' has in John become a pair of nations: the same transformation is found in the *Sibylline Oracles* (iii. 512) and frequently in the Talmud, where Gog and Magog are said to be the rebel-lious nations of Ps ii. (*Ber.* , 10a, 13a; *Shab.* 118a; *Pes.* 118a; *Meg.* 11a) . . . What does matter is that already in Ezekiel Gog and Magog are symbols of a pro-found spiritual truth.[125]

John certainly was aware of Psalms 135 and 136 in which the psalmist praises God for his deliverance of Israel from Gog, the king of Bashan and all the kingdoms of Canaan. As God had delivered his people from Gog in the past, so now too he will deliver them from any present or future "Gogs". That the nations Satan gathers are numberless as *the sand on the seashore* indicates the breadth of the resilience of evil and the willingness of people to be seduced by Satan.

Rev. 20:9. *They marched across the breadth of the earth and surrounded the camp of God's people, the city he loves. But fire came down from heaven and devoured them.* There is a tendency of futurists to equate this military move with some future battle of Armageddon, but this again is reading into Revelation a view that is neither necessary nor in keeping with the point John is making. This *demonic* army surrounds **the camp of God's people** which John describes as **the city he loves**. The camp is a term which had been used in Jewish tradition to speak of the military camp of God's people who had been purified, who were chaste, and who were ready for battle (cf. 14:4; Num 5:1-4; 31:19; Deut 23:14; and the *Qumran War Scroll*, *1QM* 3:5-9, 10:1-8).[126] It is unlikely that by **the city he loves** John had in mind the new Jerusalem that he shortly describes as coming down from heaven. At this point the end has not occurred and the new city is not yet part of the narrative. Several proposals have been made in attempts to identify this city, and Charles went so far as to propose that this expression was misplaced in his radical rearrangement of 19 and 20.[127] Caird argues against this, saying that such radical surgery is not necessary since John did not have the new Jerusalem in mind. The city God loves merely stands for the church or God's people wherever they are gathered and are subject to Satan's attacks.[128] The point John is making is that Satan still has great power and will continue to gather evil forces in attempts to destroy God's people. Revelation suggests this as Satan's *modus operandi*, for he went to war with Michael and his angels and was defeated, he went to war on the churches in Asia and was defeated, and he will continue to make war on God's people with the same result; he will be defeated and in the end be cast into the lake of fire. The **fire came down from heaven and devoured them** is a symbolic way of describing Satan's ultimate defeat at the hands of God. It recalls Ezekiel's description of God's judgment on Gog and Magog (Ezek 38:17-23) where God pours out fire and brimstone on Gog. The *Sibylline Oracles* are replete with similar outpourings of fire and brimstone on God's enemies (*Sib. Or*. 2:196-383; 3:84-386; 4:169-180; *passim*).

Rev. 20:10. *And the devil, who deceived them, was thrown into the lake of burning sulfur, where the beast and the false prophet had been thrown. They will be tormented day and night for ever and ever.* The devil, Satan, the dragon, the enemy of God's people is finally judged and brought down in defeat and judgment. I am again impressed by the striking simplicity of John's description of this significant event. It reminds us of his description of God bringing Babylon/Rome down in one hour, in fact with one word (Rev 18). Now when we come to God's judgment and destruction of Satan, John does not enter into great detail, he surprisingly merely mentions it in passing. But he does not miss the import of this event, for Satan is decisively judged and thrown into **the lake of burning sulfur** to join the beast and the false prophet whom he had used as his agent to attack God's people. The **lake of burning sulfur**, that is, hell, is the ultimate place of eternal torment and suffering prepared by God for Satan and his followers.[129] There in the lake of fire Satan joins the beast (Rome) and the false prophet (the Imperial Cult and the great harlot). Mounce adds an interesting comment here referring to the dragon, the beast, and the false prophet as the unholy trinity whose torment continues unceasingly, "day and night for ever and ever."[130] He adds a comment by Ladd observing that "this figure describes in picturesque language a 'real fact in the spiritual world: the final everlasting destruction of the forces of evil which have plagued men since the garden of Eden'."[131]

John does not go into a detailed theological description of hell other than to paint it in the worst images imaginable. The main point, however, is that it represents eternal ruin, and there Satan has been doomed for eternity. He is not in this scene bound or limited in the Abyss, but is decisively cast down into hell itself there to experience the worst kind of suffering possible, eternal torment.

Beginning with 1:1–3, Revelation has not been primarily concerned with the final judgment, but with God's judgment on Rome and his vindication of the suffering saints. In order to bring his theodicy to closure, however, John must mention the final judgment and destruction of Satan (20:11–15). Although not a major theme in Revelation, it is vital to the message in that it brings closure to the human tragedy that John portrays.

THE SEVENTH UNNUMBERED DESCRIPTION OF GOD'S WRATH: THE FINAL JUDGMENT—REV. 20:11–15.

The Text
Then I saw a great white throne and him who was seated on it. Earth and sky fled from his presence, and there was no place for them. [12] And I saw the dead, great and small, standing before the throne, and books were opened. Another book was opened, which is the book of life. The dead were judged according to what they had done as recorded in the books. [13] The sea gave up the dead that were in it, and death and Hades gave up the dead that were in them, and each person was judged according to what he had done. [14] Then death and Hades were thrown into the lake of fire. The lake of fire is the second death. [15] If anyone's name was not found written in the book of life, he was thrown into the lake of fire.

Rev. 20:11. Again, the expression *then I saw*, kai eidon, does not present a chronological sequence of events, but simply introduces a new vision.[132] John is not setting a chronological timetable, but is presenting a series of visions that explain the vindication of the saints and the judgment of the beast, the false prophet, and Satan. He connects this scene to the parenthetic statement that the rest of the dead did not come alive with the martyrs at the first resurrection (20:5), describing now in this paragraph the final judgment of all men. Up to this point John has described in graphic detail God's judgment of Rome, the beast, and the false prophet. In the previous pericope John described the judgment of Satan (20:7–15), which obviously takes place at the final judgment of the world. Now in this pericope he brings his theodicy to closure by describing the final judgment of all mankind. The description of the final judgment of Satan and all mankind is included in John's narrative in order to bring the theodicy of Revelation to meaningful closure, for God cannot be a righteous God if he does not judge evil and destroy it forever. Before a new system without evil, suffering, and death (21:1, a new heaven and a new earth) can come about, the source of all evil, Satan, and all forces opposed to God, including all men who have not honored God and submitted to his will, have to be judged and destroyed. Thus John includes a brief description of this final act of a righteous God.

The new vision John sees is a *great white throne and him who was seated on it*. Osborne correctly observes that "all are agreed that this will occur at the end of history," namely the final judgment. No description is given to the *him* that sits on the great white throne, for by now the reader knows and anticipates that it is God, the almighty sovereign of creation that sits on this throne. So majestic and awesome is he that *earth and sky fled from his presence, and there was no place for them*. Since this expression is followed by *there was no place for them* it may point forward to 21:1 where the old heaven and earth have passed away, indicating that in the aftermath of God's judgment the physical earth with all of its problems will be no more. N. T. Wright poses several challenging possibilities of what will happen to this earth and what the new heavens and earth will look like.[133] Aune[134] considers that some parallel may be found to a Greek translation of the Hebrew of Dan 2:35 which may point to a destruction of the physical earth. However, John adds this expression to magnify the awesome nature of the God who sits in judgment on all his beings. This is the only time in Revelation that the heavenly throne is described as being white, but we are by now familiar with the significance of the color white (white robes, a white horse, white clouds) which signifies purity and triumph.

John states *and I saw the dead, great and small, standing before the throne*. Aune suggests that the introductory formula *kai eidon*, *and I saw* "functions to focus on the specific group named here."[135] Why the living are not mentioned seems to indicate that John has moved forward to what follows the second coming of Christ, the *parousia*, when those that are alive will meet him in the air together with those who have died and gone ahead (1 Thess 4:13-18) and beyond the general resurrection, to the final judgment scene. Aune states that John presupposes the general resurrection but does not specifically mention it.[136] This would be in keeping with John's style of focusing on the themes that are important to his theology and not every detail and chronological concern. Variations of great and small are not uncommon in both Revelation and the Old Testament and indicate that those of both high and low position will stand before the judgment seat of God. This would be particularly pleasing to those saints who had just been degraded by the supposed great in the world and disgraced in public. Now the great are reduced to the small in one category, all standing before the throne of the Almighty Sovereign of the universe awaiting the books of judgment to be opened. The symbolism of the opened books should warn against reading too much detail into this scene.

It is not necessary to see the various judgment scenes in Revelation in a chronological order. John revisits the judgment scenes from several perspectives according to his purpose. He has no need or design to describe in detail the order of things or the precise details, only to mention the fact that all, great and small, will be judged when the books are opened.

With the statement *and books were opened* John connects with the similar statement of Daniel 7:10 and the Jewish tradition that held that books would be opened at the judgment, one for the deeds of the righteous and the other for the deeds of the wicked

(Esth. 6:1; Ps. 56:8; Isa. 4:3; 65:6; Jer. 22:30; Mal. 3:16; *Jubilees* 30:22; *Ascension of Isaiah* 9:22). The connection of 20:12 with Daniel 7:9–10 is significant in view of the similarity of words of Daniel: "As I looked, thrones were set in place, and the Ancient of Days took his seat. His clothing was as white as snow; the hair of his head was white like wool. His throne was flaming with fire, and its wheels were all ablaze. [10]A river of fire was flowing, coming out from before him. Thousands upon thousands attended him; ten thousand times ten thousand stood before him. The court was seated, and the books were opened." In addition to the general reference to books of judgment, John focuses now on one other book that would be of particular interest and meaning to the saints facing martyrdom: *another book was opened, which is the book of life. The dead were judged according to what they had done as recorded in the books.* At 13:8 and 17:8 the book of life belonged to the Lamb, and those who worshipped the beast were not written in the book of life. At 21:27 John will return to the book of life with another statement regarding the new Jerusalem, which would be of have significant meaning for the saints: *Nothing impure will ever enter it, nor will anyone who does what is shameful or deceitful, but only those whose names are written in the Lamb's book of life.* Those who had committed the lie, confessing that Caesar is Lord, will have no part in this city, only those whose names are written in the Lamb's book of life. Martyrs have no place in the city of this world, Rome; their names have been excised from the citizen roles of this city, but they will have a place in the city of heaven, the new Jerusalem.

The concept that all will be judged on that great judgment day according to their deeds is a prominent New Testament theme. However, this text is not a full theology of the atonement. John is not writing within a Pauline context of salvation by grace and not by works, but in the larger context of the Judeao-Christian view that all will be judged by God according to their life deeds. (For reference to Scriptures teaching judgment by works or deeds, cf. Matt. 16:27; Rom. 14:12; 1 Cor. 3:12-15; 1 Pet. 1:17.) John adopts the broader view without departing from either the Christian doctrine of atonement by grace or the context of Revelation, where all will be judged by their confession of faithfulness to Jesus and denial of the confession that Caesar is Lord. Surely Daniel 12:1–2 must have been in John's mind as he penned the words of 20:12: "At that time Michael, the great prince who protects your people, will arise. There will be a time of distress such as has not happened from the beginning of nations until then. But at that time your people—everyone whose name is found written in the book—will be delivered. [2] Multitudes who sleep in the dust of the earth will awake: some to everlasting life, others to shame and everlasting contempt."

Rev. 20:13. *The sea gave up the dead that were in it, and death and Hades gave up the dead that were in them, and each person was judged according to what he had done.* Death and Hades appeared in Revelation previously associated with the Fourth Horseman of the Apocalypse, 6:7. Previously at 1:18 John had written of Jesus holding the keys of death and Hades. As in 6:7 John again personifies death and Hades indicating the full realm of the dead. All of the dead, all who have ever lived, will face the final judgment. Since the sea in Revelation symbolizes a source of evil (13; 21:1) it is possible that John has in mind here that even the source of evil must relinquish its demonic world to the final judgment. Aune[137] draws attention to ancient coastal cultures (Greek, Roman, and Palestinians) who saw land and sea as abodes of the dead. There is some speculation among commentators as to what death represents, with opinions ranging from death as the last enemy to be destroyed (1 Cor 15:54), to death and Hades as symbols of demonic forces; death as a metonymy referring to the unbelievers due for perdition; or merely physical death. As mentioned above I understand death to include all who will experience the final resurrection and now stand before the judgment seat of God. Death thus includes all mankind as they stand before the great white throne. Aune sees "death from the sea and from Hades as a doublet of the judgment of all the dead before the great white throne."[138] Osborne suggests that since death and Hades may also represent the malignant forces of demonic evil this may be John's way of expressing the total judgment of all evil forces.[139]

Rev. 20:14–15. *Then death and Hades were thrown into the lake of fire. The lake of fire is the second death.* [15] *If anyone's name was not found written in the book of life, he was thrown into the lake of fire.* The lake of fire and the second death are Johannine metaphors for the final judgment. The beast and the false prophet have already been judged and thrown into the lake of fire (19:20). Satan has likewise been judged and thrown into the same "place" or condition of eternal judgment (20:10). Now all evil beings, demonic and human who are opposed to God, are condemned to this same lake of fire. We should not see these as three or two separate judgments, for it is not John's intention to set out a chronology of judgments. These are simply repeated descriptions of judgment to demonstrate that Satan and all his agents and demonic forces are judged and condemned to the fires of hell. John concludes this scene in 20:15 with the statement that everyone whose name has not been written in the Lamb's book of life will be condemned to the same fires of hell.

Summary of the Authority of God over Evil Exercised —Rev. 17:1–20:15

This section reminds us that the time for warning judgments calling on Rome and evil men to repent has passed; the seven bowls have been poured out; and now in a succession of judgment visions and scenes, John describes God's judgments of evil more specifically, including a glimpse of the final judgment. We have encountered in a succession of visions and scenes the great harlot seated on the seven-headed beast, the coming and going of seven and eight kings who all end up in perdition, the doom of Babylon/Rome described along with the lament of those who have been seduced by the power and riches of Rome. We witnessed the marriage feast of the saints and the Lamb, the binding of Satan and reign of the slain saints in heaven, the judgment of the beast, the false prophet, and the kings opposed to God, and the final judgment and condemnation of Satan. Finally, in brief symbolic terms John has described the final judgment in order to bring his theodicy to closure. It remains now in the following section to learn of the great reward of the faithful saints in the new Jerusalem with God.

Chapter 11

The New Order of Things

The Church in Perfection

21:1–22:5

Now that Satan and his agents have been condemned to the lake of fire a new system or as John puts it, a new heaven and earth, are possible. In this new system in which Satan and all demonic forces have no place, in which the sea as a source of evil is no more, there is no more suffering, tears, persecution, death, and mourning, for all things have been made new. The saints are home with God and He personally takes care of them. They are sustained by the river and tree of life. The Church in Imperfection has by the grace of a loving God become the Church in Perfection.

Osborne (*Revelation*, 726) observes that "Not just the Book of Revelation but the whole Bible has pointed to this moment. . . ." Every stage and vision has been working toward the goal of the new heaven and new earth."It is especially connected to the seven letters to the seven churches for any of the promises given to the 'overcomers' (2:7, 11, 17, 26-28; 3:5, 12, 21) are fulfilled in the vision of the 'new heaven and new earth." He cites Hemer (*The Letters to the Seven Churches*, 16) who observed that the perfected state of the church is implicitly contrasted with the imperfections of the seven churches in Rev 2 and 3.

In the penultimate level of the chiastic structure, level VII parallels level I and describes the ideal church as having reached its goal in heaven. This should be the goal of every church and Christian in every age, but in the context of first-century Asia, it would be encouragement to those uncertain of their ultimate goal.

Prologue 1:1–20
    I. The Church in Imperfection (2:1–3:22)
    Seven Letters to the Seven Churches

II. The Authority of God over Evil Explained (4:1–8:6)
  Seven Seals on the Scroll
    III. The Warning Judgments (8:1–11:19)
      Seven Trumpets
        IV. The Lamb—God's Answer to Evil (12:1–14:20)
          Seven Unnumbered Figures
        V. The Consummated Judgments (15:1–16:21)
          Seven Bowls of Wrath
      VI. The Authority of God over Evil Exercised (17:1–20:15)
        Seven Unnumbered Descriptions of God's Judgments
  VII. The Church in Perfection (21:1–22:5)
    Seven Unnumbered Descriptions of the Church in Perfection
Epilogue 22:6–21

The New Heaven and New Earth

The Text

21:1–8. *Then I saw a new heaven and a new earth, for the first heaven and the first earth had passed away, and there was no longer any sea. ² I saw the Holy City, the new Jerusalem, coming down out of heaven from God, prepared as a bride beautifully dressed for her husband. ³ And I heard a loud voice from the throne saying, "Now the dwelling of God is with men, and he will live with them. They will be his people, and God himself will be with them and be their God. ⁴ He will wipe every tear from their eyes. There will be no more death or mourning or crying or pain, for the old order of things has passed away."*

⁵ He who was seated on the throne said, "I am making everything new!" Then he said, "Write this down, for these words are trustworthy and true."

⁶ He said to me: "It is done. I am the Alpha and the Omega, the Beginning and the End. To him who is thirsty I will give to drink without cost from the spring of the water of life. ⁷ He who overcomes will inherit all this, and I will be his God and he will be my son. ⁸ But the cowardly, the unbelieving, the vile, the murderers, the sexually immoral, those who practice magic arts, the idolaters and all liars—their place will be in the fiery lake of burning sulfur. This is the second death."

21:1–8 serves as a transitional passage into the discussion of ***the new heaven and new earth*** and ***the Holy City, the new Jerusalem,*** namely, the church in its perfected state in heaven. Aune[1] points to an interesting chiastic structure in 21:1–5 regarding the new heavens and new earth that reinforces the contrast between the *new* (*kainos*), which is created by God, and the *first* (*prōtos*), which *passes away* (*apēlthan*):

a *new* (*kainos*) heaven and *new* (*kainē*) earth (1)
  b *first* (*prōtos*) heaven, earth, and sea have *passed away* (*apēlthan*) (1)
    c the sea exists *no longer* (*ouk estin*) (1)
      d the holy city descends from heaven (2)

d¹ God dwells with his people (3–4)
c¹ death exists *no longer* (*ouk estin*) (4)
b¹ *former things* (*ta prōta*) have *passed away* (*apēlthan*) (4)
a¹ God creates everything *new* (*kaina*) (5)

21:1 John draws on a rich Jewish and apocalyptic tradition in regard to the ***new heaven*** and ***new earth,*** for instance, Isa 65:17 and 66:22, where at Isa 65:17 Isaiah had prophesied that God would *create* a *new heavens* and a *new earth.*[2] The Biblical and apocalyptic tradition is divided as to whether the new heaven and new earth is to be a recreation or a renovation[3] which has led to scholars holding different views on this point. Caird, Bauckham, Prigent,[4] and others, favor a renovation, while Aune and Osborne[5] favor a new creation rather than a renovated one. Others such as Mounce, Beasley-Murray, and Beale speak of a figurative use of new and which emphasizes the *qualitative difference* between the two heavens and earth. The qualitative view is possibly reinforced by the use of the word *kainos,* for *new* which in normal New Testament usage in eschatological contexts indicates *newness in quality* rather than a *temporal* usage. Beale observes that in redemptive-historical or eschatological contexts the qualitative difference predominates. Arndt and Gingrich support this possibility, "in the sense that what is old has become obsolete, and should be replaced by what is new. In such a case *the new is, as a rule, superior in kind to the old . . . Esp. in eschatol. usage k. ouranon, k. gē* (Is 65:17; 66:22) 2 Pt 3:13; Rv 21:1."[6] Since we have throughout Revelation been in cosmic visions that are figurative I would favor the figurative usage here in regard to old and new. The ***first heaven and the first earth had passed away***, that is, *a new kind of system* is coming in which the ***sea*** as a source of evil no longer exists since Satan has been judged and cast into the lake of fire. A new system without Satan, evil, suffering, persecution, and death is what John has in mind, namely a system of qualitative difference.

21:2. In his vision John now sees ***the Holy City, the new Jerusalem, coming down out of heaven from God, prepared as a bride beautifully dressed for her husband.*** That John describes "the church in perfection" as the Holy City and the new Jerusalem is not surprising since these terms have a long tradition in Jewish literature as the ideal future place of God's people. In several texts (e.g., Isa. 52:1–2; 65:18; Ezek. 48:35; Zech. 8:3; 14:1–11) the old Jerusalem of rebellion is contrasted with the new eschatological Jerusalem of hope or the "city of truth" (Zech. 8:3), where God would dwell. Aune points out that "the earliest occurrence of the phrase 'Jerusalem the holy city' is found in Isa 51:1, and of the holy city in Isa 48:2. Thereafter there is an increasing tendency to use the term 'holy city' to mean Jerusalem.'"[7] In the context of Revelation, the new Jerusalem, the holy city, the one that comes down out of heaven in which "the church in perfection," is contrasted with Babylon the Great, "the great city allegorically called Sodom and Egypt where their Lord was crucified" (11:8). Aune adds that there is a "striking widespread reluctance" in early Jewish literature to refer to the eschatological city as Jerusalem.[8] The exact expression ***the New Jerusalem*** is found only twice in the Bible (3:12 and 21:2).

However, Jerusalem is either directly spoken of, or alluded to, as the Holy City six times on the Bible. In Revelation John speaks of the Holy City four times, but in each case it is not used of the old earthly Jerusalem but symbolically either of the people persecuted for forty-two months (11:2) or the heavenly, or eschatological city (21:2; 10; 22:19). It is obvious that the Holy City, the new Jerusalem in this text is a reference to a new heavenly system, or "place," where "the church in perfection" is found, or the city in which God dwells with his people, since John explicitly states at 21:3 that *he will live with them. They will be his people, and God himself will be with them and be their God.* There are those[9] who suggest that the city is in fact the people themselves in whom God dwells, but this is not what John writes.[10]

Pointing back to 19:7, 8 and his discussion of the Bride of the Lamb celebrating at the marriage feast, John now describes the glory of the holy city in terms of the city being *prepared as a bride beautifully dressed for her husband.* Added to this image of a bride beautifully dressed John speaks of a new Jerusalem, a holy city. The mixing of metaphors to describe the glorious future of the saints is intentional. Here at 21:2 and later at 21:9-14 John portrays the beauty of the bride as a holy city having the glory of God with radiance like precious jewels. Beale makes a significant point to the discussion of the combination of the mixed metaphors of bride and the new Jerusalem.

> John's addition of "new" to "holy city, Jerusalem" is also derived from Isaiah.
> Isa. 62:1–2 refers to "Jerusalem" as that which "will be called by a new name"
> at the time of its end-time glorification. This new name is then explained in
> Isa. 62:3–5 as signifying a new, intimate marriage relationship that Israel will
> have with God. Therefore, the marriage metaphor in Rev. 21:2 explaining the
> significance of "new Jerusalem" is not fortuitous. Already in 3:12 identification
> with Christ's "new name" has been seen to be essentially the same as identi-
> fication with "God's name" and "the name of the new Jerusalem. " All three
> names refer to the intimate, latter-day presence of God and Christ with their
> people, as expressed in 22:3–4 and 14:1–4. . . . 21:3 infers the same idea from
> "new Jerusalem" and the marriage picture: "Behold, the tabernacle of God is
> among people, and he will tabernacle among them, and they themselves will
> be his people, and God himself will be among them."[11]

Any attempt to read into this text a Premillennial or Dispensational view of a physical renewal and return to the Jerusalem of old is forcing an interpretation on the text that is extraneous to the cosmic style typical of the visions of Revelation.

21:3–4. Since it is God himself who speaks in 21:5, the voice that now speaks from the throne is either a mighty angel who speaks with divine authority or one of the four living creatures. *And I heard a loud voice from the throne saying, "Now the dwelling of God is with men, and he will live with them. They will be his people, and God himself will be with them and be their God. [4] He will wipe every tear from their eyes. There will be no more death or mourning or crying or pain, for the old order of things has passed* *away."* In the previous system of persecution, God had been with his people, providing protection for them in a spiritual sense; however, in this new system, or "place," he is with them fully and personally. The word *dwelling* regarding God's dwelling with men draws on a rich heritage from the Old Testament. *Dwelling* is a translation of *hē skēnē tou theou*, an expression from the Septuagint that translates the Hebrew *Shekinah* of God, which was used to describe the cloud and fire of his presence in the tabernacle in the wilderness. It signified that God was with his people in a different manner. He will now personally wipe away all tears of the past, and there will be no more death, mourning, crying, or pain, for the old system in which Satan exercised demonic power has passed away. No longer will there be any need for an intermediary priest or prophet, for God himself will be present.

21:5–8. Now God personally speaks directly from his throne, *"I am making everything new." Then he said, "Write this down, for these words are trustworthy and true."* [6] *He said to me: "It is done. I am the Alpha and the Omega, the Beginning and the End. To him who is thirsty I will give to drink without cost from the spring of the water of life.* [7] *He who overcomes will inherit all this, and I will be his God and he will be my son.* [8] *But the cowardly, the unbelieving, the vile, the murderers, the sexually immoral, those who practice magic arts, the idolaters and all liars—their place will be in the fiery lake of burning sulfur. This is the second death."*

21:5. Unfortunately, the NIV softens the divine announcement, for the Greek actually reads *idou, kaina poiō panta* ("behold, I make all things new"). The expression *idou* ("behold") adds a tone of dramatic seriousness that the NIV misses. By dropping *idou*, the NIV detracts from the significance of the words God now announces. Caird observes that the voice that speaks comes "from the ultimate future which has something urgent to say to the critical present, **Behold, I am making everything new.**"[12] John, as in 1:11, 19; 14:13; 19:9, is told to write words down, this time stressing the reason for writing, for God's ***words are trustworthy and true*** and should not be lost. Osborne, Beckwith, Kraft, Prigent, Mounce, and Aune[13] believe that the command to write words down, especially those that are trustworthy and true as in this verse, 1:11, 19, and 22:6, where the expressions are identical, relate to the message of the entire work of prophecy and not only to the words regarding the finality of God's present action and the bringing in of the new eschatological age. However, along with Caird, Beasley-Murray, Morris, and Beale, I hold that these words relate to the specific words of comfort and assurance God is uttering regarding the final end. Osborne[14], however, to the contrary, observes that this is the second of three statements regarding the truthfulness of the prophecy as a whole. The other two being 19:9 and 22:6. That the expressions are identical does not necessarily argue that they must relate to the same situation. I see 19:9 being specific words of comfort relating to the invitation to the marriage feast of the Lamb, and not to the message of Revelation as a whole. At 22:6 I will hold that the words that are trustworthy and true relate to the prophecy of Revelation as a whole and not to a specific word of encouragement as in 19:9 and 21:5. The statement that ***I am making everything***

new seems to favor a new creation and not a refurbished one. However, the argument regarding a refurbished earth and heaven or a new earth and heaven are a moot point since it is not possible to describe in human terms what the new existence will be like.

21:6 This verse is especially interesting in view of how the phrase *"it is done"* has been translated in our English Bibles. The Greek actually reads *gegonan* ("all things are done.") *Gegonan* is a verb in the perfect tense, third person plural. The perfect tense signifies or stresses a state of affairs resulting from a past action. The third person plural implies that *"all things are completed."* The reason our English translations have translated this as *it is done* at 21:6 is to agree with 16:17, where the Greek reads *gegonen*, correctly translated as third person singular of *ginomai*, *it is done*. What we have in the NIV, RSV, and most English translations, however, is not a good translation principle. *All things are completed* is the better translation at 21:6.[15] At 16:17 the expression related to the pouring out of the seventh bowl of plagues and judgment of Rome as Babylon the Great. Here in 21:6 it relates to God's final judgment of Satan and evil. The old system has passed away and the new has come. All things are now completed; Satan has been judged and the saints are home with Jesus and God. Thus John triumphantly records, *All things have been completed*. What we have in the NIV, RSV, and most English translations, however, is not a good translation principle. *All things are completed* is the better translation at 21:6. (Cf. the comments by Caird, Aune, and Osborne.[16]) At 16:17 the expression related to the pouring out of the seventh bowl of plagues and judgment of Rome as Babylon the Great. Here in 21:6 it relates to God's final judgment of Satan and evil. The old system has passed away and the new has come. *All things are now completed*, Satan has been judged and the saints are home with God. So, John triumphantly records, *All things have been completed*. The eschatological end has come, and the next age can begin. The statement *I am the Alpha and the Omega, the Beginning and the End* is in line with a similar one spoken by the Almighty at 1:8, *"I am the Alpha and the Omega," says the Lord God, "who is, and who was, and who is to come, the Almighty."* With a similar title *the first and the last* added to these terms the divine title is also applied to Jesus at 1:17 and 2:8. All three titles will be applied to Jesus at 22:13 where Jesus says, *I am the Alpha and the Omega, the First and the Last, the Beginning and the End*. The background to these expressions is Isaiah 41:4; 44:6 and 48:12. The full impact of these three divine titles is that God and Jesus are the sovereign beginning and end of all things.

God adds the comforting words *To him who is thirsty I will give to drink without cost from the spring of the water of life*. John will return to this concept as he describes *the river of the water of life* that flows from the throne of God in 22:1. Adding to the promises given to the conqueror at 2:7 regarding the tree of life and hidden manna, the promise of the water of life builds on a firm Jewish and Christian tradition regarding the life giving qualities of the water tradition that began with Moses and Israel in the wilderness at Rephidim (Exod. 17:1-7) and Jesus' discussion with the woman of Samaria at Jacob's well in John 4:7-15. The background to this promise is Isaiah 55:1–3.

The Jewish literary tradition is rich vis-à-vis the life sustaining qualities of living water (Isa. 12:3; 35:7; 41:17, Ps. 23:2; 36:8; Jer. 2:13; Ezek. 34:10-13; Joel 3:18; *Odes of Solomon* 30:1–2; and *Sirach* 55:23f). Drinking *without cost* (*dōrean*) obviously draws on the words of Jesus preserved in the Johannine tradition of John 4:10 and the discussion with the Samaritan woman at the well, where Jesus said to her, "If you knew the gift (*dōrean*, RSV "free gift") of God and who it is that asks you for a drink, you would have asked him and he would have given you living water." Paul also refers to the free gift (*dōrean*) of justification Christians enjoy in Christ (Rom. 3:24).

21:7. God leaves no doubt in the mind of the readers that he is primarily concerned here with the martyrs for he returns to the theme of *conquering* by promising those *who overcome* (NIV) or *who conquer* (RSV) (*nikaō, to conquer*) that they *will inherit all this, and I will be his God and he will be my son. He who overcomes*, *ho nikōn*, is a present participle of *nikaō* emphasizing the continuing process of overcoming or conquering Satan and his agents. Osborne observes that this expression is drawn from the conclusion of each of the seven letters, where it contained the eschatological promises given to all those who were "victorious" over the world with its temptations and sufferings,"[17] namely the Roman and pagan world of Asia." Beale[18] points to other parallels between the seven letters of the church in imperfection and these churches or Christians now in perfection. The seven letters and now these seven blessings promised to the conquering martyr saints forms an *inclusio* and fits in well to the chiastic structure of Revelation. They form a sort of beginning and end of the drama. Among other references Beale cites 2:7 and 22:2 and 2:11 and 21:7,8. These all accommodate the chiastic structure we have been following in our study of Revelation. The story of Revelation opened at 2 and 3 with life giving promises to those who conquer. The story now closes with the same life giving promises. Essentially what those who conquer will inherit is the life giving presence of the Almighty eternal God himself. Furthermore, God himself will be their *personal* God and they will be His *son* (*huios, child or children*). Aune suggests that the singular *huios* could be a form of inclusive language that could be translated *children*.[19] Both Aune and Beale see in this expression a link to the Jewish and Ancient Near Eastern adoption formula and find some connection to the Davidic covenant tradition reflected in 2 Sam 7:14.[20] These Christians who were facing martyrdom needed reassuring that they would be safe and secure when Jesus returned no matter whether they were dead or alive. Emphasizing the enormity of the promise to be their personal God, Osborne observes "Yet the greatest blessing of all is the incredible fact that God will be God to each of them and they will be His children. "He adds that "in a sense, this sums up both the Abrahamic and Davidic covenants."[21]

21:8. To the contrary, *the cowardly, the unbelieving, the vile, the murderers, the sexually immoral, those who practice magic arts, the idolaters and all liars—their place will be in the fiery lake of burning sulfur. This is the second death.* By contrasting those who conquer with those who are cowardly, John has in mind the cowardly who have compromised their faith with the imperial cult and worshipped the beast, or Roman emperor. By compromising their faith, they were in fact **unbelieving**. Their worship of the beast made them corporately murderers, sexually immoral, practitioners of magic arts, idolaters, and especially liars, for they had committed the worst of lies by saying "Caesar is Lord." Osborne observes regarding the cowardly, "While the rest of the list describes the unchurched and wicked who were enemies of Christianity, this term describes those in the church who fail to persevere but give in to the pressure of the world."[22] It was common among ancient philosophers such as the Stoics and Cynics to compile vice codes that are similar to that presented here. Such codes depict the depravity of mankind. Paul's outburst of indignation at pagan immorality is apparent at Romans 1:26-27. Three similar vice codes are found in Revelation (9:21; 21:8; 22:15). The intention of including such a vice code at this point is to heighten awareness of the total depravity of those who are cowardly and who follow the imperial cult[23] and worship the emperor. Therefore, God repeats the warnings of Revelation and pronounces his judgment: those who compromise their faith in Jesus by paying any kind of homage to the emperor as Lord in a religious sense will have **their place . . . in the fiery lake of burning sulfur**. Driving home the severity of this condemnation, God adds that this results in condemnation at the final judgment, for **this is the second death**. Progressively, beginning in 2:11, where Jesus promised that those who conquer would not be hurt by the second death; then at 20:6, where John added that the second death has no power over the martyrs; then at 20:14, where Death and Hades were thrown into the lake of fire; and finally here at 21:8, where the cowards and liars will be thrown into the lake of fire, which is the second death, John paints the awful picture of the end of those who compromise their faith with Satan. The first death was the physical death; the second death is the horrifying final judgment—eternal death and separation from a loving and kind God and eternal torment in the absence of all good.

The New Jerusalem—21:9–22:5

An angel gives John a detailed description of the new Jerusalem in all of its glory. Moving through a description of its gates and foundations, to its impressive measurements, to the precious stones and jewels from which it is built, to its Shekinah, he arrives at a description of its blessings. The contrast between the city of this world (Rome) and the city of God (heaven) is obvious. The destiny of the city of this world is the lake of fire. The destiny of the faithful church and Christians is the city of God. John draws on numerous Old Testament scriptures to describe the city of God, the new Jerusalem.

The Text
[9] *One of the seven angels who had the seven bowls full of the seven last plagues came and said to me, "Come, I will show you the bride, the wife of the Lamb."* [10] *And he carried me away in the Spirit to a mountain great and high, and showed me the Holy City, Jerusalem, coming down out of heaven from God.* [11] *It shone with the glory of God, and its brilliance was like that of a very precious jewel, like a jasper, clear as crystal.* [12] *It had a great, high wall with twelve gates, and with twelve angels at the gates. On the gates were written the names of the twelve tribes*

of Israel. ¹³ *There were three gates on the east, three on the north, three on the south and three on the west.* ¹⁴ *The wall of the city had twelve foundations, and on them were the names of the twelve apostles of the Lamb.*

¹⁵ *The angel who talked with me had a measuring rod of gold to measure the city, its gates and its walls.* ¹⁶ *The city was laid out like a square, as long as it was wide. He measured the city with the rod and found it to be 12,000 stadia in length, and as wide and high as it is long.* ¹⁷ *He measured its wall and it was* ¹⁴⁴ *cubits thick, by man's measurement, which the angel was using.* ¹⁸ *The wall was made of jasper, and the city of pure gold, as pure as glass.* ¹⁹ *The foundations of the city walls were decorated with every kind of precious stone. The first foundation was jasper, the second sapphire, the third chalcedony, the fourth emerald,* ²⁰ *the fifth sardonyx, the sixth carnelian, the seventh chrysolite, the eighth beryl, the ninth topaz, the tenth chrysoprase, the eleventh jacinth, and the twelfth amethyst.* ²¹ *The twelve gates were twelve pearls, each gate made of a single pearl. The great street of the city was of pure gold, like transparent glass.*

²² *I did not see a temple in the city, because the Lord God Almighty and the Lamb are its temple.* ²³ *The city does not need the sun or the moon to shine on it, for the glory of God gives it light, and the Lamb is its lamp.* ²⁴ *The nations will walk by its light, and the kings of the earth will bring their splendor into it.* ²⁵ *On no day will its gates ever be shut, for there will be no night there.* ²⁶ *The glory and honor of the nations will be brought into it.* ²⁷ *Nothing impure will ever enter it, nor will anyone who does what is shameful or deceitful, but only those whose names are written in the Lamb's book of life.*

²²¹*Then the angel showed me the river of the water of life, as clear as crystal, flowing from the throne of God and of the Lamb* ² *down the middle of the great street of the city. On each side of the river stood the tree of life, bearing twelve crops of fruit, yielding its fruit every month. And the leaves of the tree are for the healing of the nations.* ³ *No longer will there be any curse. The throne of God and of the Lamb will be in the city, and his servants will serve him.* ⁴ *They will see his face, and his name will be on their foreheads.* ⁵ *There will be no more night. They will not need the light of a lamp or the light of the sun, for the Lord God will give them light. And they will reign for ever and ever.*

⁶ *The angel said to me, "These words are trustworthy and true. The Lord, the God of the spirits of the prophets, sent his angel to show his servants the things that must soon take place."*

21:9–14. THE CITY

One of the seven angels who had the seven bowls full of the seven last plagues came and said to me, "Come, I will show you the bride, the wife of the Lamb." ¹⁰ *And he carried me away in the Spirit to a mountain great and high, and showed me the Holy City, Jerusalem, coming down out of heaven from God.* ¹¹ *It shone with the glory of God, and its brilliance was like that of a very precious jewel, like a jasper, clear as crystal.* ¹² *It had a great, high wall with twelve gates, and with twelve angels at the gates. On the gates were written the names of the twelve tribes of Israel.* ¹³ *There were three gates on the east, three on the north, three on the south and three on the west.* ¹⁴ *The wall of the city had twelve foundations, and on them were the names of the twelve apostles of the Lamb.*

21:9–10. John is taken by *one of the seven angels who had the seven bowls full of the seven last plagues* or of God's wrath (cf. 16) and is shown the glory of the new city depicted as *the bride, the wife of the Lamb.* The bride of the Lamb is now the beautiful city of God, the holy city Jerusalem. The same introduction of one of the seven angels is also found at 17:1. The similarity of the expressions is not accidental. At 17:1:4 John was introduced to an evil woman, the great harlot who seduced men to worship the beast. In contrast to this woman, the angel, possibly the same angel, introduces another woman, the bride of the Lamb. The angel of 17:1 introduced God's judgment on the harlot. He now introduces the reward of faithfulness to those who have become the bride of the Lamb. John is carried away in a spiritual *condition to a great, high mountain.* Mountain experiences in the Jewish tradition have always been significant. Mount Sinai was where the law was given to Moses; from Mount Nebo Moses was shown the promised land; and Mount Zion was a symbol of God's sovereignty and the place where his kings reigned. At 14:1 the Lamb stood with the church militant and victorious on Mount Zion. The background behind this high mountain image at 21:10 is possibly Ex 40:1f where God gave Ezekiel a vision of the new Temple. Osborne points out that Caird, Beale, et al. "have shown that Jewish tradition placed the final eschatological city on a mountain" (Isa 2:2; 4:1-5; Mic 4:1f; 1 *Enoch* 18:8; 24:1ff; 25:3; *Jub.* 4:26)[24]. It is appropriate, therefore, that John is given a mountain vision of the eschatological city in similar fashion.

21:11. Thus *the holy city Jerusalem* is described as *coming down out of heaven from God.* It is the city in which God will dwell with his saints, a city that God has prepared for them. This is not an earthly city, but a heavenly city clothed in celestial glory. The glory of the city *shone with the glory of God, its brilliance was like that of a very precious jewel, like a jasper, clear as crystal.* The nature of the jewels describes the brilliance of the city whose light is the presence of God. One should not press the transparency of the jewels. What is intended is their beauty and radiance. As already noted, at 21:2 the combination of the bride and the heavenly city are images rich in Jewish tradition of the presence of God's people with him in the eschatological age and of the "tabernacle of God with his people."

21:12–14. The point to be emphasized here is simply not the dimensions of the walls of the city that John will describe at 21:17, but that the walls have twelve gates guarded by twelve angels, three gates per wall. The walls are certainly immense and impressive, securing the city from intrusion. What is noticeable is that there are twelve gates on which *the names of the twelve tribes of Israel* were written. These gates are representative of the twelve tribes of Israel and the people of God. There are also twelve angels guarding the twelve gates. The background to the angels at the gates is possibly Isaiah 62:6, where Isaiah speaks of "watchmen upon your walls." On the gates were inscribed the names of the twelve tribes of Israel. The twelve tribes of Israel are symbolic of God's faithful people (7:4); nothing unclean may enter through the gates (21:27). The angels are apparently the guardians of the city and will grant entry permission only to those whose names have been written in the Lamb's book of life (21:27). Beale and Osborne[25] question whether these angels are guardians and suggest that they may represent the angels of the seven churches of 2 and 3. Since the angels of the seven churches were representative of the spiritual nature of the churches and since the seven letters were addressed to the seven angels, it seems possible that the twelve angels here may be similar representatives of the city who are responsible for the residents of the city. In keeping with Aune I,[26] prefer to see the twelve angels as being responsible for the residents of the city and guardian angels to the city. The walls of the city have twelve foundations with the *names of the twelve apostles of the Lamb* written on them. Including the twelve tribes of Israel and the twelve apostles indicates that God's faithful from all ages may enter and be part of this city.

21:15–21. THE MEASUREMENTS OF THE CITY.

The angel who talked with me had a measuring rod of gold to measure the city, its gates and its walls. [16] The city was laid out like a square, as long as it was wide. He measured the city with the rod and found it to be [12,000] stadia in length, and as wide and high as it is long. [17] He measured its wall and it was [144] cubits thick, by man's measurement, which the angel was using. [18] The wall was made of jasper, and the city of pure gold, as pure as glass. [19] The foundations of the city walls were decorated with every kind of precious stone. The first foundation was jasper, the second sapphire, the third chalcedony, the fourth emerald, [20] the fifth sardonyx, the sixth carnelian, the seventh chrysolite, the eighth beryl, the ninth topaz, the tenth chrysoprase, the eleventh jacinth, and the twelfth amethyst. [21] The twelve gates were twelve pearls, each gate made of a single pearl. The great street of the city was of pure gold, like transparent glass.

At 11:1 John was given a rod and told to measure the temple. The background to this is surely Ezekiel 40:1-5., where Ezekiel was instructed by God to measure the temple. The message was that God knew his people and would protect them. It also stated that the temple and the people were owned by God. In the case of 21:15, although here the angel does the measuring, not John, a similar symbolism is intended. The *measuring rod* is *of gold*, which is appropriate for a city whose roads are paved in *pure gold* (21:21), whose walls are adorned with precious jewels, and whose *gates* are *made of a single pearl*. The nature of the twelve jewels that adorn the walls and foundations has led to considerable speculation. Among the most popular proposals are that these jewels either represent the twelve signs of the Zodiac or eight of the stones on the high priest's breastplate. In either case there are problems of precise agreement, and it is possible that a combination of both major views may help. However, there are other instances in the Jewish tradition where jewels figure, and Osborne is most likely correct that the jewels symbolize the celestial majesty of this great city, depicting the glory of the saints on the basis of the presence of God.[27]

Some discussion is also found relating to the size of the city since a precise measurement of stadia is difficult to determine. The consensus is that the dimension of 12,000 stadia is probably approximately 1,500 miles, in which case the city is enormous (1,500 miles by 1,500 miles, by 1,500 miles). Likewise, the walls are 144 cubits wide or high

(John is not precise). Neither is he precise in the statement that the 144 cubits are a *man's measure, which the angel was using*. The Greek reads *metron anthrōpon, ho estin aggelou*, which can be read as "a man's measurement, which is an angel's measurement." This enigmatic expression may mean that "the angel measuring the walls is using a human measurement of a cubit."[28] Since John has used numbers throughout Revelation symbolically, one should not press the dimensions of the city and wall nor the materials of the city too far other than to conclude that the city is enormous and magnificent. As already observed, the twelve gates and twelve foundations symbolize that this city is open to the faithful from all ages.

21:22–27. THE LIGHT OF THE CITY

[22] *I did not see a temple in the city, because the Lord God Almighty and the Lamb are its temple.* [23] *The city does not need the sun or the moon to shine on it, for the glory of God gives it light, and the Lamb is its lamp.* [24] *The nations will walk by its light, and the kings of the earth will bring their splendor into it.* [25] *On no day will its gates ever be shut, for there will be no night there.* [26] *The glory and honor of the nations will be brought into it.* [27] *Nothing impure will ever enter it, nor will anyone who does what is shameful or deceitful, but only those whose names are written in the Lamb's book of life.*

21:22. Although one of the promises to the seven churches was that the conquerors would be pillars in the temple of God (3:21), now John sees no temple in the city of God, the Holy City, the new Jerusalem. No contradiction is intended other than that the visions and symbolism, like John's kaleidoscope, have changed. John explains the reason for there not being a temple in the city: for *the Lord God Almighty and the Lamb are its temple*. Jewish tradition implied that in the eschatological kingdom there would be no need for a physical temple,[29] and the Christian tradition also implied that the saints themselves would be a holy temple.[30] Osborne adds "We must remember that the major religious feature of the temple was that God resided there."[31]

21:23–26. *The glory of God gives it light, and the Lamb is its lamp*. Building on the temple theme and the temple as the presence of God, John says no light is needed in the city, for the Shekinah of the presence of God and the Lamb provide all the light that is necessary. Isaiah 60 dominates this Shekinah theme of God and Jesus as the light of nations. In particular, Isaiah 60:3, 5, 11, 19 frame John's message here. John has interpreted Isaiah's imagery to shape his vision of the eschatological glory of the saints' eternal destiny. J. N. Oswalt,[32] in his commentary on Isaiah 40–66, argues that by the first century it had become the practice in some Jewish circles to associate this messianic text with Jesus, in particular with John 1:5, 9; 3:19; 8:12; and 12:35–36. Striking among these is Jesus' statement in John 8:12, "I am the light of the world." To Jesus' light of the world expression, John substitutes Isaiah's term "nations" with the more global and inclusive term "world."

The statements of 21:24 and 26, have, however, generated considerable discussion and several divergent views. One of the views is a universalist view as in M. Rissi, J. M.

Vogelgesang, Caird[33], and others. Another in various forms is proposed by Osborne, Beale, Aune, Mounce, Beasley-Murray, and others[34] in which in various forms it is suggested that the kings and nations have somehow repented and now walk willingly into the holy city to pay homage to God. A radical view is to hold that this pericope is an interpolation into the general message of Revelation[35] and as such is an attempt to soften the harsh message of judgment. Although Caird does not support an interpolation, the reason for an interpolation certainly fits Caird's views that John was not a ruthless and pessimistic rigorist.[36]

However, Revelation is not a message of grace and atonement but one of oppression, suffering, vindication, reward, and reassuring saints undergoing cruel martyrdom for their faith. The overall message is one set in a military conflict, war, conquering, and victory. Those aligned with Michael and the Lamb are victorious and will be rewarded by God. Those aligned with Satan and the beast will be conquered and face the full dire penalty of being conquered. They have given their allegiance and wealth over to the enemy, Rome. Now they will symbolically be forced to pay homage as conquered foes to the God, the Lamb, and their army. The martyred saints will be vindicated, even in the presence of their foes (11:12).

It would seem that John's expression, *the nations will walk by its light, and the kings of the earth will bring their splendor into it. . . .*[26] *The glory and honor of the nations will be brought into it*, implies that the nations and kings who had previously opposed God's purposes and who had oppressed the saints now have open access into the holy city. However, these nations and kings have been described as those who followed the beast and the harlot and who bore the mark of the beast. They were depicted as gathering at Armageddon to oppose God and his forces in battle (16:16). Later they were described as representing the resilience of evil in Gog and Magog, who would finally be defeated by the Lamb and cast into the lake of fire (20:7ff). Although everyone unclean who practices immorality will be barred by the angels at the gates of the city from entering the holy city, they now seemingly have open access to the city! However, between 21:24 and[26] John adds *On no day will its gates ever be shut, for there will be no night there*. He then follows these expressions with 21:27: *Nothing impure will ever enter it, nor will anyone who does what is shameful or deceitful, but only those whose names are written in the Lamb's book of life*. Does this imply that the gates are now wide open without controlled access? What complicates the issue is the statement *that the nations will walk by its light*. Are we to understand by this that the nations and kings have been converted and now walk voluntarily and happily in procession into the city? Or does it mean that even the kings and nations who repent may have access into the city?

Rissi, Vogelgesang, and others propose that God's grace and mercy would provide a second chance of redemption resulting in the salvation of all the nations.[37] In agreement with Osborne and Beale, I have serious problems with this view.[38] Contrary to this view are those who propose that these kings and nations represent those kings and others who had responded to God's call for repentance and who had been converted prior to the final judgment of the Lamb (19:11ff).[39] While this is possible, there does not seem adequate indication of this conversion in the narrative of Revelation to form this opinion. Key to this view would be an understanding of how John has used Isa 60:3,"Nations will come to your light, and kings to the brightness of your dawn." 60:11, "Your gates will always stand open, they will never be shut, day or night, so that men may bring you the wealth of the nations — their kings led in triumphal procession." However, in our use of Isa 60:3-11 we should not overlook 60:12, "For the nation or kingdom that will not serve you will perish; it will be utterly ruined. "Are Isaiah and John indicating that the kings and nations have been converted prior to the procession? This does not seem to be the case.

A few commentators observe that some scholars, in an attempt to work through the problems of this text, have identified possible redactional elements or a redactional use of Jewish documents in these verses. However, this approach is unnecessary; for as difficult as this little problem may seem, such proposed redactional elements cannot be understood within the flow of Revelation and the context of the major pericope (21:22–26).[40]

Mounce proposes that John's seeming inclusion of the unregenerate nations and kings may be understood as an element of a prophetic perspective in which the Gentile nations continue on earth after the establishment of the eschatological era.[41] The problem with this view is that it fits more in the theology of a Dispensational view of the Millennium than it does in the context of the theology of Revelation.

An alternate view is suggested in the concept of defeat and plunder taken in a military victory, and we are reminded that Adela Yarbro Collins had drawn attention in her study, *The Combat Mythology in the Book of Revelation*, that Revelation should be interpreted in the context of war imagery. Oswalt has pointed out that Isa 60, notably 60:1-9 is likewise set in the context of a military victory and plunder. The plunder of the nations and their vast wealth which were brought to the altar of God in Isa 60 are symbolic of God's victory over the heathen nations, and the future Messianic glory. John apparently has adapted this war and plunder imagery to emphasize the complete victory over the nations. Beale succinctly points out that we should not interpret this imagery literally but see it in the victory symbolism of Revelation.[42] Mounce observes that the imagery of Apocalypse is inevitably spiritual and not literal.[43] Caird suggests:

> The nations are the heathen, who once had been allowed to trample the holy
> city underfoot, who once were seduced by the great whore, and who were
> finally reduced to subjection by the armies of Christ (xi. 2; xviii. 3, 23; xix. 15).
> The kings of the earth are those over whom Christ has asserted his authority
> only at the cost of untold suffering to his faithful people . . . Those who once
> brought the splendor of their luxury trade to deck the great whore now bring
> their willing tribute to adorn the holy city."[44]

While I like Caird's comment, I disagree with Caird's obvious universalist views in regard to this text. In keeping with Oswalt's observations regarding Isa 60 and the war-plunder imagery, the tribute paid here is not willing but under the constraint of

Christ's absolute victory over the kings of the earth. The concept of splendor and glory here are John's interpretation of the results of the plunder taken from the conquered enemies of God which they are now offering in submission to God as defeated enemies. This interpretation seems to be more in keeping with the symbolism of Revelation and symbolically in keeping with the combat mythology proposed by Adela Yarbro Collins. It does not imply that the nations have open access to the city, nor does it imply a universalist conversion of the nations. The symbolic imagery represents a vindication of the saints and a humiliation of the kings of the earth. Oswalt observes, "In its victory parades ancient Rome customarily displayed all the spoil of the defeated people... the victor in his chariot, leading the highest living official, preferably the king, of the defeated country as his slave. "It is this military plunder imagery that John conveys at 21:23-26 of the kings of the earth bringing their splendor into the city. Once again we see John brilliantly adapting and transforming Old Testament images to suit his needs and message.

Obviously I disagree with Beale's view that this pericope does not refer to the military plunder symbolism of the victorious army as indicated by Oswalt regarding Isa 60. However, I like Beale's observation regarding John's symbolic imagery in this pericope:

> Therefore the perpetual opened gates and the apparent ceaseless pilgrimage of Gentiles into the city throughout eternity are not intended to be understood literally . . . Neither can the image imply that unsaved Gentiles wander for a long time outside the city after Christ's coming and then enter at various times when they come to repentance . . . Implausible also is the idea that the open gates suggest that unsaved Israel will be converted and arise from the lake of fire to enter through the gates sometime after Christ's final parousia. Interestingly, the universalist view of Rissi and Vogelgesang, and others is based on an over literal interpretation of the picture of continually opened gates and the seemingly unceasing pilgrimage of the nations into the city.[45]

While I am sympathetic to the views of Mounce, Caird, Beale, and Osborne regarding the possible conversion of the some of the kings and nations, and their paying due homage to the eternal God and ruler of all, I believe that their views are reading into Revelation a theology of atonement not necessarily in keeping with the stark views of judgment outlined in Revelation. While I certainly agree that God had given the kings and nations adequate opportunity to repent and obey his eternal gospel, they had adamantly refused to do so.

The strength of John's closing observation at the conclusion of this pericope maintains and strengthens the view that only those who have not compromised their faith with the great harlot and who have not become allies with the kings and nations who had succumbed to the seduction of Rome have no part in this city, *Nothing impure will ever enter it, nor will anyone who does what is shameful or deceitful, but only those whose names are written in the Lamb's book of life.*

22:1–5. THE BLESSINGS TO BE FOUND IN THE CITY

Then the angel showed me the river of the water of life, as clear as crystal, flowing from the throne of God and of the Lamb [2] *down the middle of the great street of the city. On each side of the river stood the tree of life, bearing twelve crops of fruit, yielding its fruit every month. And the leaves of the tree are for the healing of the nations.* [3] *No longer will there be any curse. The throne of God and of the Lamb will be in the city, and his servants will serve him.* [4] *They will see his face, and his name will be on their foreheads.* [5] *There will be no more night. They will not need the light of a lamp or the light of the sun, for the Lord God will give them light. And they will reign for ever and ever.*

22:1–2. John pulls together several traditional Jewish views of God's spiritual provision. Ezekiel 47 and Zechariah 14 dominate John's imagery and flow of thought in this pericope. Blending thoughts from these two texts and the garden of Eden story (Gen. 2:4–14), John speaks of the life-sustaining *river of the water of life* (Ezek. 47:1). He adds that this new heavenly river contains no impurity, for it is *clear as crystal*. He supplements this new image with a flashback to the *tree of life* of 2:7 (cf. also Ezek. 47:12) and adds that this new heavenly river is never without fruit, for it bears *twelve crops of fruit, yielding its fruit every month*. Once again John is assuring the martyred saints that God provides eternal life and spiritual sustenance to those who are faithful and who conquer Satan and the beast. In this vision the food provided in the Holy City, coming from the presence of God and the Lamb, addresses the anguish of those facing martyrdom for their faith in Christ. This is reinforced in the statement that the *leaves of the tree are for the healing of the nations*, which also draws on Ezekiel 47 and refers to the fact that healing is available in the presence of God for people of all nations who suffer martyrdom for the worship of God and refusal to worship the emperor.

22:3. The curse of suffering and martyrdom will no longer be a concern to the martyrs, for *no longer will there be any curse* to trouble them. Zechariah 14:9-15 speaks of a curse as a plague in the context of wars against Jerusalem. Zechariah speaks of the deliverance of Jerusalem from the curse of destruction by apostate enemies and promises that the Lord will become king over all the earth. He adds that the wealth of the nations round about Jerusalem will be gathered in abundance. These images from Zechariah must have been prominent in John's thought as he describes the establishment of the new Jerusalem. *The throne of God and of the Lamb will be in the city, and his servants will serve him.* John returns to one of his major theological themes of Revelation: Jesus is fully divine. He sits on God's throne and reigns over God's kingdom, and the saints serve him and share in his reign. Jesus as sovereign king is worthy of worship. Like the Almighty God, Jesus is the first and the last, the beginning and the end, and the Alpha and the Omega. Now in the city of God, the Lamb sits on his throne alongside God, and all of *his servants will serve him.* It is interesting that John refers to the saints as *servants* (*douloi*), but the type of service they offer is that of the bond servant, for this is the meaning of *douloi*. John had introduced this thought at 1:1, when he wrote that God had given the message of Revelation *to show his servants what must soon take place*. Many of the early Christians were slaves of various kinds of masters, some good, some bad. They thus understood the full range of ramifications of the term *doulos*. Refusing slavery to the emperor, they would die as martyrs and by doing this become slaves of God. John wanted the Christians to remember that in reality they were slaves of God, purchased by the blood of Jesus (1 Cor. 6:20; 7:23), having the mark of God on their foreheads, owing allegiance only to God, not to any man, even an emperor. However, now in the Holy City, the new Jerusalem, they are seen worshipping and serving God, not the emperor.

22:4. THEY WILL SEE HIS FACE, AND HIS NAME WILL BE ON THEIR FOREHEADS.

Aune observes regarding this expression:

> The phrase "seeing the face of God" is a metaphor in Judaism and early Christianity for a full awareness of the presence and power of God (Job 33:26; Pss. 10:11; 17:15; 3 John 11), for worshiping God in the temple (Ps. 42:2), or for seeing God in the context of a prophetic vision (Isa. 6:1). . . . In early Judaism and early Christianity the privilege of seeing God is often considered an eschatological blessing (Ps. 84:7; Matt. 5:8; 1 John 3:2; Heb. 12:14; *Jub.* 1:28; 4 *Ezra* 7:91, 98; 1 *Enoch* 102:8; cf. 1 Cor. 13:12).[46]

Seeing the face of God, they now worship him. In contrast to Exodus 33:20, where God had told Moses that no one could see his face and live, now in the eschatological new Jerusalem, God's face or "person" is openly visible. Now the conquering saints, who have God's name written on their foreheads (cf. 3:12; 7:3; 14:1, a sign of ownership and protection) live and worship.

22:5. John draws his themes relating to the New Jerusalem (Rev 21:22ff)together by explaining that in the New Jerusalem **there will be no more night** for the presence of God provides all the light they need. The reference to there being **no more night** most likely draws on Isa 60:19, 20. Aune adds this interesting thought, adding Isa 60:2 as further support of his point.

> 4 *Ezra* 7:38–42 contains a lengthy list of twenty-seven things that will no longer exist in the day of judgment (*sun, moon, stars*, cloud, thunder, lightning, wind, water, air, darkness, evening, *morning*, summer, spring, heat, winter, frost, cold, hail, rain, dew, *noon*, night, *dawn, shining, brightness*, and *light*), "but only the splendor of the glory of the Most High, by which all shall see what has been determined for them." The italicized natural phenomena center on the theme of light (this list was very likely inspired by Gen 8:22 and Eccl 12:2 as well as by Isa 60:19–20).[47]

John's final thought on this topic, *they will reign for ever and ever*, summarizes the major theme of victory and conquering in Revelation, that is, that the saints would reign with Jesus as priests in God's kingdom (cf. 1:6, where John had stressed that Christ *has made us to be a kingdom and priests to serve his God and Father*. Christians are a kingdom of priests who because of Christ's victory over Satan on the cross, both reign on thrones with Christ and as priests offer their lives in sacrifice to God and Christ. John had also alluded to this twice in Jesus' letters to the churches, first at 2:26, where he recorded Jesus' promise that the conqueror would receive a rod of iron and would rule over the nations as Jesus had conquered and now ruled, and then at 3:21, where the conquerors were promised the right to sit on thrones with Christ. The climax of this theme was stressed at 20:4, where John described the conquering saints seated on thrones reigning with Christ for a thousand years, that is reigning completely with Christ. Now John summarizes this theme with the statement that the saints in the new Jerusalem, along with Christ in "fulfillment" of images in Daniel 7, *reign for ever and ever*.

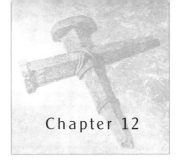

Chapter 12

The Epilogue

22:6–22:21

There is considerable discussion (cf. Aune, vol. 3, pp. 1204 ff; Charles, *Revelation*, vol. 2, pp. 211; Osborne, pp. 777f) regarding the exact parameters of the epilogue, but a reasonable consensus is that 22:6-21 forms the it. Three emphases can be identified in the prologue and epilogue: (1) the concern of God and Christ for the life of the saints, (2) the immediacy of the crisis about to fall on the churches in Asia, (3) the need for an uncompromising faithfulness to Jesus as Lord and Christ. There is some discussion regarding whether 22:6 belongs in the previous discussion of the new Jerusalem or whether it belongs in the epilogue (cf. Aune, vol. 3, pp. 1181ff). I will treat it as part of the epilogue.

The final level of the chiastic structure of Revelation is the epilogue. The epilogue serves as one of the book ends, or points of the *inclusio* in John's literary structure of Revelation. The other part of the *inclusio* is the prologue. The literary style and purpose of a prologue and an epilogue focuses attention on the major themes of the literary composition, or message. Several themes or word groups are prominent in the prologue and epilogue that focus attention on the central message of the book. Some of these are (1) the message of Revelation is sent by God to his servants through angelic intermediaries; (2) the message is in the form of a prophecy; (3) it concerns things that must soon take place; (4) John heard and saw the visions of the message; (5) there is a sense of immediacy, for the crisis time of which the message speaks is near; (6) careful attention is needed to hear the message of the book, which must be read repeatedly and heeded; (7) there is a message of urgency and judgment, for Jesus will come soon, bringing his recompense (8) Jesus is the Alpha and the Omega, the first and the last, the beginning and the end.

There is no apparent structural organization to the themes of the epilogue. Each paragraph, or section, emphasizes a theme developed in the main section of the book.

Prologue 1:1–20
> I. The Church in Imperfection (2:1–3:22)
>   Seven Letters to the Seven Churches
>   II. The Authority of God over Evil Explained (4:1–8:6)
>   Seven Seals on the Scroll
>   III. The Warning Judgments (8:1–11:19)
>   Seven Trumpets
>   IV. The Lamb—God's Answer to Evil (12:1–14:20)
>   Seven Unnumbered Figures
>   V. The Consummated Judgments (15:1–16:21)
>   Seven Bowls of Wrath
>   VI. The Authority of God over Evil Exercised (17:1–20:15)
>   Seven Unnumbered Descriptions of God's Judgments
>   VII. The Church in Perfection (21:1–22:5)
>   Seven Unnumbered Descriptions of the Church in Perfection

Epilogue 22:6–21

THE EPILOGUE

The Text[1]

[6] *The angel said to me, "These words are trustworthy and true. The Lord, the God of the spirits of the prophets, sent his angel to show his servants the things that must soon take place."* [7] *"Behold, I am coming soon. Blessed is he who keeps the words of the prophecy in this book."*

[8] *I, John, am the one who heard and saw these things. And when I had heard and seen them, I fell down to worship at the feet of the angel who had been showing them to me.* [9] *But he said to me, "Do not do it. I am a fellow servant with you and with your brothers the prophets and of all who keep the words of this book. Worship God."* [10] *Then he told me, "Do not seal up the words of the prophecy of this book, because the time is near.* [11] *Let him who does wrong continue to do wrong; let him who is vile continue to be vile; let him who does right continue to do right; and let him who is holy continue to be holy."*

[12] *"Behold, I am coming soon. My reward is with me, and I will give to everyone according to what he has done.* [13] *I am the Alpha and the Omega, the First and the Last, the Beginning and the End.*

[14] *"Blessed are those who wash their robes, that they may have the right to the tree of life and may go through the gates into the city.* [15] *Outside are the dogs, those who practice magic arts, the sexually immoral, the murderers, the idolaters and everyone who loves and practices falsehood.*

[16] *"I, Jesus, have sent my angel to give you this testimony for the churches. I am the Root and the Offspring of David, and the bright Morning Star."* [17] *The Spirit and the bride say, "Come." And let him who hears say, "Come." Whoever is thirsty, let him come; and whoever wishes, let him take the free gift of the water of life.*

[18] *I warn everyone who hears the words of the prophecy of this book: If anyone adds anything to them, God will add to him the plagues described in this book.* [19] *And if anyone takes*

words away from this book of prophecy, God will take away from him his share in the tree of life and in the holy city, which are described in this book.

²⁰ *He who testifies to these things says, "Yes, I am coming soon." Amen. Come, Lord Jesus.*

²¹ *The grace of the Lord Jesus be with God's people. Amen.*

THE AUTHENTICITY AND URGENCY OF THE BOOK.

22:6–7. *The angel said to me, "These words are trustworthy and true. The Lord, the God of the spirits of the prophets, sent his angel to show his servants the things that must soon take place."* ⁷ *"Behold, I am coming soon. Blessed is he who keeps the words of the prophecy in this book."*

22:6–7 The NIV translation here is misleading for the Greek text does not say an angel spoke. It reads *Kai eipen moi*, **And he said to me.** There is considerable debate as to the exact nature of the one who spoke to John. Charles[2] identifies the speaker as Christ, Aune[3] sees the speaker as the angel who spoke at 1:1 and 21:5, Beckwith, Beasley-Murray, and Ramsey Michaels[4] propose one of the angels with the seven bowls of wrath who introduced John to the New Jerusalem. Exactly who it is who spoke is immaterial for it is obvious that he speaks for God and Christ. What is important is his proclamation, *these words are trustworthy and true*. Although the exact or similar words were spoken at 19:9 and 21:5, one should not confuse or conflate the context of the words. At 19:9 the words applied to the blessing associated with the invitation to the marriage feast of the Lamb. At 21:5 the context was the assurance and consolation of the suffering martyrs that all things would be made new, and the expression speaks of a new existence in which there would be no more persecution, suffering, and death. Here at 22:6 the words apply to the total content of the message of the book of Revelation. Since the message of Revelation came directly from God through Jesus Christ and the angels, it obviously must be reliable and true and should be heard and followed with great care. The next statement affirms this fact, echoing the words of 1:1: *The Lord, the God of the spirits of the prophets, sent his angel to show his servants the things that must soon take place*. The message of Revelation, that is, the words spoken by God through his angel regarding what must soon take place, is true and reliable. John repeats here that the message of Revelation relates to things that *must soon take place*. The language is identical to 1:1. The message, as noted at 1:1, is not about the end of the world, but about crises *shortly* (*soon*) to take place in the life of the churches in Asia (*ha dei genesthai en tachei*, "what must soon take place"[5]). Emphasizing the certainty and authority of the prophecy regarding the events *soon* to occur in the life of the churches, John adds that it is *the Lord, the God of the spirits of the prophets* who speaks this message through his angel.

That the message comes from God stresses the urgency and certainty of the revelation that cries out to be heard with earnest attention. The one speaking, presumably an angel, speaks the words of Jesus in order to confirm Jesus' promises to be with his saints through their ordeal. In Jesus' words the angel proclaims the imminent coming of Jesus.[6] Speaking the words of Jesus, the angel promises *Behold, I am coming soon*. Throughout

Revelation John has prophesied that God through Jesus would stand by the churches in the imminent crises they would face and vindicate the saints. He promised them victory and life-giving rewards for their faithfulness. He assured them that he would judge both the unrepentant churches and Rome, the beast, the harlot, and those who worship the beast. In answer to the prayers of the martyred saints who cried out from beneath the altar (6:10), he had responded that they should be patient, for God would in his time and purpose take care of their enemies and avenge them of their blood. His promises included that through their faithfulness they would sit with Jesus on thrones and judge the nations with Jesus. Now he again reassures them of the certainty of his victory and judgment, for Jesus is *coming soon*, *bringing* his *recompense* (22:12) upon the enemies of the church. Attempts to see in these promises of *coming soon* a reference to the end of the world, or the *parousia,* are unnecessary and out of context. That he will come again at the end of the age in judgment of the whole world is certain and a fundamental teaching of the New Testament. It is upon that certainty that John builds his proleptic eschatological theology throughout Revelation.[7] This *coming* in judgment expressed in regard to the seven churches was conditional, based upon their repentance (chs. 2, 3).[8] It is described in Revelation primarily as coming on those who compromise their faith and worship the beast. The coming in judgment on those who persecute the saints and upon the beast and the false prophet is also conditional based on their repentance, which they spurned. Their judgment is sure, as sure as the final judgment at the end of the age; hence, it is pronounced in eschatological terms. At 22:6 the promise of his coming is followed by the promise of a *blessing* on those who *keep* the words of the prophecy in this book. This echoes the promised *blessing* of 1:3, and focuses attention on the urgent message of **this book**, that is, the book of Revelation.

Excursus On "I am Coming Soon": Rev 22:7

The following comments by Caird and Roberts will assist the reader to seriously keep the interpretation of this expression within the context of the socio-religious context of Revelation. I am in agreement with both Caird and Roberts. Regarding this expression at 22:6 Caird states, "After all we have read it is no more possible to think that John had a naïve attitude to this promise than it was when we first heard it proclaimed in the letters to the churches (ii. 5, 16; iii. 11; cf. xvi. 15). He will be there to meet them at their Calvary." (Caird, 283;) To follow Caird we note his comments at 3:10, "The letters are addressed to a critical situation, but do not give any hint that the author felt himself to be living on the eve of the final crisis of history. The church is under attack from inside and outside, and the attack will shortly be drastically intensified. For those who are unprepared for the testing period ahead there is the added menace of Christ's coming in judgment, but that coming is contingent and may not prove to be necessary; and, if it does happen, it will be an event in the spiritual life of the particular church, not the final event of world history. Even in the present letter [to the church in Philadelphia] the promise 'I am coming soon' is best taken with what precedes: the Christian will be kept *safe through the ordeal*, because this is the moment at which Christ will make good to them his promise to come again" (Caird, 54, 283). In a similar vein Roberts observes regarding the crisis of impending persecution, "The timing of that crisis is important to the Revelation and to an understanding of it: *And behold, I am coming soon*. How this promise was been treated in the book has been repeatedly commented on. John believed (along with the rest of the New Testament writers) that he lived in the realized Kingdom of Heaven (1:9), which was the unseen but great reality of his world (cf. Luke 17:21). John and his fellow Christians were a part of the city of the living God, which here and now comes down from heaven (3:12; 21:2). Within that sphere of the living the Lord of creation worked: he was constantly 'coming' in the events of history in fulfillment of his promise to be with his disciples always, to the end of the world. Part of the message of this book has been to warn the church (as in 2:5) that they must not fail to see the coming of the Lord in the events facing the church (cf. 16:15)," Roberts 196-97. Consequently, it is my opinion that the expression "I am coming soon" must be kept in the context of the crises coming soon on the churches in Asia and Jesus' assurance that he will constantly be present with them, walking around in their presence as "lampstand" churches, to support them, and to judge them in their weakness "unless they repent." Jesus had clearly addressed this conditional coming in his seven letters. The expression should not be interpreted in reference to the final *parousia* of Jesus and final judgment.

WORSHIP ONLY GOD, 22:8–11

The Text

[8] *I, John, am the one who heard and saw these things. And when I had heard and seen them, I fell down to worship at the feet of the angel who had been showing them to me.* [9] *But he said to me, "Do not do it. I am a fellow servant with you and with your brothers the prophets and of all who keep the words of this book. Worship God."* [10] *Then he told me, "Do not seal up the words of the prophecy of this book, because the time is near.* [11] *Let him who does wrong continue to do wrong; let him who is vile continue to be vile; let him who does right continue to do right; and let him who is holy continue to be holy."*

22:8– 9. John's words *I, John, am the one who heard and saw these things. And when I had heard and seen them, I fell down to worship at the feet of the angel who had been showing them to me*, echo the statement of 1:2, that it was John *who testifies to everything he saw—that is, the word* (or message) *of God and the testimony of Jesus Christ*. This is not the first time John records that he fell down to worship at the feet of an angel; on a previous occasion when John fell at the feet of the angel to worship (19:10), he was rebuked and told to worship only God. Here again, John is rebuked and told in forceful terms, *"Do not do it. I am a fellow servant with you and with your brothers the prophets and of all who keep the words of this book. Worship God."* Emphasizing the importance of John's role as a prophet, he is referred to as one of the *brothers* of *the prophets*, obviously referring to the circle of New Testament prophets whose ministry was primarily to affirm the message proclaimed in the name of Christ.[9] The angel, although an impressive celestial being, reminds John that he is, like John, only a fellow servant (*sundoulos*, fellow slave, or bond servant) of God. Likewise, those who *keep the words of this book* are also fellow servants of God. However, the mention of those who *keep the words of this book* is intentional and a reminder of the need to constantly read aloud, hear, keep the message of the book of Revelation (1:3). The idea of constantly keeping derives from the present active participle *tērountōn*. The force of this message to *worship* only *God* and Jesus in the context of Revelation is profound. One must not worship the beast nor even an angel.

22:10. John is instructed by the angel, *"Do not seal up the words of the prophecy of this book, because the time is near."* This command echoes Dan 8:26, "The vision of the evenings and mornings that has been given you is true, but seal up the vision, for it concerns the distant future;" Dan 10:14, "Now I have come to explain to you what will happen to your people in the future, for the vision concerns a time yet to come";and Dan 12:4, 9 "Go your way, Daniel, because the words are closed up and sealed until the time of the end." Daniel was told to seal up his message for it refers to the distant future or a time yet to come. However, John contra Daniel is told not to seal up the message for *the time is near*. Again, God through John is telling his readers that this book is not about the far distant end of the world, but is about crises that are about to break in on the church. Beale has appropriately referred to the expression *the time is near* as an exaggerated expression of imminence that includes a notion of present time.[10] Roberts makes the following perceptive comment regarding the expression *"Do not seal up the words of the prophecy. . . ."*

> The command to John **Do not seal up the words of the prophecy** is explained by **the time is near**. This is another way of saying .... That the impending "coming" is not the parousia but the beginning of the persecutions. At the end of his apocalyptic visions Daniel saw an angel lift up his hand to swear that Daniel's vision did not belong to his own day but was for a far future time. He was told to seal up the vision "for it pertains to many days hence" (Dan8:26) or to seal it up "until the time of the end" (Dan12:9). . . . John had seen this vision repeated. In the vision of the little book (ch. 10), too, he had seen an angel stand and swear by God that the days of the sounding of the seventh angel "the mystery of God" would be finished; there would be "no more delay. "This deliberate reversing of Daniel's vision was a way of saying that John's and Daniel's books differed. The sealing up until a future time became a standard literary device in the Jewish apocalypses. John's book now complete, pertains to the immediate and not distant future. The events foreseen are about to begin [11]

22:11. *Let him who does wrong continue to do wrong; let him who is vile continue to be vile; let him who does right continue to do right; and let him who is holy continue to be holy.* The message of the angel continues a theme analogous to that of Dan. 12:10. In similar fashion the angel explains to John that although doing evil, doing right, and being holy will continue, this does not change the content and authority of the message. This emphasis would help those who struggle with the difficult reality that although they are trying to be good and faithful Christians, persecution and suffering continues. The question of the theodicy is how can one believe in a God who is all powerful and full of love and still have to suffer persecution. John has already addressed this at 13:10. This is a world in which Satan operates, and in such a world evil and suffering are inevitable because of sin. However, God will in his time take care of the situation, judge Satan, and establish a new heaven and new earth in which Satan, suffering, and death have no part. Christians need to keep their faith focused on what God has done and is doing through Jesus Christ. As stated in Dan. 12:10, "Many will be purified, made spotless and refined, but the wicked will continue to be wicked. None of the wicked will understand, but those who are wise will understand." John adapts this in his expression, **Let him who does wrong continue to do wrong; let him who is vile continue to be vile; let him who does right continue to do right; and let him who is holy continue to be holy.**[12] In spite of, and in the face of, opposition and persecution, the saints are encouraged to keep their faith. One is reminded of Paul's encouragement to the Corinthians (1 Cor. 15:58), "Therefore, my beloved brethren, be steadfast, immovable, always abounding in the work of the Lord, knowing that in the Lord your labor is not in vain" (RSV).

JESUS' PROMISE OF REWARD AND RECOMPENSE, 22:12–15

The Text

[12] *"Behold, I am coming soon. My reward is with me, and I will give to everyone according to what he has done.* [13] *I am the Alpha and the Omega, the First and the Last, the Beginning and the End.* [14] *Blessed are those who wash their robes, that they may have the right to the tree of life and may go through the gates into the city.* [15] *Outside are the dogs, those who practice magic arts, the sexually immoral, the murderers, the idolaters and everyone who loves and practices falsehood."*

22:12. Jesus' promise, *I am coming soon.* It obviously involved a secondary sense of final futurity and final eschatological judgment, but it essentially stressed a sense of proleptic judgment and reward in an *exaggerated* or heightened *imminence*. When he comes he will bring both *reward* to the faithful (Cf. 2 and 3) and *recompense* to those who compromise their faith and worship the beast. He will also bring *recompense* to those who persecute the faithful. I prefer the translation of the RSV over that of the NIV at this point, *"Behold, I am coming soon, bringing my recompense, to repay every one for what he has done."* The Greek for the NIV *reward* and RSV *recompense* is *misthos* which carries with it not only positive reward but also a negative punishment.[13] John intends the concept of recompense to imply the repayment of persons for their deeds. The NIV reads *I will give to everyone according to what he has done.* The RSV more precisely reads **to repay**

everyone. Each person (NIV **everyone**) will receive their reward and repayment for their deeds; for the faithful as conquerors, spiritual food for eternal life and reigning with Christ; for the unfaithful and unregenerate idolaters, condemnation in the lake of fire.

22:13. To stress the importance and certainty of Jesus' promise, John adds the "divine" description of Jesus, *I am the Alpha and the Omega, the First and the Last, the Beginning and the End*. This series of brief parallel statements (*isocola*) occurs only once in Revelation although couplings of two have occurred elsewhere. The *I am* concept as a divine name is well known in the Judeo Christian tradition. In Revelation God has already been identified as "*the Alpha and Omega*" (1:8, 21:6) and "*the Beginning and the End*" (21:6) and Christ as "*the First and the Last*" (1:17, 2:8). The combination of these three *I am* statements relating to God and Christ emphasize the absolute divinity and sovereignty of Christ over all creation and history. Osborne notes: "The titles refer to the sovereignty of God and Christ over history. They control the beginning of creation and its end, and therefore control every aspect of history in between. Since this is the only passage to contain all three titles, it has the greatest emphasis of them all on the all-embracing power of Christ over human history."[14]

22:14. With the following beatitude Jesus and John draw the concluding remarks of the epilogue back into the context of Revelation and the message to the seven churches in Asia. The message pronounces a *blessing* on those who do not compromise their faith with Satan and Rome and who die as conquerors for their faith. The message is one of eternal reward and vindication for faithfulness. The washing of their robes points 7:14, the great multitude who had come out of the great tribulation of suffering at the hands of their enemies and had washed their robes in the blood of the Lamb. The statement that these *have the right to the tree of life and may go through the gates into the city* (cf. also 2:7 22:2) clearly establishes that John and Jesus are referring to the conquering martyrs. The following stark statement, *Outside are the dogs, those who practice magic arts, the sexually immoral, the murderers, the idolaters and everyone who loves and practices falsehood*, builds on 21:22 and clearly has reference to those who have prostituted themselves and their faith with the beast and the false prophet and who have made the confession "Caesar is Lord." Although they may not have committed sexual immorality or murder, they have in their corporate relationship with the beast become part of the corporate corrupt nature of the beast.

JESUS' FINAL WORD TO THE SEVEN CHURCHES, 22:16–19.

The Text

"I, Jesus, have sent my angel to give you this testimony for the churches. I am the Root and the Offspring of David, and the bright Morning Star." [17] *The Spirit and the bride say, "Come." And let him who hears say, "Come." Whoever is thirsty, let him come; and whoever wishes, let him take the free gift of the water of life.* [18] *I warn everyone who hears the words of the prophecy of this book: If anyone adds anything to them, God will add to him the plagues described in this*

book. [19] *And if anyone takes words away from this book of prophecy, God will take away from him his share in the tree of life and in the holy city, which are described in this book.*

It is necessary to recognize that this last pericope is in the form of a concluding statement to the book. It involves several statements intended to focus attention on the urgency of the message of Revelation. There is a message from Jesus, one from the Spirit and the bride, and one seemingly from John himself. It is also challenging in that it includes three invitations *to come.* The statements are rolled together in an almost confusing manner, yet the message is clear. The complexity of the three imperatival invitations to come[15] is seen in the fact that almost every commentator on these verses identifies several possibilities in the text and has difficulty in arriving at a final or firm resolution to the three invitations. Questions range from who it is that is issuing the invitations to precisely who is being addressed. Aune is correct in observing that the final invitation, *"Come, Lord Jesus"* at 22:20 "must necessarily be given an eschatological interpretation and should be held within the gravity of the total message of Revelation."[16]

22:16. The first statement of this pericope is from Jesus himself. John reminds the saints that the message of Revelation to the seven churches did not simply originate from within his own interests, but came with the full authority of Jesus' divine messianic being and message. John has already used the messianic expression *I am the Root and the Offspring of David, and the bright Morning Star* to describe Jesus (2:28; 5:5). The reader (or hearer) of the message would immediately be reminded of 1:1,*the revelation of Jesus Christ, which God gave him to show his servants what must soon take place*, which clearly established that this message came from God through Jesus Christ, not simply from John. The first statement therefore drives home the divine origin, concern, and urgency of the revelation.

22:17. Although the first statement, 22:16, obviously is a message from Jesus, the second message introduced at 22:17 John states as coming from *the Spirit and the bride.* This message involves an invitation to *come.* This introduces the of three invitations to *come.* There is some discussion as to whether this invitation comes from Jesus or from John speaking by inspiration of the Holy Spirit.[17] Jesus had promised at 22:12 to be *coming soon.* Now in response to that promise the Holy Spirit speaking through John and the bride encourage Jesus to *come.* This invitation is clearly stated to come expressly from both *the Spirit and the bride* and not from Jesus himself. However, does the reference to the Spirit refer to the Holy Spirit or the spirit of the prophets? Both are possibilities. And to whom does the bride refer? Does this refer to the saints of the seven churches or to the church universal? I am in agreement with Caird, Bauckham, Mounce, Beasley-Murray, and Aune[18] that the basis of the appeal comes from the Holy Spirit who incidentally also inspires the spirit of prophecy. Aune also indicates that as Paul had coupled the Christ and the Spirit in speaking of the Spirit of Christ that this is most likely a reference to the Holy Spirit who speaks through the prophets. The *bride* in the context of Revelation presumably refers to the church or at least the conquering saints in the church who have experienced the eschatological marriage of the Lamb (19:9). Osborne observes regarding the bride, "Most likely the bride is the church of 21:9-10, a literary figure seen in its victory and joy and constituting all who will inherit eternal life . . ."[19] The context of Revelation and the seven churches would seem to indicate that the plea for Christ to come bringing his recompense would come from the beleaguered church of Revelation. The bride inspired by the Holy Spirit call on Jesus to *come*, bringing his recompense and reward.

However, 22:17 includes a second invitation to *come*. The first call to *come* obviously comes from the Spirit and the bride, but the second *come* raises some other interesting possibilities. Is this an invitation *from* the churches *to* Jesus to *come*, or is it an invitation *to* the saints *from* the Spirit and the bride to *come* and experience eternity and its rewards in the new Jerusalem? Regarding the second *come*, Caird notes, "it is a summons both to join the ranks of the Conquerors and to enter the Conquerors' reward."[20] Beale proposes that the first invitation is issued by the prophetic leaders through whom the Spirit speaks, and the second imperatival invitation is from individual believers who have heard the first invitation and call to other believers who are still hearing or are in the process of making a decision.[21] That John states that that this second invitation, or exhortation, comes from *him who hears* seems to focus attention on the readers of the message of the revelation to whom the message was originally addressed. Beale's proposal has much to offer. Osborne's proposal that "both the final church and the current church call the reader to 'come' to Christ" has some relevance if we see the final church as the eschatological church seen in its victory and the current church as the churches addressed in chapters 2 and 3.[22] It would seem that the first invitation to *come* is to the conquerors to join with the bride in its heavenly realm, with the second invitation to *come* being addressed to Christians to faithfully join the ranks of the conquerors. Whichever proposal one may prefer, the invitations to *come* are invitations to join the ranks of those who have conquered through their faithful testimony to Jesus. The invitation is an open one to all, for it is addressed to *whoever wishes* to come *and let him take the free gift of the water of life*.

Several commentators[23] observe a liturgical and eucharistic flavor in these invitations, especially when they are coupled with the final invitation to Jesus to come and the liturgical statement *maranatha*[24] voiced as an early creedal confession in the early second century and later eucharistic practices. I find some merit in this thought since the Eucharist involves both a present celebration of, and a focus on, the future coming of Jesus at his *parousia*. How all three of the invitations are associated with the eucharistic prayer maranatha is uncertain, but when the second one is coupled with the invitation to the thirsty to come, this seems a possibility. I can imagine the gathering of the Christians in Ephesus or Pergamum celebrating the Eucharist, praying for loved ones taken by the powers and martyred, thinking of the Lord's promises to return both to bring recompense and to finally judge Satan, and crying "Come, Lord Jesus" both with an eye to the immediate future and the final end of time.

22:18–19. *I warn everyone.* It is possible that this warning comes from John and not from Jesus. Aune notes that the "identification of the speaker is problematic", with scholars being equally divided over whether the speaker is Jesus or John.[25] He notes that Sweet, Charles, Mounce, and others favor Jesus as the speaker. Zahn, Bousset, Lohmeyer, and Caird prefer the speaker to be John. Whoever the speaker may be, the message resounds with dramatic authority. *I warn everyone who hears the words of the prophecy of this book: If anyone adds anything to them, God will add to him the plagues described in this book.* [19] *And if anyone takes words away from this book of prophecy, God will take away from him his share in the tree of life and in the holy city, which are described in this book.* The association of this warning with an "oath" or "integrity" formula is interesting.[26] Aune notes that Käsemann[27] proposes the term "canonization formula." It is apparent, however, that the nature of this formula would have impact. Deuteronomy 4:2; 12:32; Proverbs 30:5–6, and several other similar Jewish traditional declarations form a stern backdrop to this warning not to add to or detract from God's word, law, or message.

Aune notes that such "oath" formulas are found occasionally in Jewish apocalyptic literature (*1 Enoch* 92–95; 98:1, 4, 6; 99:6; 103:1; 104:1; 49:1; *Asc. Isaiah* 1:8; 3:18; *Apoc. Moses* 18:3; 3 *Apoc. Baruch* 1:7). He adds: "The function of oath the formula in apocalyptic literature is the verification of the truth of the vision report that follows. Apocalyptists, including John, conceived of their role as witnesses to divine truth, whether they wrote under pseudonyms or not. The oath formula could therefore be more appropriately designated the "witness formula" in view of that function."[28]

Whatever the background may be, this warning embodies a reference to the divine authenticity of the message of Revelation. There can be no compromise. To compromise one's faith and worship the beast and the false prophet will bring on one the full condemnation of God pronounced on Satan, the beast, and the false prophet, and the loss of all the privileges and rewards of faithful service to God and Christ.

Several incidental thoughts relate to this warning. Some members of the Stone Campbell Restoration Movement, or Churches of Christ, refer to a slogan, "We will speak where the Bible speaks, and be silent where the Bible is silent" as a formula prohibiting practices that the Bible does not specifically propose. However, when it is pointed out that this slogan is itself nowhere stipulated in the Scripture, they argue that silence is included in the Revelation formula of 22:18–19. However, this takes 22:18–19 out of context. It says nothing about silence as the Campbellian, or silence, slogan indicates. Revelation speaks to adding or detracting from the charge of Revelation not to compromise one's faith with the imperial cult. Thomas Campbell (ca. 1890) was addressing the addition of creedal statements not specified in Scripture as binding on communion, fellowship, or salvation. The silence principle, while being a noble one, eliminates itself as a binding principle, much as the logical positivism principle negated itself. Members of Churches of Christ take seriously the admonition to honor the instructions and teachings of Scripture, but also the challenge not to bind human creeds and opinions in matters of faith and fellowship. The slogan to "Speak where the Bible speaks and remain silent where the Bible is silent" is a noble plea, but should not be translated into a hermeneutical law.

Relating to another church/theological discussion, John was not concerned with the Calvinistic/Arminian controversy over whether one could fall away from grace and salvation. He certainly indicates that apostasy from faith in Jesus is not only possible, but also probable. One should not introduce later Christian theological arguments into a work that knew nothing of the later controversies. I like Osborne's observation that Revelation's warnings can address both Calvinistic (it could not happen to the elect but could happen to other members of the church), and Arminian views (it could happen to anyone in the church).[29]

Concluding Comments, 22:20–21.

The Text

[20] *He who testifies to these things says, "Yes, I am coming soon." Amen. Come, Lord Jesus.* [21] *The grace of the Lord Jesus be with God's people. Amen.*

2:20. John concludes his message by observing that it is Jesus who is behind the testimony or warning of the preceding verses. That he is *coming soon* adds to the seriousness of the warnings. We have already noted that his imminent coming is one in which he will bring his recompense for the deeds of both the saints and their enemies. This statement of Jesus certainly authenticates the above warnings not to add to the words of the prophesy or to detract from them. By adding the expression *amen* (*amēn,* the traditional liturgical formula meaning *truly*) John testifies to the accuracy of Jesus' imminent coming and adds his plea for Jesus' coming in vindication of the saints and judgment on their enemies. Although the promise of Jesus to come soon, bringing his recompense, must not be overlooked in this *Come, Lord Jesus* cry, the eucharistic overtones surely would resonate in the minds of the worshippers and hearers with Jesus' promise to come at the end of the age and set all things right.

22:21. John concludes his message and Epilogue with the traditional Christian benedictory formula involving the *grace of the Lord Jesus*. The NIV provides the words *be with God's people* where the Greek simply reads, *pantōn,* the genitive plural of *pas, be with all*. It is most likely that John primarily had in mind in this benediction the readers or hearers of the message in the churches of Asia, but the benediction would be relevant to all readers of the Revelation.

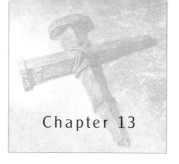

Chapter 13

The Meaning and Relevance of Revelation

It is common today to be more concerned with what a text means to the contemporary reader than perhaps with what the text meant to the author and original recipients. Failure to determine the original purpose of the text, the recipients, and the theological problems being addressed too often results in subjective speculation. One is then open to reading into the text thoughts and messages not intended by the author. Reader response criticism, however, has demonstrated the need to move beyond the historical critical method of exegesis and focus on meaning and application. Unfortunately, one result of the challenge of reader response criticism has been a neglect of the full range of biblical criticism in the interpretation of the text. This commentary has been written from a firm historical critical method in which I have also given considerable attention to the full range of critical biblical and historical concerns. Where possible I have made application of the theology of the text to contemporary situations. I leave most of the theological application of the text to well-trained pulpit ministers and teachers of the word.

Some have identified the approach I have adopted as a moderate preterist model of interpretation, and in some measures this is correct. However, I understand Revelation to be a visionary drama, set in the context of first-century churches located in Asia. The drama is played out on a cosmic set in which major theological principles can be identified. It is these theological principles that have meaning and are applicable to all ages and cultural contexts. Osborne and Beale have identified their approach to Revelation as an eclectic one in which the strengths of several approaches such as the historical context and the dramatic and philosophy of history models are incorporated into their view of the book. I am of the same persuasion and adopt a moderate eclectic approach to the text that sets the primary theology firmly in the historical context of first-century Christianity in Asia. Without careful attention to this and the historical beacons John provides in the book, it is easy to lose direction and wander from the original intention of the writer and to read into the text contemporary interests. I realize that there is a sense of futurity and finality to Revelation, but seek to keep the theological setting in its original context (John's expression, "*what must soon take place . . . for the time is near*") and eschatological dimension. I have attempted to hold the primary message in the context of proleptic eschatological genre without overlooking a futuristic view of Revelation that keeps an eye on the final end of history. I encourage the reader to read the introduction to this study carefully for fuller discussion of such an eclectic approach to Revelation and John's use of a proleptic eschatological genre.

My primary concern in the commentary has been to learn as best as possible what the original author's intention and message was, and how he intended his first-century audience to understand that message. I have tried to focus on the theological emphases and principles inherent in the text. It now remains to learn from that original message how Revelation can speak to the church in the twenty-first century.

In 1944 H. H. Rowley published his ground-breaking work, *The Relevance of Apocalyptic*,[1] in which he identified the theological principles expressed in apocalyptic and demonstrated their relevance for contemporary situations. Rowley's work sparked the thought for the title of this chapter.

The task of determining the relevance of Revelation is no different from that of determining the relevance of the Gospel of Matthew or Paul's First Epistle to the Corinthians. In the case of the gospels, one has to recognize that a gospel has to be studied at three levels, or three *Sitz im Leben*. First, there was the context of Jesus' personal ministry in which he taught his disciples the meaning of the cross and discipleship as he moved around Palestine. The careful scholar will seek to understand what was going on in the life of an ordinary Jew in Israel at the time of Jesus' life and ministry. In this manner one seeks to understand the terminology used by Jesus as a Jew in Jesus' day would have understood such. But the Gospel of Matthew, for instance, was written by an evangelist (ancient tradition holds that this was Matthew) possibly forty years after the death of Jesus. Matthew did not write his gospel as a bright idea early one Monday morning. He was writing for a community of believers, mostly of Jewish roots, probably somewhere in Syria, who needed to hear the gospel story of Jesus relevant to their own context and needs. This presents us with a different level of research, that of understanding what was going on in the life of the church in Syria some forty years after Jesus' death. Finally, we today read and study the Gospel of Matthew in an altogether different, modern culture and context. It is the responsibility of the modern interpreter, then, to interpret the original message taught by Jesus to his disciples as it was recorded forty years later by Matthew for a different group of believers. Consequently, the modern interpreter must first examine the text in its original historical context to determine those theological principles Jesus was teaching his original disciples. Second, the modern interpreter must learn how these principles were applied by Matthew to a later group in a different context and culture from Jesus' original disciples. Finally, having determined what the theological principles originally were, the modern interpreter must apply these theological principles to a modern culture and context.

Consider now Paul and his relationship with the church in Corinth. Word had reached Paul that the church was facing serious challenges and disruption. In a series of four epistles and possibly two additional visits Paul worked with the Corinthian Christians as they brought their faith back to Jesus. Without careful attention to what was going on in Corinth, what the initial problems were, and how Paul addressed them, we are impoverished in our understanding of the Corinthian epistles. Without careful historical, literary, sociological, and theological research, one is unable to understand fully the dimensions of Pauline theology as found in the Corinthian correspondence. Only after one determines what was going on in Corinth and how Paul addressed the situations can one apply the theological principles that surface in the Corinthian correspondence to contemporary situations.

We should conclude, therefore, that our biblical books, whether Old Testament or New Testament, were situational, that is, written to address specific historical and religious situations. They are also contextual in the sense that they must be examined within specific literary, cultural, and cultural contexts. Studying Revelation is no different from studying any book in the Bible. Obviously, the literary genre is radically different from that of the Gospels, but the process of determining the major theological principles remains the same. One must first set the book in its historical, literary, cultural, and theological contexts, seek to understand its literary genre, then after identifying its theological message or principles, apply them to our contemporary situation. The careful scholar, by using all the tools of biblical criticism available, will consequently seek first to determine what theological principles the original writer intended, and then finally determine how those principles might apply in a contemporary situation.

This brings us to the relevance of Revelation. In the commentary I have attempted to demonstrate careful attention to the historical and religious context of the church in Asia in the first century. I have been sensitive to the literary genre adopted by John, found in the Old Testament, the Jewish rabbinic tradition, and the apocalyptic, apocryphal, and pseudepigraphical literature. I have been careful to understand the theology of the proleptic apocalyptic eschatology adopted by John in Revelation and his use of Old Testament images and messages. I have identified certain theological themes and messages that God, through his servant John, wanted the churches in Asia to hear and learn.

John's style of presenting God's message was in the form of a cosmic drama, which he presented in the language of the Old Testament and pseudepigraphical literature, a language clearly understood by Christians in the first century. In this cosmic drama we see the ancient battle between Satan and his forces pitted against God and his forces set first in the context of heaven, then in the historical context of Christians in first-century Asia. Satan, having lost the first heavenly battle, transfers his hatred to earth against the churches, focused in Revelation on the churches in Asia. But once again, Satan is defeated, this time by Christians who refuse to compromise their faith in Jesus and who are willing to die for that faith. They conquer Satan by their uncompromising, resolute faith and by their willingness to die for that faith, empowered by the victory of Jesus at the cross over Satan especially in Jesus' resurrection. The relevance of Revelation, then, lies in Christians' understanding those theological principles of an uncompromising faith in Jesus and a willingness to die for that faith.

Although Revelation is a mysterious book, written in a unique literary genre, the mysterious apocalyptic style was clearly understood by its original readers. They understood the theological faith impact of the apocalyptic genre and were able to understand its message. Clearly, the historical situation of the churches in Asia toward the close of the first century was one of severe crises and challenges to the Christians' faith. At the hands of a pagan society aided by the political power of the Roman Empire and the Roman imperial cult, Christians were tested in the extreme, with martyrdom a reality of everyday life. In the context of increasing and severe persecution, Christians were called on to stand firm in their faith in Jesus as Lord and adamantly refused to confess Caesar as Lord. Such refusal inevitably resulted in their being forced to offer their lives as martyrs for their faith in Jesus Christ. The reward for this uncompromising faith would be sharing with God in his eternal blessings and reigning with Christ in his eternal kingdom.

Although believers throughout the ages have had to suffer and die for their faith, John reassures us that Christians can conquer Satan through their resolute faith. He affirms that Christians through their faith in Jesus are already reigning with Jesus in his eternal kingdom. *Conquering suffering, even persecution, and reigning with Christ through faith are dominant themes in Revelation.* John reassures Christians of all ages that they have within their faith the power to join others of the past and become more than conquerors through their faith in God. Likewise, he reassures us today that Jesus is already reigning in his kingdom and that faithful Christian can and will join him in that reign through their uncompromising faith in Jesus. The kingdom reign of Christ is not something that we anticipate and await for future fulfillment, but is something already active in the present. In these last days of the Christian eschaton, we already experience the future reign of God, the climax of which will come at the end of the age.

Thus the story of Revelation runs as follows: the Almighty God through his Son Jesus Christ, through his Holy Spirit, and finally through his servant John, warned the churches of Asia to examine their faith and if necessary to repent before the crises about to break in on them destroyed their heritage in Christ and their right to be lampstands or witnesses for Jesus. God warned them to get their faith sorted out and focused in the proper place in order to be able to withstand the temptation about to break in on them in the form of the Roman imperial cult. He warned them that a compromised faith would not realize for them of the promises God had in store for them in heaven. Likewise, churches today need constantly to examine their congregational and individual lives to determine whether their faith is focused on Jesus or on some other form of religious or regimented orthodoxy.

Revelation challenges churches and Christians to see clearly and understand fully the holiness, righteousness, and sovereignty of God, and to know that it is God who is in control of all life, not man, not any political power. In *The Myth of a Christian Nation* (2005),[2] Gregory Boyd warns of the danger of Christians' seeking political power as an answer to secular challenges to faith. He argues that the quest for political power of the conservative religious right in America, or anywhere else, can destroy the vital and dynamic power of the church. Boyd is not against Christians' becoming involved in the political arena, but is concerned that by seeking political power the church runs contrary to the mind of Christ, whose kingdom is not enhanced by political "clout" but by the preaching of the Christian message of Jesus. This is one dimension of what John was calling for in Revelation. The kingdom of Christ is not furthered by political alliances but by proclaiming the power of faith in Jesus Christ. In the confusion of contemporary challenges from secularism, the church enlarges the boundaries of the faith, not by political alliances, but by its commission to maintain faith and preach the message of faith, namely, Jesus Christ. Furthermore, Revelation reminds the church that God, the Holy Spirit, and Jesus are always present in the struggles of life, even against pagan and secular challenges, to give them focus and strength to endure. Thus John's apocalyptic eschatology encourages Christians not to fix their hope in human or political solutions to the real problems of life and to understand that God has already in the death and resurrection of Jesus intervened in human affairs. He will in the end intervene again and in righteousness judge Satan and his agents and reward faithful Christians with his real, glorious presence.

Revelation challenges Christians to see clearly the constant abiding love of God and Jesus for the church. In regard to the challenges of an evil world, God has a plan that he has been working from before the foundation of the world. That plan reveals that the faithful can conquer evil and that they will triumph eternally in God's plan. This plan focuses attention on what God has been working and achieving through Jesus. It is not uncommon for Christians in the context of extreme suffering to ask what God is doing regarding the problem of evil. Revelation reveals that God has already acted through Jesus Christ to deal with evil, that Christians need to be patient as God works his plan, for he will in his own time and manner judge and destroy evil.

The church is challenged to see clearly that God has already in Jesus conquered Satan. Through faith in Jesus and what God has already achieved through the death and resurrection of Jesus, the church and individual Christians today can also triumph over adversities.

Jesus, through John and Revelation, stresses that life has difficulties and challenges that are inevitable, but through faith Christians can in the present conquer Satan and in advance of the final end receive the reward of living in Jesus' presence. In the same manner, Revelation assures Christians that God has in the present already judged evil with final condemnation and judgment.

The message of Revelation challenges Christians to lift their horizons from the immediate struggles to see the hope of the future that can give them strength to endure the present. In the words of Wolfhart Pannenberg, a prominent theologian of hope, the present is already the arrival of the future.[3]

The eschatology of Revelation stresses that the present gains its meaning from the future that God has already determined and that the present is nothing more than the advance (proleptic) arrival of the future. Through faith in Jesus as the Son of God and divine ruler of all creation, we already in the present, in the face of difficulty and opposition, experience the final victory over the world and the powers of evil (1 John 5:4–5).

Final words from the Apostle Paul:

And we know that in all things God works for the good of those who love him, who have been called according to his purpose. [29] For those God foreknew he also predestined to be conformed to the likeness of his Son, that he might be the first-born among many brothers. [30] And those he predestined, he also called; those he called, he also justified; those he justified, he also glorified. [31] What, then, shall we say in response to this? If God is for us, who can be against us? [32] He who did not spare his own Son, but gave him up for us all—how will he not also, along with him, graciously give us all things? [33] Who will bring any charge against those whom God has chosen? It is God who justifies. [34] Who is he that condemns? Christ Jesus, who died—more than that, who was raised to life—is at the right hand of God and is also interceding for us. [35] Who shall separate us from the love of Christ? Shall trouble or hardship or persecution or famine or nakedness or danger or sword? [36] As it is writ-ten: "For your sake we face death all day long; we are considered as sheep to be slaughtered." [37] No, in all these things we are more than conquerors through him who loved us. [38] For I am convinced that neither death nor life, neither angels nor demons, neither the present nor the future, nor any powers, [39] neither height nor depth, nor anything else in all creation, will be able to separate us from the love of God that is in Christ Jesus our Lord. (Rom. 8:28–39).

Glossary of Terms

RESOURCES:

The following definitions of key expressions in this study of Revelation are adapted from several reference works, among them are the following: Collins, John J., *The Apocalyptic Imagination: An Introduction to the Jewish Matrix of Christianity*, (New York: Crossroad Publishing, 1984); Collins, John J., ed., *Apocalypse: The Morphology of a Genre* (Semeia 14: Society of Biblical Literature, 1979); Ferguson, Everett, ed., *Encyclopedia of Early Christianity* (New York: Garland, 1990), Hanson, Paul D., *The Dawn of Apocalyptic* (Philadelphia: Fortress, 1975), and Soulen, Richard N., *Handbook of Biblical Criticism* (Atlanta: John Knox, 1981); *The Anchor Bible Dictionary* (New York: Doubleday, 1992); *The International Standard Bible Encyclopedia* (Grand Rapids: Eerdmans, 1979); James, M. R., *The Apocryphal New Testament* (Oxford: Clarendon, 1950); Hennecke, Edgar, and William Schneemelcher, *New Testament Apocrypha*, 2 vols. (Philadelphia: Westminster, 1963); Robinson, James M., *The Nag Hammadi Library in English* (San Francisco: Harper, 1990); Goodspeed, Edgar J., *The Apocrypha: An American Translation* (Chicago: University of Chicago Press, 1938); Goodspeed, Edgar J. *The Story of the Apocrypha*, (Chicago: University of Chicago Press, 1939); Nickelsburg, G. W. E., *Jewish Literature between the Bible and the Mishna* (Philadelphia: Fortress, 1981); Stone, M., *Jewish Writings of the Second Temple Period* (Philadelphia: Fortress, 1984); and Clouse, Robert G., ed., *The Meaning of the Millennium: Four Views* (Downers Grove, Ill: InterVarsity Press, 1977).

AMILLENNIALISM

Amillennialism is one of the terms used to describe theological theories regarding the thousand-year reign, or the "anticipated" millennial reign, of Christ. Other terms falling under the category of millennial theology are premillennialism, dispensationalism, and postmillennialism. Each of these is discussed in its own right in the glossary.

As will be noticed under the discussion of millennialism, the term derives from the Latin terminology for thousand years, namely, *mille, one thousand*, and *annus, year*. Hence, the term millennial refers to theories of the thousand-year reign of Christ of Revelation 20:4.

Amillennial is the term used to refer to theories that do not see in Revelation 20:4 and the thousand years a literal period of time, or to that extent, any period of time. Amillennial theories suggest that the millennium refers rather to conditions or situations implying completeness since the figure one thousand is understood to refer to completeness. In the case of Revelation 20:4, the reign of the martyrs for a thousand years refers to the fact that they reign completely with Christ. They are conquerors (victorious) and thus share with Christ in his victory and reign. Revelation 20:4 does not say that Christ reigns for a thousand years or that his reign is on earth. It is the martyrs who reign completely with Christ (for a thousand years with the thousand figuratively referring to the completeness of their reign).

Amillennial theories do not follow a literal interpretation of the figurative language of apocalyptic and Revelation and, furthermore, are committed to setting the message of Revelation within the context of the first-century church suffering under Roman persecution. Amillennial scholars explain that the theological principles revealed in the message of Revelation to the first-century church apply today to Christians suffering persecution or affliction.

Although amillennial views differ, the following chart diagrams the amillennial view adopted in this commentary:

AMILLENNIALISM

ANTICHRIST

The term "antichrist" nowhere appears in the text of Revelation itself, but is found often in commentaries, especially those coming from some protestant, fundamentalist, or dispensationalist persuasions. The Greek term *antichristos* appears only five times in the New Testament, and only in the Johannine Epistles (1 John 2:18, 22; 4:3; and 2 John 7). In the Johannine Epistles the term is used only in regard to those who deny that Jesus is the Christ or that Jesus Christ came in the flesh. In this case the problem seems to be a gnostic-type heresy (see glossary under gnosticism) that in no way addresses the theological problem of Revelation. The use of the term "antichrist" in the context of Revelation is unfortunate, arising in most cases from a poor understanding of who the beast is in Revelation and the nature of the problem Christians were encountering with the beast. This commentary will not make reference to the "antichrist" or refer to the beast as the antichrist. Certainly, the beast is opposed to the Christian faith and in that sense is anti-Christian, but the term "antichrist," having been used in the biblical text in other contexts, is not suitable for this study.

APOCALYPTIC

Apocalyptic derives from the Greek word *apokalypsis* ("a revelation, an uncovering, a disclosure"). Apocalyptic is a broad term, appearing first in biblical criticism at the beginning of the nineteenth century. The term is used to designate those ancient visionary writings or parts of writings that, like the New Testament apocalypse from which the name is derived, namely, the book of Revelation, claim to reveal mysteries relating to the end of the world (age) and the glories of a future transcendent world (age) that is to break into human experience.

Apocalyptic literature is not, therefore, limited to the canonical Scriptures, for a vast pool of apocalyptic, or heavily apocalyptically flavored, texts are available to the biblical critic. This rich storehouse of information provided an appropriate and powerful vehicle for the authors of our biblical texts. This is particularly true of the author of Revelation, who found in the apocalyptic mindset, genre, and literature a most suitable medium for his theological message.

The term is used in a variety of ways and may refer to a range of concepts and theological motifs typical of this genre of literature. It may refer to a sociological or theological mind-set, a method of communicating, or a type (genre) of literature, all of which are heavily influenced by visions, symbols, cosmic eruptions and wars, and threatening beasts. Biblical apocalyptic is a distinctive Jewish and Christian phenomenon that flourished in the four centuries between 200 B.C. and 200 A.D. The roots of apocalyptic, however, reach back into the sixth and fifth centuries B.C. Two of the best examples of the biblical genre are Daniel and the book of Revelation. Many other biblical texts, both Old and New Testament, draw in varying degrees on the apocalyptic genre (Isa. 13:4–16; 24–27 [the "Isaiah Apocalypse"]; Joel 2; Zech. 9–11, 12–14; Ezek. 38–39; Amos 5:16–20; 9:11–15; Mark 13; Matt. 23–25; Luke 21; 1 Thess. 4–5; 2 Thess. 2:1–2; 1 Cor. 15; Rom. 1:18–32; 8:18–25).

Many of the pseudepigraphal and apocryphal writings (see glossary) are designated apocalypses or are considered to be heavily influenced by apocalyptic. Though no complete agreement exists, those so designated usually include *Apocalypse of Abraham*; *Apocalypse of Baruch* (*2* or *Syriac Baruch*); *Apocalypse of Esdras* (*IV Ezra* 3–14); *1 Enoch*; *Book of Elijah*; *1 Baruch*; *Apocalypse of Moses* (or the *Life of Adam and Eve*); *Apocalypse of Sedrach*; *Apocalypse of Elijah*; *2 Enoch*; *Assumption of Moses*; *Sibylline Oracles*; *Book of Jubilees*; *Testament of Abraham*; *Testament of the Twelve Patriarchs*; *Ascension of Isaiah*. Of this list, the first four, plus the canonical apocalyptically influenced Daniel and Revelation, are the best literary examples of this type.

Several of the Dead Sea Scrolls are also considered to be significantly influenced by apocalyptic interests. In particular the *War Scroll*, the Description of the New Jerusalem, and the Thanksgiving Psalms manifest striking apocalyptic features. Several prominent apocalyptic works found among the Dead Sea Scrolls indicate the apocalyptic interests of the Dead Sea Covenanters. They are Daniel, *1 Enoch*, and *Jubilees*.

Challenging questions arise when discussing apocalyptic: How does one define apocalyptic? What are its unique characteristics? How does it work, and what was its purpose? What unique social and religious contexts gave rise to this genre? And why was it popular among Jewish and Christian writers during the four hundred years of its zenith? Several questions have challenged scholars addressing this genre. Questions as to whether it constitutes an identifiable literary genre continue to be debated, although an apocalyptic group meeting as part of the Society of Biblical Studies study groups has made significant strides in identifying this genre. (See J. J. Collins' two works referred to below in the bibliography.) Those with somewhat negative attitudes toward an identifiable literary genre argue that apocalyptic simply uses, adapts, and transforms older traditional genres. Klaus Koch has, however, identified six general literary features that are normally present in apocalypses: 1) discourse cycles (frequently called "visions") between the apocalyptic seer and a heavenly being, revealing the secret of man's destiny; 2) formalized phraseology depicting the spiritual turmoil of the seer (trance, etc.) that accompanies the vision; 3) a paraenetic discourse conveying an eschatological ethic or an introductory legend illustrating proper behavior; 4) pseudonymity, bearing the name of some ancient worthy, although the book of Revelation is an exception; 5) mythical images rich in symbolism (animals, angels, demons, cosmic phenomena); and 6) a composite character (seventy percent of the book of Revelation is influenced significantly by previously written sources).

In terms of general content, apocalyptic is characterized by the belief 1) that the radical transcendent transformation of this world lies in the immediate future, Dan. 12:11,12; Rev. 22:20; *2 Baruch* 85:10; *4 Ezra* 2; 4:50; 2) that a cosmic catastrophe (war, fire, earthquake, famine, pestilence) precedes the end; 3) that the epochs of history leading up to the end are predetermined; 4) that a hierarchy of angels and demons mediate the events in the two worlds (this world and the one to come) and that victory is assured to the divine realm; 5) that a righteous remnant will enjoy the fruits of salvation in a heavenly Jerusalem; 6) that the act inaugurating the kingdom of God and marking the end of the present age is his (or the Son of Man's) ascension to the heavenly throne; 7) that the actual establishment of the new kingdom is effected through a royal mediator, such as the Messiah or the Son of Man, or simply an angel; 8) that the bliss to be enjoyed by the righteous can only be described as glory, Rev. 21:1; Dan. 12:3; *1 Enoch* 50:1.

The origin of apocalyptic is variously ascribed to Hebrew prophecy, Iranian religion, Hellenistic syncretism, and old Canaanite myths, with the greater number of scholars acknowledging at least the influence of eastern religion, particularly Zoroastrianism. (For a full appraisal of the question of the origins of apocalyptic and the methodology used to answer it, see Paul D. Hanson, John J. Collins in the above bibliography.) Points often debated in contemporary New Testament scholarship relate to what extent Jesus and the New Testament writers, especially Paul, were influenced by apocalyptic; to what extent was apocalyptic pessimistic about world history; and to what extent can the kingdom of God be continuous with this world or the present age or time.

John J. Collins and his associates in the apocalyptic study group propose the following working definition of an apocalypse: *"a genre of revelatory literature with a narrative framework, in which a revelation is mediated by an otherworldly being to a human recipient, disclosing a transcending reality which is both temporal, insofar as it envisages eschatological salvation, and spatial insofar as it involves another, supernatural world."*

For the purpose of this study, apocalyptic is a mind-set that expressed itself in literary form that eventually became an identifiable literary genre. The context of apocalyptic usually is a people under severe social, political, or religious opposition and persecution. Fundamentally pessimistic about human potential and the role of history (human effort) to resolve the problem, apocalyptic looks to divine or transcendent intervention as the only hope for the future. Drawing on cosmic visions in a kaleidoscopic manner and an intense symbolism, the author paints impressionistic pictures as he develops his theme. The primary theme or theology of apocalyptic, especially as it relates to the biblical texts and in particular, Revelation, is that the only hope for victory over the "enemy" is God's transcendent intervention. The persecuted are encouraged through the apocalyptic genre and its theology not to lose or compromise their faith, to be faithful to God "even unto death," and God would transform any defeat into a magnificent victory. In the words of Paul (Rom. 8:37) "we are more than conquerors through him who loved us." A major theme in Revelation is that Christians conquer Satan and the "enemy" through dying for their faith (martyr, from the Greek *martus,* means to "witness to one's faith"). Martyrs are raised by the power of God, thus vindicated by God, and reign with Christ in God's kingdom.

Apocrypha

The term Apocrypha derives from the Greek *apokruphos* ("hidden" or "concealed"). In biblical studies it has reference to a collection of writings that are considered highly spiritual, close to the biblical mindset, yet not completely in keeping with the biblical integrity. As a result, the apocryphal books of Judaism and Christianity were not included in the Protestant biblical canon (list of books received by the church or community of faith as authoritative and normative). There are both New and Old Testament apocryphal books. Although not considered "inspired" or "normative," these writings were highly esteemed at the time the New Testament books were being produced and in many cases formed the conceptual framework of the writer. We will notice this in particular in regard to Revelation, but an interesting demonstration can be found in Jude 8, 9, 14. The Apocrypha became a plentiful and significant resource of ideas and expressions for the writer of Revelation.

NT Apocrypha

The New Testament apocryphal books date from the second to the sixth centuries They are written in the form of gospels, acts (histories), epistles, and apocalypses, and claim to report events, teachings, and prophecies related to Jesus and the early apostles that are not recorded in the canonical Scriptures. These writings contain little of historical value in terms of the subjects with which they deal (e.g., the birth of Mary and the childhood of Jesus), but are of inestimable value in understanding the mind-set of both orthodox and heterodox Christianity of the early centuries. Like the books of the New Testament, the apocryphal New Testament writings derive from the life and concerns of the early Christian communities.

The great flood of new material that in recent years has enriched the field of biblical studies, much of it due to the discovery in 1945 of a hoard of Coptic gnostic texts at Nag in upper Egypt, has increased and enhanced the apocryphal materials available to scholars and provided both a sociological and religious laboratory for research into early Christian beliefs and practices.

The following list of the most important apocryphal texts, organized into the four traditional categories represented in the canonical New Testament, demonstrates the proportions of this valuable resource of pseudo-biblical material:

- Gospels: *Arabic Gospel of the Infancy; Armenian Gospel of the Infancy; Assumption of the Virgin; Gospel of Bartholomew; the Book of the Resurrection of Christ by Bartholomew; Gospel of Basilides; Gospel of Cerinthus; Gospel of the Ebionites; Gospel according to the Hebrews; Protoevangelium of James; History of Joseph the Carpenter; Gospel of Marcion; Gospel of the Birth of Mary; Gospel of Philip; Gospel of Pseudo-Matthew*; and finally possibly one of the most valuable, *Gospel of Thomas.*
- Acts: *Apostolic History of Abdias; Acts of Andrew;* fragmentary story of *Andrew; Acts of Andrew and Matthias; Acts of Andrew and Paul; Acts of Barnabas; Ascent of James; Acts of James the Great; Acts of John; Acts of John by Prochorus; Martyrdom of Matthew; Acts of Paul; Passion of Paul; Acts of Peter; Acts of Peter and Andrew; Acts of Peter and Paul; Acts of Philip; Acts of Pilate; Acts of Thaddaeus; Acts of Thomas.*
- Epistles: *Epistles of Christ and Abgarus; Epistle of the Apostles; Third Epistle of the Corinthians; Epistle of the Laodiceans; Epistle of Lentulus; Epistles of Paul and Seneca; Apocryphal Epistle of Titus.*
- Apocalypses: *Apocalypse of James; Apocalypse of Paul; Apocalypse of Peter; Revelation of Stephen; Apocalypse of Thomas; Apocalypse of the Virgin.*

Additional writings, known by little more than their name, could be included in this list of apocryphal writings, as well as some literature classified under other categories of early Christian literature.

Old Testament Apocrypha

The Old Testament Apocrypha is comprised of those books, or portions of books, included in the LXX (*Septuagint*, Greek translation of the Hebrew Old Testament, traditionally thought to be translated in Alexandria, Egypt, ca. 270 B.C.) or included in the Old Latin translation of the LXX, but not included in the Hebrew canon of the Old Testament. These writings were accepted by some sectors of the early church as sacred writings, but were never included in the Hebrew canon. They represent deeply religious writings that date from ca. 300 B.C. Some of them are as late as A.D. 70.

Jerome, in preparing his edition of the Bible in Latin (Vulgate), ca. A.D. 400, chose to follow the Hebrew canon rather than the LXX, which included the additional non-canonical books. Jerome put the additional books into a distinct corpus that he termed "apocryphal." These he also described as "ecclesiastical books" in contradistinction to the "canonical books" of the Hebrew Old Testament. Since Jerome, the theological and physical place of the Apocrypha in the Christian canon has continued to be a matter of dispute, with the Eastern and Russian Orthodox, the Roman Catholics, and the Protestants accepting differing solutions as indicated below.

Apocryphal books include:

- *Tobit*, *Judith*, the *Wisdom of Solomon*, and *Eccelesiasticus* or the Wisdom *of Jesus, the Son of Sirach*—of the apocrypha, these alone were accepted as canonical by the Eastern Church at the Synod of Jerusalem in 1672.
- *Baruch*, *Letter of Jeremiah* (or *Baruch*, ch. 6; in the LXX these two writings appear as additions to the book of Jeremiah); the *Prayer of Azariah* and *the Song of the Three Young Men* (or *Holy Children*); the *History of Susanna*, and *Bel and the Dragon* (in the LXX the last three appear as additions to the book of Daniel); and *1* and *2 Maccabees*.

The writings above were confirmed as canonical by the Council of Trent in 1548, though entitled "Deuterocanonical" since they did not appear in the Hebrew Bible.

- *1 Esdras* (called *Esdras A* in the LXX, *3 Esdras* in the Vulgate, where Ezra and Nehemiah are called *1 and 2 Esdras*), which contains portions of 2 Chronicles, Ezra, and Nehemiah plus other material; *2 Esdras* (called *4 Esdras* in the Vulgate, also known as *The Ezra Apocalypse* (spec. chs. 3–14; chs. 15–16, which are called *5 Esdras* in some manuscripts, are a composite work and do not appear in the LXX); and, the *Prayer of Manasseh*, a brief penitential prayer—these writings were not confirmed as canonical by the Council of Trent and consequently appear in Catholic Bibles in an appendix or not at all (so the Jerusalem Bible). In modern Protestant editions of the Apocrypha (RSV, NEB) all of the above are included.
- In the LXX and in the appendix to the Greek canon, one finds also Psalm 151 and *3* and *4 Maccabees*.

CHIASM

Chiasm, used in literary criticism and biblical interpretation, refers to a literary style or structure adopted by an author to add sequence, meaning, or force to the message. The background of the term is the Greek letter *chi*, which is similar to the Arabic X. The front half of the X, becomes the shape of the literary structure as indicated below in solid lines.

CHIASM

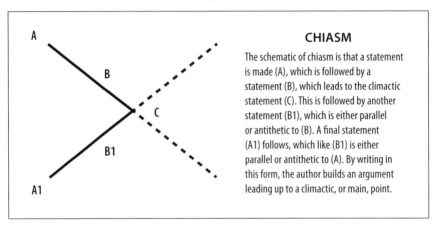

CHIASM

The schematic of chiasm is that a statement is made (A), which is followed by a statement (B), which leads to the climactic statement (C). This is followed by another statement (B1), which is either parallel or antithetic to (B). A final statement (A1) follows, which like (B1) is either parallel or antithetic to (A). By writing in this form, the author builds an argument leading up to a climactic, or main, point.

Many scholars believe that the literary structure of Revelation is best described as a chiasm in which the high point of the literary piece is chapter 12, Christ the Lamb of God. This is more fully described in the introduction to this study.

CHILIASM

Like millennialism, the term chiliasm describes kingdom views relating to the thousand-year reign suggested in 20:4–7. Chiliasm derives from the Greek word *chilias, one thousand*. Chiliasm is used to describe early views views of the millennium. There are several similarities between chiliasm and premillennialism. An important difference between the two words is that the former is used almost exclusively for first- through sixth-century theories relating to the thousand-year reign, whereas millennialism is used in reference to modern-day theories. Because of the similarity of these two terms, those such as Eldon Ladd who espouse a form of premillennialism known as historic premillennialism trace the roots of premillennialism to the first-century chiliasm. In fact, chiliasm is a form of premillennial thinking. As will be discussed below, there are, however, significant differences between chiliasm and historic premillennialism.

It seems that chiliastic views had their roots in Phrygia in western Asia Minor, now Turkey. The general sense of chiliasm is that following the death and resurrection of Jesus the church was established in what one could term the church age. Due to early persecutions and social opposition, many Christians hoped for a future period of peace in which they, together with Christ, would reign in a peaceful kingdom. Such hopes gendered heated discussion and led to considerable controversy in the early church with opinions divided over whether this future kingdom would be physically on earth or a spiritual kingdom in heaven. Because of this debate, some groups were reluctant to include Revelation in their canon since it was the source of much of this speculative theology. Primarily, chiliastic views were that, with the second coming of Christ, a kingdom would be established when the saints would be caught up to be with the Lord in his kingdom.

Chiliastic views during the first six centuries had a wide range of ideas. Fundamental to all of them, however, is the longing for a period of peace following times of stress. Some views stressed that this thousand-year reign would be centered in Jerusalem and would be followed by the general resurrection and judgment. Chiliastic thought can be found in such early prominent figures as Papias, bishop of Hierapolis (western Asia Minor), Justin Martyr, Hippolytus of Rome, Irenaeus, bishop of Lyons, and Methodius of Olympus. Both Origen of Alexandria and Caesarea, and Augustine of Rome were staunch opponents of chiliasm, preferring to see in the thousand-year reign a figurative symbol rather than a literal period of time.

CHILIASM

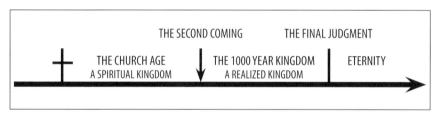

As can be seen from the above chart, basic chiliasm holds that the church age is also a period of spiritual kingdom experience. However, the peace on earth that the thousand-year kingdom promised remained unfulfilled in this life, so chiliasts looked for a future period (1000 years) of peace in a kingdom with Christ. The major difference between chiliasm and historic premillennialism is the emphasis that premillennialism gives to the Jewish nature of the fulfilled kingdom, interpreting it as a fulfillment or restoration of the Jewish kingdom, this time, however, with Christ reigning as king. Chiliasm does not make as much of the restored Jewish kingdom. Chiliasm of the early centuries was far from a unified system, but was characterized by a wide range of emphases.

CONQUEROR OR CONQUER

A repeated theme in Revelation is the one who conquers or the one who overcomes. In each of the letters to the seven churches, Jesus rewards those who overcome or conquer. The term is variously translated in the KJV, NIV, ASV, NAS, RSV, NRSV, and ESV Bibles. The KJV tradition, including the NIV, renders this as *overcometh* or *overcome* while the NAS, RSV traditions render it as *conquer*. The term is a translation of the Greek noun *nikē* or the verb *nikaō*. In a war context such as Revelation, the translation conqueror or conquer is preferred. In Revelation conquerors becomes a synonym for martyrs, those who conquer Satan by dying for their faith in Jesus.

DISPENSATIONALISM

The term "dispensationalism" derives from the Greek term *oikonomia*, which occurs eight times in the New Testament. The term in the New Testament is translated in a variety of ways depending on the context of the term. *Oikonomia* is the root of our English word "economics," which conveys the sense of the plan, or how something is carried on or brought into being. The Greek term, comprised of two words (*oikos, house* and *nomos, law,* or *principle*) literally means "principles by which a house operates." Of specific interest is Ephesians 1:10, where the RSV translates the term as "a plan" in reference to how God would unite all things in Christ. The modern theological term "dispensationalism" is derived from King James usage, where *oikonomia* is sometimes translated as "dispensation," sometimes as "stewardship." Working out of this "dispensational" King James terminology and with the unfortunate casting of God's saving work in terms of a time period rather than a system of operation, dispensationalists have developed their unique doctrinal views.

In dispensational use the term represents a period of time, differentiated from other periods of time, in which God works his plan in a specific manner. In different "dispensations" God works his plan in different ways. Each dispensation begins with an offer by God that mankind is to accept and obey and ends with rebellion, or failing to obey God. Based on a literal interpretation of several Old Testament passages, notably Daniel 9:24–27, dispensationalism holds that there will be seven dispensations, five before the incarnation, or first coming, of Christ, one representing the church age, or the age of grace, and then a final millennium or dispensation. Between the sixth and seventh dispensations, there is to be a "rapture" in which believing saints will be caught up into the air to meet Christ (1 Thess. 4:13–17). Toward the end of this sixth dispensation of grace, there will be an apostasy of the church that will introduce a period of tribulation (based on Dan. 9:24–27). The final dispensation, or the millennial kingdom, will be initiated by the second coming to earth of Christ, who will then re-establish the Jewish kingdom, over which he will reign eternally. This millennial kingdom will be on earth, centered on Jerusalem, and the finalization of God's eternal plan, or purpose. In this kingdom the law of God will be re-established along with the sacrificial system.

The following chart represents a basic dispensationalist scheme. However, dispensationalists have through the years differed significantly in their understanding of this scheme. Each dispensation begins with an offering, or promise, to man by God, is followed by man's disobedience, and finally by God's judgment on man's sinful ways.

SEVEN DISPENSATIONS

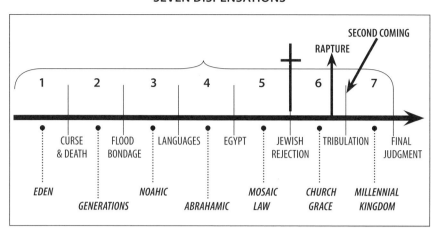

Although dispensationalists claim that this system dates back to the early doctrines of the church, especially into the second century, dispensationalism as we know it today dates from the early nineteenth century, when a new type of premillennialism was introduced by John Nelson Darby. Darby had been educated as a lawyer, graduating from Trinity College in Dublin. His academic preparation and education in the classical languages, humanities, and arts was extensive and impressive. His theological education was, however, self-learned. An ordained deacon in the Church of England, Darby became dissatisfied with what he interpreted as the apathy and lethargy of the Church of England. With several others who were disenchanted with the traditional church, Darby began a "house meeting" movement that soon became known as the Plymouth Brethren; their millennial theology was designated "Darbyism." Impressed by a literal interpretation of Dan. 9, Darby divided human history into seven periods of time, or dispensations. These periods of time, or dispensations, are listed below:

Dispensation 1: Gen. 1:28 – the period of innocence
    Dispensation 2: Gen. 3:7 – the period of conscience and moral responsibility
    Dispensation 3: Gen. 8:15 – the period of human government
    Dispensation 4: Gen. 12:1 – the period of promise
    Dispensation 5: Exod. 19:1 – the period of law
    Dispensation 6: Acts 2:1 – the period of the church
    Dispensation 7: Rev. 20:4 – the period of the kingdom

Fundamental to Darby's dispensationalism and those following him was the view that the church age is unknown to the Old Testament prophetic system since it was "unforeseen" by Daniel and the other Old Testament prophets. This is described as the "great parenthesis" inserted between the sixty-ninth and seventieth weeks of Dan. 9. In other words, the "kingdom clock" was stopped with the rejection of Jesus by the Jews and would be started again only at the second coming, at which time the kingdom would begin.

Although Darby made several visits to the United States, beginning in 1840, where his views were adopted by Charles Henry Mackintosh and William Blackstone, Darbyism was popularized on the American theological scene primarily by Cyrus Ingerson Scofield (1843–1921), a lawyer from Kansas who became a Congregationalist minister in 1882. Early in his theological career, Scofield was influenced by Mackintosh and Blackstone, and after attending the Niagara Bible Conference, where he was deeply impressed by a lecture on Darbyism, Scofield's influence spread widely with his edition of the Bible accompanied by notes interpreting the Bible along Darby's dispensational lines. So influenced was he by Darby that Scofield openly advanced the view that Darby was the most profound Bible scholar of his day. Dispensationalism in America owes much to the drive and foresight of Cyrus Ingerson Scofield, who through his ministry in the Congregational Church in Dallas, his Scofield Notes in the Scofield Reference Bible, and his relationship with Lewis Sperry Chafer, minister for the Scofield Memorial Church in Dallas and founder of the Dallas Theological Seminary, did much to shape American dispensationalism along Darbyism lines. A common thread running between Darby, Scofield, and Chafer was that none of them had formal theological training.

Other significant personalities in the American Dispensational movement have been A. C. Gaebelein, Dwight L. Moody, Charles Spurgeon, Watchman Nee, John Walvoord, and Hal Lindsey.

Clarence B. Bass has defined the basic dispensational position and view. "What, then, are the distinguishing features of dispensationalism? They are: its view of the nature and purpose of a dispensation; a rigid applied literalism in the interpretation of Scripture; a dichotomy between Israel and the church; a restricted view of the church; a Jewish concept of the kingdom; a postponement of the kingdom; a distinction between law and grace that creates a multiple basis for God's dealing with man; its view of the purpose of the great tribulation; its view of the nature of the millennial reign of Christ; its view of the eternal state, and its view of the apostate nature of Christendom." Clarence B. Bass, *Backgrounds to Dispensationalism* (Grand Rapids: Eerdmans, 1960), 19.

Problems one encounters with dispensational theology are the extreme literal interpretation of Scripture, failure to see beyond a Jewish fulfillment of Scripture, extreme speculative prophetic projections (especially of Dan. 9), the restoration of the Jewish system (which amounts to a direct challenge to the all sufficiency of Christ's atoning work), and the fact that much of its theology is based on poor biblical interpretation (for example, the rapture and the view based on Rev. 20:4-6 that the kingdom would be set up on earth).

The following is an attempt to diagram the dispensational scheme in similar fashion to other schematics developed in this study:

DISPENSATIONALISM

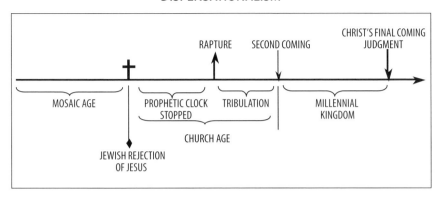

Dispensationalism is not limited to any one denominational group but cuts across religious affiliation. There are some religious movements, however, that are significantly dispensational in orientation. These would obviously include the Plymouth Brethren, but another religious group committed to dispensationalism as a fundamental tenet of faith is the Jehovah's Witness sect. As indicated above, those graduating from Dallas Theological Seminary would most likely be of this persuasion. It may not be an overstatement to observe that most followers of a literalist interpretation of Scripture, any biblical fundamentalism for example, would be of this persuasion. Many of the community Bible fellowship churches would be dispensational in theological outlook, especially in their interpretation of Revelation.

Eschatology

The term eschatology derives from two Greek words, *eschatos*, *last*, and *logos speech*, *word*, or *discussion*. As a theological term, eschatology carries the basic meaning of "the last things or the last age." It is used in a variety of different, yet related contexts such as the second coming of Christ, the final judgment, or the final days of human history. In another "timeless" sense, the term is used in regard to events that have "end-time" significance. Thus the pouring out of the Holy Spirit, repentance, baptism, and matters relating to divine activity concerning the inauguration of the kingdom are referred to as eschatological events, or matters having eschatological significance. In the context of genre such as apocalyptic, significant events such as the destruction of Jerusalem in A.D. 70 are often described in eschatological terminology. The intent is not to imply that such events inaugurate the final end time, but is intended to demonstrate that the event carries within it end-time significance.

In the context of Revelation, the author relies heavily on both apocalyptic and eschatological genres. In one sense, much apocalyptic is eschatological in that it draws heavily on the transcendent intervention of God, and in the case of Revelation such intervention bears end-time significance. Hence, in Revelation much of the apocalyptic genre has eschatological implications. The use of the eschatology of Revelation is not intended to imply that the eschatological terminology describing an event is intended as a prophecy regarding some end-time event. The intention is that the event being described in eschatological language simply bears end-time significance.

See also proleptic eschatology below.

GNOSTICISM

Gnosticism designates a wide range of thought that emerged during the late first century and became a serious threat to both Judaism and Christianity in the second century. The term stems from the Greek *gnosis, knowledge*. It referred to a doctrine that argued that "salvation," or "deliverance," came through the possession of a special intuitive knowledge that was possessed by those "enlightened" by some "deliverer" or one who would break in from "above." Gnosticism never formed a specific religion, but remained an influence or way of thinking that permeated most religions or philosophies of its day. It is not possible to define Gnosticism with any specific precision since it ranged over such a wide spectrum of thought, but a few leading concepts can be traced in most Gnostic-like communities. There was the thought derived from Platonic schools that matter was evil since matter and mankind were created by a "mischievous," or wayward, child (sometimes identified with Jehovah) of the ultimate God who is absolute light and goodness. This wayward god-child also created other spirit beings that ruled the "space" between the physical world and the ultimate god of light. In order for mankind to return to this god of light, they would have to negotiate space and escape these spirit beings (demi-gods) on their way back to the god of light. However, another child of this god of light, the deliverer, managed to make this journey from the god of light to mankind and enlighten certain ones, thus enabling them to return through space to the god of light by escaping the "spiritual beings in the heavenly places."

The evident similarities of this school of thought to the Christian faith made the Christian faith an obvious target for this philosophy. The challenge lay especially in the fact that this school views the physical creation as inherently evil. This would rise on Christian circles as a serious challenge to the resurrection of Jesus and eventually the general resurrection; otherwise, why would one want to raise an evil body and place a pure redeemed spirit back in captivity in the evil body? Another, even more serious challenge to the Christian faith, and one that John addressed in the Johannine Epistles, was the denial that Jesus the Christ had come in the flesh, since flesh is evil.

Other serious problems encountered in this gnostic mind-set were its obviously heretical cosmogony (an evil creation that was the result of the wayward god-child, Jehovah), its challenge to God's saving activity in history (notably Jesus' death on the cross and resurrection, both seen by Christians as God's saving activity in history), and its emphasis that deliverance lay exclusively in possession of some special esoteric knowledge possessed by an elite community of believers. This heresy also tended to take sin lightly since sin was something intangible resulting from the flesh. Those "spiritual beings" enlightened by *gnosis* were not responsible for these sins of the flesh. This strange concept of special "grace" led to an antinomian (no law) and lascivious, licentious (having a license to do something) attitude that was a direct contradiction to the ethical standards of both Judaism and Christianity.

Concerns over such forms of Gnostic thought (some of them Jewish forms) permeate much of the New Testament in some form, especially the Johannine Epistles. The problem in the Johannine Epistles, where John refers to this mind-set as the "antichrist," had to do with the denial that Jesus had come in the flesh, which idea lay at the very heart of Christian faith. This "antichrist" flesh problem is not what we encounter in Revelation, and it would be pushing the gnostic argument to the extreme to see Revelation as a response to this form of gnostic thought. Since Revelation was written in the context of Ephesus and Asia Minor, which was certainly a hotbed for gnostic thought, it is not surprising to find a possible reference to gnostic tendencies in the references to the Nicolaitans, of whom we know very little other than the fact that they appeared to be an antinomian and licentious challenge to the Christian faith. Obviously, Gnosticism and the "antichrist" of the Johannine Epistles are not the problem addressed by John in Revelation.

Heilsgeschichte

Heilsgeschichte is a German word that has become a theological term relating to God's plan of salvation, or scheme of redemption. The fundamental theme of *Heilsgeschichte* is that God has worked his plan of salvation in the context of real history. The idea is that God's acts of salvation have taken place in real events in history according to a plan that God has been working on since the fall. This plan reached a climax in the death, burial, and resurrection of Jesus, which all took place in history. Salvation is not something worked out in some form of specialized knowledge such as gnosticism, but is located in decisive acts of God in history that are revealed as part of the process of history. *Heilsgeschichte* does not claim that history itself is salvific but that God's acts of salvation have taken place in history.

Millennialism

Millennialism is a broad term that applies to modern interpretations of the thousand-year reign of Revelation 20:4. The term derives from the Latin *mille*, one thousand, and *annus, year*. Millennial views and theories are many. Several sub-categories are included in millennialism, namely, amillennialism, premillennialism, postmillennialism, and dispensationalism. Each of these is discussed in this glossary. Basically, these theories attempt to interpret the statement in Revelation 20:4 that the saints described in 20:4 (martyrs) will reign with Christ for a thousand years. This millennial kingdom/reign is perceived by some to follow the parousia, or second coming, of Jesus (premillennialism and dispensationalism), or to precede the parousia (postmillennialism). In either case, millennial theories have been extremely divisive in church history. One millennial view of the ancient church, chiliasm (see the glossary) was similar in some form to premillennialism. This view in a variety of forms was most likely the dominant theory of the early church and prevailed until Origen and then Augustine challenged the extreme literal interpretation of the biblical text upon which most millennial theories stand. In similar fashion today, amillennial scholars challenge most millennial theories, charging that they are not the result of careful biblical exegesis and hermeneutic (interpretation) and manifest an extreme literalist interpretation of the biblical text. Other challenges to millennial theories are that they remove the message of Revelation from the first-century church and push the message into the distant future.

MONTANISM

Montanism was a late second- and early third-century heretical Christian movement originally known as the "Phrygian heresy." In later years it was identified with, and named after, its founder, Montanus (ca. A.D. 170). The group was characterized by ecstatic prophecy and revelations, engrossment in millennial speculation, extended periods of fasting and asceticism, and an interest in eschatological conjecture. The movement engendered a bitter controversy with the mainline church that ultimately led to the excommunication of Montanus and the Montanist movement. Montanism's influence was significant enough, however, to sway the great church scholar Tertullian of Carthage, who converted to this persuasion shortly after A.D. 208. Montanism gained a considerable North African following as a result of Tertullian's influence. Because of the movement's emphasis on ecstasy, revelations, and prophecy, the book of Revelation became one of the movement's favored texts, with the result that many mainline churches became suspicious of Revelation and resisted the inclusion of this book into the church's canon. In time, however, Revelation was looked upon in its own right and was accepted into the canon. After the third century, references to Montanism in Christian literature began to ebb, with only sparse mention indicating that by the seventh century Montanism was no longer of any interest in church concerns.

Montanism's interest to Revelation studies is limited to references to early millennial thought and the role this movement played in the acceptance of Revelation into the church's cannon. In the larger context of Christian study, the reluctance of the mainline church to accept the charismatic tendencies of Montanism indicates the declining interest and suspicion of the mainline church in charismatic expressions of Christian faith.

PAROUSIA

Parousia is the combination of two Greek words, *para, alongside* in conjunction with *ousia, substance* literally means "the coming alongside in substance." In Christian dialogue *parousia* refers to the literal "coming of Jesus in substance," or the *second coming* of Jesus. The term is used in reference to the real, "bodily" or "physical" coming of Jesus in place of a spiritual coming as in the presence of Jesus with his church today. The term is eschatological in the sense that it refers to Jesus' coming in judgment at the end of the age.

POSTMILLENNIALISM

The roots of postmillennialism can be identified in Christian theology as early as the century following Origen and Augustine's allegorizing hermeneutic and the church's abandonment of chiliasm. The optimistic mindset following Constantine's "conversion" and the establishment of a universal state church paved the way for a view of the church as the arrival of the kingdom of God on earth. In the modern era, however, postmillennialism first came into prominence in England as a result of the influence of Daniel Whitby, a Unitarian minister (1638–1726). The religious fervor and revival in America following the preaching of Jonathan Edwards and others ushered in an optimistic view of the church's potential to "convert" society and prepare it for the coming of Christ to take up his reign on earth. Postmillennialism, with its optimistic view of history and progress, looks toward a "golden age of spiritual growth and prosperity" as the preaching of the gospel of Christ ushers in an age of religious, or spiritual, revival. Postmillennialists therefore interpret this period of great religious awakening and conversion as the millennial age that precedes the return and reign of Christ. The reign of Christ is thus "post-millennial." Loraine Boettner, a prominent twentieth-century postmillennialist, observes regarding postmillennialism that it is "that view of the last things which holds that the kingdom of God is now being extended in the world through the preaching of the gospel and the saving work of the Holy Spirit in the hearts of individuals, that the world eventually is to be Christianized and that the return of Christ is to occur at the close of a long period of righteousness and peace commonly called the millennium." He further observes that this period of religious awakening "is to be brought about through forces now active in the world. . . . The changed character of individuals will be reflected in an uplifted social, economic, political and cultural life of mankind. The world at large will enjoy a state of righteousness which up until now has been seen only in relatively small and isolated groups . . . it . . . means that evil in all its many forms eventually will be reduced to negligible proportions, that Christian principles will be the rule, not the exception, and that Christ will return to a truly Christianized world" (Loraine Boettner, "Postmillennialism," *The Meaning of the Millennium: Four Views*, ed. Robert G. Clouse (Downers Grove, IL: InterVarsity Press, 1977), 118-141.

Alexander Campbell, and many followers of the Restoration Movement among the Disciples of Christ and Churches of Christ prior to the American Civil War were postmillennial in theological outlook. Following the trauma of the Civil War and the subsequent division of the Restoration Movement into two distinct groups, the Disciples of Christ and the Churches of Christ, Churches of Christ vacillated between a chiliast form of premillennialism and a tentative form of postmillennialism.

POSTMILLENNIALISM

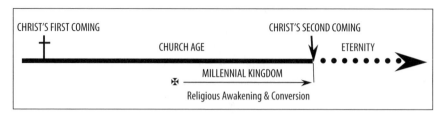

Problems encountered with the postmillennialist view are that postmillennialism cannot be sustained biblically and that it manifests an overly optimistic anthropology and an overly progressive understanding of sociology.

Premillennialism

Premillennialism is one of those terms that can be fairly widely interpreted, depending on the perspective of the interpreter. Broadly speaking, the term refers to theories of the millennium (Rev. 20:4) that consider the second coming of Christ (the parousia) to occur immediately prior to the arrival of the millennium. This doctrine teaches that Christ will return to earth and establish his kingdom on earth, most often located in Jerusalem. Sometimes premillennial theories are "moderate," meaning that they simply consider the coming of the kingdom to follow Christ's second coming. Views range from those that do not identify the church in any fashion with the kingdom, to those that see the church as a "spiritual" kingdom still to be fully realized on earth at some time in the future. Sometimes the view refers to a literal fulfillment on earth, at other times to a kingdom in heaven.

Ancient chiliasm was premillennial in thought and would be at one end of a continuum of premillennialism. Dispensationalism (for example, Darbyism, the Jehovah's Witnesses, Scofield, Hal Lindsey, and the Dallas Theological Seminary theology) would lie at the other end of that continuum with a more fully developed dispensational theory of the millennium. (These views are discussed elsewhere in the glossary). Toward the middle of the continuum would be the historic premillennialism espoused by Eldon Ladd.

A fully developed premillennial view considers the church to be a "spiritual" kingdom with Christ reigning in the hearts of the saints from heaven, but with a fulfilled kingdom to be literally established on earth, centered in Jerusalem, with the Jewish system restored. Such views consider God's promises to the Jews to have never been completely fulfilled and yet awaiting fulfillment.

HISTORIC PREMILLENNIALISM

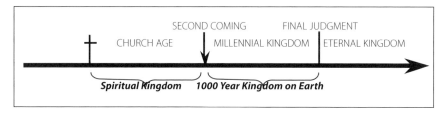

A major difference between historic premillennialism and dispensationalism is the absence of a rapture and postponement (prophetic clock stopped) theory in historic premillennialism. Both, however, stress the Jewish nature of the millennial kingdom and the fact that this kingdom will be on earth and centered in Jerusalem.

Problems encountered in historic premillennialism are the Jewish nature of the future kingdom, the expectation of an earthly kingdom centered in Jerusalem, the literal interpretation of the thousand years, the view that the kingdom must be the earthly fulfillment of the promise to the Jews of an earthly kingdom over all the world, which promise was not fulfilled in the past, and the denial of the fact that the church age is really the kingdom age, that there is something lacking in the church-kingdom.

Proleptic Eschatology

This concept derives from the word *prolepsis*, from the Greek *prolepsis* or *prolambanein*, *take place beforehand*, from *pro*, *before*, and *lambanō*, *to take* or *receive*. *Eschatology* (see above) means a discussion of end-time things. In the context of eschatology, proleptic means to describe, experience, or see something relating to the end-time in advance of the end. The Lord's Supper or communion is a proleptic eschatological experience in the sense that during this meal the Christian experiences in advance the benefits of the great eschatological banquet that all of the saints will experience around God's table. Baptism is a proleptic eschatological experience in that in baptism one experiences in advance the resurrection to a new life in Christ. In Revelation John describes imminent judgment on Rome in terms of end-of-the-world language. In this he is drawing on the concept of proleptic eschatological experience in that Rome is experiencing the final judgment in advance or that the judgment is expressed in advance in terms of end-of-the-world language.

Pseudepigrapha

The Pseudepigrapha refers to a large group of writings falsely attributed to a person other than the one penning the work. The Greek term behind our English word simply means "false writing." In regard to New Testament Pseudepigrapha, the term refers to writings ascribed to an author other than the real writer. In the case of the Old Testament, however, the term has broader reference, namely, to literature not included in the canon, but considered sacred by early Jewish and Christian groups. Pseudepigraphy includes a wide range of literature covering what may almost be authentic to what is obviously falsely attributed to an author. Pseudepigraphy was not considered literary forgery in the early years of the church since the intention of the writer was not necessarily to deceive. Early Christians considered it a matter of respect and honor to attribute their writings to one who had inspired their work. Some even argued that failure to do so was a matter of failure to honor one's predecessors. By the year 120, pseudepigraphy was the norm among many Christian groups. Correctly speaking, pseudepigraphy was not the same as anonymity; pseudepigraphy was related in some fashion through a school of thought to some great person. Scholars judge only the references to the author to be "false," with the content of the writings themselves being considered invaluable for clarifying some early Jewish and Christian problems or difficulties. Some of the pseudepigraphical works were produced by learned and respected scholars. Important questions to ask pseude-pigraphical writings relate not so much as to who wrote the work, but why the author wrote it and attributed it to another, and what the theme or theology of the book is.

Examples of literature considered pseudepigraphical would be *1 Enoch*; *Testament of Adam*; *Odes of Solomon*, *Apocalypse of Solomon*; *Apocalypse of Elijah*; *Ascension of Moses*; *3 Corinthians*; *Epistle to the Laodiceans*; *Apocalypse of Paul*; *Passions of Peter and Paul*; *Acts of Paul*; *Apocalypse of Peter*; *Gospel of Peter*; *Birth of Mary*; *Passion of Mary*; *Apocalypse of the Virgin*s. It is obvious that some of the pseudepigrapha are also listed among the apocryphal books.

The reason that the pseudepigrapha are important to Revelation studies is that much of the thought and message of Revelation is paralleled in the pseudepigrapha, and many of the conditions of the living community were similar. Such information provides a thought and conceptual background, as well as a terminological environment for understanding Revelation as a real living piece of literature addressed to a real living community of believers whose faith was under question and being severely challenged.

REBIRTH OF IMAGES OR RECAPITULATION

This is a literary style in which the writer mentions a concept without developing it but will return to it progressively as the story is developed. On each revisit to the theme, it is developed in greater specificity. In the tradition of Revelation hermeneutic reaching back to the fourth century, *recapitulatio* (recapitulation) has been explored and considered a significant literary and theological device. Austin Farrer in modern times described this device as the "rebirth of images." For instance, John introduces the expression "those who dwell on earth" early in Revelation without definition or expansion. He returns to this theme repeatedly, adding definition and specificity so that we learn that those who dwell on earth are not all those living on earth but those who belong to the world and who worship the Roman Emperor and persecute the saints.

SALVATION

In Revelation, salvation is not expressed in terms of individual salvation but of God's ultimate scheme of redemption of his created universe. The apocalyptist looks beyond individual salvation to see salvation in the big picture. In this context salvation is often expressed in Revelation as victory, that is, victory of God and the saints over Satan and the problem of evil and suffering. The Greek term is *sōtēria*, which according to context can be translated "healing, "salvation," or victory." Since the context of Revelation is a war between Satan and God and Satan and God's people, victory is a suitable translation for *sōtēria*. Apocalyptic is not focused in salvation from sin but salvation or victory of God's creation over evil.

Soon

John uses the word soon, for instance, in Revelation 1:1, where he records that God has revealed to the saints through Jesus that certain things must soon take place. The expression soon derives from the Greek *en tachei*. All of our major translations (KJV, ASV, NASV, RSV, NRSV, NIV, ESV) translate this as "soon" or shortly." Greek lexicons and grammars inform us that in the context of eschatological thought the adverbial phrase *en tachei* should be translated as soon or shortly, not swiftly or quickly. In Revelation this means that the events revealed must soon take place. This does not mean that they will take place quickly when they eventually happen, as futurists believe.

Time

Two Greek words are translated into English as time, *chronos* and *kairos*. *Chronos* is normally translated as time as it passes without significance. *Kairos* carries the sense of critical, important, or significant time. *Kairos* can be translated as crisis time. Although translated as time in Revelation, the Greek word used by John is *kairos*. The expression "the time is at hand" (Rev. 1:3) carries the sense that the crisis time, *ho kairos eggus*, is imminent or about to break in on the readers.

Theodicy

A theodicy attempts to defend the righteousness of an all-powerful, loving, and holy God in light of suffering and the persistence of evil. The term derives from two Greek words, *theos* (God) and *dikē righteousness, judgment, justice.* One definition expresses theodicy as "a vindication of God's goodness and justice in the face of the existence of evil." Revelation is a theodicy in that it attempts to explain the meaning of suffering and martyrdom by innocent people living in an evil world. Revelation seeks to encourage the persecuted to see their life in the big picture of God's scheme of redemption (*Heilsgeschichte*) and to understand that martyrdom, although evil, is not the ultimate end of life for those who maintain faith in Jesus.

Bibliography

This is not intended to be an extensive bibliography over the Book of Revelation. For a comprehensive bibliography of books, commentaries, and journal articles we recommend the bibliographies in:

Aune, *Revelation*, vols. 1, 2, 3, Dallas: Word Book Publisher, 1997, 1998, 1998.
Beale, G. K. ,*The Book of Revelation*, Grand Rapids: William B. Eerdmans, 1999.
Mounce, Robert H. , *The Book of Revelation*, Grand Rapids: William B. Eerdmans, 1977, 1998.

The following bibliography is a working list of the major books used as reference materials in this commentary:

Books:

Aland, Barbara, Kurt Aland, Johannes Karavidopoulos, Carlo Martini, and Bruce Metzger. *The Greek New Testament*. Fourth revised edition of the twenty-sixth edition. Nördlingen, Germany: United Bible Societies, 2002.
Aune, David E. *Revelation*. 3 vols. Dallas: Word, 1997, 1998, 1998.
Bass, Clarence B. *Backgrounds to Dispensationalism*. Eugene, Oregon: Wipf and Stock, 1960.
Bauckham, Richard. *The Climax of Prophecy*. Edinburgh: T & T Clark, 1993, 2000.
____. *The Theology of the Book of Revelation*. Cambridge, England: Cambridge University Press, 1993.
Beale, G. K. *The Book of Revelation*. Grand Rapids: William B. Eerdmans, 1999.
Beasley-Murray, G. R. *Revelation*. Grand Rapids: William B. Eerdmans, 1974.
Beckwith, Isbon T. *The Apocalypse of John*. Grand Rapids: Baker Book House, 1999; reprint1979. Original copyright, 1919.
Boring, M. Eugene. *Revelation*. Interpretation. Nashville: John Knox Press, 1989.
Caird, G. B. *The Revelation of St. John the Divine*. San Francisco: Harper and Row, 1966.
Charles, R. H.. *A Critical and Exegetical Commentary on the Revelation of St. John*. 2 vols. Edinburgh: T & T Clark, 1920.
Collins, Adela Yarbro. *Crisis & Catharsis*. Philadelphia: Westminster Press, 1984.
____. *The Apocalypse*. Wilmington, Delaware: Glazier, 1979.
____. *The Combat Myth in the Book of Revelation*. Missoula, Montana: Scholars Press, 1976.
Collins, J. J.. *The Apocalyptic Imagination*. New York: Crossroad, 1992.
____, ed. *Apocalypse: The Morphology of a Genre*. Semeia. Society of Biblical Literature, 1979.
Court, John M. *Myth and the Mystery of the Book of Revelation*. Atlanta: John Knox Press, 1979.
Davis, John J. *Biblical Numerology* Grand Rapids: Baker Book House, 1968.
Elior, Rachel. *The Three Temples*. Oxford, Oregon: Littman Library of Jewish Civilization, 2005.
Ellul, Jacques. *Apocalypse*. New York: Seabury, 1977.
Farrer, Austin. *A. Rebirth of Images: The Making of St. John's Apocalypse*. Boston: Beacon, 1963.
Fee, Gordon D. *Revelation*. Eugene, Oregon: Wipf & Stock Publishers, 2010.
Feuillet, A, *The Apocalypse*. New York: Alba House, 1975.
Fiorenza, Elisabeth Schüssler. *Invitation to the Book of Revelation*. New York: Doubleday & Company, 1981.
____. *The Book of Revelation: Justice and Judgment*. Philadelphia: Fortress Press, 1985.
Ford, J. Massyngberde. *Revelation*. Anchor Bible. New York: Doubleday & Company, 1975.
Frend, W. H. C. *Martyrdom and Persecution in the Early Church*. Oxford: Blackwell, 1965.
Hailey, Homer. *Revelation*. Grand Rapids: Baker, 1979.
Hamilton, Mark W. ed. *The Transforming Word One-Volume Commentary on the Bible*. Abilene, Texas: Abilene Christian University Press, 2009.
Hanson, Paul D. *The Dawn of Apocalyptic*. Philadelphia: Fortress, 1975.
Hemer, Colin J. *The Letters to the Seven Churches in their Local Setting*. Sheffield, England: Sheffield Academic Press, 1986, 1989.
Kiddle, M. and M. K. Ross. *The Revelation of St. John*. London: Hodder and Stoughton, 1940.
Metzger, B. M. *Breaking the Code*. Nashville: Abingdon, 1993.
Michaels, J. R. *Interpreting the Book of Revelation*. Grand Rapids: Baker, 1992.
____. *Revelation*. Downers Grove, Illinois: InterVarsity Press, 1997.

Minear, P. S. *New Testament Apocalyptic*. Nashville: Abingdon, 1981.
Morris, Leon. *The Revelation of St. John*. Grand Rapids: Eerdmans, 1987.
Morris, Leon. *Apocalyptic*. Grand Rapids: Eerdmans, 1972.
Mounce, Robert H. *The Book of Revelation*. Grand Rapids: Eerdmans, 1977, 1998.
Nickelsburg, George W. E. *Jewish Literature between the Bible and the Mishna*. Minneapolis: Fortress Press, 2005.
Orlov, Andrei. *The Enoch-Metatron Tradition*. Tübingen, Germany: Mohr Siebeck, 2005.
____. *Scrinium, The Theophanei School: Jewish Roots of Eastern Christian Mysticism*. Saint-Pietersbourg: Byzantinorossica, 2007.
Osborne, Grant R. *Revelation*. Baker Exegetical Commentary on the New Testament. Grand Rapids: Baker Academic, 2002.
Pannenberg, Wolfhart. *Theology and the Kingdom of God*. Philadelphia: Westminster Press, 1969.
Ramsey, W. M. *The Letters to the Seven Churches of Asia and Their Place in the Plan of the Apocalypse of John*. London: Hodder and Stoughton, 1904.
Rissi, M. *Time and History: A Study on the Revelation*. Richmond: John Knox, 1966.
Roberts, J W. *The Revelation to John*. Austin, Texas: Sweet Publishing Company,1974.
Rossing, Barbara. *The Rapture Exposed*. New York: Basic Books, 2004.
Rowley, H. H. *The Relevance of Apocalyptic*. New York: Association Press, 1963.
Sauer, Val J. *The Eschatology Handbook*. Atlanta: John Knox Press, 1981.
Smalley, Stephen S. *The Revelation to John*. Downers Grove, Illinois: IVP Academic, 2005.
Summers, Ray. *Worthy Is The Lamb*. Nashville: Broadman, 1951.
Swete, H. B. *The Apocalypse of St. John*. London: Macmillan, 1906.
Talbert, C. H. *The Apocalypse*. Louisville: Westminster Press, 1994.
VanderKam, James C. *The Dead Sea Scrolls*. Grand Rapids: Eerdmans, 1994.
Walvoord, John F. *The Revelation of Jesus Christ*. Chicago: Moody, 1966.
Weinrich, William C., ed. *Revelation*. Ancient Christian Commentary on Scripture. Downers Grove, Illinois: InterVarsity Press, 2005.
Wilcock, M. *I Saw Heaven Opened*. London: InterVarsity Press, 1975.
Wright, N. T. *The New Testament and the People of God*. Minneapolis: Fortress Press, 1992.
____. *Jesus and the Victory of God*. Minneapolis: Fortress Press, 1996.
____. *The Resurrection of the Son of God*. Minneapolis: Fortress Press, 2003.

Journals, Articles, and Encyclopedia Articles

Aune, D. E. "Eschatology." *Anchor Bible Dictionary*. Ed. David Noel Freedman. New York: Doubleday, 1992.
Bornkamm, Günter. "Die Kompositionder apokalyptischen Vision in der Offenbarung Johannes.„ *Zeitschrift fur die Neutestamentliche Wissenschaft*, 36 (1937), 132–149.
Caird, G. B. "On Deciphering the Book of Revelation." *Expository Times* (1962–1963), 13, 15, 51–53, 81–84, 103–105.
Charry, Ellen T. "A Sharp Two-edged Sword. "*Interpretation*, 53 (April 1999), 158–172.
Collins, Adela Yarbro. "Apocalyptic Themes in Biblical Literature." *Interpretation*, 53 (April 1999), 117–130.
____. "Apocalypses and Apocalypticism." *Anchor Bible Dictionary*, ed. David Noel Freedman. New York: Doubleday, 1992.
Cukrowski, Kenneth. "The Influence of the Emperor Cult on the Book of Revelation." *Restoration Quarterly*, 45, numbers 1 & 2 (2003).
Danner, Dan. "A History of the Interpretation of Revelation 20:1–10 in the Restoration Movement." *Restoration Quarterl,*. 7, 217–235.
Freedman, D. N. "The Flowering of Apocalyptic." *Journal for Theology and the Church*, 6 (1969).
Jeremias, J. "Chiasmus in den Paulusbriefen." *Zeitschrift fur die neutestamentliche Wisenschaft*, 49 (1958).
Käsemann, Ernst. "The Beginnings of Christian Theology." *Journal for Theology and the Church*, 6 (1969).
McNicol, Alan. "Revelation." In *The Transforming Word*, ed. Mark W. Hamilton. Abilene, Texas: Abilene Christian University Press, 2009.
____. "Revelation 11:1–4 and the Structure of the Apocalypse." *Restoration Quarterly*, 22, Number 4 (1979), 193–202.
Norris, Frederick W. "Alogoi." In *Encyclopedia of Early Christianity*, vol. 1, Everett Ferguson, ed. New York: Garland Publishing Co., 1997.
Patterson, Stephen J. "Apocrypha." In *Anchor Bible Dictionary*, ed. David Noel Freedman. New York: Doubleday, 1992.
Roberts, J W. "The Meaning of the Eschatology in the Book of Revelation." *Restoration Quarterly*, 15 (1972), 95–110.
Sleeper, C. Norman. "Christ's Coming and Christian Living," *Interpretation*, 53 (April 1999), 131–142.

Smylie, James H. "A New Heaven and New Earth." *Interpretation*, 53 (April 1999), 143–157.

Towner, W. Sibley. "Theological Table Talk: Rapture, Red Heifer, and other Millennial Misfortunes." *Theology Today* (October, 1999), 379–389.

Wallace, David. "The Use of Psalms in the Shaping of a Text: Psalm 2:7 and Psalm 110:1 in Hebrews." *Restoration Quarterly*. 45, numbers 1 & 2 (2003).

Notes

Preface

1   Dr. Robert's name was J W Roberts. The initials were not an abbreviated form for names, hence there are no periods following J and W as in J. W. Roberts.

Introduction

1   Eusebius, *The Ecclesiastical History*, trans. Kirsopp Lake (Cambridge, Mass.: Harvard University Press1926/1965).
2   Grant R. Osborne, *Revelation* (Grand Rapids: Baker Academic, 2002), 1.
3   J. Ramsey Michaels, *Revelation* (Downers Grove, Ill.: InterVarsity Press, 1997), 13.
4   G. B. Caird, *The Revelation of St. John the Divine* (San Francisco: Harper and Row, 1966), 2.
5   Richard Bauckham, *The Theology of the Book of Revelation* (Cambridge: Cambridge University Press, 1993, 1998), 1.
6   Cf. the above note.
7   Richard Bauckham, *The Climax of Prophecy* (Edinburgh: T & T Clark, 1993, 2000), ix–x.
8   Bauckham, *The Theology of the Book of Revelation*, 1f.
9   Cf. Rev. 2:9; 3:9.
10   Isbon T. Beckwith, *The Apocalypse of John* (1919; repr. ed., Grand Rapids: Baker Book House, 1979), 337. Beckwith has an excellent discussion on the early circulation of Revelation. Beckwith adds that "the silence of these writers (Ignatius, Barnabas, and Hermas) does not however prove their ignorance of the book."
11   Little is known of the Alogoi other than that they were a group who denied the divinity of the Word (a-logos). Frederick W. Norris, "Alogoi," *Encyclopedia of Early Christianity*, ed. Everett Ferguson (New York: Garland, 1990).
12   Cited by Caird, 2.
13   Cf. the excellent studies by John J. Collins, George W. E. Nickelsburg, Andrei Orlov, James VanderKam, and others working in the field of Jewish mysticism, apocalyptic, and the Dead Sea Scrolls.
14   Allan McNicol, "Revelation," in *The Transforming Word* (Abilene, Tex.: ACU Press, 2009), 1063.
15   See the excellent studies by G. B. Caird, Robert H. Mounce, Colin Hemer, M. Eugene Boring, Bruce Metzger, Adela Yarbro Collins, Elisabeth Schüssler Fiorenza, J. Ramsey Michaels, Michael Wilcock, G. K. Beale, Grant R. Osborne, David Aune, Richard Bauckham, and others.
16   Cf. Hal Lindsey, *The Late Great Planet Earth*, *Satan Is Alive and Well on Planet Earth*, *The Liberation of Planet Earth*, and Tim LaHaye and Jerry Jenkins, *Left Behind* and the Left Behind Series, which typify this speculative end-time focus on Revelation.
17   Cf. the excellent list of scholars listed in endnote 15.
18   Colin Hemer, *The Letters to the Seven Churches of Asia in Their Local Setting* (Sheffield, Eng.: Sheffield Academic Press, 1989), 1. Hemer cites H. B. Sweet, *The Apocalypse of St. John*, 2d ed. (London, 1907), ccxvii. Hemer's study provides an excellent resource for understanding the historical and social context of the church in first-century Roman Asia, and the serious student is encouraged to pay careful attention to this work.
19   Ibid.
20   Michaels, 22.
21   Osborne, 1.
22   Proleptic eschatological is a technical term that emphasizes something that is to be experienced at the final end of the world judgment but is experienced in advance in the present time. Proleptic derives from two Greek words, *pro* (*before*) and *lēmpsomai* (*to receive* or *experience*). Baptism is an advance experience of the final resurrection, as the Lord's Supper is an advance experience of the final eschatological banquet in heaven.
23   The idealist philosophy of history is a model of interpretation that plays down the historical context of the text, emphasizing a more contemporary approach to the text. This will be defined more succinctly under models of interpretation in the section "Interpreting Revelation" in the introduction.
24   Michaels, 21.
25   Cf. Osborne, 6; Beale. 4. The dating of Revelation will be discussed in greater detail below.
26   Cf. Colin Hemer, *The Letters to the Seven Churches of Asia in Their Local Setting*.
27   Bill Humble and Ian Fair, *The Seven Cities of Asia* (Nashville: Gospel Advocate Co., 1995), 19.
28   William M. Ramsay, *The Letters to the Seven Churches* (Grand Rapids: Baker Book House, 1979, originally published by Hodder and Stoughton, London, 1904), 114.
29   We need to draw attention again to the fine article by Kenneth Cukrowski, "The Influence of the Emperor Cult on the Book of Revelation," *Restoration Quarterly*, in which Cukrowski argues succinctly that, although the Roman

imperial cult posed a serious threat to the early church, it was only part of the social environment that opposed the spread of Christianity in the first three centuries of Christianity. We need also to note, however, that Revelation is pointing to an imminent, yet growing Roman threat that was not yet fully present, but clearly on the horizon. Yarbro Collins thinks that the social crises faced by the church, not persecution and martyrdom, are the real issue in Revelation. Osborne, however, argues correctly that Collins has overstated her case (Osborne, 11).

30   Several fine studies of persecution and martyrdom during this period enlighten our understanding of the sociological, political, and religious plight of both the Jews and Christians during this period. Cf. W. H. C. Frend, 213. Note also Eusebius, *Ecclesiastical History*, vols 1 and 2.

31   Eusebius, *Ecclesiastical History*, 1.231ff., and especially 273ff.

32   For excellent discussion on the deteriorating relations between the Christians and Rome, see Isbon T. Beckwith, *The Apocalypse of John* (Grand Rapids: Baker Book House, 1991; repr. 1979), 197ff.; Yarbro Collins, *Crisis and Catharsis*, 97ff.; and W. H. C. Frend, 151ff., 210ff.

33   Frend, 213.

34   Frend, 215.

35   Cf. Homer Hailey, *Revelation, An Introduction and Commentary* (Grand Rapids: Baker Book House, 1979), 59ff., for detailed discussion of the historical background to Roman persecutions of the church. Cf. also Elizabeth Schüssler Fiorenza, *The Book of Revelation: Justice and Judgment* (Philadelphia: Fortress, 1985), 9ff.

36   Cf. Osborne, 10ff.

37   Nickelsburg, *2 Ezra, 2 Baruch, passim*.

38   Frend, 210ff. This interesting exchange of correspondence between Pliny and the Emperor Trajan, and its consequences for Roman-Christian relations is documented in most commentaries on Christian persecution and Christian-Roman relations. See also Eusebius, *Ecclesiastical History*, 1277ff.

39   Yarbro Collins, *Crisis and Catharsis*, 84ff.

40   Cukrowski, "The Influence of the Emperor Cult on the Book of Revelation," *Restoration Quarterly*.

41   Cf. H. H. Rowley, *The Relevance of Apocalyptic* (New York: Association Press, 1963).

42   Calvin Miller, *The Singer Trilogy* (Downers Grove, Ill.: InterVarsity Press, 1975, 1990). This is a fascinating "mythology" well worth reading as an illustration of creative symbolic or figurative writing.

43   We will address the tendency to over literalize Revelation at a later point of the study as we examine the literary nature of Revelation as apocalyptic. However, at this point, cf Fiorenza, *The Book of Revelation*, 9ff., for discussion on the literary style and genre of Revelation.

44   Cf. Schüssler Fiorenza, *The Book of Revelation*, 1ff., for an excellent introduction to the literary genre of Revelation and its rich Judeo-Christian heritage. For excellent comments and discussion on the use of the apocalyptic traditions in Revelation, see Richard Bauckham, *The Climax of Prophecy* (Edinburgh: T & T Clark, 1993), 38ff. Cf. also Nickelsburg, *Jewish Literature between the Bible and the Mishna*.

45   Cf the works of John J. Collins and George Nickelsburg listed in the bibliography.

46   Yarbro Collins shapes the theology of her doctoral dissertation on Revelation around a structural analysis of the book. Adela Yarbro Collins, *The Combat Myth in the Book of Revelation* (Missoula, Mont.: Scholars Press, 1976). Cf. 5–56. Although considerable discussion has been generated regarding the structure of Revelation, almost all serious commentaries on Revelation have given considerable attention to structural forms. Richard Bauckham, *The Climax of Prophecy*, devotes the first chapter of his book to structure, (1–37). The biblical literary tradition and environment of the closing centuries of the Old Testament era and of the first century of the Christian era have provided us with an extensive library of apocalyptic literature against which we can evaluate and interpret the book of Revelation. Without sensitivity to this rich literary tradition, expositions of Revelation are denied some vital corrective parameters and much enriching symbolism.

47   Cf. also H. B. Swete, *The Apocalypse of John*. Even in recent times some have preferred to refer to Revelation as an apocalypse; cf. C. H. Talbert, *The Apocalypse* (Louisville: Westminster John Knox, 1994); D. E. Aune, "The Apocalypse of John and Greco-Roman Revelatory Magic," *New Testament Studies* 33 (1987); D. L. Barr, "The Apocalypse as a Symbolic Transformation of the World: A Literary Analysis," *Interpretation* 38 (1984).

48   The recent resurgence of interest in J. R. R. Tolkien's Ring trilogy and J. K. Rowling's Harry Potter series, along with a continuing fascination with C. S. Lewis's Narnia works is an indication that Western readers can make the transition to myth and legend. The difficulty encountered in regard to literature such as Revelation is the fundamentalist reluctance to view Scripture adopting myth and cosmic symbolism to convey theological truth. A reasonable understanding of the fundamental nature of myth in expressing otherworldly reality is often lacking in fundamentalist views of Scripture.

49   The term "rebirth of images" is one made popular by Austin Farrer, *A Rebirth of Images* (Westminster: Dacre Press, 1949). It refers to the particular style of the author of Revelation of repeating images previously used or understood in either new contexts or in a more detailed manner than previously. This rebirth of images accounts for the many repetitions of themes that commentators have for centuries noted in Revelation. Any structural analysis of Revelation must take into consideration the unique linking, or hooking, style John builds into his narrative thereby linking one vision or image to another.

50   Allan J. McNicol, "Revelation," in *The Transforming Word* (Abilene, Tex.: ACU Press, 2009), 1064.

51   Cf. G. K. Beale, *The Book of Revelation* (Grand Rapids: Eerdmans, 1999), 76ff., for an excellent discussion of this.

52   Cf. the excellent article by David Wallace, "The Use of Psalms in the Shaping of a Text: Psalm 2:7 and Psalm 110:1 in Hebrews," *Restoration Quarterly* 45.1 & 2 (2003): 41ff., demonstrates how New Testament writers creatively used the Old Testament.

53   R. H. Gundry, *The Use of the Old Testament in St. Matthew's Gospel* (Leiden: Brill, 1967).

54   Cf. Beale, 86ff., for an excellent discussion on types of fulfillment references in the New Testament.

55   Cf. the discussion of this in the arguments for an authorship other than the same author of the Gospel of John in Robert H. Mounce, *The Book of Revelation* (Grand Rapids: Eerdmans, 1977), 13; Caird; *The Revelation of St. John the Divine*, 5; Beckwith, *The Apocalypse of John*, 341; Beale, 34ff.; and R. H. Charles, *Revelation*, vol. 1 (Edinburgh: T & T Clark, 1920), xxixff. Charles, in the modern era, popularized Dionysius's arguments. Dionysius "the Great," bishop of Alexandria (ca. 247–64), was possibly the first scholar of Revelation and the Johannine literature to point out that the Greek of the Gospel of John and of Revelation were vastly different, indicating that these two books could not have been written by the same author.

56   Cf. Nickelsburg, *Jewish Literature between the Bible and the Mishna*.

57   Caird, 5.

58   G. K. Beale, 86ff.

59   Ernst Käsemann, *Journal for Theology and the Church*, 6 (1969), 40. Cf. also R. H. Charles, *The Apocrypha and Pseudepigrapha of the Old Testament*, 2:1.

60   D. N. Freedman, *Journal for Theology and the Church* 6 (1969): 167.

61   John himself explicitly states this in Rev. 1:10, "I was in the Spirit on the Lord's day, and I heard behind me a loud voice like a trumpet saying, 'Write what you see in a book.'"

62   Although the text of this study will be based on the *New International Version*, 1973, 1978, 1984, certain quotations as in this case are from the *Revised Standard Version* (Grand Rapids: Zondervan, 1971).

63   Bauckham, ix and 1.

64   See Yarbro Collins, *The Combat Myth in the Book of Revelation*, in which Collins demonstrates that the genre of combat myth plays a significant role in the composition and meaning of Revelation.

65   Bauckham, 210ff.

66   "Mythological" implies that the language is "otherworldly," or cosmic. The Satanic battle fought between Michael and the dragon is otherworldly and cannot be described in human "this worldly" terms. The term myth does not imply that the battle is not real, only that it cannot be described in normal human constructs. Hence we have dragons and beasts engaged in a battle with archangels and angels on a cosmic screen.

67   Yarbro Collins, *Crisis and Catharsis: The Power of the Apocalypse* (Philadelphia: Westminster, 1984), 20, 21.

68   As a beginning point, for example, see the research and publications of John J. Collins and the circle of scholars of which he is a primary leader. John J. Collins, ed.,: *Apocalypse, The Morphology of a Genre, Semeia* 14 (Society of Biblical Literature, 1979), and John J. Collins, *The Apocalyptic Imagination* (New York: Crossroad, 1984). Cf. also George W. E. Nickelsburg, *Jewish Literature between the Bible and the Mishna*. A considerable bibliography has formed around this discipline in recent years, much of it due to the work of an Apocalypse and Pseudepigrapha Group of the Society of Biblical Literature's Genres Project. Notable other works in this study are James H. Charlesworth, ed., *The Old Testament Pseudepigrapha: Apocalyptic Literature and Testaments* (New York: Doubleday, 1983). Two small, yet excellent works are Paul S. Minear, *New Testament Apocalyptic* (Nashville: Abingdon, 1981), and Leon Morris, *Apocalyptic* (Grand Rapids: Eerdmans, 1972). A number of excellent references can be found in scholarly journal articles and publications.

69   Ernst Käsemann, "The Beginnings of Christian Theology," *Journal for Theology and the Church*, 6 (1969).

70   R. H. Charles, *The Apocrypha and Pseudepigrapha of the Old Testament* (Oxford: Clarendon, 1913), 2:1.

71   D. N. Freedman, "The Flowering of Apocalyptic," *Journal for Theology and the Church* 6 (1969).

72   Leon Morris, *Apocalyptic*, 10.

73   Klaus Koch, *Ratlos von der Apokalyptik* (Gutersloh: Mohn, 1970), English translation, *The Rediscovery of Apocalyptic* (Naperville, Ill.: Alec R. Allenson, 1972). Like many other terms that inherently involve multiple meanings and uses, we retain the term apocalyptic simply because we do not have an alternate term that represents our concerns better than the one we have, problematic though it may be. Cf. also the discussion of this in Beale, 37ff., and Aune, *Revelation* 1.lxxviff.

74   John J. Collins, *The Apocalyptic Imagination*, 1.

75   See Minear, 15ff.; Collins, *Apocalypse: The Morphology of a Genre*, 3ff.; and M. Eugene Boring, *Revelation* (Louisville: John Knox, 1989), 35ff.

76   Minear, *New Testament Apocalyptic*, 17.

77   It is important to stress here again that the persecution faced by the early church was not simply that of Rome. The persecution was much broader and more complex than a simple Roman persecution. Admittedly, the Roman civil and religious power played an important part in this persecution, especially as we move from the second into the third centuries, but the persecution can be traced to several sources, all of which drew on the power or Rome to raise objections to the Christian faith. There were local cultural differences between Christians and their pagan neighbors, and Jewish opposition was already present in the first century. It was apparent from both the New Testament and early Christian history (cf. Eusebius and Frend) that the Christian's pagan and Jewish neighbors were skilful in manipulating the situation so that Rome was involved.

78   Minear, *New Testament Apocalyptic*, 27.

79   Yarbro Collins, *Crisis and Catharsis*, 84ff. We have already observed that Osborne feels that although Collins has stuck on a major theme in Revelation she has possibly overstated her case against Roman persecution.

80   The Apocrypha can be found in most Bibles of the Roman Catholic tradition, and now between the Old Testament and New Testament of some modern ecumenical Bibles. The books in the Apocrypha fall mostly within the period after the close of the writing of the Old Testament canon and before the beginning of the Christian era. The apocryphal writings were not included in the Protestant canon of Scripture, but were nevertheless highly prized by the early church as intensely spiritual. The Pseudepigrapha refers to an extensive library of Jewish and early Christian writings that were also prized by the early church as enlightening spiritual texts. The pseudepigraphaphic writings were so called because they were understood to have been written under pseudonymous names.

81   See the excellent discussion of this in John Collins, *Apocalypse: The Morphology of a Genre*, and *The Apocalyptic Imagination*.

82   Paul Hanson, *The Dawn of Apocalyptic* (Philadelphia: Fortress, 1975); D. S. Russell, *The Method and Message of Jewish Apocalyptic* (Philadelphia: Westminster, 1964); and H. H. Rowley, *The Relevance of Apocalyptic* (London: Athlone, 1944).

83   A list of Jewish and Christian apocalyptic works can be found following the bibliography for this study, together with a list of Jewish and Christian pseudepigraphic and apocryphal writings.

84   The story of Little Red Riding Hood dates back as far as the seventeenth century European folk tales. It has come down to us in various forms. The meaning of the folk tales range from innocent lessons of little girls' being wise as to where they go unattended to warnings against sexual prostitution and the dangers of sexual awakening of young girls. The lessons are not set in time constructs but in symbolic narrative lessons.

85   John Collins, *The Apocalyptic Imagination*, 4, 5.

86   John Collins, *The Apocalyptic Imagination*, 4.

87   For an excellent account of how millennial thinking has impacted the American psyche, see James H. Smylie, "A New Heaven and New Earth: Uses of the Millennium in American Religious History," *Interpretation*, 53. 2. 1999: 143 ff.

88   Richard Hughes, *Reviving the Ancient Faith: The Story of Churches of Christ in America* (1996; new edition, Abilene, Tex.: Abilene Christian University Press, 2008).

89   Eschatology is the theological discipline that discusses either matters that relate to the end-time or matters that have end-time significance. The term derives from the Greek words *eschatos* ("last things") and *logos* ("word, discourse, discussion"). The word has a wide-ranging application and must be understood in the context of the discussion.

90   Cf. J W Roberts, "The Meaning of the Eschatology in the Book of Revelation," *Restoration Quarterly*, 15 (1972), 95110; Val J. Sauer Jr., *The Eschatology Handbook* (Atlanta: John Knox, 1981); Oscar Cullmann, *Christ and Time: The Primitive Christian Concept of Time* (Westminster: John Knox; rev. ed., Oct. 1964); and David C. Sim, *Apocalyptic Eschatology in the Gospel of Matthew* (Cambridge: Cambridge University Press, 1996), for an excellent discussion of the relationship of apocalyptic and eschatology.

91   For an interesting accounting of the development of Jewish linear time with a beginning and end, cf. Thomas Cahill, *The Gifts of the Jews* (New York: Doubleday, Anchor Books, 1998).

92   Cf. inaugurated eschatology in Oscar Cullmann, *Christ and Time* (New York: Gordon, 1977).

93   N. T. Wright, *The New Testament and the People of God* (Minneapolis: Fortress, 1992), 333.

94   N. T. Wright, *Jesus and the Victory of God* (Minneapolis: Fortress, 1996), 208.

95   For a discussion on the conditional coming of Jesus and his coming soon in the life of the churches of Asia, cf. the discussion at Rev. 2:5; 2:16; 3:11.

96   Cf. again J W Roberts, "The Meaning of the Eschatology in the Book of Revelation," 95–110.

97   Cf. the discussion of this two-fold view of Revelation in two Acts under structure and outline below.

98   In addition to John's own statement to this effect in Rev. 1:3 where the RSV correctly translates this as "read aloud," we have the comment of many commentators to the effect that Revelation was intended to be an oral composition. Cf. Richard Bauckham, *The Climax of Prophecy*, 1f., where Bauckham observes that the structure of the book "must have been intended to be perceptible in oral performance."

99   In a dramatic audio-visual presentation of Revelation, "Revelation Illustrated," Pat Marvenko Smith demonstrates the dramatic audio-visual impact of Revelation. Cf. www.revelationillustrated.com. I highly recommend this video to those interested in a serious study of Revelation.

100   Michael Wilcock, *I Saw Heaven Opened* (Downers Grove, Ill.: InterVarsity Press, 1975); Calvin Miller, *The Singer Trilogy* (Downers Grove, Ill.: InterVarsity Press, 1975–1990).

101   John D. W. Watts, *Isaiah 1–33* (Dallas: Word, 1985).

102   Cf. the discussion of this under interpreting revelation below.

103   Grant R. Osborne, *Revelation* (Grand Rapids: Baker Academic, 2002), 5.

104   Osborne records that Carson, Moo, and Morris observe that four dates were customarily proposed by early Christian writers, Claudius (41–54), Nero (54–68), Domitian (81–96), and Trajan (98–117). As indicated in the text, most modern commentators propose three dates.

105   For detailed discussion on the dating of Revelation, see G. K. Beale, 4ff., and Yarbro Collins, *Crisis and Catharsis*, 54ff.

106   It should be noted that there are no periods following J W as J W was his name and not an abbreviation of a name.

107   J W Roberts, *The Revelation to John* (Abilene, Tex.: Abilene Christian University Press, 1974), 13.

108   Observe the comment on Roberts at n. 79.

109   J W Roberts, *The Revelation to John*, 9.

110   Cf. the discussion of this in the pertinent literature, as in Osborne, *Revelation*, 617ff.; Aune, *Revelation*, 3:945ff.; and the discussion of Rev. 17:8ff. in this commentary.

111   G. B. Caird, 218–19.

112   Yarbro Collins, *Crisis and Catharsis*, 58ff.

113   Elisabeth Schüssler Fiorenza, *Research Perspectives on the Book of Revelation* (Philadelphia: Fortress, 1985), 20. See also discussion on this in G. K. Beale, *The Book of Revelation*, 21ff. Cf. also David Aune, *Revelation*, 1.lviff.

114   J W Roberts, 141, suggests this possibility. In lectures and class notes Roberts apparently considered this alternative possible.

115   Yarbro Collins, *Crisis and Catharsis*, 76–77. Collins devotes a whole chapter to exploring the various views of authorship and concludes, as indicated above, that a Domitian date best fits both the internal and external evidence.

Regarding the external evidence, Collins disagrees with most commentators in regard to the circumstances that gave rise to John's Revelation. Collins argues that it was the general cultural antipathy of the Roman pagan society towards the church that lay behind the crisis faced by the church rather than any pressure on Christians to worship the emperor. Cf also G. K. Beale, 5ff.; David Aune, *Revelation*, 1.lviff.

116   For an excellent detailed survey of the history of the interpretation of Revelation, see Isbon T. Beckwith, 318ff. Cf. also John M. Court, *Myth and History in the Book of Revelation* (Atlanta: John Knox, 1979), 1ff.; Grant R. Osborne, 18ff.; G. K. Beale, 44ff.; Robert H. Mounce, 44ff.

117   Cf. G. K. Beale, Robert H. Mounce, Steve Gregg, eds., *Revelation: Four Views* (Nashville: Thomas Nelson, 1997); and Robert G. Clouse, *The Meaning of the Millennium: Four Views* (Downers Grove, Ill.: InterVarsity Press, 1977), for discussion on this and examples of how the various views shape interpretation.

118   G. K. Beale, 48, describes his approach to the methods of interpreting Revelation as "eclecticism," as does Homer Hailey, *Revelation* (Grand Rapids: Baker Book House, 1979), 50. Cf. also Osborne, 21. It will become apparent that I also adopt a form of eclecticism in my approach to Revelation.

119   Isbon T. Beckwith, 318ff., gives an excellent survey of the chiliast views.

120   George Eldon Ladd, "Historic Premillennialism," in *The Meaning of the Millennium*, ed. Robert Clouse, 17ff.

121   Dennis E. Groh, "Montanism," *Encyclopedia of Early Christianity*, 2d ed., ed. Everett Ferguson, (New York: Garland, 1997), 778–79.

122   Robert J. Daly, "Origen," *Encyclopedia of Early Christianity*, 835ff., for discussion on Origen and his impact on biblical interpretation.

123   Gerald Bray, *Biblical Interpretation, Past and Present* (Downers Grove, Ill.: InterVarsity Press, 1996), 78, 104–110.

124   Pamela Bright, "Tyconius," *Encyclopedia of Early Christianity*, 1148.

125   William Hendriksen, *More Than Conquerors* (Grand Rapids: Eerdmans, 1962).

126   Austin M. Farrer, *A Rebirth of Images*.

127   See under discussion of structure in Revelation.

128   That is, dealing with the expected or imminent end of the world and millennial age.

129   Cf. Beckwith, 331–32. Cf. also Mounce, 26–27.

130   Cf. the discussion of eschatology above, 37ff.

131   For further information on the continuous historical, cf. Beckwith, 334ff.; Beale, 46; Mounce, 27; Steve Gregg, *Revelation: Four Views*, 36ff.; Court, 1ff.

132   Cf. Court, 11.

133   In Church of Christ circles, John Hinds, *Commentary on Revelation* (Nashville: Gospel Advocate, 1937), followed this model.

134   They are unbiblical in the sense that they introduce subjective modern historical issues into their view of biblical history. There are no biblical controls or guidelines to their model of interpretation that limit the extremes of subjectivity.

135   The Western bias of this approach is evident in that the historical figures identified in this approach are mostly drawn from Western history, with some reference to Eastern historical figures, but only insofar as they have relevance for Western concerns, and the total absence of African historical figures truncates the meaning of Revelation to Western church concerns. In contrast to this, Revelation was written to Eastern churches.

136   Futurist's view Rev. 4–21 to be distinct from Rev. 1–3 in that Rev. 1–3 relates to the time of the church in Asia and Rev. 4–21 to the final end, or distant future. Cf. Court, 8ff.; Steve Gregg, ed., 40ff.; Mounce, 27ff.; Beale, 40ff.

137   This tendency in Beale is a flaw in his otherwise excellent commentary. As will be noticed later in this study, this is due to a poor understanding of the eschatological style used by John in Revelation. Cf. J W Roberts, "The Meaning of the Eschatology in the Book of Revelation,"95–110.

138   Osborne, 22.

139   Osborne, 20.

140   J W Roberts, "The Meaning of the Eschatology in the Book of Revelation," 95-110.

141   Cf again the discussion of the use of eschatological language in Revelation in J W Roberts, "The Meaning of the Eschatology in the Book of Revelation," 95-110, and the discussion of 37ff. of this commentary.

142   Wolfhart Pannenberg, *Theology and the Kingdom of God* (Philadelphia: Westminster Press,1969), 127ff.

143   Robert G. Clouse, ed., *The Meaning of the Millennium: Four Views*; Steve Gregg, ed., *Revelation: Four Views*.

144   George Eldon Ladd, *A Commentary on the Revelation of John* (Grand Rapids: Eerdmans, 1972); Ladd, "Historic Premillennialism," in *The Meaning of the Millennium: Four Views*; Ladd, *The Presence of the Future* (Grand Rapids: Eerdmans, 1974).

145   G. R. Beasley-Murray, *The Book of Revelation* (Grand Rapids: Eerdmans, 1981).

146   Clarence B. Bass, *Backgrounds to Dispensationalism* (Grand Rapids: Eerdmans, 1960); Steve Gregg, 40ff.; Herman A. Hoyt, "Dispensational Premillennialism," in *The Meaning of the Millennium: Four Views*, 63ff.

147   Clarence B. Bass, *Backgrounds to Dispensationalism*, 19. Bass gives a detailed definition of the origins and major doctrines of dispensationalism. Charles Caldwell Ryrie, a prominent dispensationalist, has criticized Bass's arguments on the grounds that Bass offers a biased view of dispensationalism. Charles Caldwell Ryrie, *Dispensationalism Today* (Chicago: Moody, 1965). Ryrie's criticisms of Bass are sarcastic and harsh, and not in keeping with Bass's criticisms of dispensationalism, but are not unexpected since Bass had at one time held dispensational views but upon further study had taken another direction in his views of the millennium. Ryrie's comment is typical of his criticism of Bass: "There is the 'intellectual' attack. The process of earning a doctor's degree has delivered the person from the dispensational teaching in which he was reared" (Ryrie, 13). Bass's comments in this regard are typical of others who upon careful scriptural analysis of dispensationalism have found difficulty with its hermeneutic. "When I began a doctoral program of research on J. N. Darby's doctrine of the church (Post-Graduate School of

Theology, New College, University of Edinburgh), I was a confirmed dispensationalist. As I began to understand the basis in which this system of interpretation is rooted, I began also to see what seemed to be a basic hermeneutical pattern of interpretation that is broadly divergent from that of the historic faith" (Bass, 9). The same hermeneutic criticism is raised by most critics of dispensationalism and its extreme literalist interpretation of Scripture. See George Eldon Ladd, Loraine Boettner, and Anthony Hoekema, in Robert G. Clouse, ed., *The Meaning of the Millennium: Four Views*, 93–114. Jim McGuiggan, *The Kingdom of God and the Planet Earth* (published by the author, 1978), is a readable discussion and appraisal of dispensationalism.

148   See the fine overview of millennial interpretation in Robert G. Clouse, ed., *The Meaning of the Millennium: Four Views;* and Clarence B. Bass, *Backgrounds to Dispensationalism.*

149   Loraine Boettner, "Postmillennialism," in *The Meaning of the Millennium*, 117ff.

150   For discussion on the preterist model and the two types of preterist thinking, see Gregg, 37ff. Cf. also G. K. Beale, 44ff.

151   We have already noted, however, that Beale prefers to identify his approach to Revelation as eclectic in that, although he is primarily a moderate preterist, he combines with this a significant futurist interpretation regarding the last days.

152   Beale, 48ff.; Gregg, 43ff., calls this view the spiritual approach; Michael Wilcock, *I Saw Heaven Opened*, 20ff. We find considerable appeal in the dramatic approach in that it illustrates the literary style adopted by John.

153   Anthony A. Hoekema, "Amillennialism," in *The Meaning of the Millennium: Four Views*, 155ff.

154   Elisabeth Schüssler Fiorenza, "Composition and Structure of the Book of Revelation," *Catholic Biblical Quarterly*, 39.3 (July 1977): 344ff.

155   Beale, 108ff.

156   Richard Bauckham, *The Climax of Prophecy*, 1–2.

157   Richard Bauckham, *The Climax of Prophecy*, 2, citing D. L. Barr, "The Apocalypse as a Symbolic Transformation of the World: A Literary Analysis," *Interpretation* 38 (1984): 111–120.

158   Richard Bauckham, *The Climax of Prophecy*, 2.

159   Richard Bauckham, *The Climax of Prophecy*, 2, n. 1.

160   Beale, 108ff.

161   Isbon T Beckwith, 322. For detailed discussion of recapitulation, cf. J. Lambrecht, *L'Apocalypse Johannique et Apocalyptique dans le Nouveau Testament* (Leuven: Leuven University Press, 1980), 78ff., Charles Homer Giblin, S. J., *Recapitulation and the Literary Coherence of John's Apocalypse, Catholic Biblical Quarterly* 56.1 (Jan. 1994); Elisabeth Schüssler Fiorenza, "Composition and Structure of the Book of Revelation," *Catholic Biblical Quarterly* 39.3 (July 1977); Yarbro Collins, *The Combat Myth in the Book of Revelation*, 32ff.; David Aune, *Revelation*, 1:xciff.; Beale, 121ff.

162   Yarbro Collins, *The Combat Myth in the Book of Revelation*, 32ff.

163   Günter Bornkamm, "Die Komposition der apokalyptischen Vision in der Offenbarung Johannes," *Zeitschrift fur die neutestamentliche Wissenschaft* 36 (1937): 132–149.

164   Austin Farrer, *A Rebirth of Images: The Making of Saint John's Apocalypse.*

165   William Hendriksen, *More Than Conquerors*. In similar fashion to Hendriksen, Beale also refers to recapitulation in Revelation as progressive recapitulation or progressive parallelism (121).

166   Yarbro Collins, *The Combat Myth in the Book of Revelation*, 21.

167   This two–section structure is only a broad generalization of two section proposals. The chief contribution it makes to the structure is the two-fold division of Rev. 1–11 and Rev. 12–22.

168   Hendriksen, *More Than Conquerors.*

169   Ronald E. Man, "The Value of Chiasm for New Testament Interpretation," *Bibliotheca Sacra* 141.562 (April–June 1984): 146ff.

170   Nils Wilhelm Lund, *Chiasmus in the New Testament* (Chapel Hill: University of North Carolina Press, 1942).

171   J. Jeremias, "Chiasmus in den Paulusbriefen," *Zeitschrift fur die neutestamentliche Wisenschaft* 49 (1958).

172   Jaques Ellul, *Apocalypse, The Book of Revelation* (New York: Seabury, 1977). This is an English translation of Ellul's original work in French.

173   Yarbro Collins, *The Combat Myth in the Book of Revelation*; Elisabeth Schüssler Fiorenza, "Composition and Structure of the Book of Revelation," *Catholic Biblical Quarterly* 39 (July 1977); Charles Homer Giblin, "Recapitulation and the Literary Coherence of John's Apocalypse," *Catholic Biblical Quarterly* 56 (Jan. 1994).

174   The phenomenon of unnumbered septets has been noted by several of the scholars referred to above. The rationale behind the unnumbered septets is uncertain. The fact of the unnumbered septets is obvious.

175   For excellent comments on the theology of Revelation, cf. Bauckham, *The Theology of the Book of Revelation*, and Osborne, 31ff.

176   Witness the trauma experienced in the USA following September 11, 2001, Muslim extremism and terrorism, and the radical secularization of modern society.

177   From my perspective there have been times in God's dealings with his people, due to the stubbornness of their hearts and disobedience, that God has adapted or revised his original plan.

178   Note Paul's reference to an eternal preordained plan of God that he is able to execute: Eph. 1:3–1.

Chapter 1

1   All references to the text of Revelation are from the Holy Bible, New International Version. Copyright ©1973, 1978, 1984 International Bible Society. Used by permission of Zondervan Bible Publishers.

2   Cf. Aune, 1:22. For a discussion of the literary genre identified by scholars as apocalyptic, see the section on apocalyptic in the introduction to this book.

3   The Greek construction "of Jesus" is in the genitive case and could be either a subjective genitive or an objective genitive. The context calls for a subjective genitive implying that Jesus is the source of this revelation.

4   This comment will have more relevance when we consider 1:9 and 6:9: "*because of the word of God and the testimony they had maintained.*"

5   The emphasis that John's message or the message of Revelation came from both God and Jesus Christ will become apparent at discussions at 1:2; 1:9; and 6:9.

6   The 1534 William Tyndale New Testament, "shortly"; the Douay-Rheims Bible, 1899, "shortly"; the 1901 American Standard Version, "shortly"; the 1971 New American Standard Version, "shortly"; the 1971 Revised Standard Version, "soon"; the 1984 New International Version, "soon"; the 1989 New Revised Standard Version, "soon." It is interesting to note that the 1966 and 1985 Jerusalem Bibles translate this phrase as "are now to take place." Cf. comments on this in Boring, 71; Mounce, 65; and Beale, 153 ff., where Beale translates *en tachei* as *quickly*, but explains that John expected the events to happen quickly "in his day"; cf. also 181ff.. where in opposition to Walvoord, Beale argues in regard to the parallel language between Rev. 1:1 and Dan. 2:28–30, 45–47 that *en tachei in* conjunction with Daniel "connotes neither the speedy manner in which the Daniel prophecy is to be fulfilled nor the mere possibility that it could be fulfilled at any time, but the definite, imminent time of fulfillment, which likely has already begun in the present." Although Beale strangely prefers "quickly" in place of "soon" in Rev. 1:1, he nevertheless understands to take place "imminently" (soon) within John's lifetime. I find Beale's discussion on Dan. 2 and Rev. 1:1 to be meaningful, insightful, and extremely important to the understanding of this text (Rev. 1:1), but also for understanding and interpretation of Revelation as a theological whole. Beale observes that the phrase *en tachei* in Rev. 1:1 "appears to indicate that fulfillment has begun (that it is being fulfilled) or will begin in the near future. Simply put, John understands Daniel's reference to a distant time as referring to his own era, and he updates the text [Dan. 2] accordingly. . . . What Daniel expects to occur in the distant "latter days" . . . John expects to begin "quickly," in his own generation, if it has not already begun to happen" (153). Beale adds, "Given the strong textual and thematic parallels between Rev. 1:1, 3 and Daniel, the very least that can be said is that the wording of these texts refers to the immediate future" (154). He adds, "Furthermore, that the events of Rev. 1:6, 9, 13–15 are all present realities indicates that the fulfillment of Daniel 2 is not merely imminent, but is taking place in John's very presence" (154). However, in spite of Beale's insightful exegesis of Rev. 1:1, 3 and Dan. 2, I differ with Beal's translation of *en tachus* as "quickly, and prefer to maintain the meaning of soon as an appropriate translation of *en tachei* in Rev. 1:1. Cf. most major English translations of Rev. 1:1 and Caird, 12, where Caird asks, "What then was it that John expected to happen **soon**?" Interestingly, the King James Version and the American Standard Version translate this as "must shortly come to pass."

7   Beckwith, 419.

8   Timothy Friberg, Barbara Friberg, and Neva F. Miller, *Analytical Lexicon of the Greek New Testament* (Grand Rapids: Baker Books, 2000).

9   Caird, 12. Paul S. Minear, in a critical review of Caird's commentary, observed that it is "the single best critical commentary on the English text of Revelation," *Journal of Biblical Literature*, 86 (1967): 230.

10   Caird, 11.

11   Beale, 182.

12   It is evident that one's understanding of eschatology and the use of eschatological language will shape one's attitude to the use of eschatology in Revelation. This commentary is written in the tradition of inaugurated eschatology (cf. Oscar Cullmann), which posits that the eschaton broke in during the ministry of Jesus, that we are now living in the eschatological age (or the last days), and that one should see any event in the Christian age as an eschatological event that can be described in eschatological language. The kingdom of Christ began to break in with the ministry of Jesus, and it became a reality with his resurrection and the pouring out of the Holy Spirit on the day of Pentecost. Furthermore, the New Testament pictures the last days or the eschatological age to have begun with the death and resurrection of Jesus, and that the Christian age is the eschatological age (Acts 2:17, Heb. 1:2). I do not believe that Revelation is primarily concerned with a supposed expectation of tribulation at the final end. Tribulation was and is a part of the Christian experience living in the last days or the eschatological age. As already indicated and will be established in the fuller context of Rev. 1:1-3, Revelation is not substantially concerned with the final end of the world, although that will play a minor role in the theodicy of Revelation. Revelation is primarily concerned with a crisis about to break in on the church in Asia, and the reaction of the church to this poses eschatological considerations. The crisis is described in eschatological terminology which that heightens the urgency of the crisis.

13   Cf. the discussion of analogous and typological fulfillment in the introduction and Beale's comments regarding these types of fulfillment.

14   Mounce, 41.

15   J W Roberts, "The Meaning of the Eschatology in the Book of Revelation," 95–110.

16   Oscar Cullmann, *Christ and Time: The Primitive Christian Conception of Time and History*, trans. Floyd V. Wilson (Philadelphia: Westminster, 1950).

17   The term "last days" (*eschatais hēmerais*) is very similar to the term eschatology in that the word *eschatos* means "the last." Eschatology is the discussion of the "last things." "The last days" has refers to the final days, or age, of world history. Christians believe that these "final days," or the last epoch, of world history began with the coming of Jesus. This understanding of world history adds a sense of urgency and demonstrates the importance Christians believe is inherent in the Christian message, or gospel. The advanced student is encouraged to refer to the glossary of terms in the appendix for a more detailed discussion of eschatology. The use of eschatological references to time in Revelation has profound significance in understanding Revelation. The advanced student should read the article by J W Roberts, "The Meaning of the Eschatology in the Book of Revelation," 95-110, and the four articles by G. B. Caird, "On Deciphering the Book of Revelation," *Expository Times* (1962–1963), 13–15, 51–53, 81–84, 103–105.

18   See previous note on Roberts and Caird.

19   J. Christiaan Beker has argued strongly for an appreciation of apocalyptic in Paul. However, Vincent Bavink has argued that Paul's use of apocalyptic may not be as simple as Beker believes. Bavink commends Beker's emphasis on apocalyptic in Paul but warns "Beker has correctly pointed out the apocalyptic framework of Paul's thought. Any interpretation of Paul which completely overlooks this framework will necessarily be unfaithful to Paul. However, Beker fails to appreciate the complexity . . . of this framework. " For Beker's position, see J. Christiaan Beker, *Paul, the Apostle: The Triumph of God in Life and Thought* (Philadelphia: Fortress, 1980), and *Paul's Apocalyptic Gospel: The Coming Triumph of God* (Philadelphia: Fortress, 1982).

20   Cf. discussion in James D. G. Dunn, *Romans 1–18*, Word Biblical Commentary (Dallas: Word, 1988), 52.

21   Caird, "On Deciphering the Book of Revelation," 83.

22   Caird, "On Deciphering the Book of Revelation," 84.

23   Beale, 182.

24   Cf. again to the interesting and insightful discussion in Beale, 152.

25   Caird, "On Deciphering the Book of Revelation," 51.

26   Aune, 1:15.

27   The Greek construction *Iesou Christou* is a genitive noun construction. This could be a subjective genitive or an objective genitive. As a subjective genitive it would refer to the message that came from Jesus. As an objective genitive it could refer to a message concerning Jesus. Both possibilities are inherent in the syntax of the construction, but the context seems to favor the meaning that the message concerning Jesus. Beale suggests with some validity that the intention might include some ambiguity, implying that both meanings are inherent in the expression *Iesou Christou*. Beale proposes that the genitives could simply be a general genitive, which includes both subjective and objective genitive meanings (Beale, 184). Aune 1.19 appropriately suggests that the *kai* (and) connecting "the word of God and the testimony of Jesus" is epexigetical, in which case Aune's suggestion is similar to that proposed by Mounce, who suggests that the genitives stand in apposition, the second genitive emphasizing or enlarging on the first. I prefer to see the testimony of Jesus as one concerning Jesus' Lordship, an objective genitive, and like Aune's suggestion that the *kai* is epexegetical, having the second statement regarding Jesus define what the message of Revelation is all about.

28   Mounce, 66.

29   Caird, 12, where Caird interprets this as the testimony "already attested by Jesus Christ in his life and teaching, when 'the Purpose took human flesh.'"

30   Mounce, 66.

31   I have already referred and will later refer to the tantalizing question of the use of the possible subjective, objective, general, or possessive genitives in these statements.

32   Cf. Aune, 1:20.

33   Beckwith, 422; Mounce, 43.

34   J. Massyngberde Ford, *Revelation* (Garden City, N.Y.: Doubleday , Anchor Bible, 1975), 374.

35   Aune, 1:20, where he traces this expression to possibly Luke 11:28 and 1 Enoch 99:10. Aune finds similar interest in apocalyptic blessings in Dio Cassius 62.20.5.

36   Note the comment by H. Preisker, "Thus the terms have an ordinary sense *but also express the hope of the imminent eschatological act of God either in commencement or consummation*." Preisker adds, "The NT usage is based on Dt. Is. In the older writings the distinctive feature of both *eggus* and *eggidzein* is that they express the characteristic aspect of the early Christian situation, being used of the eschatological fulfillment, of the great turning point in world history, of the coming of the kingdom of God directly into the present as the miracle of God. . . . In Hb., as in OT prophecy, *eggus* refers to eschatological judgment. In Hb. 6:8 defection from Christ brings destruction in the imminent judgment. 8:13 speaks of the overthrow of the OT order by the new established in Christ. On the other hand, in Hb. 7:19 and Jm. 4:8 we have the formula *eggidzein tō theō* from the LXX and Philo, except that the certainty of the actualization of the drawing near is now stronger and surer and more complete than in the OT and later Judaism. Like the Synpt., Rev. uses *eggus* only as a term for the near coming of the kingdom of God. Thus we have *ho gar kairos eggus* in 1:3; cf. 22:10." *Eggus, Theological Dictionary of the New Testament*, ed. Gerhard Kittel and Gerhard Friedrich, trans. Geoffrey W. Bromiley (Grand Rapids: Eerdmans, 1964), 2:330–32.

37   Rudolf Bultmann argued for a timeless eschatology in which eschatology has no reference to time, but stresses those matters that are ultimate, or ultimately significant. It is in this sense that we should understand John's use of this expression in Rev. 1:3. Cf. the discussion of *chronos* in Gerhard Delling, *Theological Dictionary of the New Testament*.

38   Osborne, 444.

39   Caird aptly translates *kairos* as *crisis* in this context (9). Karl Barth and Rudolf Bultmann were certainly correct in stressing that the eschatology of the New Testament was more than merely an historical eschatology. Both called for a significant, or timeless, eschatology in place of an eschatology of history. Barth and Bultmann's reaction to the role of history in faith caused them to reject historical concerns in favor of a timeless eschatology, thus resulting in an unnecessary overreaction to history. We should not, however, reject their sound emphasis on a significant eschatology on the grounds of their overreaction to the role of history in the development of faith.

40   Aune, 1:21.

41   Elisabeth Schüssler Fiorenza, *The Book of Revelation: Justice and Judgment* (Philadelphia: Fortress, 1985), 49.

42   Boring, 74, Mounce, 67.

43   Everett Ferguson, "Dionysius of Alexandria," *Encyclopedia of Early Christianity* (New York: Garland, 1990).

44   J W Roberts, *The Revelation to John* (Austin: Sweet Publishing Company, 1974, now owned by ACU Press, Abilene, Texas), 11.

45   Caird, 5.

46   Yarbro Collins, *Crisis and Catharsis*, 49, 50.

47   Mounce, 31. The innovative proposal by J. Massyngberde Ford, *Revelation,* Anchor Bible Commentary (Garden City, N.Y.: Doubleday, 1975) that the author was from the circle of John the Baptist has not met with favorable comment from scholars in this field.

48   R. H. Charles, *The Revelation of St. John,* 2 Vols. (Edinburgh: T&T Clark, 1920), I. xxxix.

49   Beale, 186.

50   Beckwith, 253, and 423–24; Beale, 186; Mounce, 45; Caird, 14.

51   Aune, 1:29; Yarbro Collins, "Numerical Symbolism in Jewish and Early Christian Apocalyptic Literature," *Aufstieg und Niedergang der römischen Welt* 2.21. 1221–22. Rachel Elior, *The Three Temples: On the Emergence of Jewish Mysticism* (Portland Ore.: Littman Library of Jewish Civilization, 2005), *passim,* draws attention to the symbolism of seven in ancient cultures and cosmic order, and in Jewish mysticism.

52   W. M. Ramsey, *The Letters to the Seven Churches in Asia* (Grand Rapids: Baker Book House, 1963, first pub. 1904), 183.

53   Colin Hemer, 14.

54   Mounce, 68.

55   "Grace and peace" was the standard greeting in the Pauline corpus, with the exception of 1 & 2 Tim., in which "mercy" was added.

56   Aune, 1:29; Beale, 187; Mounce, 45.

57   Richard Bauckham, *The Theology of the Book of Revelation* (New York: Cambridge University Press, 1993), 23.

58   Most of the better commentaries will discuss this in varying degrees of detail. Cf. Beckwith, 424; R. H. Charles, *The Revelation of St. John,* 1. 10; Caird, 16; Mounce, 45; Beale, 188; Beasley-Murray, 54; Aune, 1:30; Massyngberde Ford, 376.

59   *"Apo ho ōn kai ho ēn kai ho erchomenos"* is the first major case of solecism or supposedly "poor" Greek referred to when questioning the authorship of Revelation. It is normally incorrect in good Greek to use the preposition *apo* with a noun form in the nominative case, for correct Greek requires that *apo* take a noun form in the genitive case. Here John follows *apo* with a nominative participle rather than a genitive. For the "purist" this is not good Greek form. However, in this case this is not poor Greek, but stylistic, expressive, idiomatic, and creative Greek. Had John followed the norms of Greek grammar, he would have completely lost the power of the Hebrew expression and heritage of the Semitic Old Testament. Only an author familiar with the Semitic idiom could have handled this with such style. Cf. Beale, 188, where Beale observes that this particular Greek construction found in Rev. 1:4 "is one of the characteristic solecisms in the Apocalypse, since a genitive construction should follow *apo.*"

60   Caird, 16.

61   Beale, 189; cf also Beasley-Murray, 54; Beckwith, 424, where Beckwith concludes that "It appears certain then that the Holy Spirit is meant."

62   Mounce, 69, Boring, 75.

63   Boring, 75; Aune, 1:33.

64   Beasley-Murray, 54.

65   Mounce, 93.

66   Aune, 1:31; Beale, 190.

67   Mounce, 70.

68   The text base adopted by the New International Version is based on an eclectic majority Byzantine type text reading. This text reading is not preferred and is not adopted by most major English translations. The variant addition of *ek,* which is the majority reading adopted by the NIV, is not even displayed as a viable text variant in the Kurt Aland, et al., *The Greek New Testament,* 2001, text published by the United Bible Society.

69   Beale, 191; Aune, 1:37.

70   The technique of repeatedly returning to a theological principle was identified as early as Victorinus (ca. 300) as recapitulation. Austin Farrer defined this more precisely as the rebirth of images, in which a concept is progressively reborn in greater or fuller detail as the work develops.

71   See the discussion of Rev. 2:11.

72   Mounce, citing Charles, warns the reader not to make too much of the change from the present participle "loves" to the aorist participles "freed" and "has made."

73   Boring, 77.

74   Caird, 17; Beale, 193; Aune, 1:47.

75   Mount Zion is a euphemism for the place or event of God's sovereign reign over Israel and the nations. God's king traditionally reigned from Mount Zion. Zion originally referred to a fortress in Jerusalem that David captured from the Jebusites. A strong theology of enthronement after victory was built around the term Mount Zion. This theology also incorporated visions of future peace. Jon D. Levenson, "Zion Traditions," *Anchor Bible Dictionary* 6 (New York: Doubleday), 1992.

76   Aune, 1:53.

77   Beasley-Murray, 58.

78   I have previously commented on John's unique use of the Old Testament in Revelation. In a midrashic style John breathes new meaning into well-known OT Scriptures as he weaves them together in a new context. His use of OT Scriptures is not intended to imply that the new setting is a temporal or historical fulfillment of the Old. His typological or theological use of the Scripture intends the focus on similar theological patterns in new contexts.

79   Boring, 27, 28; Beale, 196.

80   Aune, 1:54.

81   Beale, 196; Aune, 1:53.

82   Mounce, 72.

83   Beale, 197. Beale is correct in shifting the focus of the coming of Jesus away from an exclusive end-of-the-world *parousia* and setting it in a proleptic eschatological expectation in which present comings and judgments in the context of the churches in Asia take on final eschatological significance. This is especially relevant in regard to the judgments pronounced on Rome, the beast, and the false prophet.

84   Roberts, *The Revelation of John*, 32; Aune, 1:57.

85   See Yarbro Collins, *The Combat Myth in the Book of Revelation, passim*.

86   For a detailed discussion of John's "exile" on Patmos, see Aune, 1. 76. Cf. also Yarbro Collins, *Crisis and Catharsis*, 102.

87   The question relating to the subjective/objective genitive construction is difficult and must be considered based on the repetition of this formula throughout Revelation. Some have suggested that the genitive construction could be a general genitive while others have suggested that John deliberately included both subjective and objective genitives in his creative style of using double meanings to certain thoughts.

88   The Greek word *basileia*, normally translated in our English Bibles as "kingdom," would be better understood in the biblical context if it were translated "reign." In fact, the primary meaning of the term is usually given as "kingship, royal power, royal rule, kingdom," with kingdom being the secondary meaning. Cf. William F. Arndt and F. Wilbur Gingrich, *A Greek-English Lexicon of the New Testament* (Chicago: University of Chicago Press, 1957). Because of the monarchial system prevailing in England when the King James translation was made, "kingdom" has been the common translation in the English tradition.

89   Caird, 20.

90   Beale, 201.

91   We should not confuse this with the eschatological term "the day of the Lord," first, because the terminology is different, second, because the context here does not demand an eschatological interpretation. Cf. Beale, 203, where Beale dismisses the possibility that this may refer to the eschatological day of judgment. Cf. also Aune, 1:83. Both Beale and Aune dismiss the suggestion of some that this may refer to Easter Sunday.

92   Caird's translation of Rev. 1:10, 19; Mounce, 55, where Mounce describes this as "a spirit of exaltation best described as a trance."

93   Aune, 1:82.

94   The Greek words *biblos/biblion* can be translated either book or scroll. In keeping with the themes of Daniel and Ezekiel, and Rev. 5:1, I prefer scroll in the context of Revelation.

95   E.g. Ramsay, *The Letters to the Seven Churches of Asia*.

96   Mounce suggests that Ramsey's point is "attractive and quite plausible," 76.

97   Mounce, 57.

98   Cf. Beckwith, 437; Aune, 1:87; and Mounce, 57.

99   Beale, 207; see also Aune, 1:88, for comments on lampstands in the Old Testament and Jewish tradition.

100   Aune, 1:90ff., questions whether there is a connection to the Christian or Gospel tradition of the Son of Man sayings.

101   Charles, *The Revelation of St. John*, 1, 27.

102   The reader is encouraged to read Ps. 2; Dan. 7; Ezek. 1–3:3, and Zech. 4 several times in preparation for this study of Revelation. These passages are favored by John for providing much of the imagery of his writing.

103   Beale, 209. Cf. also the discussion of the son of man in Aune, 1:90.

104   Caird, 25.

105   Caird, 25.

106   Aune, 1:97.

107   There is an interesting tradition that may also draw on the fact that Roman coins have been found with seven stars depicted on them. There are coins from Domitian's reign depicting his infant son, who had died in childhood, playing with the stars. Some think that this Roman tradition of seven stars on Roman coins meant that the destiny of the universe lay in the emperor's hands. Caird, 15, and Beasley-Murray, 67, 71; Boring, 84.

108   Beckwith, 440; Beale, 211; Boring, 84.

109   Beale, 216. Beale devotes a whole section in his introduction to this text; cf. 152. Cf. also Aune, 1. 105; Caird, 28.

110   Charles, *The Revelation of St. John*, 1:33; Henry B. Swete, *The Apocalypse of St. John* (1906; reprinted., Grand Rapids: Eerdmans, 1951), 21.

111   Beasley-Murray, 68.

112   110 Caird, 26.

113   Beale, 216, 152, and notably, 161; Aune, 1:105.

114   Beckwith, 443; Aune, 1:105, "Therefore write down what you will see, that is, the events which are now happening and the events which will happen later." Aune also observes that the *kai* in this text is epexegetical, 106; Mounce, 62.

115   Beckwith, 443; Caird, 26; Mounce, 62; Beale, 152–70; Aune, 1:105; Boring, 84.

116   Martin Kiddle, *Revelation* (N. Y.: Harper and Brothers, 1940), 12.

117   Mounce, 82.

118   William F. Arndt and F. Wilbur Gingrich, *A Greek-English Lexicon of the New Testament* (Cambridge: University of Chicago Press, 1957), *mellō* with the aorist infinitive, 502.

119   Beale, 216.

120   Beale, 216. Cf. Beal's extensive discussion of Rev. 1:19 at 152.

121   Aune, 1:106.

122   Aune, 1:106, and Beale, 216.

123   Cf the discussion of angels in 1:20 and the seven letters in the major commentaries, but especially in Aune, 1:108.

124   See the detailed discussion on this in Beckwith, 445.

125   Boring refers to this view as "pedestrian," arguing that it ignores the meaning of "angel" throughout the book of Revelation (86).

126   Caird, 24; Beasley-Murray, 68; Mounce, 63; Boring, 86.

127   Beale, 217. Beale includes an interesting discussion of angels and stars in the Jewish tradition.

128   Aune, 1. 107. Like Beale, Aune includes a brief interesting discussion on angels in Jewish tradition.

129   Caird, 24; Mounce, 82; Beasley-Murray, 68.

Chapter 2

1   Those interested may find stimulating information on the seven churches in Asia in a set of video lessons prepared by Dr. Bill Humble, former professor of Bible, biblical archaeology, and Restoration Studies at Abilene Christian University, and Dr. Ian A. Fair, and published by the Gospel Advocate Publishing Company, Nashville, Tennessee. This set of lessons may be obtained from the publisher or from ACU Press, 1626 Campus Court, Abilene, Texas, 79601. In these videotaped lessons Dr. Humble and Dr. Fair visit the ancient sites of the seven churches and narrate the historical and religious background of each of the churches.

2   Cf. Aune, 1:119 for a detailed discussion on the literary structure of the seven letters.

3   See the discussion on angels at Rev. 1:20.

4   Beckwith, 445.

5   Beale, 217.

6   See the discussion of angels in this commentary on Rev. 1:20, and in particular in Boring, 86; Beasley-Murray, 68; and Caird, 24, 25.

7   Aune, 1:136.

8   For detailed discussion on the importance of Ephesus and the church at Ephesus, see Hemer, *The Letters to the Seven Churches of Asia in Their Local Setting*; and Aune, 1. 136 ff. Cf. also William M. Ramsay, *The Letters to the Seven Churches in Asia and Their Place in the Plan of the Apocalypse* (London: Hodder and Stoughton, 1904).

9   Aune, 1:139; Flavius Josephus, *Antiquities of the Jews*, 12.125, 166, 172.

10   Helmut Koester, "GNOMAI DIAPHOROI: The Origin and Nature of Diversification in the History of Early Christianity," *Trajectories through Early Christianity* (Philadelphia: Fortress, 1971), 154.

11   Cf. the comments by Eusebius in his *Ecclesiastical History*, 5.8.4.

12   Caird, 30; Mounce concurs with Caird, 68.

13   Caird, 15; cf. also Helmut Koester, *History and Literature of Early Christianity* (New York: De Gruyter, 1982/1987), 289, where Koester includes a coin of Domitian as the son of "divinized Augustus Vespasian."

14   Cf. the standard Greek grammars on the epexegetical use of *kai* and Aune, 1:143. One of the *kai* coordinating conjunctions in the text following "apostles" is better translated "but." This, however, does not diminish the force of the epexegetical *kai* in the first clause. On the challenging interpretation or translation of this verse, cf. also Beale, 216 and 152–70; Mounce, 62; and Caird, 26, where Caird observes that a threefold interpretation of this verse is a "grotesque over-simplification."

15   In the past scholars have questioned the apostolic authorship of the Gospel of John and Revelation. However, this is no longer the case, with several fine scholars accepting the apostolic authorship of both. Cf. the discussion under authorship in the introduction.

16   Both Paul's and John's epistles written to Ephesus or to churches in the regions surrounding Ephesus indicate trials, false teachers, and sundry difficulties.

17   Cf. Koester, "GNOMAI DIAPHOROI" at n. 10 above.

18   Beale, 230, equates the loss of love in the Ephesian church to their apparent failure to witness for him in the present. Originally, they had been zealous to witness for Jesus, but now in the face of impending social opposition, their failure to witness effectively is described as a loss of the love for Jesus that they had originally experienced and practiced.

19   Roberts, *The Revelation to John*, 38.

20   Caird, 31f.

21   Mounce, 88.

22   Mounce, 88.

23   William Barclay, *The Revelation of John* (Philadelphia: Westminster, 1960), 77.

24   Aune, 1:147.

25   The Greek is *ta prōta erga poiēson*, "the first works do." One wonders whether John is in fact referring to the primary works of the Christian life, or the works the Ephesians did at first. In either case, they both refer to works characterized by love.

26   Beale, 232: "the activities of both "removing" *and* "coming" are conditional. . . . Therefore, it is unlikely that the "removing" is conditional while the "coming" is not.

27   Aune, 1:147, demonstrates that in Hebrew the term lamp was used as a metaphor for the tribe of Benjamin. Losing one's right to be a lampstand in Revelation would therefore be equivalent to losing one's right to be a tribe of God's people.

28   Aune, 1:147.

29   Beale, 232.

30   Beasley-Murray, 75. Caird adds, "If we take this view (the use of apocalyptic language) we shall take the conditional threats to Ephesus, Pergamum, and Sardis as evidence that an imminent Parousia was *not* one of the

428   CONQUERING WITH CHRIST

events which John believed were 'bound to happen soon' (i: I), and that even in the apocalyptic visions his immediate concern is the martyrdom rather than the end" (32).

31   *Heilsgeschichtlichen* is a term I have adapted from the German *Heilsgeschichte* to refer to God's eternal plan of redemption, which plan God set in motion before the creation of the world, and through which he will redeem both his saints and his creation.

32   Dana and Mantey speak of the futuristic present in which "the present tense denotes an event which has not yet occurred, but which is regarded as so certain that it may be contemplated as already coming to pass." H. E. Dana and Julius R. Mantey, *A Manual Grammar of the Greek New Testament* (Toronto: Macmillan, 1927, 1957), 185. They cite Thayer's translation of Luneman's revision of Winer: *Grammar of the Idiom of the New Testament* (7th ed.), 265: "While the present is thus used 'in appearance for the future,' it in reality retains its own temporal and essential force, being employed to denote a future action 'either because it is already firmly resolved upon or because of some unalterable law.'"

33   Mounce, 70.

34   Caird, 32.

35   Caird, 31.

36   See the discussion of this in Elisabeth Schüssler Fiorenza, "Apocalyptic and Gnosis in the book of Revelation," *Journal of Biblical Literature* 92 (1973): 565–81. The fundamental point here for the theology of Revelation is that this group, as well as those following Balaam (2:14) and Jezebel (2:20), practiced compromise with pagan society and the fertility cults. For further discussion on the Nicolaitans see Aune, 1:148.

37   Mounce, 71.

38   For a detailed discussion on this formulaic expression, see Beale, 236.

39   Cf. Yarbro Collins, *The Combat Myth in the Book of Revelation* (Missoula, MT: Scholars Press, 1976), in which Collins argues correctly for a literary genre of combat myth for the Book of Revelation. Cf. also Bauckham, "The Apocalypse as a War Scroll," in *The Climax of Prophecy*, 210.

40   Aune, 1:151.

41   The NIV translation of *nikaō* as "overcome" as mentioned above is unfortunate and misses the impact of combat language. The RSV and NRSV translation of *nikaō* as "conquer" is more in keeping with the context of Revelation, and we should understand the term in this sense rather than merely overcome.

42   On the Greek *nikaō*, see Caird, 33; Aune, 1:151ff; Beale, 234.

43   Cf. Beasley-Murray, 77; Kiddle, 61.

44   Cf. Beckwith, 451; Aune, 1:151; Beasley-Murray, 79; Beale, 236; and Hemer, 42.

45   Hemer, 57.

46   "Izmir," *Britannica 2001* (Britannica.com).

47   Aune, 1:159.

48   Mounce, 73.

49   Hemer, 57.

50   The serious student of Revelation is encouraged to read the account of the martyrdom of Polycarp in Eusebius, *Eccles. Hist.* IV, XIV, vol. 1, pp. 337-355.

51   Eusebius, *Eccles. Hist.* IV, XIV, Loeb 1. 345.

52   Aune, 1:161.

53   Cf. Yarbro Collins, *Crisis and Catharsis*, 84–106; Hemer, 58; Aune, 1:161.

54   Eusebius records that, together with the heathens, the Jews cried out for Polycarp's death, and that, being particularly zealous for the death of Christians, they were responsible for gathering the wood for Polycarp's immolation. Eusebius, *Eccles. Hist.* IV, XIV, Loeb 1. 351.

55   Beale, 239.

56   See the *Martyrdom of Polycarp*, which documents this Jewish hostility against the Christian community: "The multitude of heathen and Jews living in Smyrna cried out with uncontrollable wrath and a loud shout . . . and the crowd came together immediately, and prepared wood and faggots from the work-shops and baths and the Jews were extremely zealous, as is their custom, in assisting at this." "Martyrdom of Polycarp," *Apostolic Fathers*, Vol. II, XII. 2-XIII. 1:329.

57   Cf. Aune, 1:162, for a discussion on this harsh rebuke. Aune is sensitive to point out that this is not a broad condemnation on all Jews, only on those who oppose God's plans as also in Philadelphia (Rev. 3:9); Beale *Revelation*, 240; Caird, 35; Mounce, 75; Beasley-Murray, 81–82; Craig S. Keener, *The NIV Application Commentary* (Grand Rapids: Zondervan, 2000), 118.

58   Although in a study such as this, it should not be necessary to observe that no anti-Semitism is intended here. Jesus and John are merely commenting on an historical fact in Smyrna.

59   Ray Summers, *Worthy Is the Lamb* (Nashville: Broadman, 1951), 113; Mounce, 76.

60   Kiddle, 28; Caird, 35.

61   Cf. Beale, 242.

62   Mounce, 76; Caird, 36; Homer Hailey, *Revelation*, 128, translates this as "even to the point of dying for the faith."

63   See the discussion in Colin J. Hemer, 70–76; Beasley-Murray, 82; Arndt and Gingrich, *stephanos*, *A Greek-English Lexicon of the New Testament*.

64   Aune, 1:166.

65   Beale, 244.

66   Charles, 1. 59; Aune, 1:168; Beasley-Murray, 83; Massyngberde Ford, 393.

67   *Pergamos*, Liddell and Scott, *Greek-English Lexicon*: "Pergamus, the citadel of Troy, generically, a citadel or acropolis."

68   Beale, 245; Aune, 1:180.
69   Cf. Hemer, 78.
70   Beale, 245, 247.
71   Aune, 1:182.
72   Cf. Aune, 1:182 and following for a discussion on the various suggestions in regard to locating the "throne of Satan." Aune lists eight possible locations, but favors the Roman judge's bench or tribunal, or place where the proconsul would pass judgment. Also included in Aune's list are the Temple of Augustus and Roma, the Great Altar of Zeus, the Temple of the Asklepios, and Pergamum as a center of the imperial cult.
73   Beckwith, 457; Caird, 37; Mounce, 78; Beale, 245; Aune, 1:182; Hemer, 82.
74   Mounce, 97; Aune, 1:184; Beale, 247.
75   R. H. Charles, 1. 62, and F. F. Bruce, "The Revelation to John," *A New Testament Commentary*, ed. G. C. D. Howley (London: Pickering and Inglis, 1969), 638.
76   Aune, 1:185; Beale, 247.
77   Everett Ferguson, *Early Christians Speak* (Abilene, Tex.: ACU Press, 2002), 202. Origen's reference to Acts 1:8 is in regard to Jesus' command to the apostles to go and be his witnesses from Jerusalem to the ends of the earth.
78   Aune, 1:185.
79   Colin J. Hemer, 86; Helmut Koester, *History, Culture and Religion of the Hellenistic Age* (New York: De Gruyter, 1992), 370.
80   Aune, 1:185.
81   Aune, 1:185.
82   Caird, 39.
83   E. M. Blaiklock, *The Seven Churches* (London: Marshall, Morgan and Scott, 1951), 39.
84   Aune, 1:186.
85   Mounce, 81. See also Caird, 38–39.
86   We have already encountered the Nicolaitans at Rev. 2:6 in the letter to the Ephesians, where we noticed that little is known about this group. They were probably a licentious group, possibly of a gnostic nature, who indulged in immoral sexual activity. For further discussion on the Nicolaitans, cf. Aune, 1. 148ff.
87   Aune, 1:188.
88   Aune, 1:185.
89   Mounce, rev. ed., 81.
90   Caird, 39. Cf. also Beale, 250.
91   Aune, 1:188.
92   Arndt and Gingrich, *porneuō*.
93   Caird, 41: "The one thing clear is that, when John speaks of an imminent coming of Christ, he is not necessarily thinking of the Parousia." Aune, 1. 188, declares that "Rev. 2:16; 3:11 must be interpreted as 'comings' in judgment preceding the final and decisive coming of Christ." Beale, 251, where Beale also refers to Rev. 2:5 and implies that Rev. 2:5 is a conditional coming and therefore not a reference to the final *parousia*. Cf. my comments at Rev. 2:5.
94   Mounce, rev. ed., 60.
95   Beale, 211; Aune, 1. 98, where both discuss this in the context of Rev. 1:16. Beale draws attention to similar language at Isa. 11:4 and 49:2.
96   Beckwith, 460–61; Caird, 82; Beale, 252; Aune, 1:189; Mounce, 82.
97   Cf. n. 96.
98   See the discussion in Beckwith, 461; Caird, 42; Beasley-Murray, 88; Beale, 252; Aune, 1:189.

Chapter Three

1   Cf. Beckwith, 483; Ramsay, *Letters*, 318; Hemer, 106; Beale, 259; and Aune, 1:201, for details regarding the social and business makeup of Thyatira.
2   For detailed discussion, cf. Beckwith, 462; Aune, 1:95; and Beale, 259. Both Aune and Beale draw attention to Daniel's prophecy of the image with feet of iron and clay, which image represented world kingdoms or powers. In contrast to this image, Jesus' feet are like "burnished bronze." Cf. also Hemer, 111.
3   Beckwith, 466; Beasley-Murray, 90.
4   Cf. Aune, 1:203; Mounce, 86; Beale, 260.
5   Aune, 1:204; Beale, 262; Mounce, 87.
6   Boring, 92–93.
7   Caird, 44. Beale, 250, agrees with Caird that the fornication is most likely spiritual fornication. Although we recognize that there is Old Testament backing for seeing fornication in a spiritual sense (Jer. 3:6), in the context of the nature of pagan worship in Asia, this is better interpreted as physical or sexual immorality as is translated in the NIV.
8   Beasley-Murray, 91.
9   Mounce, 1998, 87; Aune, 1. 188 sees a "close association . . . between idolatry and sexual immorality."
10   There is some reference made in the Jewish tradition to such a curse being used in judgment on those who fornicate, and an amulet in the Cairo Geniza might reinforce this concept; cf. Aune, 1:205. Possibly Jesus drew on a Hebraism in this expression that emphasized the seriousness of sexual immorality and adultery. Cf. also Beckwith, 467.
11   2 Sam. 12:14–18.
12   Mounce, 88; Beasley-Murray, 91 draws attention to a similar text in Ezek. 33:27.
13   Aune, 1:207.

14   Mounce, 89, J. Moffatt, *An Introduction to the Literature of the New Testament*, (New York: Scribner, 1927), 362.
15   Cf. Aune, 1:207.
16   Koester, *History and Literature of Early Christianity*, 2. 249–57.
17   The stress on the issues faced by the church in the imperial cult does not remove the suffering, opposition, and persecution from the context of the pagan cultural and Jewish synagogue problems faced by the church at the time of writing Revelation. There was a synergy in the interaction of the pagan idolatry, the Jewfish synagogue opposition, and the imperial cult in which all three drew on each other to oppose the Christian movement. Each cultural setting was motivated by its own interests, but each worked within the dynamic provided by the Roman concern for unity that manifested itself in the imperial cultus. One should not focus attention exclusively on the imperial cultus as the only problem faced by the churches, but one should see the three working in a synergistic way to oppose the church, or at least to provide difficult faith issues for the church.
18   Caird, 46.
19   Beale, 266.
20   Beale, 266.
21   C. Craigie, *Psalm 1–50*, (Dallas: Word Books, 1983), 57.
22   See the discussion in Aune, 1:209.
23   Mounce, 91.
24   Caird, 46: "We are compelled therefore to look for the fulfillment of this promise within the present order; and since the Christian becomes a conqueror in this world only in the moment of his leaving it, the fulfillment must be the actual death of the martyrs."
25   Mounce, 90; Hemer, 125.
26   Beasley-Murray, 94.
27   Hemer, 129; Aune, 1:218.
28   For an excellent discussion of Sardis and its history, see Hemer, 129.
29   Cf. the excellent, although dated study by William M. Ramsay, "The Jews in the Asian Cities," *The Letters to the Seven Churches* (1904; reprint ed., Grand Rapids: Baker Book House, 1979), 142, 354; and Hemer, 129.
30   Mounce, 93.
31   Aune, 1:219.
32   W. M. Ramsay, *The Letters to the Seven Churches of Asia*, updated ed. (Peabody, Mass.: Hendrikson, 1994), 272.
33   Beasley-Murray, 94.
34   Caird, 48; Osborne, 173.
35   Ramsay, *The Letters to the Seven Churches*, 354.
36   The Greek has the imperative form *ginou* of the verb *ginomai*, which when used in conjunction with the participle *grēgorōn* could be translated more as "be watchful." However, "wake up" is more in keeping with the strident challenge of Jesus. The RSV translates this as "Awake" while the NIV translates it as "Wake up."
37   Mounce, 95.
38   Aune, 1:221.
39   Caird, 49. Beale, 278, adds that the white robes draw from the broader biblical and pagan background symbolizing purity, festivity, and triumph.
40   Beasley-Murray, 97.
41   Cf. Rev. 10:8–10.
42   Beale, 279; cf. also Beasley-Murray, 98.
43   Beale, 279.
44   Aune, 1:223.
45   Cf. Mounce, 97; Beale, 278; for comment by Caird, 49; Walvoord, *The Revelation of Jesus Christ*, 82.
46   Cf. the discussion regarding the naming of the city in Hemer, 153ff., for discussion of the city of Philadelphia, Osborne, 184.
47   Hemer, 154; Ramsay, 391.
48   Cf. Hemer, 168ff.; Aune, 1:234.
49   Eusebius, *Ecclesiastical History*, Vol. I, Book V, xviii.
50   Hemer, 172.
51   W. M. Ramsay, 391–92.
52   Hemer, 174.
53   Hemer, 158.
54   Aune, 1:234f. Hemer, 157, adds that after the reign of Claudius (41–54) there is no record of the name Neocaesareia being used of the city.
55   Cf. Beckwith, 478ff.; Beasley-Murray, 99; Beale, 283; Aune, 1:235.
56   Beckwith, 479; Beale, 284; Aune, 1:235.
57   Caird, 51.
58   Mounce, 100.
59   Although no archaeological work has been possible since a modern city lies over the site of ancient Philadelphia, resulting in no archaeological evidence of a synagogue in the city, there is evidence of an active Jewish community and the existence of a synagogue in the city during the second century; see Hemer, 175; Aune, 1:234.
60   Beckwith, 481; Beale, 285; Aune, 1:236.
61   Hemer, 160.
62   Beale, 286.

63   Such statements in Revelation that the synagogue of the Jews became the synagogue of Stan are not intended to be anti-Semitic and a rejection of Jews, for many of the Christians in Asia were in fact Jewish Christians, and in all probability John the writer of Revelation was a Jew, as was the apostle Paul, the writer of the Roman letter. Such observations are theological in that they speak out against the mindset of the synagogue in Asia, but beyond that they are statements of historical record (cf. Eusebius's observations regarding the Jews in Smyrna who betrayed Polycarp and assisted in his martyrdom, *Eccl. Hist.*, IV, xiv. 1-xv. 30) rather than comments of ethnic rejection.

64   Caird, 61; cf. also Beckwith, 481–82; Beale, 288; Aune, 1:237ff.: N. T. Wright, *Jesus and the Kingdom of God* discusses at length Jesus' eschatological claims that Israel's messianic hopes were being fulfilled in his ministry, that the disciples of Jesus (the kingdom or church) had become the Israel (messianic) of God.

65   Aune, 1:240.
66   Cf. Beale, 289; Aune, 1:238; Mounce, 102, for further discussion on related issues in this text.
67   Cf. the works cited above by Beale and Aune.
68   Beale, 290.
69   Aune, 1:240.
70   Mounce, 103.
71   Roberts, *The Revelation to John*, 49.
72   For discussion on the phrase "hour of trial," cf. Beale, 289; Aune, 1:240; Beasley-Murray, 101.
73   See the map in Ramsay.
74   Ramsay, 413; Hemer, 178.
75   Hemer, 178.
76   Hemer, 182; Ramsay, 420.
77   Cf. Aune, 1:255.
78   On Old Testament references to first-born cf. Gen. 43:33; 48:18; Exod. 4:22.
79   Cf. Aune, 1:255; Mounce, 108; Beale, 297; Beasley-Murray, 103; Caird, 57; Beckwith, 488.
80   Cf. the discussion on the bad taste of the water in Hemer, 186; Mounce, 108; Beale, 303; Aune, 1:257.
81   E. M. Blaiklock, *The Seven Churches* (London: Morgan and Scott, 1951), 77.
82   Mounce, 111.
83   Ramsey, 431.
84   Mounce, 112 ; Hemer, 465; Beale, 307; Osborne, 210.
85   Beasley-Murray, 106–7.
86   Cf. the discussions in Aune, 1:260; Beale, 307; Mounce, 113; Caird, 58.

Chapter 4

1   Caird, 60.
2   Beale, 317.
3   Beale, 317.
4   Beale, 152-168.
5   Beasley-Murray, 108.
6   Caird, 60.
7   Mounce, 116.
8   Beale takes specific issue here with Hal Lindsey, *Late Great Plane Earth*, and other futurists. Cf. n. on 318.
9   I will comment more fully below on John's use of Jewish mysticism and in particular with Merkabah chariot mysticism in his visionary scenes.
10   Beale, 426.
11   Beale, 314.
12   Bogdan G. Bucor, "The Angelomorphic Spirit in Early Christianity: *Revelation, The Shepherd of Hermas,* Clement of Alexandria"; and Andrei Orlov, "Celestial Choirmaster: The Liturgical Role of Enoch-Metatron in 2 Enoch and the Merkabah Tradition," Scrinium, (Saint Petersburg: Byzantinorossica, 2007), 3. 4 and 279.
13   Cf. Aune, 1:276; Beale, 311; Andrei A. Orlov, *The Enoch-Metatron Tradition* (Tübingen, Germany: Mohr Siebeck, 2005).
14   Yarbro Collins, *The Combat Myth in the Book of Revelation*.
15   Caird, 60.
16   Yarbro Collins, *The Combat Myth in the Book of Revelation*.
17   Beale, 316.
18   Caird, 60, Beale, 316.
19   Cf. the articles by Roberts and Caird to this effect: Roberts, "The Meaning of the Eschatology in the Book of Revelation," *Restoration Quarterly*, 15 (1972): 95-110; Caird, "On Deciphering the Book of Revelation," *Expository Times* (1962-1963): 13-15, 51-53, 81-84, 103-105.
20   The occasion of an open door into heaven is discussed at length by Aune, 1:275. He draws attention to the widespread use of this imagery in Judaism and the Jewish apocalyptic tradition, including a discussion of Merkavah (chariot) mysticism, citing 1 Enoch 14; 2 Enoch, et al. Cf. Also Beasley-Murray, 111, and Beale, 118.
21   Beckwith, 495; Kiddle, 80; Charles, *Revelation*, 1:108; Beasley-Murray, 111; Beale, 317; Mounce, 118.
22   Caird, 60.
23   Mounce, 118.
24   Beale pulls together the realized eschatology of C. H. Dodd and the inaugurated eschatology of Oscar Cullmann in a manner that explains the unique nature of Revelation as both present and imminent future.
25   Beale, 317.

26   Cf. Orlov, *The Enoch-Metatron Tradition*); Rachel Elior, *The Three Temples; On the Emergence of Jewish Mysticism* (Portland, Ore.: Littman Library of Jewish Civilization, 2005).

27   Caird, 63; cf. also Beale, 321.

28   Beasley-Murray, 113.

29   Cf. Beckwith, 498; Caird, 63; Beasley-Murray, 113; and Mounce, 121 devote a full excursus to the many approaches to these twenty-four elders, 120ff. Most agree that the number twenty-four does not have Old Testament or Jewish parallels, but that the concept of elders around the throne of God draws on the Jewish apocalyptic tradition.

30   Beale, 322.

31   Both Beale, 327, and Aune, 1. 295, defer the interpretation of the seven spirits to Rev. 5:6. Mounce "tentatively" interprets the seven spirits in this text as a reference to angelic beings (122). Beasley-Murray sees in the seven spirits a reference to the Holy Spirit (115).

32   Cf. the discussion of the lightning, etc., in Beale, 326, and Aune, 1. 293.

33   Caird, 65. For a list of variant views of the sea, cf. Mounce, 123. Aune, 1. 296 proposes an alternate view of the brazen laver in the presence of the temple of Solomon, while also being aware of mythological references to the sea as a realm of chaos and evil.

34   Beale, 327.

35   Akkadian and Sumerian creation myths suggest that creation came about as a result of the mixing of sweet and salty waters. "A far more trustful and committed attitude toward the powers that rule existence finds expression in the seemingly slightly later Babylonian creation story *Enuma elish*, which may be dated to the latter part of the first dynasty of Babylon (ca. 1894–ca. 1595 B.C.). Babylon's archenemy at that time was the Sealand, which controlled Nippur and the country south of it—the ancestral country of Sumerian civilization. This lends political point to the battle of Marduk (thunder and rain deity), the god of Babylon, with the Sea, Tiamat." "The conception of a primal body of water from which everything is derived is especially prevalent among peoples living close to coasts or in river areas—e. g., the Egyptian Nu (the primordial ocean) and the Mesopotamian Apsu (the primeval watery abyss) and Tiamat (the primeval chaos dragon)" (*Encyclopædia Britannica*, 1994–2001).

36   Beale, 328. Cf. Yarbro Collins, *The Apocalypse*, 86: "So the 'waters' are symbolic of chaos and destruction," and "the sea before the throne shows that the rule of god is always in tension with the opposing forces of disorder and disintegration."

37   Cf. Beckwith, 500; Caird, 64; Mounce, 124; Beasley-Murray, 116; Beale, 328; Aune, 1:296, for a full discussion on the four living creatures.

38   Alan J. McNicol, "Revelation," in *The Transforming Word* (Abilene, Tex.: ACU Press, 2009), 1072.

39   Osborne, 236.

40   McNicol, "Revelation" *The Transforming Word*, 1068, 1073.

41   Osborne, 236.

42   Beale, 332.

43   Beale, 332.

44   Mounce, 125.

45   Beale, 332.

46   Cf. Beckwith, 502; Beale, 334; Mounce, 8; Beasley-Murray,118; Aune, 1:302, for excellent discussion of this hymn of praise.

47   Osborne, 239.

48   G. M. Stevenson, "Conceptual Background to Golden Crown Imagery in the Apocalypse of John," *Journal of Biblical Theology* 114 (1995): 268.

49   Mounce, 126. Cf also Aune, 1:308.

50   Beale, 336.

51   Beale, 334.

Chapter 5

1   Osborne, 245.

2   Osborne, 245, 246.

3   Aune, 1. 338. For other remarks relating to the coordinating and continuation function of 5:1 and its relationship with 4:1–11, cf. Aune, 1:329, and Beale, 337.

4   Cf. Aune, 1:332.

5   William F. Arndt and F. Wilbur Gingrich and Frederick W. Danker, *A Greek-English Lexicon of the New Testament and Other Early Christian Literature*.

6   McNicol, "*Revelation*," 1064.

7   Both Beale and Aune discuss the nature of scrolls in considerable detail, Beale, 339; Aune, 1:339.

8   Caird, pp. 70ff; Beale337ff; Aune, vol. 1, pp. 341ff; Beckwith , pp. 504ff, Osborne, pp. 247ff. Aune adds that there "has been a great deal of speculation about the contents of the sealed scroll. . . ." Aune, 1:343.

9   Caird, p. 72.

10   Beale, pp. 340ff.

11   Aune, 1:345. Aune cites Sweet, Caird, Beasley-Murray, and Lohse as proponents of this view.

12   Beckwith, 505.

13   Aune, 1:338.

14   Osborne, 247.

15   Cf. the comments at n. 5.

16   Aune, 1:346; Beale, 337; Osborne, 250.

17   Cf. Beale, 86, on how the concept of Old Testament fulfillment is used in Revelation.
18   Cf. John J. Davis, *Biblical Numerology* (Grand Rapids: Baker, 1968), 122; Beckwith, 253; Beale, 58.
19
20   For an additional detailed discussion of the scroll and its sevenfold sealing, see Beale, 337; Aune, 1. 338; Osborne, 246; Bauckham, *The Climax of Prophecy*, 243.
21   Cf Osborne, 251.
22   That the final eschaton is discussed in brief in Revelation does not imply that the eschatological message of Rev. 6–22 refers to the final eschaton. What we encounter in Revelation is an inaugurated eschatological message that presents events in the immediate future of the church in eschatological genre for effect and dramatic emphasis. God is treating the crises faced by the church with the utmost seriousness, which involves eschatological implications; hence the churches must treat the events of the immediate impending crises with eschatological concern. The eschaton must be mentioned in the theodicy of Revelation, as in Rev. 20:10–15, in order to bring closure to the theodicy of Revelation.
23   Cf. the above n. and Beale, 341.
24   Beale, 340.
25   Beale, 342.
26   Beale, 342.
27   See Caird, 74; Aune, 1:349; Beale, 349; Osborne, 252.
28   Aune, 1:349.
29   Osborne, 254. I disagree with Osborne's comments regarding Armageddon, but will discuss that at Rev. 16:16.
30   Osborne, 254.
31   Cf. the rich discussion of these metaphors in Osborne, 254ff.; Aune 1:336; Beale, 350; Caird, 74; and Bauckham, *The Theology of the Book of Revelation*, 60. Bauckham adds that the word lamb, referring to Christ, occurs 28 times in Revelation, thus indicating that this is an important image of Christ in Revelation.
32   Caird, 74.
33   Osborne, 255.
34   Osborne, 256.
35   Caird, 75.
36   Beale, 350.
37   Beale, 351; Osborne, 254; Mounce, 132.
38   See the discussion of this text in Caird, 75; Mounce, 132; Beale, 354; and Aune, 1:353; Osborne, 256; Bauckham, *The Climax of Prophecy*, 150. The discussion in Beale is worth serious consideration. At the conclusion of his comments on the seven spirits of God and the Holy Spirit, Beale observes, "The seven spirits of God . . . are agents only of God operating throughout the earth. . . . But as a result of the death and resurrection, these spirits also become Christ's agents throughout the world, who figuratively represent the Holy Spirit himself. The Spirit carries out the sovereign plan of God," 355.
39   Osborne, 257.
40   Osborne, 257f.
41   Beale, 356.
42   Beale, 357.
43   Aune, 1:355; Osborne, 258.
44   We are reminded of William Hendriksen's views of progressive parallelism in described in his commentary *More Than Conquerors* and Austin Farrar's views of recapitulation in *A Rebirth of Images*.
45   Osborne, 259.
46   Mounce, 135.
47   Aune, 1:356.
48   Aune, 1:358.
49   Beale, 358; Aune, 1:355.
50   See the discussion of this in Caird, 77; Beale, 360; Aune, 1:363.
51   The textual issue of whether the pronoun us (*hēmas*) should be part of the text is well discussed in Beale, 360. The United Bible Society Greek text of 1966/2001 omits *hēmas*.
52   Henry Swete, *The Apocalypse of John* (Grand Rapids: Eerdmans, 1906), 82; Mounce, 136.
53   Caird, 77.
54   Beale, 360; Osborne, 261.
55   For an excellent and detailed discussion of this problem, cf. Beale, 362. Mounce prefers the future tense here but is aware that the verb can represent a "futuristic present."
56   Caird, 77; Beale, 362; Aune, 1:362.
57   It is generally recognized that the description "myriads of myriads and thousands of thousands" is taken from Dan. 7:10 (cf. also 1 *En.* 40:1; 60:1; 71:8, which also allude to Dan. 7:10; cf. further 1 *En.* 14:22; Num. 10:36). That such a clear picture of Dan. 7:10 should arise here is not surprising in light of the observations of Dan. 7 influence in 5:2–10. The repeated mention of Ezekiel's cherubim is now in 11a combined with the scene of Dan. 7:10. Beale, 364.

Chapter 6

1   Beale, 370. Serious students of Revelation should read this section of Beale, 370ff.
2   Caird, 78.

3   Osborne, 269.
4   Cf. the discussion in Caird, 79; Beale, 374; Osborne, 277.
5   Beale, 377, Aune, 2:394, Osborne, 277.
6   Beale, 374.
7   Cf. Beale, 375; Osborne, 275. Some who hold this view are Henry Alford, William Hendriksen, and Z. C. Hodges.
8   Beale, 377; cf. also the discussion in Osborne, 276, and Aune, 2:393.
9   Caird, 79; Osborne, 276; H. B. Swete, *The Apocalypse of John*, 1911; Leon Morris, *Revelation* (Grand Rapids: Eerdmans/InterVarsity Press, 1967), 101; Bruce M. Metzger, *Breaking the Code* (Nashville: Abingdon, 1993), 57; Beazley-Murray, 131; Mounce. 141; Aune, 2:394.
10   Cf. Osborne, 276. Osborne considers this horseman to represent the ultimate depravity of humanity. I am persuaded, however, that the point of representing this army as an evil agent is that God can use even evil agents and war to achieve his purpose.
11   Osborne, 274; Beale, 378; Caird, 80; Beasley-Murray, 130; Metzger, 55.
12   Mounce, cites Cicero, *Verr.* 3:81, in support of this figure.
13   Beckwith, 520.
14   Osborne, 280; Beale, 380; Aune, 2:398.
15   Arndt and Gingrich, *A Greek-English Lexicon of the New Testament*.
16   Metzger, 57.
17   Aune, 2:406; Beale, 390.
18   Cf. Rev. 5:6, Beale, 391, Osborne, 285.
19   Osborne, 284; Mounce, 146.
20   I recognize that the difference between *maintained, borne*, and *made* is marginal, but I prefer the sense of borne.
21   Timothy Freiberg, Barbara Freiberg, and Neva F. Miller, *Analytical Lexicon of the Greek New Testament* (2000).
22   Cf. the discussion in Beckwith, 421, 434, 526; Aune, :19, 80; Beale, 184, 202; Osborne, 56, 82; 285.
23   Osborne, 285.
24   Osborne, 285.
25   Cf. the discussion in Aune, 1:12, 19, 81; 2:406; Beale, 183, 390.
26   Beckwith, 418, 421; Charles, 1:6; Aune, 1:12, 19, 81; 2:406.
27   Beckwith, 526; Charles, 1. 174; Aune, 2:406.
28   Unfortunately, this does not altogether resolve the issue, for 12:17 is also fraught with genitive issues, as are 1:2, 9; 6:9.
29   Osborne, 285.
30   Beckwith, 526; Aune, 2:407; Osborne, 286. Osborne claims that it is used 19 times in the LXX of God.
31   Osborne, 286.
32   Beale, 394; Osborne, 289; Mounce, 149; and Aune, 2:412.
33   Bauckham, *The Climax of Prophecy*, 48–56.
34   Caird, 88; Aune, 2:413; Beale, 396; Osborne, 290.
35   Bauckham, 209. In fact, Bauckham devotes a whole chapter, "The Eschatological Earthquake," to this discussion.
36   Beale, 398.
37   Beale, 398.
38   Osborne, 292–93.
39   Beasley-Murray, 137.
40   Osborne, 293.
41   Osborne, 294.
42   Osborne, 294.
43   Caird, 79; Morris, 110; Roberts, 70; Beasley-Murray, 142; Beale, 406; Osborne, 305.
44   Beale, 407; Osborne, 305.
45   Cf. the discussion in Osborne, 306.
46   Osborne, 307; Beale, 408.
47   Aune, 2:455.
48   Beale, 416.
49   Osborne, 313.
50   Caird says Irenaeus attributed this to Manasseh's being substituted because the rabbinic tradition held that the antichrist would come from the tribe of Dan. Caird adds that this may be a reason the Chronicler omitted Dan from his list of the twelve tribes, 99. Bauckham, however, thinks that John's omission was purely arbitrary and not sinister, 223. Osborn nevertheless believes that the idolatry theory may be viable, 314.
51   Osborne, 314, comments: "The presence of Joseph and Manasseh is also interesting. Ephraim and Manasseh were the two sons of Joseph, and normally their listing depended on whether Levi was mentioned. If Levi was omitted, Joseph was also omitted and both Ephraim and Manasseh were named among the twelve tribes (cf. Deut. 27:12–13 [with Levi] and Num. 1:5–15 [without Levi]. Here, however, Levi is included and so is Joseph, but Manasseh seemingly replaces Dan. Cf. also Beale, 416ff. and most commentators on this text.
52   Boring, 130. Beale refers to "the implausibility of a literal view of Rev. 7:3-8, p. 420.
53   Cf. the discussion of the listing of the twelve tribes in Beckwith, 534; Caird, 98; Mounce 158; Aune, 2:459; Bauckham, 215; Morris, 112; Beale, 416; Osborne, 310; Boring 130.
54   Cf. Beale's citing of Walvoord, *Revelation*, 140, Roberts, *Revelation*, 1–7, 473–482.

55   Beale, 416; Osborne, 310; Caird, 94; Roberts, 71.
56   McNicol, "Revelation," *The Transforming Word*, 1064.
57   Beckwith, 135; Boring, 129; Morris, 111; Metzger, 61; Roberts, 71; Mounce, 158; Beasley-Murray, 140.
Several, Sweet, 148; Boring, 129, find allusion to Christian baptism in this analysis of the 144,000 as the church,
but most discard this since baptism is not a theme John develops in Revelation. Cf. Caird, 96; Beasley-Murray, 143;
Osborne, 310.
58   Kiddle, 136; Caird, 97.
59   Beale, 422; Osborne, 312; Bauckham 215; Boring, 128.
60   Yarbro Collins, *The Combat Myth in the Book of Revelation*, and Richard Bauckham, *The Climax of Prophecy*.
61   Caird, 95; Bauckham, 215; Osborne, 312; Beale, 422; Boring; 128; McNicol, "Revelation," *The Transforming
Word*, 1073. Bauckham identifies some connection of John's military images with the Holy War concepts of the
Qumran and Jewish Second Temple mysticism. He recognizes that John is not calling for a Holy War against the
enemies of the church, but is using these images in a "non-military" understanding of the spiritual battle in which the
church is engaged.
62   Boring, 128.
63   Bauckham, 215.
64   Beale, 424; cf. also Bauckham, 215, who sees a connection between the lion and the lamb at 5:5–6. Cf. also
Osborne, 316; Mounce, 161; Aune, 2:466; Caird, 100; Boring, 131.
65   McNicol, "Revelation," *The Transforming Word*, 1073.
66   I see in this a Jewish *Merkavah* mystical concept of Ezekiel's chariot taking him into the throne room of God.
Cf. Elior, *The Three Temples*.
67   Osborne, 320; Beale, 427; Aune, 2:467.
68   Caird, 100, argues appropriately that the Greek word *sotēria* in Rev. 7:10 should be translated *victory*. Cf. also
Bauckham, 225 and Aune, 2:470; Osborne, 10, who are in accord with Caird, and who add the concept of deliverance
to the meaning of *sotēria*.
69   Bauckham, 224–225.
70   Beale, 431.
71   Osborne, 323. Osborne cites Charles, Beckwith, Thomas, and Aune in support of his conclusion.
72   Osborne, 324.
73   Beale, 433.
74   Beale, 440, Osborne, 328; Beasley-Murray, 148.
75   Aune, 2:476.
76   For a detailed discussion on these possibilities, cf. Beale, 445; Osborne, 336; Aune, 2:507.
77   Beale, 451; Osborne, 338.
78   Beale, 452.
79   Cf. Beckwith, 550; Charles, 1:225; Aune, 2:508; Caird, 107; Morris, 117; Mounce, 172; Beale, 454; Osborne,
342. There is some discussion among the commentators regarding the articular construction of the seven angels,
indicating that John was identifying these angles with a well-known Jewish tradition.
80   Osborne, 339.
81   Osborne and Mounce observe that this was the view of early commentators, as well as Beale, but both disagree with this interpretation of the "other angel." Cf. Osborne, 343, and Mounce, 173. Both Osborne and Mounce
identify Bede, Elliott, Walvoord, Beale, and possibly Hendriksen as those opting for Christ as this 'other angel.'
Beckwith, 552; Caird, 107, agree with Osborne and Mounce. Aune, 2. 511, although he does not discuss the identity of
this "other angel" in detail, falls in line with the interpretation of Osborne, Mounce, Caird, and others.
82   J. Ramsey Michaels, *Revelation* (Downers Grove, Ill.: InterVarsity Press, 1997), 117.
83   Caird, 107.
84   Osborne, 346; Beale observes that this verse (Rev. 8:5) "formally interpreted the scenes of woe in 6:12–17
and 8:1 as the answer to the prayer of 6:10." Osborne correctly comments that Beale is wrong, however, in connecting
8:5 with the last judgment.
85   Beale, 457. Cf also Beasley-Murray, 150; Kiddle, 147; Osborne, 346; Mounce, 174.
86   Michaels, 118.
87   Bauckham, 201. In addition to Bauckham's comment, I might add that the judgments about to be trumpeted
are not in regard to the final judgment, but are proleptic expressions of God's judgment on the oppressors of the
saints in Rev. 6:10. His judgment on those who dwell on earth, the oppressors of the saints, is announced in final
eschatological terms to emphasize the extent of God's wrath.
88   Bauckham, 204. Bauckham's comments on the theophanies of Rev. 8:5,6 are from his chapter "The
Eschatological Earthquake."
89   Cf. the discussion of trumpets in Caird, 107; Beasley-Murray, 152; Mounce, 176; Beale, 468; Aune, 2:518.
90   Osborne, 349.
91   Beale, 468.
92   Roberts, 74.

Chapter 7

1   Cf. the similar location in the structure of Revelation of this pericope in Beale, 445, 465, and Osborne, 336,
349.
2   Cf . Beale, 465; Osborne, 349; Aune, 2:494 ; Beasley-Murray,154, 166; Mounce, 176.
3   Mounce, 177.

4   Mounce, 176. Cf. Osborne, 346, who argues contra Beale that these judgments are not the last judgment.
5   On Rev. 8:3–5 there is considerable discussion among scholars regarding the angel, the altar, and the prayers of the saints.
6   Cf. Beale, 457; Osborne, 343ff.
7   The Greek text does not mention an angel in 8:7, but the context suggests this.
8   Aune, 2:519.
9   Osborne, 350; Aune, 2:519. Mounce dismisses the possibility of contemporary experiences of desert rain as "unlikely", 178, n. 10.
10   Cf Mounce, 178; Osborne, 351; Beale, 473.
11   Aune, 2:520.
12   Osborne, 352.
13   A few commentators argue that Jerusalem is intended by Babylon, but these views are not well attested by scholarly research into the use of Babylon in early Christian literature, where every reference for five centuries is to Rome, not Jerusalem.
14   Beckwith, 557; Charles, 1:234.
15   Beale, 479; cf also Osborne, 354.
16   Caird, 114.
17   Osborne, 360.
18   Beale, 489.
19   Osborne, 361.
20   Beale, 489.
21   Beale, 490.
22   Osborne, 349.
23   Mounce, 183.
24   Caird, 141.
25   Beasley-Murray, 188.
26   Osborne, 361.
27   Osborne, 361.
28   Beale, 491.
29   Beale, 491. Cf. also Aune, 2:525.
30   Caird, 118.
31   Mounce, 185.
32   Beale, 492.
33   Osborne, 362.
34   S. Thompson, "The End of Satan," *Andrews University Seminary Studies*, 37:257–268.
35   Mounce, 185; Aune, 2:525; J. Ramsey Michaels, 124.
36   Osborne, 362.
37   Aune, 2:521; Beale, 493; Osborne, 362.
38   Beale, 495; Aune, 2:495; Osborne, 365.
39   Cf. Aune, 2:530; Beale, 497; Osborne, 367; Mounce, 188; Beasley-Murray, 161; Caird, 120; Charles, 1:243; Beckwith, 562.
40   Beckwith, 562.
41   Mounce, 188.
42   For detailed discussion of this scorpion/locust army cf. Osborne, 369ff; Beale, 499 ff; Aune, 2:531ff; Mounce, 188 ff; Beckwith, 562f.
43   Beale, 502f.
44   Osborne, 374; Mounce, 191; Aune, 2, 532ff; Beasley-Murray, 162; Caird, 120. Others simply see a reference to the god Apollo, the destroyer or god of destruction, Beckwith, 563; J. Ramsey Michaels, 127f.
45   Bauckham, *The Climax of Prophecy*, 65.
46   Beale, 506.
47   Osborne, 378; Beale, 505; cf. also comments by Aune, 2:536.
48   Mounce, 193; Beale, 505.
49   Beale, 378.
50   Osborne, 378.
51   Cf. Caird, 121; Mounce, 193; Beale, 508; Aune, 2:596, for discussion of the troops being held at the Euphrates and their significance to John's message in revelation.
52   Cf. the discussion of pagan idolatry in Aune who speaks of a stereotypical Jewish or Semitic phrase that connects idolatry with demon worship and immoral practices, vol. 2, pp. 541ff; Osborne, pp. 386f; Mounce, 198; Beale, 517ff; Caird, 123f., where Caird compares this litany of pagan degeneration to Rom. 1:18ff.
53   Cf. Aune, 2:555 and Osborne, 390.
54   Osborne, 390.
55   Bauckham, 238ff.
56   Cf. the discussion in Osborne, 393; Aune, 2:555; Bauckham, *The Climax of Prophecy*, 254; Beale, 523; Mounce, 201; Beasley-Murray, 170.
57   Caird, 126; Mounce, 202.
58   Beckwith, 580. Cf. also Osborne, 394; Beale, 522; Caird, 125; Mounce, 201; Aune, 2:557; Beasley-Murray, 169.
59   Aune, 2:556; Osborne, 395.

60   Osborne, 396; Beale, 529.
61   Bauckham, *The Climax of Prophecy*, 244, questions whether it has a diminutive force in Revelation.
62   Beckwith, 580.
63   Caird, 126.
64   Leon Morris, *The Revelation of St. John*, Tyndale New Testament Commentaries (Grand Rapids: Eerdmans, 1987), 138.
65   Mounce, 202.
66   Beasley-Murray, 171.
67   Beale, 527.
68   Osborne, 394.
69   Osborne, 396.
70   Cf. Osborne, 398; Aune, 2:564.
71   Aune, 2:568.
72   Aune, 2:568.
73   Timothy Friberg, Barbara Friberg, and Neva F. Miller, *Analytical Lexicon of the Greek New Testament* (Grand Rapids: Baker), 2000.
74   Beckwith, 581; Charles, 1:263; Caird, 127; Beasley-Murray, 170; Beale, 539; Aune, 2:567; Osborne, 400; Mounce, 205; et al.
75   Whether one agrees with Caird regarding the temporal setting of Daniel or one prefers the traditional setting of Babylonian captivity makes little difference at this point. This is not the place to debate the historical or temporal setting of Daniel. The same argument Caird makes can, however, be made from either temporal setting for Daniel, namely that Daniel is set in the context of persecution and oppression, which context is paralleled in Revelation.
76   Caird, 127.
77   The terms analogous and typological are mine in keeping with Beale's discussion of how John uses the Old Testament. Cf. the discussion in the introduction.
78   Caird, 127.
79   For various views on this complex text see Beckwith, 582 where Beckwith rejects earlier (KJV) translations; Sweet, 129 and the translation "interval of time"; Caird, 128 where Caird connects this statement with 6:10; Charles, 1. 263; Beale, 538, where Beale refers this to God's termination of history; Osborne, 398 where Osborne considers this a reference to the time of the eschaton predicted by Daniel; Aune, 2, 567 and his lengthy offering of "no more interval of time and rejection of the translation "delay"; Beasley-Murray, 174, and his reference to the mystery as "the completion of God's purpose in creation and in the history of man in particular"; and Mounce, 205, where he rejects the translation of *chronos* as time, preferring the use of "delay," *contra* Aune.
80   Mounce, 206.
81   Beale, 541.
82   Caird, 128.
83   Osborne, 401.
84   Osborne, 401.
85   Cf. N. T. Wright, *Jesus and the Victory of God* (Minneapolis: Fortress), 1996.
86   Osborne, 402.
87   Osborne, 401, who speaks of two levels to this pericope.
88   Osborne, 402; Bauckham, 246; Beale, 549.
89   Sweet, 131; Krodel, 216.
90   Beale, 552.
91   Aune, 2:572.
92   Caird, 130.
93   Osborne, 403.
94   Cf. also Osborne, 403.
95   Aune, 2:573.
96   Beale, 554, cf. also Osborne, 404.
97   Aune, 2. 573, "It is of critical importance to decide how the preposition *epi* is used in this verse"; Osborne, 404; Beale, 554.
98   Bauckham, *The Climax of Prophecy*, 265.
99   Bauckham, *The Climax of Prophecy*, 265.
100   Cf. Beale, 557; Aune, 2:585; and Osborne, 409, who summarize the many proposals identifying the temple.
101   Caird, 130.
102   Bauckham, *The Climax of Prophecy*, 272.
103   Beale, 559.
104   Beale, 563.
105   Osborne, 411.
106   Aune, 2:598.
107   Aune, 2:597.
108   Frederick W. Norris, "Andrew of Caesarea," in *Encyclopedia of Early Christianity*, ed. Everett Ferguson (New York: Garland, 1997), and Aune, 2:597.
109   Cf. Sweet, Caird, Mounce, Beale, Aune, Osborne, Bauckham.
110   Bauckham, *The Theology of the Book of Revelation*, 126. Cf. also Aune, 2:598, on John's reinterpretation of the Jewish symbols. Cf. also McNicol, "Revelation," *The Transforming Word*, 1064, on John's predilection for the intertextuality of Old Testament and Revelation terms and ideas.

111   Beale, 558.

112   Caird, 132.

113   Osborne, 413.

114   Beale, 565.

115   Osborne, 414. I am not too excited about referring to the antichrist in that his term is alien to Revelation.

116   Caird, 132. Caird appropriately refers to Daniel's use of the symbolic time periods as "Daniel's cryptic estimate" of the duration of persecution.

117   Cf. also Osborne, 414, "Finally, the three-and-a-half year period refers to a limited period that is strictly under God's control."

118   Cf. the discussion in Osborne, 417.

119   Osborne, 421.

120   Mounce, 218.

121   Aune, 2:599.

122   Caird, 134; Mounce, 218; Osborne, 419; Beale, 573; Morris, 144; Beasley-Murray, 184.

123   Beale, 575.

124   Beale, 582.

125   Aune, 2:617ff. It is surprising that Aune would expect specific information regarding how the saints were killed or the details of the street or square in Rome where this would have taken place, 620. The specifics in a metaphor or symbolism are not the point in the dramatic narrative.

126   Osborne, 424; Caird, 137; Beasley-Murray, 185; Mounce, 219; Aune, 2:616.

127   There is some discussion on how the Greek term *pneumatikōs* should be translated. The word literally means *spiritually*. The NIV prefers figuratively, the RSV prefers allegorically, the NRSV prefers *prophetically*. Cf. the discussion in Bauckham, 168; Aune, 2:619.

128   Beckwith, 601, "Jerusalem is certainly meant"; Beasley-Murray, 186; Aune, 2:620; Osborne, 426. Some prefer to identify the great city as any city opposed to God, as in John Bunyan, *The Pilgrim's Progress* or C. S. Lewis, *The Pilgrim's Regress*, Ramsey-Michaels, 142, Morris, 146.

129   Caird, 138.

130   Beale, 591.

131   Cf. the discussion of Rome in Osborne, 426; Beale 591; Aune, 2:616.

132   Beckwith, 602.

133   Beckwith, 252.

134   Beckwith, 602; Caird, 138; Beasley-Murray, 186; Aune, 2:621.

135   Osborne, 428.

136   Beale, 594.

137   Aune, 2:621.

138   Osborne, 428.

139   Osborne, 428; Beale 595; Aune, 2:621.

140   Osborne, 429.

141   Beale, 598ff; Osborne, 430ff; Aune, 2:624ff.

142   Beale, 599, where Beale speaks of acceptance, divine approval, and vindication. Beale however, sees in this action a reference to prophetic commissioning of both Ezekiel and John. Like Osborne, I question that prophetic commissioning is necessary in this case.

143   Caird, 139.

144   Osborne, 433.

145   Osborne, 434.

146   Osborne, 439; Beale, 609, prefers to translate "soon" as "quickly," which is linguistically possible, but in keeping with John's use in Revelation is unlikely. Aune, 2:630, translates soon as shortly which retains the sense of imminence.

147   The expression is a play on the ten plagues on Egypt, which in our narrative refers to the plagues on Rome, calling on the new pharaoh, Domitian, to repent.

148   Caird, 141.

149   Osborne, 438.

150   Osborne, 438.

151   Beale, 609.

152   Osborne, 442.

153   Aune, 2. 642.

154   Osborne, 444.

155   Osborne, 445.

Chapter 8

1   Mounce, 231.

2   Beale, 621, cites Prigent, *Apocalypse 12*, 1959, in support of this. See also Osborne, 452; Mounce, 229; Beasley-Murray, 191.

3   I will clarify these references below in the commentary of the text.

4   Beale, 622.

5   Beale, 621.

6   For discussion on the possibilities in structuring this section, cf. Beale, 621; Mounce, 229; Kiddle, 215; Morris, 44, 155; Osborne, 452; Aune, 2:657.

7   Beckwith, 612; Charles, 1:310; Caird, 147; Beale, 624; Osborne, 454; Beasley-Murray, 192.

8   Caird, 147.

9   Beasley-Murray, 193.

10   Beale, 625.

11   Osborne, 457.

12   Charles, 1. 316. However, here Charles identifies the twelve stars with the twelve tribes of Israel, not the signs of the zodiac.

13   Beckwith, 622ff. However Beckwith sees a possible reference to the twelve tribes of Israel connecting to the signs of the zodiac.

14   Beasley-Murray, 197.

15   Aune, 2:681.

16   Beale, 626.

17   Mounce, 232, n. 5. Mounce, however, sees a possible reference to both the twelve tribes of Israel and the twelve apostles.

18   Osborne, 457.

19   Beasley-Murray, 194.

20   Beale, 627.

21   Cf. the discussion in Beckwith, 612; Caird, 149; Beale, 631; Mounce, 231; Aune, 2:680; Osborne, 457.

22   In the discussion of the woman as "mother Zion," the reference is to a symbolic woman, not a literal person.

23   Beale, 628; Osborne, 457; Caird, 149; Mounce, 231; Yarbro Collins, *The Combat Mythology in the Book of Revelation*, 106.

24   Yarbro Collins, *The Combat Myth in the Book of Revelation*, 107.

25   Cf. Mounce, 232; Osborne, 458; Beale, 632; Aune, 2:682. For an excellent discussion of the dragon, cf. Bauckham, *The Climax of Prophecy*, 185.

26   Beale, 635; Osborne, 460.

27   Mounce, 233; Osborne, 461.

28   Mounce, 233.

29   Mounce, 233, where Mounce argues that this is not a theology of fallen angels but merely a demonstration of Satan's great power.

30   Osborne, 461.

31   Beale, 635.

32   Beale, 637.

33   Caird, 147.

34   Beale, 639, and Osborne, 462.

35   Cf. the discussion in Osborne, 463; Beale, 639; Yarbro Collins, *The Combat Myth in the Book of Revelation*, 105.

36   Mounce, 234; Morris, 155.

37   Aune, 2:691.

38   Cf. the discussion in Caird, 151; Beale, 637; Osborne, 462.

39   Cf. Yarbro Collins, *The Combat Myth in the Book of Revelation*, *passim*. Cf. also Collins, *The Apocalypse*, xiv and 82.

40   Bauckham, *The Theology of the Book of Revelation*, 66ff. and *The Climax of Prophecy*, 210.

41   Bauckham, *Climax*, 210. Cf. also Caird, 153; Mounce, 234; Beasley-Murray, 201; Beale, 650; Osborne, 467; Aune, 2:691.

42   Beale, 650.

43   James M. Charlesworth, ed., *Jesus and the Dead Sea Scrolls*, Anchor Bible Reference Library (New York: Doubleday, 1992), 12, 33, passim.

44   Aune, 2:695. Cf. also Beale, 650, and Osborne, 468, for discussion of the cosmic and primordial nature of this battle and the fall of Satan and his angels.

45   Beale, 651.

46   Duane F. Watson, "Michael," in *Anchor Bible Dictionary* (New York: Doubleday, 1992).

47   Cf. Duane F. Watson, "Devil," *Anchor Bible Dictionary*.

48   Beckwith, 625, Beasley-Murray, 203; Osborne, 473; Aune, 2:699.

49   Osborne, 473.

50   Cf. Caird, 153; Beasley-Murray, 202; Osborne, 473; Aune, 2:699. This victory sense of *sōtēria* is found three times in Revelation: 7:10; 12:10; 19:1.

51   F. Wilbur Gingrich and Frederick W. Danker, *A Greek English Lexicon of the New Testament* (1957).

52   Cf. Beale, 665; Osborne, 477; Aune, 2:703.

53   Osborne, 475.

54   Osborne, 480.

55   Cf. Beale, 669ff, and Aune, 2, 704f, for fuller discussion of this, notably in the Egyptian and Jewish Midrashic and Dead sea Literature Traditions.

56   *The Greek New Testament*, 4th rev. ed. of the 26th ed. of *the Novum Testamentum Graece*, Barbara Aland, Kurt Aland, Johannes Karavidopoulos, Carlo Martini, Bruce Metzger (Stuttgart: United Bible Societies), 2001.

57   Osborne, 489. For a good discussion on the role of this expression and its place in the various manuscripts, cf. Osborne, 489; Beale, 681; Aune, 2:731.

440   CONQUERING WITH CHRIST

58   Cf. the discussion in Bruce Metzger, *A Textual Commentary on the Greek New Testament* (United Bible Society, 1971), 748; Osborne, 489; Beale, 681; Aune, 2:716.
59   Aune, 2:732.
60   Cf. my comments at Rev. 4:6, and Beckwith, 633; Osborne, 489; Aune, 2:732.
61   Beale, 684.
62   Beale, 682.
63   Cf. Osborne, 490–91.
64   Cf. Osborne, 490; Beale, 682.
65   Beale, 683.
66   Osborne, 491. Cf. also Beale, 684.
67   Cf. Aune, who gives an impressive survey of the imperial cult of the first century.
68   Osborne, 492.
69   Cf. also Yarbro Collins, *The Apocalypse*, 91.
70   Osborne, 492.
71   Cf. Beckwith, 635; Beasley-Murray, 210; Osborne, 496; Aune, 2:736.
72   Cf. Beasley-Murray, 212; Osborne, 499.
73   Cf. Osborne, 500.
74   Cf. Beale, 697; Osborne, 500.
75   Beale, 701; Aune, 2. 746; Osborne, 503.
76   Cf. Beale, 703.
77   Mounce, 252.
78   Beale, 703.
79   Beale, 707.
80   Beale, 707.
81   Mounce, 256. Cf. also Beale 707; Osborne, 512; Aune 2:752.
82   Caird, 171; Beasley-Murray, 216; Osborne, 513; Aune, 2:756.
83   Charles, 1. 357.
84   Aune, 2:756.
85   Beasley-Murray, 216; Helmut Koester, *Introduction to the New Testament*, vol. 1, *History, Culture and Religion of the Hellenistic Age*, 317-317, 370; and *Introduction to the New Testament*, vol. 2 , *History and Literature of Early Christianity*, 249-251, 288.
86   Eusebius, *Ecclesiastical History*, vol. 1, Book IV, XV. 18-24.
87   Aune, 2:766.
88   Mounce, 262; Aune, 2:770; Osborne, 521.
89   Cf. the discussion in Aune, 2:769, and Beale, 718.
90   Caird, 176.
91   "Sibylline Oracles," *Sibylline Oracles*, Book 1, line. 324ff.; J. J. Collins, *The Old Testament Pseudepigrapha*, ed. James H. Charlesworth (New York: Doubleday, 1983). There are several versions of the *Sib. Or.* available on the internet. The one used in this study is by Milton S. Terry, *The Sibylline Oracles* (New York: Eaton & Mains, 1899; digitized 2001), Book 1, line 393ff. at http://www. sacred-texts.com/cla/sib/sib. pdf. Note fn. 6 in the text copied above, "396. *Four vowels.* —The name Jesus in Greek, (Grk *Iēsous*), contains four vowels and the consonant is twice told, and the numerical value of all the letters is 888."
92   Caird, 172; Osborne, 516; Beale, 715; Aune, 2:765.
93   Beasley-Murray, 221.
94   Beasley-Murray, 222.
95   Aune, 2:803; Beale, 731.
96   Cf. "Zion," *Anchor Bible Dictionary*.
97   Mounce, 265.
98   Osborne, 526.
99   Osborne, 526.
100   Caird, 179, Bauckham, *The Climax of Prophecy*, 229.
101   Arndt and Gingrich on *parthenos*.
102   Osborne, 529, cites Lohmeyer, Farrer, Caird, Beasley-Murray, Schüssler Fiorenza, Chilton, Bauckham, Harrington, Giesen, Michaels in support of this view.
103   Osborne, 530.
104   Cf. the discussion of this point in Beale, 745; Osborne, 531.
105   Osborne, 533.
106   Aune, 2:823, but Aune misses the angel of vs. 9 in his count.
107   Aune, 2:823.
108   Arndt and Gingrich, *Geek-English Lexicon of the New Testament* on *mesouranēma*.
109   Cf. Eusebius, *Eccles. Hist.* Book II: xv, citing Clement. Cf. also Aune, 2:829; Osborne, 538; Beale, 757. Cf. also *2 Baruch* 11:1; 67:7; 79:1; *Sib. Or.* 5:143, 159; *2 Esdras* 3:2.
110   Cf. Beale, 754; Osborne, 537; Aune, 2:829.
111   Osborne, 540; Aune, 2:833.
112   Cf. the footnotes on paragraphing in Aland, et. al., *The Greek New Testament*, 4th ed.
113   Osborne, 543. Where necessary I have transliterated the Greek into English.
114   Osborne, 543, and Beale, 766, set this obedience to God's commandments in a larger context, but I am inclined to limit this to worshipping only God, not the beast.

115   Cf. Aune, 2:839; Beasley-Murray, 227.
116   Dana and Mantey, *A Manual Grammar of the Greek New Testament*, *gar*, 242; Arndt and Gingrich, *A Greek-English Lexicon of the New Testament*, *gar*; Osborne, 545. *Gar* may be either causal or explanatory. In the case of 14:13, it should be explanatory.
117   Cf. also Osborne, 546.
118   Osborne, 551. For his detailed discussion, see 550.
119   Osborne, 550.
120   Osborne, 551; cf. also Beale, 774.
121   Cf. Aune, 2:844.
122   Beckwith, 664; Beasley-Murray, 229; Mounce, 279; Osborne, 553; Beale, 775.
123   Cf. Caird, 192; Osborne, 554.
124   Cf. the discussion in Osborne, 555; Beale, 780; Aune, 2. 847; Caird, 192; Mounce, 281.
125   Beale, 782; Osborne, 556.
126   Mounce, 281; Beasley-Murray, 230; Beale, 782; Osborne, 556.
127   Bauckham, 40ff.

Chapter 9

1   Caird, 196f.
2   Caird, 200.
3   Cf. Beale, 784; Osborne, 560; Aune, 2:869; Beasley-Murray 233.
4   Beale, 787. Beale sites Beasley-Murray, 234.
5   Beale, 788.
6   Cf. the discussion in Caird, 197; Mounce, 284; Osborne, 561; Beale, 512; Aune 2:870; Beasley-Murray, 235.
7   Cf. the discussion in Beale, 793; Osborne, 563; Caird, 197, and others understand this as a subjective genitive, which would translate as "harps that God gave them." The NIV along with Caird favors the subjective genitive.
8   Cf. Beale, 792; Osborne, 564.
9   Mounce, 285; Beale, 793, finds reference to the resurrection of Jesus in this expression of the song of the Lamb.
10   Cf. Beale 801, and Osborne, 569, for the genitive construction, and Mounce, 288, and Beasley-Murray 237.
11   Metzger, *Textual Commentary on the Greek New Testament*, 756. Cf. the discussion in Beale, 804–5; Osborne, 569; Aune, 2:878.
12   Lev. 16:4, 23; Ezek. 9:2, 3, 11; and *Joseph and Aseneth* 3:6 (dated between 1st century B.C. and 2nd century).
13   Beale, 804. Cf. also Exod. 40:34; Isa. 6:4; 2 Chron. 5:13.
14   Beasley-Murray 237.
15   Osborne, 570.
16   Beale, 806.
17   Beale, 807; cf. also Osborne, 570.
18   Mounce, 289.
19   Cited by Osborne, 572.
20   Beckwith, 679; Caird, 200; Beasley-Murray, 237.
21   Caird, 200; Osborne, 572.
22   Osborne, 576.
23   Beckwith, 679; Osborne, 576; Beale, 808; Beasley-Murray, 238; Mounce, 290; Caird, 201.
24   Osborne, 578; Beale, 812.
25   Cf. Beasley-Murray, 242.
26   Cf. Beale, 821, on the symbolic nature as opposed to the literal.
27   Hermann Wolfgang Beyer in Kittel, *Theological Dictionary of the New Testament*, *blasphēmia*.
28   Aune, 2:888.
29   Caird, 203.
30   Osborne, 587.
31   Beale, 825.
32   Beale, 828.
33   Cf. the discussion in Beale, 828.
34   Cf. Beale, 832ff., where he cites several sources in the rabbinic tradition.
35   Beckwith, 683.
36   Osborne, 592.
37   Aune, 2:895.
38   Aune, 2:896.
39   Aune, 2:896.
40   Cf. the discussion in Aune, 2:896; Osborne, 892; Beale, 834; Mounce, 300.
41   Roberts, 130.
42   Caird, 206.
43   Beale, 838.
44   Roberts,130.
45   This seduction will be spelled out in Rev. 17 and the figure of the great harlot.
46   Beasley-Murray, 245.

47   Osborne, 594ff. N. A. Silberman, "Armageddon, Megiddo, and the End of the World," *Archaeology*, 52/6:36, 37.

48   Osborne, 595f.

49   Caird, 206.

50   Beasley-Murray, 245.

51   Mounce, 301 and Beale 838f make similar observations.

52   Beale, 838f.

53   In Israel very few "mountains" would be considered mountains in Colorado. In Texas, what in Colorado are called hills are commonly known as mountains. The size of a mountain is, I expect, relative to where one lives.

54   Beasley-Murray, 246. Although I may have some concern or difference with Beasley-Murray over his comment that Armageddon may" have been a symbol for the last resistance of anti-god forces prior to the kingdom of Christ", his statement is otherwise cogent.

55   Caird, 207.

56   Osborne, 596.

57   Beale, 841.

58   Beale, 842.

59   Aune, 3:1111, discusses some textual variant forms at 21:6, but these do not relate to the immediate discussion of singular and plural endings.

60   Osborne, 596.

61   Beckwith, 686.

62   Caird, 209.

63   Beckwith, 686.

64   Roberts, 132.

65   For excellent discussion of the Old Testament theophany images and apocalyptic background to this pericope, cf. Bauckham, "The Eschatological Earthquake," *The Climax of Prophecy*, 199ff.

66   Bauckham, "The Eschatological Earthquake" and "The Economic Critique of Rome in Revelation," in *The Climax of Prophecy*, 199 and 338. I will discuss the great harlot in greater detail in the next section on Rev. 17–19.

67   Mounce, 303. Mounce cites Bruce, Kiddle, and Morris as separating the two cities, "that great city" and Babylon. Morris does not believe that the great city should have any geographical connection. Mounce points out, and I concur, that the three repetitions of *kai* separating the three mentions of a city in this verse should be read as an epexegetical *kai* and could be read as "and so." Aune, 2:900, recognizing that identifying the great city has been problematic, agrees with Mounce and Bauckham that the great city should be understood as Rome, the new Babylon.

68   Osborne, 599.

69   Osborne, 599.

70   Osborne, 600.

71   Cf. the discussion in Caird, 209; Mounce, 304; Beasley-Murray, 247; Osborne, 600; Beale, 844; Bauckham, *The Climax of Prophecy*, 204; Aune, 2:901.

Chapter 10

1   Hendriksen, *More than Conquerors*.

2   Bauckham, 349.

3   Bauckham, 338.

4   Osborne, 605.

5   Mounce, 308.

6   Caird, 212.

7   Cf. the discussion in Caird, 212; Mounce, 308; Osborne, 608; Beasley-Murray, 251; Beale, 848; Aune, 3:919. Aune includes a illustration of the *Dea Roma* coin of Vespasian's era.

8   Osborne, 608.

9   Osborne, 609; Beale, 849; Mounce, 309. Mounce refers to this representing "the apostate nations who have entered into illicit relations with Rome . . . enticed into idolatrous worship of herself and the beast."

10   Cf. Osborne, 610; Beale, 851, Beckwith, 692.

11   Caird, 213.

12   Charles, 2. 64.

13   Mounce, 310.

14   Aune, 3:935.

15   Cf. the discussion in Osborne, 612, who cites Lohmeyer, Walvoord, Johnson, Ladd, Chilton, Giesen, and Michaels in agreement with the RSV translation. Cf also Mounce, 311; Beasley-Murray, 253; Aune, 3:936.

16   Beale, 858; Mounce, 311; Aune, 3:936.

17   Osborne, 613.

18   Aune, 3:937.

19   Osborne, 614.

20   Osborne, 617.

21   Beale, 868 ; Osborne, 618; Aune, 3:944; Yarbro Collins, *Crisis and Catharsis*, 58; Fiorenza, 20; Mounce, 314; Beasley-Murray, 256.

22   Caird, 218.

23   Yarbro Collins, *Crisis and Catharsis*, 58.

24 Fiorenza, *Research Perspectives on the Book of Revelation*, 20. Cf. Also Aune, 1:lviff., and 3:945ff; and Osborne, 617ff.
25 Cf. the discussion in Aune, 3:944; and Osborne, 617.
26 Cf. Osborne, 619.
27 Cf. Caird, 217.
28 Cf. the discussion of this in Caird, 217f, Aune, 3:946f; Adela Yarbro Collins, *Crisis and Catharsis*, 58ff; Osborne, 617ff.
29 Osborne, 617ff.
30 Aune, 3:946.
31 Caird, 218f.
32 Aune, 3. 952; W. C. von Unnik, "*Mia Gnōmē*, Apocalypse of John xvii, 13,17," in *Studies in John*, Novum *Testamentum Supplement* 24, 209–20.
33 Cf. Osborne, 631; Beale, 895; Aune, 2:879; C. R. Smith, "Reclaiming the Social Justice Message of Revelation: Materialism, Imperialism and Divine Judgment in Revelation 18." *Transformation* 7:28-3; A. D. Callahan, "Apocalypse as Critique of Political Economy: Some Notes on Revelation 18," *Horizons in Biblical Theology*, 29 (1999), 46–65.
34 Aune, 3:976.
35 Osborne, 634.
36 Cf. Osborne, 641, who cites Beckwith, Ladd, Hughes, Ford, Sweet, Kline, Krodel, Chilton, Mounce, and Thomas as holding this view.
37 Cf. Beale, 641, and Callahan, 59; D. C. Chilton, *The Days of Vengeance: An Exposition of the Book of Revelation* (Fort Worth, Tex.: Dominion, 1987), 450.
38 Cf. the discussion of this challenging concept of retribution in Aune, 3:992.
39 Cf. Caird, 232.
40 Cf. Aune, 3:1027; Osborne, 666; Beale, 930.
41 Cf. the discussion in Aune, 3:1027; Osborne, 666.
42 Heinrich Schlier, *aineō*, Gerhard Kittel, *Theological Dictionary of the New Testament*.
43 Caird, 236.
44 Caird, 235.
45 Osborne, 672.
46 Beale, 199. Cf the discussion of *ho pantokratōr*, in Aune, 1:306.
47 Cf. the discussion of the aorist tense in Dana and Mantey, *A Manual Grammar of the Greek New Testament*, 193; F. Blass, A. Debrunner, and Robert W. Funk, *A Greek Grammar of the New Testament*, 171, James H. Moulton and Nigel Turner, *A Grammar of New Testament Greek*, 3:68.
48 It is not surprising that futurists or premillennialists would prefer to translate the aorist in the case of Rev. 19:6 regarding the reign of God as an ingressive aorist, indicating that in the final judgment, which is how they read this pericope, God has now begun to reign.
49 Osborne, 672.
50 Cf. Beckwith, 729; Caird, 237; Beasley-Murray, 275; Mounce, 349; Beale, 947; Osborne, 677; Aune, 3:1038.
51 Mounce, 350f.
52 Osborne, 679.
53 Cf. Beckwith, 732; Caird, 242; Beasley-Murray, 279; Mounce, 353; Beale, 952; Osborne, 681; Aune, 3:1055, for discussion on the wide-ranging proposals to this mystery.
54 Beasley-Murray, 279.
55 Cf. the discussion of this in Beale, 957; Caird, 242–43; Beasley-Murray, 280; Mounce, 353; Aune, 3:1057.
56 Osborne, 682.
57 Mounce, 354.
58 Cf. Beale, 960; Osborne, 684.
59 Osborne, 684; Aune, 3:1059.
60 Beale, 965.
61 Osborne, 687; cf. also Aune, 3:1063; Beale, 965.
62 Osborne, 682.
63 Osborne, 691; Timothy Friberg, Barbara Friberg, Neva F. Miller, *Analytical Lexicon of the Greek New Testament*.
64 Mounce, 360.
65 Michael Wilcock, *I Saw Heaven Opened: The Message of Revelation* (Downers Grove, Ill.: InterVarsity Press, 1975), 175.
66 Caird, 249.
67 Morris, 227.
68 Osborne, 696.
69 Osborne, 697. Osborne states that he takes a premillennial approach to this pericope. I, however, take an amillennial approach to Revelation.
70 J W Roberts, *The Revelation to John*, 169.
71 Osborne, 697.
72 Osborne, 697.
73 Cf. Yarbro Collins, *The Combat Myth in the Book of Revelation*.
74 Mounce, 360.
75 Beale, 973.
76 Mounce, 361. Mounce argues for a chronological sequence of visions ranging from 19:11 through 21:1.
77 Osborne, 699.

78   Beale, 974. Beale calls for a "nonsequential temporal relationship."
79   As in Rev 12:7ff., Satan has been defeated on several occasions already in Revelation.
80   Elisabeth Schüssler Fiorenza, *Priester für Gott, Studien zum Herrschafts und Priestermotief in der Apokalypse* (Munster, Germany: Aschendorf, 1972), 295.
81   Aune, 3:1081.
82   Aune, 3:1082.
83   See my comments on the abyss at Rev 9:1.
84   Osborne, 700.
85   Mounce, 361.
86   Cf. Beckwith, 736f; Roberts, 170f; Aune, 3:1082ff; Beale, 984ff; Osborne, 700ff; Beasley-Murray, 286f; Mounce, 360f.
87   Beckwith, 736.
88   Beasley-Murray, 286.
89   R. H. Charles, *The Apocrypha and Pseudepigrapha of the Old Testament* (Berkley, Ca.: Apocryphile Press, 2004. Orig. publication 1913.
90   E. Isaac in *The Old Testament Pseudepigrapha*, ed. James H. Charlesworth (New York: Doubleday and Company, 1983), translates the ending of 1 Enoch 18:16 as "in the year of mystery" with a footnote "for a myriad years." R. H. Charles, *The Book of Enoch* (London: Society for Promoting Christian Knowledge, 1917), translates this last verse as "*And He was wroth with them, and bound them till the time when their guilt should be consummated (even) for ten thousand years.*"
91   R. H. Charles, *The Book of Enoch*.
92   Harold Hazelip, *Restoration Quarterly*, 18, no. 4 (1975). Cf. also Jim McGuiggan, *The Book of Revelation*, (West Monroe, La.: William C. Johnson, Inc. 1976), 274.
93   Ray Summers, *Worthy Is the Lamb* (Nashville: Broadman Press, 1951), 204.
94   Wilfred J. Harrington, *The Apocalypse of St. John* (London: Geoffrey Chapman, 1969), 199.
95   Beale, 995.
96   All of these commentaries are referenced prominently in this study.
97   Aune, 3:1089f.
98   Dan Danner, "A History of the Interpretation of Revelation 20:1-10 in the Restoration Movement," *Restoration Quarterly*, 7, No. 4 (1963).
99   Beale, 995. Cf. also Jim McGuiggan, *The Book of Revelation*, 276.
100   Osborne, 985.
101   Osborne, 985.
102   McGuiggan disagrees with Roberts who suggests that Satan is limited, arguing that limited Is not strong enough. McGuiggan argues for the completeness of Satan's power being taken away in regard to Rome. I feel that this is very the point Roberts is making.
103   Roberts, 171.
104   Cf. Osborne, 702; Beale, 986. Beale takes issue with those who would give the *hina* clause a wider application than limited to Rome. I agree with Beale that the *hina* clause limits the application to the nations who are deceived by Satan and the beast.
105   Osborne, 703.
106   Beale, 991, citing Bauckham, *The Theology of the Book of Revelation*, 107.
107   Beale, 995.
108   United Bible Society, Fourth Revised Edition (2002), The Greek New Testament, or the Nestle Aland, Deutsche Bibelstiftung, Stuttgart, 26th edition of Novum Testamentum Graece (1979).
109   Aune, 3:1071, 1073.
110   Aune, 3:1086, cites several references to support his view that decapitation was a fairly common means of martyrdom among early Christians under the Roman system.
111   Osborne, 706.
112   Beale, 995.
113   Beale, 995.
114   Aune, 3:1090.
115   Aune, 3:1090.
116   Aune, 3:1090.
117   Beale, 1004 ff.
118   Morris, 231.
119   Roberts, 174. Bold text in the citation by Roberts.
120   Caird, 254.
121   Aune, 3:1090.
122   Beale, 1022. Beal speaks of John's universalizing the Ezek. 38–39 prophecy.
123   Osborne, 711f.
124   Aune, 3:1095; Osborne, 713.
125   Caird, 256. Cf. also the discussion of this in Charles, 2, 188ff.
126   Beckwith, 746; Aune, 3:1098f; Beale,1026.
127   Charles, 2, 144ff where Charles engages in a lengthy discussion of the order of these verses in Revelation.
128   Caird, 257; cf. Beckwith who suggests an allegory made of the old Jerusalem in favor of an idealized city of God's people, 746.
129   Cf. the discussion of this at Rev 19:20.

130   Mounce, 374.
131   Ladd, George Eldon, *A Commentary on the Revelation of John*, (Grand Rapids: Eerdmans, 1972), 270f.
132   Osborne, 719.
133   N. T. Wright, *Simply Christian* (New York: Harper-Collins, 2006).
134   Aune, 3:1101.
135   Aune 3:1101.
136   Aune, 3:1101. Cf. also Beckwith, 748; Beasley-Murray, 301; Beale, 1033, who adds that this shows John's preoccupation with the final judgment.
137   Aune, 3:1102.
138   Aune, 3:1103.
139   Osborne, 723.

Chapter 11

1   Aune, 3:1114.
2   Cf. Aune's discussion of translation issues in Isa 65:17 and the possibility that John is using an independent Greek text at this point. The Septuagint does not have the word create whereas the Masoretic text does. Aune, 3:116.
3   Cf. 2 Pet 3:13; *1 Enoch* 72:1; 91:16; *Sib. Or.* 5:212; *Jub.* 1:29; and *Apoc. of Elijah*, 5:38 for recreated, and *1 Enoch* 45:4f; *2 Apoc. of Baruch*, 44:12; *4 Ezra* 7:30f for a renewed heaven or earth.
4   Caird, 265; Bauckham, *Theology*, 49f; Prigent, 324f.
5   Aune, 3:1117; Osborne, 730f.
6   Arndt and Gingrich, *kainos, Greek English Lexicon of the New Testament*. Italics mine (IAF) for emphasis.
7   Aune, 3:1121.
8   Aune, 3:1121.
9   Robert H. Gundry, "The New Jerusalem: People as Place, not Place for People," *Novum Testamentum* 29:254 ff.; Mounce, 382.
10   Cf. Osborne, 733; Aune, 3:1120.
11   Beale, 1044. Cf also Aune, 3:1121.
12   Caird, 265. My translation stresses the word "behold" and reads the verb *poiō* ("make") as a present tense in the indicative active mood rather than a subjunctive. I agree with Beale that this is most likely a "prophetic present that reinforces the certainty that the future will occur." Cf. Beale, 1052–53.
13   Osborne, 737.
14   Osborne, 737.
15   Cf. Caird, 266, "All is over"; Aune, 3:1111 and 1126, where Aune observes that "the eschatological events . . . are part of the eternal plan." Beale, 1054 translates this as "they are done" and observes this "underscores the climactic nature of the fulfillment of the prophecies woven throughout vv 1–5." Osborne, 737–38, similarly translates this as "they are over" and observes that the perfect tense stresses a state, which "means salvation history is at an end and the future age can begin."
16   Cf. Caird, 266, "All is over"; Aune, 3:1111 and 1126 where Aune observes that "the eschatological events...are part of the eternal plan." Beale, 1054 translates this as "they are done" and observes this "underscores the climactic nature of the fulfillment of the prophecies woven throughout vv 1-5." Osborne, 737f similarly translates this as "They are over", and observes that the perfect tense stresses a state" which "means salvation history is at an end and the future age can begin."
17   Osborne, 739.
18   Beale, 1058.
19   Aune, 3:129.
20   Aune, 3:1129; Beale, 1058.
21   Osborne, 740. I have paraphrased Osborne's comments.
22   Osborne, 741. Cf. also Caird, 267; Beale, 1059; Beasley-Murray, 314; Mounce, 386.
23   Osborne, 741.
24   Osborne, 748; Caird, 269f; Beale, 1065ff. Cf also Aune, 3:1151.
25   Beale, 1069; Osborne, 750.
26   Aune, 3:1154.
27   Osborne, 758. For discussion on the various proposals regarding the jewels, cf. Osborne, 756; Beale, 1079; Caird, 274; Mounce, 393; Aune, 3:1164; Beasley-Murray, 324; Charles, *Revelation*, 2:1675; Beckwith, 762, who observes that the precise identification of the jewels is impossible.
28   Cf. the discussion in Caird, 273; Beale, 1077; Ramsey Michaels, 241; Osborne, 752.
29   Cf. Beale, 1092; Aune, 3:1066; Osborne, 760.
30   Eph. 2:21; 1 Cor. 3:15; 6:19; 2 Cor. 6:16.
31   Osborne, 759.
32   J. N. Oswalt, *The Book of Isaiah, Chapters 40–66*, New International Commentary on the Old Testament (Grand Rapids: Eerdmans, 1998), 557. Cf. also Beckwith, 763; Ramsey Michaels, 244; Bauckham, *The Climax of Prophecy*, 241; Osborne, 761; Beale, 1093; Aune, 3:1168.
33   Caird, 279 and contrary to the general thrust of the message of Revelation surprisingly observes, "He did not believe that God would be content to save a handful of martyrs and allow the rest of mankind, along with all their achievements of culture and civilization, to perish in the abyss."
34   Cf. the discussion of this in Beale, 1094-1099; Osborne, 767; Aune, 3:1170-1174; Mounce, 396, 397; Beasley-Murray, 328, 329.

35   Aune, 3:1173.
36   Caird, p. 279.
37   M. Rissi, *The Future of the World: An Exegetical Study of Revelation 19:11-22:15,* Studies in Biblical Theology, 2. 23 (London: SCM, 1972), pp. 73f; J. M. Vogelgesang, *The Interpretation of Ezekiel in the Book of Revelation*, Unpublished Dissertation, Harvard University, 1985.
38   Osborne, 767; Beale, 1099.
39   In some measure this view is seen in Beale, 1096ff; Osborne, 761ff.
40   Cf. Aune, 3. 1173; Beasley-Murray, 328, regarding W. Bousset; Mounce, 396, regarding older views of scholars such as E. Vischer, P. Pfleiderer, and J. Weiss.
41   Mounce, 396f.
42   Beale, 1099.
43   Mounce, 397.
44   Caird, 279.
45   Beale, 1099.
46   Aune, 3:1179.
47   Aune, 3:1181.

Chapter 12

1   I have adopted the paragraphing of *The Greek New Testament*, Kurt Aland, et al., 4th rev. ed., 1983.
2   Charles, 2:445.
3   Aune, 3:1182.
4   Beckwith, 772; Beasley-Murray, 334; Ramsey Michaels, 249.
5   Cf. the discussion at Rev. 1:1–3.
6   Cf. Rev. 2 and 3 for the discussion of the conditional coming of Jesus to remove the lampstand of the five churches unless they repent.
7   Cf. the discussion in the introduction.
8   Cf. the discussion at Rev. 2 and 3.
9   There is some discussion on whether the text here might link the prophets to those who keep the words of the prophecy. Beale makes a similar suggestion. Cf. Beale, 1128; and Osborne, 784.
10   Cf. the discussion of tis in the Introduction to this study and at Rev 1:3, and Beale, 185.
11   Roberts, 198.
12   Cf. Mounce, 406; Morris, 252; Ramsey Michaels, 252; Beasley-Murray, 337; Osborne, 785, for discussion on various approaches to this text.
13   Cf. Arndt and Gingrich, *A Greek English Lexicon of the New Testament* on *misthos*.
14   Osborne, 789. Cf. also Beale, 1138; Aune, 3:1219; Caird, 285.
15   Aune, 3:1208.
16   Aune, 3:1235.
17   Cf. the discussion of this pericope and the three imperatival invitations in Beale, 1148ff; Osborne, 793ff; Aune, 3:1227.
18   Caird, 287; Bauckham, *The Climax of Prophecy: Studies on the Book of Revelation*, 167f; Mounce, 409, Beasley-Murray, 344f; Aune, 3:1127.
19   Osborne, 794.
20   Caird, 287.
21   Beale, 1148.
22   Osborne, 793.
23   Caird, 288; Roberts, 201; Osborne, 797; Beale, 1155; Beasley-Murray, 348.
24   *Maranatha* is a word found in 1 Cor. 16:22, the *Didache*, and the Apostolic Fathers, associated in the second century with the prayer "Come, Lord Jesus" prayed during the Lord's Supper, or Eucharist. *Maranatha* is believed to have its origin in the Aramaic expression *marana tha* when the Aramaic is transliterated into the Greek alphabet. Cf. Aune, 3. 1234.
25   Aune, 3:1229; cf. also Osborne, 794
26   Aune, 3:1208 and 1229.
27   Aune, 3:1208.
28   Aune, 3:1229.
29   Osborne, 796f.

Chapter 13

1   H. H. Rowley, *The Relevance of Apocalyptic* (London: Lutterworth, 1944).
2   Gregory A. Boyd, *The Myth of a Christian Nation* (Grand Rapids: Zondervan, 2005).
3   Wolfhart Pannenberg, *Theology and the Kingdom of God*, ed. Richard John Neuhaus (Philadelphia: Westminster, 1969), *passim*, but specifically, 127.